Economic Integration and Multinational Investment Behaviour

NEW HORIZONS IN INTERNATIONAL BUSINESS

Series Editor: Peter J. Buckley
Centre for International Business,
University of Leeds (CIBUL), UK

The New Horizons in International Business series has established itself as the world's leading forum for the presentation of new ideas in international business research. It offers pre-eminent contributions in the areas of multinational enterprise – including foreign direct investment, business strategy and corporate alliances, global competitive strategies, and entrepreneurship. In short, this series constitutes essential reading for academics, business strategists and policy makers alike.

Titles in the series include:

Alliance Capitalism for the New American Economy
Edited by Alan M. Rugman and Gavin Boyd

The Structural Foundations of International Finance
Problems of Growth and Stability
Edited by Pier Carlo Padoan, Paul A. Brenton and Gavin Boyd

The New Competition for Inward Investment
Companies, Institutions and Territorial Development
Edited by Nicholas Phelps and Philip Raines

Multinational Enterprises, Innovative Strategies and Systems of Innovation
Edited by John Cantwell and José Molero

Multinational Firms' Location and the New Economic Geography
Edited by Jean-Louis Mucchielli and Thierry Mayer

Free Trade in the Americas
Economic and Political Issues for Governments and Firms
Edited by Sidney Weintraub, Alan M. Rugman and Gavin Boyd

Economic Integration and Multinational Investment Behaviour
European and East Asian Experiences
Edited by Pierre-Bruno Ruffini

Strategic Business Alliances
An Examination of the Core Dimensions
Keith W. Glaister, Rumy Husan and Peter J. Buckley

Investment Strategies in Emerging Markets
Edited by Saul Estrin and Klaus E. Meyer

Multinationals and Industrial Competitiveness
A New Agenda
John H. Dunning and Rajneesh Narula

Foreign Direct Investment
Six Country Case Studies
Edited by Yingqi Annie Wei and V.N. Balasubramanyam

Japanese Multinationals in Europe
A Comparison of the Automobile and Pharmaceutical Industries
Ken-ichi Ando

Economic Integration and Multinational Investment Behaviour

European and East Asian Experiences

Edited by

Pierre-Bruno Ruffini

Professor of Economics, University of Le Havre, France

NEW HORIZONS IN INTERNATIONAL BUSINESS

Edward Elgar

Cheltenham, UK • Northampton, MA, USA

Published by
Edward Elgar Publishing Limited
Glensanda House
Montpellier Parade
Cheltenham
Glos GL50 1UA
UK

Edward Elgar Publishing, Inc.
136 West Street
Suite 202
Northampton
Massachusetts 01060
USA

A catalogue record for this book
is available from the British Library

ISBN 1 84376 652 3

Printed and bound in Great Britain by MPG Books Ltd, Bodmin, Cornwall

Contents

Contributors

Nathalie Aminian, Senior Lecturer in Economics, is at the Centre d'Etudes et de Recherches en Economie et Gestion Logistique (CERENE), University of Le Havre, France (nathalie.aminian@univ-lehavre.fr)

João Dias, CEDIN/ISEG/Technical University of Lisbon, Portugal (jdias@iseg.utl.pt)

John Malcolm Dowling, Department of Economics, Melbourne University and Singapore Management University, Australia (johnmd@unimelb.edu.au)

João Paulo Filipe, CEDIN/ISEG/Technical University of Lisbon, Portugal (Joao.Paulo.Filipe@oninet.pt)

Maria Paula Fontoura, CEDIN/ISEG/Technical University of Lisbon, Portugal (mpfontoura@mail.telepac.pt)

Tran Van Hoa, Associate Professor, Department of Economics and Director, Vietnam Focus Research Program, University of Wollongong, Australia (tvheco@uow.edu.au; http://www.uow.edu.au~tvheco/tvh.htm)

Chen-Min Hsu is Professor at the Department of Economics, National Taiwan University, Republic of China (chenmin@ccms.ntu.edu.tw and chenmin@npf.org.tw)

Camilla Jensen is an Assistant Professor with the Centre for East European Studies, Department for International Economics and Management, Copenhagen Business School, Denmark (cj.cees@cbs.dk)

Jong-Kil Kim is Professor at the Department of Economics and International Trade, Inha University, Incheon, The Republic of Korea (jongkim@inha.ac.kr)

Fukunari Kimura is Professor at the Faculty of Economics, Keio University, Tokyo, Japan (fkimura@econ.keio.ac.jp)

Kozo Kiyota is Associate Professor at the Faculty of Business Administration, Yokohama National University, Yokohama, Japan (kiyota@ynu.ac.jp)

Jong-Hwan Ko is Professor of Economics at the Faculty of International & Area Studies, Pukyong National University, Pusan, Korea (jonghko@pknu.ac.kr) and Visiting Professor, Columbia University, New York, USA (jk2386@columbia.edu)

Mudrajad Kuncoro, Faculty of Economics and Master of Management Program, Godjah Mada University, Indonesia (Mudrajadk@yahoo.com)

You-il Lee is a Senior Lecturer in International Business at the School of Management, Faculty of Business and Public Management, Edith Cowan University, Australia (y.lee@ecu.edu.au)

Gilliane Lefebvre, Research Assistant, CNRS, Université de Paris 10 Nanterre and FORUM-GIFT, France (gilliane.lefebvre@u-paris10.fr)

Jung Duk Lim is Professor of Economics at the Department of Economics, Pusan National University, Pusan, Korea (jdlim@pusan.ac.kr)

Wan-Chun Liu is Assistant Professor at Department of International Trade, Takming College, Republic of China (shane@takming.edu.tw)

Bernadette Madeuf, Professor of Economics, Université of Paris 10 Nanterre and FORUM-GIFT, France (bernadette.madeuf@u-paris10.fr)

Thierry Mayer, Professor of Economics, TEAM-Université de Paris 1 and CNRS (ESA 8059), France (tmayer@univ-paris1.fr)

Jean-Louis Mucchielli is Professor of Economics and Director of the Centre of International Economics (CESSEFI-TEAM), University of Paris 1, Panthéon-Sorbonne, France (jlmuc@univ-paris1.fr)

Françoise Nicolas is a Senior Research Fellow at the French Institute of International Relations (IFRI), Paris and an Assistant Professor at Marne-la-Vallée University, France (nicolas@ifri.org)

Young-il Park is Professor, School of International Trade and Regional Studies, Inha University, Incheon, Korea (parkyoil@inha.ac.kr)

Etienne Pfister is Assistant Professor of Economics at the University of Nancy 2, member of CREDES and member of TEAM-University of Paris I and CNRS (ESA8089), France (Etienne.Pfister@univ-nancy2.fr)

Florence Puech is Research Assistant at the TEAM-CNRS, University of Paris 1, Panthéon-Sorbonne, France (Puech@univ-paris1.fr)

Pierre-Bruno Ruffini, Professor of Economics, is at the Centre d'Etudes et de Recherches en Economie et Gestion Logistique (CERENE), University of Le Havre, France (pierre-bruno.ruffini@univ-lehavre-fr)

Philippe Saucier, Professor of Economics, is at the Laboratoire d'Economie d'Orléans (LEO), University of Orléans, France (Philippe.Saucier@univ-orleans.fr)

Yoko Sazanami is Professor at the Faculty of Comprehensive Business Administration, Toyogakuen University, Professor Emeritus at Keio University and Meikai University, Japan (ZUD05755@nifty.ne.jp)

Dong-Chon Suh is Professor, Division of International Trade and Regional Studies, Inha University, Incheon, Korea (dchon@chollian.net or dcsuh@inha.ac.kr)

Seiji Yoshimura is Directeur du CEDIMES-Tokyo, Institut CEDIMES, Université Paris 2 Panthéon-Assas, France (seiji-yoshimura@nifty.com)

Preface and Acknowledgements

The chapters in this volume were originally presented and discussed at the international conference *Location of economic activity, regional development and the global economy – European and East Asian experiences* held at the Faculté des Affaires Internationales of the University of Le Havre (France) on 26–27 September 2001. This conference took place under the patronage of the Centre d'Etudes et de Recherche en Economie et Gestion Logistique (CERENE, University of Le Havre). It was jointly organized by the University of Le Havre and Inha University (Republic of Korea) within the context of their long standing and valued cooperation. The organizers of this conference are most grateful to the City Council and the Port Authority of Le Havre, the General Council of Seine-Maritime, the General Council of Upper Normandy, the French Embassy in Korea, Crédit Agricole Indosuez, Hanjin Shipping, Hyundai Merchant Marine and SCAC Le Havre for their financial support.

We gratefully thank all members of the scientific committee, speakers and participants at the conference and owe a special debt to Claire Dissaux (Crédit Agricole Indosuez), Michel Fouquin (Deputy Director, Centre d'Etudes Prospectives et d'Informations Internationales, Paris), Jai-Ryong Jang (Ambassador of the Republic of Korea, Paris), Jong-Kil Kim (Professor at Inha University), Jung-Duk Lim (President of Pusan Developement Institute), Sang-Gon Lee (President of the Korea Energy Economics Institute), Philippe Saucier (Professor at the University of Orléans, France) and Yoko Sazanami (Professor at Mekai University and Keio University).

We extend our thanks to Annick Barbot, Eun-Sook Chabal, Pierre Chabal, Katia Meziani and Fabien Fruteau for their able assistance in organizing the conference and preparing the publication.

We would like to dedicate this work to the memory of Professor Sang-Gon Lee, President of the Korean Energy Economic Institute, who died on 2nd May 2004. He was the instigator of the conferences which are co-organized every two years by Le Havre and Inha, and, as such, he made a major contribution both to their success and to the cooperation between our two universities.

1. Introduction

Pierre-Bruno Ruffini

This book brings together studies in economic integration and multinational investment behaviour and is divided into three parts, each with six chapters. The first part of the volume offers a firm-oriented approach to global integration, and sheds light on the location decisions of firms in relation to their global performance. The second part turns to foreign direct investment (FDI) and gives special attention to East Asia as a major recipient zone for such inflows. The third part of the book complements the picture with the presentation of studies on regional economic integration.

The opening part of this volume pays special attention to spatial factors in economic activity and deals with some aspects of the location decisions of multinational enterprises (MNEs) and their impact on the spatial organization of these enterprises on a world wide scale. In Chapter 2, T. Mayer and E. Pfister analyse the relation between the existence in potential host countries of legislation for protecting intellectual property rights (such as patents, trademarks…) and the location choices of multinational enterprises. The chapter attempts at measuring the role of intellectual property rights in shaping the direction of foreign direct investment. In order to assess empirically the influence of intellectual property rights protection on FDI, the authors use a conditional logit model to analyse 755 location decisions made by French MNEs in 37 countries between 1980 and 1992. Beside standard determinants of location choices (such as demand, trade openness and labour costs), the results emphasize agglomeration forces as well as corruption and political rights as primary factors in location decisions. Regarding intellectual property rights, the authors find that their impact is limited to countries with a sufficiently high imitation capacity and to industries with a high propensity to patent (such as the pharmaceutical industry). They also find that this impact is non-linear in the sense that it is positive for low levels of protection and then negative for higher levels.

In Chapter 3, J.-L. Mucchielli and F. Puech contribute other material for understanding location decisions of MNEs and test whether foreign subsidiaries of French firms are geographically concentrated or dispersed in the European area at national and regional levels. They measure the degree of geographic concentration for each industrial sector of activity by using the random location model of Ellison and Glaeser. For each sector they test if the observed concentration or dispersion of plants deviates significantly from a random distribution of French foreign direct investments. The originality of Mucchielli and Puech's study is to take into account at the same time two different geographic levels for evaluating the degree of spatial concentration of multinational firms. They show first that the distribution of French FDI is very different across sectors of activity and also with regard to the geographic level considered. Second, they show that, for a given sector, foreign investments can be concentrated at the regional level and not necessarily concentrated at the national one, or vice versa. The overall picture, the authors conclude, is rather balanced: a significant level of agglomeration of French subsidiaries exists for some sectors of activity but for other sectors, there is clearly a dispersion phenomenon.

In Chapter 4, B. Madeuf and G. Lefebvre turn to the globalization of technology and innovative activities by multinational groups, and give specific attention to French groups. The globalization of industrial research now forms a central part of the strategy of MNEs. But, as the authors point out, this does not imply that the specific characters of territories at the local level have become irrelevant. Rather, they are playing a reinforced role, as demonstrated by the study presented in the chapter. This investigation is based on a survey conducted on a sample of 27 French industrial groups during the first months of 2000. The authors provide first a measure of the R&D activities conducted by these groups in their foreign locations and second, analyse the motives, functions and organization of R&D activities located abroad. The choice of French firms in this case study is particularly relevant, as these firms have been significantly less studied than enterprises originating from other countries, as far as R&D policy is concerned.

One central result of this chapter concerns the important role played by local and territorial factors in the global technological strategy of multinational firms. The authors draw this conclusion from an in-depth study of the regional specializations of foreign located R&D centres of French companies. They identify two different models and show that centres located in European countries differ from centres in the USA in many respects. US centres illustrate a so-called 'technology-focused' strategy, with scientific and technical factors playing a prominent role, whereas European centres are more 'market strategy'-oriented. Furthermore, the survey shows that a link exists between the orientation of R&D conducted abroad and the intensity of the company's integration into the local scientific systems. These findings may appear somewhat paradoxical: the more global the R&D objectives of the centres are – in terms of targeted markets and technological breakthroughs – the more these centres are involved in local partnership networks. What we learn from this chapter is the power of R&D conducted within multinational groups for linking territories, from local to global.

The following two chapters introduce into the overall picture the intra-firm dimension of multinational enterprises' global activity. Trade is a major activity among those conducted 'within' multinational groups: in Chapter 5, J. P. Filipe, M. P. Fontoura and P. Saucier study the evolution and determinants of US intra-firm trade between 1989 and 1998. The authors complete econometric testing done previously by using the most recent data and also by considering inter-country differences in addition to inter-sectoral variation of intra-firm trade. Using information relative to the intra-firm trade between US parent companies and their majority-owned foreign affiliates (excluding trade between MNEs and their US affiliates) and considering the case of the manufacturing industry, the authors establish two sets of results. At the sectoral level, relevant factors for explaining intra-firm trade appear to be technology intensity, the level of vertical integration, economies of scale and the level of international production, as well as the impact of the geographic concentration of US parent firms. At the country level, the size of the market and some country-specific factors appear to favour intra-firm trade. On the contrary, increasing levels of the tax rate on profits in the foreign country and increasing economic distance are disincentives to intra-firm trade. Country-specific factors appear to impact positively in some cases, such as being a member of the North America Free Trade Area (NAFTA) or displaying cultural affinities, like in the European Union (EU) case. And, as expected, US parents prefer to transact internally with less distant countries.

Chapter 6 brings other original conclusions drawn from the observation of Japanese MNEs, starting with a question put by K. Kiyota and F. Kimura: does the fragmentation of the production process of MNEs have an effect on their corporate performance? Fragmentation is the splitting of a production process into two or more steps that can be undertaken in different locations but that lead to the same final product. Fragmentation, the authors recall, is conducted not only by establishing affiliates but also by preparing various forms of contracts with other firms, such as commissioned production arrangements for instance. The chapter introduces a distinction between intra-firm fragmentation (establishing affiliates) and arm's length fragmentation (through commissioned production). Differences between national and international fragmentation are also examined. The study is based on firm-level longitudinal data concerning Japanese corporate firms from 1994 to 1997.

Regression results indicate that firms with a fragmented production process grow faster than others. Moreover, the growth rate of firms' profit–sales ratio is by far higher for firms with international fragmentation than firms without. Another important result drawn from the data analysis is that the number of cases of firms with commissioned production fluctuates over time more drastically than the number of cases of firms with affiliates, especially in overseas activities. Commissioned production is a relatively easy way to enter in and to exit from foreign markets. Following a logic similar to the one suggested by Aoki (1990), Japanese firms might use commissioned production as a buffer for business cycles, while retaining the stability of intra-firm activities. This may imply that the expansion of arm's length type fragmentation as opposed to intra-firm type fragmentation contributes to the improvement of corporate performance.

The initial question put by Y. Sazanami, S. Yoshimura and K. Kiyota in Chapter 7 is the following one: why did Japanese FDI to East Asian countries decline sharply after the Asian financial crisis of 1997 and why has it remained stagnant since then, which is in contrast with the FDI response of other countries? In order to answer this question, the authors enlarge the scope of their study: they investigate the importance of changes in real exchange rates between the yen and East Asian currencies in determining Japanese foreign direct investment outflows to East Asian countries from 1978 to 1999.

In general terms, a decline in the real exchange rate is ordinarily supposed to promote FDI outflows. The authors' findings over the period are consistent with this widely accepted assertion. The estimates reveal that Japan's FDI outflows have been stimulated by the fall in the real exchange rates of East Asian currencies against the yen and the subsequent rise in Japan's relative labour cost. But the study sheds light on another important explanatory factor: the accumulation effect of FDI, which promotes further ouflows, reflecting Japanese firms' preference to locate affiliates in regions where they have built up production networks that generate 'agglomeration' effects. In order to explain why the Japanese FDI responded poorly to the sharp fall in the real exchange rate at the time of the Asian financial crisis, the authors refer to the general trend of Japanese outwards FDI: Japanese FDI to East Asia tends to have a strong positive trend when total annual FDI flows are growing strongly as they did in the first half of the 1990s. But they tend to stagnate once annual FDI flows decline, as in 1998. A policy implication is drawn by the authors: countries willing to attract FDI should avoid the overvaluation of exchange rates, and also promote intra-regional trade to construct more efficient production networks within Asian countries. With this last remark, attention is moving towards the recipient-countries' perspective, which constitutes the core of the second part of the volume.

What is the impact of FDI on host country economies? How does FDI help their growth and development? How can it facilitate the way towards regional integration? These fundamental questions are of particular relevance in the post-crisis East Asian context. Chapters in the second part of this volume bring original and up-to-date views on some aspects of these major issues.

The geographic concentration of economic activity is the subject of Chapter 8. The island of Java, in which most of Indonesia's large and medium manufacturing industries have located overwhelmingly, is the subject of the case study conducted by M. Kuncoro and J. M. Dowling. Java is the part of Indonesia where most investments, either foreign or domestic, have concentrated. Geographic concentration is measured with the regional specialization index, which indicates from employment data the relative industrial specialization of districts or regions. By pooling data on manufacturing industry over the period 1991–1996, the authors show that there has been a natural market-led tendency towards the spatial concentration of manufacturing industry in metropolitan regions. Manufacturing firms in Java seek to locate in more densely populated areas to enjoy both localization economies and urbanization economies, as witnessed by the significance in the regressions of scale economies and income per capita variables. The former variable is associated with the size of a particular industry, while the latter reflects the size of the market of a district in a particular urban area. More importantly, the results suggest that synergy effects are at work between the thickness of market and the agglomeration forces. The interplay of agglomeration economies is intensified by the imperfect competition of Java's market structure. One can find in the broad scope of this chapter arguments which are relevant for the purpose of this volume: FDI is tested as one of the potential determinants of the geographic concentration of manufacturing industry. However, the authors show that foreign direct investment does not rank among the factors playing an important role in explaining the concentration of manufacturing activity, neither encouraging nor retarding regional specialization.

T. V. Hoa focuses in Chapter 9 on a major OECD newly industrializing economy (NIE), namely Korea. The author studies the interaction between investment and the other major economic activities in the Korean economy. He develops and estimates for this purpose a new multisectoral econometric model of FDI in flexible functional form and determines the impact of this variable on the country's economic growth in recent years (including the contagion of the 1997 financial crisis). Hoa investigates the causal structure and empirical forecast of investment in Korea, a major Asian NIE and the second Asian member of the OECD. This investigation implies two practical applications: the causal effect being established, remedies can be looked for in order to restore investment in Korea in the post-Asia crisis period. Second, the findings of the chapter help to understand how regional integration and globalization will impact on Korea's investment. Apart from its particular interest in the field of applied econometric modelling and statistical theory of forecasting, this chapter contributes a useful macro economic background for understanding the situation of the Korean economy, and complements in this way other chapters of this volume.

In Chapter 10, J.-K. Kim addresses the changes that the economic crisis have brought to the characteristics of inward foreign direct investment in East Asia. Due mainly to the low cost of acquiring firms and to deregulating attractive policies, a sharp rise in foreign direct investment occurred in Asia after the 1997 crisis. Changes occurred in the distribution of foreign direct investment drawn by Asian recipient countries, with a rise in the share of first tier newly industrializing economies (especially Korea) and a set-back in the share of ASEAN countries. The countries of origin of investors have also changed: Japanese investments in the region, that were overwhelmingly dominant in the seventies and eighties, have dwindled as a consequence of prolonged economic recession in Japan. Meanwhile, investments from the USA and Europe have surged to take advantage of the weakening position of Japan. The changing nature of foreign direct investment can also be noticed in the move from greenfield investment to cross-border mergers and acquisitions, which have become the dominant form of foreign entry in the post-Asian financial crisis era. Lastly, the sectoral composition of these capital inflows has changed, with a rise of investments in the service sector and a decline of investments in the manufacturing sector. The chapter explores the implications of these changes on the domestic economic conditions of Asian recipient countries. According to Kim's view, foreign direct investment is supportive of strong (or supposedly strong) sectors, such as electronics-related industries, and weak sectors, such as banking and finance. But it is also worth noticing that the industrial organization is changing, from the 'full-set' industrial structure, which was the trade mark of Japanese style industrial organization before the financial crisis, to the so-called 'network type' of Western organization. Another positive consequence of the increase in foreign direct investment to Asian economies is the strengthening of financial stability in the regional area, as FDI has proved to be more stable than other types of financial flows. Finally, a third beneficial effect is characteristic of foreign direct investment: its positive influence on the dynamics of Korean domestic investment.

Chapter 11, by N. Aminian, depicts foreign direct investment as a major factor in Asian regional development and focuses more specifically on the link between FDI and growth. What the theory has to say about the contribution of FDI to growth is generally positive, the author recalls: FDI is supposed to enhance economic growth in the host country through two main channels, the diffusion of technology and the accumulation of capital. However, empirical studies have so far led to more balanced conclusions: the effects of FDI on recipient countries are not always positive, and may often be negative. The study presented in this chapter tries to challenge the diverging conclusions of the empirical literature about the true effects of capital inflows. It examines the long run impact of FDI on domestic investment and economic growth in selected East Asian economies over the period 1979–1999. Causality tests between FDI and real domestic variables are also part of the picture and they suggest that a strong association exists between the two sets of variables.

But the author's results do not support the theoretical claim that FDI inflows *per se* accelerate economic growth. FDI does not seem robustly linked with economic growth. FDI is associated with domestic investment, especially in the 1980s. But this tendency weakens in the 1990s. Various factors have weakened the link between FDI and domestic investment in the 1990s; among them the author mentions the rise in integration of international markets, which distends the link between domestic savings and investment decisions, and the growing importance of cross-border mergers and acquisitions in the total volume of foreign direct investment.

Chapter 12, by Y.-I. Lee, offers an original case study about South Korea as a FDI recipient country. One original feature of this chapter comes from the author's 'political economic' approach: a strong emphasis is put on the role of domestic political structures in shaping policy implementation and, ultimately, determining economic growth. The theoretical background of this chapter is that economic development and performances are the results of a conscious State choice to achieve economic and political objectives, rather than the result of market forces. This seems an appropriate hypothesis for dealing with the Korean example, if one considers the overwhelming role that the State has traditionally played in economic structures and policy in this country. This also offers up an interesting starting point for revisiting explanations of the Korean financial crisis with original arguments: the author expresses the view that the crisis was the unexpected result of a rapid growth in which various but detrimental factors were embedded in the institutions that stimulated growth.

This background is helpful to a good understanding of the results of the survey presented in the second part of the chapter, and which is an investigation into the features of the past and present Korean market environment as seen by major multinational investors. This empirical study is based on extensive survey work, including over 80 face to face interviews with senior executives of multinational corporations. In contrast to the pre-crisis period, the post-97 era contributed to the change in the Korean market image among multinational corporations. In 1998, Korea was ranked as the least favourable destination among Asian countries in which to invest, the complex and difficult procedure with bureaucracy and the strong nationalism being major barriers which foreign investors had to face. Since then, the perception of market opportunities (size and potential of the Korean economy), the ongoing and progressive process of deregulation and restructuring, have stimulated favourable decisions to acquire or locate productive assets in Korea. This helps to explain the revival of FDI in this country from 1997 onwards (also studied by Kim in Chapter 10).

With F. Nicolas's Chapter 13, we turn to the relation between FDI and foreign exchange related factors. Can exchange rate policy help in reviving FDI inflows? How could such policies be coordinated at a regional level? Chapter 13 sheds light on these issues in the case of ASEAN countries. The author starts by recalling in general terms the various ways in which exchange rates affect FDI inflows. According to the literature, the impact of a real depreciation of the host country's currency is theoretically indeterminate. This is also the case when exchange rate volatility and uncertainty are observed: they may both stimulate and hinder FDI, depending on the location and the orientation of FDI. Finally, the literature does not provide any clear-cut conclusion: the direction of foreign exchange impact on FDI inflows, as well as the channels through which it operates, are ambiguous both theoretically and empirically. Nevertheless, general policy implications can be drawn from the literature survey: as far as exchange rate levels are concerned, the policy recommendation for a FDI-seeking economy would be to avoid a real appreciation as a primary objective. But with regard to exchange rate volatility, the implications are not as clear-cut: an optimal exchange regime depends very much on the kind of FDI a country is willing to attract.

When considering FDI to ASEAN countries, empirical evidence shows that Japanese FDI is strongly affected by changes in real bilateral exchange rates, while this is not the case for FDI from the USA. Also, exchange rate policies adopted by ASEAN countries during the pre-crisis period were not absolutely identical, all of them followed a de facto nominal peg to the dollar. The depreciation of the host countries' currencies with respect to the yen, coupled with the appreciation of the yen with respect to the dollar, led to an increase in Japanese FDI in South East Asia.

Attracting FDI inflows has always ranked high in the priority list of ASEAN governments, and the choice of an exchange rate regime is not neutral, although not determined exclusively by the authorities' desire to stimulate FDI inflows. The major policy implication from the literature reviewed in this chapter is that an exchange rate strategy allowing governments to preserve competitiveness while minimizing nominal volatility could be instrumental in luring foreign investors. The author's opinion is that pegging to a basket of currencies would be the best choice for the countries in the region, given their relatively balanced but complex set of partners. And a common exchange rate policy could be an optimal choice in order to avoid the risk of beggar-my-neighbour strategies. The author concludes by stressing the importance of regional cooperation in the monetary sphere, the consistency of this policy being more important than the type of exchange rate policy that could come out of the cooperation.

In the third part of this volume, international trade and investment issues are approached through their impact on regional economic integration. Two chapters illustrate this topic in the European context and four chapters are drawn from analyses of East Asian experiences. Chapter 14 by J. Dias analyses some of the effects of economic integration of the Iberian peninsula on the trade relations between Portugal and Spain. Owing to the teaching of the 'New economic geography', this study stresses the importance of spatial factors for the understanding of trade relations between Portugal and Spain. These relations have changed radically since 1986, when the two countries joined the European Community, starting from an abnormal and insignificant level of bilateral trade to the present situation, where Portugal and Spain are important commercial partners. For Portugal, which was before a rather insulated domestic market, EU membership particularly favoured the normalization of trade relations with Spain.

Generally speaking, a well-known consequence of economic integration is the promotion of specialization not between industries but within industries. The ongoing integration of the two Iberian economies confirms this tendency, with still an important share of inter-industry trade. This chapter proposes an application of a gravity-type equation, which explains the relations between any two countries as a function of some forces of attraction and repulsion. A model is estimated, in the spirit of this gravity equation, and applied to trade between forty-seven provinces of Continental Spain and Portugal. According to the author's conclusions, some of the forces described by the New economic geography concerning the location of economic activity in the Iberian peninsula are apparent. Some of them tend to concentrate production in Spain and may lead to the marginalization of Portugal (or large areas in both countries) in terms of industrial activity. However, there are also institutional forces in motion to counteract the purely economic ones, tending to impose a more even distribution of population and economic activity over the Iberian space. An important aspect of this institutional intervention is the slow but persistent integration of the neighbouring regions from both sides and the operation of distance in an economically consistent way. As a result of the operation of both types of forces, the Iberian territory has reached a reasonably high degree of integration, in particular at the regional level.

Chapter 15, by C. Jensen, analyses the ongoing real integration through trade and FDI between the EU and Central and Eastern European (CEE) countries. Focus is placed on changes in the content and competitiveness of trade since 1993 from the viewpoint of CEE host countries. Since FDI has been a major factor behind firm restructuring in the region, cross-border intra-firm trade with EU home activities is expected to have played a dominant role in shaping bilateral trade. This chapter discusses how motivations for FDI and the factors behind intra-firm trade may be related. The analysis of the contents of trade confirms that considerable upgrading has taken place in bilateral trade, both in terms of structure (increasing shares of manufactured exports) and through reduction of price–quality gaps.

Upgrading is often to be associated with subsidiaries where technology and marketing resources are created in the subsidiary, since this may result in global product mandates emanating from the CEE region. With the model applied in this chapter it is found that a positive relationship exists between FDI increases and the bilateral shares of manufactured exports, and a negative relationship between FDI and bilateral terms of trade and trade balances. On the other hand, the results suggest little causal link between quality upgrading and FDI.

In Chapter 16, Y.-I. Park analyses the changing pattern of intra-regional trade in Northeast Asia and aims at explaining the source of the rapid growth of bilateral trade between Korea, Japan and China. Three broad sets of factors are generally stressed for explaining intra-regional trade: the increase in the region's share in world trade; the underlying complementarity between the commodity structures of regional countries' global trade; and the differential degree of trade resistances between trading routes, causing trade diversion. Lee's Chapter 12 confirms that these factors have played their role in the increase of intra-regional trade in Northeast Asia.

The study is based on the 'intensity approach' and emphasizes those trade resistances which cause a diversion between trading routes, which is more frequent in a multi-country real world. The author uses the intensity approach and focuses on two elements: trade potentials resulting from the commodity composition of each country's global trade in the absence of trade resistances, and the deviation of effective trade from potential trade resulting from the differential degree of trade resistances. The study provides an in-depth analysis of the changing pattern of trade specialization of Japan, Korea and China over the last twenty years and highlights the greater interdependence of industrial structures among these countries. The author measures the increasing trade intensity between these trading partners, by calculating trade intensity indexes, complementary indexes and country-bias indexes. The study interestingly shows that complementarity in intra-regional trade is high, although these three countries have a comparative advantage in the manufacturing sector, and hence are potentially competitors against each other. Lee's analysis shows also how imbalances in bilateral trade are netted out in the intra-regional framework: bilateral imbalance is favourable to Japan in Korea–Japan trade, favourable to Korea in Korea–China trade and favourable to China in China–Japan trade.

In Chapter 17, J.-H. Ko and J. D. Lim simulate the potential economic effects of a free trade agreement between Korea and Singapore. Korea is one of the very few world major trading partners to have so far stayed apart from significant regional economic arrangements, but is on the verge of joining the global trend in forming regional trade blocs. For the purpose of their study, the authors use a multi-region and multi-sector computable general equilibrium (CGE) model. This model is a standard one, depicting the behaviour of firms, private households, governments and global sectors across each region in the world. The application consists in selecting three regions (Korea, Singapore and the rest of the world) that are linked through international trade, and 26 economic sectors. Nine different scenarios are examined to capture the static and dynamic effect of a Korea–Singapore free trade area. Compared to static effects (changes of allocative efficiency) caused by tariff elimination as a result of the establishment of the free trade area, dynamic effects (changes in productive capacity) are projected to be much larger in terms of bilateral trade, trade balance, per capita utility, equivalent variation (i.e., change in welfare level converted into income change) and real GDP.

The authors explain the mechanism by which an increase in total factor productivity creates such positive dynamic effects on economic growth as follows: a Korea–Singapore free trade area can generate an investment expansion effect, as firms will increase new investment to gain further access to regional markets after tariff elimination and shift their production facilities from non-member countries to member states according to the existence of preferential rules of origin. A comprehensive free trade agreement, which includes investment protection clauses, investment liberalization measures and a dispute settlement mechanism, will make trade liberalization policies internationally binding and thus enhance investors' confidence and profitability in the partners' investment environment, thereby resulting in an expansion of intra-regional investment. In the long run, the economic growth to be achieved by a Korea–Singapore free trade agreement will increase the competitiveness of firms and enable the more efficient allocation of resources, thus stimulating further investment in both economies. In assessing the economic impact of the FTA, the authors draw attention to the long-run dynamic effects and recommend securing strong impetus for the pursuit of the FTA. They advise both economies to seek the means by which to achieve closer cooperation and coordination in the highly competitive structures of their industries.

In Chapter 18, C.-M. Hsu and W.-C. Liu connect the FDI logic to the debate on regional integration. They examine first the allocation of FDI flows to the East Asian region among Southeast Asian countries and China. The authors particularly emphasize the Taiwanese case, since Taiwan has been one of the main FDI contributors in this region. Taiwanese firms started to make substantial direct investment in Southeast Asia in 1980 and in China in 1991. Firms that invest abroad are mostly small and medium sized ones, and their competitive edge relies on their ability to achieve small scale and flexible production. The chapter investigates also the role of public policy and private firms during the foreign direct investment process in the 1990s.

The authors show the dynamics of the FDI industry types during the 1990s. It appears that FDI is a major vehicle for economic integration between Taiwan and China. The driving force of economic integration between Taiwan and China is technology rather than public policy. This trade integration will be accelerated by World Trade Organization agreements in the future, and by the relaxation of limits of Taiwanese investment in China. The originality of Hsu and Liu's chapter is to shed light on the effects of FDI on the home country. The Taiwanese case is particularly relevant as, the authors say, in this country FDI may be suspected of exerting adverse effects on domestic production and investment and hollowing-out Taiwanese industries. The authors run regressions to check the complementary or substitution effect of Taiwanese FDI. The conclusion is that FDI has little substitution effect on domestic investment.

Chapter 19 concludes the volume and broadens the overall reflexion on economic integration and multinational investment behaviour with an overview of the problems and prospects of regional integration in Northeast Asia (Japan, China, South and North Korea). In this last chapter, D.-C. Suh stresses first the singularity of Northeast Asia, which has up to now kept away from the proliferation of regional integration arrangements on the global scene.

According to Suh, there has been no serious attempt at institutional integration in the region. The main reason for this was the lack of political consensus on the necessity of integration, a pre-condition for establishing regional economic arrangements according to most writers. Economic factors such as the diversity of economic systems and ideologies, the structure of industry and trade, and informal barriers to trade were also obstructions. The author then points out the significant changes that have recently taken place in the region's political economy. The East Asian economic crisis had an impact on the market integration, one of the aspects of this impact being, according to Suh, that countries realized that the IMF and USA were powerless in crisis prevention and management, which in turn awakened regionalism and provided a powerful rationale for institutional cooperation in the wake of the crisis.

Recent changes have also come from the improvement in North–South relations in the Korean peninsular since the North–South summit of June 2000, from China's entry into the World Trade Organization in 2001 and the fact that the Japanese economy is moving towards a closer integration with the Asian economies. But Suh also points out that the change of US policy towards Asian integration is still to come – the USA being suspicious of any strengthening of Asia's institutional autonomy, that would favour a move from a two-bloc towards a three-bloc world. The chapter concludes by considering prospects for regional integration in Northeast Asia. Although there may be a growing optimism that institutional integration can be launched, the prospects are still uncertain. The uncertainties about North–South Korean reconciliation and the absence of regional political leadership are negative factors. Suh considers that forming a free trade agreement between countries in Northeast Asia would bring poor economic gains. On the contrary, physical rather than trade integration is the most promising area of cooperation, for instance in the field of infrastructure (regional transportation and the physical distribution network).

REFERENCES

Aoki, M. (1990), 'Toward an economic model of the Japanese firm', *Journal of Economic Literature*, **28** (1), 1–27.

PART I

Location Decisions and the Global Performance of Firms

2. Foreign Direct Investment and Intellectual Property Rights: Evidence from French Multinationals' Location Decisions

Thierry Mayer and Etienne Pfister

INTRODUCTION

How the protection of intellectual property rights (IPRs) may influence the location choices of transnational firms is a relatively recent research field, mainly stirred by the implementation of the Trade Related Intellectual Property Rights (TRIPs) agreement. Signed in 1994 under the auspices of the World Trade Organization (WTO), this agreement forces each member to implement and enforce minimum standards of IPR protection. While it may not bring forth any significant reform in most industrialized countries, drastic changes are to be introduced in most developing countries.

Indeed, until very recently, most developing countries did not have any legislation regarding the protection of patents, trademarks and their likes. The lack of protection allowed these economies to imitate, as long as their own technological capacities were up to that task, products and processes that were still under protection in industrialized countries. For some economies, imitation permitted an industrialization of some sort (Vaitsos, 1971): the Indian and Brazilian pharmaceutical industries, as well as the textile industry in Turkey or Asia, are examples of such industrialization by imitation (*The Economist*, 1999, 2000; Commission Européenne, 1998).

For developing countries, the impact of this strengthening in IPR protection remains hard to assess. The price increases that may follow the implementation of patent protection remain hard to assess, as both product and industry characteristics interact to either minimize or maximize the market power of the patent/trademark holder. For pharmaceutical products, which have attracted most of the empirical work so far, Maskus and Eby-Konan (1994) mention price increases ranging from 2 per cent (if patent protection does not yield great market power) up to 60 per cent (if the patent holder can act like a monopolist). Corresponding deadweight losses range from $110 million for Argentina to more than $2 billion for India[1].

These losses should ideally be compared to the dynamic gains stemming from an increase in the innovation rate and, more specifically, from an increase in the number of therapies targeting diseases specific to developing countries. Of the 132 development projects currently sponsored in pharmaceutical firms, only eight focus on diseases specific to developing countries (Lanjouw and Cockburn, 2000). A strengthening of IPR protection in these countries may encourage greater R&D efforts being devoted to these diseases, although the effect remains theoretically ambiguous (Helpman, 1993). Yet, only few empirical studies have established a convincing relationship between patent reforms and innovation efforts (Kortum and Lerner, 1999; Sakikabara and Branstetter, 2001). Arguably, there have been only few remarkable patent reforms susceptible to modifying innovation strategies and estimating this relationship poses several econometric problems (Jaffe, 2000). As Lanjouw (1998) and Lanjouw and Cockburn (2000) point out, in the case of the TRIPs agreement, there is some evidence of a change in attitude of pharmaceutical firms from both developed and developing countries. As they point out, however, this evidence remains suggestive at best and should be further examined once firms have assessed which opportunities the promotion of IPR protection will really yield. In any case, the low revenues of these countries and the near absence of an insurance system probably limit the extent of revenues that might be earned through greater patent protection.

Given these limitations, the study of the dynamic impact of the TRIPs agreement has shifted from innovation incentives to the patterns of trade and foreign direct investment (FDI). The supporters of the TRIPs agreement have long stressed that in making imitation more costly, stronger IPR laws will encourage inflows of goods and capital. Following Lai (1998), Markusen (2001) and others, firms may prefer FDI to trade as the risks of imitation decrease and as the costs of FDI decrease. Further strengthening of IPR laws may finally lead firms to substitute licensing for FDI, as market-based contracts such as technology licensing are better enforced (Fosfuri, 2000). The jobs and spillovers associated with trade, FDI and licensing may then compensate developing economies for the deadweight loss associated with price increases. Moreover, several theoretical models (Helpman, 1993; Lai, 1998) have stressed that the impact of stronger IPR laws is not without influence on its impact towards innovation: basically, stronger IPR laws will stimulate innovation more if they are also associated with productivity gains, materialized, for instance, through FDI or licensing.

There are, however, several counterarguments to this story, as many examples tend to demonstrate. Maskus and Penubarti (1995) indicate that in the 1980s, the investment by pharmaceutical firms in Brazil and India exceeded $700 million (against exports of only $50 million) even though these countries regrouped the most competitive pirating firms. Indeed, FDI can be a weapon against imitators. Therefore, an increase in IPR protection may also tilt the trade-off between exports and FDI towards exports.

More generally, the real question regarding the relationship between IPR protection and FDI hinges more on its existence than merely on its sign. First, the above stories implicitly assume that imitating a product/process is easier when the firm is located near in the same country - as the potential imitator. It remains uncertain whether this assumption bears any empirical relevance, at least in the case of product innovations. Second, R&D units are seldom international and especially not in developing countries which often do not have the necessary required competences to make the good. Finally, IPR protection will only matter when the potential host countries have the ability to imitate the good.

This chapter seeks to assess the empirical relevance of these arguments. There are only few empirical studies that have considered this relationship before. Lee and Mansfield (1996) consider the flows of FDI in 14 emerging countries (mainly from South America or South East Asia) and find a positive correlation between these flows and the strength of IPR protection in these host countries. Similarly, for these 14 countries, the technological intensity of the investments made by American chemical firms increases with IPR strength. Maskus (1998) pursues these conclusions by showing that IPR protection matters only for developing countries, not for developed economies. These encouraging results are somewhat contradicted by Kumar (1996), who considers the R&D intensity of FDI. He finds that it bears no significant relationship to IPR strength in developing countries, though it does so for developed economies. As he suggests, the investments made in these countries may be essentially incremental and therefore relatively insensitive to patent protection.

This chapter introduces two distinct dimensions. First, it considers individual location choices rather than aggregated FDI inflows. Second, it tries to distinguish what stems from IPR protection itself from what may stem from other parameters of the host country, possibly correlated with IPR protection, such as corruption, R&D intensity or political freedom. As Ginarte and Park (1998) and Lerner (2000) have demonstrated, patent protection is essentially endogeneous to the development level attained by the country. An economy with a high R&D capital generally promotes innovation. Similarly, economic and political freedom are correlated with patent protection because a patent protects the rights of an individual relative to those of the community or of the State. Clearly, the omission of such parameters would result in a specification bias, as the role played by IPR would be overestimated.

The next section presents our dataset as well as the variables that have been assembled to assess the impact of IPR protection on location choices and the econometric procedure we use. The following section presents and discusses the results.

DATASET, VARIABLES AND ECONOMETRIC PROCEDURE

A Dataset on Location Choices

We consider the determinants of 755 location choices by French multinationals in 37 countries during the years 1981, 1982 and 1988–1992[2]. A conditional logit is used to analyse the choice of country j at date k among all other possible locations. Formally, location j among the 36 other countries generates a profit π_j depending on the set of variables U_j with $U_j = [\ln X_{j1},\ldots, \ln X_{jk}]$ denoting the vector of the observable characteristics (X) of location j. Thus, we can write:

$$\pi_j = bU_j + \epsilon_j \tag{2.1}$$

where b denotes a vector of coefficients to be estimated and ϵ_j the inobservable advantage of location j. The probability that country j is chosen is:

$$P_j \equiv \text{Prob}(\pi_j > \pi_l) = \text{Prob}(\epsilon_l < \epsilon_j + U_j - U_l) \ \forall l \neq j \tag{2.2}$$

When the error terms are distributed according to a double exponential law, we obtain a logit-like probability:

$$P_j = \frac{e^{bU_j}}{\sum_{i=1}^{37} e^{bU_i}}$$

The coefficient associated with each of the variables is estimated by maximum likelihood. The independent variables as well as the expected sign of their coefficient are discussed below.

The Independent Variables

Potential demand is measured by the GDP of the host country (*GDP*). The higher the demand, the more a firm should locate in this country. Conversely, the higher the production costs in this country, the less likely it is that this country gets chosen. Because we did not get production costs for most developing countries, we use a consumption price index (*PC*) as a proxy. The openness of the host country (*OPEN*) is measured through the sum of its exports and imports divided by its GDP. Openness exerts an ambiguous influence on location choices. On the one hand, it can stimulate FDI because the country is well inserted into international trade flows. On the other hand, tariff and non-tariff barriers could stimulate tariff-jumping FDI. Previous empirical results do reflect this ambiguity: Wheeler and Mody (1992) find a negative impact of openness on FDI while Kumar (1996) and Maskus (1998) conclude a positive impact. A dummy indicating whether the country belongs to the European Union is also used (*UE*): French firms are probably more prone to locate in markets that are politically, culturally and economically close to their home one. To assess potential agglomeration or dispersion effects, we use the DREE dataset to calculate the number of firms of the same industry that are already located in the host country under consideration. We distinguish firms from the same group and competitors. Most studies (Wheeler and Mody, 1992; Mayer and Mucchielli, 1999) have outlined the existence of agglomeration effects, but from a theoretical standpoint, dispersion remains possible if competition increases strongly with proximity.

Our regressions also include the development level of the host country (either GDP per capita, *GDP/c*, or a dummy variable, *LDC*, indicating whether the host country is a developing economy), R&D intensity and secondary school attainment (*EDUC*). These variables are used for two reasons. First, location choices may well depend on the development level of the host country and on its technological/human capital. Second, these variables are necessary to check the influence exerted by intellectual property rights. Indeed, several studies (Maskus, 1998; Ginarte and Park, 1998; Lerner, 2000) have outlined the possible link between development and IPR protection.

With few exceptions, most studies conducted on the impact of IPR protection on trade and/or FDI rely on the indexes developed by Rapp and Rozek (1990) and Ginarte and Park (1998) (hereafter, G&P). Noteworthy enough, these indexes are not meant to evaluate the effectiveness of IPR protection. First, they only consider patent protection. Second, they are based on the laws rather than on how these laws are enforced. However, patent, trademark and copyright laws are usually linked one to the other. Also, G&P note that, so far, firms complain more about the absence of laws than about how these laws are enforced[3]. The G&P index has been preferred to the Rapp and Rozek one as it considers a higher number of countries and years and because its evaluation of patent law is based on a continuous scale (rather than dummy indexes). This entails a greater variability across countries. The G&P index ranges from 0 (low protection) to 5 (strong protection).

Several studies have stressed the link between economic and political freedom and IPR protection. As we shall see, it is indeed crucial to integrate these dimensions in order not to overestimate the impact of patent protection in developing countries. We measure economic freedom through a corruption index (*CORP*) built by *Transparency International*, an international consultancy that measures and fights corruption the world over. Established for 99 countries and ranging from 0 (least corrupt) to 10 (most corrupt), this index is built through 17 different polls and ten different surveys by ten independent institutions. Finally, we measure political freedom (*POL*) through an index of the World Bank which ranges from 0 (no freedom) to 6 (large freedom)[4]. A country where corruption is high and where political freedom is weak should receive less investment[5].

Table 2.1 summarizes our variables, their sources as well as the expected signs of their coefficients.

Tables 2.2 and 2.3 present the descriptive statistics of each of these variables and the correlation matrix, respectively. For developing countries, the variables *POL*, *EDUC* and *RD/GDP* could only be gathered sporadically. To get a significant sample, each available year was used for the two preceding and the two subsequent years. Also, the corruption index used for the years 1981–1982 is the mean of this index for years 1980–1985; the index used for the years 1988–1992 is the mean of these indexes for years 1988–1992 (yearly indexes were unavailable). The correlation matrix points to strong correlations between GDP per capita, consumption prices, R&D intensity, secondary school attainment, political freedom, corruption and IPR protection. All the variables are used in log forms.

The correlation matrix in Table 2.3 raises the question of the multicollinearity of our variables. The value inflation factors calculated for the baseline model indeed reveal that the GDP per capita is a linear approximation of the other variables in the model (Table 2.4). To overcome this problem, we will use two sets of regressions: in the first one, the variable *GDP/c* is maintained. In the other one, we substitute a dummy variable

Table 2.1 Variables

Variable	Definition	Source	Expected impact
NC	Number of French competitors already located in the host country	DREE	?
NG	Number of affiliates from the same group already located in the host country	DREE	?
OPEN	Openness to trade	Pennworld	?
GDP	Host country GDP	Chelem	+
PC	Consumption price index	Pennworld	–
GDP/c	GDP per capita	Chelem	+
UE	Dummy variable –1 if the host country belongs to the European Union		+
RD/GDP	Research investment/GDP ratio	UNESCO	?
EDUC	Secondary education enrollment rate	World Bank; Barro and Lee (1994)	?
IPR	Index of patent strength	Ginarte and Park (1998)	?
POL	Index of political rights	World Bank	+
CORP	Index of corruption	Transparency International	–

Table 2.2 Summary statistics

Variable	Mean	Standard deviation	Min.	Max.
DEPVAR	0.020	0.142	0	1
NC	0.923	2.042	0	26
NG	0.202	0.676	0	13
OPEN	66.985	61.358	12.66	412.76
GDP	486129	952358.2	28292	565.200
GDP/c	10.249	8.946	0.261	29.904
PC	78.80	40.96	19.60	170.91
EDUC	0.669	0.278	0.04	1
RD/GDP	1.107	0.819	0.090	3.20
CORP	4.469	2.775	0.7	9.8
POL	4.701	1.811	0	6
IPR	2.805	1.017	0.33	4.523

indicating whether the host country is a developing country or a developed one (*LDC*). In this latter case, as Table 2.5 demonstrates, the risk of multicollinearity is sufficiently low to be neglected.

Table 2.3 Correlation matrix

Variable	*DEPVAR*	*NC*	*NG*	*OPEN*	*GDP*	*PC*	*GDP/c*	*RD/GDP*	*EDUC*	*POL*	*CORP*	IPR
DEPVAR	1.000											
NC	0.122	1.000										
NG	0.103	0.231	1.000									
OPEN	–0.21	0.044	–0.028	1.000								
GDP	0.191	0.466	0.316	–0.257	1.000							
PC	0.056	0.193	0.130	0.064	0.164	1.000						
GDP/c	0.076	0.255	0.175	0.074	0.0274	0.871	1.000					
RD/GDP	0.104	0.279	0.190	–0.057	0.459	0.791	0.827	1.000				
EDUC	0.077	0.239	0.154	0.100	0.221	0.782	0.802	0.646	1.000			
POL	0.075	0.216	0.128	–0.160	0.174	–0.638	–0.611	0.419	0.588	1.000		
CORP	–0.059	–0.151	–0.104	–0.310	–0.102	–0.796	–0.788	–0.679	–0.737	–0.577	1.000	
IPR	0.099	0.311	0.197	0.076	0.309	0.764	0.733	0.765	0.645	–0.374	–0.704	1.000

Table 2.4 Variance inflation (VIF)

Variable	VIF
GDP/c	23.32
PC	16.27
CORP	5.50
POL	4.04
EDUC	3.44
RD/GDP	3.30
OPEN	3.21
GDP	3.00
IPR	2.86
UE	1.63
NC	1.37
NG	1.12
VIF mean	5.75

Table 2.5 Variance inflation (VIF)

Variable	VIF
GDP/c	6.18
PC	4.74
CORP	3.86
POL	3.57
EDUC	3.54
RD/GDP	3.04
OPEN	2.82
GDP	2.78
IPR	2.50
UE	1.72
NC	1.37
NG	1.12
VIF mean	3.12

However, this variable is probably less satisfying to assess the development level of a country. Therefore, we expect some of the other variables, which may probably be correlated with this one, to be significant in one model but not necessarily in the other.

RESULTS

The Baseline Model

The model (a) in Tables 2.6 and 2.7 considers the traditional determinants of location choices. Table 2.6 uses the GDP per capita as an approximation of the development level. Market size, openness, GDP per capita and belonging

Table 2.6 Location choices (variable GDP/c)

	Dependent variable: chosen country					
Model	(a)	(b)	(c)	(d)	(e)	(f)
NC	0.24***	0.22***	0.24***	0.27***	0.23***	0.24***
	(0.07)	(0.07)	(0.07)	(0.07)	(0.07)	(0.07)
NG	0.30***	0.30***	0.29***	0.33***	0.30***	0.32***
	(0.10)	(0.10)	(0.10)	(0.10)	(0.10)	(0.10)
OPEN	0.27**	0.51***	0.26**	0.42***	0.52***	0.58***
	(0.12)	(0.15)	(0.12)	(0.13)	(0.15)	(0.15)
GDP	0.62***	0.85***	0.61***	0.73***	0.86***	0.89***
	(0.07)	(0.08)	(0.07)	(0.08)	(0.09)	(0.09)
PC	−1.97***	−1.19***	−2.04***	−1.59***	−1.13***	−1.01**
	(0.37)	(0.40)	(0.38)	(0.41)	(0.42)	(0.43)
GDP/c	1.16***	0.63***	1.16***	1.01***	0.62***	0.61***
	(0.18)	(0.21)	(0.18)	(0.19)	(0.21)	(0.21)
UE	0.75***	0.66***	0.75***	0.73***	0.66***	0.65***
	(0.10)	(0.11)	(0.10)	(0.09)	(0.11)	(0.11)
RD/GDP	−0.02	−0.45***	−0.03	0.01	−0.46***	−0.38***
	(0.10)	(0.11)	(0.10)	(0.09)	(0.11)	(0.11)
EDUC	−0.15	−0.44**	−0.16	−0.15	−0.44**	−0.40*
	(0.20)	(0.21)	(0.20)	(0.20)	(0.21)	(0.21)
CORP		−1.01***			−1.04***	−0.89***
		(0.23)			(0.24)	(0.25)
POL		0.82***			0.83***	0.75***
		(0.26)			(0.26)	(0.26)
IPR			0.14	0.61*	−0.10	0.21
			(0.19)	(0.33)	(0.22)	(0.33)
IPRSQ				−0.56***		−0.30
				(0.19)		(0.19)
N	25688	25688	25688	25688	25688	
R^2	0.191	0.196	1.191	0.193	1.196	0.196

Note: Standard errors in parentheses. ***, ** and * denote the 1%, 5% and 10% levels of significance, respectively.

Table 2.7 Location choices (variable LDC)

	Dependent variable: chosen country					
Model:	(a)	(b)	(c)	(d)	(e)	(f)
NC	0.30***	0.23***	0.30***	0.33***	0.24***	0.26***
	(0.07)	(0.07)	(0.07)	(0.07)	(0.07)	(0.07)
NG	0.34***	0.30***	0.34***	0.38***	0.31***	0.33***
	(0.10)	(0.10)	(0.10)	(0.10)	(0.10)	(0.10)
OPEN	0.59***	0.81***	0.57***	0.79***	0.84***	0.90***
	(0.13)	(0.14)	(0.13)	(0.14)	(0.15)	(0.15)
GDP	0.80***	1.02***	0.79****	0.95***	1.04***	1.08***
	(0.07)	(0.08)	(0.07)	(0.09)	(0.08)	(0.09)
PC	0.03	–0.08	–0.04	0.30	0.02	0.13
	(0.21)	(0.20)	(0.22)	(0.24)	(0.23)	(0.24)
LDC	–0.05	0.15	–0.06	–0.02	0.17	0.16
	(0.17)	(0.18)	(0.17)	(0.18)	(0.19)	(0.19)
UE	0.61***	0.52***	0.61***	0.61***	0.53***	0.53***
	(0.09)	(0.11)	(0.09)	(0.09)	(0.11)	(0.11)
RD/GDP	–0.07	–0.55***	–0.09	–0.02	–0.55***	–0.48***
	(0.10)	(0.13)	(0.10)	(0.10)	(0.13)	(0.13)
EDUC	0.46**	–0.30	0.43**	0.33*	–0.31	–0.27
	(0.18)	(0.20)	(0.18)	(0.18)	(0.20)	(0.20)
CORP		–1.25***			–1.30***	–1.16***
		(0.22)			(0.23)	(0.24)
POL		1.18***			1.17***	1.08***
		(0.24)			(0.24)	(0.25)
IPR			0.16	0.63**	–0.20	0.09
			(0.17)	(0.30)	(0.22)	(0.32)
IPRSQ			–0.72***			–0.30
			(0.17)			(0.19)
N	25688	25688	25688	25688	25688	25688
R^2	0.182	0.194	0.1822	0.186	0.194	0.195

Note: Standard errors in parentheses. ***, ** and * denote the 1%, 5% and 10% levels of significance, respectively.

to the European Union exert a positive influence on the probability of locating in a given country. Conversely, high consumption prices deter location. Neither the education level, nor the R&D intensity, appear to have a significant impact on the probability of location. The agglomeration variables also display the usual positive signs, thus reflecting the strong propensity of firms to locate in countries where firms of the same industry (be they firms from the same group or competitors) also locate. The model (a) of Table 2.7 substitutes a dummy variable indicating whether the host country is a developed (= 0) or a developing economy (= 1). This change induces an increase in the coefficients of the openness and market size variables. Education now reaches the 5 per cent level of significance. Finally, the price consumption index is no longer significant. As development is less precisely measured by the dummy variable than by GDP per capita, the variables that are positively correlated with the development level gain more weight[6].

Introducing the corruption and political freedom indexes somewhat alters these results (model (b), Tables 2.6 and 2.7). Both coefficients are of the expected sign, negative and positive respectively, and are significant at the 1 per cent level of significance. They are also higher when the development level of the host country is measured through the dummy variable (Table 2.7). Also note that in Table 2.6, the coefficient associated with the development level is almost halved compared to model (a). The R&D intensity and the education level are both negative and significant, at the 1 and 5 per cent level of significance respectively. Similar modifications are to be noted in Table 2.7: the R&D intensity is negative and significant, the education level is no longer significant. Therefore, a significant part of the influence of these variables was to be attributed to the absence, in model (a), of the corruption and political freedom indexes.

Models (c) and (d) of Tables 2.6 and 2.7 reveal that, when *CORP* and *POL* are omitted from the regressions, there is a non-linear relationship between IPR protection and location probability: the *IPR* variable as well as *IPRSQR* (the square of the variable *IPR*) are significant at the 10 and 1 per cent level of significance, respectively. More precisely, the probability of location increases up to a threshold of 1.71; it decreases thereafter. Admittedly, one interpretation of this result could be the following: an intermediary level of patent protection encourages foreign firms to locate in a country, but it still deters them from licensing their technologies to this country. Only when the patent protection regime is strong enough does this effect come into play and licensing tend to substitute to FDI. These results are also coherent with those obtained by Yang and Maskus (2001) regarding licensing fees: they concluded that licensing fees tend to increase once patent protection exceeds a certain threshold.

Note first that this positive impact would be relevant for only a minority of countries, such as India, Mexico, Columbia, Venezuala or Indonesia. But more importantly, the influence exerted by IPR protection is no longer significant once the corruption and political rights index are included in the regressions (models (e) and (f)). Substituting the variable *LDC* for *GDP/c* does not greatly alter these results. Absent corruption and political freedom, IPR protection exerts a non-linear influence on the probability of location. The positive influence is stronger than before and the threshold now stands at 1.55. But again, introducing the *CORP* and *POL* variables reduces this influence to insignificance.

The following subsections attempt to deepen this preliminary analysis first by distinguishing patent sensitive and insensitive industries. In a second step, we separate technologically able countries from those less likely to have the technological knowledge needed to imitate.

Patent Protection and Foreign Direct Investment on a By-Industry Basis

As all business surveys made in the last 20 years tend to demonstrate, the effectiveness of patents in deterring imitators varies greatly across industries. Generally, they are even rated as less effective than 'economic' (as opposed to legislative) appropriation strategies such as lead-time or secrecy[7]. Therefore, the use of patents, and by extension of other IPRs, varies greatly across industries. We would naturally expect patent protection to matter mostly in those industries where patents are considered as a tool against imitators.

To distinguish patent sensitive from patent insensitive industries, we use the SESSI dataset on the firms' patent propensities. This survey, conducted on 2000 firms, asks firms what percentage of their innovation they choose to patent. The more effective the patent, the higher the rate of patenting. We use the mean patent propensity (products and process innovations) for each of our 16 industries. The median patent propensity is 25 per cent, so that all industries with patent propensity of more (resp. less) than 25 per cent are considered as patent sensitive (resp. patent insensitive). In the former group, we find, in descending order, electrical and electronic equipment, cars, cosmetics and drugs, transport equipment, electric and electronic components, household equipment, steel, utilities and oil refineries. The latter group comprises, in descending order, mechanical equipment, chemicals and plastics, publishing and printing, wood and paper, textile and leather, and clothes.

Tables 2.8 and 2.9 present the results that were obtained for patent sensitive industries. We note that, compared to the baseline model, agglomeration effects (*NC* and *NG*) are no longer significant. The firms belonging to this industry are less sensitive to the labour costs (proxy: *PC*). Finally, they also turn out to be less sensitive to the political rights awarded to the host country citizens. When the *POL* and *CORP* variables are omitted, the influence exerted by IPR protection is non-linear, first positive and then negative. The turning point locates at 1.76. More importantly, this influence is robust to the inclusion of the corruption and political rights variables. This influence is negative but is significant only above a certain threshold. Substituting the dummy variable *LDC* for the GDP per capita does not modify these conclusions (Table 2.9).

Tables 2.10 and 2.11 consider the results that are obtained for patent insensitive industries. As expected, the protection granted to innovators is not

Table 2.8 Location choices – high propensity to patent (variable GDP/c)

	Dependent variable: chosen country					
Model	(a)	(b)	(c)	(d)	(e)	(f)
NC	0.16*	0.14	0.16	0.21**	0.15	0.19*
	(0.10)	(0.09)	(0.10)	(0.10)	(0.10)	(0.10)
NG	0.16	0.15	0.15	0.21*	0.16	0.20
	(0.13)	(0.12)	(0.13)	(0.13)	(0.13)	(0.13)
OPEN	0.42***	0.59***	0.41***	0.60***	0.62***	0.72***
	(0.15)	(0.18)	(0.15)	(0.16)	(0.19)	(0.19)
GDP	0.66***	0.88***	0.65***	0.82***	0.90***	0.96***
	(0.09)	(0.11)	(0.09)	(0.10)	(0.11)	(0.12)
PC	–1.56***	–0.80	–1.62***	–1.00*	–0.64	–0.44
	(0.47)	(0.51)	(0.48)	(0.52)	(0.54)	(0.55)
GDP/c	1.06***	0.50*	1.06***	0.85***	0.48*	0.46*
	(0.24)	(0.27)	(0.24)	(0.24)	(0.27)	(0.26)
UE	0.63***	0.59***	0.63***	0.62***	0.60***	0.59***
	(0.12)	(0.14)	(0.12)	(0.12)	(0.14)	(0.14)
RD/GDP	–0.11	–0.55***	–0.12	–0.04	–0.56***	–0.43**
	(0.13)	(0.16)	(0.13)	(0.13)	(0.16)	(0.17)
EDUC	–0.11	–0.38	–0.12	–0.11	–0.39	–0.33
	(0.26)	(0.26)	(0.26)	(0.26)	(0.27)	(0.27)
CORP		–1.20***			–1.27***	–1.00***
		(0.29)			(0.31)	(0.32)
POL		0.69**			0.70**	0.57*
		(0.33)			(0.33)	(0.32)
IPR			0.11	1.07*	–0.22	0.52
			(0.24)	(0.60)	(0.27)	(0.55)
IPRSQ				–0.94***		–0.63**
				(0.31)		(0.29)
N	15229	15229	15229	15229	15229	15229
R^2	0.162	0.169	0.162	0.167	0.169	0.171
RMSE	.	.	.	.	.	.

Note: Standard errors in parentheses. ***, ** and * denote the 1%, 5% and 10% levels of significance, respectively.

significant even when the *CORP* and *POL* are omitted from the regressions. Compared to the baseline results, these industries are less sensitive to the openness ratio, the R&D intensity or the educational level. Corruption also seems to matter less than in patent sensitive industries. When the *LDC* dummy is substituted for *GDP/c*, no significant change can be noted beyond those already outlined for the baseline model.

Patent sensitive industries appear to pay attention to the patent protection offered in host countries. On the contrary, industries that make a low use of the patent system are less influenced. Interacting the *IPR* and *IPRSQR* variables with industry dummies allows us to test whether the location choices of each industry are sensitive or not to the patent system of the host

Table 2.9 Location choices – high propensity to patent (variable LDC)

	Dependent variable: chosen country					
Model	(a)	(b)	(c)	(d)	(e)	(f)
NC	0.23**	0.14	0.23**	0.27***	0.16*	0.20**
	(0.09)	(0.09)	(0.09)	(0.09)	(0.09)	(0.10)
NG	0.20	0.15	0.20	0.26**	0.17	0.21
	(0.12)	(0.12)	(0.12)	(0.13)	(0.12)	(0.13)
OPEN	0.76***	0.94***	0.75***	1.01***	0.99***	1.08***
	(0.16)	(0.19)	(0.16)	(0.18)	(0.19)	(0.20)
GDP	0.84***	1.05***	0.83***	1.04***	1.10***	1.16***
	(0.09)	(0.10)	(0.09)	(0.11)	(0.11)	(0.11)
PC	0.35	0.18	0.30	0.73**	0.37	0.55*
	(0.26)	(0.26)	(0.28)	(0.30)	(0.30)	(0.31)
LDC	0.15	0.39*	0.14	0.22	0.44*	0.42*
	(0.21)	(0.23)	(0.21)	(0.23)	(0.24)	(0.24)
UE	0.49***	0.44***	0.49***	0.50***	0.45***	0.45***
	(0.12)	(0.14)	(0.12)	(0.12)	(0.14)	(0.14)
RD/GDP	–0.10	–0.56***	–0.11	0.00	–0.55***	–0.43***
	(0.12)	(0.15)	(0.13)	(0.13)	(0.16)	(0.16)
EDUC	0.40*	–0.30	0.39*	0.24	–0.32	–0.27
	(0.22)	(0.24)	(0.22)	(0.23)	(0.25)	(0.25)
CORP		–1.41***			–1.51***	–1.24***
		(0.28)			(0.29)	(0.31)
POL		1.02***			1.00***	0.84***
		(0.31)			(0.31)	(0.31)
IPR			0.09	0.92*	–0.36	0.31
			(0.21)	(0.51)	(0.27)	(0.51)
IPRSQ				–1.05***		–0.60**
				(0.28)		(0.28)
N	15229	15229	15229	15229	15229	15229
R^2	0.155	0.169	0.155	0.163	0.169	0.171
RMSE	.	.	.	.	.	.

Note: Standard errors in parentheses. ***, ** and * denote the 1%, 5% and 10% levels of significance, respectively.

country. This specification does not modify the coefficients obtained with the baseline model, so we left it unreported. The industry variables reveal that the impact of IPR protection is limited to a few industries. The case of the pharmaceutical industry stands out as particularly striking, but coherent with most survey data suggesting that patents are particularly important in this industry. The coefficients indicate that an increase in protection would first entail an increase in the probability of location. However, above a threshold of 2.45, a further strengthening of patent protection would actually decrease the probability of location: firms may indeed find licensing a more profitable strategy.

Table 2.10 Location choices – low propensity to patent (variable GDP/c)

	Dependent variable: chosen country					
Model	(a)	(b)	(c)	(d)	(e)	(f)
NC	0.37***	0.35***	0.36***	0.36***	0.35***	0.34***
	(0.11)	(0.11)	(0.11)	(0.11)	(0.11)	(0.11)
NG	0.52***	0.51***	0.51***	0.52***	0.51***	0.50***
	(0.15)	(0.15)	(0.15)	(0.16)	(0.15)	(0.15)
OPEN	0.00	0.34	–0.01	0.03	0.33	0.29
	(0.21)	(0.25)	(0.21)	(0.23)	(0.25)	(0.26)
GDP	0.55***	0.79***	0.54***	0.57***	0.78***	0.76***
	(0.12)	(0.14)	(0.12)	(0.14)	(0.15)	(0.15)
PC	2.71***	–1.92***	–2.79***	–2.69***	–1.95***	2.02**
	(0.61)	0.65)	(0.63)	(0.68)	(0.69)	(0.70)
GDP/c	1.35***	0.84**	1.34***	1.31***	0.85**	0.85**
	(0.30)	(0.33)	(0.30)	(0.31)	(0.33)	(0.34)
UE	1.00***	0.82***	1.00***	0.99***	0.82***	0.83***
	(0.16)	(0.18)	(0.16)	(0.16)	(0.18)	(0.18)
RD/GDP	0.14	–0.27	0.12	0.13	–0.27	–0.31
	(0.16)	(0.22)	(0.17)	(0.17)	(0.22)	(0.23)
EDUC	–0.20	–0.52	–0.22	–0.21	–0.52	–0.56
	(0.33)	(0.35)	(0.33)	(0.33)	(0.35)	(0.36)
CORP		–0.69*			–1.068*	–0.75*
		(0.38)			(0.39)	(0.42)
POL		1.11**			1.11**	1.17**
		(0.44)			(0.44)	(0.45)
IPR			0.18	0.25	(0.38)	–0.08
			(0.33)	(0.40)		(0.43)
IPRSQ				–0.11		0.15
				(0.26)		(0.28)
N	10459	10459	10459	10459	10459	10459
R^2	0.241	0.246	0.242	0.242	0.246	0.246

Note: Standard errors in parentheses. ***, ** and * denote the 1%, 5% and 10% levels of significance, respectively.

There are some other industries sensitive to patent protection, but the levels of significance as well as the estimated coefficients are less outstanding. The impact of patent protection is positive in the printing and publishing industry; it is significant at the 5 per cent level of significance. A non-linear impact can be noted when the squared IPR variable is introduced. In that case, the influence is first positive and then negative with a threshold at about 3.38. The printing and publishing industries do not stand out as particularly innovating and they are not particularly sensitive to patent protection. On the other hand, it comprises most of the artistic activities generally protected by copyrights. As far as this form of protection is correlated with patent protection, firms in this industry will appear as sensitive to patent protection in host countries. The transport industry is also

Table 2.11 Location choices – low propensity to patent (variable LDC)

	Dependent variable: chosen country					
Model	(a)	(b)	(c)	(d)	(e)	(f)
NC	0.42***	0.37***	0.41***	0.43***	0.37***	0.36***
	(0.11)	(0.11)	(0.11)	(0.11)	(0.11)	(0.11)
NG	0.56***	0.53***	0.55***	0.57***	0.53***	0.52***
	(0.15)	(0.15)	(0.15)	(0.16)	(0.15)	(0.16)
OPEN	0.30	0.59**	0.27	0.39*	0.59**	0.55**
	(0.21)	(0.23)	(0.22)	(0.23)	(0.24)	(0.25)
GDP	0.73***	0.96***	0.72***	0.80***	0.96***	0.94***
	(0.12)	(0.12)	(0.12)	(0.14)	(0.13)	(0.14)
PC	–0.49	–0.56*	–0.60*	0.42	0.56	0.63
	(0.33)	(0.33)	(0.36)	(0.38)	(0.38)	(0.39)
LDC	–0.39	–0.26	–0.41	–0.40	–0.26	–0.25
	(0.29)	(0.30)	(0.28)	(0.29)	(0.31)	(0.30)
UE	0.84***	0.68***	0.84***	0.83***	0.68***	0.69***
	(0.15)	(0.17)	(0.15)	(0.15)	(0.17)	(0.17)
RD/GDP	–0.02	–0.56***	–0.06	–0.04	–0.56***	–0.59***
	(0.16)	(0.21)	(0.16)	(0.16)	(0.21)	(0.23)
EDUC	0.58*	–0.26	0.54*	0.50	–0.26	–0.30
	(0.31)	(0.35)	(0.31)	(0.31)	(0.35)	(0.36)
CORP		–0.99***			–0.99***	–1.07***
		(0.38)			(0.38)	(0.41)
POL		1.57***			1.57***	1.63***
		(0.42)			(0.42)	(0.44)
IPR			0.24	0.41	0.01	–0.13
			(0.29)	(0.37)	(0.37)	(0.42)
IPRSQ				–0.33		0.16
				(0.25)		(0.28)
N	10459	10459	10459	10459	10459	10459
R^2	0.232	0.243	0.232	0.233	0.243	0.243

Note: Standard errors in parentheses. ***, ** and * denote the 1%, 5% and 10% levels of significance, respectively.

sensitive to IPR laws: Pfister (2000), for instance, has shown that this industry suffered important losses due to trademark infringement. A strengthening of patent protection has a positive impact, significant at the 10 per cent level of significance. The same story goes for the steel industries and oil refineries.

Technological Capital of the Host Country

In this section, we distinguish potential host countries on the basis of their technological capital. We assume that the impact of patent protection depends on whether the host country is able to imitate the products or processes of the multinational. Presumably, strengthening patent protection will only favour one country relative to another if these countries have sufficient technological capital so as to be able to imitate the products and processes. Like Smith (1999), we approximate the technological capital and the ability to imitate through an R&D investment to GDP ratio. This author has shown that American exports increase with IPR protection when the receiving country has an R&D to GDP ratio above 0.5 per cent, while they tend to diminish when the country has a low R&D to GDP ratio. Our own empirical results regarding location choices of French multinationals do confirm that the impact of IPR protection varies with the technological capital of the host country. However, compared to Smith, our results indicate that 1) the R&D to GDP ratio above which the impact of patent protection is modified is closer to 1 per cent than to 0.5 per cent; 2) IPR protection does

Table 2.12 Location choices – nested choice between technology strong countries (RD/GDP > 0.5%) and technology weak countries

	Dependent variable: chosen country							
Model	(a)	(b)	(c)	(d)	(e)	(f)	(g)	(h)
NC	0.21***	0.19**	0.22***	0.20***	0.28***	0.21***	0.29***	0.22***
	(0.08)	(0.08)	(0.08)	(0.08)	(0.07)	(0.07)	(0.07)	(0.08)
NG	0.36***	0.36***	0.38***	0.37***	0.41***	0.37***	0.43***	0.38***
	(0.10)	(0.10)	(0.10)	(0.10)	(0.10)	(0.10)	(0.10)	(0.10)
OPEN	0.35***	0.53***	0.37***	0.56***	0.66***	0.84***	0.73***	0.85***
	(0.13)	(0.15)	(0.13)	(0.16)	(0.13)	(0.15)	(0.14)	(0.15)
GDP	0.70***	0.87***	0.73***	0.89***	0.87***	1.05***	0.93***	1.06***
	(0.08)	(0.09)	(0.08)	(0.09)	(0.08)	(0.09)	(0.09)	(0.09)
PC	–1.98***	–1.35***	–1.99***	–1.39***	0.02	–0.12	0.05	–0.24
	(0.40)	(0.44)	(0.44)	(0.46)	(0.23)	(0.26)	(0.27)	(0.30)
UE	0.79***	0.68***	0.78***	0.65***	0.66***	0.53***	0.64***	0.52***
	(0.10)	(0.12)	(0.10)	(0.12)	(0.10)	(0.11)	(0.09)	(0.11)
GDP/c	1.13***	0.68***	1.10***	0.65***				
	(0.18)	(0.21)	(0.19)	(0.22)				
LDC					–0.14	0.11	–0.09	0.11
					(0.18)	(0.19)	(0.18)	(0.18)
RDGDP	0.00	–0.48***	0.02	–0.44***	–0.06	–0.64***	–0.03	–0.59***
	(0.13)	(0.17)	(0.13)	(0.17)	(0.13)	(0.16)	(0.14)	(0.16)
EDUC	–0.06	–0.32	–0.08	–0.30	0.53***	–0.20	0.45**	–0.17
	(0.21)	(0.21)	(0.21)	(0.21)	(0.19)	(0.21)	(0.19)	(0.21)
CORP		–0.93***		–0.86***		–1.29***		–1.19***
		(0.26)		(0.27)		(0.25)		(0.25)
POL		0.79***		0.81***		1.19***		1.15***
		(0.27)		(0.28)		(0.25)		(0.26)
*HRD*IPR*	–0.51*	–0.28	1.29	1.35	–0.57**	–0.24	1.35	1.69
	(0.30)	(0.33)	(1.35)	(1.53)	(0.28)	(0.33)	(1.36)	(1.59)
*LRD*IPR*	0.52*	0.08	0.61**	0.21	0.49**	–0.13	0.63**	0.06
	(0.27)	(0.29)	(0.30)	(0.33)	(0.23)	(0.28)	(0.30)	(0.33)
*HRD*IPRSQR*			–0.88	–0.76			–1.01*	–0.91
			(0.60)	(0.68)			(0.60)	(0.70)
*LRD*IPRSQR*			–0.17	–0.20			–0.67**	–0.38
			(0.34)	(0.35)			(0.33)	(0.35)
N	16347	16347	16347	16347	16347	16347	16347	16347
R^2	0.193	0.197	0.194	0.198	0.183	0.195	0.186	0.196

Note: Standard errors in parentheses. ***, ** and * denote the 1%, 5% and 10% levels of significance, respectively.

Table 2.13 Location choices – nested choice between technology strong countries (RD/GDP > 1%) and technology weak countries

	Dependent variable: chosen country							
Model	(a)	(b)	(c)	(d)	(e)	(f)	(g)	(h)
NC	0.22***	0.20***	0.26***	0.24***	0.29***	0.23***	0.34***	0.27***
	(0.08)	(0.08)	(0.08)	(0.08)	(0.08)	(0.08)	(0.08)	(0.08)
NG	0.35***	0.34***	0.39***	0.38***	0.41***	0.36***	0.45***	0.41***
	(0.10)	(0.10)	(0.10)	(0.10)	(0.10)	(0.10)	(0.10)	(0.10)
OPEN	0.32**	0.61***	0.41***	0.76***	0.59***	0.82***	0.76***	1.03***
	(0.13)	(0.16)	(0.13)	(0.16)	(0.13)	(0.15)	(0.14)	(0.16)
GDP	0.66***	0.89***	0.76***	1.00***	0.82***	1.03***	0.93***	1.16***
	(0.08)	(0.09)	(0.08)	(0.09)	(0.08)	(0.08)	(0.09)	(0.09)
PC	–2.00***	–1.05**	–2.04***	–1.43***	–0.05	0.03	0.34	–0.02
	(0.38)	(0.43)	(0.44)	(0.44)	(0.22)	(0.24)	(0.25)	(0.26)
UE	0.74***	0.63***	0.57***	0.27**	0.60***	0.52***	0.58***	0.20
	(0.09)	(0.12)	(0.11)	(0.14)	(0.09)	(0.11)	(0.11)	(0.14)
GDP/c	1.22***	0.66***	1.31***	0.84***				
	(0.19)	(0.21)	(0.21)	(0.22)				
LDC					–0.32	–0.12	–0.16	–0.05
					(0.21)	(0.25)	(0.22)	(0.25)
RDGDP	0.11	–0.34**	0.10	–0.43***	0.00	–0.51***	0.03	–0.60***
	(0.12)	(0.15)	(0.12)	(0.15)	(0.11)	(0.14)	(0.11)	(0.14)
EDUC	–0.25	–0.50**	–0.11	–0.37	0.38**	–0.32	0.45**	–0.12
	(0.20)	(0.21)	(0.22)	(0.24)	(0.18)	(0.21)	(0.21)	(0.23)
CORP		–1.04***		–1.11***		–1.32***		–1.41***
		(0.27)		(0.27)		(0.25)		(0.26)
POL		0.95***		1.28***		1.29***		1.60***
		(0.26)		(0.29)		(0.25)		(0.29)
*HRD*IPR*	0.24	0.02	26.48***	39.67***	–0.45	–0.05	9.39	33.51***
	(0.42)	(0.41)	(7.61)	(8.04)	(0.43)	(0.41)	(7.01)	(7.81)
*LRD*IPR*	0.20	–0.17	0.54	–0.01	0.27	–0.24	0.62*	–0.08
	(0.22)	(0.26)	(0.33)	(0.34)	(0.20)	(0.25)	(0.32)	(0.33)
*HRD*IPRSQR*			–10.49***	–15.48***			–3.98	–13.13***
			(2.94)	(3.10)			(2.73)	(3.02)
*LRD*IPRSQR*			–0.48*	–0.11			–0.88***	–0.20
			(0.25)	(0.25)			(0.24)	(0.25)
N	12120	12120	12120	12120	12120	12120	12120	12120
R^2	0.188	0.195	0.193	0.202	0.178	0.192	0.182	0.198

Note: Standard errors in parentheses. ***, ** and * denote the 1%, 5% and 10% levels of significance, respectively.

not appear to play any role in countries with a low technological capital; and 3) the difference between our and her results may well be attributed to the omission of certain key variables such as corruption and political rights.

Consider Tables 2.12 and 2.13. They present the estimation results of a nested logit model where firms only compare countries of the same group (able to imitate or unable to imitate). Using a threshold of 0.5 per cent to distinguish between these two groups of countries, we note that when the *CORP* and *POL* variables are omitted (Table 2.12), the impact of patent protection is negative for technologically able countries while it is non-linear (positive and then negative) for countries with a low technological base.

*Table 2.14 Location choices – IPR/IPR*HDR, 0.5 % threshold.*

	Dependent variable: chosen country							
Model	(a)	(b)	(c)	(d)	(e)	(f)	(g)	(h)
NC	0.24***	0.27***	0.22***	0.24***	0.30***	0.33***	0.24***	0.25***
	(0.07)	(0.07)	(0.07)	(0.07)	(0.07)	(0.07)	(0.07)	(0.07)
NG	0.30***	0.34***	0.30***	0.32***	0.35***	0.35***	0.31***	0.33***
	(0.10)	(0.10)	(0.10)	(0.10)	(0.10)	(0.10)	(0.10)	(0.10)
OPEN	0.30**	0.39***	0.52***	0.59***	0.63***	0.79***	0.83***	0.89***
	(0.13)	(0.13)	(0.15)	(0.15)	(0.13)	(0.14)	(0.15)	(0.15)
GDP	0.63***	0.74***	0.86***	0.91***	0.82***	0.96***	1.04***	1.09***
	(0.07)	(0.08)	(0.09)	(0.09)	(0.08)	(0.09)	(0.08)	(0.09)
PC	–1.90***	–1.76***	–1.14***	–1.0**	0.08	0.29	–0.02	0.07
	(0.39)	(0.42)	(0.43)	(0.45)	(0.23)	(0.24)	(0.24)	(0.25)
UE	0.77***	0.73***	0.65***	0.62***	0.65***	0.61***	0.51***	0.49***
	(0.10)	(0.09)	(0.11)	(0.12)	(0.09)	(0.09)	(0.11)	(0.11)
GDP/c	1.13***	1.07***	0.61***	0.61***				
	(0.19)	(0.19)	(0.21)	(0.21)				
LDC					–0.04	–0.02	0.17	0.15
					(0.18)	(0.18)	(0.18)	(0.18)
RDGDP	0.08	0.01	–0.50***	–0.48***	0.07	–0.02	–0.63***	–0.62***
	(0.12)	(0.12)	(0.17)	(0.17)	(0.12)	(0.13)	(0.16)	(0.16)
EDUC	–0.20	–0.18	–0.44**	–0.40*	0.38**	0.34*	–0.32	–0.27
	(0.20)	(0.20)	(0.21)	(0.21)	(0.18)	(0.18)	(0.20)	(0.20)
CORP			–1.07***	–0.88***			–1.36***	–1.22***
			(0.25)	(0.28)			(0.24)	(0.26)
POL			0.86***	0.82***			1.22***	1.12***
			(0.27)	(0.27)			(0.25)	(0.26)
*HRD*IPR*	0.27	0.63**	–0.15	0.18	0.31	0.63**	–0.28	0.01
	(0.22)	(0.29)	(0.25)	(0.33)	(0.19)	(0.29)	(0.24)	(0.33)
*LRD*IPR*	–0.35	0.76	0.11	0.67	–0.48**	0.22	0.20	0.41
	(0.23)	(0.53)	(0.25)	(0.54)	(0.22)	(0.51)	(0.24)	(0.54)
*HRD*IPRSQR*		–0.07		–0.15		–0.60*		–0.38
		(0.34)		(0.35)		(0.32)		(0.35)
*LRD*IPRSQR*		–0.89*		–0.43		–0.24		–0.02
		(0.52		(0.56)		(0.50)		(0.54)
N	25688	25688	25688	25688	25688	25688	25688	25688
R^2	0.191	0.193	0.196	0.197	0.183	0.187	0.194	0.195

Note: Standard errors in parentheses. ***, ** and * denote the 1 %, 5 % and 10 % levels of significance, respectively.

However, once the *CORP* and *POL* variables are included, there is no longer any impact of IPR protection, whatever the technological capital of the host country.

However, we do observe a differentiated IPR impact when the threshold distinguishing imitating from non-imitating countries is at 1 per cent (Table 2.13). In that case, technologically able countries regroup most of the industrialized countries. Patent protection exerts a non-linear (positive and then negative) influence on the probability of a country being chosen when technologically able countries are compared. The turning point stands at 3.59 when the *GDP/c* variable is used and at 3.56 when the *LDC* dummy is used instead. Also note that, again, IPR protection in technological unable

*Table 2.15 Location choices – IPR/IPR*HRD, 1% threshold*

	Dependent variable: chosen country							
Model	(a)	(b)	(c)	(d)	(e)	(f)	(g)	(h)
NC	0.22***	0.24***	0.22***	0.22***	0.29***	0.31***	0.24***	0.24***
	(0.07)	(0.07)	(0.07)	(0.07)	(0.07)	(0.07)	(0.07)	(0.07)
NG	0.29***	0.31***	0.29***	0.30***	0.33***	0.36***	0.31***	0.32***
	(0.10)	(0.10)	(0.10)	(0.10)	(0.10)	(0.10)	(0.10)	(0.10)
OPEN	0.33***	0.44***	0.63***	0.65***	0.59***	0.77***	0.87***	0.89***
	(0.12)	(0.13)	(0.16)	(0.16)	(0.13)	(0.14)	(0.15)	(0.15)
GDP	0.66***	0.74***	0.90***	0.92***	0.81***	0.93***	1.05***	1.07***
	(0.07)	(0.08)	(0.09)	(0.09)	(0.07)	(0.09)	(0.08)	(0.09)
PC	–2.01***	–1.56***	–1.14***	–0.95**	–0.06	0.37	0.00	0.18
	(0.38)	(0.42)	(0.42)	(0.44)	(0.22)	(0.25)	(0.23)	(0.26)
UE	0.73***	0.74***	0.61***	0.64***	0.60***	0.64***	0.50***	0.54***
	(0.09)	(0.09)	(0.11)	(0.12)	(0.09)	(0.09)	(0.11)	(0.11)
GDP/c	1.21***	1.06***	0.69***	0.66***				
	(0.19)	(0.19)	(0.21)	(0.21)				
LDC					–0.33*	–0.16	–0.09	–0.08
					(0.20)	(0.22)	(0.23)	(0.25)
RDGDP	0.12	0.13	–0.30**	–0.27*	0.01	0.03	–0.48***	–0.44***
	(0.12)	(0.12)	(0.15)	(0.15)	(0.11)	(0.11)	(0.13)	(0.14)
EDUC	–0.22	–0.17	–0.49**	–0.44**	0.44**	0.38**	–0.31	–0.26
	(0.20)	(0.20)	(0.21)	(0.21)	(0.18)	(0.19)	(0.20)	(0.21)
CORP			–0.90***	–0.87***			–1.19***	–1.14***
			(0.25)	(0.26)			(0.24)	(0.25)
POL			0.92***	0.82***			1.26***	1.12***
			(0.26)	(0.27)			(0.25)	(0.26)
IPR	0.19	0.56*	–0.01	0.16	0.23	0.62	–0.09	0.09
	(0.20)	(0.33)	(0.23)	(0.34)	(0.18)	(0.32)	(0.23)	(0.33)
*HRD*IPR*	–0.35***	–0.78	0.32**	–0.84	–0.37***	–1.06*	0.30*	–0.96
	(0.12)	(0.59)	(0.13)	(0.58)	(0.14)	(0.63)	(0.17)	(0.63)
IPRSQR		–0.57**		–0.33		–0.86***		–0.38
		(0.25)		(0.25)		(0.24)		(0.25)
*HRD*IPRSQR*		0.42		0.45		0.70		0.56
		(0.45)		(0.45)		(0.47)		(0.46)
N	25688	25688	25688	25688	25688	25688	25688	25688
R^2	0.192	0.194	0.197	0.197	0.184	0.187	0.195	0.195

Note: Standard errors in parentheses. ***, ** and * denote the 1%, 5% and 10% levels of significance, respectively.

countries appears to have either a negative or a non-linear (positive and then negative) influence on the probability of location when the *CORP* and *POL* variables are omitted from the regressions. This impact becomes non-significant once these variables are taken into account.

Tables 2.14 and 2.15 consider to what extent IPR protection matters more in countries with the ability to imitate when these countries are compared to the other group of countries. Again, there does not seem to be any difference in the IPR impact when a 0.5 per cent threshold is used (Table 2.14): though a significant impact does appear in models (b), (e) and (f), it disappears once the corruption and the political rights variables are included. When the 1 per cent R&D ratio is used, a negative and significant impact appears for the group of technologically able countries. The coefficient is significantly negative at the 10 per cent level of significance (Table 2.15).

CONCLUSION

This chapter has considered the impact of IPR protection on the location decisions of French multinationals. A conditional logit model allowed us to analyse the determinants of 755 location decisions in 37 countries. Besides traditional determinants such as demand, openness, labour costs and agglomeration effects, this analysis also demonstrated the extremely significant influence exerted by the level of corruption and of political rights granted in the potential host country.

These variables also matter when it comes to measuring the impact of patent protection. When they are omitted, patent protection seems to exert a non-linear, positive and then negative, influence on the probability of a country being chosen. However, once corruption and political rights are taken into account in the regressions, patent protection no longer plays any role.

Further analysis reveals, however, that patent protection matters significantly in patent sensitive industries as well as in countries that are able to imitate the process and products of the multinationals.

In both cases, the influence is non-linear. For patent sensitive industries, it is first insignificant and then negative. The impact is particularly important for the pharmaceutical industry as well as the publishing, transport, steel and oil refinery industries. For countries with a large R&D capital, the influence is also non-linear, first positive and then negative. The impact of patent protection is higher when these countries are compared one with another than when they are compared to the whole set of countries.

These results tend to contradict those of Lee and Mansfield (1996) or Maskus (1998), who found that higher patent protection stimulated inward FDI into developing countries. Instead, our regressions tend to suggest that a large part of this impact may stem from omitted variables such as corruption or political rights. Rather, we may conclude that IPR protection only matters for FDI targeted towards countries with sufficient imitative capabilities, i.e., industrialized countries. It is also restricted to a few key industries such as pharmaceuticals. The impact of IPR protection is non-linear, first positive and then negative. Two alternative and complementary explanations can be proposed. The first relies on the trade-off between exports, FDI and licensing. The second hinges on how FDI may be used to deter imitation and on how, therefore, stronger protection may lower the incentives to locate in a country. More work, both theoretical and empirical, is needed to test the empirical relevance of each of these assumptions.

NOTES

1. See also Watal (1998), Fink (2000) and Dumoulin (2000) for a survey.
2. Originally, the dataset comprised 2756 location decisions made between 1959 and 1994. The lack of appropriate data led us to reduce drastically the size of our sample.
3. This is especially true of the years at which we conducted this study. Recently, pharmaceutical firms have complained about how the Brazilian and South African courts implement the TRIPs agreement.
4. See Easterly (1997) for another use of this index.
5. The importance of corruption in explaining FDI has been stressed, among others, by Hines (1996) and Wei (2000).
6. Similar modifications will appear frequently but we will no longer comment on them.
7. See Mansfield *et al.* (1986), Levin *et al.* (1987), Cohen *et al.* (1997), Brouwer and Kleinknecht (1999).

REFERENCES

Barro, R. and J. Lee (1994), 'Sources of economic growth', *Carnegie-Rochester Conference Series on Public Policy*, **40**, 1–46.

Brouwer, E. and A. Kleinknecht (1999), 'Innovative output and a firm's propensity to patent: An exploration of CIS Micro Data', *Research Policy*, **28**, 615–24.

Cohen, W., R. Nelson and J. Walsh (1997), *Appropriability conditions and why firms patent and why they do not in the American manufacturing sector*, Unpublished Working Paper, Carnegie Mellon University.

Commission Européenne (1998), *Intellectual Property Textile Infringements in Asia*, DG I, mimeo.

Dumoulin, J. (2000), 'Les brevets et le prix des médicaments', *Revue Internationale de Droit Economique – Numéro spécial: Brevets Pharmaceutiques, Innovations et Santé Publique* (1), 45–69.

Easterly, W. (1997), 'Life during growth', World Bank discussion paper.

Fink, C. (2000), 'How stronger patent protection in India might affect the behavior of transnational pharmaceutical industries', World Bank discussion paper.

Fosfuri, A. (2000), 'Patent protection, imitation and the mode of technology transfer', *International Journal of Industrial Organisation*, **18**, 1129–49.

Ginarte, J. and W. Park (1998), 'Determinants of patent rights: a cross-national study', *Research Policy*, **28**, 283–301.

Helpman, E. (1993), 'Innovation, imitation and intellectual property rights', *Econometrica*, **61**, 1247–80.

Hines, J. (1996), 'Forbidden payment: Foreign bribery and American business after 1977', NBER Working Paper 5266.

Jaffe, A. (2000), 'Policy innovation and the innovation process', *Research Policy*, **29**, 531–55.

Kortum, S. and J. Lerner (1999), 'What is behind the recent surge in patenting?', *Research Policy*, **28**, 1–22.

Kumar, N. (1996), 'Intellectual property protection, market orientation and location of overseas R&D activities by multinational enterprises', *World Development*, **24**, 673–88.

Lai, E. (1998), 'International intellectual property rights protection and the rate of product innovation', *Journal of Development Economics*, 55, 131–51.

Lanjouw, J. (1998), 'Patent protection in the shadow of infringement: simulation estimations of patent value', *Review of Economic Studies*, 65, 671–710.

Lanjouw, J. and I. Cockburn (2000), 'Do patents matter? Empirical evidence after GATT', NBER Working Paper 7495.

Lee, J. and E. Mansfield (1996), 'Intellectual property protection and US foreign direct investment', *Review of Economics and Statistics*, **78**, 181–6.

Lerner, J. (2000), '150 years of patent history', NBER Working Paper 7476.

Levin, R., A. Klevorick, R. Nelson and S. Winter (1987), 'Appropriating the returns from industrial research and development', *Brookings Papers on Economic Activity*, **3**, 783–820.

Mansfield, E., M. Schwartz and S. Wagner (1986), 'Imitation costs and patents: an empirical study', *Economic Journal*, **91**, 907–18.

Markusen, J. (2001), 'Contracts, intellectual property rights and multinational investment in developing countries', *Journal of International Economics*, **53**, 189–204.

Maskus, K. (1998), 'The international regulation of intellectual property', *Weltwirtschaftliches Archiv*, **134**, 186–208.

Maskus, K. and D. Eby-Konan (1994), 'Trade-related intellectual property rights: issues and exploratory results, in Deardoff A.V. and R.M. Stern (eds), *Analytical and Negotiating Issues in the Global Trading System*, Ann Arbor: University of Michigan Press, pp. 401–54.

Maskus, K. and M. Penubarti (1995), 'How trade-related are intellectual property rights?', *Journal of International Economics*, **39**, 227–48.

Mayer, T. and J.-L. Mucchielli (1999), 'La localisation à l'étranger des entreprises multinationales', *Economie et Statistiques*, **326-7**, 159–76.

Pfister, E. (2000), *The legal enforcement of intellectual property rights: an empirical investigation of French trademarks conflicts*, mimeo, Université de Paris I.

Rapp, R. and R. Rozek (1990), 'Benefits and costs of intellectual property protection in developing countries', *Journal of World Trade*, **24**, 75–102.

Sakikabara, M. and L. Branstetter (2001), 'Do stronger patents induce more innovation? Evidence from the 1988 Japanese patent law reforms', *RAND Journal of Economics*, **32**.

Smith, P. (1999), 'Are weak patent rights a barrier to US exports?', *Journal of International Economics*, **48**, 151–77.
The Economist (1999), 'The Politics of Piracy', 20 February, 81–3.
The Economist (2000), 'Generic Genius – A Problem of Patents', 30 September, 80–4.
Vaitsos, C. (1971), 'Patents revisited: their function in developing countries', *Science, Technology and Development*, 71–97.
Watal, J. (1998), *Product Patents, Pharmaceutical Prices and Welfare Losses: The Indian Numbers Revisited*, mimeo.
Wei, S. (2000), 'How taxing is corruption on international investors?, *Review of Economics and Statistics*, 82, 1–11.
Wheeler, D. and A. Mody (1992), 'International investment location decisions', *Journal of International Economics*, **33**, 57–76.
Yang, G. and K. Maskus (2000), 'Intellectual property rights and licensing: an econometric investigation', *Weltwirtschaftliches Archiv*.

3. Location of Multinational Firms: An Application of the Ellison and Glaeser Index to French Foreign Direct Investment in Europe[1]

Jean-Louis Mucchielli and Florence Puech

INTRODUCTION

With the renewal of interest in spatial geography, there is an increasing amount of articles in economic literature which are devoted to multinational firms' location. Even if in economic theory there subsist some debates on the location of economic activity[2], at an empirical level, it seems that geographic concentration is an unquestionable fact. A number of recent econometric studies do not reject the hypothesis of geographic concentration of multinationals at a national level (Wheeler and Mody, 1992; Devereux and Griffith, 1998; Mayer and Mucchielli, 1998; Ford and Strange, 1999) or at a more disaggregated geographic level, i.e. at regional or county scales (Woodward, 1992; Head and Ries, 1996; Ferrer, 1998; Jianping, 1999; Mayer and Mucchielli, 1999; Guimarães *et al.*, 2000; Crozet *et al.*, 2003; Mucchielli and Puech, 2004).

In this chapter, we assess at national and regional levels the existence of spatial concentration of French industrial firms in the European area. Using an index proposed by Ellison and Glaeser (1997), we determine the degree of geographic concentration for each industrial sector of activity. Consequently, according to the 'random location model' of Ellison and Glaeser, we test for each sector if the observed concentration or dispersion level deviates significantly from that of a random distribution of French foreign direct investments (FDI).

The chapter is organized as follows. The first section briefly overviews the distribution of French FDI in Europe. The second section provides reasons for the use of the Ellison and Glaeser index and presents this geographic concentration measure and empirical results regarding French multinationals in the European area.

STYLIZED FACTS

In 2001, France became the second most important foreign direct investor ($82.8 billion) behind the United States ($114 billion) (UNCTAD, 2002). A descriptive analysis based on the database *Enquête-Filiales* 2000 of the French Directory of Economic and Foreign Relationships (DREE) of the French Ministry of Economics, Finance and Industry indicates that, during the nineties, around 40 per cent of French FDI was located in the European Union. Nevertheless, the distribution of French firms is not equivalent throughout European countries. At a national level, some host countries were able to attract more FDI than others (in terms of subsidiaries located in the country). The most favoured destinations were the United Kingdom, Germany, Spain, Belgium and Italy. These five countries accounted for more than 75 per cent of French international investments in Europe. Moreover, within countries, one can easily observe a strong intra-national disparity of the distribution of French FDI. Generally, industrial regions or regions which contain the capital city have an important attractiveness and they 'catch' a large part of French investments. Considering the main host European regions in terms of the number of French FDI until 2000, the respective shares of the Eastern region in Spain, Lombardy in Italy or the South East in the United Kingdom were 8.1 per cent, 5.1 per cent and 3.9 per cent, and those of Madrid, Brussels and London were respectively equal to 7.1 per cent, 7 per cent and 6.5 per cent[3]. Besides, for some countries, there was only one region which attracted more than half of the French subsidiaries within this country: for instance the region of Brussels (51.9 per cent), Lisbon (66.7 per cent), Athens (75.3 per cent) or Lombardy (60.8 per cent).

If we now focus on industrial sectors, the five main important sectors in terms of French industrial firms located in the European area in the same period were electric and electronic products (17.9 per cent), the chemical industry (13.1 per cent), mechanical engineering (11 per cent), metallurgy and metal transformation (10.3 per cent) and the food, drink and tobacco industry (9.7 per cent). Again, the geographic distribution of French industrial FDI highlights some geographic disparities across countries and regions. For instance, the most represented industrial sector in Germany, Denmark, Italy, the Netherlands, Portugal, the United Kingdom and Sweden is electric and electronic products; for Austria, non-metallic mineral products are preponderant; the chemical industry for Belgium, Finland and Ireland; and last, for Luxembourg, Greece and Spain, the food, drink and tobacco industry is dominating[4].

In summary, considering the empirical findings of this brief descriptive analysis, it seems that some geographic concentration of French investments exists in Europe at national and regional levels. Nevertheless, an attempt to quantify the degree of spatial concentration for each industrial sector is worthwhile. It will enable us to determine whether the observed concentration applies to all industrial sectors or if there are some geographic dispersion effects for specific activities.

THE ELLISON AND GLAESER INDEX

Why did we Choose this Index?

To analyse the spatial distribution of firms, the Gini coefficient is one of the most frequently used measures for evaluating the geographic concentration of industries (See, for instance, Amiti, 1997; Audretsch and Feldman, 1996; Brülhart and Torstensson, 1996; Midelfart-Knarvik *et al.*, 2000; Brülhart, 2001). The Gini coefficient is computed as follows. Consider a sector s and a territory divided into regions. For each region, we calculate the ratio of the share of total employment in sector s to the share of total employment in all sectors (in the considered region). Next, we rank the ratios to construct the Lorenz curve. We respect the order of magnitude of the ratios and we represent the regions' cumulative shares of total employment in sector s (on the vertical axis) and the regions' cumulative shares of total employment in all sectors (on the horizontal axis). The ratio of the area between the resulting curve and the first bisector to the area under the first bisector is the Gini coefficient. If the shares of total employment in sector s across all regions are equal to the share of employment in all sectors, the Gini coefficient is equal to zero (the location curve and 45-degree line coincide). Inversely, the more the spatial distribution in sector s is concentrated, the further the Lorenz curve is away from the bisector, and the closer the Gini coefficient is to 1.

Consequently, this index does not take into account the industrial concentration (size of firms). Nevertheless, if we want to evaluate the geographic location of French FDI in Europe, we have to pay attention at the same time to firm sizes and to the number of FDI because some important differences exist between the distribution of employees and the number of firms across areas. For example, in terms of employment some sectors are very well represented by large firms, while other industries have mainly small firms. We are compelled to integrate two different situations: 1) a sector of activity is concentrated because there are very few affiliates which have a large number of employees in a given area; 2) the spatial clustering results from numerous small sized FDI located in the same geographical area (Devereux *et al.*, 1999). Ellison and Glaeser (1997) introduced an index which includes this distinction. Moreover, the theoretical background of those two indices is not the same. As we have shown, the Gini index evaluates the concentration of firms of a sector in an area (country, region or county for example) against the distribution of firms of all sectors in the same area, whereas the Ellison and Glaeser index tests the concentration of plants in an area against a theoretical random location of firms in the same area. In what follows, the random location model proposed by Ellison and Glaeser is more explicitly presented.

The Ellison and Glaeser Index

This index determines the deviation of the geographic concentration of an industry from the one which would result if firms chose to settle independently and randomly. According to the random location model of Ellison and Glaeser, an industry is concentrated (or dispersed) if the observed concentration (or dispersion) deviates significantly from a random distribution of firms. Ellison and Glaeser compare the phenomenon of firms' location to a 'dartboard approach' because they imagine a process where the different areas of the target represent the possible host regions and where investments are represented by darts drawn on this target. Theoretically, the more important a host region is, the greater the number of firms that will be found.

The construction of the index is as follows. In a first step, for a given sector, Ellison and Glaeser define a raw geographic concentration measure, denoted by G. It is computed as the squared sum of all the differences (in each region) between the share of employment in the considered sector (s_i) and the total employment of all manufacturing sectors (x_i), thus $G=\Sigma_i(s_i-x_i)^2$. Moreover, the expected value of G for a completely random distribution of firms, denoted by $E(G)$, is equal to $E(G)=DH$ where D measures the economic activity across locations[5] ($D=1-\Sigma_i x_i^2$) and H is the Herfindahl index of industry firms' sizes, that is $H=\Sigma_k z_k^2$. Consequently, the value $(G-DH)$ measures the difference between the observed value of G and the one resulting from chance. To control for the sector size, the exact expression of the Ellison and Glaeser index, denoted by γ, is: $\gamma = (G-DH) / D(1-H)$.

In those conditions, we can easily determine if the observed values of the distribution are significantly different from random distributed values. In other words, we can study if the distribution of investments is significantly concentrated or dispersed across locations. The significance of our results will be calculated by the formula of Ellison and Glaeser (1997), given by:

$$V(G) = 2\left\{H^2\left[\sum_i x_i^2 - 2\sum_i x_i^3 + \left(\sum_i x_i^2\right)^2\right] - \sum_j z_j^4\left[\sum_i x_i^2 - 4\sum_i x_i^3 + 3\left(\sum_i x_i^2\right)^2\right]\right\}$$

For instance, if the value (*G–DH*) for a sector is positive, the gamma value will be positive. Consequently, the observed value of *G* is superior to the random value: subsidiaries which belong to the considered sector are geographically concentrated. And thanks to the calculation of the variance, we can show whether this spatial concentration is significant or not.

Empirical Study

This index has been applied at the national level for the United States (Ellison and Glaeser, 1997; Rosenthal and Strange, 2001), Spain (Callejón, 1997) and France (Maurel and Sédillot, 1999; Houdebine, 1999), or, at the international level, to French and Japanese FDI in Asia (Head *et al.*, 2002). In this subsection, we are going to study the distribution of French multinationals in the European area considering two geographic scales: national and regional levels.

The database

We used the database *Enquête-Filiales DREE* which registers French multinationals over the world at an individual level. The French Directory of Economic and Foreign Relationships (DREE) of the French Ministry of Economics, Finance and Industry annually records French multinationals or multinational firms with a French participation (over 10 per cent) in the world. This survey records international French establishments created until 2001. In the sample, we only retained French industrial firms in the European Union countries (14 countries) created between 1980 and 2000, and which had at least 5 employees. Concerning the sectors of activity, we chose the NAF 31, which is a French nomenclature that lists the main sectors of economic activity. Industrial activities are classified into 14 sectors: food, drink and tobacco industry (DA); textiles (DB); leather and footwear industry (DC); wood and wooden products (DD); paper products, printing and publishing (DE); coking, refining, nuclear industry (DF); chemical industry (DG); rubber and plastics industry (DH); non-metallic mineral products (DI); metallurgy and metal transformation (DJ); mechanical engineering (DK); electric and electronic products (DL); transportation equipment (DM); and miscellaneous manufacturing industries (DN). Moreover, at the regional scale, the NUTS 1 level is chosen (standard regions) except for Finland, Ireland, Portugal, Sweden (NUTS 2) and for Luxembourg and Denmark (NUTS 0, national level). According to this, the sample is composed of 1294 French location decisions in 14 countries and 75 regions.

Results at national and regional levels

Tables 3.1 and 3.2 present the results of the Ellison and Glaeser index respectively at national and regional scales. At the national level, each share of the target represents a country (France being omitted).

Table 3.1 Results of the different variables (with D=0.82) at national level

Sectors	*H*	*G*	*DH*	$\sigma(G)$	$Z=(G-DH)/\sigma(G)$	Significance	Gamma
DA	0.20	0.23	0.17	0.06	1.04	68%	0.09
DB	0.42	0.33	0.35	0.09	−0.21	16%	−0.04
DC	0.13	0.14	0.11	0.06	0.52	39%	0.04
DD	0.47	0.48	0.38	0.15	0.67	48%	0.23
DE	0.11	0.09	0.09	0.04	0.09	7%	0.00
DF	0.30	0.45	0.24	0.10	2.11	95%	0.36
DG	0.07	0.01	0.05	0.02	−1.83	91%	−0.06
DH	0.16	0.28	0.13	0.05	3.08	99%	0.22
DI	0.06	0.08	0.05	0.02	1.26	77%	0.04
DJ	0.06	0.08	0.05	0.02	1.48	84%	0.04
DK	0.20	0.27	0.17	0.07	1.46	83%	0.16
DL	0.07	0.04	0.06	0.03	−0.71	51%	−0.02
DM	0.04	0.05	0.03	0.02	1.27	77%	0.03
DN	0.20	0.12	0.16	0.06	−0.70	50%	−0.07

Table 3.2 Results of the different variables (with D=0.96) at regional level

Sectors	*H*	*G*	*DH*	$\sigma(G)$	$Z=(G-DH)/\sigma(G)$	Significance	Gamma
DA	0.20	0.18	0.20	0.06	−0.30	23%	−0.02
DB	0.42	0.44	0.40	0.12	0.28	22%	0.06
DC	0.13	0.14	0.12	0.04	0.46	35%	0.02
DD	0.47	0.49	0.45	0.13	0.34	27%	0.09
DE	0.11	0.13	0.11	0.03	0.76	55%	0.03
DF	0.30	0.33	0.29	0.08	0.57	43%	0.07
DG	0.07	0.06	0.06	0.02	−0.39	30%	−0.01
DH	0.16	0.16	0.15	0.04	0.28	22%	0.02
DI	0.06	0.06	0.06	0.02	0.00	0%	0.00
DJ	0.06	0.07	0.05	0.02	1.08	71%	0.02
DK	0.20	0.12	0.20	0.06	−1.27	79%	−0.09
DL	0.07	0.04	0.07	0.02	−1.22	77%	−0.03
DM	0.04	0.06	0.04	0.01	2.65	99%	0.03
DN	0.20	0.19	0.19	0.06	0.01	1%	0.00

Considering the empirical findings, the index values and significances associated with each sector of activity have to be examined at the same time. In other words, the observed values of the Ellison and Glaeser index (denoted by γ) need to be significantly different from random distributions of investments. Hence, at the 5 per cent significance level, we can be 95 per cent confident that the distribution does not result from chance. At this threshold, only two sectors are concentrated: the coking, refining, nuclear industry (DF) and the rubber and plastics industry (DH). At the 10 per cent significance level, only one sector is significantly dispersed: the chemical industry (DG). Results at the national level can perhaps mask some geographic concentration or dispersion at a regional level. At this smaller scale, taking a 10 per cent significance level, only one sector of activity is regionally concentrated (transportation equipment, DM).

We have to mention that the Ellison and Glaeser index results only constitute a descriptive analysis of the industrial concentration of French industrial firms in European countries and regions and therefore they are not able to give any explanation of the observed phenomena. It is worth noting that the empirical results do not depend on the nature of the agglomeration forces. Ellison and Glaeser consider two factors (natural advantages and positive externalities generated by the concentration of firms) which could prompt firms to locate their affiliates in the same place. In both cases of agglomeration forces, the theoretical model leads to the same formalization of the index. Therefore, we do not know which force comes into play. Empirical findings simply indicate the geographic concentration/dispersion degree of sectors of activity. Consequently, resulting explanations can only be arguments. Our study is first to consider two geographic levels to evaluate the industrial concentration of multinationals thanks to the Ellison and Glaeser index. The spatial distribution of French subsidiaries in Europe could be significantly concentrated (or dispersed) at regional and national levels, or at only one geographic level, and for some sectors, the spatial distribution could not be significantly different from chance.

Firstly, it is quite surprising that the number of sectors significantly concentrated is less important at the regional scale and index values are higher at the national level. For instance, agglomeration effects take place in a close environment (externalities generated by the geographic proximity such as externalities of knowledge occuring at short distances). Thus, one could have been expected to find more sectors concentrated at the regional level. The average and the median of the index are higher at the national scale (resp. equal to 0.074 and 0.040) than the regional one (0.013 and 0.017). However, the increase of the average of the Ellison and Glaeser index with the level of spatial aggregation has already been underlined by previous studies (Ellison and Glaeser, 1997: from 0.044 at the state level to 0.078 at the census region level; Rosenthal and Strange, 2001: 0.010, 0.019 and 0.049 at the zip code, county or state level; Maurel and Sédillot, 1999: 0.06 and 0.09 at the *département* and regions scale).

However, we do not find any geographically concentrated sector of activity both at national and regional levels. Concerning the coking, refining, nuclear industry (DF) or the rubber and plastics industry (DH), empirical findings indicate that multinationals are only sensitive to national features whereas for the sector of transportation equipment (DM), regional characteristics seem to play an important role for French firms' location choice. Finally, one sector is significantly more dispersed at the national level than we expect to find from chance: the chemical industry (DG). This last result indicates that the French affiliates are evenly located across countries.

CONCLUSION

Taking into account the location of French investments in Europe, the purpose of this chapter was twofold: to assess the degree of spatial concentration of French FDI and to show whether the area of industrial activity alters the level of concentration. The originality of the chapter is to consider at the same time two geographic levels to evaluate the degree of spatial concentration of multinational firms using the Ellison and Glaeser index.

Firstly, applying this measure, we show that the distribution of French investments is strongly different across industrial sectors and according to the geographic level considered. Secondly, taking into account two geographic levels allows us to find that if one sector is concentrated at one level, it is not necessarily agglomerated at the other level. This fact proves that when we study the geographic location of French multinationals, we are compelled to consider at the same time regional and national levels. Finally, the Ellison and Glaeser index is a measure of concentration and cannot provide an explanation for the observed results. Consequently, this chapter paves the way for future research in the area of modelling the behaviour of French FDI, which would explain the results obtained in this study.

NOTES

1. We are grateful to the Direction des Relations Economiques Extérieures (DREE) of the French Ministry of Economics, Finance and Industry, for enabling us to work on the database *Enquête-Filiales DREE 2000*. We also want to thank Eric Marcon. This study received support from the Commissariat Général au Plan, research convention N° 4/1998.
2. See for example Duranton (1997), Fujita and Thisse (1997), Fujita *et al.* (1999), Ottaviano and Puga (1998) for an explanation of the different agglomeration or dispersion forces.

3. Estimations calculated from the *Enquête-Filiales DREE 2000.*
4. *Les Notes Bleues de Bercy* (2002).
5. Notations '*D*' and '*Z*' are taken from Head *et al.* (2002).

REFERENCES

Amiti, M. (1997), 'Specialisation patterns in Europe', *Centre for Economic Performance*, Discussion Paper 363.

Audretsch, B.D. and M.P. Feldman (1996), 'R&D spillovers and the geography of innovation and production', *American Economic Review*, **86** (3), 630–40.

Brülhart, M. (2001), 'Evolving geographical concentration of European manufacturing industries', *Weltwirtschaftliches Archiv*, **137** (2), 215–43.

Brülhart, M. and J. Torstensson (1996), 'Regional integration, scale economies an industry location in the European Union', *Centre for Economic Policy Research*, Research Paper 1435.

Callejón, M. (1997), 'Concentración geográphica de la industria y economías de aglomeración', *Economia Industrial*, **0** (5), 61–68.

Crozet, M., T. Mayer, and J.-L. Mucchielli (2003), 'How do firms agglomerate? A study of FDI in France', *Regional Science and Urban Economics*, forthcoming.

Devereux, M.P. and R. Griffith (1998), 'Taxes and the location of production: evidence from panel of US multinationals', Journal of Public Economics, **68** (3), 335–67.

Devereux, M.P., R. Griffith and H. Simpson (1999), 'The geographic distribution of production activity in the UK', *The Institute for Financial Studies*, Working Paper 26/99.

Duranton, G. (1997), 'La nouvelle économie géographique: agglomération et dispersion', *Economie et Prévision*, **131** (5), 1–24.

Ellison, G. and E.L. Glaeser (1997), 'Geographic concentration in U.S. manufacturing industries: A dartboard approach', *Journal of Political Economy*, **105** (5), 889–927.

Ferrer, C. (1998), 'Patterns and determinants of location decisions by French multinationals in European countries', in J.-L. Mucchielli (ed.), *Multinational Location Strategy, Research in Global Strategic Management*, Greenwich, CT: JAI Press, pp. 117–38.

Ford, S. and R. Strange (1999), 'Where do Japanese manufacturing firms invest within Europe and why?', *Transnational Corporations*, **8** (1), 117–40.

Fujita, M. and J.-F. Thisse (1997), 'Economie géographique, problèmes anciens et nouvelles perspectives', *Annales d'Economie et de Statistique*, **0** (45), 37–87.

Fujita, M., P. Krugman and A. Venables (1999), *The Spatial Economy*, Cambridge: MIT Press.

Guimarães, P., O. Figueiredo and D.P. Woodward (2000), 'Agglomeration and the location of foreign direct investment in Portugal', *Journal of Urban Economics*, **47** (1), 115–35.

Head, K. and J. Ries (1996), 'Inter-city competition for foreign investment: static and dynamic effects of China's incentive areas', *Journal of Urban Economics*, **40** (1), 38–60.

Head, K., T. Mayer and J. Ries (2002), 'The geographic concentration of FDI in Asia', in J.H. Dunning and J.-L. Mucchielli (eds), *Multinational Firms: The Global and the Local Dilemma*, London: Routledge, pp. 159–77.

Houdebine, M. (1999), 'Concentration géographique des activités et spécialisation des départements français', *Economie et Statistique*, **326–327** (6–7), 189–204.

Jianping, D. (1999), 'Agglomeration effects in manufacturing location, are there any country's preferences?', *Economia Internazionale*, **52** (1), 59–78.

Les Notes Bleues de Bercy (2002), 'L'implantation des entreprises françaises en Europe', N° 241.

Maurel, F. and B. Sédillot (1999), 'A measure of the geographic concentration in French manufacturing industries', *Regional Science and Urban Economics*, **29** (5), 575–604.

Mayer, T. and J.-L. Mucchielli (1998), 'Strategic location behaviour: the case of Japanese investments in Europe', in J.-L. Mucchielli, P.J. Buckley and V.V. Cordell (eds), *Globalization and Regionalization: Strategies, Policies and Economic Environments*, The Haworth Press, pp. 131–67.

Mayer, T. and J.-L. Mucchielli (1999), 'La localisation à l'étranger des entreprises multinationales: une approche d'économie géographique hiérarchisée appliquée aux entreprises japonaises en Europe', *Economie et Statistique*, **326–327** (6–7), 159–76.

Midelfart-Knarvik, K.H., H.G. Overman, S.J. Redding and A.J. Venables (2000), 'The location of European industry', *European Commission*, Economic Paper 142.

Mucchielli, J.-L. and F. Puech (2003), 'Internationalisation et localisation des firmes multinationales: l'exemple des entreprises françaises en Europe', *Economie et Statistique*.

Ottaviano, G.I.P. and D. Puga (1998), 'Agglomeration in the global economy: A survey of the new economic geography', *World Economy*, **21** (6), 707–31.

Rosenthal, S.S. and W.C. Strange (2001), 'The determinants of agglomeration', *Journal of Urban Economics*, **50** (2), 191–229.

UNCTAD (2002), *Transnational Corporations and Export Competitiveness*, United Nations Publications: United Nations, New York and Geneva.

Wheeler, D. and A. Mody (1992), 'International investment location decisions, the case of U.S. firms', *Journal of International Economics*, **33** (1–2), 57–76.

Woodward, D.P. (1992), 'Location determinants of Japanese manufacturing start-ups in the United States', *Southern Economic Journal*, **58** (3), 690–708.

4. Globalization of R&D and Local Scientific Systems: Regional Patterns and Local Integration[1]

Bernadette Madeuf and Gilliane Lefebvre

INTRODUCTION

This chapter deals with the globalization of technology and innovative activities by multinational groups, particularly in the case of French groups. The growing trend in the globalization of technology presents two salient features: the first is the regional specialization of foreign research units, the second is the integration of these units in local scientific and technological systems. In other words, globalization of technology does not imply that local specific characteristics of territories are becoming meaningless. On the contrary, they are playing a reinforced role.

Globalization of industrial research now forms a central part of the strategy of multinational enterprises. Until recently, the globalization of industrial research has been regarded as either a specific feature of some multinationals originating from small countries (like Swedish companies, for instance) or a condition for product adaptation to local demand peculiarities. But it has now received full attention as a general trend. Compared with the case of companies in other countries, the case of French companies is far less documented: the research conducted abroad by French companies has been indirectly estimated by patents deposits in the United States (USPO, Cantwell and Kotecha, 1994; Cantwell and Janne, 2000); on the other hand, the research conducted in France by foreign companies, even if the Ministry of Research is providing general information, has not been frequently studied (Madeuf *et al.*, 1993).

The survey we conducted during the first months of 2000 on behalf of the French Ministry (MERT) constitutes a first direct appraisal of the internationalization of R&D by French multinational enterprises[2]. The first objective was to provide a measure of the R&D activities conducted in foreign locations, the second was to analyse the motives, functions and organization of the foreign located R&D. Since recent studies in the field have resulted in a growing number of competing models for the technological strategy and the organization of foreign research centres, the survey allowed us to assess their relevance (Niosi, 1999). The analysis of the French case also shows the role that national systems of innovation, or rather local systems of innovation, are playing as determining factors in the choice of location and specialization of laboratories. One particular issue is the trade-off between spatial proximity and organizational proximity in strategic decisions by multinationals (Blanc and Sierra, 1999; Lawson, 1999).

Relationships between national, or local, scientific and technical systems on the one hand and, on the other, the internationalized R&D in multinational enterprises represent a prominent issue for scientific and technological policy (Archibugi and Iammarino, 1999; Madeuf and Lefebvre, 1999; Meyer-Krahmer and Reger, 1999). Location decisions of foreign R&D centres are based on existing scientific and technical resources and skills; but the activities of the centres reinforce these local capacities, and therefore the technological comparative advantages of foreign locations (either at the national or local level). Another possible consequence of foreign controlled R&D is the crowding out effect resulting from the use of (relatively) scarce resources by the research centres: these local resources, particularly skilled labour, are employed to produce innovations contributing to reinforce the mother companies' competitive edge, but not the competitive advantage of the national economies where centres are operating. On the contrary, the location of research centres in a foreign environment particularly well endowed with scientific and technical resources and characterized by dynamic innovative activities, could compensate for deficiencies in the innovation system of the country of origin of mother companies.

The first part of this chapter is devoted to the main features of the foreign located R&D centres of the French companies of the survey. These features are connected with the conclusions, or outstanding questions, raised in the literature on this topic. The second part deals with the regional specialization of the centres. Two models may be distinguished according to the location of the centres in European countries or in the United States. Beyond regional differences, the issue examined in the third part deals with the local integration of the research centres. In a way that may appear somewhat paradoxical, there is a relationship between the orientation of the foreign located R&D activities and the strength of their integration in the local scientific and technical systems. The more global are the objectives of the R&D activities in the centres (in terms of worldwide markets and technological breakthroughs aimed at), the more frequent and intense are their co-operative links with local partners. These relationships imply not only that international flows of scientific and technical knowledge are intensifying inside the multinational enterprises among their different units (this trend is consistent with the growing globalization), but also that local flows are multiplying through the local integration of globalized R&D centres.

GLOBALIZATION OF INDUSTRIAL R&D: THE FRENCH CASE IN PERSPECTIVE

Recent Growth, Geographic and Industrial Concentration

In order to measure how much industrial research is globalizing, two methods may be used: the first measures the input of innovative activities through R&D expenses, the other is based on patents statistics, mainly patents deposits in the US Patent Office, considered as a fair proxy of innovative output[3]. Generally the direct method is used for limited samples comprising a few dozen enterprises (for instance Gassmann and von Zedwitz, 1999; Gerybadze and Reger, 1999), whilst the patents statistics method has made possible analyses of larger populations comprising several hundred multinational enterprises (Cantwell and Janne, 1999, 2000; Patel and Vega, 1999). Our survey belongs to the first approach (see the presentation of the survey, note 1). Despite the advantages presented by the patents statistics (data from the USPO are homogeneous, allow for international comparisons and offer time series), their use might result in underestimating foreign R&D activities of either smaller companies that do not apply for patents in the USA, or companies operating in industries where patents are of less extensive use. On the other hand, R&D expenses do not cover the total efforts geared towards innovations in the firms (there is knowledge coming from outside, and resources devoted to innovations that are not located in the R&D centres themselves). Nevertheless, R&D expenses are not only used for international comparisons (see OECD, 1998), but may also be compared with national data, regularly collected, on R&D expenses of the business sector. Thus, in the case of the surveyed groups, taking into account their weight in the total R&D budgets of the business sector in France, the proportion of the globalized industrial research might be estimated to be at least 25 per cent of the total amount of business R&D. This proportion appears to be close to figures measuring the share of globalized research for German or Finnish enterprises, but larger than the corresponding figure for US enterprises (according to data from the OECD Secretariat, covering a limited number of countries).

Comparisons with measures based on US patents statistics are more complex. According to a recent study, the share of globalized research of French companies is estimated to reach 26.9 per cent of the total research, for the years 1987–95 (Cantwell and Janne, 2000). This figure is lower than the figure of 34.5 per cent corresponding to the share of globalized research of the 27 multinational groups of our survey (as for 1999). But the figure based on patents statistics exhibits a very fast growth (it was still 8.1 per cent in the years 1978–86). This trend parallels our own observations on the accelerating progress in the globalization of research expenses by French companies during the last decade.

In fact, the growing trend of internationalization of R&D by French companies appears as a recent phenomenon: 60 per cent of the foreign located centres have been implanted during the last ten years. Moreover, this trend shows two accelerating phases: the first from 1986 to 1990 during which 26 new research centres were established and the second from 1996 to 1999 with 41 new centres, out of which there were 24 in the years 1998 and 1999. These two phases parallel two periods of acceleration in international direct investment flows at the world level (CNUCED, 2000). The globalization of French companies not only reflected this evolution, but also resulted in catching up (Ministère de l'Economie, des Finances et de l'Industrie, 2001).

Industrial and geographic distributions of the research centres controlled by French groups appear to be close to observations from previous studies on country cases. The industrial distribution confirms that the globalization of research mainly concerns high technology industries. A few companies operating in two industries – chemical and pharmaceutical products, electronics, computers and telecommunications – exhibit the most globalized industrial research: they correspond to 18 groups controlling 148 out of the 214 research centres of the survey, amounting to 90.5 per cent of the total foreign R&D expenses, presenting a ratio of foreign R&D to total R&D higher than average (respectively 40 and 37.5 per cent).

The geographic distribution of the research centres shows that foreign located R&D is mainly concentrated in advanced economies, firstly in European countries then in the USA; the French companies appearing very close to other European companies. The regional distribution of the 214 centres (or the distribution of the foreign R&D budgets) shows that Europe is the first region, with 101 centres (and 64.8 per cent of the total foreign budget), before North America (in fact the USA, since Canada hosts only one centre) with 52 centres (and 29.5 per cent of the budget). The recently growing number of centres implanted in the USA, and the prospect of future development in this country, correspond to the trend emerging from analyses based on patents statistics (Cantwell and Janne, 2000). Until recently, the globalization of industrial research by European firms, more advanced than it is for US or Japanese firms, might have been considered as a mere 'regionalization' resulting from both the process of regional economic integration and the relatively small size of national economies of origin. But there appears to be an actual 'globalization', meaning that the location of foreign research centres is not limited to other European countries, and the case of French firms is not different from other European firms.

Emphasis on the geographic or spatial factors determining the globalization of industrial research might lead us to underestimate the part played by the globalization of industries and markets in this process. Motives explaining the implantation of research centres, as well as the functions they are implementing, are useful to understand how the foreign located research is integrated within group strategies.

Globalizing R&D: Towards the 'Technology-Focused' Strategy

Is the globalization of industrial research resulting from decisions geared to optimally locate the firm's technological and innovative activities taking into account the worldwide distribution of available scientific and technical resources (Doz *et al.*, 2001; Sachwald, 2000)? Or is this globalization determined by choices related to productive or commercial strategies of the firm? In this second view, the globalization of the technology function would result from the globalization of the production itself (Patel and Vega, 1999; Patel and Pavitt, 1998). The circumstances and motives of the implantation of the centres provide some answers to this central issue.

According to studies on the factors determining the globalization of research in non-French firms, the first possibility, sometimes labelled as 'technology sourcing' orientation, appears more frequently associated with industries characterized by rapid technological change (pharmaceuticals, electronics), whilst the second corresponds to less R&D intensive industries. Emphasis put on either orientation might result from the size of the samples and the industrial activities of the firms on which the studies are based. Thus, analyses of relatively small samples, comprising 20 or 30 highly globalized enterprises operating in high tech industries, present conclusions which differ from those of studies based on large populations of several hundred firms covering a wider range of industrial activities. The discussion of the French case will lead to a balanced proposal, which, furthermore, takes into account the current evolution.

At first, it appears that in the surveyed sample, the groups showing the larger foreign R&D ratio (as a share of their total R&D expenses) also have the more globalized profile (as measured by the share of foreign sales). Globalization of industrial research therefore appears to go along with global involvement of firms. This is reinforced by the circumstances surrounding implantation of the centres. Actually, a very large number of the centres have been taken over: the average proportion is one creation against four acquired centres through international merger and acquisitions. The acquisition of research capacities is thus the by-product of a wider strategic move decided for motives which are not mainly of a technical or scientific nature. This is the case for 95 per cent of the centres which have been acquired. Nevertheless, for a minority of the acquired centres (for almost 20 per cent), the possibility of buying R&D assets has also played a part in motivating the merger–acquisition, in parallel with the acquisition of productive and marketing assets. Anyway, in every case the main objective is to enter or reinforce the presence on the market, or to reach the critical size in order to face competition in the global or regional marketplace. It can be observed that the proportion of acquisitions is rising for the more recently implanted centres, with some regional or industrial variations: this trend is consistent with the international merger and acquisitions wave which has been spreading worldwide from 1996 to 2000.

The motives behind the implantation of the centres are presented below in order to complete the picture of the factors determining the research globalization. It must be stressed that in the case of the acquired centres, the implantation motives are to be understood as motives for maintaining the centres after they have been acquired (actually, only a small proportion of the acquired centres have been experiencing a cut in their budget or staff).

Whether the centres are created or acquired, two main categories of motives come first. These are the support to production (with adaptation of the product or process of production) and the exploitation of local scientific or technical resources (high skilled, or low wage, scientific manpower, R&D co-operation with business or academic sector). These two motives are both presented for more than 43 per cent of the total number of centres. The support to production motive appears of particular importance for the centres of the electronic–computer industry (66 per cent) and the centres located in the USA (52 per cent). Conversely, in the chemical–pharmaceutical industry this motive is less frequent. Behind the support to production different elements are to be found, such as the necessity to meet local standards, either technical, health or environment related, or to answer the technical needs of specific customers (electronic equipment). All these elements are associated with the local demand peculiarities and market competitive pressure.

The possibility to take advantage of local scientific and technical resources includes three main different advantages. The availability of high skilled labour plays a role for more than 33 per cent of the 148 centres; the possibility to enter into co-operative agreements with public or academic laboratories is mentioned for almost 30 per cent of them; and the possibility of co-operative research with enterprises appears for 22 per cent of them. We shall mention that one third of the foreign located centres are actually co-operating with the public or academic sector, showing that local co-operation forms an important dimension of the globalization of research.

The weight of the various motives shows that implantation of foreign research centres is not predominantly oriented towards the exploitation of local scientific and technical capacities in order to reinforce and mobilize innovatory capabilities of the multinational groups. This should not be interpreted as the rejection of such a strategy, that might be labelled 'technology-focused'. But this strategy is not the only possible explanation of the international dissemination of industrial research. Furthermore, this strategy presents some peculiar features: the technology-focused orientation is more pronounced in the case of the centres created, in the electronic–computer–telecommunications industry and in the case of larger centres. Eventually, comparison of motives according to the period of implantation of the centres reveals that local scientific and technical advantages and technology-focused strategy are more frequent in the case of more recently established centres. Future prospects, which include a rise in the share of research property, as opposed to development (in R&D), as well as an intensified specialization of the centres, tend to confirm that the technology-focused strategy will progressively be more asserted.

World Market: First Target of the Global Organization of Research

Competences and functions of foreign research centres determine the part they play in the global strategy of firms. Different kinds of information are used: nature of the R&D activities, type of technology field (generic, key and advanced technologies) and targeted markets. In fact, the main objective of the research activities of the centres is the world market, far more than the local or regional market, even if the centres have originally been taken over during mergers and acquisitions motivated by the conquest of market shares abroad. This orientation is accompanied by rather centralized management methods giving the centres a very limited autonomy. Such is the answer that the French groups' experience gives to a recurrent question in the literature, either economic or more management oriented: this is the 'centralization versus decentralization' issue, which is a key issue in the management of technology and innovation at the world level (Gerybadze and Reger, 1999;

Chiesa, 1996; Zander, 1999). It is generally dealt with by analysing centripetal and centrifugal forces in order to find how to balance them. Whilst the former take into account local factors (local demand, technical adaptation, use of local skills, or local co-operation), the latter mainly correspond to specific features of the production of new technological knowledge (tacit and not codified knowledge, economies of scale, preservation of proprietary assets through central control, synergy between functions inside firms, strategic dimension of the technology).

At first, it must be noted that the most important part of the foreign located research is dedicated to experimental development. It amounts to 84.3 per cent of the total R&D expenses, while applied research is about 15.1 per cent and fundamental research 0.6 per cent. On average, the distribution of industrial research in France gives 67.6 per cent for development, 28 per cent for applied research and 4.4 per cent for fundamental research in 1998 (Ministère de l'Education Nationale, 2000). The leading share of experimental development is observed in every industry, but is larger in low tech industrial activities. This corresponds to the short term concern of producing rapid R&D results to be used in local production and markets. It furthermore confirms that enterprises are trying to maintain the most critical R&D activities as close as possible to their headquarters in order to keep control over the technological evolution.

Nevertheless, there is a recent change. On the one hand, the distribution of foreign R&D activities shows that the share of research activities, either fundamental or applied, is growing. On the other hand, the type of R&D research work inside the centres is changing according to the period of their implantation: the more recent the centres, the more their research work is geared towards key technologies and, conversely, less towards generic technologies. This evolving profile reflects a change in the functions of the centres, which are becoming closer to the technological frontier in accordance with the technology-focused strategy.

Simultaneously, the market orientation of their objectives shows that the mission of a large majority of centres corresponds to innovating for the global world market, even if the innovation may also be geared to markets close to the centres. The world market is the main target of the research work of the centres in every industry and region: more than 60 per cent of the centres devote part of their research work to innovation for the world market. Adaptation of products or processes of production, also for the world market, is the second objective of the centres.

The competences and functions of the centres, in terms of markets and technical change aimed at, may be put together through a classification of the centres in a typology containing four categories: the centre devoted to technical support for local production, i.e. 'local support'; the centre dedicated to local innovation, i.e. 'local innovation'; the 'global laboratory' aimed at the development of products or processes for the world market in a particular product or technological field; and the 'excellence centre' oriented to basic research or key technologies for the whole group. Any centre may belong to one or more categories. Half of the 148 foreign research centres are of the 'global laboratory' type, one third are 'excellence centres'. Less than 25 per cent are devoted to 'local support' and less than 6 per cent are dedicated to 'local innovation'. A comparison of the origins and motives of implantation of the 'excellence centres' shows that they have been more frequently created than taken over, and motivated by local scientific and technical advantages. They thus correspond to the technology-focused strategy.

For all categories of research centres, their autonomy varies according to the kind of decision, but generally remains very limited. Concerning the origin of the research projects, the group's demand plays a leading part since the central research unit and the product division (or regional division) are involved in the definition of projects (for respectively 38.5 and 45.3 per cent of the centres). The centres themselves also take part in the decision process (for 37.8 per cent of the centres). Concerning the definition and management of the budgets of the centres, the decision process is even more centralized. Several responsibility levels intervene, but the headquarters, or at least its approval, remains a necessary step in the determination of the budget for more than half of the centres. In the case of the budget distribution among projects, if the centres seem to recover part of their autonomy *vis-à-vis* the headquarters, they remain under the control of the product division (or the regional division).

For the labour management, concert and decentralization go in parallel. The choice of the manager of the centre is jointly decided by the local affiliate and the headquarters, for more than 40 per cent of the centres. The centres intervene in 22 per cent of the cases, and always in accordance with the headquarters or local affiliate or product (or regional) division. Recruitment of research staff is the most decentralized decision. It is decided at the local level in 88.6 per cent of the centres. Eventually, all matters pertaining to the industrial property field are controlled by the central legal department, sometimes in concert with the local affiliates, but more rarely with the research centres themselves.

REGIONAL SPECIALIZATION: PROFILES OF US AND EUROPEAN RESEARCH CENTRES

The globalization of R&D by the French groups is characterized by geographic concentration, with 94.3 per cent of the research budgets of the 148 centres located in the USA and in Europe. Foreign located R&D appears slightly more concentrated than French direct investment abroad (the total share of the USA and Europe is 79.7 per cent of the total stock of direct investment). But American and European centres differ in many respects, which are explored in this section.

Industrial Specialization, Size and Periods of Implantation of the Centres

Industrial distribution of the centres, measured by either the number of centres or the amount of their budgets, reveals that European centres are mostly operating in the electronic–computer–telecommunication industry (with 44 centres and 71.4 per cent of the total R&D budget in Europe) and American centres are mostly in the chemical–pharmaceutical products (with 16 centres and 47.1 per cent of the total American R&D budget). In each region, the centres pertaining to the industry of specialization are larger than average. The industrial distribution is evolving in the USA: the more recently implanted centres are more frequently operating in the electronic activities.

Sizes and periods of implantation of centres also differ between the two regions. European centres are on average larger (47 per cent of the centres have budgets over 100 FF millions) than US centres (60 per cent of the centres have budgets less than 50 FF millions). This size difference is linked to the historical trend of the implantations. European centres have generally been established earlier than American ones. In 1995, there were 43 European centres, but still only 18 in the USA. But the regional distribution is evolving. Up to 1995, the number of new European centres was steadily growing; it has stabilized since then. The centres established in the USA multiplied during the two phases of acceleration already mentioned (1986–90 and 1996–99), and particularly during the second phase. This should not be a surprise, since the USA has become the first host country for world direct investment during these years.

The industrial specialization of the regions and its evolution are comparable to the results of studies using the patents statistics. These trends are in a way reflecting the local scientific advantages of the two regions; they may also result from the technology-focused strategy implemented by multinationals. But simultaneously, the historical trend of implantations appears closely related to direct investment and international merger and acquisitions trends. And therefore research globalization seems to be mainly a by-product of the production and marketing globalization. These two apparently opposed views might be reconciled by taking into account the evolution of the strategies of the firms.

Market Strategy in Europe versus Technology-Focused Strategy in the USA

European centres result from acquisitions in a much larger proportion than US centres (82.3 and 73.9 per cent). Conversely, the share of centres which have been created is higher in the USA (23.9 and 11.4 per cent). These differences show that French companies have been taking an active part in the competitive size race which has developed in various European industries in order to consolidate market shares. On the other hand, the implantation of US centres through creation may be associated with strategies more oriented to 'technology sourcing'.

The circumstances of acquisitions confirm this difference between strategies. In both regions the acquisition of a research centre is generally explained by the acquisition of productive assets. Nevertheless, a small proportion of the acquisitions are motivated by the existence of technological assets, and this is more frequently the case in the USA.

Motives to implant foreign research centres differ between the two regions. For the American centres of the French companies, two categories of motives are mentioned in higher proportion than is the case for the European centres: motives related to demand conditions and competitive pressure on the one hand, and on the other hand, motives of local scientific advantages. Thus production support, in the form of product adaptation (52.2 per cent for US and 44.3 per cent for European centres), reaction to local demand (one third of US centres and one tenth of European centres) and to local and international competitors are reaching higher percentages in the USA (see Table 4.1). On average, the presence of local scientific advantage, of any kind, plays a slightly larger part in the case of US centres (46 versus 42 per cent), but there are regional variations in the weight of each specific advantage. Surprisingly, the presence of high skilled scientific and technical labour is more frequently mentioned for European centres (39 and 31 per cent). But, for the possibility to enter into co-operative agreement with the academic or business sector, the reverse is true. Fiscal reduction for R&D expenses and flexibility of legal dispositions are also ranked higher in the case of the US centres (see Table 4.1).

The analysis of the motives of implantation reveals two regional profiles of research centres. US centres correspond to a strategy wherein scientific

Table 4.1 Comparing European to American centres: motives (%)

Motives for implantation of centres	Europe	USA
Support to production		
Product adaptation	44.3	52.2
Process adaptation	32.9	26.1
Reaction to demand conditions		
Local demand	13.9	32.6
Regional demand	11.3	32.6
Reaction to competition		
Local competitors	27.8	50
International competitors	39.2	45.6
Local scientific advantages		
Scientific skilled labour	39.2	30.4
Wages level	5.1	8.9
Co-operation with academic R&D	29.1	34.8
Co-operation with business R&D	17.7	28.3
Financial and legal advantages		
Taxation	6.3	15.2
Subsidies	5.1	8.7
Legislation	3.8	10.8

and technical factors play a prominent role. But at the same time, French firms stress that intense competition in the US market makes their local presence necessary to face this competition.

The content and orientation of the R&D activities, the importance of the global market as their main goal and the resulting typology of the centres, all confirm the differing strategic orientations of the research conducted in each region.

Whilst research in the European centres is more oriented to experimental development and generic technologies, in the US centres it is marked by a larger part of applied research and advanced and key technologies. In the total budgets, the development shares are 83.3 per cent in European centres and 77.5 per cent in US centres, applied research shares amount to 11 and 22.2 per cent. This general orientation is confirmed by the distribution of R&D among technological fields. European centres' activities are relatively balanced among the three considered fields – generic technologies, key technologies and advanced technologies – with a slightly less marked share for the third one. In the USA, the advanced technologies field is the most important, and conversely the generic technologies field represents a lower share than in European centres (see Table 4.2).

Table 4.2 Comparing European to American centres: composition of R&D (%)

Distribution of R&D expenses	Europe	USA
Basic research	0.7	0.3
Applied research	11.0	22.2
Development	88.3	77.5
Nature of technologies*		
Generic technologies	39.2	32.6
Key technologies	29.1	32.6
Advanced technologies	26.6	47.8

Note: *Answering ratio 72%.

The US technology leadership is surely the main factor determining the attractiveness of the country in recent years. The development of French direct investment, via merger and acquisitions, as well as the orientation of the activities of the R&D centres reinforce the technology-focused strategy of the French multinationals (Florida, 1997; Serapio and Dalton, 1999).

The world market is the first target of the research work of the centres in both regions, for either innovation or adaptation of existing products. This orientation seems to be more pronounced in the European centres. Furthermore, innovation or adaptation for local markets is rarely considered as a significant goal in Europe, whilst technology adaptation for local markets is the third goal for US centres (after innovation and adaptation for world markets). This is explained by the need to satisfy specific customer demands (technical standards) and to capture a growing share in this competitive market.

The distribution of the centres among the categories of the typology is a reflection of their whole missions. The centres of the 'global laboratory' type form the most frequent category in both regions, with a slightly larger share in Europe. Differences concern the 'excellence centres' and 'local support' types: US centres more often belong to these two categories (excellence centres 43.5 versus 35.4 per cent, local support 30.4 versus 22.8 per cent, see

Table A.6). This distribution of the US centres among categories may be explained by two trends: the first corresponding to a more decentralized advanced research, the second to R&D aimed at the satisfaction of local standards and demands. This distribution also reflects the possibility to co-operate with local R&D, which constitutes a motive more frequently cited in the US case. In other words, the technology-focused strategy is confirmed for US located centres.

GLOBALIZATION AND LOCAL CO-OPERATION ARE CONNECTED

Establishing research centres abroad and entering into international technological alliances constitute two complementary forms of the globalization of technology and innovative activities. Most multinational firms simultaneously use both methods. At the world level, the more the multinational firms develop an international network of research centres, the more they are involved in strategic technological partnerships (Narula and Hagedoorn, 1997). Nevertheless, the main targets aimed at by each method are not exactly the same. Compared to the internationalization of R&D, international technological partnership is mostly implemented by firms seeking complementary specific assets, trying to share the growing costs and risks of innovations; access to markets and collective agreements for defining technological standards also play a part.

One central question could be whether technological partnership might result in, or be a substitute for, the implantation of foreign research centres. The answer depends on the type of the alliances. Thus co-financed research projects do not imply the constitution of a foreign laboratory, as opposed to alliances for joint laboratories. Relationships between the two forms of globalization of technology seem to be complex.

Our survey allowed us to study the topic of the relationship between foreign located R&D and international technological partnership at the level of the research units abroad, and not at the global level of the multinational headquarters. The main result is that the more the foreign research units are integrated into technology-focused strategies, the stonger is their participation in local partnerships. Thus, research centres with R&D geared towards research, more than development, and oriented to innovation for the world market, also multiply co-operation agreements with enterprises, academic or public research laboratories located nearby. In other words, the globalization process does not involve territorial, or spatial, factors having become meaningless, as could be implied by an overstated use of the adjective 'footloose' to describe activities with shallow local rooting. On the contrary, the deepening of local partnerships accompanies the globalization process.

Co-operation with Academic and/or Business R&D

Local partnerships are analysed under their various forms. Regional and industrial differences are presented as examples illustrating the relationships between research globalization and local integration.

The first information confirms the important role played by co-operation: centres with actual co-operative agreements (67 per cent of the answering centres) outnumber centres with the motive of co-operation. A second surprising point is related to the respective weight of two forms of partnership, partnership with public or academic research and partnership with business R&D. The proportion of centres with the latter form is higher (82 per cent) than the share of centres with the former (64 per cent). Eventually, almost half of the total number of centres have entered into both forms of partnership.

The gap between the frequency of co-operation as a motive and the frequency of co-operative agreements as actually implemented, is explained by the number of agreements with business R&D. The centres with agreements only with other enterprises are in majority centres for which co-operation was not presented as a motive for implantation. This may give rise to two explanations. Either local co-operation with enterprises is not considered as a local scientific advantage conditioning the location decision; or if co-operation with business R&D is a local scientific advantage, this is considered as attainable without being locally present, but by remote contracting (it is possible, too, that co-operation with business is considered as mere evidence, not to be discussed or mentioned). Therefore, if the latter is confirmed, the two forms of technology globalization – foreign located centre and international partnership – are alternatively used in the case of co-operation with enterprises, but playing complementary parts in the case of co-operation with academic research.

The frequency of partnership, orientation of agreements towards academic or business R&D, and complementary roles of these two forms show industrial and geographic differences giving rise to contrasting features.

Geographic and Industrial Profiles

For European centres, the importance and orientation of the co-operative agreements are close to the average of the total surveyed population. But American centres present a more specific profile.

Generally, centres located in the USA have more often contracted local agreements, since almost 75 per cent of them are involved (this confirms the information related to co-operation as a motive). Centres co-operating only with R&D laboratories in universities are fewer than elsewhere, but it must be noted that 57.7 per cent of the co-operating centres are engaged in both forms of agreement. These forms thus play complementary parts in the US case.

Concerning industrial differences, there is a sharp contrast between the two large groups of industries that are the most active in the field of technological change. In the chemical–pharmaceutical industry, centres appear to be less geared towards local partnership (57.8 against an average of 67.2 per cent). There are a few centres with co-operative agreements only with enterprises; but conversely, co-operation with academic centres is more frequent than in other industries (see Table 4.3). In the same industry, more than half of the co-operating centres have both forms of partnership. The centres in the electronic–computer industry are characterized by a higher rate of partnership (83.3 per cent of the centres), a stronger trend to enter agreements with business R&D (94 per cent of the co-operating centres), but lower links with academic research (only 6 per cent of the centres have only this kind of co-operation).

Table 4.3 Co-operation agreements of foreign R&D centres (%)

	Number of centres	Per cent of co-operating centres (total)	With the academic sector	With the business sector	With both sectors
Total	119	67.2	17.5	36.3	46.2
USA	35	74.3	7.7	34.6	57.7
Europe	61	68.3	21.4	35.7	42.9
Other areas	23	52.2	25.0	41.7	33.3
Chemical-Pharma.	45	57.8	30.8	11.5	57.7
ECT*	42	83.3	5.7	51.4	42.9
MEE**	25	48	16.7	58.3	25
Other industries	7	100	28.6	14.3	57.2

Notes: *ECT=Electronics, computers, telecommunications.
**MEE=Mechanical engineering, electrical equipment.

The emerging picture is the following: the more the centres are conducting 'high tech' activities oriented to world innovation, the more they have developed local co-operation agreements with academic and business sectors. Partnership with business R&D is particularly intense in the case of products for which firms have to adapt their technologies to local demand in order to face competition.

Characteristic Features of the Centres with Local Partnership

In order to refine the analysis of the link between local partnership and functions of the foreign research centres, this last subsection deals with the specific features of co-operating centres. Actually, centres which have entered local research agreements constitute a very peculiar part of the whole population of our survey. Compared to the centres with no agreement, they differ in many respects examined in the study: motives of implantation, nature of the R&D activities, research project orientation, management style and distribution among classes in the typology. The profile of centres with local partnership shows that they are conducting R&D activities oriented to scientific topics, or at the leading edge of technological change, aimed at scientific or technological breakthrough and this research work is deeply integrated into the global competitive strategies of the whole groups.

Thus, by comparison, centres with partnership agreements have been more frequently created than centres without partnership (31.2 against 8.8 per cent). Among the various motives for implantation, local scientific advantages play a relatively more important part: existing local highly skilled labour has been taken in account for 57.5 per cent of the co-operating centres (13 per cent for the centres with no partnership), the possibility of local partnership with academic research appears ranked second with 53.6 versus 2.6 per cent) and local partnership with enterprises is ranked third (with 40 versus 2.6 per cent). Centres with partnership correspond closely to the technology-focused strategy.

The size of their budgets and the preponderance of research over development in their R&D activities confirm the role played by the co-operating centres. First, these centres (80) altogether represent 78.2 per cent of the total amount of foreign R&D expenses and their average size is larger than the average size of the population (of the 148). Together they spend 100 per cent of the basic research, 94 per cent of the applied research and 75.6 per cent of the development expenditures abroad. Their R&D activities are mainly aimed at the enlargement and deepening of scientific and technological capabilities of their group, and not only at the exploitation of technological knowledge already produced by central research units (Kuemmerle, 1999).

Besides production of new technological knowledge, the R&D work of centres with partnership agreements is oriented towards innovation (far more than adaptation) designed for the world market which comes first in their objectives, far before innovation or adaptation for regional or local markets representing very secondary goals. Conversely, centres with no co-operation are leading R&D works less oriented to the world market and more to local market.

Orientation to world markets of research activities of centres with partnership is related to their key position in the global technology strategy of the multinationals they are part of. One last specific feature of these centres offers a general synthetic view: it is their distribution among the various categories of the typology. Two categories appear as predominant, the 'global laboratory' and the 'excellence centre'. Compared to centres with no co-operation, the share of the 'excellence centre' appears particularly high: more than half of the co-operating centres are of this type (52.5 per cent), whilst they are less than 18 per cent among the centres without partnership (17.6 per cent). The relationship between local integration in research systems and global technological vocation of the foreign R&D centres is thus confirmed.

CONCLUSION

As a concluding point it seems important to stress that globalization of industrial research and technology is a dynamic process presenting changing features as it progresses. Three elements are probably going to influence the global dissemination of research by French companies and direct it to the technology-focused strategy. First comes the progress of the share of research, basic and applied, which is appearing in the total R&D expenses of the most recently implanted centres. Second, for the immediate future the French firms are planning to develop their foreign R&D, particularly in the USA and in the electronic–computer–telecommunication industry and less in Europe and in the chemical–pharmaceuticals. Eventually, the multinationals are generally going to 'redesign' the attributions of the centres, in the direction of a sharper specialization. This new orientation of centres' activities can be easily understood, taking into account the large number of acquired centres. In order to prevent the duplication of R&D efforts, to reach economies of scale, to optimize resources allocation according to local scientific potentials, rationalizing the industrial research and innovative capacities is regarded by firms as a necessary step to enhance their innovative edge at world level.

NOTES

1. The text of this chapter was previously published by the journal *Sciences de la Société*, 54, October 2001, pp. 29–50, Toulouse, Presses Universitaires du Mirail,

under the title: 'Les liens paradoxaux entre stratégie technologique globale et intégration locale. Le cas des groupes français'. It is reprinted here with the permission of the editor.

2. A direct survey on foreign located R&D activities of French groups has been conducted for the French Ministère de l'Education Nationale during the year 2000. The sample has been formed on the basis of the companies with the largest R&D budgets in the annual survey on business R&D expenses conducted by the Ministry in 1998–99 (concerning R&D expenses for 1997). After correction (exluding foreign controlled firms, public companies and a few firms refusing to participate in our survey), the sample contains 27 large industrial companies amounting together to more than half (57.6 per cent) of the total R&D expenses of the French business sector, excluding R&D under foreign control. The 27 groups have been classified according to their activities (and taking into account confidentiality of data) into four large industries based on generic technologies: chemical–pharmaceutical products (10 groups), mechanical engineering–electrical equipment (6 groups), electronic–computer–telecommunications (8 groups) and other industries (3 groups). One of the difficulties of the survey is that these global companies have been experiencing multiple international mergers and acquisitions and restructuring of their operations. From 1997 to 2000, 12 of them have been involved in large international M&As, with following adaptations which are not yet wholly stabilized. Together in 1999 these 27 global firms were controlling 214 research centres located abroad (and 138 in France) and spending a foreign R&D budget representing 34.8 per cent of their total R&D budget. Quantitative and qualitative detailed data have been gathered for 148 foreign research centres, amounting to 78 per cent of the total foreign R&D budgets of our sample (Madeuf *et al.*, 2000).
3. Globalization of R&D presents two sides: R&D conducted by foreign companies inside the country (inward) and R&D conducted abroad by national companies (outward). Quantitative data are less frequent in the second case.

REFERENCES

Archibugi, D. and S. Iammarino (1999), 'The policy implications of the globalization of innovation', *Research Policy*, **28** (2–3), 317–36.

Blanc, H. and C. Sierra (1999), 'The internationalization of R&D by multinationals: a trade-off between external and internal proximity', *Cambridge Journal of Economics*, **23** (2), 187–206.

Cantwell, J. and U. Kotecha (1994), 'L'internationalisation des activités technologiques: le cas français en perspective', in F. Sachwald (ed.), *Les défis de la mondialisation*, Paris: IFRI /Masson, pp. 107–52.

Cantwell, J. and O. Janne (1999), 'Technological globalization and innovative centres: the role of corporate technological leadership and locational hierarchy', *Research Policy*, **28** (2–3), 119–44.

Cantwell, J. and O. Janne (2000), 'The role of multinational corporations and national states in the globalization of innovatory capacity: the European perspective', *Technology Analysis and Strategic Management*, **12** (2), 243–62.

Chiesa, V. (1996), 'Managing the internationalization of R&D activities', *IEEE Transactions on Engineering Management*, **43** (1), 7–23.

CNUCED (2000), *World Development Report*, Genève.

Doz, Y., J. Santos and P. Williamson (2001), *From Global to Metanational: How Companies Win in the Knowledge Economy*, Boston, MA: Harvard Business School Publishing.

Florida, R. (1997), 'The globalization of R&D: results of a survey of foreign-affiliated R&D laboratories in the USA', *Research Policy*, **26** (1), 85–104.

Gassmann, O. and M. von Zedtwitz (1999), 'Organizing industrial R&D on a global scale', *R&D Management*, **28** (3), 147–62.

Gerybadze, A. and G. Reger (1999), 'Globalization of R&D: recent changes in the management of innovation in transnational corporations', *Research Policy*, **28** (2–3), 251–74.

Kuemmerle, W. (1999), 'Foreign direct investment in industrial research in the pharmaceutical and electronic industries – Results from a survey of multinational firms, *Research Policy*, **28** (2–3), 179–93.

Lawson, C. (1999), 'Towards a competence theory of the region', *Cambridge Journal of Economics*, **23** (2), 151–66.

Madeuf, B. and G. Lefebvre (1999), 'La globalisation de la recherche industrielle face aux systèmes nationaux d'innovation', *Sciences de la Société*, **48**, 91–112.

Madeuf, B., G. Lefebvre and L. Chentouf (2000), *La globalisation de la recherche-développement. Le cas des entreprises françaises*, Rapport pour le Ministère de l'Education Nationale, Paris.

Madeuf, B., G. Lefebvre and A. Savoy (1993), *Les activités de recherche en France des sociétés étrangères*, Rapport pour le Ministère de la Recherche et de l'Enseignement, Paris.

Meyer-Krahmer, F. and G. Reger (1999), 'New perspectives on the innovation strategies of multinational enterprises: Lessons for technology policy in Europe', *Research Policy*, **28** (2–3), 751–76.

Ministère de l'Economie, des Finances et de l'Industrie (2001), 'Les investissements directs dans le monde', *Les Notes bleues de Bercy*, 199.

Ministère de l'Education Nationale (2000), *Recherche & Développement en France, Résultats 1998*, Paris.

Narula, R. and J. Hagedoorn (1997), *Globalization, Organizational Modes and the Growth of International Strategic Technology Alliances*, MERIT Research Memorandum, Maastricht.

Niosi, J. (1999), 'The internationalization of industrial R&D: from technology transfer to the learning organization', *Research Policy*, **28** (2–3), 107–17.

OECD (1998), *L'internationalisation de la R&D industrielle: structure et tendances*, Paris.

Patel, P. and K. Pavitt (1998), 'The wide (and increasing) spread of technological competencies in the world's largest firms: a challenge to conventional wisdom', in A.D. Chandler, P. Hagström and O. Sölvell (eds), *The Dynamic Multinational Firm*, Oxford: Oxford University Press, pp. 192–213.

Patel, P. and M. Vega (1999), 'Patterns of internationalization of corporate technology: location vs. home country advantages', *Research Policy*, **28** (2–3), 145–55.

Sachwald, F. (2000), 'The new American challenge and transatlantic technology sourcing', *Les Notes de l'Ifri, Série Transatlantique*, 24.

Serapio, M. and D. Dalton (1999), 'Globalization of industrial R&D: an examination of foreign R&D in the United States, *Research Policy*, **28** (2–3), 303–16.

Zander, I. (1999), 'How do you mean « global » ? An empirical investigation of innovation networks in the multinational corporation', *Research Policy*, **28** (2–3), 195–213.

APPENDIX TABLES

Table A4.1 Comparing European to American centres: objectives of R&D (%)

Targeted markets	Europe	USA
Local market		
Adaptation	17.7	37.0
Innovation	1.3	2.2
Regional market		
Adaptation	5.1	
Innovation	3.8	15.2
World market		
Adaptation	53.2	45.6
Innovation	67.1	52.2

Table A4.2 Comparing co-operating to not co-operating centres: motives (%)

Motives for implantation of centres	With local co-operation	Without local co-operation
Support to production		
Product adaptation	48.8	38.2
Process adaptation	46.3	10.3
Reaction to demand conditions		
Local demand	11.3	33.8
Regional demand	33.8	4.4
Reaction to competition		
Local competitors	22.5	51.5
International competitors	55	23.5
Local scientific advantages		
Scientific skilled labour	57.5	7.4
Wages level	13.9	2.9
Co-operation with academic R&D	53.8	1.5
Co-operation with business R&D	40	1.5
Financial and legal advantages		
Taxation	16.3	0
Subsidies	11.3	0
Legislation	11.3	1.5

Table A4.3 Comparing co-operating with not co-operating centres: composition of R&D (%)

Distribution of R&D expenses of the centres	With co-operation	Without co-operation
Basic research	0.7	0.1
Applied research	18.2	4
Development	79.5	95.9
Nature of Technologies		
Generic technologies	43.8	38.2
Key technologies	53.8	10.3
Advanced technologies	53.8	13.2

Table A4.4 Comparing co-operating with not co-operating centres: goals of R&D (%)

Targeted markets	Centres with co-operation (80)	Centres without co-operation (68)	All centres (148)	Excellence centres with or without co-operation (54)
Local market				
Adaptation	10.5	45.6	26.3	1.9
Innovation	2.5	2.9	2.7	0
Regional market				
Adaptation	17.5	8.8	13.5	11.1
Innovation	15	2.9	9.5	13
World market				
Adaptation	65	29.4	48.6	34.8
Innovation	85	33.8	61.5	81.5

Table A4.5 Comparing co-operating to not co-operating centres: typology (%)*

Centres classified as:	Co-operating (80)	Not co-operating (68)	All centres (148)
Global laboratory	52.5	47.1	50
Excellence centre	52.5	17.6	36.5
Local support	15	35.3	24.3
Local innovation	10	1.5	6.1

Note: *Column total percentages higher than 100%, multiple answers are possible.

Table A4.6 Comparing European to American centres: typology (%)*

Centres classified as:	Europe	USA
Global laboratory	48.1	45.7
Excellence centre	35.4	43.5
Local support	22.8	30.4
Local innovation	3.8	6.5

Note: *Column total percentages higher than 100%, multiple answers are possible.

5. US Intra-firm Trade: Sectoral, Country and Location Determinants in the 1990s

João Paulo Filipe, Maria Paula Fontoura and Philippe Saucier

INTRODUCTION

In almost every year since the end of the 1940s, the volume of international trade has grown faster than the volume of world production and, as a result, the degree of interdependence of the world economy has increased. A large share of this rapid growth of international trade has been accomplished under the control of multinational corporations (MNCs) and a good proportion of MNCs' imports and exports consists of intra-firm trade.

Despite this increasingly important role of intra-firm trade in international commerce, this phenomenon has not attracted much investigation in the academic community. The reasons are twofold.

Firstly, intra-firm trade presents a substantial challenge to traditional trade theories. Most theorizing on international trade assumes explicitly or implicitly that it is undertaken by unrelated buyers and sellers in world markets. However, motivation for the international exchange of goods on open markets may differ for transactions within the MNCs. While in the former decisions are relatively decentralized, in the latter they tend to be centralized – 'hierarchical' transactions in Williamson's terminology (1975). Apparently we need a new and specific theoretical framework to grasp the phenomenon, not yet available.

Secondly, data on intra-firm trade is scarce, and when it exists it is usually too aggregated. The United States (US) and Japan[1] are the only countries that systematically report on related party trade, but in the latter case data are too aggregated for the purposes of this chapter. In the US case, the Bureau of Economic Analysis (BEA) of the US Department of Commerce reports annually on intra-firm trade but disaggregated data available for consultation are restricted to the majority-owned foreign affiliates (MOFAs). For other countries only rarely is it possible to get a figure for the importance of total intra-firm trade.

These shortcomings explain the few studies we have on this subject. Those available aim mainly at identifying at an empirical level, and in spite of the data limitations, the possible sources of intra-firm trade[2]. This chapter belongs to this line of research.

We aim to investigate the factors determining the intra-firm trade of US firms in the period 1989–1998. We will extend previous similar econometric testing not only by using more recent data but also by considering inter-country differences in addition to inter-sectoral variation of intra-firm trade. Besides, among the factors considered we will also analyse the specific role of the concentration/proximity factors suggested by the Economic Geography theory. Our results will be conditioned by the high level of aggregation of our study (32 sectors and 34 countries) imposed by our data source. However, the panel nature of the data allows us to partially overcome the reduced number of observations.

The chapter goes as follows: the next section presents a brief description of intra-firm trade of US firms between 1989 and 1998; the third section makes a short review of some contributions to the hypotheses to be tested; the models and the variables used are described in the fourth section; in the fifth section we present and discuss the results and a final section concludes.

EMPIRICAL EVIDENCE

In what follows we use the information of the BEA of the US Department of Commerce to analyse the major trends of US intra-firm trade (IFT) for the period between 1989 and 1998. Data for 1998 are preliminary.

Table 5.1 presents statistics for the share of US intra-firm trade in the US trade. As we can observe, the intra-firm trade represents a weight close to 40 per cent of total US trade in all years. From 1989 to 1998, intra-firm trade varied between 37 per cent and 44.1 per cent. This means that US foreign trade data are probably highly sensitive to variations in the transfer pricing of MNCs. This fact in itself justifies paying special attention to this phenomenon, as its implications involve not only the balance of payments but also tax revenue considerations.

Since the value of this indicator varied very little in the period, we can assume that US intra-firm trade increased roughly at the same rate as the US trade. This is also true for the share of US intra-firm imports in the total of US imports and for the US intra-firm exports in the total of US exports. The indicator varied, in the latter case, between 32.7 and 38.1 per cent (respectively, in 1991 and 1989) and, in the former, between 39.3 per cent (in 1998) and 49.8 per cent (in 1990).

Table 5.1 Share of US IFT in the total US trade, 1989–1998 (%)

	Exports	Imports	Total
1989	38.1	48.7	44.1
1990	36.5	49.8	43.9
1991	32.7	43.1	38.3
1992	33.4	41.5	37.8
1993	33.5	39.8	37.0
1994	36.5	43.4	40.4
1995	35.1	41.6	38.8
1996	35.5	41.6	39.0
1997	36.0	39.8	38.1
1998	35.4	39.3	37.6

Source: US Bureau of Economics Analysis, US Department of Commerce.

We can divide this US intra-firm trade into two major categories: one that corresponds to IFT between US parent firms and their affiliates[3] in the rest of the world, and another relative to IFT between foreign parent firms and their affiliates[4] in the US (US affiliates, in what follows). There is, obviously, a third category that refers to the trade between US affiliates and foreign affiliates of the same group, but the BEA does not report these data.

From Table 5.2 we can observe the average share of intra-firm trade, in these two groups for the period analysed. For the total intra-firm trade the values are similar: 20.4 per cent for trade between US parents and their foreign affiliates and 18.6 per cent for trade between foreign firms and their US affiliates. But the nature of this trade is different. The intra-firm trade between US parents and their foreign affiliates is, essentially, intra-firm exports (on average, 25.3 per cent of total US exports) while the US affiliates' intra-firm trade is, basically, intra-firm imports (on average, 25.5 per cent of total US imports).

Comparing intra-firm exports of US affiliates with the intra-firm imports of US parents, we can observe that this value is higher (almost double) in the latter case. In order to understand this result, we have to take into consideration that US affiliates export to several markets, while US parents are importing into a single, large and well developed market.

Table 5.2 Share of US IFT in the total US trade reported between US parents and US affiliates from foreign MNCs (1989–1998 average, %)

	US parents	US affiliates	Total
Exports	25.3	9.8	35.1
Imports	16.5	25.5	42.0
Total	20.4	18.6	39.0

Source: US Bureau of Economic Analysis, US Department of Commerce.

The intra-firm trade statistics disaggregated by country are described in Tables 5.3 and 5.4. These tables report the US intra-firm trade in the total US trade but now at the bilateral level. This means that they describe the propensity of each US partner to trade through related parties instead of at arms' length. We analyse the case of the NAFTA members (Canada and Mexico), the European Union (EU), Brazil (the major developing economy with data available for all years) and Asia 5, that includes Hong Kong, South Korea, Taiwan, Singapore and Thailand.

Table 5.3 Share of US bilateral IFT in the total US bilateral trade 1989–1998 (%)

	1989	1990	1991	1992	1993	1994	1995	1996	1997	1998
Brazil	23.2	22.7	21.8	27.4	31.3	31.0	27.4	32.9	29.7	30.8
Canada	44.3	41.5	42.3	41.8	39.8	41.9	39.9	39.4	39.5	38.2
Japan	70.9	75.6	75.0	75.9	72.2	80.4	78.2	82.2	77.5	75.6
Mexico	25.1	25.5	28.2	28.8	29.0	32.0	30.9	31.9	29.3	28.2
EU	44.2	41.2	42.3	44.1	45.3	48.1	48.8	48.4	49.3	48.7
Asia 5	20.1	21.1	21.3	20.2	23.7	26.2	26.3	29.5	30.5	33.3

Source: US Bureau of Economic Analysis, US Department of Commerce.

Data show this propensity is higher in the Japanese case. The share of US intra-firm trade with Japan in the US bilateral trade with this country is, on average, 75.6 per cent, reaching 82.2 per cent in 1996. The EU is second in this ranking, and presents a stabilized tendency at the end of the period, with around 48 per cent of total trade with US corresponding to intra-firm trade. Canada and Mexico have propensities of intra-firm trade around 40 and 30

Table 5.4 Share of US/EU countries' bilateral IFT in the total bilateral trade 1989–1998 (%)

	1989	1990	1991	1992	1993	1994	1995	1996	1997	1998
Austria	26.9	40.1	39.9	34.9	36.3	36.7	36.8	46.7	36.2	32.0
Denmark	23.6	20.2	20.7	23.8	27.7	22.6	25.0	27.5	26.5	27.2
Finland	16.3	22.5	22.8	33.4	27.3	48.7	50.1	39.0	48.5	51.8
France	52.5	49.0	46.9	50.0	50.8	59.3	59.5	55.3	47.4	42.2
Germany	55.0	52.6	52.3	53.9	57.7	62.05	61.8	60.4	63.9	61.0
Greece	5.2	3.4	2.4	2.1	2.8	2.5	4.8	3.0	2.7	2.2
Ireland	43.4	44.9	43.6	40.2	34.9	34.1	41.3	39.3	44.2	54.4
Italy	23.2	19.9	21.3	21.3	22.0	26.4	25.4	25.3	26.9	22.7
Netherlands	48.2	47.1	51.5	58.5	62.3	59.8	59.9	60.7	78.8	93.3
Portugal	6.4	8.9	7.4	8.1	9.6	5.2	9.4	9.0	10.8	10.4
Spain	30.7	16.3	17.9	17.6	19.9	19.8	18.5	21.3	20.8	19.9
Sweden	61.3	61.3	60.8	65.6	68.9	77.6	64.3	63.2	73.7	72.4
UK	47.7	45.2	48.3	48.5	46.4	49.8	51.0	49.9	45.5	42.1
Bel.+Lux.	30.1	27.6	28.1	29.4	28.6	27.5	28.0	27.5	27.3	29.0

Source: US Bureau of Economic Analysis, US Department of Commerce.

per cent respectively between 1989 and 1998. Considering that these countries have a free trade agreement with the US since 1994 (with the launching of NAFTA), we may conclude that NAFTA's impact on the members' intra-firm trade and on the members' arms' length trade was similar.

In what concerns EU members, Sweden, Germany, Netherlands and the United Kingdom (UK) display the highest shares of bilateral intra-firm trade in the bilateral US trade, with values higher that 50 per cent in almost all years. On the other hand, Portugal and Greece are the EU members with the lower shares of intra-firm trade with the US economy, with values never higher than 11 per cent. The remaining members have stable and moderate values for their intra-firm trade.

Next we analyse for the US partners signalled in the previous two tables, the weight of bilateral intra-firm trade in the total US intra-firm trade (Tables 5.5 and 5.6).

We can observe in Table 5.5 that for all years, but the last one, Japan was the major US intra-firm trade partner, even if, during the period analysed, the relative importance of this country decreased. Canada is second in this

Table 5.5 IFT by country in the total US IFT, 1989–1998 (%)

	1989	1990	1991	1992	1993	1994	1995	1996	1997	1998
Brazil	1.0	0.9	0.8	1.0	1.1	1.1	1.1	1.3	1.3	1.3
Canada	22.9	21.4	21.4	21.4	21.7	21.4	21.0	20.7	21.2	21.0
Japan	30.5	30.9	30.1	29.8	29.0	29.2	28.6	27.2	24.4	22.6
Mexico	4.1	4.4	5.2	5.9	6.1	6.8	6.5	7.6	7.7	8.1
EU	23.6	23.1	23.0	23.5	22.9	21.6	24.2	23.7	24.8	26.4
Asia 5	6.7	6.8	7.0	6.7	7.9	8.1	8.9	9.4	9.5	9.3
Other	10.2	12.5	12.5	11.7	11.3	11.8	9.7	10.1	11.1	11.3
Total	100	100	100	100	100	100	100	100	100	100

Source: US Bureau of Economic Analysis.

Table 5.6 IFT by EU countries in the total US IFT, 1989–1998 (%)

	1989	1990	1991	1992	1993	1994	1995	1996	1997	1998
Austria	0.17	0.26	0.27	0.24	0.26	0.24	0.28	0.36	0.27	0.25
Denmark	0.19	0.18	0.19	0.20	0.20	0.16	0.17	0.19	0.17	0.19
Finland	0.12	0.16	0.13	0.18	0.17	0.29	0.34	0.34	0.34	0.39
France	4.02	3.87	3.87	3.97	3.74	3.78	3.64	3.31	2.92	2.94
Germany	7.14	7.27	7.13	7.28	7.09	6.70	7.11	6.82	7.26	7.78
Greece	0.02	0.01	0.01	0.01	0.01	0.01	0.02	0.01	0.01	0.01
Ireland	0.55	0.57	0.58	0.56	0.47	0.45	0.66	0.60	0.78	1.27
Italy	1.38	1.22	1.24	1.21	1.12	1.22	1.25	1.24	1.28	1.13
Netherlands	2.43	2.50	2.71	3.01	2.95	2.47	2.68	2.55	3.60	4.13
Portugal	0.03	0.05	0.03	0.04	0.04	0.02	0.04	0.03	0.04	0.04
Spain	0.78	0.41	0.43	0.41	0.37	0.34	0.34	0.38	0.35	0.34
Sweden	1.53	1.51	1.37	1.34	1.23	1.23	1.17	1.21	1.32	1.41
U.K.	5.80	5.84	5.62	5.61	5.78	5.44	5.53	5.41	5.29	5.19
Bel.+Lux.	1.24	1.22	1.20	1.17	1.10	1.03	1.04	0.98	1.02	1.13

Source: US Bureau of Ecomic Analysis.

ranking. Between 1989 and 1998, the share of this country in total US intra-firm trade varied between 21.4 and 22.9 per cent, displaying a clear stable tendency. For the other NAFTA member (Mexico), the share of US intra-firm trade is much lower, with values between 4.1 per cent (in 1989) and 8.1 per cent (in 1998), even if in this case there is a clear increasing trend.

The EU is, undoubtedly at the end of the period, the first major US intra-firm trade partner. The weight of this group of countries in the total US intra-firm trade is relatively stable until 1995, but starts increasing afterwards. Table 5.6 allows us to have a picture of this analysis by EU country.

In Table 5.6 we observe that Germany, the United Kingdom, France and the Netherlands dominate EU intra-firm trade with the US. These four countries are responsible for almost 75 per cent of total intra-firm trade between the EU and US in all years and represent about 30 per cent of total US intra-firm trade. As noted above, Portugal and Greece have poor intra-firm trade shares, with less than 0.1 per cent of total US intra-firm trade. We can also identify a third group of EU countries with moderate intra-firm trade shares that includes Spain, Sweden, Ireland, Italy and Belgium plus Luxembourg.

For all EU countries the values reported in Table 5.6 are relatively stable during the period analysed except for the Netherlands and Ireland, which display a significant increase. In the Irish case, the observed trend is related to the increasing volume of US foreign direct investment in this country.

The remaining table allows us to have a sectoral picture of the phenomenon. Table 5.7 shows the shares of sectoral intra-firm trade in the total US intra-firm trade in the period analysed. The most important remark is that about 50 per cent of the US intra-firm trade occurs in the manufacturing industry. In this respect, transportation equipment had the largest share (17.5 per cent, on average) denoting the role of the automobile producers in

Table 5.7 Share of industry IFT in the total US IFT, 1989–1998 (%)

	1989	1990	1991	1992	1993	1994	1995	1996	1997	1998
Petroleum	5.4	7.0	6.6	5.5	4.8	5.2	4.7	4.7	4.7	4.7
Manufacturing	47.8	46.7	47.9	48.9	48.9	51.1	52.6	57.0	57.0	57.7
Food and kindred products	1.2	1.2	1.3	1.4	1.5	1.4	1.2	1.1	1.1	1.3
Chemicals and allied products	5.6	5.5	5.8	6.1	5.9	6.1	6.3	4.3	4.3	4.4
Primary and fabricated metals	2.1	1.7	1.7	1.9	1.8	1.9	2.0	2.1	2.1	2.0
Machinery, except electrical	8.6	9.1	9.4	8.8	8.7	8.9	9.7	13.3	13.3	13.1
Electric and electric equipment	6.8	7.4	7.7	8.3	8.3	9.1	9.5	7.8	7.8	7.9
Transportation equipment	18.5	16.5	16.4	16.6	17.1	18.3	18.4	19.0	19.0	16.0
Other manufacturing	5.2	5.4	5.6	5.7	5.5	5.3	5.5	9.8	9.8	13.4
Wholesale trade	45.4	45.0	44.1	44.0	44.9	42.3	41.4	37.5	37.5	36.8
Services	1.4	1.3	1.4	1.6	1.4	1.4	1.3	1.4	1.4	0.8
Total	100	100	100	100	100	100	100	100	100	100

Source: US Bureau of Economic Analysis.

multinational activities and, as a consequence, in related parties' trade. Machinery and electric and electronic equipment also have substantial shares of US intra-firm trade.

US wholesale intra-firm trade also represents a large share of US intra-firm trade (42 per cent, on average), indicating that a substantial part of US intra-firm trade is in final goods.

In our empirical modelling we will resort to the database of this section but with a restriction. We will use only information relative to the intra-firm trade between US parents and their majority-owned foreign affiliates MOFAs[5]. This means that we are excluding trade between foreign MNCs and their US affiliates, i.e., around 50 per cent of total US intra-firm trade and 20 per cent of total US trade. The reason for confining our analysis to these data is the more detailed information we can get, indispensable to our modelling (like in the case of research and development and taxes paid by the affiliates). Tables 5.3 to 5.7 were rebuilt for this reduced sample[6]. Comparing the intra-firm values we get when we limit our analysis to MOFAs with the previous ones suggests some noteworthy remarks.

First, in what concerns the share of the US bilateral intra-firm trade in the total US bilateral trade, the main alteration is the downfall of the prevalent role of Japan (a drop from more that 70 per cent to values never higher than 10 per cent). This means that in the case of this country, intra-firm trade with the US is mainly due to the activity of US affiliates of Japanese MNCs, the US parents bearing a small role. In the case of the EU, US parents' and US affiliates' shares are similar on average. There are remarkable reductions in the values of bilateral IFT with the USA in the cases of Denmark, Finland, France, Germany, the Netherlands, Sweden and the United Kingdom, pointing to the relevant role of US affiliates in the intra-firm trade of these countries.

Second, analysis of the weight of intra-firm trade by country in the total US intra-firm trade for MOFAs confirms the particular case of Japan, which displays very small values for MOFAs, but is among the most important US partners when US affiliates are also considered.

Third, when we take into consideration sectoral information for MOFAs, the weight of the manufacturing industry in the total US intra-firm trade increases, from an average value of 50 per cent to around 70 per cent. The reason is the fact that, by considering MOFAs only, we are excluding the intra-firm trade between foreign parent firms and their affiliates in a developed economy (the USA), precisely the type of intra-firm trade that we would expect to include a substantial amount of wholesale intra-firm trade.

THEORETICAL GUIDELINES

In order to understand the motivations for intra-firm trade it is necessary to consider the reasons for vertical and horizontal integration across international boundaries. What leads a MNC to buy inputs and finished goods within the international corporate structure instead of acquiring them through the market? And why should purchases be done abroad and not in the national economy?

We do not dispose of formalized modelling that embodies in a systematic way the two aspects. However, it is possible to find relevant contributions in some conventional economic frameworks.

The literature on MNCs postulates that the expansion of firms abroad occurs in response to certain 'monopolistic advantages' which allow quasi-rents such as scale economies, product differentiation, skills of various sorts, access to capital, advanced technology and so on. The fact that internalization is preferred to open market sales of these advantages has been taken to reflect imperfections in what may broadly be labelled 'information markets' (Hymer, 1960; Arrow, 1974). These imperfections are 'market failures' which raise the cost of transacting open market sales, because of the difficulties inherent in fully appropriating the gains from the possession of superior 'information' in open markets. Internalization can also be analysed in the context of the transaction costs theory (Coase, 1937), in the sense that it is a matter of comparing the marginal cost associated with transacting through the open market with the marginal cost of the internalized trade.

Internalization in the sense we have described offers unquestionably a good reason for investing abroad, but what we aim to explain is why trade is internalized. Lall (1978) suggests that the choice of a MNC to resort to intra-firm trade may also be viewed as a response to a market failure in commodity markets which renders recourse to external transactions either impossible or relatively costly. If failure in commodity markets involves commodities which embody new information (i.e., they are produced with superior technology), the reasons for investing abroad (technological superiority) will be similar to the reasons for intra-firm trade (highly specific products not available on open markets).

Another relevant theoretical body of analysis to our subject is the theory of vertical integration. Vertical integration is basically a matter of internalization, when the latter occurs between different stages of the value-added chain. It is possible, however, to stipulate the following basic distinction. While the internalization of trade by MNCs refers to the choice between external and internal markets of firms that are already under common ownership and control, vertical integration can be seen as the act of merging of ownership (or taking over of one firm by another), independently of location considerations[7].

Both theories provide a number of plausible reasons for the fact that a firm may prefer to rely on affiliates for their transactions. All sources of quasi-rents like scale economies, advertising expenditures or technological intensity, should stimulate intra-firm trade. As a particular case of quasi-rent, Lall (1978) mentions the specificity of the product, in the sense of the 'uniqueness' of high-technology products made by the MNC, not available in open markets. Uncertainty, like political instability, price changes, variation on quality of the inputs, may either impact positively or negatively, depending on whether it is associated with domestic conditions or external ones. For instance, factors deferring repatriation of foreign profits may constitute a disincentive to related parties' trade.

Intra-firm trade is, however, also a matter of location. In fact, the issue is what leads a MNC to locate its related party in a foreign country instead of resorting to domestic trade, whether intra-firm or market trade. Several reasons have been offered in this respect but with an *ad hoc* nature. Some of these factors are systematized by Cho (1990) in a kind of eclectic approach, which incorporates product, region, government and firm-specific factors. Among them, transfer pricing should be underlined. It has been recognized, for example, that firms may employ transfer-pricing techniques in order to maximize their after-tax earnings. In Horst (1973), the firm chooses either the lowest or the highest transfer price possible depending on a comparison of the relative differential in tax rate on profits between the importing and the exporting countries with the tariff rate, and Eden (1998) has shown that such transfer pricing can affect intra-firm trade. In any case one should expect a country's tax rate on profits to have influence on the magnitude of intra-firm trade flows and it is well known that one method for shifting profits between countries is to underprice goods sold to high tax countries and overprice goods sold to low tax countries. Such a strategy should imply that intra-firm trade flows to (from) high tax countries' affiliates are low (high) relative to intra-firm trade flows to (from) low tax countries' affiliates. Clausing (1998) offered empirical evidence on this assumption for the US MNCs.

Intra-firm trade may also respond to exchange rate variations. Some authors argue that MNCs should be highly sensitive on this respect, due to superior international networks that allow informational advantages. By operating in different countries, they are able to alter sourcing and pricing decisions in response to exchange rate changes, insulating themselves from dramatic fluctuations. Cross-border investments and production facilities are thus likely to make fluctuations in exchange rates more tolerable for firms.

The concept of international and spatial division of labour has also been associated with intra-firm trade. Multinational firms allocate different phases of the production process to different countries on the basis of regional characteristics in terms of technology and knowledge. The pattern that usually occurs is high-tech and managerial tasks allocated to core regions, while labour intensive standardized and non-qualified activities are allocated to the periphery, and trade occurs between different regions but internally to the firms.

Finally, one should also consider factors suggested by the Economic Geography. It is possible that multinational firms, when searching for parent and/or foreign affiliate locations, focus particularly on areas which their rivals have already explored and found satisfactory[8]. The reason might be a combination of centrifugal and centripetal effects, along the lines of Fujita *et al.* (1999). Agglomeration is viewed here as a matter of external economies of scale, the hypothesis being that the profitability of each firm can be higher if other firms are nearby and this could be due either to vertical linkages – i.e., it is advantageous to be near suppliers of intermediates and buyers of final goods – or to horizontal linkages, such as direct knowledge spillovers between firms and indirect knowledge links through a common, local pool of skilled labour or specialized management, for instance[9]. If this concentration effect occurs, it may impact negatively on the level of intra-firm trade, reducing the need for vertical/horizontal integration between related parties located in different countries.

However, in the context of the spatial division of labour, if geographical concentration occurs in particular parts of the value added chain of multinational production, the relation of industrial agglomeration and the level of intra-firm trade may be positive. For instance, if semi-finished products and other kinds of inputs are produced in local industrial networks and sent to other plants in other locations and agglomerations (Scott and Storper, 1992). In this context, agglomeration economies will stimulate intra-firm trade of the vertical type.

Finally, geographical distance should act as a disincentive to trade of related parties, not only by increasing risk and uncertainty but also on account of the fact that it can diminish market accessibility.

EMPIRICAL MODELLING

Taking support from the theoretical references mentioned above and also the empirical evidence from several studies, it is possible to formulate some hypothesis on the impact of the determinant factors of intra-firm trade of US firms between 1989 and 1998.

As previously explained, our dataset confines the estimates to intra-firm trade between US parents and the MOFAs, thus excluding the trade between foreign MNCs and their affiliates in the USA.

Besides, we had to consider only the case of the manufacturing industry, which according to our data represents more than two thirds of intra-firm trade. A larger sample was not treatable due to missing data[10]. This means that we excluded distributional activities and other services, including the case of the typical trade with an affiliate that engages in nothing but sales activity.

Finally, our data also preclude the possibility of separating the finished products relative to the intermediate ones used in production.

We will explore the industry and country characteristics associated with intra-firm trade but with distinct models. Alternatively we could have introduced simultaneously in the same equation both national and industry-specific variables. However, we are sceptical about the advantage of doing this when the observation for the industry (product) is the same for every country involved in each bilateral transaction. In fact, due to the data requirements, both home and foreign country conditions on industry characteristics have to be proxied with just home-country conditions on the equivalent industry for every country involved in the bilateral trade. Of course, separate estimations do not overcome this shortcoming, but at least we do not have to explicitly attribute a value at the industry level for each bilateral transaction[11].

The 'Industry Model'

In the 'industry model' we considered 34 sectors and the following five hypotheses:

H1.1. The propensity of an industry to intra-firm trade is positively related to the extent of vertical integration (*VI*) in that industry.

H1.2. The propensity of an industry to intra-firm trade is positively related to the intensity of international production (*IP*) (as a pre-condition to intra-firm trade) of that industry.

H1.3. The propensity of an industry to intra-firm trade is positively related to the technology intensity (*TI*) of that industry.

H1.4. The propensity of an industry to intra-firm trade is positively related to the level of economies of scale (*ES*) in that industry.

H1.5. The propensity of an industry to intra-firm trade is related to the level of US parent firm spatial (geographic) concentration (*GC*) on that industry. This variable aims to capture agglomeration economies and the expected sign is ambiguous, depending on whether the industry concentration concerns only a part of the value added chain (for instance, intermediate inputs, traded with final products in the foreign market) or covers a significant part of the production process. In the former case, geographical concentration may stimulate intra-firm trade; in the latter, it will tend to produce low or even null levels of intra-firm trade (considering that the distribution activities are not included in our data).

Thus, five regressors compose the 'industry model':

Vi_{it} is an indicator of the extent of vertical integration for industry *i* in *t*, and is the ratio of value added in industry *i* to industry *i*'s total sales during year *t*. We build the variable without profits in the numerator and denominator to get the 'adjusted vertical integration index' of Tucker and Wilder (1977).

IP_{it}, the intensity of international production, is proxied by the simple average between year *t*–1 and *t* of the ratio of total assets of US parents' foreign affiliates in industry *i* over total assets of US parents in the same industry.

TI_{it} is an indicator of the technology intensity given by the ratio of R&D expenditure in industry *i* to industry *i*'s total sales during year *t*.

ES_{it} is an indicator of the level of economies of scale of an industry proxied by the ratio of the average sales per firm in industry *i* to the average sales per firm in all industries.

GC_{it} is the Gini coefficient for industry *i* in year *t*. It was built considering five major regions in the USA: New England, Mideast, Great Lakes, Plains, Southeast, Southwest, Rocky Mountains and Far West.

Given these variables, the basic 'industry model' is expressed as:

$$IFT_{it} = \beta_0 VI_{it} + \beta_1 IP_{it} + \beta_2 TI_{it} + \beta_3 ES_{it} + \beta_4 GC_{it} + E_{it} \qquad (5.1)$$
$$(i = 1, 2, \ldots, 32; t = 1, 2, \ldots, 10)$$

where the dependent variable is an indicator of the propensity to intra-firm trade, that is, IFT_{it} is the share of industry *i* intra-firm trade in the total sales[12] of industry *i* during year *t*. E_{it} stands for the disturbance term for the *i*th unit (industry) at time (year) *t*.

The 'Country Model'

In the 'country model' we consider 36 countries and the following hypotheses:

H2.1. The intra-firm trade between the USA and country *j* is positively related to the market size of trade partners (*GDP*).

H2.2. The intra-firm trade between the USA and country *j* is negatively related to the tax rate on profits in country *j* (*PTR*)[13].

H2.3. The intra-firm trade between the USA and country *j* is related to the exchange rate (*EXR*) between the US dollar and country *j*'s currency. A negative sign should be expected if we are considering the import flows but positive for the export side. Thus, if we take both flows, the expected sign is ambiguous.

H2.4. The intra-firm trade between the USA and country *j* is negatively related to the distance between the two nations (*DIST*).

H2.5. The intra-firm trade between the USA and country *j* is negatively related to the risk increase in country *j* (*RISK*).

In order to control for the effect of risk on bilateral IFT, we added a proxy for risk constructed for each one of the countries of our sample with the Risk Country Index published every six months by the European Review. It was built as the difference between the value of the index for the USA and for each one of the partner countries, lagged for one or more years. The expected impact of this variable on IFT is negative, because if the risk differential in the market of the US parents' foreign affiliates increases, the US parents will tend to decrease their presence by reducing foreign direct investment.

Accordingly, the following regressors compose the 'country model':

GDP_{jt}, the product of the US Gross Product and the Gross National Product of country *j* in year *t*.

PTR_{jt}, the tax rate on profits of country j at year t, which is proxied by the share of income taxes paid by MOFAs in their total income for country j during year t.

EXR_{jt}, the real exchange rate between the US dollar and country j's currency at year t.

$DIST_{jt}$, the distance between Chicago and the major trading city in country j.

$DUMMIES_{jt}$, the country dummies with value one for the country considered and zero otherwise.

$RISK_{j,t-1}$ the difference between risk in the USA and in the foreign partner lagged for one (or more) years.

Considering the explanatory variables, the 'country model' is expressed as:

$$IFT_{jt} = \beta_0 GDP_{jt} + \beta 1 PTR_{jt} + \beta_2 DIST_j + \beta_3 EXP_{jt} + \beta_4 DUMMIES_j + \beta_5 RISK_{j,t-1} + E_{jt} \quad (i = 1, 2, .., 36; t = 1, 2, .., 10) \tag{5.2}$$

where IFT_{jt} is an indicator of intra-firm trade constructed in two different ways. First, we will use the total volume of intra-firm trade between the USA and country j in year t at 1993 constant (market) prices. In a second step, we will use, alternatively, the share of US bilateral intra-firm trade in total bilateral trade between the USA and country j in year t. The reason to consider the second measure is the fact that we should not depreciate intra-firm imports and exports with the import and export market price index, but with an index based on transfer prices, which, nonetheless, is not available.

The second indicator is also however subject to criticism. In fact, on the one hand, it allows us to by-pass the fact that an appropriate price level deflator is not available; but, on the other hand, being a measure for the propensity of the US to have intra-firm trade with country j, the level of intra-firm trade may be increasing while this ratio is decreasing, if a higher proportional increase is occurring in the total bilateral trade level.

The proxies were built using the IMF data for GDP, real exchange rate and price indexes for the 1989–1997 period. US Bureau of Economic Analysis (BEA) data is used for the other indicators. Distance is calculated between Chicago and the major city in the partner country. GDP and trade data are in constant 1993 prices using the GDP and the import/export price indexes published by the IMF and US Labor Department, respectively.

The various equations are estimated in terms of a panel sample. The fundamental advantage of a panel set over a cross section is that it will allow the researcher far greater flexibility in modelling differences in behaviour across individuals. In both models we tested the hypothesis that the constant terms are all equal with an F test. If the null hypothesis is accepted, the efficient estimator is pooled least squares. But if we accept the existence of fixed effects, the ordinary least squares still provides consistent and efficient estimates of the regressors provided that we include dummy variables for the specific effects. The t-statistics are corrected for heteroscedasticity with the White method. Examination of the correlation coefficients of the explanatory variables does not suggest multicollinearity.

In the industry model, our dependent variable assumes values in the interval [0,1]. The correctness of the functional form of the *OLS* regression in this case is questionable considering the possibility that the predicted value for the dependent variable may fall outside the feasible interval. However, following other authors who faced a similar problem, we opt for the *OLS* estimation for three reasons. First, it is not clear which alternative functional form should be used[14]. Second, this problem is less critical if the purpose is 'hypothesis testing', as it is in this case, than if the equation is used for forecasting/prediction. Third, in the light of the data deficiencies and proxy problems encountered in such work, it is questionable whether it is worth trying to sophisticate the OLS method, as also pointed out in the intra-industry trade literature (Greenway and Milner, 1986, p. 131).

It is possible that some of the factors determining intra-firm trade impact differently according to whether we are considering exports or imports. We also estimated both models disentangling the dependent variable according to this distinction. In the country model the results are similar to the model with the intra-firm trade balance, suggesting that the same factors affect both sides. In the industry model, we face serious data limitations and, perhaps on account of that, the explanatory power of the regression is very poor.

EMPIRICAL RESULTS

The 'Industry Model'

Results for the 'industry model' are presented in Table 5.8. The explanatory power of the model is high. The technological intensity and vertical integration coefficients are statistically significant with the expected sign. The economies of scale and international production variables are significant, the former with a positive sign and the latter with a negative one. These results are reasonable in economic terms if we consider that the economies of scale are a well known source of quasi rents and the world is more and more featured by the volatility of the installed firms.

The result for the degree of spatial concentration of parent firms appears to be negatively correlated with intra-firm trade. The reason for a negative

Table 5.8 Industry model regression

Dependent variable regressors	Intra-firm trade
C	−0.07***
	(−2.51)
TI	0.896***
	(77.293)
ES	0.003**
	(2.276)
VI	0.063**
	(2.494)
IP	−0.0001***
	(−3.109)
GC	−0.007*
	(−1.856)
R^2	0.979
R^2 adj.	0.961
N	320
$F(\alpha, \beta = \alpha_\iota, \beta)$	1.238
	(H0 accepted 5%)

Notes: *t*-statistics (between brackets) White-corrected.
* 10% significance level.
** 5% significance level.
*** 1% significance level.

correlation may be that parent firms in the USA, if they search for agglomeration economies and therefore geographically concentrate, tend to 'clusterize' (in the sense of Porter, 1990), that is to say, the spatial concentration of an industry concerns a significant part of the value added production process. Of course we cannot exclude that intra-firm trade of these firms occurs in the distribution and other service activities not included in our data.

There might exist industry individual effects, which are taken to be constant over time and specific to the individual cross-sectional unit. However, with the F test performed to the equality of these coefficients, the null hypothesis is not rejected.

The 'Country Model'

Table 5.9 shows the results for the country model when the dependent variable is the total volume of intra-firm trade between the USA and country *j* (at constant prices). The explanatory power of the model is good (the adjusted R^2 is 0.570). We confirm that the dimension of the markets' impact, as measured by their GDP, is positive and significant. The tax rate on profits displays the negative expected result.

The exchange rate variable was not significant, and this led us to exclude it from the results. The reason might be the fact that US parent firms envisage the external markets as basically stable in what concerns exchange rate variations. However, the most plausible reason is the fact that an opposite sign should be expected depending on whether we are considering the import flows (negative) or the export side (positive), the effect being cancelled when the trade balance is considered.

The distance variable has the expected negative impact on intra-firm trade.

We added two dummies to capture country idiosyncrasies. This was suggested, on the one hand, by the above-mentioned *F* test to the equality of the coefficients. In fact, the null hypothesis is rejected. On the other hand, the descriptive analysis of an earlier section clearly suggests the existence of country asymmetries in bilateral intra-firm trade with US firms. We included dummies for the case of countries with trade agreements – NAFTA and EU countries – but only in the first case do we get a significant result (and positive, as expected)[15]. The fact that the EU variable is not significant can be related to the heterogeneity of the countries that belong to this block in terms of the phenomenon we are analysing (see Table 5.6). We also included a dummy for the UK case, to capture whether the particular historical, cultural and linguistic relations impact positively on the level of intra-firm trade, as in fact is statistically confirmed.

Finally, we do not confirm the negative impact of the risk proxy. However, countervailing effects may be expected if we take into consideration that US parents will probably overprice exports and underprice imports in their intra-firm trade with MOFAs, in order to transfer profits from the country where risk, in relative terms, has increased, to the US parents; the expected decrease in intra-firm trade based on FDI considerations may thus be, at least in part, annihilated, in what concerns the intra-firm trade of exports or even of both flows (exports and imports).

Table 5.9 displays only the estimation with the significant variables, considering that inclusion of the EU dummy and the risk variable, similarly to what occurs with the exchange rate variable, does not have a remarkable effect on the remaining variables.

Table 5.9 Country model regression

Dependent variable Regressors	Intra-firm trade
C	12.207*** (3.084)
GDP	0.045*** (14.310)
PTR	–72.7544*** (–3.709)
DIST	–0.008** (–2.323)
NAFTA dummy	56.467*** (5.671)
UK dummy	5.907*** (3.287)
R^2	0.574
R^2 adj.	0.570
N	340
$F(\alpha, \beta = \alpha_i, \beta)$	91.348 (H0 rejected)

Notes: *t*-statistics (between brackets) White-corrected.
* 1% significance level.
** 5% significance level.
*** 10% significance level.

As we have previously explained, we also used, as an alternative to the dependent variable of Table 5.9, the share of bilateral intra-firm trade in the bilateral trade. The explanatory power of the model diminishes dramatically however (the adjusted R^2 is only 0.089). Criticism of this second measure may explain this disappointing result.

CONCLUSION

This chapter studies the evolution and determinants of US intra-firm trade between 1989 and 1998 reported by the Bureau of Economic Analysis of the US Department of Commerce.

In what concerns the main characteristics of US intra-firm trade, it is worthwhile mentioning that Japan is the country with the highest values for bilateral intra-firm trade with the USA in the total US bilateral trade, followed by the EU and Canada, and these three partners also represent the highest shares of total US intra-firm trade. However, when we consider only intra-firm trade of MOFAs (thus excluding intra-firm trade managed by US affiliates of foreign parent firms), the prevalent role of Japan drops dramatically and the values for the EU decrease to half, thus pointing to the relevant role of US affiliates in intra-firm trade of these countries. Considering MOFAs only, the weight of the manufacturing industry in the total US intra-firm trade increases from an average of 50 per cent to around 70 per cent, suggesting that intra-firm trade between foreign parent firms and their affiliates includes a substantial amount of wholesale intra-firm trade.

Our attempt to explain the determinant factors of the US intra-firm trade was conditioned by the quality of the data. In fact, our figures have some obvious limitations and suggest some prudence for general conclusions. First of all they concern only MOFAs, excluding from our sample the intra-firm trade conducted by US affiliates of foreign parent firms. Second, they do not allow us to distinguish trade of finished goods from trade of intermediate products. Third, they concern only manufacturing activities, thus excluding sales and after-sales activities, even if they represent only a unilateral flow (imports or exports) of intra-firm trade. Fourth, some apparently relevant factors could not be tested due to lack of data (such as excess capacity and other host governments' policies). Finally, work with data at the firm level would be relevant as firms can be highly heterogeneous in a given sector. In spite of these shortcomings, the empirical results of both the model to explain inter-sectoral variation and the model for inter-country differences appear to be in general interesting and work well in terms of their explanatory power.

Summarizing our statistical results, the factors that affect the US intra-firm trade managed by MOFAs are technology intensity, the level of vertical integration, economies of scale, the level of international production, as well as the impact of the geographic concentration of US parent firms. The fact that location considerations related to agglomeration economies appear to impact negatively on intra-firm trade is not surprising. It is reasonable to assume that industries that search for agglomeration economies tend to geographically concentrate a significant part of the value added production process. This does not mean that the spatially concentrated industries do not transact on related parties. If we take into consideration that wholesale trade and services are excluded from our data, it is possible that 'clusterized' industries engage in related party trade in sales and after-sales activities. In any case, this is a subject for further research.

At the country level we also identified some relevant factors. The size of the market appears to favour intra-firm trade while the level of the tax rate on profits of the foreign country disincentives this trade. As expected, country specificities appear to impact positively in some cases, such as being a member of NAFTA or displaying cultural affinities, like in the UK case.

Finally, US parents prefer to transact internally with less distant countries, as expected.

As regards specification, some further points can be raised. First, more theory before pursuing the empirical work would be most valuable. There is still a long theoretical path to run to prove the relation between intra-firm trade and factors related to characteristics of the foreign markets internalized, such as the sensitivity of trade to exchange rate variations, the role of transfer pricing and restrictive business practices, or the role of geographical factors. Second, a most relevant question seems to be not whether intra-firm trade occurs more or less in an industry or a country but rather if it behaves differently from trade between unrelated parties, as pointed out by Helleiner since his seminal paper of 1979. Third, much more detailed data should be provided in order to allow new and better insights on the phenomenon.

NOTES

1. Jetro is the Institution responsible for this kind of statistics.
2. See Lall (1978), who represents one of the first systematic attempts to explain inter-industry differences in the US intra-firm exports, and Helleigner and Lavergne (1979), who explained inter-industry differences in the US intra-firm imports.
3. A 'foreign affiliate of a US parent firm' is defined by the US Department of Commerce as a foreign business enterprise in which a US person owns or controls 10 per cent or more of the voting securities or the equivalent.
4. According to the US Department of Commerce, a US affiliate of a foreign parent firm is a US business enterprise in which a single foreign person owns or controls, directly or indirectly, 10 per cent or more of the voting securities or equivalent.
5. According to the Department of Commerce, this concept includes all foreign affiliates in which the direct and indirect ownership interest of all US parents exceeds 50 per cent.
6. Data will be supplied on request.
7. See Lall (1978) for this distinction.
8. Preliminary evidence of this possibility is supported by Barrell and Pain (1999) on the concentration of the stock of US manufacturing FDI in Europe.
9. See, for this purpose, Flôres *et al.* (2000), p. 22 and following.
10. In the non-manufacturing industry, we have several 'missing values' due to protection of information.
11. See a similar argumentation but for the case of an intra-industry model, in Crespo and Fontoura (2001).
12. It was not possible to use total trade due to the missing values of the dataset in the case of some sectors.
13. The tax rate is the foreign income tax paid by affiliates in a given country relative to their net (before tax) income.

14. We tested for an alternative functional form which restricts the predicted value to the limited range: the logistic function, estimated with non-linear least squares. Similarly to the OLS model, we verify a positive impact of technology intensity and the level of vertical integration.
15. We also run a least squares dummy variable model, with a dummy variable for each country, but this grouping significantly increases the explanatory capacity of the model.

REFERENCES

Arrow, K.J. (1974), *Limits of organization*, New York: W. W. Norton.

Barrell, R. and N. Pain (1999), 'Domestic institutions, agglomerations and foreign direct investment in Europe', *European Economic Review*, **43**, 925–34.

Bureau of Economic Analysis, *Foreign Direct Investment in the United States*, Various years.

Bureau of Economic Analysis, *US Direct Investment Abroad*, Various years.

Cho, K.R. (1990), 'The role of product-specific factors in intra-firm trade of US manufacturing multinational corporations', Journal of International Business Studies, **21** (2), 319–30.

Clausing, K.A. (1998), 'The impact of transfer pricing on intra-firm trade', *NBER Working Papers*, 6688.

Coase, R. (1937), 'The nature of firm', *Economica*, **4**, 386–405.

Crespo, N. and M.P. Fontoura (2001), 'Determinants and pattern of horizontal and vertical intra-industry trade: what can we learn from Portuguese data', *Working Papers*, Department of Economics, ISEG/UTL, WP 9/2001/DE/CEDIN.

Eden, L. (1998), *Taxing Multinationals: Transfer Pricing and Corporate Income Taxation in North America*, Toronto: University of Toronto Press.

Euromoney, Various years.

Flôres, R., M.P. Fontoura and R. Santos (2000), 'Foreign direct investment spillovers: what can we still learn from country studies?', *Working Papers*, Department of Economics, ISEG/UTL, WP 4/2000/DE/CEDIN.

Fujita, M., P.R. Krugman and A. Venables (1999), *The Spatial Economy: Cities, Regions and International Trade*, Cambridge, London: MIT Press.

Greenway, D. and C. Milner (1986), *The Economics of Intra-Industry Trade*, Oxford: Basil-Blackwell.

Helleiner, G.K. (1979), 'Transnational corporations and trade structure: the role of intra-firm', in H. Giersh (ed.), *On the Economics of Intra-industry*, Institut für Weltwirtschaft an der Univers.

Helleiner, G.K. and R. Lavergne (1979), 'Intra-firms trade and industrial exports to US', *Oxford Bulletin of Economic and Statistics*, **41** (4), 297–311.

Horst, T. (1973), 'The theory of multinational firm: optimal behaviour under different tariff and tax rates', *Journal of Political Economy*, **79** (5), 1059–72.

Hymer, S. H., (1960, published 1976), *The International Operations of National Firms: A Study of Direct Foreign Investment*, Cambridge, MA: MIT Press.

International Monetary Fund, *International Financial Statistics*, Yearbook, Various issues.

Lall, S. (1978), 'The pattern of intra-firm exports by US multinationals', *Oxford Bulletin of Economic and Statistics*, **40** (3), 209–22.

Porter, M.E. (1990), *The Competitive Advantage of Nations*, New York: Free Press.

Scott, A. and M. Storper (1992), 'Regional development considered', in Ernste and V. Meier (eds), *Regional Development and Contemporary Industrial Response*, London: Belhaven.

Tucker, Irvin B. and Ronald P Wilder (1977), 'Trends in Vertical Integration in the US Manufacturing Sector', *The Journal of Industrial Economics*, **26**, 81–94.

Williamson, O.E. (1975), *Markets and Hierarchies, Analysis and Antitrust Implications: A Study in the Economics of Internal Organization*, New York: Free Press.

6. Fragmentation and Corporate Performance of Japanese Firms in Globalization: Evidence from Micro Data[1]

Kozo Kiyota and Fukunari Kimura

INTRODUCTION

With the recent expansion of the activities of multinational enterprises (MNEs), the fragmentation of their production process has been examined extensively in the theoretical studies of international trade such as Jones and Kierzkowski (1990), Deardorff (2001a, 2001b), Venables (1999) and Jones (2001). These works have made substantial contributions in analysing the relationship between fragmentation and recently emerging international trade patterns of intermediate products. However, another important dimension of foreign direct investment (FDI), namely a 'firm', has not been fully explored in the literature, and thus we have not yet specified differences and connections between 'intra-firm' fragmentation and 'arm's-length' fragmentation.

The fragmentation of the production process is conducted not only by establishing affiliates but also by preparing various forms of contracts with other firms, an example of which is a commissioned production arrangement. It is well known that traditional Japanese firms have extensively utilized a stable and efficiency-enhancing inter-firm relationship called 'subcontracting[2]'. On the other hand, the recently emerging form of inter-firm arrangement called commissioned production is more foot-loose than subcontracting though not completely a spot-market-type contract, which includes original equipment manufacturing (OEM) contracts and contracts with electronics manufacturing service (EMS) firms[3]. The reduction in the cost of service links enables firms to conduct arm's-length fragmentation such as commissioned production in addition to intra-firm fragmentation through establishing affiliates.

A long-lasting recession after the burst of the asset market bubble in Japan forced corporate firms to reorganize intra-firm structure and inter-firm relationships. One of the important aspects of corporate restructuring was the development of international as well as national fragmentation of Japanese firms[4]. Table 6.1 presents the trend of commissioned production from 1994 F/Y to 1997 F/Y. Commissioned production had an increasing trend as a whole with some fluctuations. A notable change is found in commissioned production abroad, which grew faster than domestic commissioned production and expanded the share from 3.4 per cent in 1994 F/Y to 7.2 per cent in 1997 F/Y in all industries.

This chapter empirically examines the effect of fragmentation on the corporate performance at the firm level. We focus on two types of fragmentation: having affiliates and commissioning production. Differences between national and international fragmentation are also examined. Data used in this chapter are Japanese firm-level longitudinal data between 1994 F/Y and 1997 F/Y. Our analysis suggests that firms that fragmented their production process grow faster than firms that did not. In particular, firms with international fragmentation present higher performance than firms without.

Another important finding is that the number of commissioned production arrangements fluctuates more than the number of affiliates, especially in overseas activities. It is well known that FDI barely moves, at least in the short run, even if faced with large economic shocks such as the Asian crisis. Commissioned production arrangements, on the other hand, may be utilized as a buffer for business cycles. This may imply that the expansion of arm's-length type international fragmentation contributes to the improvement of corporate performance.

The chapter plan is as follows: the next section briefly reviews the related empirical works to provide a reference point for the Japanese case. The third section explains our empirical methodology as well as our longitudinal dataset. The fourth section reports our findings for the relationship among fragmentation, globalization and corporate performance. The fifth section focuses on differences in fragmentation patterns across industries. The last section presents concluding remarks.

Table 6.1 Trends of commissioned production arrangements

		Value (billions of yen)			Share (%)			Index (1994 F/Y = 100)		
		Total	Domestic	Abroad	Total	Domestic	Abroad	Total	Domestic	Abroad
All industry	1994	44 379	42 849	1 530	100.0	96.6	3.4	100.0	100.0	100.0
	1995	48 233	45 729	2 504	100.0	94.8	5.2	108.7	106.7	163.6
	1996	51 508	48 246	3 263	100.0	93.7	6.3	116.1	112.6	213.2
	1997	47 280	43 861	3 418	100.0	92.8	7.2	106.5	102.4	223.4
		Total	Domestic	Abroad	Total	Domestic	Abroad	Total	Domestic	Abroad
Manufacturing	1994	36 831	35 732	1 100	100.0	97.0	3.0	100.0	100.0	100.0
	1995	40 821	38 869	1 952	100.0	95.2	4.8	110.8	108.8	177.5
	1996	43 507	40 844	2 663	100.0	93.9	6.1	118.1	114.3	242.2
	1997	40 282	37 553	2 729	100.0	93.2	6.8	109.4	105.1	248.2

Source: The MITI dataset.

PREVIOUS EMPIRICAL LITERATURE

Empirical Analysis of Fragmentation

Most previous empirical studies regard the volume of trade in intermediate goods or components as a proxy for the degree of fragmentation and examine the causes and effects of international fragmentation. Baldone *et al.* (2001), focusing on the textiles and apparel industry in EU countries as a typical example of international delocalization, investigate the determinants of trade flows of textiles and apparel between EU countries and Central European countries. In this chapter, the fragmentation is measured by the outward processing trade, which consists of exports of intermediate goods, both intra-firm and arm's-length, for the processing in a foreign country, after which the goods are re-imported under tariff exemption. Their econometric exercise confirms that the most important factor for the choice of a country as a processing partner is labour costs along with geographic and cultural proximity. However, once the process has been activated, EU firms do not necessarily keep looking for the lowest labour cost country as the preferred partner.

Not only the determinants but also the impacts of fragmentation are examined in the recent empirical literature. Egger *et al.* (2001) investigate the impacts of international fragmentation of Austrian manufacturing on total factor productivity and mandated factor prices. They define fragmentation as outward processing trade, which is the same as that of Baldone *et al.* (2001), and the data cover processing trade from Austria to Eastern European countries for the period 1990–1998. The econometric analysis reveals that outsourcing to the East significantly improves domestic growth in total factor productivity. Under the assumption of perfect competitive factor markets, wages of Austrian manufacturing would become lower for low-skilled workers and higher for high-skilled workers in response to the outsourcing[5]. Egger and Egger (2001) also examine the effects of outward processing trade on the skill ratio, the employment of skilled labour divided by that of unskilled labour, in the European Union. Using outward processing trade data for the EU15 countries from 1995 to 1997, they found that the outward processing is more prevalent in import-competing industries than export industries. Although the skill intensity was higher in exporting industries than in import competing counterparts, the impact of outward processing on skilled-to-low-skilled employment ratio in export industries is significantly negative.

These studies confirm the importance of international fragmentation, but there is some room to investigate further. For instance, the analysis on intermediate products trade does not take into account the difference between intra-firm and arm's-length fragmentation. Moreover, the impacts of fragmentation at the firm level are not thoroughly examined yet.

The concept of fragmentation, 'the splitting of a production process into two or more steps that can be undertaken in different locations but that lead to the same final product' (Deardorff, 2001a), covers the broad range of organizational structure. A recently emerging form of inter-firm relationship in Japan is commissioned production (*seisan itaku*). Commissioned production is a sort of outsourcing, in that a firm separates two (or more) production processes into two or more production blocks that can be undertaken by other firms. Although commissioned production sounds very similar to subcontracting, they are quite different from one another in Japan in at least following two senses.

First, subcontracting includes long-term commitment between contracting firms while commissioned production does not have to be a long-lasting relationship. Although the costs of long-term arrangements between contracting firms are often pointed out in the theoretical literature, Japanese firms preferred subcontracting to short-term spot-market type contracts in the past. On the other hand, commissioned production leads to more foot-loose type contracts than subcontracting but not fully spot-market type.

Second, in subcontracting, outsourced firms are smaller in scale (in terms of employment, sales or value-added) than outsourcing firms. Therefore, outsourcing firms tend to have strong bargaining power in the process of negotiating and implementing contracts. On the other hand, in commissioned production, outsourced firms are not necessarily smaller. Outsourcing and outsourced firms typically have equal bargaining power. Subcontracting in Japan, once highly recognized, is now under fire in the long-lasting recession since it lacks the flexibility and therefore loses efficiency. Japanese firms start restructuring not only their intra-firm structure but also their inter-firm relationships.

Globalization and Corporate Performance

The relationship between foreign exposure and corporate performance is one of the important topics worth being investigated in the context of the microstructure of international fragmentation. The openness–growth nexus has long been an important subject for both academic research and policy studies. The standard microeconomic model supports the link between openness and the static efficiency of resource allocation, but the dynamic implication of openness has not yet been documented in a convincing manner. Casual cross-country regression analysis so far suggests a weak positive correlation between openness and growth[6]. In the past decade, we observed an emerging empirical literature on the relationship between exports and corporate performance by using micro or longitudinal data at the firm or establishment level. The pioneering work was Aw and Hwang (1995). They used the micro data of the Taiwanese electronics industry in 1986 and found significant differences in productivity between exporters and non-exporters.

In the case of American firms, Bernard, Jensen and their colleagues extensively examined the benefits of exports at the plant level (Bernard and Jensen, 1995a, 1995b, 1997, 1999a, 1999b; Bernard *et al.*, 2000). One of the major findings of their work is that the effect of exports on the firm's performance is not clear. The regression analysis does not confirm a statistically significant relationship between firms' prior export activities and the growth performance in subsequent years.

In case of Japanese firms, however, the story is totally different. Following the approach of Roberts and Tybout (1997) and Bernard and Jensen (1999a), Kimura and Kiyota (2003) investigate the relationship between foreign exposure of firms and corporate performance by using the Japanese micro panel data for the fiscal year of 1994 to 1997 at the firm level. They found that Japanese firms with foreign exposure, i.e., conducting FDI as well as exports, were more successful in corporate restructuring in the distress period of the Japanese economy than firms without[7].

Previous empirical works have made a substantial contribution in explaining the pattern of fragmentation and the relationship between globalization and corporate performance. However, the impact of fragmentation at the micro level is still ambiguous, and more detailed analysis is called for. Based on the growing importance of firm-level analysis and the recent expansion in the global fragmentation, the effects of fragmentation on corporate performance at the firm level seem to be worth investigating to clarify the microstructure of fragmentation. The following sections examine the impact of fragmentation on corporate performance, based on the analytical framework in line with Bernard and Jensen (1999a) and Kimura and Kiyota (2003).

METHODOLOGY AND DATA

Methodology

We now examine the performance of Japanese enterprises after conducting fragmentation, particularly focusing on fragmentation in the international context. We focus on two types of fragmentation: having affiliates and commissioning production. To clarify the microstructure of connection between fragmentation and economic performance, we utilize firm-level data rather than industry-level data, which enables us to conduct detailed analysis on each firm's performance. We examine the effects of international activities on the growth of enterprises, following Bernard and Jensen (1999a) and Kimura and Kiyota (2003).

The performance of affiliates holders (AFHs) and commissioned production users (CPUs) is examined by regressing the growth of firms on the affiliate and the commissioned production status at initial year ($t = 0$)[8]. In evaluating the growth of firm i, $\%\Delta X_{iT}$, we focus on changes in five indicators related to firms' performance: sales per regular worker (*SALES*), capital–labour ratio (*KLRATIO*), average wage (*WAGE*), the number of regular workers (*L*) and profit–sales ratio (*PROFIT*). The affiliate and commissioned production status, AFH_i^g and CPU_i^g, take the value of one if firm i has at least one affiliate and one partner of commissioned production respectively, and zero otherwise. Superscript g is used to identify the fragmentation status. It takes D in analysing national fragmentation and F in doing international fragmentation.

We run regressions together with firms' characteristics, Z_{ik0}, including ownership[9] size, age, and others in the initial year as

$$\%\Delta X_{iT} = \frac{1}{T}\ln\left(\frac{X_{iT}}{X_{i0}}\right)\times 100 = \alpha_0 + \alpha_1 \text{AFH(CPU)}_{i0}^{D} + \sum\nolimits_{k=2}^{K} \alpha_k Z_{ik0} + \varepsilon_{iT}$$

in analysing the national fragmentation and

$$\%\Delta X_{iT} = \frac{1}{T}\ln\left(\frac{X_{iT}}{X_{i0}}\right)\times 100 = \beta_0 + \beta_1 \text{AFH(CPU)}_{i0}^{F} + \sum\nolimits_{k=2}^{K} \beta_k Z_{ik0} + \mu_{iT}$$

in analysing the fragmentation abroad, where ε_{iT} and μ_{iT} are the error terms. The coefficients α_1 and β_1 provide differences in average annual growth rates between AFHs (CPUs) and non-AFHs (non-CPUs) for national and international arrangements, respectively. At the same time, three-digit industry dummies are introduced in order to control possible effects of industry-level characteristics such as comparative advantage, tariff and non-tariff measures, and market conditions[10].

Data

We use the micro database of *Kigyou Katsudou Kihon Chousa Houkokusyo* (*The Results of the Basic Survey of Japanese Business Structure and Activities*) by the Research and Statistics Department, Minister's Secretariat, Ministry of International Trade and Industry (MITI) (1996, 1997, 1998, 1999 and 2000). This survey was first conducted in the 1991 F/Y, then in the 1994 F/Y and annually afterwards. The main purpose of the survey is to statistically capture the overall picture of Japanese corporate firms in light of their activity diversification, globalization and strategies on R&D and information technology. The strength of the survey is its census coverage of samples and the reliability of figures. From this survey, we develop a longitudinal (panel) data set between 1994 and 1998, based on each firm's permanent number.

In the following, an affiliate is defined as a firm where more than 20 per cent of its equity share is owned by a parent firm. On the other hand, commissioned production arrangement is defined as a contract in which production process is committed to other firms. Commissioned production includes contracts such as OEM and ones with EMS firms but excludes subcontracting[11]. In this chapter, therefore, a commissioned production arrangement captures a relatively foot-loose type of arm's-length fragmentation.

Based on the MITI's survey, we develop a longitudinal (panel) dataset between 1994 and 1997, using each firm's permanent number. Our dataset includes firms that were continuously in operation between 1994 and 1997 and with the information on sales, total wages, the number of regular workers, affiliates, commissioned production arrangements and tangible assets for those years. We drop the firms from the sample set for which the data of capital (tangible assets), labour (the number of regular workers), age (questionnaire-level year minus establishment year), or the number of affiliates/commissioned production arrangements are not positive due to incomplete replies[12]. Firms whose annual average growth rate in sales per regular worker, capital–labour ratio, average wage, total employment or profit (operating surplus) is by more than 3σ (absolute terms) deviated from its mean are also dropped from our samples because they disturb our arithmetic averages. The number of samples ends up with 7409 each year.

EFFECTS OF FRAGMENTATION ON CORPORATE PERFORMANCE

This section examines whether firms that use fragmentation (having affiliates or arranging commissioned production) perform better than firms that do not. We also investigate differences between national and international fragmentation. Let us start from checking static differences in corporate characteristics between firms with fragmentation and firms without. Table 6.2 reveals sharp contrasts in basic indicators between AFHs and non-AFHs and between CPUs and non-CPUs in 1994 F/Y and 1997 F/Y. AFHs are older, larger in terms of sales and employment, spending more on advertisement and paying higher wages. In particular, differences in R&D expenditure to sales (*RRD*) and profit to sales (*PROFIT*) are notable. Overall, firms with AFHs are bigger and more competitive than non-AFHs though we cannot confirm definite differences between firms with domestic affiliates and firms with foreign affiliates. As for the comparison between CPUs and non-CPUs, we observe weaker but similar differences. Again, CPUs are larger in size and more competitive than non-CPUs.

These are static observations with cross section data, simply indicating that AFHs and CPUs perform better than non-AFHs and non-CPUs at some point in time. We next check the dynamic aspects: whether or not firms with fragmentation at a time period would perform better in the following periods than firms without. Before going into the regression, we would like to check how the firm's status changes.

Table 6.3 presents a sort of Markov matrices for AFHs/non-AFHs and CPUs/non-CPUs between 1994 F/Y and 1997 F/Y. Compared with national AFHs/CPUs, the number of firms with foreign AFHs/CPUs tends to increase from 1994 F/Y to 1997 F/Y though there are some fluctuations. The number of firms that have domestic affiliates slightly increases from 5023 in 1994 F/Y to 5066 in 1997 F/Y while the number of firms that conduct domestic commissioned production arrangements decreases from 5159 to 4837 during the same period. On the other hand, the number of firms that have affiliates abroad and that conduct commissioned production abroad increase throughout the period. Specifically, the number of firms that have affiliates abroad grows from 1802 to 2154 while those that conduct commissioned production abroad goes from 538 in 1994 F/Y to 598 in 1997 F/Y[13].

In Tables 6.2 and 6.3, we focus on whether the firm has an affiliate or not and whether firms commission their production or not. Such analysis is useful in analysing the difference between firms with fragmentation and firms without, but the analysis drops some of the important information such as how many affiliates does the firm have. To take into account the degree of fragmentation, next we examine the changes in the number of firms' affiliates/commissioned production arrangements and make comparisons between national and international fragmentations, using a similar matrix to Table 6.3. We also investigate the combination between affiliates and commissioned production to identify the difference between them.

Table 6.4 classifies firms by the changes in the number of affiliates and commissioned production arrangements between 1994 F/Y and 1997 F/Y. Figures in the table present the percentage share of firms (the total number of firms in the sample is 7409). The table clearly presents differences between national and international fragmentation: the number of firms that increase affiliates/commissioned production arrangements abroad and decrease domestic affiliates/commissioned production arrangements is larger than those who decrease affiliates/commissioned production arrangements abroad and increase domestic affiliates/commissioned production arrangements. Firms that increase the number of affiliates abroad and decrease that of domestic affiliates account for 3.6 per cent of total number of firms (7409) while those that decrease the number of affiliates abroad and increase that of domestic affiliates account for 1.0 per cent. Firms that increase the number of commissioned production arrangements abroad and decrease that of domestic commissioned production arrangements are 2.5 per cent while those that decrease the number of commissioned production arrangements abroad and increase that of domestic commissioned production arrangements are only 0.8 per cent.

The combination of commissioned production and affiliates also indicates that the trends of Japanese firms' fragmentation directs to globalization. Firms that increase the number of affiliates abroad and decrease that of domestic commissioned production arrangements account for 6.8 per cent while those that decrease the number of affiliates abroad and increase that of domestic commissioned production arrangements account for 1.4 per cent. Firms that increase the number of commissioned production arrangements abroad and decrease that of domestic affiliates are 1.8 per cent while those that decrease the number of commissioned production arrangements abroad and increase that of domestic affiliates are only 0.9 per cent of total firms.

It is also notable that many firms change the number of domestic commissioned production arrangements from 1994 F/Y to 1997 F/Y. The share of firms that change the number of commissioned production accounts for 65.6 per cent, which is more than six times as large as that of commissioned production abroad. The corresponding value of domestic affiliates is 38.9 per cent while that of affiliates abroad accounts for 19.6 per cent.

Table 6.5 presents our regression results, reporting the gaps in annual average growth rates of selected performance indicators between AFHs and non-AFHs and between CPUs and non-CPUs. The figures indicate how much faster AFHs/CPUs in 1994 F/Y grew in terms of selected indicators in the period of 1994–1997 F/Y than non-AFHs/non-CPUs did. For control variables Z_{ik0} in the 'with control' regressions, we use R&D sales ratios, advertisement expenditure sales ratios, capital–labour ratios, average wages, foreign owned dummy (that takes one if more than 50 per cent equity share is owned by foreigners and zero otherwise), the firm's age, and three-digit industry dummies in 1994 F/Y though the estimated coefficients are not reported in the table.

For both domestic and international holdings of affiliates and arrangements of commissioned production, AFHs/CPUs grow faster than

Table 6.2 Differences in static corporate characteristics across AFH/CPU status

		Affiliate(s) (AFHs)				Commissioned production arrangements (CPUs)			
		Domestic		Abroad		Domestic		Abroad	
1994 F/Y	All firms	Yes	No	Yes	No	Yes	No	Yes	No
KLRATIO	10.32	**11.65**	**7.54**	**12.69**	**9.57**	9.74	11.67	10.35	10.32
[millions of yen per person]	(16.81)	**(15.89)**	**(18.29)**	**(14.35)**	**(17.46)**	(11.95)	(24.50)	(11.46)	(17.16)
SALES	50.86	**56.33**	**39.33**	**64.99**	**46.31**	39.99	75.77	49.89	50.93
[millions of yen]	(89.15)	**(100.19)**	**(57.92)**	**(139.77)**	**(64.36)**	(44.19)	(144.26)	(63.66)	(90.85)
WAGE	4.86	**5.02**	**4.52**	**5.29**	**4.72**	4.81	4.96	**5.14**	**4.83**
[millions of yen]	(1.58)	**(1.59)**	**(1.50)**	**(1.62)**	**(1.55)**	(1.51)	(1.74)	**(1.55)**	**(1.58)**
RRD	0.95	**1.09**	**0.64**	**1.80**	**0.68**	**1.06**	**0.69**	**1.69**	**0.89**
[%]	(2.04)	**(2.16)**	**(1.74)**	**(2.51)**	**(1.79)**	**(2.13)**	**(1.80)**	**(2.25)**	**(2.02)**
RAD	0.57	**0.65**	**0.39**	**0.83**	**0.48**	0.55	0.61	**0.82**	**0.55**
[%]	(1.60)	**(1.61)**	**(1.58)**	**(2.03)**	**(1.43)**	(1.58)	(1.66)	**(1.86)**	**(1.58)**
PROFIT	4.03	4.01	4.06	4.52	3.87	**4.19**	**3.65**	4.05	4.03
[profit–sales ratio %]	(4.26)	(4.36)	(4.03)	(4.50)	(4.16)	**(4.33)**	**(4.04)**	(3.81)	(4.29)
AGE	35.42	**38.81**	**28.28**	**40.59**	**33.75**	**35.82**	**34.49**	**39.12**	**35.13**
[year]	(13.09)	**(11.55)**	**(13.26)**	**(10.90)**	**(13.30)**	**(12.98)**	**(13.28)**	**(11.70)**	**(13.15)**
L	709	**912**	**282**	**1 810**	**356**	**755**	**605**	**2 284**	**586**
[number of regular wokers]	(2 662)	**(3 168)**	**(780)**	**(5 073)**	**(761)**	**(2 845)**	**(2 182)**	**(6 629)**	**(1 999)**
ESTAB	12	**15**	**6**	**23**	**9**	11	16	**19**	**12**
[number of establishments]	(35)	**(41)**	**(11)**	**(62)**	**(17)**	(24)	(50)	**(30)**	**(35)**
Number of observations	7 409	5 023	2 386	1 802	5 607	5 159	2 250	538	6 871

1997 F/Y									
KLRATIO	11.20	**12.70**	**7.97**	**13.91**	**10.10**	10.61	12.32	11.08	11.22
[millions of yen per person]	(17.92)	**(16.28)**	**(20.65)**	**(25.10)**	**(13.79)**	(12.81)	(24.78)	(12.79)	(18.30)
SALES	55.12	**60.87**	**42.71**	**68.08**	**49.81**	42.89	78.14	48.32	55.72
[millions of yen]	(95.19)	**(104.38)**	**(69.81)**	**(137.09)**	**(70.56)**	(45.48)	(146.31)	(42.35)	(98.47)
WAGE	5.39	**5.55**	**5.03**	**5.85**	**5.20**	5.38	5.40	**5.78**	**5.35**
[millions of yen]	(1.68)	**(1.69)**	**(1.58)**	**(1.71)**	**(1.63)**	(1.58)	(1.84)	**(1.65)**	**(1.67)**
RRD	0.97	**1.10**	**0.68**	**1.76**	**0.64**	**1.10**	**0.72**	**1.97**	**0.88**
[%]	(2.11)	**(2.07)**	**(2.17)**	**(2.51)**	**(1.82)**	**(2.05)**	**(2.19)**	**(2.54)**	**(2.04)**
RAD	0.60	**0.69**	**0.39**	**0.75**	**0.53**	0.55	0 67	**0.83**	**0.58**
[%]	(2.34)	**(2.66)**	**(1.43)**	**(1.70)**	**(2.56)**	(2.60)	(1.76)	**(1.83)**	**(2.38)**
PROFIT	2.68	**2.77**	**2.47**	**3.78**	**2.22**	**2.84**	**2.36**	**3.70**	**2.59**
[profit–sales ratio %]	(4.95)	**(4.87)**	**(5.11)**	**(5.28)**	**(4.73)**	**(4.90)**	**(5.02)**	**(4.89)**	**(4.95)**
AGE	39.48	**43.78**	**30.17**	**46.18**	**36.73**	**39.88**	**38.71**	**44.23**	**39.06**
[year]	(16.08)	**(15.22)**	**(13.79)**	**(15.46)**	**(15.51)**	**(15.89)**	**(16.40)**	**(16.44)**	**(15.98)**
L	680	**870**	**270**	**1 527**	**333**	**733**	**580**	**1 992**	**565**
[number of regular workers]	(2 513)	**(2 932)**	**(1 069)**	**(4 334)**	**(893)**	**(2 770)**	**(1 939)**	**(5 901)**	**(1 912)**
ESTAB	12	**15**	**5**	**21**	**9**	11	15	**17**	**12**
[number of establishments]	(40)	**(47)**	**(10)**	**(63)**	**(24)**	(30)	(53)	**(37)**	**(40)**
Number of observations	7 409	5 066	2 343	2 154	5 255	4 837	2 572	598	6 811

Notes: 1. All figures except the number of observations are arithmetic means. Standard deviations are in parentheses.

2. *KLRATIO*: the capital–labour ratio, which is defined as tangible assets (millions of yen) divided by the number of regular workers; *SALES*: per capita sales, which is defined as total sales (millions of yen) divided by the number of regular workers; *WAGE*: average wage, which is defined as total wages (millions of yen) divided by the number of regular workers; *RRD*: the ratio of advertisement expenditure (%), which is defined as advertisement expenditures (millions of yen) divided by total sales (millions of yen); *L*: the number of regular workers; *ESTAB*: the number of establishments; *AGE*: the firm's age.

3. Shaded cells mean that the mean of 'yes' is statistically larger than that of 'no' at the 5% level.

4. AFHs: affiliate holders; CPUs: commissioned production users.

Source: The MITI dataset.

Table 6.3 Status changes from 1994 F/Y to 1997 F/Y

Affiliates (AFHs)		Domestic Yes	Domestic No	Domestic Total			Abroad Yes	Abroad No	Abroad Total
1994 F/Y	Total	5 023	2 386	7 409	1994 F/Y	Total	1 802	5 607	7 409
1995 F/Y	Yes	4 912	334	5 246	1995 F/Y	Yes	1 715	280	1 995
	No	111	2 052	2 163		No	87	5 327	5 414
1996 F/Y	Yes	4 865	375	5 240	1996 F/Y	Yes	1 712	394	2 106
	No	158	2 011	2 169		No	90	5 213	5 303
1997 F/Y	Yes	4 694	372	5 066	1997 F/Y	Yes	1 703	451	2 154
	No	329	2 014	2 343		No	99	5 156	5 255
Status change between 1994–1997					Status change between 1994–1997				
	Yes	414	457	871		Yes	177	503	680
	No	4 609	1 929	6 538		No	1 625	5 104	6 729
Commissioned production arrangements (CPUs)		Domestic Yes	Domestic No	Domestic Total			Abroad Yes	Abroad No	Abroad Total
1994 F/Y	Total	5 159	2 250	7 409	1994 F/Y	Total	538	6 871	7 409
1995 F/Y	Yes	4 816	444	5 260	1995 F/Y	Yes	424	167	591
	No	343	1 806	2 149		No	114	6 704	6 818
1996 F/Y	Yes	4 759	513	5 272	1996 F/Y	Yes	400	278	678
	No	400	1 737	2 137		No	138	6 593	6 731
1997 F/Y	Yes	4 359	478	4 837	1997 F/Y	Yes	301	297	598
	No	800	1 772	2 572		No	237	6 574	6 811
Status change between 1994–1997					Status change between 1995–1997				
	Yes	973	656	1 629		Yes	264	449	713
	No	4 186	1 594	5 780		No	274	6 422	6 696

Notes: *AFHs*: affiliate holders; CPUs: commissioned production users.

Source: The MITI dataset.

Table 6.4 Changes in the number of affiliates and commissioned production between 1994 F/Y and 1997 F/Y

CPUs Domestic	Commissioned production arrangements (CPUs) abroad				Affiliate(s) (AFHs) domestic				Affiliate(s) (AFHs) abroad			
	–	0	+	Total	–	0	+	Total	–	0	+	Total
–	2.9	30.4	2.5	35.7	6.9	21.5	7.4	35.7	1.5	27.4	6.8	35.7
0	0.4	33.4	0.6	34.4	6.0	21.3	7.1	34.4	1.0	29.5	3.9	34.4
+	0.8	26.0	3.0	29.9	5.4	18.3	6.1	29.9	1.4	23.5	4.9	29.9
Total	4.1	89.8	6.1	100.0	18.2	61.1	20.7	100.0	3.9	80.4	15.7	100.0

CPUs Abroad	AFHs domestic				AFHs abroad			
	–	0	+	Total	–	0	+	Total
–	1.1	2.0	0.9	4.1	0.5	2.2	1.3	4.1
0	15.3	56.4	18.1	89.8	2.8	75.2	11.9	89.8
+	1.8	2.7	1.6	6.1	0.7	3.0	2.5	6.1
Total	18.2	61.1	20.7	100.0	3.9	80.4	15.7	100.0

AFHs Domestic	AFHs abroad			
	–	0	+	Total
–	1.7	12.8	3.6	18.2
0	1.2	53.8	6.2	61.1
+	1.0	13.8	5.9	20.7
Total	3.9	80.4	15.7	100.0

Notes: Figures are percentage of total number of firms (7 409=100.0).
For other notes, see Table 6.2.

Source: The MITI dataset.

Table 6.5 Differences in dynamic corporate performance across AFH/CPU status: annual average growth rate of various indicators (%)

	Domestic affiliates (domestic AFHs)					Affiliates abroad (international AFHs)				
	SALES	KLRATIO	WAGE	L	PROFIT	SALES	KLRATIO	WAGE	L	PROFIT
All firms										
without control	0.02	0.61	–0.36	–0.79	0.60	1.67	0.36	0.55	–0.36	4.31
	(0.09)	(2.15)	(–1.93)	(–6.81)	(0.65)	(9.62)	(1.42)	(2.60)	(–2.93)	(4.51)
with control	0.05	0.52	0.17	–0.22	1.33	1.09	0.09	0.63	0.09	3.23
	(0.26)	(1.66)	(0.90)	(–1.69)	(1.30)	(5.78)	(0.34)	(2.98)	(0.69)	(3.03)
Manufacturing firms										
without control	0.01	0.59	–0.27	–0.79	0.70	1.75	0.20	0.53	–0.32	4.91
	(0.07)	(1.95)	(–1.23)	(–5.92)	(0.64)	(8.70)	(0.70)	(2.12)	(–2.23)	(4.37)
with control	0.02	0.40	0.18	–0.23	1.31	1.25	–0.16	0.47	0.01	3.81
	(0.07)	(1.22)	(0.81)	(–1.54)	(1.08)	(5.69)	(–0.54)	(1.86)	(0.07)	(3.03)
	Domestic commissioned production arrangements (domestic CPUs)					Commissioned production arrangements abroad (international CPUs)				
	SALES	KLRATIO	WAGE	L	PROFIT	SALES	KLRATIO	WAGE	L	PROFIT
All firms										
without control	0.57	–0.61	0.52	–0.13	2.21	1.63	–0.16	0.81	–0.61	3.08
	(3.47)	(–2.27)	(2.76)	(–1.07)	(2.41)	(5.24)	(–0.41)	(2.25)	(–3.06)	(1.96)
with control	–0.16	–0.27	–0.05	0.01	1.46	0.68	–0.29	0.63	–0.32	0.63
	(–0.87)	(–0.91)	(–0.25)	(0.09)	(1.44)	(2.18)	(–0.73)	(1.91)	(–1.56)	(0.39)
Manufacturing firms										
without control	0.07	–0.31	–0.15	0.10	1.91	1.57	–0.10	1.01	–0.68	2.11
	(0.33)	(–0.94)	(–0.55)	(0.63)	(1.51)	(4.59)	(–0.23)	(2.56)	(–3.14)	(1.21)
with control	–0.12	–0.26	–0.40	0.03	1.49	0.76	–0.37	0.76	–0.60	–0.44
	(–0.52)	(–0.76)	(–1.52)	(0.20)	(1.11)	(2.24)	(–0.88)	(2.08)	(–2.71)	(–0.24)

Notes: Figures represent the extra annual average growth rate (1994–1997) of firms with status 'yes' in 1994 compared with status 'no'.
The regression coefficient for status dummy is reported. Estimation method is the ordinary least squares with robust standard deviations.
As for 'with control', regression equations include firm's characteristics and industry dummies in addition to each status dummy.
t-statistics are in parentheses.
For other notes, see Table 6.2.

Source: The MITI dataset.

non-AFHs/non-CPUs in terms of profit–sales ratio, and AFHs grow faster than non-AFHs in terms of per-worker sales and capital–labour ratio. This result implies that firms with fragmentation, both domestic and foreign, are likely to become more profitable than firms without.

We must stress that the firms with affiliates/commissioned production abroad tend to present higher growth rates in profit–sales ratio than firms without. In particular, firms with affiliates abroad present higher figures. The difference of annual average growth rate in profit–sales ratio between firms with affiliates abroad and firms without accounts for 3.23 per cent to 4.91 per cent. The difference in the growth rate of per-worker sales between firms with affiliates abroad and firms without also indicates significant difference, presenting from 1.09 per cent to 1.67 per cent. These results clearly indicate that firms with international fragmentation present a better performance than those without.

Table 6.6 is in the same format as Table 6.4 but presents average profit ratios in 1997 F/Y. There are three notable points in this table. First, firms that increase the number of commissioned production arrangements between 1994 F/Y and 1997 F/Y tend to present higher profit than those that decrease it. For instance, firms that increase their domestic commissioned production arrangements present 3.08 per cent while those that decrease it present 2.57 per cent. The corresponding values of firms that increase the number of commissioned production arrangements abroad indicate 3.76 per cent while those that decrease it indicate 2.74 per cent. Second, the firms that increase the number of affiliates abroad and commissioned production arrangements abroad tend to present a higher profit ratio than the average firms (2.68 per cent). Finally, the firms that do not change their number of affiliates and commissioned production arrangements tend to present the lowest profit ratios in the matrices.

The findings of this section are summarized as follows. First, the overall trend is in the direction of globalization: more firms start having affiliates abroad and conducting commissioned production abroad than firms start having domestic affiliates and conducting domestic commissioned production. Second, firms with fragmentation tend to have faster growth than firms without. In particular, the firms with international fragmentation are likely to grow faster in profit–sales ratio than the firms without. Third, all firms that increase the number of affiliates abroad and/or the number of commissioned production arrangements abroad present higher values in profit–sales ratio than the average firms. Finally, the firms that do not change either the number of affiliates or commissioned production arrangements are likely to present the lowest profit–sales ratios.

Table 6.6 Firm's profits by the changes in the number of affiliates and commissioned production arrangements

CPUs Domestic	Commissioned production arrangements (CPUs) abroad –	0	+	Total	Affiliate(s) (AFHs) domestic –	0	+	Total	Affiliate(s) (AFHs) abroad –	0	+	Total
–	2.33	2.52	3.43	2.57	2.54	2.50	2.79	2.57	3.73	2.32	3.30	2.57
0	3.85	2.41	3.47	2.44	2.54	2.38	2.54	2.44	3.69	2.23	3.73	2.44
+	3.67	2.94	4.09	3.08	3.28	2.93	3.34	3.08	4.38	2.76	4.20	3.08
Total	2.74	2.60	3.76	2.68	2.76	2.59	2.87	2.68	3.95	2.42	3.69	2.68

CPUs Abroad	AFHs domestic –	0	+	Total	AFHs abroad –	0	+	Total
–	2.35	2.86	2.95	2.74	3.07	2.44	3.12	2.74
0	2.68	2.53	2.74	2.60	3.91	2.36	3.79	2.60
+	3.62	3.57	4.24	3.76	4.77	3.75	3.49	3.76
Total	2.76	2.59	2.87	2.68	3.95	2.42	3.69	2.68

AFHs Domestic	AFHs abroad –	0	+	Total
–	4.06	2.27	3.84	2.76
0	4.38	2.41	3.75	2.59
+	3.26	2.55	3.54	2.87
Total	3.95	2.42	3.69	2.68

Note: Figures are operating surplus-sales ratio (%) in 1997 F/Y, which are the same as PROFIT shown in Table 6.2.
Source: The MITI dataset.

THE PATTERN OF FRAGMENTATION ACROSS INDUSTRIES

In the regression analysis in the last section, we control industry-specific characteristics by using industry dummies. The industry dummy is useful in controlling the overall effects of each industry but does not allow us to examine the detailed characteristics of fragmentation. To identify the industry-level characteristics of fragmentation, we examine the pattern of Japanese firms' fragmentation across industries.

Table 6.7 presents the pattern of fragmentation across industries from 1994 F/Y to 1997 F/Y[14]. Overall, the number of affiliates abroad steadily increases throughout the period while that of domestic affiliates stays at almost the same level. At the industry level, the number of affiliates is large in the chemical industry, machinery industries and wholesale trade. In 1997 F/Y, the number of affiliates abroad in the chemical industry, general machinery, electric machinery, transportation machinery, and wholesale trade is 1149, 1183, 1843, 1185 and 5434, respectively.

As for the ratio of the number of affiliates abroad to that of total affiliates, in addition to the chemical industry, machinery industries and wholesale trade, plastic products and rubber products also present relatively high figures. Moreover, these ratios grow in almost all industries from 1994 F/Y to 1997 F/Y with some fluctuations. The ratio of all industries increases from 22.7 per cent to 27.1 per cent during the same period. These figures support the previous sections' results: as for affiliates, the overall trend is in the direction of globalization.

Table 6.8 presents the pattern of commissioned production arrangements across industries. The number of domestic commissioned production arrangements is quite large compared with the number of affiliates. Moreover, as indicated by the large fluctuations, incumbent effects or sunk costs seem to be small compared with having affiliates. Domestic commissioned production is mainly conducted by manufacturing firms. In 1997 F/Y, for instance, 80.4 per cent of domestic commissioned production arrangements are conducted by manufacturing firms. We can also confirm that the total number of domestic commissioned production arrangements decreases throughout the period in almost all industries.

As for commissioned production arrangements abroad, the number is small compared with domestic commissioned production arrangements. Indeed, for all industries' total, the ratio of commissioned production arrangements abroad to total commissioned production arrangements is around 5 per cent. Major sectors conducting commissioned production

Table 6.7 The pattern of fragmentation across industries: affiliates

	Number of domestic affiliates				Number of affiliates abroad				Affiliates abroad/total affiliates (%)			
Industry	1994	1995	1996	1997	1994	1995	1996	1997	1994	1995	1996	1997
Agriculture, forestry and fishery	0	2	2	0	0	0	0	0	n.a.	0.0	0.0	n.a.
Construction	522	796	845	849	33	57	73	76	5.9	6.7	8.0	8.2
Food products	1 552	1 767	1 675	1 583	200	254	273	267	11.4	12.6	14.0	14.4
Beverages	756	780	811	753	167	156	171	180	18.1	16.7	17.4	19.3
Textile products	869	911	873	808	102	147	175	159	10.5	13.9	16.7	16.4
Timber, wooden products and furniture	573	191	213	198	65	45	48	45	10.2	19.1	18.4	18.5
Pulp, paper and paper products	1 802	1 806	1 828	1 959	128	146	137	147	6.6	7. 5	7.0	7.0
Chemical products	2 844	3 189	3 140	3 165	845	935	1 008	1 149	22.9	22.7	24.3	26.6
Petroleum refinery and coal products	381	363	330	337	40	37	38	37	9.5	9.3	10.3	9.9
Plastic products	621	650	670	632	156	201	225	219	20.1	23.6	25.1	25.7
Rubber products	458	536	491	475	124	136	163	179	21.3	20.2	24.9	27.4
Ceramic, stone and clay products	1 246	1 304	1 320	1 356	96	135	160	168	7.2	9.4	10.8	11.0
Iron, steel and metal roducts	3 087	3 320	3 273	3 279	597	711	768	804	16.2	17.6	19.0	19.7
General machinery	2 768	2 631	2 754	2 580	1 017	1 060	1 162	1 183	26.9	28.7	29.7	31.4
Electric machinery	4 067	3 681	3 662	3 659	1 740	1 791	1 779	1 843	30.0	32.7	32.7	33.5
Transportation machinery	3 011	2 962	3 065	2 852	906	1 057	1 110	1 185	23.1	26.3	26.6	29.4
Precision machinery	390	380	403	342	179	216	224	238	31.5	36.2	35.7	41.0
Other manufacturing	406	417	426	334	179	167	197	198	30.6	28.6	31.6	37.2
Electricity, gas and water supply	113	116	121	123	9	7	9	8	7.4	5.7	6.9	6.1
Transportation	54	55	68	52	4	5	5	5	6.9	8.3	6.8	8.8

Communication	26	28	30	31	5	0	0	0	16.1	0.0	0.0	0.0
Wholesale trade	9 456	9 874	9 706	10 061	3 993	4 317	4 711	5 434	29.7	30.4	32.7	35.1
Retail trade	1 428	1 380	1 428	1 421	174	166	170	169	10.9	10.7	10.6	10.6
Restaurants	13	8	9	14	2	0	0	1	13.3	0.0	0.0	6.7
Finance and insurance	10	8	6	9	0	0	0	0	0.0	0.0	0.0	0.0
Real estate	11	17	16	24	0	0	1	3	0.0	0.0	5.9	11.1
Information, advertisement and software	142	137	140	81	12	14	19	21	7.8	9.3	11.9	20.6
Other services	102	143	121	179	27	31	33	84	20.9	17.8	21.4	31.9
Education and research	0	0	0	0	0	0	0	0	n.a.	n.a.	n.a.	n.a.
Others	301	265	229	76	53	53	63	59	15.0	16.7	21.6	43.7
All industry	37 009	37 717	37 655	37 232	10 853	11 844	12 722	13 861	22.7	23.9	25.3	27.1

Note: Industrial classification is based on the source with some aggregation.

Source: The MITI dataset.

Table 6.8 The pattern of fragmentation across industries: commissioned production arrangements

	Number of domestic commissioned production arrangements				Number of commissioned production arrangements abroad				Commissioned production arrangements abroad / total commissioned production arrangements (%)			
Industry	1994	1995	1996	1997	1994	1995	1996	1997	1994	1995	1996	1997
Agriculture, forestry and fishery	0	4	0	0	0	0	0	0	n.a.	0.0	n.a.	n.a.
Construction	5 669	6 909	11 473	8 915	29	20	76	59	0.5	0.3	0.7	0.7
Food products	2 656	2 674	2 830	2 322	12	44	104	57	0.4	1.6	3.5	2.4
Beverages	972	1 148	1 203	1 130	9	10	11	8	0.9	0.9	0.9	0.7
Textile products	10 516	9 670	9 978	9 663	69	118	219	102	0.7	1.2	2.1	1.0
Timber, wooden products and furniture	5 166	4 361	3 864	3 627	28	13	30	22	0.5	0.3	0.8	0.6
Pulp, paper and paper products	34 080	32 834	35 878	33 318	58	52	92	69	0.2	0.2	0.3	0.2
Chemical products	5 814	6 175	6 137	5 365	34	59	65	58	0.6	0.9	1.0	1.1
Petroleum refinery and coal products	92	104	105	45	4	4	4	1	4.2	3.7	3.7	2.2
Plastic products	10 703	11 062	12 331	10 343	85	103	110	103	0.8	0.9	0.9	1.0
Rubber products	2 858	2 594	2 100	2 085	48	45	48	42	1.7	1.7	2.2	2.0
Ceramic, stone and clay products	1 635	2 218	2 894	2 350	18	34	58	55	1.1	1.5	2.0	2.3
Iron, steel and metal roducts	36 348	33 404	34 651	34 333	141	162	164	150	0.4	0.5	0.5	0.4
General machinery	72 590	74 525	73 136	62 053	9 578	10 705	11 765	12 578	11.7	12.6	13.9	16.9
Electric machinery	59 949	62 449	62 357	55 068	7 601	3 280	1 564	1 446	11.3	5.0	2.4	2.6
Transportation machinery	42 673	45 207	44 584	38 587	493	997	1 105	890	1.1	2.2	2.4	2.3
Precision machinery	9 177	11 604	10 289	11 822	162	224	226	151	1.7	1.9	2.1	1.3
Other manufacturing	6 660	8 166	7 340	4 937	89	150	195	207	1.3	1.8	2.6	4.0
Electricity, gas and water supply	230	163	180	169	0	0	0	0	0.0	0.0	0.0	0.0
Transportation	54	56	109	71	0	0	0	0	0.0	0.0	0.0	0.0

Communication	11	0	0	0	0	0	0	0	0.0	n.a.	n.a.	n.a.
Wholesale trade	48 762	52 087	48 040	39 250	935	1 516	1 086	912	1.9	2.8	2.2	2.3
Retail trade	8 487	8 944	9 549	7 629	92	152	154	193	1.1	1.7	1.6	2.5
Restaurants	11	12	12	12	0	0	0	0	0.0	0.0	0.0	0.0
Finance and insurance	0	0	0	0	0	0	0	0	n.a.	n.a.	n.a.	n.a.
Real estate	5	1	4	9	0	0	0	0	0.0	0.0	0.0	0.0
Information, advertisement and software	2 770	995	975	935	1	0	0	0	0.0	0.0	0.0	0.0
Other services	1 948	2 441	2 338	2 421	555	599	642	760	22.2	19.7	21.5	23.9
Education and research	0	0	0	0	0	0	0	0	n.a.	n.a.	n.a.	n.a.
Others	939	1 998	2 542	2 885	0	0	1	0	0.0	0.0	0.0	0.0
All industry	370 775	381 805	384 899	339 344	20 041	18 287	17 719	17 863	5.1	4.6	4.4	5.0
All industry exclude electronics machinery	310 826	319 356	322 542	284 276	12 440	15 007	16 155	16 417	3.8	4.5	4.8	5.5

Notes: Industrial classification is based on the source with some aggregation.
Source: The MITI dataset.

Table 6.9 Industrial distribution of the number of affiliates and commissioned production arrangements: machinery industries

Industry	Domestic affiliates				Affiliates abroad				Domestic commissioned production arrangements				Commissioned production arrangements abroad			
	1994	1995	1996	1997	1994	1995	1996	1997	1994	1995	1996	1997	1994	1995	1996	1997
29 General machinery	**2 768**	**2 631**	**2 754**	**2 580**	**1 017**	**1 060**	**1 162**	**1 183**	**72 590**	**74 525**	**73 136**	**62 053**	**9 578**	**10 705**	**11 765**	**12 578**
Metal molds and bearing machinery	212	213	216	195	113	127	138	136	8 101	7 763	8 368	6 912	21	28	47	36
Special industrial machinery	899	938	947	910	209	258	271	299	15 332	18 787	16 330	11 682	147	249	266	202
Machinery for office and service industry	426	300	338	323	178	131	173	168	6 904	4 931	5 452	5 346	110	71	89	70
Other general machinery	1 231	1 180	1 253	1 152	517	544	580	580	42 253	43 044	42 986	38 113	9 300	10 357	11 363	12 270
30 Electronics machinery	**4 067**	**3 681**	**3 662**	**3 659**	**1 740**	**1 791**	**1 779**	**1 843**	**59 949**	**62 449**	**62 357**	**55 068**	**7 601**	**3 280**	**1 564**	**1 446**
Industrial, household and communication equipment	1 479	1 817	1 455	1 530	560	694	477	561	27 071	30 031	30 061	25 203	2 301	2 498	517	328
Applied electric equipment	1 127	631	1 023	986	421	345	496	505	13 065	10 700	12 441	11 643	234	336	550	578
Semi-conductor devices and integrated circuits	1 116	887	825	800	650	636	693	662	14 755	15 495	14 682	13 783	5 012	264	305	368
Other eelectrical machinery	345	346	359	343	109	116	113	115	5 058	6 223	5 173	4 439	54	182	192	172
31 Transportation machinery	**3 011**	**2 962**	**3 065**	**2 852**	**906**	**1 057**	**1 110**	**1 185**	**42 673**	**45 207**	**44 584**	**38 587**	**493**	**997**	**1 105**	**890**
Cars	2 359	2 409	2 514	2 398	798	932	974	1 078	32 143	33 296	33 784	30 559	404	428	527	821
Other transport equipment	652	553	551	454	108	125	136	107	10 530	11 911	10 800	8 028	89	569	578	69
32 Precision machinery	**390**	**380**	**403**	**342**	**179**	**216**	**224**	**238**	**9 177**	**11 604**	**10 289**	**11 822**	**162**	**224**	**226**	**151**
Medical instruments	85	68	102	37	34	72	44	40	2 068	4 359	2 689	2 184	13	45	39	12
Optical instruments	43	38	20	20	32	33	36	40	2 066	1 919	1 994	2 493	14	10	7	19
Watches and clocks	100	83	81	104	36	24	30	50	1 028	908	874	702	23	13	14	32
Other precision machinery	162	191	200	181	77	87	114	108	4 015	4 418	4 732	6 443	112	156	166	88

Notes: Industrial classification is based on the source with some aggregation.
Source: The MITI dataset.

abroad are general machinery, electric machinery, wholesale trade and other services. In 1997 F/Y, these four industries present 87.9 per cent of the total number of commissioned production arrangements abroad.

Contrary to the results for affiliates abroad, the total number of commissioned production arrangements abroad gradually decreases from 1994 F/Y to 1997 F/Y. However, a notable decline is observed in electric machinery, and the total number of commissioned production arrangements excluding those of electric machinery is rather increasing. The detailed pattern of fragmentation in machinery industries is tabulated in Table 6.9. As was mentioned, commissioned production shows large fluctuations compared with the holdings of affiliates. Moreover, the decline in commissioned production abroad was mainly attributed to the decline in semiconductor devices and integrated circuits from 1995 F/Y to 1996 F/Y. Other industries such as general machinery, transportation machinery and other electronics machinery such as applied electric equipment had a larger number of

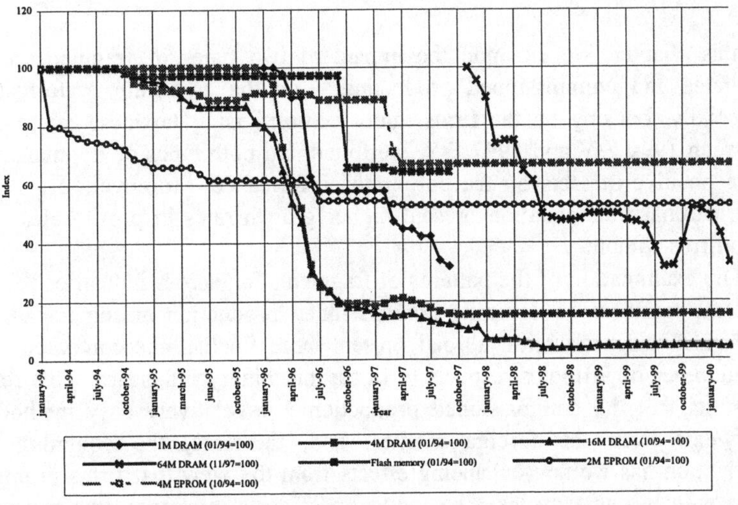

Note: The price in 1994 F/Y or in initial year (semi-conductor appears in the market) is normalized as 100.

Source: Nikkei NEEDS database (accessed date 08/15/2001).

Figure 6.1 Changes in semi-conductor wholesale prices

commissioned production arrangements abroad. Taking into consideration the fact that the semi-conductor wholesale prices radically declined from 1995 F/Y (Figure 6.1), the commissioned production abroad seemed to be used as a buffer against negative demand shocks by Japanese firms. The results indicate a similar logic to what Aoki (1990) suggested: Japanese firms might use commissioned production abroad as well as domestic commissioned production as a buffer for business cycles[15].

Firms that internationally fragment their production process, both by having affiliates and arranging commissioned production, tend to perform better than firms that do not. In addition, the examination of the patterns of fragmentation across industries reveals that the numbers of domestic commissioned production arrangements and commissioned production abroad present large fluctuations compared with the number of affiliates, especially in the machinery industries. This result suggests that the commissioned production is a relatively easy method to entry/exit from the foreign markets. The results imply that the cost of coordination among production blocks might be lower in commissioned production than in having affiliates.

CONCLUDING REMARKS

In this chapter, we examine the impact of two types of fragmentation – affiliates and commissioned production – on the corporate performance, especially focusing on the firms' globalization. Using Japanese micro data between 1994 F/Y and 1997 F/Y, we found that both types of fragmentation have positive impacts on the corporate performance. Moreover, firms with international fragmentation present higher growth rates in profit–sales ratio than firms without.

The examination of the patterns of fragmentation across industries reveals that the numbers of domestic commissioned production arrangements and commissioned production abroad present large fluctuations compared with the number of affiliates, especially in the machinery industries. This result suggests that the commissioned production is a relatively easy method to entry/exit from the foreign markets and, therefore, the commissioned production has welfare-enhancing effects from the view that firms promptly cope with business cycles. The reduction of costs in service link promotes Japanese firms' commissioned production abroad, which results in the good performance of the firms with international fragmentation.

NOTES

1. The MITI database was prepared and analysed in cooperation with the Research and Statistics Department, Minister's Secretariat, Ministry of International Trade and Industry (currently called the Ministry of Economy, Trade, and Industry or

METI), Government of Japan. An earlier version of this chapter was presented at the international conference *Location of Economic Activity, Regional Development and the Global Economy* at the University of Le Havre, France on September 26–27, 2001. We are thankful to Professor Yoko Sazanami and other participants for important comments and suggestions at the conference. However, opinions expressed in this chapter are those of the authors.

2. As for subcontracting, see Aoki (1990), Taylor and Wiggins (1997) and Kimura (2002).
3. OEM is defined as the production of another firm's brand products while EMS is defined as the firm that does not have their own brand and specializes in IT related manufacturing works. The importance of commissioned production in recent business activities is also pointed out by JETRO (2000, p. 46).
4. As Jones and Kierzkowski (2001, p. 17) suggested, fragmentation can take place across borders and/or within the same country: 'Breaking down the integrated process into separate stages of production opens up new possibilities for exploiting gains from specialization. Although such fragmentation is likely to occur first on a local or national basis, significant cuts in costs of international coordination often allow producers to take advantage of differences in technologies and factor prices among countries in designing more global production network.' Ruane and Gorg (2001, p. 146) also state that 'while international fragmentation arguably offers more possibilities for exploiting differences in comparative advantages across countries, fragmentation within the same country may, on the other hand, involve lower transaction costs.'
5. Under the assumption of perfect competitive factor markets, changes of factor costs are often called 'mandated' since the changes are required to maintain zero profits across sectors. For more detail, see Leamer (1998) and Feenstra and Hanson (1999).
6. See, for example, Sachs and Warner (1995), Harrison (1996) and Rodriguez and Rodrik (1999).
7. Blomström *et al.* (2000) also found that Japan's FDI contributed to the restructuring of the Japanese economy.
8. In the following sections, a MNE is defined as a firm that has one or more affiliates abroad.
9. The recent empirical literature confirmed the fact that differences in a firm's activity are partly explained by differences in ownership of nationalities. See, for example, Aitken *et al.* (1995), Globerman *et al.* (1994) and Doms and Jensen (1998).
10. Note that the industry dummies also control the effects due to the degree of foreign exposure at the industry level.
11. Subcontracting data is only available in the 1994 F/Y survey.
12. Since the information on equipment investment is not available for many firms, the estimation of capital stock by perpetual inventory method would result in an unbearable reduction in the number of observations. We therefore use tangible assets data as a proxy of capital stock.
13. Note that Table 6.3 focuses on the number of firms that commission production rather than the values of commissioned production as in Table 6.1. Also, Table 6.3 uses the firms that were continuously in operation between 1994 F/Y and 1997 F/Y.

14. A firm's industrial classification is specified by its major products/services in the year concerned. There is a possibility that some firms change their industrial classification between 1994 and 1997.
15. Strictly speaking, Aoki (1990) focuses on the Japanese subcontracting system rather than commissioned production.

REFERENCES

Aitken, B., A. Harrison and R. Lipsey (1995), 'Wages and foreign ownership: comparative study of Mexico, Venezuela and the United States', *NBER Working Paper*, 5102.

Aoki, M. (1990), 'Toward an economic model of the Japanese firm', *Journal of Economic Literature*, **28** (1), 1–27.

Aw, B.-Y. and A.R. Hwang (1995), 'Productivity and the export market: a firm level analysis', *Journal of Development Economics*, **47** (2), 313–32.

Baldone, S., F. Sdogati and L. Tajoli (2001), 'Patterns and determinants of international fragmentation of production: evidence from outward processing trade between the EU and Central Eastern European countries', *Weltwirtschaftliches Archiv*, **137** (1), 80–104.

Bernard, A.B. and J.B. Jensen (1995a), 'Exporters, jobs, and wages in U.S. manufacturing: 1976–1987', *Brookings Papers on Economic Activity: Microeconomics*, Washington, D.C.: The Brookings Institution.

Bernard, A.B. and J.B. Jensen (1995b), 'Why some firms export: experience, entry costs, spillovers and subsidies', Yale University mimeo.

Bernard, A.B. and J.B. Jensen (1997), 'Exporters, skill upgrading, and the wage gap', *Journal of International Economics*, **42** (1/2), 3–31.

Bernard, A.B. and J.B. Jensen (1999a), 'Exceptional exporter performance: cause, effect, or both?', *Journal of International Economics*, **47** (1), 1–26.

Bernard, A.B. and J.B. Jensen (1999b), 'Exporting and productivity', *NBER Working Paper*, 7135.

Bernard, A.B., J. Eaton, J.B. Jensen and S. Kortum (2000), 'Plants and productivity in international trade', *NBER Working Paper*, 7688.

Blomström, M., D. Konan and R.E. Lipsey (2000), 'Foreign direct investment in the restructuring of the Japanese economy', *NBER Working Paper*, 7693.

Deardorff, A.V. (2001a), 'Fragmentation in simple trade models', *North American Journal of Economics and Finance*, **12** (2), 121–37.

Deardorff, A.V. (2001b), 'International provision of trade in services, trade and fragmentation', *Review of International Economics*, **9** (2), 233–48.

Doms, M. and J.B. Jensen (1998), 'Comparing wages, skills and productivity between domestically and foreign-owned manufacturing establishments in the United States', in R.E. Baldwin, R.E. Lipsey and J.D. Richardson (eds), *Geography and Ownership as Bases for Economic Accounting*, Chicago: University of Chicago Press.

Egger, H. and P. Egger (2001), 'Cross-border sourcing and outward processing EU manufacturing', *North American Journal of Economics and Finance*, **12** (3), 243–56.

Egger, P., M. Pfaffermayr and Y. Wolfmayr-Schnitzer (2001), 'The international fragmentation of Austrian manufacturing: the effects of outsourcing on productivity and wages', *North American Journal of Economics and Finance*, **137** (3), 257–72.

Feenstra, R.C. and G.H. Hanson (1999), 'The impact of outsourcing and high-technology capital on wages: estimates for the United States, 1979–1990', *Quarterly Journal of Economics*, **114** (3), 707–1084.

Globerman, S., J.C. Ries and I. Vertinsky (1994), 'The economic performance of foreign affiliates in Canada', *Canadian Journal of Economics*, **27** (1), 143–56.

Harrison, A. (1996), 'Openness and growth: a time-series, cross-country analysis for developing countries', *Journal of Development Economics*, **48**, 419–47.

Japan External Trade Organization (JETRO) (2000), *JETRO Boueki Hakusho 2000* (*White Paper on Trade 2000*), Tokyo: JETRO. [In Japanese]

Jones, R.W. (2001), *Globalization and the Theory of Input Trade* (The Ohlin Lectures, 8), Cambridge, MA: The MIT Press.

Jones, R.W. and H. Kierzkowski (1990), 'The role of services in production and international trade: a theoretical framework', in R.W. Jones and A.O. Krueger (eds), *The Political Economy of International Trade: Essays in Honor of Robert E. Baldwin*, Cambridge, MA: Basil Blackwell.

Jones, R.W. and H. Kierzkowski (2001), 'A framework of fragmentation', in S.W. Arndt and H. Kierzkowski (eds), *Fragmentation: New Production Patterns in the World Economy*, Oxford: Oxford University Press.

Kimura, F. (2002), 'Subcontracting and the performance of small and medium firms in Japan', *Small Business Economics*, **18** (1–3), 163–75.

Kimura, F. and K. Kiyota (2003), 'Exports and foreign direct investment accelerate corporate reforms: evidence from the Japanese micro data', in R.M. Stern (ed.), *Japan's Economic Recovery: Commercial Policy, Monetary Policy, and Corporate Governance*, Cheltenham, UK and Northampton, MA: Edward Elgar.

Leamer, E.E. (1998), 'In search of Stolper–Samuelson linkages between international trade and lower wages', in S.M. Collins (ed.), *Imports, Exports and American Worker*, Washington, D.C.: Brookings Institution Press.

Research and Statistics Department, Minister's Secretariat, Ministry of International Trade and Industry (MITI) (various years), *Kigyou Katsudou Kihon Chousa Houkokusho* (*The Results of The Basic Survey of Japanese Business Structure and Activities*). [In Japanese]

Roberts, M.J. and J.R. Tybout (1997), 'The decision to export in Colombia: an empirical model of entry with sunk costs', *American Economic Review*, **87** (4), 545–64.

Rodriguez, F. and D. Rodrik (1999), 'Trade policy and economic growth: a skeptic's guide to the cross-national evidence', *NBER Working Paper*, 7081.

Ruane, F. and H. Gorg (2001), 'Globalization and fragmentation: evidence for the electronics industry in Ireland', in S.W. Arndt and H. Kierzkowski (eds), *Fragmentation: New Production Patterns in the World Economy*, Oxford: Oxford University Press.

Sachs, J. and A. Warner (1995), 'Economic reform and the process of global integration', *Brookings Papers on Economic Activity*, **1**, 1–118.

Taylor, C.R. and S.N. Wiggins (1997), 'Competition or compensation: supplier incentives under the American and Japanese subcontracting systems', *American Economic Review*, **87** (4), 598–618.

Venables, A.J. (1999), 'Fragmentation and multinational production', European Economic Review, **43** (4–7), 935–45.

7. Japanese Foreign Direct Investment Flows to East Asia and the Real Exchange Rate: Lessons from the Asian Financial Crisis[1]

Yoko Sazanami, Seiji Yoshimura and Kozo Kiyota

INTRODUCTION

The Japanese influx of foreign direct investment (FDI) to East Asia[2] peaked in 1995 reaching 12.2 billion dollars (Table 7.1). The appreciation of the yen against the dollar after the Plaza Accord in 1985 motivated Japanese multinational enterprises to relocate their domestic affiliates to East Asia as the real exchange rate (RER) of East Asian currencies depreciated against the yen in countries adopting a *de facto* dollar pegged exchange rate regime. Japanese firms continued to invest heavily in East Asia even after the RERs of some East Asian currencies appreciated against the yen, reflecting the depreciation of the yen against the dollar from 1995 (Sazanami and Yoshimura, 2002). At the end of the Asian financial crisis of 1997–98, Japanese FDI to East Asia declined sharply. It fell from 11.2 billion dollars in 1997 to 6.0 billion dollars in 1998. Japanese FDI outflows to East Asia remained stagnant in 1998, 1999 and 2000.

The Japanese FDI response in 1997–98 seems to differ from the FDI responses of other countries. According to a study by the World Bank (1999, p. 59), 'FDI flows were relatively stable to four of the five East Asian countries most affected by the crisis, although these countries

Table 7.1 Regional distribution of Japanese FDI outflows, 1978–2000 (thousands of US dollars)

	1978	1979	1980	1981	1982	1983	1984	1985	1986	1987	1988	1989
World	**4 541 869**	**4 931 767**	**4 632 737**	**8 858 815**	**7 649 567**	**8 103 357**	**10 113 146**	**12 180 685**	**22 270 115**	**33 311 056**	**46 973 115**	**65 481 872**
North America	1 386 207	1 439 811	1 602 185	2 554 101	2 909 786	2 714 933	3 572 938	5 643 244	10 456 881	15 393 304	22 665 280	33 184 177
Europe & Central Asia	321 080	418 418	572 734	793 153	865 734	981 759	1 926 123	1 918 150	3 456 539	6 566 356	9 099 299	14 280 958
East Asia	1 337 369	967 002	1 177 204	3 316 645	1 378 070	1 769 423	1 602 366	1 414 433	2 309 025	4 838 754	5 526 397	7 855 531
China	n.a.	13 500	11 863	25 795	18 493	2 955	114 194	99 858	226 356	1 226 499	296 234	425 319
Korea	222 133	94 759	35 083	73 194	103 165	129 042	106 702	133 767	435 533	646 858	482 904	578 900
Hong Kong	158 494	224 715	155 805	329 101	401 013	562 524	411 723	131 068	502 301	1 072 488	1 661 781	1 813 874
Taiwan	39 549	38 667	47 217	54 437	54 645	103 023	64 691	114 142	290 525	367 401	372 367	479 683
Singapore	173 945	255 381	139 888	266 338	180 256	322 065	224 810	338 969	302 176	494 399	747 102	1 864 743
Indonesia	610 182	149 780	529 396	2 434 148	409 650	373 562	373 825	408 266	249 769	545 445	585 507	609 111
Malaysia	47 942	33 457	146 337	31 047	82 534	139 637	142 143	79 296	158 035	163 324	387 135	654 146
Philippines	53 476	102 200	78 318	71 947	34 139	64 948	45 655	60 654	20 581	72 379	134 480	195 209
Thailand	31 648	54 543	33 297	30 638	94 175	71 667	118 623	48 413	123 749	249 961	858 887	1 234 546
Latin America & Caribbean	541 397	1 154 922	555 080	1 124 571	1 451 115	1 787 879	2 189 374	2 399 843	4 643 118	4 575 337	5 914 383	4 730 647
Others	955 816	951 614	725 534	1 070 345	1 044 862	849 363	822 345	805 015	1 404 552	1 937 305	3 767 756	5 430 560

	1990	1991	1992	1993	1994	1995	1996	1997	1998	1999	2000
World	**57 688 280**	**42 211 340**	**34 987 999**	**37 333 091**	**41 883 453**	**52 698 502**	**49 728 192**	**54 738 724**	**39 852 221**	**65 307 654**	**49 821 463**
North America	27 962 684	19 359 276	15 237 077	16 346 013	19 155 369	24 262 957	24 365 107	21 891 033	10 719 232	24 397 939	13 143 692
Europe & Central Asia	14 461 731	9 470 436	7 241 182	8 277 451	6 383 884	8 795 604	7 634 580	11 363 449	13 686 643	25 267 543	25 030 158
East Asia	7 033 773	5 945 972	6 322 587	6 769 825	9 478 886	12 153 496	11 387 952	11 251 465	6 033 689	6 682 952	5 857 384
China	352 890	584 134	1 090 524	1 757 001	2 625 147	4 592 142	2 599 316	2 015 076	1 041 282	735 266	1 019 942
Korea	289 081	264 693	229 465	260 167	411 367	460 633	430 478	448 430	295 978	959 186	834 167
Hong Kong	1 802 348	935 586	762 489	1 301 579	1 153 755	1 175 999	1 539 543	704 937	588 580	950 424	959 532
Taiwan	450 729	411 493	296 879	308 396	285 985	467 066	539 782	456 373	219 121	279 430	522 758
Singapore	850 653	621 556	690 559	661 289	1 077 264	1 215 495	1 154 809	1 849 683	622 459	942 295	434 417
Indonesia	1 115 685	1 208 905	1 690 985	856 472	1 768 609	1 645 893	2 500 060	2 549 752	1 052 366	899 040	424 377
Malaysia	736 591	892 656	725 348	801 858	755 117	589 584	591 879	802 407	502 723	514 613	237 777
Philippines	264 597	205 275	166 086	211 865	668 607	735 555	578 880	531 023	370 490	603 905	469 336
Thailand	1 171 200	821 672	670 251	611 198	733 035	1 271 130	1 453 203	1 893 785	1 340 690	798 792	955 078
Latin America & Caribbean	3 272 443	2 525 370	2 392 646	2 904 396	4 091 637	3 375 222	3 295 572	5 537 561	6 131 072	6 022 466	4 795 666
Others	4 957 649	4 910 287	3 794 506	3 035 405	2 773 677	4 111 223	3 044 981	4 695 217	3 281 586	2 936 755	994 562

Table 7.1 (continued) Regional distribution of Japanese FDI outflows, 1978–2000 (%)

	1978	1979	1980	1981	1982	1983	1984	1985	1986	1987	1988	1989
World	**100.0**	**100.0**	**100.0**	**100.0**	**100.0**	**100.0**	**100.0**	**100.0**	**100.0**	**100.0**	**100.0**	**100.0**
North America	30.5	29.2	34.6	28.8	38.0	33.5	35.3	46.3	47.0	46.2	48.3	50.7
Europe & Central Asia	7.1	8.5	12.4	9.0	11.3	12.1	19.0	15.7	15.5	19.7	19.4	21.8
East Asia	29.4	19.6	25.4	37.4	18.0	21.8	15.8	11.6	10.4	14.5	11.8	12.0
China	n.a.	0.3	0.3	0.3	0.2	0.0	1.1	0.8	1.0	3.7	0.6	0.6
Korea	4.9	1.9	0.8	0.8	1.3	1.6	1.1	1.1	2.0	1.9	1.0	0.9
Hong Kong	3.5	4.6	3.4	3.7	5.2	6.9	4.1	1.1	2.3	3.2	3.5	2.8
Taiwan	0.9	0.8	1.0	0.6	0.7	1.3	0.6	0.9	1.3	1.1	0.8	0.7
Singapore	3.8	5.2	3.0	3.0	2.4	4.0	2.2	2.8	1.4	1.5	1.6	2.8
Indonesia	13.4	3.0	11.4	27.5	5.4	4.6	3.7	3.4	1.1	1.6	1.2	0.9
Malaysia	1.1	0.7	3.2	0.4	1.1	1.7	1.4	0.7	0.7	0.5	0.8	1.0
Philippines	1.2	2.1	1.7	0.8	0.4	0.8	0.5	0.5	0.1	0.2	0.3	0.3
Thailand	0.7	1.1	0.7	0.3	1.2	0.9	1.2	0.4	0.6	0.8	1.8	1.9
Latin America & Caribbean	11.9	23.4	12.0	12.7	19.0	22.1	21.6	19.7	20.8	13.7	12.6	7.2
Others	21.0	19.3	15.7	12.1	13.7	10.5	8.1	6.6	6.3	5.8	8.0	8.3
	1990	1991	1992	1993	1994	1995	1996	1997	1998	1999	2000	
World	**100.0**	**100.0**	**100.0**	**100.0**	**100.0**	**100.0**	**100.0**	**100.0**	**100.0**	**100.0**	**100.0**	
North America	48.5	45.9	43.5	43.8	45.7	46.0	49.0	40.0	26.9	37.4	26.4	
Europe & Central Asia	25.1	22.4	20.7	22.2	15.2	16.7	15.4	20.8	34.3	38.7	50.2	
East Asia	12.2	14.1	18.1	18.1	22.6	23.1	22.9	20.6	15.1	10.2	11.8	
China	0.6	1.4	3.1	4.7	6.3	8.7	5.2	3.7	2.6	1.1	2.0	
Korea	0.5	0.6	0.7	0.7	1.0	0.9	0.9	0.8	0.7	1.5	1.7	
Hong Kong	3.1	2.2	2.2	3.5	2.8	2.2	3.1	1.3	1.5	1.5	1.9	
Taiwan	0.8	1.0	0.8	0.8	0.7	0.9	1.1	0.8	0.5	0.4	1.0	
Singapore	1.5	1.5	2.0	1.8	2.6	2.3	2.3	3.4	1.6	1.4	0.9	
Indonesia	1.9	2.9	4.8	2.3	4.2	3.1	5.0	4.7	2.6	1.4	0.9	
Malaysia	1.3	2.1	2.1	2.1	1.8	1.1	1.2	1.5	1.3	0.8	0.5	
Philippines	0.5	0.5	0.5	0.6	1.6	1.4	1.2	1.0	0.9	0.9	0.9	
Thailand	2.0	1.9	1.9	1.6	1.8	2.4	2.9	3.5	3.4	1.2	1.9	
Latin America & Caribbean	5.7	6.0	6.8	7.8	9.8	6.4	6.6	10.1	15.4	9.2	9.6	
Others	8.6	11.6	10.8	8.1	6.6	7.8	6.1	8.6	8.2	4.5	2.0	

Note: Data is notification and fiscal year basis.

Source: http://www.mof.go.jp (accessed date 08/07/2001).

differed in some respects. FDI flows to Thailand and Korea rose in 1998, despite the severity of recession in these countries, while flows declined slightly to Malaysia and the Philippines, continuing downward trends during the 1990s'. The overall FDI flows to crisis-hit countries thus contrast with Japanese FDI flows in 1998, which fell as much as 29 per cent in Thailand, 34 per cent in Korea, 37 per cent in Malaysia and 30 per cent in the Philippines from the previous year.

Our study aims to investigate the reasons why Japanese firms responded differently from the firms of other countries. We estimate equations drawn from a partial equilibrium framework using time-series data on RERs between the yen and the East Asian currencies and Japanese FDI outflows to East Asian countries. The data employed for estimation covers the period from 1978 to 2000.

After a brief overview of Japanese FDI outflow to East Asia between 1978 and 1999, the chapter is organized as follows. The second section presents several studies that focus on the relationships between RER and FDI that are particularly related to our work. The third section describes our research design and data used for estimation and the fourth section presents results of the estimation. A summary of our findings and some policy implications are given in the final section.

RELATIONSHIP BETWEEN EXCHANGE RATE AND FOREIGN DIRECT INVESTMENT

Selling of America

The depreciation of the dollar from the late 1970s generated a dramatic increase in FDI inflows to the United States. During this period, US assets became cheaper to Japanese investors who held the yen. The acquisition of the RCA (Radio Corporation of America) building in New York City by Mitsubishi Estate Company in 1989 was typical of the 'selling of America'.

Froot and Stein (1991) found that, between 1973 and 1988, a regression of de-trended FDI as a per cent of US GNP against the US RER implied that a 10 per cent depreciation brought in about 5 billion dollars additional FDI to the United States (Froot and Stein, 1991).

- The study was based on a model that assumed an improvement in the wealth position of foreign investors because they hold more assets in non-dollar dominated form.
  The depreciation of the dollar thus improves the relative wealth position of the foreign investors and subsequently lowers their relative cost of

capital compared to domestic investors. Total foreign capital inflows into the United States were divided into foreign-official and foreign-private inflows. The latter was further subdivided into FDI, foreign investment in US Treasury securities and foreign portfolio investment in corporate stocks and bonds. Each item was deflated by US GNP and regressed on the real value of the dollar and a time trend.

- Empirical results indicated that the value of the dollar was significantly negative only for FDI among the various types of capital inflows. When FDI inflows were subdivided into thirteen separate industries[3], all of the thirteen coefficients on the exchange rate were negative and five of them were statistically significant. Among the eight types of inflows[4] whose sensitivity to RERs were tested, mergers and acquisitions (M&A), new plants and joint ventures transactions were statistically significant.

Klein and Rosengren (1994) also examined whether the large increase in foreign ownership of land and capital in the United States since the early 1970s was caused by the depreciation of the dollar that lowered the cost of acquisition to foreign investors (relative wealth hypothesis). In addition, the study questioned whether the depreciation of the dollar made foreign investors choose the United States as a production base (relative labour cost hypothesis). In their study, FDI was divided into four data subsets for inflows[5] to the United States. The correlation coefficients of RER (between the dollar and the currencies of seven industrial countries investing in the United States) and FDI indicated that depreciation (appreciation) of RER increased (decreased) FDI during the period from 1979 to 1991. All estimated correlation coefficients except those for the real estate industry were statistically significant at the 5 per cent level. Regression results also revealed that in addition to the RER, a real wealth variable[6] promoted FDI inflows to the United States at a 5 per cent level of significance. Regression on foreign M&A of the US assets relative to total M&A in the United States revealed a strong negative relationship with the RER. The relative wage cost variable, represented by the ratio of wage costs in the United States to wage costs in the investing country, was statistically insignificant in all four data subsets on FDI inflows to the United States.

Hollowing out of Japan

Until the Thai government let the baht float in July 1997, most of the countries in East Asia had adopted *de facto* dollar-pegged exchange rate systems. These benefited Japanese investors by assuring macro-economic policy discipline in East Asian countries that kept prices of tradable goods in line with world prices in the US dollar. Provided that the yen/dollar rate remained stable or that the yen appreciated against the dollar, *de facto* dollar-pegged exchange rate systems helped Japanese firms to reduce exchange rate risks when establishing affiliates to produce export goods to the United States. The sharp appreciation of the yen against the dollar after the Plaza Accord in 1985 motivated Japanese manufacturing firms to continue to shift their manufacturing affiliates to East Asian countries. When Japanese FDI outflow to East Asia increased from 1.4 billion dollars in 1985 to 12.2 billion dollars in 1995 (Table 7.1), the share of manufacturing in total FDI increased from 27.1 per cent to 56.1 per cent. In Japan, a rapid shift in domestic industrial location to ASEAN countries and to China was perceived as a threat to domestic employment and industrial competitiveness. The danger of the 'hollowing out of Japan' caused by the yen appreciation became one of the important issues from the mid-1990s.

Bayoumi and Lipworth (1998) tested the determinants of FDI outflows from Japan to twenty Asian trading partners, focusing on the business conditions of Japan and the host country[7] as well as the RER. The study found that the RER and business conditions of Japan and the host country (lagged) were statistically significant determinants of FDI for a sample period of 1982–1995. During this period, bilateral FDI flows significantly affected trade patterns between Japan and host countries in East Asia. While Japanese FDI outflows influenced Japanese exports to host countries in the short-term, the high stock of Japanese FDI in the host countries had a long-term positive effect on Japanese imports from host countries. One of the interesting findings of the study was that poor business conditions in Japan could more than offset the stimulating effect of a fall in the RER on FDI to East Asia.

Ito (2000) attributed the increased FDI outflows from Japan to Asia from the late 1970s to the cost conscious behaviour of Japanese manufacturing firms. The persistent appreciation of the yen against the dollar motivated these firms to shift their production sites to Asian countries. The study employed the yen/dollar exchange rate lagged one year as an independent variable to reflect the persistency of changes in the exchange rate. It also used the growth of the host country to reflect expectation for future growth as another independent variable determining Japanese FDI to eight countries in East Asia[8]. For the sample period from 1976 to 1996, only the growth rate variable was statistically significant in the pooled sample of eight countries. Individual country analysis revealed that only the exchange rate variable was statistically significant in the case of Singapore and Hong Kong. Both growth and exchange rate variables were statistically significant in the case of the Philippines, and for the remaining five countries, only the growth variable was statistically significant.

CHOOSING APPROPRIATE EXCHANGE RATE REGIMES IN EAST ASIA

From the first quarter of 1995, East Asian countries' RERs started to appreciate against the yen, reflecting the rise of the dollar against the yen and dollar-pegged exchange rate regimes. Appreciation weakened the export competitiveness of East Asian countries and subsequently resulted in the deterioration of their current account. In the following year, bank loans and other short-term capital inflows increased while portfolio investment and FDI accounted for merely 19 per cent of total capital inflows (Institute of International Finance, 1998). After the fall of the Thai baht in 1997, the financial crisis contagion forced currency devaluation in neighbouring East Asian countries. Countries were forced to choose alternative exchange rate regimes after abandoning de facto dollar-pegged systems.

Ito, Ogawa and Sasaki (1998) advocated pegging East Asian currencies to the optimal basket weights of the yen and the dollar that would minimize the fluctuation of the growth rates and of trade balances. They found that economic fluctuations and trade imbalances would be reduced from 1981 to 1996 if optimum currency weights that gave higher weights to the yen relative to the dollar had been applied instead of the actual currency weights. In fact, Beng (2000) pointed out that East Asian monetary authorities assigned a greater weight to the yen at the expense of the US dollar in their currency baskets from July 1997. He concluded that East Asian currency markets became more stable as authorities allowed their exchange rates to float in response to their economic fundamentals.

Sazanami and Yoshimura (2002) estimated misalignments of RERs from the long-run equilibrium rates for the peso, the rupiah, the won and the baht against the dollar and the yen for the period from January 1995 to November 1998. They found that the monetary authorities of the Philippines, Indonesia, Korea and Thailand terminated their dollar-pegged exchange rate regime in the third quarter of 1997. Instead, they managed their exchange rates to adjust the misalignment of the RER against both the yen and the dollar[9]. The ringgit was excluded from the estimation because Malaysia controlled capital flows from September 1998 and at the same time pegged the ringgit to the dollar. From July 1997 to January 1998, four countries let their currencies float in a surprisingly similar way, adjusting misalignments against the yen as well as the dollar. When the adjustment of misalignment to the long-run equilibrium rates was over, the RERs of four currencies against the yen and the dollar regained relative stability towards the end of 1998.

Questions related to the choice of appropriate exchange rate regimes for emerging countries have recently been the centre of discussion among academics, monetary authorities and international organization officials.

Corden (2001) in a seminar at the International Monetary Found stressed that developing countries should choose their exchange rate regimes according to specific economic circumstances. Since East Asian monetary authorities failed to maintain their pegs during the 1997–98 crises, they must look for the alternative exchange rate regime. A free float for East Asian currencies can cause excessive exchange rate volatility that may undermine export growth as well as FDI inflows. If the East Asian experience of 1997–98 has any lesson, it is that keeping RERs roughly in line with their long-run equilibrium rates is necessary to avoid the overvaluation that can invite currency crises.

RESEARCH DESIGN AND DATA

Benchmark Model

Our model aims to assess the statistical significance of RERs as determinants of FDI from Japan to East Asian countries during the sample period of 1978 to 1999. In our study, the RER is defined as:

$$RER = \frac{S/P}{1/P^*} = \frac{SP^*}{P}, \qquad (7.1)$$

where S is the nominal exchange rate of an East Asian currency against the Japanese yen, P stands for the producer price index or wholesale price index of the host country and P^* indicates the wholesale price index of Japan. The benchmark regression equation used in our analysis is:

$$\ln\frac{FDI_t^i}{GDP_t^i} = \alpha_1 \ln RER_t^i + \alpha_2 \ln RLC_t^i + \alpha_3 \ln\frac{CUMFDI_{t-1}^i}{GDP_{t-1}^i} + \alpha_4 Trend_t^i + \varepsilon_t^i, \qquad (7.2)$$

where superscript i refers to the country and subscript t refers to time. The dependent variable FDI_t^i / GDP_t^i is the ratio of real FDI outflows from Japan to a respective East Asian country relative to the host country's real GDP, GDP_t^i. In addition to the RER, we exploit Klein and Rosengren (1994) to include a relative labour cost variable GDP_t^i as an independent variable in equation (7.2).

Recent international trade theories emphasize the importance of 'region' in trade (Krugman, 1991). In Europe where national boundaries have become less important, the regional factor has gained importance for multinational enterprises in choosing their production site locations (Yamawaki *et al.* 1998). This 'regional' or 'agglomeration' effect is also observed for Japanese firms. According to Head *et al.* (1995), Japanese firms preferred to locate their manufacturing affiliates in regions where Japanese production has 'agglomerated'. In order to capture this 'agglomeration' effect, equation (7.2) also includes $CUMFDI_{t-1}^{i} / GDP_{t-1}^{i}$ that is defined as the one-year lagged cumulative total of Japan's FDI to the host country scaled by host country's GDP.

Because the depreciation of the host country's currency will improve the foreign investors' wealth position (Froot and Stein, 1991) and lower the cost of acquisition (Klein and Rosengren, 1994), the sign of α_1 is expected to be negative. The sign of α_2 is expected to be positive since a rise in Japanese per capita income relative to the host country's income motivates Japanese manufacturing firms to shift their production location to save production costs (Ito, 2000). We also expect a positive sign for α_3 since 'agglomeration' effects in East Asia accelerate Japanese FDI.

Additional Variables to Control East Asia Specific Effects

It is important to examine whether factors specific to East Asia, namely ASEAN rationalization and the Asian financial crisis, affect the relationships in our benchmark regression equation (7.2). To capture regional and time-specific effects, we introduced three types of dummy variables: $RERA_t^i$, $ASEAN4_t^i$ and $ASEAN4S_t^i$.

The dummy variable, $RERA_t^i$, is one after 1997 and zero otherwise. This dummy variable captures the effect of the Asian crisis through the RER on FDI. Sazanami and Yoshimura (2002) found sharp declines in the RERs of East Asian currencies against the yen in 1997. As East Asian countries abandoned *de facto* dollar pegs at the time of the Asian crisis, these declines reflected the adjustment of misalignments of East Asian RERs from their long-run equilibrium rates with the yen. These misalignments started from 1995 when the dollar appreciated against the yen. $RERA_t^i$ tries to ascertain whether financial market turmoil in 1997 had a statistically significant influence on Japanese FDI outflow to East Asia.

The dummy variables $ASEAN4_t^i$ and $ASEAN4S_t^i$ are used to capture ASEAN-specific rationalization effects. $ASEAN4_t^i$ takes one for ASEAN-4 countries – Indonesia, Malaysia, the Philippines and Thailand – and zero otherwise. $ASEAN4S_t^i$ takes one for ASEAN-4 plus Singapore and zero for other East Asian countries. $ASEAN4_t^i$ is introduced in our study for two reasons. Firstly, we found very high cross-country correlations in Japanese outward FDI to ASEAN countries for the sample period of 1979–2000 (Table 7.2). Cross-country correlation coefficients ranged between 0.504 in the case of Malaysia and Indonesia to 0.871 in the case of Thailand and Singapore. Such a close link between Japanese FDI and member countries must reflect a preference by Japanese firms to locate affiliates in ASEAN countries where

Table 7.2 Cross-country correlations of Japan's outward FDI between 1979 F/Y and 2000 F/Y

	China	Korea	Hong Kong	Taiwan	Singapore	Indonesia	Malaysia	Philippines	Thailand
China	1.000								
Korea	0.339	1.000							
Hong Kong	0.395	0.530	1.000						
Taiwan	0.456	0.726	0.646	1.000					
Singapore	0.567	0.503	0.650	0.538	1.000				
Indonesia	0.571	0.037	0.223	0.216	0.529	1.000			
Malaysia	0.546	0.352	0.660	0.572	0.717	0.504	1.000		
Philippines	0.830	0.487	0.417	0.421	0.684	0.616	0.627	1.000	
Thailand	0.600	0.416	0.635	0.565	0.871	0.600	0.790	0.734	1.000

For notes and sources, see Table 7.1.

they have built a production network that generates strong 'agglomeration' effects.

Secondly, the recent emergence of China as a major industrial centre in East Asia is threatening ASEAN member countries' vested advantage in inviting Japanese FDI (Kuroda, 2001). China's joining the WTO might provide an opportunity for the opening-up of its potential domestic market to ASEAN countries. However at the same time, ASEAN countries must strengthen regional co-operation to compete with China in attracting Japanese FDI. In our study, we try to investigate the level of statistical significance of the ASEAN dummies for different manufacturing industries – precision machinery, general machinery, electrical machinery and transportation machinery – to assess the importance of the 'regional' factor as a determinant of Japanese FDI outflow to East Asian countries.

Data

The nominal exchange rates are annual averages expressed in local currency units against the US dollar quoted from IMF (2001, line *rf*). Exchange rates of East Asian currencies against the yen are obtained by applying the US dollar rates against the Japanese yen. For the tradable price-based deflator, we used producer price index or wholesale price index data, reported in IMF (2001, line 63). The Indonesian producer price index data excludes petroleum products (IMF 2001, line 63a). The Malaysian producer price index data are missing for a number of years. The RER is computed based on equation (7.1) and normalized assuming a value in 1990 as 100.

Nominal FDI data is obtained from the website of the Japanese Ministry of Finance (http://www.mof.go.jp), and converted into dollars by applying annual average nominal exchange rates for respective years. In our regression analysis, we follow Bayoumi and Lipworth (1998) in deflating real FDI by the GDP deflator. The nominal exchange rate is based on IMF (2001, line *rf*), except for Taiwan. For Taiwan, it is based on the Council for Economic Planning and Development, Republic of China (2000). The GDP deflators are from the World Bank (2001) except for Taiwan where the GDP deflator was from the Council for Economic Planning and Development, Republic of China (2000).

Relative labour cost is measured by taking the ratio between Japanese per capita GDP to the host country's per capita GDP in 1995 prices. Per capita GDP for host countries is obtained from the World Bank (2001). Taiwan's per capita GDP is from the Council for Economic Planning and Development, Republic of China (2000). Although we find the International Labour Office (ILO) wage index is a more desirable one for our analysis, the limited availability of data on East Asia made it difficult to use the ILO wage index in our estimation. FDI_t^i, RLC_t^i, GDP_t^i and $CUMFDI_t^i$ are in 1995 prices.

ESTIMATION RESULTS

Table 7.3 provides the summary statistics of the five variables included in estimating equation (7.2) in a partial equilibrium macroeconomic framework

Table 7.3 Basic indicators and correlation matrix of variables

Basic indicators	*N*	Mean	S.D.	Min.	Max.
ln(*FDI/GDP*) =ln(*FDI/GDP*)	189	–5.51	1.25	–11.25	–2.77
ln(real exchange rate) =ln*RER*	161	4.60	0.20	4.05	5.23
ln(relative labour cost) =ln*RLC*	189	2.49	1.32	0.47	5.13
ln(cumulative FDI/FGDP) =ln(*CUMFDI/GDP*)	188	–3.66	1.43	–9.47	–1.54
Trend	189	11.00	6.07	1.00	21.00

Correlation matrix	ln(*FDIGDP*)	ln*RER*	ln*RLC*	ln(*CUMFDI/GDP*)	*Trend*
ln(*FDI/GDP*)	1.000				
ln*RER*	–0.069	1.000			
ln*RLC*	–0.179	0.200	1.000		
ln(*CUMFDI/GDP*)	0.708	–0.274	–0.424	1.000	
Trend	0.134	–0.705	–0.171	0.558	1.000

Notes: *FDI*: Japanese outward FDI to each country (1995 prices).
GDP: Foreign partner country's GDP (at 1995 prices).
RER: Real exchange rate, *RLC*: real exchange rate.
RLC: Japanese per capita GDP relative to each country's per capita GDP (at 1995 prices).
CUMFDI: cumulative value of Japan's outward FDI (1995 prices).

Sources: World Bank (2001) *World Development Indicators* (CD-ROM), Washington, D.C.: World Bank.
Council for Economic Planning and Development (2000) *Taiwan Statistical Databook*.
International Monetary Fund (2000) *International Financial Statistics* (CD-ROM), Washington, D.C.: IMF.
Ministry of Finance (2000) http://www.mof.go.jp/1c008.htm (accessed date 12/24/00).

(Ito, 2000). This table also presents the correlation matrix between these five dependent and independent variables. The correlation coefficients between the variables ranged between –0.705 and 0.708. Such results indicate a small probability of serious multicollinearity in estimating the relationship between RERs and Japan's FDI outflows. In what follows, we drop both superscript *i* that refers to the country and subscript t to simplify notation.

Table 7.4 reveals the estimated relationship between the RER and Japanese FDI outflows to East Asia (*FDI/GDP*) obtained by feasible generalized least square estimation with heteroskedastic error term[10]. In addition to RER, estimated relationships that include relative labour costs (*RLC*), the 'agglomeration' variable (*CUMFDI/GDP*), the financial market turmoil dummy (*RERA*) and the trend variable ($Trend_t^i$) are presented. The estimated coefficients of *RER* are negative at a 1 per cent level of significance, implying that the decline in RER promotes Japanese FDI to East Asia. The estimated coefficients of *RLC* have positive signs as expected at a 1 per cent level of significance, indicating that a rise in labour costs in Japan relative to East Asia promotes Japanese FDI. Estimated coefficients of *CUMFDI/GDP* are significantly positive at a 1 per cent level. This implies that Japanese firms try to locate affiliates in East Asia to enjoy the advantages of 'agglomeration' that arise from the accumulation of production networks.

Table 7.4 Regression of real exchange rate on Japan's outward FDI

Dependent variable	ln*RER*	ln*RERA*	ln*RLC*	ln(*CUMFDI* /*GDP*)	*Trend*	*N*	Log-L	AIC
ln(*FDI/GDP*)	–0.339***		0.179***	0.935***	–0.087***	161	–137.9	1.76
	[6.91]		[4.18]	[19.21]	[10.96]			
ln(*FDI/GDP*)	–0.351***	–0.03	0.178***	0.929***	–0.083***	161	–137.5	1.77
	[7.00]	[0.90]	[4.16]	[19.01]	[8.63]			

Notes: 1) Feasible generalized least squares are used for estimation. Figures in brackets are t-values.

2) ***, ** and * indicate statistically significant at the 1%, 5% and 10% level, respectively.

3) AIC means Akaike's information criteria and Log-L means log-likelihood.

4) ln*RERA*: ln*RER* times (after the Asian financial crisis dummies), which takes one if year > 1997 and zero otherwise.

5) For other notes and sources, see Table 7.3.

On the other hand, the coefficients of *RERA* are not statistically significant. The East Asian financial market turmoil after 1997 did not change the relationship between Japanese FDI outflows and the RER or between FDI and other variables included in the estimation. The trend variable has a statistically significant negative sign at the 1 per cent level.

Table 7.5 presents the estimated relationships between five independent variables (*RER*, *RLC*, *CUMFDI/GDP*, *RERA* and *Trend*) and Japanese FDI outflows to East Asia for four machinery industries – precision, electrical, general and transport machinery industries. The estimated coefficients of *RER* are negative and those of *CUMFDI/GDP* are positive at the 1 per cent level of significance for all four machinery industries. Estimated coefficients of *RLC* have positive signs at the 1 per cent level of significance for general machinery, electric machinery and transportation machinery and at the 5 per cent level for precision machinery. The coefficient of *RERA* is also positive at the 10 per cent level of significance only for transportation machinery.

Table 7.6 assesses ASEAN regional effects on the relationship between Japan's total FDI outflows and RERs. It also presents these effects for the four machinery industries. We find estimated coefficients of the *RER* are negative at the 1 per cent level of significance for total FDI outflows as well as for all four machinery industries. All estimated coefficients of *CUMFDI/GDP* are positive at the 1 per cent level of significance. The estimated coefficients of *RLC* were statistically significant at the 1 per cent level for general machinery, electrical machinery and transportation machinery. In the case of total FDI outflows, *RLC* became statistically significant when the ASEAN-4 dummy, *ASEAN*4, was included in the estimation while in case of the precision machinery industry *RLC* became statistically significant only when ASEAN plus the Singapore dummy, *ASEANS*, was added to the estimation. The transportation machinery industry was the only industry where *RERA* was statistically significant. This implies changes in Japanese FDI behaviour after the financial crisis in 1997.

Regional effects estimated by including *ASEAN*4 and *ASEAN*4*S* differ across industries. *ASEAN*4*S* coefficients are statistically significant at the 1 per cent level for total FDI outflows and significant at the 5 per cent level for the precision machinery and electrical machinery industries. *ASEAN*4 coefficients are statistically significant at the 10 per cent level for the precision machinery and transportation machinery industries.

Table 7.5 Regressions of real exchange rate on Japan's outward FDI: machinery industry

Dependent variable	ln*RER*	ln*RERA*	ln*RLC*	ln(*CUMFDI/GDP*)	*Trend*	*N*	Log-L	AIC
Precision machinery								
ln(*FDI/GDP*)	–0.927***		0.155**	0.597***	–0.062***	157	–237.5	3.08
	[9.78]		[2.51]	[9.96]	[4.44]			
ln(*FDI/GDP*)	–0.923***	0.071	0.156**	0.591***	–0.071***	157	–237.3	3.09
	[9.50]	[1.14]	[2.52]	[9.76]	[4.23]			
General machinery								
ln(*FDI/GDP*)	–0.578***		0.339***	0.920***	–0.067***	156	–227.6	2.97
	[5.71]		[4.21]	[12.96]	[5.05]			
ln(*FDI/GDP*)	–0.598***	–0.061	0.340***	0.918***	–0.057***	156	–227.2	2.98
	[5.83]	[0.99]	[4.29]	[12.91]	[3.54]			
General machinery								
ln(*FDI/GDP*)	–0.579***		0.281***	0.853***	–0.056***	160	–213.4	2.72
	[7.48]		[4.16]	[15.08]	[4.94]			
ln(*FDI/GDP*)	–0.608***	–0.077	0.271***	0.839***	–0.044***	160	–212.7	2.72
	[7.60]	[1.46]	[4.04]	[14.70]	[3.13]			
Transportation machinery								
ln(*FDI/GDP*)	–1.459***		0.485***	0.431***	–0.042**	142	–233.9	3.35
	[10.48]		[4.79]	[6.09]	[2.31]			
ln(*FDI/GDP*)	–1.441***	0.142*	0.489***	0.426***	–0.059***	142	–232.6	3.35
	[10.24]	[1.68]	[4.82]	[6.03]	[2.80]			

Notes: Feasible generalized least squares are used for estimation. Figures in brackets are *t*-values.
***, ** and * indicate statistically significant at the 1%, 5% and 10% level, respectively.
AIC means Akaike's information criteria and Log-L means log-likelihood.
For other notes and sources, see Table 7.3.

Table 7.6 Regressions of real exchange rate on Japan's outward FDI: regional effects

Dependent variable	ln*RER*	ln*RERA*	ln*RLC*	ln(*CUMFDI* /*GDP*)	*ASEAN4*	*ASEN4S*	*Trend*	*N*	Log-L	AIC
All industry (total FDI outflows)										
ln(*FDI*/*GDP*)	–0.360***	–0.03	0.143**	0.908***	0,106		–0.082***	161	–137.2	1.78
	[7.03]	[0.91]	[2.28]	[16.61]	[0.81]		[8.51]			
ln(*FDI*/*GDP*)	–0.468***	–0.033	0.081	0.802***		0.376***	–0.072***	161	–133.2	1.73
	[7.83]	[1.03]	[1.59]	[13.12]		[3.32]	[7.17]			
Precision machinery										
ln(*FDI*/*GDP*)	–1.051***	0.093	0.061	0.501***	0.491*		–0.068***	157	–236.1	3.08
	[8.28]	[1.46]	[0.73]	[6.20]	[1.89]		[3.95]			
ln(*FDI*/*GDP*)	–1.193***	0.09	0.151**	0.467***		0.537**	–0.061***	157	–235.3	3.07
	[7.45]	[1.43]	[2.39]	[5.49]		[2.20]	[3.55]			
General machinery										
ln(*FDI*/*GDP*)	–0.598***	–0.063	0.415***	0.927***	-0,305		–0.057***	156	–226.1	2.98
	[5.86]	[1.04]	[4.65]	[13.05]	[1.51]		[3.52]			
ln(*FDI*/*GDP*)	–0.566***	–0.063	0.361***	0.937***		–0,114	–0.058***	156	–227.0	2.99
	[4.70]	[1.02]	[4.17]	[11.67]		[0.60]	[3.53]			
Electrical machinery										
ln(*FDI*/*GDP*)	–0.599***	–0.75	0.235***	0.840***	0,168		–0.046***	160	–212.3	2.73
	[7.43]	[1.43]	[2.98]	[14.78]	[0.95]		[3.21]			
ln(*FDI*/*GDP*)	–0.681***	–0.076	0.251***	0.809***		0.326**	–0.042***	160	–210.1	2.70
	[7.86]	[1.45]	[3.73]	[13.84]		[2.31]	[2.93]			
Transportation machinery										
ln(*FDI*/*GDP*)	–1.574***	0.149*	0.347***	0.339***	0.539*		–0.049**	142	–231.3	3.34
	[10.20]	[1.80]	[2.75]	[4.06]	[1.81]		[2.34]			
ln(*FDI*/*GDP*)	–1.524***	0.147*	0.438***	0.380***		0.253	–0.054**	142	–232.2	3.35
	[9.10]	[1.75]	[3.76]	[4.36]		[0.88]	[2.51]			

Notes: 1) Feasible generalized least squares are used for estimation. Figures in brackets are *t*-values.

2) ***, ** and * indicate statistically significant at the 1%, 5% and 10% level, respectively.

3) AIC means Akaike's information criteria and Log-L means log-likehood.

4) ASEAN indicates ASEAN-4 (Indonesia, Malaysia, the Philippines and Thailand) dummy variable while ASEANS indicates ASEAN-4 plus Singapore dummy variable.

5) For other notes and sources, see Table 7.3.

SUMMARY OF OUR FINDINGS AND POLICY IMPLICATIONS

In this chapter, we attempt to identify the factors responsible for stagnant Japanese FDI to East Asia after the Asian financial crisis. Estimation is based on a partial equilibrium framework that focuses on the relationship between the RERs of East Asian currencies and the yen and Japanese FDI to East Asia for the period from 1978 to 1999. We estimate the determinants of total FDI and FDI in four machinery industries – precision machinery, general machinery, electrical machinery and transport machinery – from Japan to East Asia.

Our estimation results on Japanese total FDI are consistent with previous studies that show a decline in the RER promotes FDI outflows, with coefficients significant at the 1 per cent level. In addition to the RER, both an increase in Japanese labour costs relative to East Asia as well as Japanese cumulative FDI in the host country relative to its GDP (reflecting the advantage of 'agglomeration') positively impact Japanese total FDI. Such findings imply that Japanese FDI to East Asia tends to have a strong positive trend when annual FDI flows are growing strongly as they did in the first half of the 1990s. However, Japanese FDI tends to stagnate once annual FDI flows decline as in 1998. Another reason for the poor response of Japanese FDI to the sharp fall in RER at the time of the Asian financial crisis could be the extremely small share of Japanese M&A to the world total at that time. In 1998, the share of Japan's cross-border M&A to the world accounted for only 1.4 per cent as a seller and 0.2 per cent as a purchaser (UNCTAD, 2001). In line with the Bayoumi and Lipworth (1998) study that finds a strong negative relationship between M&A and the RER, the response of Japanese FDI to the fall in the RERs of East Asian currencies might be smaller than the response of other countries' FDI that includes large shares of M&A.

To distinguish the changes in Japanese FDI strategy after the Asian financial crisis, we introduced dummy variables in the estimation of equations for a subset of four manufacturing industries. We find that the transportation machinery industry is the only one where FDI outflows are significantly affected by policy changes after the financial crisis. After the financial crisis, ASEAN members introduced policies aimed to promote the sales of cars produced by domestic assemblers, namely so-called 'Domestic Car' policy. Reflecting the policy change, automobile parts account for as much as 80 per cent of the regional complementary scheme for liberalization in the ASEAN Industrial Cooperation Scheme, or AICO[11]. Such a liberalization scheme for intra-regional trade can promote Japanese FDI strategy in transportation machinery (Kimura *et al.*, 2002, p. 240) as revealed by the positive coefficient on the Asian financial turmoil dummy variable.

The recent surge of FDI inflows in China has motivated ASEAN member countries to strengthen their industrial ties by accelerating the formation of the ASEAN Free Trade Area (AFTA). Two types of regional dummy, ASEAN4 and ASEAN4 plus Singapore, are estimated for total FDI flows and for data subsets for four manufacturing industries. The ASEAN4 plus Singapore dummy was statistically significant for total FDI, precision machinery and electrical machinery. The ASEAN4 dummy was statistically significant for precision machinery and transportation machinery. In all cases, the coefficients of the dummy variable were positive which implies the importance of AFTA in inviting FDI from Japan. The close relationship between Singapore and ASEAN4 is important for these countries in promoting FDI from Japan. The exception is transportation machinery where only the ASEAN4 dummy was significant. The transportation machinery case might reflect the importance of the recent changes in 'Domestic Car' policy measures since Singapore never had any.

In conclusion, our study indicates the importance of both RERs as well as the accumulation of Japanese FDI that creates strong positive 'agglomeration' benefits in stimulating Japanese FDI to East Asia. From an East Asian host country perspective and especially for ASEAN member countries, policy should avoid overvaluation of exchange rates if the host country wishes to attract FDI from Japan. For the same goal, policy should also promote intra-regional trade to construct more efficient production networks within Asian countries.

NOTES

1. An earlier version of this chapter was presented at the international conference titled 'Location of Economic Activity, Regional Development and the Global Economy', at the University of Le Havre (France) on 26–27 September 2001. We are grateful to the discussants and other participants at the conference for helpful comments on an earlier draft.
2. East Asia includes China, Hong Kong, Indonesia, Korea, Malaysia, the Philippines, Singapore, Taiwan and Thailand.
3. The thirteen industries are 1) all industries, 2) petroleum, 3) manufacturing – subdivided into 4) food, 5) chemicals, 6) fabricated metals, 7) machinery, 8) other manufacturing – 9) trade, 10) finance, 11) insurance, 12) real estate and 13) other industries.
4. The eight types of inflows are 1) mergers and acquisitions (M&A), 2) equity increases, 3) real estate, 4) new plant, 5) joint ventures, 6) plant expansion, 7) other expansion and 8) no type listed

5. Four types of inflows are 1) total outlays in International Trade Administration (ITA) data, 2) total outlays in Bureau of Economic Analysis data, 3) M&A in ITA and 4) real estate purchase subset data in ITA.
6. The real wealth variable is defined as an index of the value of the US stock market relative to an index of value of the stock market of the investing countries.
7. Business conditions in Japan and the host country are defined as domestic investment in Japan and the host country, respectively.
8. These eight countries are Hong Kong, Indonesia, Korea, Malaysia, the Philippines, Singapore, Taiwan and Thailand.
9. Sazanami and Yoshimura (1999) defined the degree of misalignment as $M = (S' - S'LA) / S'LA$, where *S*' is the actual nominal exchange rate and *S*'*LA* is the equilibrium rate of long-run average rates.
10. This means that the variance for each country is assumed to differ. As for FGLS, see, for instance, Baltagi (2001).
11. 'The ASEAN Industrial Cooperation Scheme (AICO) is an industrial cooperation mechanism to promote joint manufacturing activities among companies based in ASEAN. The scheme, which became effective on 1 November 1996, offers companies located in different ASEAN member countries, the opportunity to benefit from economies of scale through resource sharing and industrial complementation. Qualified participating companies will benefit from the Common Effective Preferential Tariff (CEPT) rates immediately, instead of waiting for the CEPT rates to reach the final range of 0–5 per cent by 2003.' (The website of Malaysian Ministry of International Trade and Industry, http://www.miti.gov.my /asean-matter3.html, accessed date 09/19/2002).

REFERENCES

Baltagi, B.H. (2001), *Econometric Analysis of Panel Data*, 2nd ed., West Sussex, UK: John Wiley and Sons.

Bayoumi, T. and G. Lipworth (1998), 'Japanese foreign direct investment and regional trade', *Journal of Asian Economics*, **9** (4), 581–607.

Beng, G.W. (2000), 'Exchange-rate policy in East Asia after the fall: how much have things changed?', *Journal of Asian Economics*, **11** (4), 403–30.

Corden, W.M. (2001), 'Developing countries' choice of exchange rate regimes', *IMF Survey*, **30** (3), 44–6.

Council for Economic Planning and Development, Republic of China (2000), *Taiwan Statistical Databook*, Taipei: Council for Economic Planning and Development, Republic of China.

Froot, K.A. and J.C. Stein (1991), 'Exchange rates and foreign direct investment: an imperfect capital markets approach', *Quarterly Journal of Economics*, **106** (4), 1191–217.

Head, K., J. Ries and D. Swenson (1995), 'Agglomeration benefits and location choice: evidence from Japanese manufacturing investments in the United States', *Journal of International Economics*, **38** (3–4), 223–47.

Institute of International Finance (IIF) (1998), *Capital Flows to Emerging Market Economies*, Washington, D.C.: IIF.
International Monetary Fund (IMF) (2001), *International Financial Statistics* [CD-ROM], Washington, D.C.: IMF.
Ito, T. (2000), 'Capital flows in Asia', in S. Edwards (ed.), *Capital Flows and the Emerging Economies*, Chicago and London: University of Chicago Press, pp. 255–96.
Ito, T., E. Ogawa and Y.N. Sasaki (1998), 'How did the dollar peg fail in Asia?', *Journal of the Japanese and International Economies*, **12** (4), 256–304.
Kimura, F., T. Maruya and K. Ishikawa (2002), *International Production Networks in East Asia and China (Higashi Ajia no kokusai Bungyo to Chuugoku)*, Tokyo: JETRO. [In Japanese].
Klein, M.W. and E. Rosengren (1994), 'The real exchange rate and foreign direct investment in the United States: relative wealth vs. relative wage effects', *Journal of International Economics*, **36** (3–4), 373–89.
Krugman, P.R. (1991), *Geography and Trade*, Cambridge, MA: MIT Press.
Kuroda, A. (2001), *Made in China (Meido in China)* Tokyo: Toyokeizai Shinnposha. [In Japanese]
Sazanami, Y. and S. Yoshimura (1999), 'Restructuring East Asian exchange rate regimes', *Journal of Asian Economics*, **10** (4), 509–23.
Sazanami, Y. and S. Yoshimura (2002), 'Exchange rate misalignment before and after the Asian crisis', in P.-B. Ruffini (ed.), *International Trade and Capital Flows in Economic Restructuring and Growth: European and East Asian Experiences*, Rouen: Publications des Universités de Rouen et du Havre, pp. 240–50.
United Nations Conference on Trade and Investment (UNCTAD) (2001), *World Investment Report 2001*, New York: United Nations.
World Bank (1999), *Global Development Finance*, Washington, D.C.: World Bank.
World Bank (2001), *World Development Indicators* [CD-ROM], Washington, D.C.: World Bank.
Yamawaki, H., L. Barbrito and J.-M. Thiran (1998), 'US and Japanese multinationals in European manufacturing: location patterns and host region/country characteristics', in K. Fukasaku, F. Kimura and S. Urata (eds), *Asia and Europe: Beyond Competing Regionalism*, Brighton, UK: Sussex University Press, pp. 161–79.

PART II

Foreign Direct Investment and Economic Development of Recipient Countries

8. The Dynamics and Causes of Agglomeration: An Empirical Study of Java, Indonesia

Mudrajad Kuncoro and John Malcolm Dowling

INTRODUCTION

During the last century, geographers, economists, urban planners, business strategists, regional scientists and other social scientists have developed explanations as to why and where economic activities locate (for example Krugman, 1991; Kuncoro, 2000a; O'Sullivan, 1996; Porter, 1998). An uneven regional distribution of economic activity within a nation has been a primary concern, and hence, encouraged increasing research in this field. There are three major theories that explain *why* and *where* firms tend to concentrate geographically in a certain region: neo-classical, new economic geography and new trade theory. From a theoretical perspective, we expect that some basic agglomeration forces are at work in the region. Each theory has offered some valid hypothesis. Yet there is virtually no rigorous empirical work that assesses the relative importance of these three theories.

This chapter examines which theory is best at explaining the geographic concentration in Java, in particular in the period of trade liberalization. There has never been a comprehensive study on industrial agglomeration that takes Indonesia (that is, Java) as a case study and uses the recent framework of the new economic geography and the new trade theory. We focus our analysis on Java for the following reasons. First, the main industrial areas in Indonesia have been located overwhelmingly in Java. Most Indonesian modern manufacturing establishments have continued to be predominantly located on

Java and to a much lesser extent, Sumatra island during 1976–1995. Even when we classify 27 provinces of Indonesia into five main islands (that is Sumatra, Java, Kalimantan, Sulawesi, Eastern Islands), Java and Sumatra provided more than 90 per cent of Indonesia's employment over the period (see Table 8.1 and Map 8.1). The share of Java's employment tended to decline slightly, while Sumatra's share tended to increase substantially. Java's share declined from 89 per cent in 1976 to 82 per cent in 1995. Sumatra's share grew from 7 to 11 per cent in the same period. Other main islands in Indonesia played a minor role in Indonesian manufacturing employment. Even when we sum up the share of Kalimantan, Sumatra and Eastern Island, their share in Indonesian employment was about 4 per cent in 1976 and 7 per cent in 1995.

Table 8.1 Employment distribution of manufacturing LME by main islands (% of total), 1976–1995

Main island	1976	1980	1985	1990	1995
Sumatra	6.7	8.7	12.1	13.0	10.8
Java	89.1	85.8	78.6	78.0	82.2
Kalimantan	1.8	3.5	5.6	5.3	3.9
Sulawesi	0.9	1.0	1.7	1.5	1.4
Eastern Islands	1.5	1.0	1.9	2.2	1.8
INDONESIA	100	100	100	100	100

Source: Calculated from BPS, Industrial Survey.

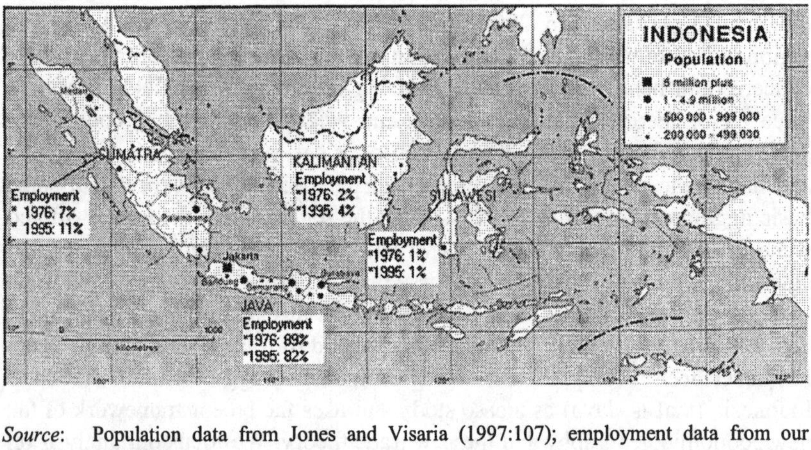

Source: Population data from Jones and Visaria (1997:107); employment data from our compilation

Map 8.1 Employment distribution by main islands and urban centres in Indonesia

Second, Java with more than half of Indonesian inhabitants offers a huge potential market and is important by its own rights. In terms of total population, Indonesia is the fourth biggest country in the world after China, India and USA. The number of Indonesian population was 179.4 million in 1990 and became 194.8 million in 1995 (BPS, 1999, p. 61). Yet the increasing number of inhabitants, with an annual average increase of 1.7 per cent between 1990 and 1990, was not followed by an equal distribution of population geographically. In 1995, according to the Central Bureau of Statistics (BPS), Java island included around 59 per cent of the Indonesian population (that is around 115 million) but had an area of only 7 per cent of the total area of Indonesia.

Third, most investments, either foreign or domestic, have been concentrated in Java. During the period 1967–1994, around 63 per cent of total approved domestic investments were located in Java, while 66 per cent of total foreign investment flowed to Java (Kuncoro, 1996). Finally, perhaps more importantly, not only are most firms privately owned, in contrast to government-owned or joint venture firms in the Outer Islands, but also most firms belong to footloose and more modern industries, while most industries in the Outer Islands are resource-based such as timber and petroleum (Hill, 1997; Kuncoro, 1994).

Our previous studies on Java have found that there was a stable – albeit increasing – trend and persistent geographic concentration in Java over the period 1976–1995 (Kuncoro, 1999, 2000b). Yet some critical and unresolved questions exist: why did the geographic concentration in Java persist during this period? To what extent can relevant theories and empirical literature be used as an explicit test of competing theories on agglomeration forces?

This chapter will attempt to address these unresolved questions. At the onset, three major competing theories of geographic concentration will be reviewed critically. This review will provide a guide for developing some testable hypotheses. This study will test these hypotheses in the Java context. An econometric model will be developed and tested using pooling time-series and cross-sectional data.

THEORETICAL FRAMEWORK

Neoclassical Theory

One of the most important contributions of the neoclassical theory (NCT) is its early recognition of agglomeration advantages (Preer, 1992, p. 34). Arguably an agglomeration arises from the behaviour of agents to seek agglomeration economies, either localization or urbanization economies[1].

Traditional location theories argue that clusters of industries arise mainly because of either transport or production costs (Isard, 1956; Weber, 1909). These theories rest on some assumptions in which the geographical basis of raw material, size of consumption location and the immobile and unlimited supply of labour are regarded as given[2].

Cities offer various advantages in terms of higher productivity and income that attract new investment, new technology and educated and skilled workers to a disproportionate degree (Kuncoro, 2000a). Neoclassical urban systems model the centripetal forces for agglomeration as pure external economies and the centrifugal forces as arising from the need to commute to a central business district within each city.

The literature highlights two NCT theories of trade, namely the theory of comparative advantage and the Heckscher–Ohlin (H–O) model. The former is derived from the work of Ricardo in the early part of the nineteenth century, which was reinforced by Mill's reciprocal demand analysis and extended by Marshall's and Edgeworth's neoclassical graphical presentations. The theory of comparative advantage postulates that: (1) countries trade in order to take advantage of their differences in natural resources; (2) regions will specialize according to their comparative advantage.

The latter is the result of Heckscher's article *Foreign trade and the distribution of income* (1919) and Ohlin's book *International and Interregional Trade* (1933). The H–O analysis establishes that 'comparative advantage is determined by the absolute distribution of resources between countries and particularly by the relative factor endowment ratios between countries' (Johns, 1985, pp. 178–81).

One of the most serious problems with NCT is its failure to capture the dynamics of geographic changes at the global level. As pointed out by Preer, the major geographic changes include: (1) the decline of the traditional manufacturing belts in Europe and North America, and the rise of new industrial regions in Sun Belts; (2) the decline of cities and the growth of suburban and rural areas; (3) the emergence of large cities as centres of corporate, producer and personal services; (4) the rise of the technopolis – propulsive regional centres of technological innovation (Preer, 1992, pp. 46–50).

The New Economic Geography

The recent state of play in the empirical agenda has been stimulated by the emergence of the new economic geography (NEG). The basic argument of NEG is that increasing returns, economies of scale and imperfect competition are far more important than constant returns to scale, perfect competition and comparative advantage in explaining trade and uneven distribution of economic activity. Indeed there are at least three reasons why economists start doing economic geography and incorporating space dimension. As Krugman points out:

> First, the location of economic activity within countries is an important subject in its own right. Second, the lines between international economics and regional economics are becoming blurred... however, the most important reason to look again at economic geography is the intellectual and empirical laboratory it provides (Krugman, 1991, p. 8).

Central to the recent development of the NEG is Krugman's work (Krugman, 1995, 1996, 1998). As has been identified by Martin and Sunley (1996), the main Krugman contributions involve first, his effort to link external economies and regional industrial agglomeration with trade. Krugman's geographical economics is a hybrid combination of the models of imperfect competition and scale economies used in new trade theory with location theory's emphasis on the significance of transport costs. Second, the recognition that regional economic development is a historical, path-dependent process. Third, region-specific shocks can have long-term growth consequences.

Although NEG offers interesting insights on the uneven geographic distribution of economic activities, the approach still has significant drawbacks. A recent critical survey on the new 'geographical turn' in economics concludes that NEG is neither new nor is it geography, instead it is a reworking (or re-invention) of traditional location theory and regional science (Martin, 1999). Moreover, the direct testing of the spatial agglomeration models using NEG frameworks is still in an infant stage (Ottaviano and Puga, 1998).

New Trade Theory

The new trade theory (NTT) offers a different perspective from that of the new economic geography (Table 8.2). Its basic belief is that the nature and character of international transactions have changed so much in recent years that contemporary cross-border flows of goods, services and assets are poorly understood by the traditional trade theories. Major criticism of NTT on the 'old' trade theory focuses largely on the assumption of perfect competition and constant returns, devotion of too much time to the data and theory rather than the issues that drive economics, and failure to pander to protectionist causes (Dodwell, 1994).

Proponents of the new trade theory argue that market size is determined fundamentally by the size of the labour force in a certain country and labour

Table 8.2 A comparison of three major grand theories of geographic concentration

	NCT	NTT	NEG
Seminal paper	Ricardo (1817), Heckscher (1919), Ohlin (1933), Weber (1909), Vanek (1986)	Krugman (1979, 1980, 1981), Dixit and Norman (1980), Helpman and Krugman (1985), Weder (1995)	Marshall (1920), Krugman (1991a, 1991b, 1993), Krugman and Venables (1995a, 1995b), Venables (1996), Markusen and Venables (1996), Puga and Venables (1997), Fujita *et al.* (1998)
Market structure	Perfect competition	Monopolistic competition	Monopolistic competition
Determinants of location	Technological differences Natural resource endowment and factor intensities	Degree of plant-level increasing returns Substitutability of differentiated goods Size of home markets	Pecuniary externalities (labour-market pooling, input–output linkages, migration induced demand linkages) Technological externalities Trade costs
Location of industry	Overall distribution of economic activity (labour) determined by given endowments Inter-industry specialization Unique equilibria	Overall distribution of economic activity (labour) exogenously given Intra- and inter-industry specialization Unique equilibria	Overall distribution of economic activity (labour) endogenous Centripetal agglomeration forces Intra- and inter-industry specialization Multiple equilibria 'U curve'
Trade structure	Inter-industry trade	Intra- and inter-industry trade	Intra- and inter-industry trade
Welfare effects of non-discriminatory trade liberalization	Net welfare gain All countries gain Owners of scarce factors lose	Net welfare gains Large countries benefit more than small ones Possibility that owners of all factors gain	

Source: Brulhart (1998, p. 778).

is immobile across countries. They believe that the main determinants of location are the degree of plant-level increasing returns, substitutability of differentiated products and size of home markets (Brulhart, 1998, pp. 777–8). As trade barriers are reduced substantially, it was predicted that increasing return industry would concentrate on the large market (Krugman, 1980). Krugman and Venables (1990) show that the tendency to locate in a larger market is stronger for values of trade costs that are neither too high nor too low[3].

Despite its attractiveness, NTT still has some significant shortcomings. Ottaviano and Puga (1998) identified three major shortcomings. First, NTT, like traditional theory, explains differences in production structures through differences in underlying characteristics. Second, it does not explain why firms in a particular sector tend to locate close to each other, leading to regional specialization. Third, it presents industrial development as taking place gradually and simultaneously in all developing countries, while in practice, industrialization often takes the form of waves of rapid industrialization in which industry spreads successively from country to country.

VARIABLES AND HYPOTHESES

Most of the empirical studies on agglomeration forces, as can be seen in Table 8.3, have not tried to assess the relative merits of competing theories across industries or regions. Previous empirical studies vary considerably according to the following respects. First, we may discriminate between studies which use sectorally disaggregated production data (for example: Henderson and Kuncoro, 1996) and those which use aggregate production data (for example: Krugman, 1991). Second, we can differentiate between studies that apply regression analysis (for example: Gelder, 1994; Mody and Wang, 1997), location choice model (for example: Kuncoro, 1994) or descriptive empirics (for example: Amiti, 1998).

Perhaps the most intutive method to estimate the relative merit of various location theories or models is to regress a measure of industry concentration over a set of determinants as identified in the theories or previous empirical studies (Brulhart, 1998; Kim, 1995, 1999). We believe that there is no single theory that may become the most 'suitable' explanation of the geographic concentration in a particular region, such as Java, and at a particular time. We will explore rigorously the nature and dynamics of agglomeration forces underpinning the uneven geographic distribution of manufacturing activities in Java by testing some key variables below. The 'nature' of those variables is derived either from theories or previous studies that have been discussed.

Table 8.3 Summary of existing studies

Study by	Method	Dependent Variables	Independent Variables	Conclusion
Mody and Wang (1997)	OLS, pooling time-series and cross section	Output growth of 23 industrial sectors in seven provinces and counties of China 1985–1989	Industry specific (specialization index) Regional specific (secondary school enrollment, FDI per person, roads, population/km, telephones, GDP per capita) Regional spillover (growth in industry in region, growth in industry outside region)	Low specialization promote growth in light industries; specialization is conducive to growth in heavy industry. Foreign investment is a spur to growth Only for light industries, secondary school enrollment is influential Growth of an industrial sector in any region is influenced by the growth of the same industry in other region
Kim (1995)	OLS, panel data	US regional localization, 1880, 1914, 1947, 1967, 1987	Resource (raw material intensity) Scale (plant size by production workers) Year specific effect Industry dummies	Changes in resources use and in scale economies, rather than external economies, explain the long-run trends in US regional localization
Henderson *et al*. (1995)	Location choice, OLS	Employment growth in 8 industries in 224 metropolitan areas between 1970 and 1987 in US	Diversity Labour force in higher education Past concentration (HHI)	Employment growth in traditional industries is higher in cities with past employment concentrations Jacobs externalities (diversity) are not important for mature industries but play an important role in high tech sector
Kuncoro (1994)	Conditional Logit	Profit of Large, Medium Small in Java using 1986 Economic Census	Log of other industries wage Distance Past employment Diversity index (HHI) Past population Age index Electricity (old firm with generator)	Wages are only important in textile, wood, and miscellaneous industry The impact of history is mixed Diversity does not affect location decision, except in textile Age is significant : new firms are more likely to locate in Kabupaten (districts) with older firms Unreability of electricity provision is unimportant in wood, paper, chemical, and machinery industry

Table 8.3 (continued)

Gelder (1994)	OLS Cobb–Douglas	Output of L&M 3-digit ISIC industry 1986–1989 in Indonesia	Capital (total horse power of all motorized machinery and equipment) Labour in industry j Average labour employed	Reject constant return to scale assumption and Henderson approach Results are not robust due to data aggregation and nonspherical disturbances, and spatial correlation.
Wang (1994)	Translog Production	Log (value added : labour) of Taiwanese 1983–87	Labour (L) Physical capital stock (K) Scale (K/L) Dummy (state-owned, foreign owned, top exporters, location in EPZs)	Higher exporting industries tend to facilitate faster productivity progress State-owned firms are more productive than domestic ones Export-led prosperity is not confined to EPZ
Glaeser *et al.* (1992)	OLS	City industry employment growth between 1956 and 1987 in US	Specialization Competition Initial conditions (wage, employment in 1956) Diversity Concentration Dummy (South)	At the city-industry level, specialization hurts, competition helps, and city diversity Support Jacobs–Rosenberg–Bairoch model (inter-industry knowledge spillover are less important for growth than spillover across industries).
Amiti (1998)	OLS	Log of the EU countries Gini coefficient	Time trend	The average increase in specialization is 2% for all countries except Italy

The 'dynamic' perspective attempts to incorporate explicitly the behaviour of the variables over time (for example Gujarati, 1995, p. 485; Matyas and Sevestre, 1992, pp. 311–3).

Dependent Variable

Which variable can be used as a measure of geographic concentration of manufacturing industry? Although there have been various spatial concentration indices (see Table 8.4), only a few of them are used in econometric analysis. The existing empirical-based econometric analyses usually utilize from among the following dependent variables:

- Employment or growth of employment (Glaeser *et al.*, 1992; Keeble, 1976);
- Growth in value added (Sjoholm, 1999);
- Output growth (Mody and Wang, 1997);
- Localization coefficient and/or locational (industry) Gini coefficient (Amiti, 1998; Kim, 1995; Krugman, 1991);
- Regional specialization index (Aziz, 1994; Kim, 1995);
- Growth quotient (modified form of location quotients) (Shilton and Stanley, 1999).

The dependent variable in our model is the regional specialization index (*LQ*). This index is a measure for determining the extent to which an industry is concentrated in a district relative to Indonesia, a benchmark region. Indeed it is either based on Hoover's coefficient of localization (Hoover, 1971, pp. 156–8 and pp. 209–11) or is popularly called a location quotient (for example Hayter, 1997, p. 435). The regional specialization index of industry *i* in district *r* (LQ_{ir}) is calculated by:

$$LQ_{ir} = \frac{E_{ir}/E_r}{E_{iINDO}/E_{INDO}} \tag{8.1}$$

where E_{ir} is employment in industry *i* for district *r*; E_j is total employment in district *r*; E_{iINDO} is employment in industry *i* for all districts in Indonesia; E_{INDO} is total employment for all districts in Indonesia. A rising LQ_{ir} for a region–industry indicates an increasing specialization of that industry in that region, and *vice versa*. We believe that high specialization of an industry in a region may speed growth of that industry in that region. This stems from the fact that knowledge gained by a firm may benefit other firms, in particular, those in the same industry. As far as the regional perspective is concerned,

Table 8.4 Existing spatial concentration or dispersion index

Name of index	Author	Distribution of dispersion index
Coefficient of geographic association	Florence *et al.*	Shares of manufacturing employment by states: industry *i* versus industry *j*
Coefficient of concentration of population	Hoover	Shares by states: population versus areas
Coefficient of redistribution	Hoover; Florence et al.	Shares of population (or total wages earners, or employment in selected manufacturing industries) by states: year α versus year β
Coefficient of deviation	Hoover	Shares of population by states: White versus Negro
Index of dissimilarity	Duncan	Shares of workers by areas: occupation group *A* versus *B*
Index of segregation	Duncan	Shares of workers by areas: specific occupation group versus all other occupation groups
Coefficient of specialization (Location Quotient, LQ)	Malecki	Shares of employment *i* in region *r* versus shares of industry *i* to total employment in the nation
Geographic concentration	Ellison and Glaeser	The index tries to captures localized industry-specific spillovers and natural advantages
Index of regional/national divergence	Krugman	The sum of absolute difference between share of industry *i* and other industry in total employment
Industry (locational) Gini coefficient	Krugman, Amiti	(1) for each locational unit, calculate both the share of total national manufacturing employment and the share of national employment in the industry; (2) rank the units by the ratio of these two numbers; (3) run down the ranking, keeping a cumulative total of both the sum of employment share and the sum of employment share in the industry

Source: Amiti (1998); Ellison and Glaeser (1997); Isard (1960); Krugman (1991); Malecki (1991).

the specialization index could provide: (1) a foundation for a preliminary and tentative judgment for industries to seek and encourage further (Isard, 1960, pp. 251–4); (2) an indicator whether a region is self-sufficient, importing or exporting products (Malecki, 1991, pp. 39–40).

Explanatory Variables

Some key explanatory variables that determine the regional specialization of manufacturing activities will be discussed. Those variables are selected on the basis of analytical considerations and an attempt to test various location models. More specifically, we will employ some principal explanatory variables as follows (Table 8.5).

Table 8.5 Key variables in the empirical study

Variables	Explanation	Hypothesis
Scale economies (*ISIZE*)	Average plant size by production workers	Size tends to be larger at industrial centres but smaller firms tend to operate in areas farther away from industrial centres
Resource intensity (*RESOURCE*)	Cost of raw materials divided by value added	Industries intensive in resources should be more localized given that resources are relatively immobile
Import content (*IMPOR*)	Ratio of imported inputs to total raw materials	Higher import content will induce higher specialized industry in a region
Income per capita (*YCAP*)	Gross Regional Domestic Product (GRDP) per capita	Increasing returns industry concentrates in the large market
Competition (*CI*)	Competition index as a proxy of market structure	Higher CI will tend to encourage regional specialization
Labour cost (*WAGES*)	Average annual wage for production workers in manufacturing establishments	Higher wage rates are negatively associated with the location of new manufacturing establishments on both US-owned and foreign manufacturing establishments, but Japanese automotive-related manufacturers prefer location with high wages
Path dependency (*AGE*)	Age distribution of firm	New firms in all industries are more likely to locate in the district with older firms
Export orientation (*EXPORT*)	Percentage of output that was exported	Higher export of specific industry in a region will reinforce greater agglomeration forces
Foreign investment (*FDI*)	Percentage of foreign ownership	Foreign investment tend to spur or retard geographic concentration
D1, …D8	Industry dummy	Different industry influence regional specialization differently
Rjkt, *Rsby*	Regional Dummy for Greater Jabotabek and Greater Surabaya	Regional variation matters in regional specialization
T91, …T95	Time dummy	Different time influence regional specialization

Scale economies

Scale economies are interpreted as a key variable by both the new economic geography and the new trade theory. Both theories argue that geographically concentrated industry is subject to scale economies. We measured scale economies (*ISIZE*) by average plant size in terms of the number of production workers as suggested by Kim (1995) and Amiti (1998). In addition, plant size may provide information about factor intensity and location behaviour in a particular industry: small firms with flexibility in adjusting their scale operations could operate in isolated regions where infrastructure is still poor (Kuncoro, 1994, pp. 10–11); whereas large and medium firms tend to agglomerate in and around metropolitan areas. Based on this measure, we will test whether scale economies can explain the industrial concentration in Java: size tends to be larger at industrial centres but smaller firms tend to operate in areas further away from industrial centres.

Resource intensity

Resource intensity represents the forces that are highlighted by NCT economists such as Heckscher–Ohlin. A measure of resource intensity will be used: cost of raw materials as a proportion of value added (*RESOURCE*) (Kim, 1995). We will test whether industries intensive in resources should be more localized given that resources are relatively immobile.

Import content

NTT advocates the importance of vertical linkages in the international context. More specifically, high proportions of intermediate inputs are found in geographically specialized industries. There has been a growing debate as to whether the share of intermediate inputs also includes raw materials, whether these inputs are domestically produced or imported, or whether vertical linkages only relate to downstream firms (Amiti, 1998, pp. 50–1).

Since we are concerned about raw materials and their sources, we use the imported inputs as a proportion of total raw material (*IMPOR*). We argue that a higher import content will induce higher industry specialized in a region.

Home market effect

The NTT emphasizes the existence of home-market effects. We include either the total population by district (*POPULATION*) or gross regional domestic product per capita (*YCAP*), as a proxy of market size. Krugman (1991, pp. 23–4) argued that the more populated locations will attract a concentration of manufacturing production, assuming that the location offers a sufficiently larger local market than others and fixed costs are large enough relative to transport costs. We will test this Krugman hypothesis.

Market structure

Both the NEG and NTT believe that monopolistic competition helps to explain geographic concentration of manufacturing activities (see Table 8.2). We will use competition index (*CI*) as a possible measure of entrepreneurial strength and the degree of competition index for industry *i* in a district *r* (CI_{irt}) is calculated by the following formula (Glaeser *et al.*, 1992, p. 1138; Mody and Wang, 1997, pp. 301–2):

$$CI_{irt} = \frac{(firm/output)_{ir}}{(firm/output)_{iINDO}} \tag{8.2}$$

where 'firm' refers to number of firms; 'output' refers to total output; iINDO is industry *i* in all districts in Indonesia; *t* indicates that the index is in a given year. A high CI_{irt} implies greater competition, meaning more firms for a given output in that district relative to the average number of firms divided by output in the industry across all districts. We argue that a higher competition index will tend to encourage regional specialization.

Labour market condition

Labour market factors, particularly wage rates or labour cost and labour skills, are viewed by the NCT as a central factor in the location decision of manufacturing establishments. We include labour cost variable (*WAGES*), which is measured as the average annual wage for production workers in manufacturing establishments. The empirical studies indicate that higher wage rates are negatively associated with the location of new manufacturing establishments on both US owned and foreign manufacturing establishments, but Japanese automotive related manufacturers prefer locations with high wages (Smith and Florida, 1994). Kuncoro (1994, pp. 51–2) found that wages are important in the textile, wood and miscellaneous industry, but turn out to be less important variables in more modern industries such as machinery, chemical and paper. We will test whether our data support or reject the finding of previous studies.

Path dependency

Historical patterns can be explained by the age distribution of firms. Instigated by Krugman (1995, 1998), the NEG believes that history matters in explaining the persistence of unequal distribution of economic activity. The age profile of an industry can provide some inferences about the nature of entry and exit process (Henderson and Kuncoro, 1996; Kuncoro, 1994). Using a location choice model, Kuncoro (1994) found that new firms in all industries – except paper, chemical and machinery – are more likely to locate in the district with older firms. We may calculate the *AGE* from the starting year of production. We will test the NEG hypothesis that history does matter, in particular: new firms are more likely to locate in districts with older firms. In other words, the older the *AGE* of a firm the more likely that there will be greater regional specialization.

Export orientation

NTT and NEG postulate that greater export orientation enhances spatial concentration. This has been an emerging view among the international economists, in which much trade represents arbitrary specialization based on increasing returns, rather than exploiting exogenous differences in resources or productivity (for example: Helpman and Krugman, 1985; Krugman, 1990). An empirical study in Taiwan, for example, shows that high exporting industries tend to facilitate faster productivity progress of an individual firm than low-exporting industries (Wang, 1994). Other evidence from the Brazilian *supercluster* in Sinos Valley indicates that export growth increased the demand for local inputs and machinery, thus contributing to the development of the cluster (Schmitz, 1995, p. 14). We use percentage of production exported (*EXPORT*). We will test to what extent the higher *EXPORT* of a specific industry in a region will reinforce agglomeration forces.

Foreign investment

NTT recognizes that there has been a convergence between trade theory and the theory of the multinational enterprises (MNEs). The focus is not only on the institutional form of overseas involvement, but also on the decision of the MNEs to locate in a particular country (for example Dunning, 1997, 1998). A number of studies of geography of Japanese investments in the UK and Australia found that foreign investors have generally preferred to invest in core regions and adjoining border regions (Fuchs and Pernia, 1989). The open door policies and special economic zones in China have successfully attracted foreign investment mainly in the coastal regions (Mody and Wang, 1997, p. 320). However, policy factors are found to be unimportant in the location decision process of 134 Japanese MNEs in Singapore, Australia, Thailand, Malaysia, Indonesia, the Philippines (Nicholas *et al.*, 1999). We will use percentage of foreign ownership (FDI) to examine whether greater foreign investment spurs retard regional specialization.

MODEL SPECIFICATION AND DATA

Model

Based on theoretical and empirical studies that have been explained above, we may derive the following model:

$$Y_{irt} = \beta 1_{irt} + \sum_{1}^{k} \beta_{kirt} X1_{kirt} + \sum_{1}^{n} \beta_{nrt} X2_{nrt} + D_i + T_t + R_{jkt} + R_{sby} + e_{irt} \quad (8.3)$$

where Y_{irt} is the specialization index;
i=1,...,9 refers to a two-digit industry sector;
r=1,...,107 refers to a district unit;
t=1,...,6 refers to a given time period;
k=number of industry-specific variables;
n=number of regional-specific variables;
$X1$ is a vector of industry-specific variables including *ISIZE*, *RESOURCE*, *WAGES*, *AGE*, *EXPORT*, *FDI*, *CI*, *IMPOR*;
$X2$ is a vector of region-specific variables consisting of *POP* and *YCAP*;
D_i is industry dummy; T_t is time dummy;
R_{jkt} and R_{sby} are regional dummy for Greater Jabotabek and Greater Surabaya respectively.

Data

The model attempts to highlight three dimensions of our data: industry, region and year. Industry in our data is two-digit industrial sectors, that are food (ISIC31), textile (ISIC32), wood (ISIC33), paper (ISIC34), chemicals (ISIC35), non-metal (ISIC36), basic metal (ISIC37), fabricated metal (ISIC38) and others (ISIC39) industry. The region is *kabupaten* or *kotamadya*, or approximately a district-county, of which Java has 107. Years include the period from 1991 to 1996.

Most of the data are from the *Annual Industrial Survey* data collected by BPS (Central Bureau of Statistics) of Indonesia. The surveys provide the plant level data of large and medium manufacturing firms, with more than 20 workers, that can be disaggregated by industry code (ISIC) and district, providing all data of industry specific variables. We also use the population data either from the 1990 Population Census and the 1995 Intercensal Population Survey. Data from the gross regional domestic product of regencies/municipalities in Indonesia supply the regional specific variable such as income per capita.

Given the three dimensions of our data, we deal with a model that pools time series and cross-sectional data. In theory, there are five cases of pooling model: (1) all coefficients are constant and the disturbance is assumed to capture differences over time and individuals; (2) slope coefficients are constant and the intercepts vary over individuals; (3) slope coefficients are constant and the intercepts vary over individuals and time; (4) all coefficients vary over individuals; (5) all coefficients vary over time and individuals (Judge *et al.*, 1980, pp. 326–59). We should identify which case is the most appropriate for our model.

EMPIRICAL RESULTS

Specification

The empirical results estimating equation (8.3) are sensitive to the variable included. We apply some methods suggested by Belsley *et al.* (1980). These methods have proved useful in a sensitivity analysis of empirical study of industrial growth in Coastal China (Mody and Wang, 1997). First, to what extent dropping one observation at a time or sets of observations (excluding from regression a province, a year, an industry, a district-industry, a year-industry and a year district) influence the coefficients. Second, to what extent adding or dropping independent variables brings an effect on the signs and magnitude of the coefficients. We perform the sensitivity analysis tests by using White heteroskedasticity test, redundant and omitted variable(s) test. As we introduce either industry dummies, regional dummies or time dummies, the results show some improvement in the goodness of fit.

In the reported regressions, as shown in Table 8.6, we weight the observation by the district population. With this weighting, the goodness of fit of the models improved substantially. In addition this weighting procedure is conducted to solve the problem of what the *spatial econometricians* call spatial heterogeneity due to the lack of 'stability' over space of the behaviour/relationship under study (for example Anselin and Florax, 1995; Paelinck and Klaassen, 1979). This is relevant to our study as the data shows dissimilar spatial units, such as the huge agglomeration of Jakarta and Surabaya, and far smaller districts such as Surakarta[4].

Principal Results

Table 8.6, which provides estimation results for 4179 observations during the period 1991–1996, presents an empirical support for models of regional specialization based on industry-specific and regional-specific variables. Scale economies (ISIZE), import content (IMPORT), labour cost (WAGES), export orientation (EXPORT), foreign investment (FDI), competition index

Table 8.6 Determinants of regional specialization, 1991–96

Variable	1	2	3	4	5
Constant	–0.769	–0.683	–0.761	–0.529	–0.664
	(–12.02)**	(–6.78)**	(–6.38)**	(–5.07)**	(–5.55)**
Resource intensity (*RESOURCE*)	0.0005				
	(1.06)				
Import content (*IMPORT*)	0.3835	0.4073	0.3959	0.6729	0.6422
	(3.65)**	(3.28)**	(3.15)**	(5.20)**	(4.96)**
Labour costs (*WAGES*)	0.0003	0.0006	0.0006	0.0006	0.0006
	(2.06)*	(5.45)**	(5.29)**	(5.47)**	(5.34)**
Scale economies (*ISIZE*)	0.0207	0.0143	0.0142	0.0179	0.0179
	(8.23)**	(8.89)**	(8.79)**	(8.67)**	(8.80)**
Export orientation (*EXPORT*)	0.2561	0.5838	0.8137	0.6496	0.8137
	(3.75)**	(6.06)**	(6.36)**	(7.12)**	(6.58)**
Foreign investment (*FDI*)	0.0029	–0.0009	–0.003	0.0021	0.0014
	(1.37)	(–0.36)	(–1.05)	(0.76)	(0.49)
Competition index (*CI*)	–0.005	–0.004	–0.005	–0.006	–0.006
	(–5.12)**	(–4.32)**	(–4.30)**	(–4.35)**	(–4.35)**
Path dependency (*AGE*)	0.0183	0.0159	0.0160	0.0102	0.0088
	(5.88)**	(3.56)**	(3.51)**	(2.34)*	(1.97)*
Income per capita (*YCAP*)	–0.059	0.0039	0.0047	0.0383	0.0491
	(–5.74)**	(0.41)	(0.45)	(3.56)**	(4.26)**
Dummy					
Industry	No	Yes	Yes	Yes	Yes
Time	No	No	Yes	No	Yes
Regional	No	No	No	Yes	Yes
Adjusted R^2	0.1575	0.2974	0.2995	0.333	0.336
Number of observations	4179	4179	4179	4179	4179
DW	1.837	1.675	1.767	1.835	1.836
F	92.947	111.510	86.097	117.19	92.947

Note: * indicates statistical significance at the 0.05 level.
** indicates statistical significance at the 0.01 level.
The dependent variable is log of LQ_{irt}. All regressions are weighted by district population and are tested by White heteroskedasticity-consistent standard errors and covariance test. The *t*-statistics are in parentheses.

(CI) and path dependency (AGE) constitute industry-specific variables that influence regional specialization significantly. Likewise, the regional income per capita (*YCAP*) as a regional specific variable also explains the regional specialization well.

As far as the underlying theory is concerned, most of the results are consistent with the NTT and NEG theories, but not the NCT. Column 1 of Table 8.6 shows that the relevance of NCT is only supported by the scale economies, while resource intensity is rejected by the insignificance of *RESOURCE*. The omitted test of *RESOURCE* indicates that dropping this variable does not bring any effect on both *F* and LR (likelihood ratio). At face value this result implies that regional specialization in Java is not based on the comparative advantage of factor endowments, but on other factors such as labour cost. Interestingly the positive coefficient of *WAGES* indicates that higher wages induce higher regional specialization. This result contradicts the prediction of traditional location theory that establishments will locate in low wage areas to minimize costs. On the other hand it supports an empirical study of Japanese automotive related manufacturers in which they are locating in areas with higher wages (Smith and Florida, 1994, p. 36). One explanation is that our sample firms are likely to pay higher wages to more highly skilled labour.

When we consider the role of imported inputs in raw materials, our result shows that the coefficient of import content is positive and significant in all cases. The result supports the NTT suggesting high import content occurs in more specialized industries. It implies that most specialized industries in Java have advantages in terms of vertical integration with foreign suppliers and relatively better access to infrastructure.

Export orientation (*EXPORT*) plays an important role in this study. The coefficient of *EXPORT* shows a positive, very statistically significant coefficient in all of the equations, suggesting that higher export orientation has reinforced greater regional specialization. The evidence confirms the argument of NTT and findings of previous studies.

Industry size (*ISIZE*) and regional income per capita (*YCAP*) show positive and very statistically significant coefficients in all of the equations. The positive coefficient of *ISIZE* and *YCAP* shows that both scale economies and large market size explain regional localization over time, confirming the prediction of NTT and NEG: scale economies and home market do matter. These results suggest that manufacturing firms in Java seek to locate in more populous and densely populated areas to enjoy both localization economies, which are associated with the size of a particular industry and agglomeration economies, which reflect the size of market of a district, in a particular urban area.

The statistical significance of the coefficients for competition index (*CI*) are negative and statistically significant. The general thrust of the results is consistent across various specifications and hence worth noting: increasing competition has a detrimental effect on regional specialization. In other words, Java's market structure may restrict competition so that firms tend to specialize geographically. It is true that the Indonesian industrial structure can be generally classified as an oligopoly industry where the four biggest firms control almost every industry (Hill, 1997; Kuncoro *et al.*, 1997; Pangestu, 1997). This structure is likely to augment further regional specialization. Our finding is consistent with NTT and NEG rather than NCT, with respect to the role of imperfect competition in explaining the uneven distribution of economic activity.

The role of path dependency in this study is strong. This is indicated by the positive and statistical significance of the coefficients for AGE across various specifications. The thrust of the results is clear: older firms tend to enhance regional specialization. This finding supports the NEG, in particular Krugman's hypothesis, with respect to the persistence of regional specialization in many cases.

The statistical significance of foreign investment is weak. In all equations, the coefficient of PMA is insignificant implying that direct foreign investment has not played an important role in regional specialization. This result challenges the finding of a study of foreign investment in Indonesia over the period 1980–1991 (Sjoholm, 1999) arguing inter-industry knowledge spillover from foreign investment. Instead the evidence supports a number of studies of geography of Japanese investments in the UK and Australia which found that foreign investors have generally preferred to invest in the core regions and adjoining border regions (Fuchs and Pernia, 1989).

Industry dummies

When the industry dummies are added to the model, the goodness of fit improves considerably (Table 8.7). Adding industry dummies increases the *F* and R^2, indicating their high explanatory power. Since other industry (ISIC39) is omitted, the omitted category becomes a base or benchmark to which the others are compared. The statistical significance of industry dummy is sensitive to whether the regression includes or excludes regional dummies. D31, D34 and D36 are not significant statistically, indicating that there is no substantial difference between regional specialization of other industry and the food industry, between other industry and the paper industry, and between other industry and the non-metallic industry respectively. The significance of other dummies (D32, D33, D35, D37, D38) indicates that

Table 8.7 Industry dummy coefficients, 1991–1996

Industry dummy	Regression with time dummies but without regional dummies[a]	Regression with regional dummies but without time dummies[b]	Regression with time and regional dummies[c]
D31: Food	–0.089624	–0.082325	–0.047483
	(–0.72882)	(–0.726969)	(–0.41843)
D32: Textile	–0.987586	–1.125870	–1.112544
	(–8.90945)**	(–9.46847)**	(–9.37692)**
D33: Wood	–0.991117	–0.924627	–0.941147
	(–8.50260)**	(–8.14060)**	(–8.46991)**
D34: Paper	–0.205902	–0.153521	–0.110666
	(–1.96000)*	(–1.439137)	(–1.02513)
D35: Chemicals	–0.263138	–0.317772	–0.274330
	(–2.63302)**	(–3.278217)**	(–2.76484)**
D36: Nonmetallic	–0.030956	–0.033466	0.010501
	(–0.28799)	(–0.313637)	(0.09676)
D37: Basic metal	–0.474058	–0.379882	–0.345648
	(–3.10293)**	(–2.57492)**	(–2.32736)*
D38: Fabricated metal	–0.462573	–0.525136	–0.48575
	(–4.40165)**	(–4.95109)**	(–4.49374)**

Note: * indicates statistical significance at the 0.05 level.
** indicates statistical significance at the 0.01 level.
The *t*-statistics are in parentheses.
a. Overall regression results are given in column 3, Table 8.6.
b. Overall regression results are given in column 4, Table 8.6.
c. Overall regression results are given in column 5, Table 8.6.

regional specialization of textile, wood, chemicals, basic metal and fabricated metal do differ from that of other industry.

Time dummies

Applying a redundant variable test for the time dummies of equation in column 5 (Table 8.6), Table 8.8 shows that time variation does matter in explaining regional specialization. This is reflected by the high value of F and likelihood ratio that is statistically significant at α=1%. Since year 1996 is omitted, the omitted category becomes a base or benchmark to which the other times are compared. The statistical significance of industry dummy is sensitive to whether the regression includes or excludes regional dummies. Table 8.8 indicates that the inclusion of industry dummies and regional dummies cause T92 statistical significance, a sharp contrast with the exclusion of regional dummies. The significance of T92 can be interpreted as regional specialization in 1992 does differ from that of 1996.

Table 8.8 Time dummy coefficients, 1991–1996

Time dummy	Regression with industry dummies but without regional dummies[a]	Regression with industry and regional dummies[b]
T91	–0.213161	–0.061385
	(–1.8737)	(–0.5447)
T92	0.054115	0.184660
	(0.6206)	(2.2098)*
T93	0.058495	0.153294
	(0.6713)	(1.8687)
T94	0.058344	0.115858
	(0.7238)	(1.5262)
T95	0.054529	0.087069
	(0.6759)	(1.1372)

Note: * indicates statistical significance at the 0.05 level.
** indicates statistical significance at the 0.01 level.
The *t*-statistics are in parentheses.
a. Overall regression results are given in column 3, Table 8.6.
b. Overall regression results are given in column 5, Table 8.6.

Regional Dummies

Table 8.9 exhibits the coefficient for regional dummies, using non-agglomeration area as the base of comparison. The coefficients of R_{jkt} and R_{sby} in the first column are positive and significantly different from 0 (at least at the 5 per cent level of confidence), implying that both Greater Jabotabek and Greater Surabaya areas do differ substantially from non-agglomeration areas in terms of regional specialization. Indeed adding industry and regional dummies improves the goodness of fit (see column 4 in Table 8.6). When we add time dummies, the second column of Table 8.6 shows it makes little

Table 8.9 Region dummy coefficients, 1991–1996

Region dummy	Regression with industry dummies but without time dummies[a]	Regression with industry and time dummies[b]
R_{jkt}	–0.6166	–0.6184
	(–8.668)**	(–8.631)**
R_{sby}	–0.1228	–0.1443
	(–1.904)*	(–2.241)*

Note: * indicates statistical significance at the 0.05 level.
** indicates statistical significance at the 0.01 level.
The *t*-statistics are in parentheses.
a. Overall regression results are given in column 4, Table 8.6.
b. Overall regression results are given in column 5, Table 8.6.

difference to the results. These results provide some confidence that regional dummies are good explanatory variables for differences in the regional specialization.

CONCLUSIONS

One of the big issues of economic geography and regional studies is to what extent the industrial concentration towards LME and metropolitan regions is driven by market forces. This chapter attempts to address this unresolved question in Java by using the regional specialization index as a measure of geographic concentration of manufacturing industry and pooling data over the period 1991–1996. Indeed, it integrates the perspectives of industry, region (space) and time. More importantly, it also explores which theory - the Neo-Classical Theory (NCT), the New Economic Geography (NEG) or the New Trade Theory (NTT) - is best at explaining geographic concentration in Java.

Our findings suggest that there has been a natural market led tendency towards the spatial concentration of manufacturing industry in metropolitan regions. From the supply side, we find that import content, export orientation, scale economies and labour costs have played a key role in LME spatial concentration. High import content and export orientation imply that most specialized industries in Java have advantages in terms of vertical integration with foreign suppliers and greater access to the international market. The positive and significant coefficient of scale economies suggests that manufacturing firms in Java enjoyed localization economies. The positive coefficient of labour costs indicate that higher wages induce higher regional specialization. From the demand side, size of market has explained spatial concentration in the manufacturing industry. It implies that manufacturing firms in Java seek to locate in more populous and densely populated areas to enjoy urbanization economies, as reflected by the size of the market of a district in a particular urban area. Furthermore the interplay of the market forces is intensified by the imperfect competition of Java's market structure. Java's market structure may restrict competition so that firms from the same group tend to concentrate geographically to optimize the benefits of agglomeration. Yet further detailed research is needed to identify which business groups are able to and exploit the agglomeration economies in metropolitan regions.

The most striking result is that most of the NCT hypothesis can be rejected. This conclusion is supported by the econometric results that resource intensity is insignificant and that the coefficient on labour costs is positive. The former implies that regional specialization in Java is not based on the comparative advantage of factor endowments. The latter suggests that the prediction of NCT – that establishments will locate in low wage areas to minimize costs – is not supported by our data. Instead our sample firms are likely to pay higher wages to more highly skilled labour. We may conclude that regional specialization in Java is based on neither natural resources nor low labour costs.

Most of the findings support the NTT and NEG hypotheses. Proponents of NTT argue that increasing returns to industry lead to concentration in the large market, while NEG has identified linkages, thick markets, knowledge spillover and other pure external economies as major centripetal forces that pull industries to urban regions (Fujita *et al.*, 1999, pp. 345–46; Krugman, 1996). Yet the results are not strong enough to enable us to differentiate between these two theories. Our findings suggest that manufacturing firms in Java seek to locate in more populous and densely populated areas to enjoy both localization economies and urbanization economies, as shown by the significance of scale economies and income per capita. The former is associated with the size of a particular industry, while the latter reflects the size of a market of a district in a particular urban area. More importantly, the results suggest that there is a synergy between thickness of market and agglomeration forces. The interplay of agglomeration economies is intensified by the imperfect competition of Java's market structure. We find that Java's market structure may restrict competition so that firms tend to concentrate geographically.

This chapter gives empirical evidence with respect to path dependency hypotheses. Krugman points out that history clearly determined what happened in the case of the US manufacturing belt and has become a self fulfilling prophecy (Krugman, 1991, pp. 27–33). Our econometric analysis finds the robust role of path dependency, as shown by the positive and statistical significance of the coefficients for age of firms across various specifications. This finding supports the New Economic Geography's belief that history matters: older firms tend to enhance regional specialization. Java has been long known as a centre of economic activity since the nineteenth century (Dick *et al.*, 1993; Dick, 1996; Sato, 1994). In addition the results, as shown by statistical significance of its regional dummy, suggest that most of the specialized industries in Java have better access to infrastructure. This is more prevalent in Greater Jabotabek and Greater Surabaya metropolitan regions that have far superior infrastructure such as seaports, airports, toll roads, than other regions in Java or even other areas in Indonesia.

NOTES

1. *Localization economies* occur if the production costs of firms in a given industry decrease as the total output of the industry increases. In contrast, *urbanization economies* occur if the production cost of the individual firm decreases as the total output of the associated urban area increases. These economies result from the scale of the entire urban economy, not just the scale of a particular industry. For further detailed discussion: see Henderson (1988), also O'Sullivan (1996).
2. Further detailed discussion of methodological aspects on conventional theories: see for example Johns (1985, chap. 4), Krugman (1990).
3. When trade costs are high, location is mainly determined by product market competition. When trade costs are low, factor market competition takes over. For further detailed discussion: see Krugman and Venables (1990).
4. Further detailed discussion on the different size of industrial areas in Java can be seen in Kuncoro (2000b: chap. 3).

REFERENCES

Amiti, M. (1998), 'New trade theories and industrial location in the EU: A survey of evidence', *Oxford Review of Economic Policy*, **14** (2), 45–53.

Anselin, L. and R.J.G.M. Florax (eds) (1995), *New Directions in Spatial Econometrics*, New York: Springer.

Aziz, I.J. (1994), *Ilmu Ekonomi Regional dan Beberapa Aplikasinya di Indonesia (Regional Economics and Its Some Applications in Indonesia)*, Jakarta: Lembaga Penerbit Fakultas Ekonomi Universitas Indonesia.

Belsley, D.A., E. Kuh and R.E. Welsch (1980), *Regression Diagnostics*, New York: John Wiley and Sons.

BPS (1999), *Statistical Yearbook of Indonesia 1998*, Jakarta: Biro Pusat Statistik.

Brulhart, M. (1998), 'Economic geography, industry location and trade: the evidence', *The World Economy*, **21** (6), 775–801.

Dick, H., J.J. Fox and J. Mackie (eds) (1993), *Balanced Development: East Java in the New Orde*, Singapore: Oxford University Press.

Dick, H.W. (1996), 'The emergence of a national economy, 1808–1990S', in J.T. Lindblad (ed.), *Historical Foundations of a National Economy in Indonesia*, 1890s–1990s, Amsterdam: Royal Netherlands Academy of Arts and Science, pp. 21–51.

Dodwell, D. (1994), 'New trade theory: A look at the empirical evidence', in CEPR (ed.), *New Trade Theories: A Look at the Empirical Evidence*, Milan: Centre for Economic Policy, 1–10.

Dunning, J.H. (1997), *Alliance Capitalism and Global Business*, London and New York: Routledge.

Dunning, J.H. (1998), 'Location and the multinational entrerprise: A neglected factor?', *Journal of International Business Studies*, **29** (1), 45–66.

Ellison, G. and E.L. Glaeser (1997), 'Geographic concentration in U.S. manufacturing industries: a dartboard approach', *Journal of Political Economy*, **105** (5), 889–927.

Fuchs, R.J. and E.M. Pernia (1989), 'The influence of foreign direct investment on spatial concentration', in F.J. Costa, A.K. Dutt, L.J.C. Ma and A.G. Noble (eds), *Urbanization in Asia: Spatial Dimension and Policy Issues*, Honolulu: University of Hawaii Press.

Fujita, M., P. Krugman and A.J Venables (1999), *The Spatial Economy: Cities, Regions, and International Trade*, Cambridge and London: MIT Press.

Gelder, L.V. (1994), *Industrial Agglomeration and Factor Market Segmentation with Empirical Applications to Indonesia*, Unpublished PhD dissertation, Cornell University, US.

Glaeser, E.L., H.D. Kallal, J.A. Scheinkman and A. Shleifer (1992), 'Growth in cities', *Journal of Political Economy*, **100** (6), 1126–52.

Gujarati, D. (1995), *Basic Econometrics*, New York: McGraw Hill, Inc. (3rd ed.).

Hayter, R. (1997), *The Dynamic of Industrial Location: The Factory, the Firm, and the Production System*, Chichester: John Wiley and Sons.

Helpman, E. and P. Krugman (1985), *Market Structure and Foreign Trade*, Cambridge, MA: MIT Press.

Henderson, J.V. (1988), *Urban Development, Theory, Fact, and Illusion*, New York: Oxford University Press.

Henderson, J.V. and A. Kuncoro (1996), 'Industrial Centralization in Indonesia', *The World Bank Economic Review*, **10** (3), 513–40.

Hill, H. (1997), *Indonesia's Industrial Transformation*, Singapore: Institute of Southeast Asian Studies.

Hoover, E.M. (1971), *An Introduction to Regional Economics*, New York: Alfred A. Knopf, Inc. (1st ed.).

Isard, W. (1956), *Location and Space Economy*, Cambridge: MIT Press.

Isard, W. (1960), *Methods of Regional Analysis: An Introduction to Regional Science*, Cambridge and London: MIT Press.

Johns, R.A. (1985), *International Trade Theories and the Evolving International Economy*, London: Frances Pinter.

Judge, G.G., W.E. Griffiths, R.C. Hill and T.-C. Lee (1980), *The Theory and Practice of Econometrics*, New York: John Wiley and Sons.

Keeble, D. (1976), *Industrial Location and Planning in the United Kingdom*, London: Methuen & Co Ltd.

Kim, S. (1995), 'Expansion of markets and the geographic distribution of economic activities: The Trends in U.S. Regional Manufacturing Structure, 1860–1987', *Quarterly Journal of Economics*, **110**, 881–908.

Kim, S. (1999), 'Regions, resources, and economic geography: sources of U.S. regional comparative advantage, 1880–1987', *Regional Science and Urban Economics*, **29**, 1–32.

Krugman, P. (1980), 'Scale economies, product differentiation, and the pattern of trade', *American Economic Review*, **70**, 950–9.

Krugman, P. (1991), *Geography and Trade*, Cambridge: MIT Press.

Krugman, P. (1995), *Development, Geography, and Economic Theory*, Cambridge and London: MIT Press.

Krugman, P. (1996), 'Urban concentration: the role of increasing returns and transport costs', *International Regional Science Review*, **19** (1–2), 5–30.

Krugman, P. (1998), 'Space: the final frontier', *Journal of Economic Perspectives*, **12** (2), 161–74.

Krugman, P. (1990), *Rethinking International Trade*, Cambridge and London: MIT Press.

Krugman, P.R. and A.J. Venables (1990), 'Integration and the competitiveness of peripheral industry', in C. Bliss and J.B. de Macedo (eds), *Unity with Diversity in the European Community*, Cambridge: Cambridge University Press.

Kuncoro, A. (1994), *Industrial Location Choice in Indonesia*, Unpublished PhD dissertation, Brown University, US.

Kuncoro, M. (1996), 'Regional development in Indonesia: some notes towards 21st Century', *UNISIA*, (31).

Kuncoro, M. (1999), *Trade liberalization and the geographic distribution of manufacturing activities: the trends in Indonesia's regional manufacturing, 1986–1995*, Paper presented at the international business dynamics of the new millennium, the 1999 ANZIBA Annual Conference, Sydney.

Kuncoro, M. (2000a), 'Beyond agglomeration and urbanization', *Gadjah Mada International Journal of Business*, **2** (3).

Kuncoro, M. (2000b), *The Economics of Industrial Agglomeration and Clustering, 1976–1996: the Case of Indonesia (Java)*, Unpublished PhD thesis, the University of Melbourne, Melbourne.

Kuncoro, M., A. Adji and R. Pradiptyo (1997), *Ekonomi Industri: Teori, Kebijakan, dan Studi Empiris di Indonesia (Industrial Economics: Theory, Policy, and Empirical Studies in Indonesia)*, Yogyakarta: Widya Sarana Informatika.

Malecki, E.J. (1991), *Technology and Economic Development: the Dynamics of Local, Regional, and National Change*, New York: John Wiley and Sons.

Martin, R. (1999), 'The new 'geographical turn' in economics: some critical reflections', *Cambridge Journal of Economics*, **23**, 65–91.

Martin, R.P. and P. Sunley (1996), 'Paul Krugman's geographical economics and its implications for regional development theory: A critical assessment', *Economic Geography*, **72** (3), 259.

Matyas, L. and P. Sevestre (eds) (1992), *The Econometrics of Panel Data: Handbook of Theory and Applications*, Dordrecht: Kluwer Academic Publishers.

Mody, A. and F.-Y. Wang (1997), 'Explaining industrial growth in coastal China: economic reform and what else', *The World Bank Economic Review*, **11** (2), 293–325.

Nicholas, S., S.J. Gray and W.R. Purcell (1999), *The Role of Incentives: Japanese FDI in Singapore and the Region*, Paper presented at the ANZIBA 1999 Annual Conference: International Business Dynamics of the New Millennium, Sydney.

O'Sullivan, A. (1996), *Urban Economics*, Chicago: Richard D. Irwin (3rd ed.).

Ottaviano, G.L.P. and D. Puga (1998), 'Agglomeration in the global economy: a survey of the 'New Economic Geography', *The World Economy*, **21** (6), 707–32.

Paelinck, J.H.P. and L.H. Klaassen (1979), *Spatial Econometrics*, Farnborough: Saxon House.

Pangestu, M. (1997, December 17–18), *Domestic Competition Policy*, paper presented at the Sustaining Economic Growth in Indonesia: A Framework for the Twenty-First Century, Jakarta.

Porter, M.E. (1998), 'Clusters and the new economics of competition', *Harvard Business Review*, November–December (**6**), 77–91.

Preer, R.W. (1992), *The Emergence of Technopolis: Knowledge-intensive Technologies and Regional Development*, New York: Praeger Publishers.

Sato, S. (1994), *War, Nationalism and Peasants: Java under the Japanese occupation 1942–1945*, St Leonards: Allen and Unwin Pty, Ltd.

Schmitz, H. (1995), 'Small Shoemakers and Fordist Giants: A Tale of a Supercluster', *World Development*, **23** (1), 9–28.

Shilton, L. and Stanley, C. (1999), 'The survival and birth of firms', *Journal of Real Estate Research*, **17** (1/2), 169–87.

Sjoholm, F. (1999), 'Productivity growth in Indonesia: the role of regional characteristics and direct investment', *Economic Development and cultural Change*, **47** (3), 559–84.

Smith, D.F. Jr. and R. Florida (1994), 'Agglomeration and industrial location: an econometric analysis of Japanese-affiliated manufacturing establishments in automotive-related industries', *Journal of Urban Economics*, (**36**), 23–41.

Wang, F.-Y. (1994), 'Reconsidering export-led growth: Evidence from firm performance, Taiwan, 1983–1987', in J.D. Aberbach, D. Dollar and K.L. Sokoloff (eds), *The Role of the State in Taiwan's Development*, New York: M.E. Sharpe, Inc., pp. 26–46.

Weber, A. (1909), *Theory of the Location of Industries*, Chicago: University of Chicago Press.

9. Modelling Foreign Direct Investment and its Impact on Regional Growth and Globalization in Major Asian Economies

Tran Van Hoa

INTRODUCTION

The standard theories of economics, international finance, transnational corporations, and within the accounting framework of the United Nations System of National Accounts (for example SNA93) stipulate that investment plays a crucial role in influencing microeconomic decisions and macroeconomic activity, national output growth and economic development, and in shaping fiscal and monetary policy (Dornbusch and Fischer, 1990) and economic reforms in many developed, newly industrialized (NIE) and especially developing countries (World Bank, 1991). Corporate and private strategies for business development and expansion in a home or host economy depend on this crucial role in a Wiener–Granger short-term causal sense. As a result, a rigorous study and discussion of the movements or trends of these economic aggregates and their empirical relationships, either in a historical context or in future predictions, are amply justified. The justification is stronger since there is currently a lack of empirical econometric studies in this area. In our observational study of a major East Asian economy, namely Korea, there were distinct subperiods of investment fluctuations: the fairly stable pre-1990 and the widely unpredictable post-1990 (see ICSEAD, 2002). These observed structural breaks could be attributed to external pressure and subsequent capital market liberalization in the country by the end of the 1980s. This and other more recent developments such as the Asian financial crisis of 1997 would make econometric modelling and accurate forecasting for Korea's investment trend and pattern and its impact on regional growth and international trade more acute and challenging for practical policy studies and also in an academic context.

The purpose of our chapter is threefold. First, it contributes to macroeconomic analysis in general and to international business, financial studies, transnational corporations, development economics and investment strategies in major Asian economies in particular. It does this by rigorously investigating the causal structure and empirical forecasts of a major SNA macroaggregate, namely, investment in Korea, a major Asian NIE and the second Asian member of the OECD (the other is Japan). Once a causal effect has been established, remedies may be found for restoring investment in Korea even in the post-Asia crisis period to a pre-crisis level that would be conducive to promotion of growth and other activities dependent on investment. Another application extension is to use the findings to study how regional integration and globalization, under different plausible scenarios, will impact on Korea's investment. The testable causal structure epistemologically is based upon the conventional dynamic multi-equation multi-sectoral Keynesian theory in flexible functional form of the computing general equilibrium (CGE) kind and consistent with the SNA data framework.

The second purpose is methodological in nature in that the chapter departs from the applied econometric modelling approaches that use conventional multiple regressions, simultaneous equations, or seemingly unrelated regressions and makes use of a fairly simple and flexible economy-wide multi-equation modelling approach (see also Tran Van Hoa, 1986b and 1992c). This approach is based on the calculus of differential analysis in economics (Tran Van Hoa, 1992a, 1992d) to provide the fundamental equations in the reduced form for better estimation and forecasting of investment (or other endogenous or endogenized variables) in the model. The success of this new approach is further assessed via its applied modelling and forecasting performance.

Finally, the chapter contributes to important practical applications of recent advances in the statistical theory of forecasting to better formulate forward planning policies and strategies in finance, economics and business in a major NIE, namely Korea. It does this by providing forecasts of Korean private investment, consumption and growth based on the empirical Bayes or two-stage hierarchical information (2SHI) theories (Tran Van Hoa, 1985, 1986a, 1993a, 1993b; Tran Van Hoa and Chaturvedi, 1988, 1990, 1997) under different plausible time-frame scenarios and comparing them to other conventional methods. More specifically, the *ex post* performance (or accuracy) of these forecasts in the context of average mean squared forecasting errors (MSE) or Wald risk criteria is then evaluated against more traditional forecasts based on the ordinary least squares (OLS), the maximum likelihood or the explicit (Baranchik, 1973) positive Stein-like (Anderson, 1984) methodologies.

The implications from our chapter's findings are fivefold. First and foremost, it provides rigorous empirical findings on Korea's investment, its impact on growth and international trade before and after the Asia crisis, and on future ramifications of globalization. Second, it provides empirical evidence on whether our method is conceptually more appropriate to studying major economic activities and engines of growth such as investment (domestic and foreign). Third, while the 2SHI is, in theory, universally superior to other conventional methods (OLS, ML, Stein) for a linear model with two or more regressors, the chapter provides numerical evidence on the improved accuracy of our new forecasts of Korea's investment for better investment policy uses. Fourth, if the modelling and forecasting success of our approach is relatively superlative – in terms of its empirical fit and accurate turning-point predictions – its superiority is further enhanced.

Finally, if, based on the same model and dataset, a substantial improvement is achieved by the 2SHI method in relation to other conventional procedures currently in use, then our findings will in addition point to a new direction of rigorous forecasting methodology for finance, economics and business analysts in their everyday or long-term strategic corporate and individual planning applications to investment or other endogenous activities of interest in the model.

TRENDS IN INVESTMENT, CONSUMPTION, GOVERNMENT EXPENDITURE, TRADE AND GROWTH IN KOREA

The quarterly movements of Korea's main macroaggregates (GDP, private consumption, gross fixed investment, government expenditure, exports and imports – all at 1995 prices) are depicted in Figure 9.1. The figure shows a very strong trend in all but one of the variables under study, starting at the take-off stage in 1970 and peaking in 1996 for investment and in 1997 for GDP, consumption and imports. All these activities show a very sharp decline even in aggregates in 1998 as a result of the 1997 Asia crisis. Exports and government expenditure continued, on the other hand, to grow for the whole 30 years but the latter at a lower stationary rate. The low proportion of government expenditure to GDP, especially in recent years, reveals the lesser part (share) the Korean government had been playing in the economy.

Suddenly high volumes of exports were achieved for 1980 (before the second oil crisis) and 1991–92 after market liberalization.

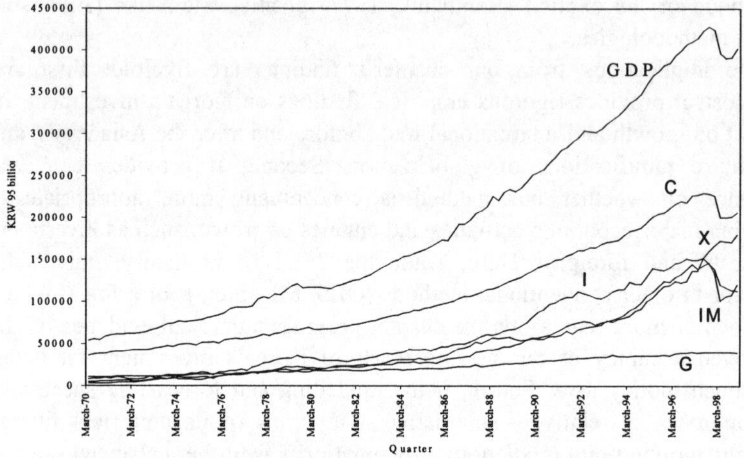

Figure 9.1 Major trends in Korea's economy (1970–1998)

The roles in international trade played by Korea as compared to those by three other major Asian countries or groups of countries (Japan, extended China and ASEAN) are depicted in Figures 9.2 and 9.4 (in USD million) and in Figures 9.3 and 9.5 (as a percentage). From Figure 9.2, we note the

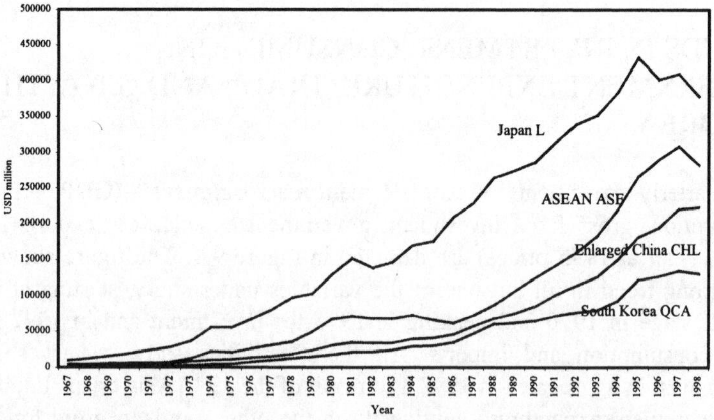

Figure 9.2 Shares of major Asian economies in world exports

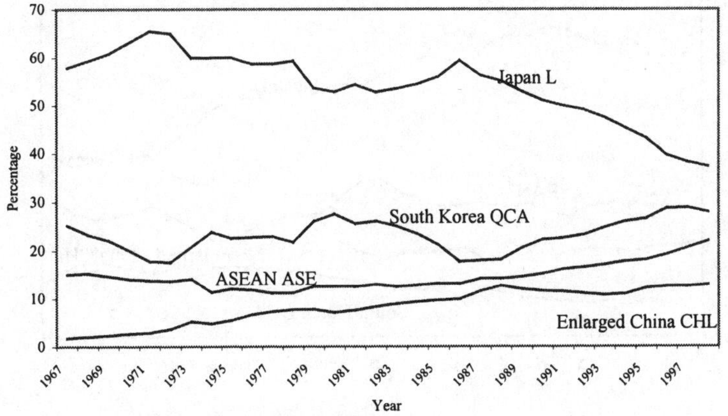

Figure 9.3 Shares of major Asian economies in world exports (%)

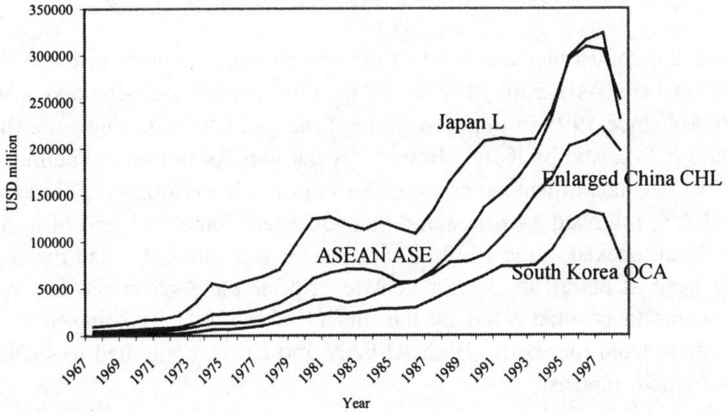

Figure 9.4 Imports of major Asian economies from the world

dominant role in exports to the world by Japan since 1967 to even after the Asia crisis of 1997. This was followed in the second place by ASEAN, then by enlarged China and finally Korea. However in Figure 9.3, this dominance by Japan had slipped considerably from nearly 70 per cent in the 1970s to less then 40 per cent in the late 1990s.

From Figure 9.3 we note that while Korea had managed a fairly steady increase in its share of exports to the world, enlarged China appears to be the only trading block with increasing export share.

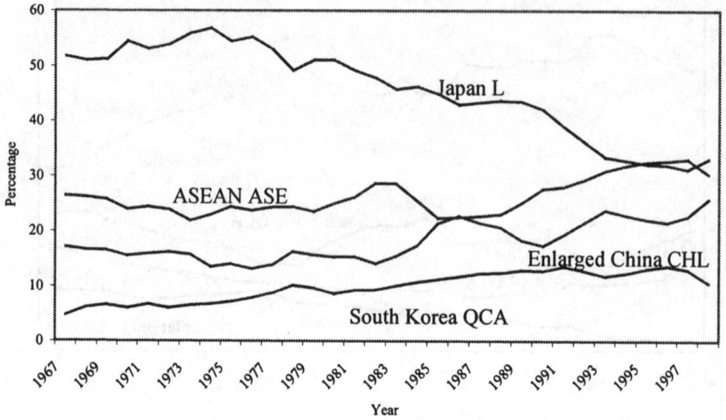

Sources: Data in Figure 9.1 are from the 2001 OECD database, and Figures 9.2 to 9.5 from 2000 CEPII-CHELEM

Figure 9.5 Imports of major Asian economies from the world (%)

Figure 9.4 shows that while Japan dominated world exports to these four trading blocks in Asia from 1967 to 1994, its dominance had been taken over by ASEAN since 1995 in import volume. Enlarged China occupies the third place and is followed by Korea. Imports by the four Asian blocks declined as a result of the Asian financial crisis. The sharpest fall was observed for Japan and ASEAN, followed by Korea and then enlarged China. In terms of import shares, Japan peaked in the 1970s at close to 60 per cent but it had managed only to keep at about the 30 per cent level after the Asia crisis. Enlarged China seems to be unaffected by the impact of the crisis, posting a strong import trend from the world. Both ASEAN and Korea continued to suffer a decline in their imports.

MODELLING INVESTMENT AND GROWTH IN KOREA: A MULTI-SECTORAL ECONOMETRIC APPROACH

Modelling and forecasting Korea's investment (or even that in the other major Asian trading block in our figures) poses a real challenge for a number of reasons. First, in Korea, the pace of deregulation of international capital flows proceeded in a manner closely linked to macroeconomic developments. The government had always been reluctant to allow liberalization of Korea's financial system to move too fast, fearing that an inflow of foreign funds would push up the nominal and real exchange rates and undermine competitiveness with its trading rivals (Smith, 1998). Three principal changes (the limit on foreign ownership raised to 15 per cent borrowings for capital good imports permitted and constraints on the ownership of foreign currency deposits eased) between 1993 and 1995 however were responsible for net capital inflow explosion (as mentioned earlier). Second, despite progress in the deregulation of capital flows, Korea's regulations remained extensive for a country whose share of international trade was very large. Third, there were two great crisis turning points in investment statistics in Korea during 1981–2000 (late 1989 and 1997) attributed by some authors to the yen appreciation, trade friction between Japan and Asian NIEs and the US and European Union, and increasing wages in Japan and the Asian NIEs (Seo and Suh, 1999).

The challenging situation above (and other economic, non-economic or policy factors) may have explained why studies of Korean investment have been limited in number, scope and methodologies. For example, most previous studies on Korea's investment were either focused on a macroeconomic or microeconomic analysis of a descriptive kind (Smith, 1998; Kwon and Suh, 2001; Asian Development Bank, 2001) or on modelling, by a single-equation approach, the impact of foreign direct investment on trade or growth from the OLI (ownership–location–internalization) theoretical underpinning of Dunning and other authors (Seo, 1998; Seo and Suh, 1999). Studies on Korea's investment and even on Korea's economy were not even covered in the 1999 OECD member country report. In view of this neglect and also of Korea's importance in the world economy and world trade under increasing globalization however, a serious study of its investment in a multi-equation multi-activity framework is fully justified.

It is well known that an empirical study of the Korean economy's major activities (such as investment) can involve a descriptive analysis of the graphs of these macroaggregates, their means and standard deviations, their shifts over time and their turning points and cycles. But a study involving the interaction between investment and other major economic activities in the Korean economy is more realistic and therefore more appropriate. We adopt the economy-wide multi-sectoral modelling approach because, first, of the inherent Marshallian nature of economic activities in which all are interrelated or interdependent as they should be, and second and methodologically, of the now well-known Haavelmo theorem on simultaneous-equation inconsistency and bias.

In an economy with interdependent sectors and activities, investment could be argued to be dependent on many varied internal and external, economic and non-economic factors in a linear, non-linear or mixed form.

Consider for illustration in this chapter a simple well-known generic five-equation Keynesian macroeconomic model of the Korean open economy in the linear form as

$$C_t = \alpha_{11} + \alpha_{12}Y_t + \alpha_{13}C_{t-1} + u1_t \quad (9.1)$$
$$I_t = \alpha_{21} + \alpha_{22}Y_t + \alpha_{23}Y_{t-1} + \alpha_{24}R_t + \alpha_{25}R_{t-1} + u2_t \quad (9.2)$$
$$X_t = \alpha_{31} + \alpha_{32}Y_t + \alpha_{33}YW_t + \alpha_{34}PW_t + \alpha_{35}XR_t + u3_t \quad (9.3)$$
$$IM_t = \alpha_{41} + \alpha_{42}Y_t + \alpha_{43}YW_t + \alpha_{44}PW_t + \alpha_{45}XR_t + u4_t \quad (9.4)$$
$$Y_t = C_t + I_t + G_t + X_t - IM_t \quad (9.5)$$

where C = private final consumption expenditure, Y = gross domestic product or GDP, I = private gross fixed investment, G = government expenditure, X = exports of goods and services, IM = imports of goods and services, YW = US income (as a proxy for world income), PW = general price deflator in the US (as a proxy for world prices), R = US prime rate (as a proxy for world interest rate), and XR = Korean won/USD exchange rate. The α's denote the structural parameters, and the u's the error terms. All value (or indexed) variables are expressed in terms of their constant 1995 prices, therefore filtered of the inflationary effect.

The model (9.1)–(9.5) is a simple dynamic macroeconomic model (Pindyck and Rubinfeld, 1991) for an open economy and takes into account (a) a partial adjustment process in consumption behaviour encompassing the hypotheses of relative and permanent income, liquid assets, wealth and life cycles in the sense of Duesenberry, Friedman and Modigliani, (b) a flexible accelerator investment behaviour, augmented by foreign capital borrowings (see for further detail Tran Van Hoa and Harvie, 2000) and user's costs, (c) trade openness through exports and imports regulated by foreign and domestic demand conditions and price relativities (via the exchange rates) and (d) relevance of the government sector expenditure (a feature prominent in many contemporary Asian economies).

In the model, consumption, investment, exports, imports and GDP are endogenous and there are nine exogenous and predetermined variables.

It can be verified that, using the order condition for identifiability or mathematical consistency in the theory of econometrics, the investment equation (9.2) in the model is over-identified. As a result, it can be written, instead of its linear form given traditionally in (9.1)–(9.5), in its complete differential form (see Allen, 1960) in the reduced form as (see Tran Van Hoa, 1992a, 1992d; Harvie and Tran Van Hoa, 1993)

$$I\%_t = a_{11} + a_{12}\,C\%_{t-1} + a_{13}Y\%_{t-1} + a_{14}R\%_t + a_{15}R\%_{t-1} + a_{16}YW\%_t + a_{17}PW\%_t + a_{18}XR\%_t + a_{19}G\%_t + e_{1t} \quad (9.6a)$$

where $I\,\%$, $C\,\%$, $Y\,\%$, $R\,\%$, $YW\,\%$, $PW\,\%$, $XR\,\%$ and $G\,\%$ indicate the rate of change of I, C, Y, R, YW, PW, XR and G respectively. The a's indicate the reduced form parameters and e_1 is the new error term. The GDP growth $Y\,\%$ equation is similarly obtained as

$$Y\,\%_t = a_{21} + a_{22}\,C\,\%_{t-1} + a_{23}Y\,\%_{t-1} + a_{24}R\,\%_t + a_{25}R\,\%_{t-1} + a_{26}YW\,\%_t + a_{27}PW\,\%_t + a_{28}XR\,\%_t + a_{29}G\,\%_t + e_{2t} \qquad (9.6b)$$

Equations (9.6a) and (9.6b) characterize the investment and growth relationships from the five-equation macroeconomic model given in (9.1)–(9.5). By conventional definition, the parameters from this equation are in fact either static (or dynamic) elasticities associated with either current (or lagged) variables included in it.

The derivation of (9.6a) and (9.6b), based on the total differentiation of an arbitrarily functional relationship, is simple and, more importantly, consistent with the procedure usually adopted for the neo-classical macroeconomic models of the applied or computable general equilibrium Johansen kind. In these neo-classical models, the endogenous and exogenous variables in the economy are linked by a (usually first order) approximate transmission mechanism in terms of the elasticities. There are however at least five important differences between our investment and growth equations given in (9.6a) and (9.6b) above and the investment specification from applied or computable general equilibrium Johansen-class models.

First, in our case, the important linking elasticities have to be estimated for the model as a whole using economic time series data and possibly other extraneous (prior) information such as policy switches or external non-economic factors. Our equation given in (9.6a) or (9.6b) thus is completely data-based, although clearly we do not preclude the use of prior or extrancous information (in the form of an oil or financial crisis or a major war for example) in the equation in other theoretical or judgemental contexts.

Secondly, in view of the above arguments, our model is capable of accommodating sub- and add-factors as well as structural change and other institutional considerations (for a discussion supporting the use of these factors in macroeconomic models, see Johansen, 1982).

Thirdly, our equation must be mathematically consistent as required by the identifiability conditions for complete systems of structural simultaneous equations in the theory of econometrics.

Fourthly, by its construct, our modelling approach encompasses a wide class of linear, non-linear or mixed multi-equation econometric models in which the exact functional form of each of the individual structural equations is, as usual, unknown or need not be specified.

Finally, for an important group of economic variables whose first differences in logs are approximately equivalent to the rates of change, our equations by their construct include as special cases the Granger–Wiener short-term causality if these rates of change are I(0) and the co-integration or long-term equations of the Engle–Granger (1987) class (see Tran Van Hoa, 1993b; Harvie and Tran Van Hoa, 1993, for further detail) if the rates of change are I(1). Our approach also avoids the awkward situation of using log-changes in applied econometric studies encountered by many econometricians when the variables involve measurements of deficits (e.g. government budget) or negative current account in national accounts or negative real rates of interest (nominal rate of interest is lower than inflation rate) in finance.

To evaluate the performance of (a) the investment equation in this macroeconomic model and (b) our forecasting methodology using official data from Korea in recent years, we have fitted the equation (9.6a) to data for the period 1970 to 1998, covering the damaging Asia crisis of 1997. This will optimally produce the necessary elasticity estimates. These estimates are then used in a comparative study which is based on stochastic simulation to measure the relative MSE performance or operational accuracy of our modelling investment equation and also of our new forecasting approach in relation to other current methodologies. The new methodology and its well-known characteristics are briefly described below.

REVIEW OF CURRENT ESTIMATING AND FORECASTTING METHODOLOGIES

The investment equation in differential and reduced form as given in (9.6a) can be written more generally with a sampling size T and k independent variables (possible causes) in matrix notation as

$$\underset{(T\text{x}1)}{y} = \underset{(T\text{x}k)}{Z} \, . \, \underset{(k\text{x}1)}{\beta} + \underset{(T\text{x}1)}{u} \tag{9.7}$$

where $y = I\,\%$ or $Y\,\%$, Z = the rate of change of the exogenous and predetermined variables (both static and dynamic), β = the parameters and u = the disturbance satisfying all standard statistical assumptions.

To estimate (9.7) which is essentially a general linear model for structural or behavioural analysis or for direct forecasting and policy analysis (see Pindyck and Rubinfeld, 1991), we can use the OLS, or at a more efficient level, any of the explicit (Baranchik, 1973) Stein or Stein-rule methods as described below.

More specifically, using (9.7), the basic and most well known method to produce estimates and forecasts of y (or I %) is the OLS estimator of β (denoted by b) and is written as

$$b = (Z'Z)^{-1}Z'y \tag{9.8}$$

A more sophisticated and efficient method is the explicit Stein estimator of β (Baranchik, 1973) that is given by

$$\begin{aligned}\beta s &= [1 - c(y-Zb)'(y-Zb)/b'Z'Zb]\, b \\ &= [1 - c(1-R^2)/R^2]\, b \end{aligned} \tag{9.9}$$

where c is a characterizing scalar and defined in the range $0 < c < 2(k-2)/(T-k+2)$, and R^2 is the square of the sample multiple correlation coefficient.

A still more efficient method is the explicit positive-part Stein estimator of β (Anderson, 1984) which is defined as

$$\begin{aligned}\beta{+}s &= [1 - \min\{1\,,\, c(y-Zb)'(y-Zb)/b'Z'Zb\}]\, b \\ &= [1 - \min\{1\,,\, c(1-R^2)/R^2\}]\, b \end{aligned} \tag{9.10}$$

A new method to obtain estimates and forecasts of β in (9.7) with better properties has been proposed (see Tran Van Hoa, 1985, 1993a; Tran Van Hoa and Chaturvedi, 1988, 1990, 1997). It is in a class of explicit improved Stein-rule or empirical Bayes (also known as 2SHI) estimators for some linear regression models. This estimator includes the explicit Stein and the double k-class (Ullah and Ullah, 1978) estimators as subsets (Tran Van Hoa, 1993a,1993b). Other applications of the Stein, Stein-rule and 2SHI estimators to linear regression models with non-spherical disturbances and to Zellner's seemingly unrelated regression model have also been made (see Tran Van Hoa *et al.*, 1993, in the case of regressions with non-spherical disturbances, and Tran Van Hoa, 1992b, 1992d, in the case of seemingly unrelated regressions).

The explicit 2SHI estimator is defined as

$$\beta h = [1 - c(1-R^2)/R^2\} - c(1-R^2)/\{R^2(1+c(1-R^2)/R^2)\}]\, b \tag{9.11}$$

and its positive-part counterpart (Tran Van Hoa, 1986a) is given by

$$\beta{+}h = [1 - \min\{1\,,\, c(1-R^2)/R^2\} - \{1/((R^2/c(1-R^2)) + 1)\}]\, b \tag{9.12}$$

While all the estimators given above can be applied to the general linear model (9.7) for structural and forecasting analysis, their relative performance in terms of historical, *ex post* or *ex ante* (Pindyck and Rubinfeld, 1991) forecasting MSE can differ. Thus, it is well known that, in MSE and for $k \geq 3$ and $T \geq k + 2$, *ßs* dominates (that is it performs better in forecasting MSE) *b*, and *ßs* is dominated by *ß+s* (Baranchik, 1973; Anderson, 1984). However, it has also been demonstrated (Tran Van Hoa, 1985; Tran Van Hoa and Chaturvedi, 1988) that, in MSE, *ßh* dominates both *b* and *ßs*, and more importantly, *ß+h* dominates *ß+s* (Tran Van Hoa, 1986a).

A further important path-breaking result of the 2SHI theory has recently been proved (see Tran Van Hoa and Chaturvedi, 1997): the dominance of the 2SHI over the OLS and Stein exists anywhere in the range $0 < c < 2(k-1)/(T-k)$. This indicates that the 2SHI method produces better (in terms of smaller Walk risk or generalized Pitman nearness) estimates and forecasts even if the estimating and forecasting equation has only one independent variable in it. *The condition for the optimal Stein dominance in the linear equation up to now requires that* $0 < c < 2(k-2)/(T-k+2)$ (see Anderson, 1984).

While some application of these forecasting methodologies to predictions of economic activity in some developed countries such as Australia (see Tran Van Hoa, 1992d) has been made, the extent of the significance of the MSE dominance, or equivalently, the informational gain or relative forecasting success between the alternative estimators above has not been investigated explicitly within an open trade theoretical framework and an empirical context using more recent economic data for the major economies in East Asia. This issue is taken up in the study below for one of the fastest growth economies in the world in recent years but with highly fluctuating investment and being very sensitive to foreign trade and capital flows in the region (see Tran Van Hoa and Harvie, 2000).

Another interesting feature of our study is that, since all data are annual and have as usual a small sample size, our study is therefore designed to look at the finite sample performance of alternative forecasting methods.

Finally, since the poor quality of economic data from the Asian countries and other less developed country (LDC) economies is well known, one by-product of our study is that we in fact investigate the performance of the alternative forecasts in the case of serious measurement errors on the variables of the macromodel of an economy however it is defined.

The substantive findings for Korea's investment reported below are based on the five-equation macroeconomic model described earlier in (9.1)–(9.5), and the appropriate estimating equation to produce elasticity parameters or the forecasting equation to produce policy impact is given in (9.6a) for investment. In addition, a number of well known forecasting methods that are currently popular among quantitative economists are used to compare their relative performance for decision analysis.

ALTERNATIVE FORECASTS AND THEIR PERFORMANCE

In our study, we have fitted the investment equation as given in differential and reduced form (9.6a) of the model (9.1)–(9.5) to annual official data collected for Korea. The original dataset is from 1960 to 1998, but the effective (i.e., after allowing for missing or statistically incompatible data) sample period is 1972 to 1998, giving, when the dynamic (lag) structure is taken into account, a sample size of up to 27 observations for each variable. In our comparative study, only the OLS or ML, the positive-part Stein and the positive-part 2SHI forecasts of Korea's investment are used.

The data are in real terms at the constant 1995 prices and obtained from the 2000 World Bank World Tables OECD and East Asia and Pacific databases, using Australia's data express (DX) extracting and transforming procedures. The performance of our reduced form investment equations is determined solely from their goodness of fit, correct turning point predictions and *ex post* forecasting MSE.

The research strategy of our study includes a number of important features.

First, to investigate the possible accuracy improvement or informational gain under different situations from the data, the *ex post* forecasts (Pindyck and Rubinfeld, 1991) of investment from our macroeconomic model are derived rather pragmatically for a lack of larger samples, for two (short-term), four (medium-term) and six (long-term) years only ahead. These are called subsamples 1, 2 and 3 respectively. In other words, for our investment equation which has 27 annual observations and nine elasticity parameters to be estimated, the *ex post* forecasts are made respectively two, four and six years ahead from 1992. The consistency of our *ex post* forecasts (which are based on the same historical simulation period), if existent, describes to some extent the possible presence of rationality (i.e., the forecasts match the data generating process) in our forecasting investment equations.

Secondly, for each of these subsamples, the MSE of the forecasts from (9.6a) is computed from a stochastic simulation and is based on 100 (smaller or larger simulations yielded similar results) statistical trials. In stochastic simulation, both the estimated parameters and the disturbances are allowed to vary from trial to trial (see Pindyck and Rubinfeld, 1991, for further detail). The distributions used to generate these parameter and disturbance trial-to-trial variations are based upon their OLS-based (Monte Carlo) sample distributions with 500 repetitions.

Finally, in the case of the disturbance or error term distribution, the simulation for each subsample takes respectively the value of s^2, $10s^2$ and $100s^2$, where s^2 is the sample disturbance variance. This strategy is adopted to investigate the impact of the size of the disturbance variances (or the size of the measurement errors on the possible causes or the misspecification of the investment function) on the relative performance of the various forecasting methodologies in our investment equation. This kind of analysis is particularly applicable to data from the LDCs, as is well known.

Thus, in our empirical study, the *ex post* forecasting MSE is obtained, by stochastic simulation, for a total of nine sets of investment forecasts in differential and reduced form, different from each other in terms of the forecasting sample size and σ^2 (the disturbance variance).

The relative performance of the OLS, positive-part Stein $\beta{+}s$, and positive-part 2SHI $\beta{+}h$ estimators for each of these equations and for Korea between 1992 and 1998 is given in Table 9.1. Relative performance between say the OLS and the positive-part Stein is defined formally as $R(b/\beta{+}s) = 100[\text{MSE}(b) / \text{MSE}(\beta{+}s) - 1]$, and dominance or informational gain in *ex post* forecasting MSE of $\beta{+}s$ over b exists whenever *ex post* forecasting $R(b/\beta{+}s) \geq 0$, with equality somewhere in the parameter space. Similar results are used for other comparisons $R(b/\beta{+}h)$ and $R(\beta{+}s/\beta{+}h)$.

It can be further verified that, for the forecasting equation of the functional form defined in (9.6a) or (9.7), when historical and future values of Z (the possible causes) are known, dominant *ex post* forecasting MSE implied dominant *ex ante* forecasting MSE. *This extension is useful for policy analysis into the future.*

For *ex post* forecasting, the relative performance of the OLS, $\beta{+}s$, and $\beta{+}h$ estimators for each of these models is also expressed in terms of its standard criteria such as mean per cent errors, RMS per cent errors and per cent improvement in *ex post* forecasting MSE or informational gain (see Pindyck and Rubinfeld, 1991). Only the informational gain or forecasting accuracy improvement is given in Table 9.1.

The relative performance in *ex post* forecasting MSE between say the OLS-based forecasts and the positive-part Stein-based forecasts, as reported in Table 9.1, is in fact defined as $R(b/\beta{+}s) = 100[(\text{MSE}(yb-y) / \text{MSE}(ys-y)) - 1]$ with $\text{MSE}(yb-y)$ being the MSE of the forecasting errors based on the OLS estimates, and $\text{MSE}(ys-y)$ being the MSE of the forecasting errors based on the positive-part Stein. The calculation of $\text{MSE}(yh-y)$ is similar.

Table 9.1 Improved modelling and forecasting investment in Korea: results of stochastic simulation

Investment in Korea: 1972 to 1998									
Average R^2									
	0.873	0.706	0.710	0.863	0.728	0.736	0.865	0.746	0.724
OLS-based disturbance variance or measurement errors									
	σ_1^2			σ_2^2			σ_3^2		
	83.1579			831.579			8315.79		
Estimation period				1972 to 1992					
Forecasting period									
	1993 to 1994 (short-term)			1993 to 1996 (medium-term)			1993 to 1998 (long-term)		
	σ_1^2	σ_2^2	σ_3^2	σ_1^2	σ_2^2	σ_3^2	σ_1^2	σ_2^2	σ_3^2
Ex post forecasting relative MSE – Informational or accuracy gain (%)									
	1993 to 1994 (short-term)			1993 to 1996 (medium-term)			1993 to 1998 (long-term)		
	σ_1^2	σ_2^2	σ_3^2	σ_1^2	σ_2^2	σ_3^2	σ_1^2	σ_2^2	σ_3^2
Ex post forecasting relative MSE – Informational or accuracy gain (%)									
R(ML/S)	18.76	50.30	42.00	17.80	49.76	40.96	21.24	47.19	43.69
R(ML/H)	39.23	96.54	89.54	37.21	106.54	92.08	44.88	105.46	93.78
R(S/H)	17.23	30.76	33.48	16.48	37.92	36.26	19.50	39.59	34.86

IMPLICATIONS FOR BETTER POLICY ANALYSIS ON INVESTMENT IN KOREA

For comparative purposes with other similar studies, the OLS estimates of the reduced form investment equation (9.6a) (and two other similarly specified equations, namely growth in (9.6b) and private consumption) fitted to Korea's annual data for 1972 to 1998 have been obtained and their historical forecasts for this period plotted in Figure 9.6. Similar forecasts for private consumption are given in Figure 9.7 and for GDP growth in Figure 9.8. Only the estimates of investment are given below:

$$I\%_t = -2.22 + 1.73C\,\%_{t-1} - 1.10Y\,\%_{t-1} - 0.01R\,\%_t + 0.05R\,\%_{t-1} + 0.93YW\,\%_t + 1.81PW\,\%_t + 0.88XR\,\%_t + 0.40G\,\%_t \quad (9.6a')$$

R^2=0.60, adjusted R^2=0.42, F=3.36, DW=1.69

Judged from conventional statistical tests, the historical forecasts of Korea's investment are efficient and emulate well its actual fluctuations (peaks and troughs) during the period under study (see Figure 9.6). Of special interest to us is the ability of our estimated model to accurately mimic the turning points of the observed investment data (especially the activity leading to the economic meltdown since 1997), even though we conceded earlier that our model is simply an illustration of our modelling and forecasting methodologies.

Also from the reported results in (9.6a'), investment in our study seems positively affected by lagged consumption, lagged world income, world prices, Korea's exchange rates and government expenditure. But it is negatively affected by lagged GDP and both current and lagged US interest rates. The strongest and most significant positive influences on Korea's investment are world prices and exchange rates. This seems to show the volatility of the Korean economy that can be attributed to principally external factors outside Korea's control and the importance of the large share of its international trade (Smith, 1998) and international reserves (see also Kwack, 2001). The findings also show the relevance of part of the OLI approach (i.e., via GDP and exchange rates) to studying Korea's investment (Seo and Suh, 1999). More importantly, they point out further forces that have been overlooked by the OLI approach but which are inherent and crucial in understanding investment behaviour in Korea in the past few decades. These are the government sector, world demand and world prices, US interest rate movements and domestic private consumption. The effect of globalization is subsumed in the movements of international trade factors in our study. In this context, the slow-down of growth and investment in Korea would have important implications for economic regionalism (such as ASEAN) and the globalization process in the country.

The superiority of our multi-sectoral and flexible approach can also be empirically evaluated and measured in terms of its better elasticity estimates and forecasts of Korea's investment in the context of the MSE criterion. More importantly, it is the ability of our forecasts to accurately foreshadow the exact downturn in investment (and output growth – see Figure 9.8

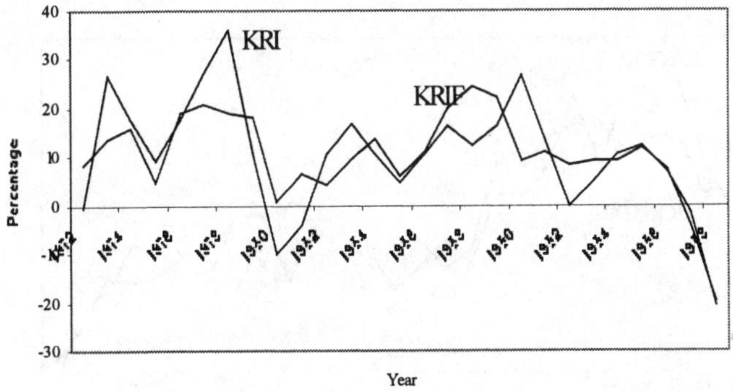

Figure 9.6 Korea's actual and forecast investment (1972–1998)

– and private consumption – see Figure 9.7) during the whole period under study (1972–1998) especially during and immediately after the Asia crisis of 1997 that indicates that a multi-sectoral model of this kind and functional form is far better, for practical policy analysis, than its alternative models of investment such as the OLI approach. Our further discussion below on the findings of our new approach is focused on more numerical detailed analysis of Korea's 2SHI investment forecasts and their informational gain or forecasting accuracy relative to other conventional estimation and forecasting methods (OLS or ML and Stein).

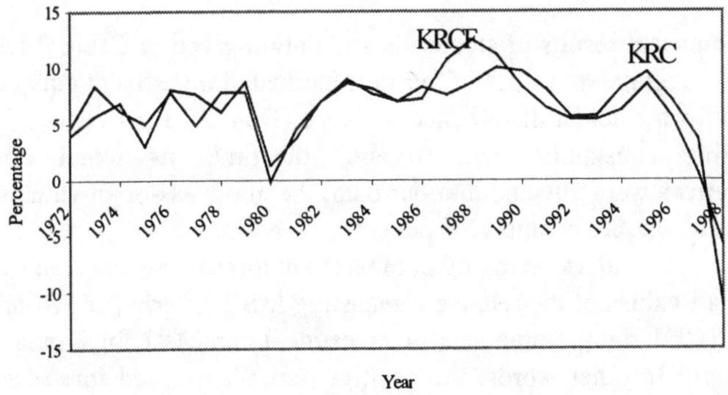

Figure 9.7 Korea's actual and forecast private consumption (1972–1998)

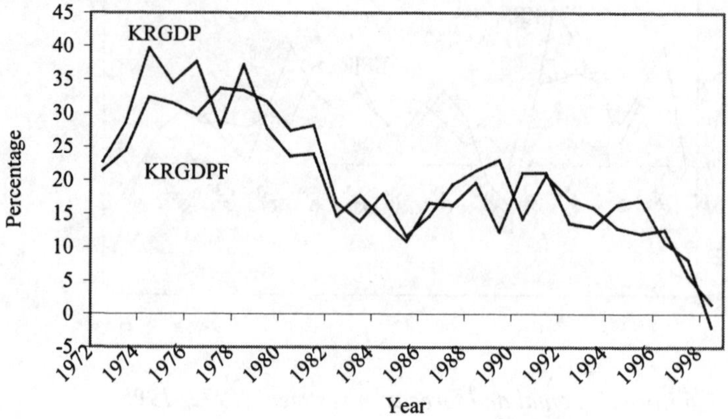

Figure 9.8 Korea's actual and forecast growth (1972–1998)

We note that our 2SHI estimation and forecasting method described earlier uniformly dominates in average MSE or under Wald risk the OLS, ML and Stein methods for all linear models having two or more RHS variables and for any finite sampling sizes, regardless of whether these variables are measured with or without errors, stochastic or non-stochastic. The discussion is based on the simulation results for Korea's investment *ex post* forecasts under a number of plausible scenarios for the short, medium and long terms.

From the empirical results of stochastic simulation given in Table 9.1, we observe that the average R^2 values of our nine estimated investment equations are fairly high for the actual disturbance variance (from 86.3 per cent to 87.3 per cent). When substantial (i.e., 10 and 100 times its actual value) measurement errors were injected into our data, the goodness-of-fit value still ranges well from 70.1 per cent to 73.6 per cent.

From Table 9.1, and in terms of comparative forecasting accuracy and improvement, all values of the relative forecasting MSE criteria [i.e., *R*(*ml*/*s*), *R*(*ml*/*h*) and *R*(*s*/*h*)] for the nine sets of investment forecasts for Korea are greater than zero. In other words, the positive-part Stein-based forecasts of investment uniformly dominate (or perform better than) the OLS-based forecasts. More spectacularly and significantly, the positive-part Stein-based forecasts of investment which have been claimed in the statistical literature to be unbeatable are in turn uniformly dominated by the positive-part 2SHI forecasts. Our findings establish the optimal hierarchy for selection of an appropriate forecasting theory for making better forward planning investment strategies.

Some other interesting forecasting and methodological features about the observed investment behaviour and trends in Korea for the period 1972 to 1998 are briefly described below (detailed comments on the investment behaviour and trends as well as trade and business opportunities from our empirical results will be reported elsewhere).

The estimated investment equation for Korea during the historical estimation period 1972–1992 has the highest R^2 value among the nine equations in our study (at 87.3 per cent). This indicates some measure of success of our multi-sectoral econometric modelling approach for the available data.

Using our 2SHI methodologies for forecasting investment in the short (two years), medium (four years) and long term (six years) for Korea, the informational gain or improved accuracy can be as high as 106.54 per cent in relation to the OLS and 50.30 per cent in relation to the positive-part Stein. The gain increases with the size of the measurement errors on investment. This establishes the superiority of our methods over other traditional methods, especially with economic and finance data where measurement errors are suspected to be large in practice.

An outstanding finding from our comparative study here is that our modelling and forecasting methodologies are able to produce better medium and long-term *ex post* forecasting results than their short-term counterpart. Usually, the opposite is true in empirical studies of this kind.

IMPLICATIONS FOR GROWTH, ASIAN ECONOMIC REGIONALISM AND GLOBALIZATION

In order to investigate more clearly the contribution of foreign direct investment to growth in the Korean economy during the period 1972–1998, we have regressed reduced-form-based forecast GDP growth on forecasts of growth in (a) investment and (b) private consumption. The exercise is rather pragmatically Friedmanian to delineate in a simple way the contribution by both investment and consumption to growth. This trivariate equation seemed affected by serious autocorrelation, reflecting in our view the inertia or long-term effect of GDP fluctuations in Korea during the period under study. The equation was then re-estimated by the AR1 maximum likelihood method.

The results of this AR1 estimation are given in equation (9.13) where the standard *t*-values are found to be highly significant. The goodness-of-fit seems excellent and the historical estimates of *Y*% emulated very well the fluctuations and turning points of our target *Y*% (see Figure 9.9). An extrapolation of our $Y\%$ estimates in this case would indicate a declining trend for Korea's growth in the short to medium terms at the same level as that of investment and consumption growths. In this equation (9.13), investment did have a strong positive impact of almost unitary elasticity on Korea's output growth. Consumption was however found to satisfy the Friedmanian intuition that it hampered growth and, in our case, with a fairly large elasticity of –1.65. The decomposition of this counter-growth consumption into even broadly defined different kinds of consumption (e.g., luxuries and necessities) would provide another important study on the determinant mechanism of growth however.

$$Y\%_t = 18.8 + 0.95I\%_t - 1.68C\%_t \qquad (9.13)$$
$$(4.87)\ (5.79)\qquad (-4.02)$$
$$R^2{=}0.90,\quad R^2{=}0.88,\quad DW{=}1.65,\quad \text{serial corr. coeff. } ro{=}0.88\ (9.56)$$

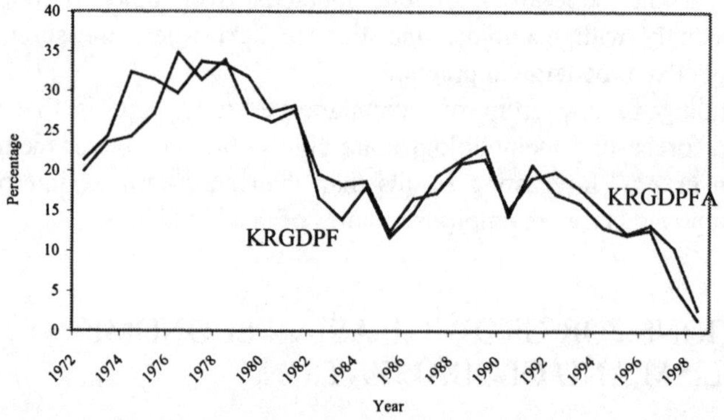

Figure 9.9 Effect of investment on Korea's growth (1972–1998)

Our simple empirical results from (9.6a') and (9.13) provide useful information on the determinants of investment and growth in Korea during the past 30 years or so, and also their effects on a country's international trade, economic regionalism and hence globalization. In (9.6a'), US prime rates appear to have only a small (about 5 per cent) impact on Korea's investment, reflecting the fact that US prime rates may be a poor substitute for user's costs of international borrowings in Korea. Korean won/USD exchange rate, world income and world inflation seem however to have an impact of almost unity on Korea's investment.

External factors that affect Korea's investment and growth will have an adverse impact on its economic regionalism that was reinforced by the advent of the Asia crisis and the inability of the IMF or WTO to resolve quickly the crisis and its contagion. Other concepts of economic regionalism that may be affected by a Korean economic slow-down include the proposal to set up an Asian Monetary Fund and the establishment of an ASEAN+3 (China, Japan and Korea) economic integration by Korea. An new international economic society, the Asia Pacific Economic Forum (APEF) was set up in May 2001 at Kangwon National University in Chunchon, Korea, to look at these issues and a report by its members was presented at a conference in Sydney in 2002.

In addition, if the effect of the current globalization process is transmitted to Korea's investment and then growth through the same external factors, then a slow-down in world economy as we are witnessing as at late 2001 will ultimately hamper Korea's investment and growth. The contagion of this effect will affect not only the Korean economy but the East Asian region and, from our earlier analysis in this chapter, even the ASEAN+3 (extended China, Korea and Japan) economic area as proposed by Korea.

To arrest a slow-down in investment into Korea and its damaging consequences to a wider economic region or group of economies in this case would require an international and national collaboration through organizations such as the WTO and IMF, a favourable economic and trade climate from major trading blocks such as AFTA, the European Union, APEC and ASEAN. Major trading countries of the world such as the USA and Japan play a special role in particular. But with their present economic woes (such as economic slow-down and corporate debts and bankruptcies), these two economic giants seem unable to offer much to either Korea or their other major trading countries and blocks to improve the predicted world-wide economic slow-down in the next year or two.

An Asia recovery is in this context a few years away (see Tran Van Hoa, 2001) and a real recovery depends crucially on formulating and adopting suitable and efficient economic crisis or slow-down management (Tran Van Hoa, 2002). This seems lacking however at both national and international levels world-wide.

REFERENCES

Allen, R.G.D. (1960), *Mathematical Analysis for Economists*, London: Macmillan.

Anderson, T.W. (1984), *An Introduction to Multivariate Statistical Analysis*, 2nd ed., New York: Wiley.

Asian Development Bank (2001), 'Asian development outlook 2001: publication highlights', *www.adb.org/*, May.

Baranchik, A.J. (1973), 'Inadmissibility of maximum likelihood estimators in some multiple regression problems with three or more independent variables', *Annals of Statistics*, **1**, 312–21.

Chaturvedi, A. and Tran Van Hoa (1997), 'The dominance of the 2SHI estimator under generalized Pitman nearness', *Communications in Statistics*, **26**, Issue 5, 1227–38.

Dornbusch, D. and S. Fischer (1990), *Macroeconomics*, 5th ed., Sydney: McGraw-Hill.

Engle, R.F. and C.W.J. Granger (1987), 'Co-integration and error correction: representation, estimation and testing', *Econometrica*, **55**, 251–76.

Harvie, C. and Tran Van Hoa (1993), 'Long term relationships of major macrovariables in a resource-related economic model of Australia: a cointegration analysis', *Energy Economics*, **15**, 257–62.

ICSEAD (2002), *Recent Trends and Prospects for Major Asian Economies*, International Centre for the Study of East Asian Development, Kitakyushu, Japan.

Johansen, L. (1982), 'Econometric models and economic planning and policy: some trends and problems', in M. Hazewinkle and A.H.G. Rinnooy Kan (eds), *Current Developments in the Interface: Economics, Econometrics, Mathematics*, Boston: Reidel.

Kwack, S. (2001), 'Factors contributing to the financial crisis in Korea', in I. Kim, S. Kwack and S. Park (eds), *Growth, Productivity and Vision for the Korean Economy*, Seoul: Pakyoungsa, pp. 44–64.

Kwon, S.-H. and C.-S. Suh (2001), 'Globalization strategies of south Korea corporations after the 1997 economic crisis: a casestudy of Samsung, LG and Hyundai Electronics', Discussion Paper No. 1, Vol. 2, Korea-Australasia Research Centre, University of New South Wales.

OECD (1999), *Measuring Globalization: The Role of Multinationals in OECD Economies*, Paris: OECD.

Pindyck, R.S. and D.L. Rubinfeld (1991), *Econometric Models and Economic Forecasts*, Sydney: McGraw-Hill.

Seo, J.-S. (1998), *Dynamics of Comparative Advantage and Foreign Direct Investment: An Analysis of the Relationship between FDI and Trade*, Unpublished PhD Thesis, University of New South Wales.

Seo, J.-S. and C.-S. Suh (1999), 'Foreign Direct Investment in East Asia: A Comparison between European, American and Asian Investments', in S.-G. Lee and P.-B. Ruffini (eds), *The Global Integration of Europe and East Asia: Studies of International Trade and Investment*, Cheltenham: Edward Elgar.

Smith, H. (1998), 'Korea', in R.H. McCleod and R. Garnaut (eds), *East Asia in Crisis: From Being a Miracle to Needing One*, London: Routledge.

Tran Van Hoa (1985), 'The inadmissibility of the Stein estimator in normal multiple regression equations', *Economics Letters*, **19**, 39–42.
Tran Van Hoa (1986a), 'The inadmissibility of the Stein estimator in normal multiple regression models: analytical and simulation results', *15th Anniversary of the NBER-NSF Seminar on Bayesian Inference in Econometrics*, ITAM, Mexico City, 16–18 January.
Tran Van Hoa (1986b), 'Effects of monetary and fiscal policy on inflation: some evidence from the J-Test', *Economics Letters*, **22**, 187–90.
Tran Van Hoa (1992a), 'Modelling output growth: a new approach', *Economics Letters*, **38**, 279–84.
Tran Van Hoa (1992b), 'Energy consumption in Thailand: estimated structure and improved forecasts to 2000' (in Thai), *Thammasat Economic Journal (Thailand)*, **10**, 55–63.
Tran Van Hoa (1992c), 'A multi-equation model of energy consumption in Thailand', *International Journal of Energy Research*, **16**, 381–5.
Tran Van Hoa (1992d), 'A new and general approach to modelling short-term interest rates with application to Australian data 1962–1990', *Journal of Economics and Finance: Proceedings*, **16**, 327–35.
Tran Van Hoa (1993a), 'The mixture properties of the 2SHI estimators in linear regression models', *Statistics and Probability Letters*, **16**, 111–5.
Tran Van Hoa (1993b), 'Effects of oil on output growth and inflation in developing countries: the case of Thailand 1966:1 to 1991:1', *International Journal of Energy Research*, **17**, 29–33.
Tran Van Hoa (2001), *The Asia Recovery*, Cheltenham: Edward Elgar.
Tran Van Hoa (2002), *Economic Crisis Management*, Cheltenham: Edward Elgar.
Tran Van Hoa and A. Chaturvedi (1988), 'The necessary and sufficient conditions for the uniform dominance of the two-stage Stein estimators', *Economics Letters*, **28**, 351–5.
Tran Van Hoa and A. Chaturvedi (1990), 'Further results on the two-stage hierarchical information (2SHI) estimators in the linear regression models', *Communications in Statistics (Theory and Methods)*, **A19** (12), 4697–704.
Tran Van Hoa and A. Chaturvedi (1997), 'Performance of the 2SHI estimator under the generalized Pitman nearness criterion', *Communications in Statistics (Theory and Method)*, **26** (5), 1227–138.
Tran Van Hoa and C. Harvie (eds) (2000), *Causes and Impact of the Asian Financial Crisis*, London: Macmillan.
Tran Van Hoa (with A. Chaturvedi and G. Shukla) (1993), 'Performance of the Stein-rule estimators when the disturbances are misspecified as spherical', *Economic Studies Quarterly (Japan)*, **44**, 601–11.
Ullah, A. and A. Ullah (1978), 'Double k-class estimators of coefficients in linear regression', *Econometrica*, **46**, 705–22.

World Bank (1991), 'The challenge of development', *World Development Report*, Oxford: Oxford University Press.
World Bank World Tables (2000), Washington D.C.

10. Foreign Investments in Asia after the Asian Economic Crisis

Jong-Kil Kim

INTRODUCTION

During the heydays of Asian growth, foreign investments to Asian countries, particularly those to Southeast Asian countries and China, contributed greatly to the phenomenal growth of these economies. The supply condition of the investment fund worldwide was abundant, the demand for foreign funds in these economies was insatiable, and the 'globalization' of economic activities was the catch-phrase all over the world in those days. However, since the financial (or economic) crisis in Asia in the second half of 1997, the supply and demand conditions of foreign investment towards Asia have been affected. For example, a downfall in business activities, shrinkage of domestic market, reduced business credibility at both national and firm levels, etc. may have turned off foreign investors. But at the same time, a drastic fall in wages and rents, fall in the value of local currencies and fall in asset prices have probably attracted foreign investors.

The economic crisis in Asia has thus, indeed, changed the character of foreign investment to Asia in many important ways. For example, the national composition of foreign investors in Asia has been affected. The Japanese investments in this region have dwindled as a consequence of prolonged economic recession in Japan, while investments from the USA and Europe have surged to take advantage of the weakening position of Japan. Also, the nature of foreign investments has also changed. Before the crisis, most foreign direct investment (FDI) was greenfield investment. Since the crisis, cross-border mergers and acquisitions (M&As) have become an increasingly important form of foreign investments in Asia.

In this chapter, we will look into the changing nature of foreign investments in Asia in the 1990s, especially that of the post Asian financial crisis, to capture new trends and characteristics. In particular, we will investigate the supply and demand conditions of foreign investments that have been changed in Asia roughly since 1990. Based on this finding, we will attempt to derive new characteristics of foreign investments, which were formed after the crisis. Next, implications of these changes on industrial structure, on financial stability and on domestic investment and growth of these economies will be investigated. Finally, we will explore future prospects of foreign investments in this region.

CHANGING ENVIRONMENT OF FOREIGN INVESTMENT IN ASIA AFTER THE CRISIS

Asian firms after the currency crisis had to restructure their corporate financial structure in part as a condition for IMF subsidy loans, and in part to improve their financial positions and to provide new capital funds. However, under the financial strain that was caused by increasing pressure for loan repayment, high interest rates and the plunging stock market, provision of new capital loans from both domestic and foreign financial markets became increasingly difficult. This caused firms to sell off not only bad assets or non-performing affiliate firms but also assets and rights of the core businesses and financially sound affiliate firms. The simultaneous and large-scale restructuring of corporate and financial sectors in the crisis countries provided a good environment for overseas multinational corporations which were trying to expand their Asian entry. There were plenty of business opportunities that were on 'firesale' (Park, 2000, p. 25). Let us look into changing supply and demand conditions of foreign investment in Asia at the time in detail.

Supply Condition of FDI Outflows by Advanced Economies

Most of the crisis-hit countries faced macroeconomic management difficulties because of a rise in local currency burden from depreciations and a sharp reduction in domestic demand. They thus were forced to sell their businesses and assets. On the other hand, for foreign firms it was a good opportunity to enter the Asian market not only because the acquiring cost was kept low but also because a deregulating process had been going on aimed at foreign firms. The fall in the currency value was quite attractive to foreign investors because it reflected lower dollar-based production costs and asset prices of their stocks. But the Asian currency crisis also brought negative influences to foreign investors as well. Negative influences were an economic recession and resulting shrinkage of domestic demand, a fall in national credit ratings and a rise in investment risk as a consequence, etc. However, positive influences must have outweighed negative influences, considering a sharp rise of foreign investments in Asia after the crisis.

Change in international capital flows

The net resource flows to developing countries in East Asia and the Pacific had risen steadily in the 1980s and 1990s, peaking at $109 billion in 1997. However, it had dropped sharply to $25 billion immediately after the crisis in 1998, before it rose again to the $42–48 billion level around 2000 (Table 10.1). The major form of international capital flows before the Asian crisis had been foreign loans, reflected as 'debt flows' in that table. For instance, the net flow of foreign debts occupied a lion's share of 77.7 per cent of total net capital inflow to developing countries in East Asia and the Pacific, while FDI constituted only 11.6 per cent and grants occupied the remaining 10.7 per cent in 1980. This was changed to FDI after the crisis, as the level and the share of FDI increased markedly and steadily to be a predominant component lately. At the same time, the figures for net debt flows showed minus signs, meaning that outflows of loans – mainly repayments of short and medium-term loans – were exceeding inflows of loans.

Table 10.1 Net resource flows to East Asia and the the Pacific, 1980, 1990, 1997–2001 (US$ billion)

	1980	1990	1997	1998	1999	2000	2001
Net resource flows	11.2	27.7	109.1	24.8	44.6	47.9	42.0
Debt flows	8.7	12.2	44.5	–32.5	–11.6	–18.0	–12.0
FDI flows	1.3	11.1	62.2	57.6	48.9	44.0	48.9
Portfolio equity flows	0.0	2.3	0.0	–2.8	4.6	19.3	2.9
Grants	1.2	2.1	2.4	2.5	2.7	2.6	2.2

Source: World Bank, *Global Development Finance*, 2001 and 2003.

The sharp drop in this loan form of capital inflow reflects the riskiness of bank loans which was proven during the Asian crisis. The rise of FDI in Asia in turn reflects a switch of world capital to East Asia, which began even before the Asian economic crisis erupted. The Mexican financial crisis in 1994 and other subsequent crises (such as the Russian, Brazilian and Argentinean) necessitated world capital to look for other areas for profitable investment, and the East and Southeast Asian region seemed to be a perfect choice. Similarly, portfolio investment to this region also rose in the first half of the 1990s, before the crisis. However, portfolio flows had also dropped sharply right after the crisis, before they picked up again and amounted to 40 per cent in 2000.

Change in international production system

The rise in FDI through Trans-National Corporations (TNCs) reflects the expansion of international production by overseas affiliates of the TNCs. As the globalization proceeds rapidly, the internationalization of production systems and the integration of international economies deepen as well. This means that most business activities, including development of new products, provision of parts and components, and sales and financing, are increasingly conducted within a cross-border context. The expansion of international production by TNCs is often carried out by an international division of the production process, and the process is forcefully activated not only by an increasing liberalization of trade barriers but also by an increasing mobility of factors of production, especially capital and technology.

Advances in technology, liberalization and changes in capital markets in recent years have been quite interactive. For example, the rapid pace of technical change has intensified competitive pressures on the world's technological leaders, most of which are TNCs. By merging with other TNCs with complementary capabilities, TNCs can share the costs of innovation, access new technological assets and enhance their competitiveness. The spreading and deepening of the international production system through cross-border M&As have further been facilitated by the ongoing removal or relaxation of restrictions on FDI[1].

There are three distinctive characteristics in the entry of Western firms into Asia after the financial crisis (Park, 2000, p. 58): 1) M&A is actively used to accelerate an entry to the Asian market; 2) despite a severe economic downturn in the Asian market after the financial crisis, Western firms are expanding production facilities to secure a production base for new products, including semi-conductors and automobiles; 3) there has been a rapid move by Western firms to China, to take advantage of the opening of the Chinese market after China's entry to the World Trade Organization (WTO). In short, Western firms with global scale are aiming for the potential demand of the Asian market, which in turn reflects their strong anticipation for economic recovery in Asia.

Demand Condition of FDI Inflows by Asian Economies

Increased competition for FDI inflows among Asian economies and the resulting acceleration of deregulation on FDI inflows

The good performance of the US economy and the growing perception of the inadequacy of their financial systems during the 1990s encouraged East Asian economies to shift to Western style financial systems, where investments are largely financed by capital markets rather than the banking system. And as they have adopted more features from the Western system, the East Asian systems are now becoming more integrated into global capital markets. The trend is accelerating as American and European financial institutions increase their presence in the region, in part to take advantage of the weaker financial positions of East Asian financial institutions and of the more liberal investment environment in the wake of the Asian crisis. The acceleration of liberalization and deregulation in both trade and investment, and the globalization of capital markets, have stimulated mergers and acquisitions of East Asian companies, particularly by US and European firms.

In their attempt to activate their economies, crisis-hit countries of Asia in particular were aggressively inducing foreign capital, especially through M&As. The wholesale financial liberalization after the Asian financial crisis in countries such as Korea and Thailand under the influence of the IMF accelerated this change. During and after the worst period of the financial crisis, they judged that foreign capital inflow was necessary in order to recover their economies fundamentally. Accordingly, they began mitigating various regulations placed on foreign capital (Table 10.2). For example, Korea reversed its legal and institutional framework for inward FDI from one of the most 'closed' to one of the most 'open' systems. Moreover, it legalized hostile corporate acquisitions.

Declining costs of production

As was emphasized earlier, a downfall in business activities, shrinkage of domestic market, reduced business credibility at both national and firm levels, etc. may have turned off foreign investors. But at the same time, a drastic fall in wages and rents, fall in the value of local currencies, and fall in asset prices have probably attracted foreign investors. According to a study with respect to Japanese firms that operate in Asian countries by the Japan External Trade Organization (JETRO), there was a change among Asian cities in terms of investment costs after the financial crisis in 1997. The rental cost of offices and factories as well as the costs of wages in the crisis-hit countries fell drastically, whereas in China wage costs rose and land and

Table 10.2 Movements of deregulation on foreign capital since the currency crisis

Country	Timing	Major contents
Thailand	Nov. 1997	For projects that have already been approved by the Board of Investment (BOI), foreign capital can be extended to half of the total if agreed by Thai partner. The 25% limit of foreign capital in a financial institution is removed in the next 10 years. A firm in the promotional industry is allowed to own land, even if not approved by the BOI.
	May 1998	A limit of foreign capital is removed until the end of 1999, to a firm in the new promotional line of industries.
	Dec. 1998	Foreign retail trade firms already in Thai can extend capital investment up to 100% with BOI approval (by notifying BOI until the end of 2000).
	Oct. 1999	A law on foreign firm regulation was amended. The number of industries that are regulated has been reduced to 43 from previous 63.
Malaysia	Aug. 1998	A regulation of foreign capital investment in manufacturing has been removed temporarily until the end of 2000, except for a few industries. Previously, the foreign capital ratio was set by the export ratio.
Indonesia	Sept. 1997	A limit on stock purchase (49%) by a foreign investor was removed, except banks and insurance companies.
	July 1998	A reduction of negative-list firms that are subject to foreign capital regulation. Practically, a 100% foreign capital investment is allowed to wholesale and retail trade firms.
	Oct. 1998	Removal of foreign investment limit in the domestic banks.
	June 1999	An establishment of foreign holding company is approved.

Philippines	Oct. 1998	A removal of foreign capital ratio (40%) in the construction industry. Up to 40% of foreign investment is allowed to ocean fishing management, restructuring firms, and owning condominiums. A limit on foreign capital ratio in investment firms was raised from 40% to 60%.
Korea	Dec. 1997	A limit on stock ownership by a foreign investor is raised from 26% to 55%.
	Feb. 1998	Up to 33% of stock ownership is allowed for hostile M&As (previously 10%).
	Apr. 1998	Liberalization of M&A by foreigners, except for defence related industries.
	Sept. 1998	Establishing a foreign investment promotion law that does not regulate foreign investors in principle.

Source: JETRO, *White Paper on Foreign Investment* (2000), p. 41.

office rental costs remained as the pre-crisis level. This has resulted in a sharp reduction of investment cost gap between Peking and other Southeast Asian cities after the crisis (Table 10.3).

OVERVIEW AND CHARACTERISTICS OF FOREIGN INVESTMENTS IN ASIA AFTER THE CRISIS

Overview

Total FDI inflows

The year-on-year rise of FDI inflows in East and Southeast Asia before the financial crisis was quite high: 6.7 per cent in 1995 and 22.9 per cent in 1996. However, in the year of the crisis, 1997, the ratio slowed down to 5.0 per cent, and in the midst of a deep crisis, the ratio declined drastically, reaching –5.8 per cent in 1998. As the region recovered from the initial shock of the crisis, the ratio climbed up again to 11.3 per cent in 1999 (Table 10.4). However, the performance among three tiers was quite different. The most

Table 10.3 Changes in wages and rental costs in major Asian cities before and after the financial crisis (US$)

Major cities	June 1997	Dec. 1998
Wage for a factory worker, monthly wage		
China (Peking)	60–97	131–144
Thailand (Bangkok)	164–368	128–264
Malaysia (Kuala Lumpur)	218–439	138–290
Indonesia (Jakarta)	103–149	56–66
Philippines (Manila)	242–284	155–189
Vietnam (Ho Chi Minh city)	86–160	77–104
Wage for middle management, monthly wage		
China (Peking)	217–603	479–544
Thailand (Bangkok)	849–2019	542–1446
Malaysia (Kuala Lumpur)	1285–2402	1111–1689
Indonesia (Jakarta)	317–2264	261–1229
Philippines (Manila)	454–1202	535–946
Vietnam (Ho Chi Minh city)	354–545	358–529
Purchasing cost of industrial complex		
China (Peking)*	84.4	72.5
Thailand (Bangkok)	85	60.8
Malaysia (Kuala Lumpur)	170	99–1113
Indonesia (Jakarta)	90	75–98
Philippines (Manila)	115	120
Vietnam (Ho Chi Minh city)**	2.25	2.3
Office rental cost, monthly office rental		
China (Peking)	25.3	27
Thailand (Bangkok)	19	13.6
Malaysia (Kuala Lumpur)	21.3–25.6	18.4–19.8
Indonesia (Jakarta)	25	24–25.5
Philippines (Manila)	31	24.5
Vietnam (Ho Chi Minh city)	40	23.1–29.7

Notes: Purchasing cost of industrial complex and office rental cost are based on per square metre.

Sources: * Using right for 50 years.
**Annual using fee.

JETRO, *SENSOR* (1997.10 and 1999.4). Reprinted from Park (2000, p. 24).

Table 10.4 FDI inflows in East and Southeast Asian economies, 1988–1999 (US$ million)

	1988–93 yr. ave.	1994	1995	1996	1997	1998	1999
First tier NIEs	9,787	18,744	16,335	23,616	24,789	25,706	43,318
Second tier NIEs							
China	8,852	33,787	35,849	40,180	44,236	43,751	40,400
ASEAN4	7,258	9,624	13,621	17,415	16,171	11,545	7,077
Third tier NIEs	510	2,190	2,865	3,187	3,386	2,453	2,123
Total	26,407	64,345	68,670	84,398	88,582	83,455	92,918

Notes: First tier NIEs are Hong Kong, Singapore, Korea and Taiwan.
Second tier NIEs are China and ASEAN4 that includes Indonesia, Malaysia, Philippines and Thailand.
Third tier NIEs are Cambodia, Laos, Myanmar and Vietnam.
Total figures are different from those in Table A10.1, which include additional amounts by South Asian countries.

Source: UNCTAD, *World Investment Report* (2000) and Table A10.1.

significant change is that the share of ASEAN (Association of South East Asian Nations) in the total inflows of FDI to the region declined noticeably after the financial crisis (from 20.6 per cent in 1996 to 7.6 per cent in 1999), whereas the share of first tier Newly Industrializing Economies (NIEs) rose considerably, from 28.0 per cent to 46.6 per cent during the same period. The shares of both China and the third tier NIEs declined slightly, but China still occupies slightly less than half of the total. Among the first tier NIEs, the rise of FDI inflows to Korea was noteworthy after the crisis. So was Thailand among the second tier NIEs. However, the sharp drop of FDI inflows to the second tier NIEs was largely because of Indonesia, where FDI inflows registered minus in both 1998 and 1999 (see Table 10.A1 for more details).

Looking at 1999 alone, FDI inflows to East and Southeast Asia increased by 11 per cent from the previous year, to reach $93 billion in 1999. The increase was mainly due to the first tier NIEs, where the FDI inflows increased by almost 70 per cent. Particularly in the Republic of Korea, the FDI inflows nearly doubled to reach another record level of over $10 billion, or four times its pre-crisis level of 1996. China, the principal FDI recipient in developing countries throughout the 1990s, retained its lead, but saw a drop (nearly 8 per cent) to just over $40 billion in 1999, compared with $44 billion in the previous year. In the longer run, China can still be expected to remain an attractive location for FDI, particularly in the light of its accession to the

World Trade Organization (WTO) and a further liberalization of its services sector. In ASEAN4, the FDI inflows continued to decrease by nearly 40 per cent in 1999. Indonesia suffered divestment in 1998 for the first time since 1974. Divestment continued in Indonesia, about $3 billion in 1999. Southeast Asian low income countries (or third tier NIEs), which are dependent on other countries in the region for FDI inflows, continue to be adversely affected by the negative impact of the Asian economic crisis.

Shares of FDI inflows as a percentage of gross domestic product and as a percentage of gross fixed capital formation

The inward FDI as a percentage of Gross Domestic Product (GDP) rose in most of the Asian economies after the currency crisis (Table 10.5). In fact, this ratio rose twofold; from 11.6 per cent in 1990 to 23.3 per cent in 1998. However, the rise is more pronounced in the crisis-hit countries of Korea, Indonesia, Malaysia and Thailand. A similar trend can also be found in the inward FDI as a percentage of gross fixed capital formation in Asia as a whole. Nevertheless, the figures for this ratio have a great variation from country to country and from period to period. Traditionally, both of these ratios were quite high in Hong Kong, Singapore, Malaysia and relatively high in the rest of ASEAN-4 and first tier NIEs except Korea and Taiwan. The rising trend of these ratios means, therefore, that the role of FDI as a source of external capital and as a contributor for growth has been intensifying in recent years after the Asian crisis.

Characteristics

Rising shares of USA and Europe, and declining share of Japan

First of all, the regional composition of FDI inflows has changed. That is, the rising shares of the USA and Europe and the declining share of Japan have become one of the significant changes in the characteristics of FDI inflows to Asia in the 1990s (Table 10.6). Japan's investment to this region was dominant in the 1970s and 1980s, whereas the interest of Western economies in Asia was relatively insignificant compared to that in Latin America or Eastern Europe. However, as the Asian economies expanded dynamically in the 1990s, USA and European firms began taking a part in Asian investment. This is particularly true for European firms, especially after the Asian financial crisis when conditions for Asian investment became much more favourable.

What are the reasons underlying this change? One obvious explanation is the prolonged economic recession in Japan in the 1990s. Japanese investment in Asia, which peaked in the second half of the 1980s, began declining after

Table 10.5 Inward FDI as a percentage of gross domestic product or gross fixed capital formation, by region and economy, 1990, 1995, 1997 and 1998

Region/economy	1990	1995	1997	1998
South, East and	11.6	14.8	18.4	23.3
Southeast Asia	4.3	7.6	9.1	10.5
Hong Kong	75.0	50.6	54.6	65.7
	9.9	7.7	9.9	29.6
Korea	2.3	2.3	3.5	6.1
	1.1	1.1	1.8	5.5
Singapore	78.2	71.2	81.6	85.8
	32.2	25.6	27.3	17.6
Taiwan	6.1	6.0	7.0	7.8
	5.6	2.9	6.8	0.4
Indonesia	36.6	25.6	28.6	77.3
	2.7	6.7	7.0	–0.8
Malaysia	24.1	31.8	38.1	67.0
	18.1	11.1	12.2	13.9
Philippines	7.4	8.2	10.2	14.3
	6.0	9.0	6.1	12.8
Thailand	9.6	10.5	8.5	17.5
	5.6	2.9	6.8	25.1
China	5.2	18.8	23.5	27.6
	4.0	14.7	14.3	12.9

Notes: Upper figures are percentages of FDI inflow from gross domestic product.
Lower figures are percentages of FDI inflow from gross fixed capital formation.
Percentages of gross fixed capital formation in 1990 are annual averages during 1987 and 1992.

Sources: UNCTAD, *World Investment Report* (1999) for figures up to year 1997.
UNCTAD, *World Investment Report* (2000) for figures in 1998.

the 'bubble' collapsed in the 1990s. In its place, Western investments from the USA and Europe began expanding to get involved with dynamic growth of these economies in the mid-1990s. After a short interval immediately following the Asian financial crisis, this change has further accelerated again as these economies were eager to attract foreign sources of capital in the process of their economic revitalization and restructuring.

Table 10.6 Inward FDI to East Asia from Japan, US and EU4

	FDI source	1990–92 US$ million	Inflows relative to Japan	1993–95 US$ million	Inflows relative to Japan	1996–98 US$ million	Inflows relative to Japan
China	Japan	3,442	1.00	14,993	1.00	11,281	1.00
	USA	4,027	1.17	20,294	1.35	18,336	1.63
	EU4	1,662	0.48	13,703	0.91	14,480	1.28
Korea	Japan	617	1.00	1,133	1.00	1,024	1.00
	USA	993	1.61	1,297	1.14	7,040	6.87
	EU4	1,098	1.78	823	0.73	4,906	4.79
Taiwan	Japan	1,795	1.00	1,247	1.00	1,940	1.00
	USA	1,414	0.79	1,866	1,50	1,933	1,00
	EU4	444	0.25	706	0,57	682	0.35
ASEAN5	Japan	17,008	1.00	23,119	1.00	33,269	1.00
	USA	10,245	0.60	18,509	0.80	12,611	0.38
	EU4	13,868	0.82	27,387	1.18	31,683	0.95
Total Asia	Japan	22,862	1.00	40,491	1.00	47,514	1.00
	USA	16,679	0.73	41,966	1.04	39,920	0.84
	EU4	17,072	0.75	42,619	1.05	51,751	1.09

Notes: EU4 includes France, Germany, the Netherlands and the UK combined.
ASEAN includes Indonesia, Malaysia, Philippines, Singapore and Thailand.

Source: Masuyama and Vandenbrink (2001, p. 25).

European firms have increased their presence in East Asia, perhaps as a catch-up process. A case in point is Korea. Foreign investment in Korea has diversified recently from the traditional source of Japan to especially Europe. In 1998, over half of inward FDI to Korea came from the EU countries compared with 8 per cent from Japan. In addition to this new development of liberalized environment for foreign capital inflows in Korea, European and American firms that were targeting emerging markets in China and India were also using Korea as a strategic regional base[2]. Whereas FDI from American and European firms had previously been directed primarily to the domestic market in Korea, it has recently focused on building export platforms in Korea.

Another possible explanation is a change in the structure of technology and a resulting change in the strategy of TNCs, which has been suggested by Masuyama and Vandenbrink. In the 1990s, as information technology replaced industrial technology and the source of innovation moved from Japan to the United States, the production networks of East Asia began reshaping and the amount of FDI into the region from Europe and especially the United States increased relative to the amount coming from Japan:

> 'Compared to networks based on industrial technology, ones based on information technology tend to be more widely dispersed geographically because the delivery of information is much cheaper and faster than the delivery of physical goods. For example, the software industry in Bangalore, India is now closely linked to Silicon Valley. Because the United States, and Silicon Valley in particular, is the center of innovation in information technology and Japan plays only a limited role, networks based on information technology link Asia more with the United States (and Western Europe) and less with Japan than did in traditional production networks', (Masuyama and Vandenbrink, 2001, p. 24).

Rising importance of M&A mode

Lately, the international direct investment has increasingly been propelled by cross-border M&As[3]. Cross-border M&As were mostly used among developed advanced countries as important and widely used means for entering overseas markets in the past. But in the 1990s, the trend has extended to developing regions including Asia. For example, the worldwide M&As were $150.6 billion in 1990. They rose 4.8 times since then and reached $720 billion in 1999. In East and Southeast Asia, they rose 6.1 times, from $3.95 billion to $24.16 billion during the same period (Table 10A.2). Indeed, cross-border M&As have become an important mode of entry in developing Asia especially since the worst year (1998) of the Asian crisis was over (from $13 billion in 1998 to $24 billion in 1999). In particular, 'the most significant increases occurred in the five crisis-hit countries. Their share of total cross-border M&As in developing Asia jumped to 68 per cent in 1998 compared to 19 per cent in 1996. Cross-border M&As in the five countries as a whole reached a record level of $15 billion in 1999'[4].

In Table 10.7, we can see the amount of M&As and its share in FDI inflows in each different region in East Asia[5]. In the region as a whole, the total M&As increased slightly less than 3 times in just three years; from $8.4 billion in the pre-crisis year of 1996 to $24 billion in the post-crisis year of 1999. The share of M&As in FDI inflows similarly rose 3 times from 8.5 per cent to 26 per cent during the same period. The rise in share is particularly significant in the ASEAN-4 countries, and to a lesser extent in the first tier NIEs, compared to that in China. However, if we look into the most recent period of 1998–99, this rise is most significant for the first tier NIEs and China.

Furthermore, the ratio of M&As to the FDI inflow didn't show a single pattern: rising for Korea, Malaysia and the Philippines, but falling in Thailand. An entering pattern in these countries after the currency crisis has also changed, in that instead of greenfield investment the acquiring and re-capitalizing M&As for the existing firms increased. Two types of cross-border M&As can be distinguished: acquisitions of local firms by new foreign investors and acquisitions of shares in existing joint ventures by foreign partners. The first was encouraged by such factors as the low prices of firms when translated into foreign currencies, the new openness to M&As, and the favourable long-term prospects of the crisis-affected countries. The second took place either through acquiring more equity from a domestic partner or through buying new issues, motivated by changes in the law or to prevent a joint venture from collapse. Many domestic joint-venture partners were either in serious financial difficulties or had undertaken restructuring, spinning off their non-core businesses.

Table 10.7 M&As and their share of FDI inflows in East and Southeast Asia, 1995–1999 (US$ million, %)

	1995	1996	1997	1998	1999
E&SEA	5,854 (8.5)	8,374 (9.5)	16,390 (18.5)	13,094 (15.7)	24,156 (26.0)
First tier NIEs	3,175 (19.4)	4,474 (18.9)	9,061 (36.6)	5,403 (21.0)	16,339 (37.7)
ASEAN-4	2,276 (16.7)	1,994 (11.5)	5,473 (33.8)	6,893 (59.7)	5,662 (80.0)
China	403 (1.1)	1,906 (4.7)	1,856 (4.2)	798 (1.8)	2,155 (5.3)

Note: Numbers in parentheses are percentages of M&A sales in the total FDI inflows in each region in each year.
Source: UNCTAD, *World Investment Report* (2000) and Table 10.1.

The foreign joint-venture partners were willing to acquire equities held by their local partners, even if they were not immediately profitable. This category of acquisitions accounted for 39 per cent of all M&A deals in the Republic of Korea in 1998. Such acquisitions were also popular in Thailand, typically in component manufacturing in the automobile or electronic and electrical appliances industries (WIR 2000, 52). Cross-border M&As were especially active in industries where the degree of industrial globalization is high: namely, automobiles, chemicals, electrical and electronics in the manufacturing sector and information technology and financing in the service sector (Park, 2000, p.14).

Changing sectoral composition of FDI inflows

The sectoral composition of FDI inflows to Asia also changed in the ten years from 1988 to 1997. During this period, the share of FDI inflows to the manufacturing sector declined from 76.6 per cent to 59.5 per cent. Similarly, the share of FDI inflows to the primary sector also declined from 5.7 per cent to 2.8 per cent. But the share of FDI inflows to the service sector rose from 16.2 per cent to 35.8 per cent (Table 10.8).

Table 10.8 FDI inflows in South, East and Southeast Asia, by industry (values in US$ million and shares in percentages)

Sector/industry	1988		1997	
	Value	Share	Value	Share
All industries	18,457	100.0	118,799	100.0
Manufacturing	14,100	76.6	70,696	59.5
Primary	1,044	5.7	3,379	2.8
Services	2,994	16.2	42,472	35.8
Unspecified	279	1.5	2,252	1.9

Source: *World Investment Report* (1999).

Among various industries in the service sector, the rise was most noteworthy in transport and storage, real estate and trade industries in 1997. However, after the financial crisis, FDI into services, particularly the finance industry, increased markedly. This can be witnessed by the sales of cross-border M&As of inefficient financial institutions in the region. As can be seen in Table 10.9, cross-border sales of finance companies in the tertiary sector increased sharply after 1997, from less than $1 billion in 1996 to more than $6 billion in 1999. Accordingly, the share of finance industry in the total cross-border sale of M&As in Asia increased from 9.2 per cent in 1997 to 15.9 per cent in 1998 and further to 24.5 per cent in 1999.

IMPLICATIONS OF THESE CHANGING CONDITIONS AND CHARACTERISTICS

Unfortunately, it is too early to examine the impacts and implications of these changing conditions and characteristics of foreign investment in East Asia on macroeconomic indices such as growth, employment, exports, etc. A quantitative analysis would also be meaningless, if not impossible, because of a shortage of observable data points and a lack in consistent data series.

However, we can at least speculate for some impacts or implications of these changes in foreign investments in Asia on the following three dimensions – namely industrial structure, financial stability and growth prospects.

Table 10.9 Sales of cross-border M&As in South, East and Southeast Asia by sector and industry, 1987, 1990, 1995–1999 (US$ million)

Sector/industry	1987	1990	1995	1996	1997	1998	1999
Primary	–	15	82	3	1,705	247	167
Secondary	56	1,621	1,668	3,344	7,035	8,689	11,274
Tertiary	200	2,324	4,528	6,398	9,846	6,906	13,563
Gas, electricity, water	–	–	4	1,012	4,904	819	1,496
Construction	–	35	330	394	222	13	129
Trade	7	275	384	619	132	495	662
Hotels, restaurants	91	71	1,168	99	487	275	604
Transport, storage		1,388	780	3,135	1,188	2,062	2,914
Finance	25	122	876	928	1,704	2,522	6,136
Business services	77	433	404	212	1,175	691	1,335
Public administration	–	–	–	–	–	8	243
Education	–	–		–	1	–	1
Health - social serv.	–	–	10	–	1	8	2
Community serv.	–	–	571		34	13	42
Total	256	3,960	6,278	9,745	18,586	15,842	25,003

Source: UNCTAD, *World Investment Report* (2000).

Industrial Structure

As is well known, East Asian industrial structure is heavily geared towards manufacturing activities. During the 1970s and 1980s, Japanese investment to developing countries in Asia contributed greatly for industrialization and economic growth in these countries, especially in the first tier NIEs. For about ten years before the Asian financial crisis, the first tier NIEs also began joining Japan in this pattern of foreign direct investment to second tier NIEs, particularly to ASEAN-4 and China. Even the ASEAN-4 countries, which are relatively resource-rich, have begun switching to manufacturing and exporting labour intensive products since the mid-1980s. These developments helped to raise the image of this whole region as the most dynamic and 'miraculous' one. Indeed, as the region gets an access to additional investment sources from Western countries of Europe and the USA in the 1990s, it appeared that industrial deepening or upgrading has been taking place in this region. To reflect this, their manufacturing and exporting activities began turning from traditional textile and clothing activities to assembling activities of electronic products since the mid-1990s.

Not surprisingly, Western investments to this area began focusing on both strong and weak sectors of the economy after the Asian financial crisis. The strong sector was electronics-related industries, where Western TNCs could utilize the abundant semi-skilled workforce for assembling and exporting information technology (IT) related products. The weak sector was finance and banking industries, where Western conglomerates could easily buy these near-bankrupt financial institutions sometimes at bargain prices. Thus, as far as manufacturing industries are concerned, East Asian industrial structure has an appearance of extreme high-tech orientation. However, the recent trend of Western investment by large TNCs through M&As casts the following implications for the industrial structure in these countries.

First, the real foundation of East Asian industries is much weaker than it appears, because of a lack in technological base and innovational capacity within these countries. Their high-tech industries grew on the basis of foreign direct investment and imported key components. Consequently, they rely on external sources of innovation and these economies have not developed local industrial clusters in sufficient depth. This may relegate East Asian industries to the less profitable areas in the international division of labour ceded by external innovators and it may deprive them of opportunities to move within the international division of labour to higher order activities.

Second, the shift to IT industries as the basis for industrial production is also forcing a change in industrial organization in the region. That is, the 'full-set' industrial structure, which was the trade-mark of Japanese style industrial organization before the financial crisis, is giving way to the so-called 'network type' of Western organization. As Masuyama and Vandenbrink point out:

> 'Economic globalization together with the IT revolution are undermining the competitiveness of the large, vertically integrated industrial organizations that had been the mainstays of East Asian industry in the age of industrial technology. Networked organizations that utilize out-sourcing and supply-chain management are more suited to the new IT environment than self-contained organizations such as keiretsu and chaebol. In electronics, American corporations, which have already adopted a decentralized, network-type organization, have gained a competitive

edge over Japan's integrated corporations and they are providing a model for East Asian corporations to emulate' (Masuyama and Vandenbrink, 2001, p. 23).

Third, the recent upsurge of M&A wave in Asia, especially where it has taken the form of hostile acquisitions or 'fire-sale', has heightened concerns on such matters as ownership transfer and competition. The basis of concern is that M&As represent a change of ownership from domestic to foreign hands, while greenfield FDI represents an addition to the capital stock. This leads to such worries as: the extent to which M&As (when compared to greenfield FDI) bring resources to host countries that are needed for development; the denationalization of domestic firms; employment reduction; loss of technological assets; crowding out of domestic firms and increased market concentration and its implication for competition. Among these, perhaps the most common concern about cross-border M&As – in distinction to greenfield FDI – is their impact on domestic competition. The sheer size of many of the firms involved and their large share of global markets raise fears about growing international oligopolies and market power[6].

Financial Stability

The liberalization of capital markets and the resultant increase in portfolio investment, in addition to the increase of M&As in the FDI, raise concern for financial stability in Asian economies. In fact, as we saw in Table 10.1, the share of portfolio equity investment in the total net resource flows in Asia and the Pacific increased from 8.3 per cent in 1990 to 40 per cent in 2000. We also saw in Table 10.7 that the share of M&As in total FDI inflows in Asia had steadily increased from 8.5 per cent in 1995 to 26.0 per cent in 1999. Because of the concern, most Asian economies have reduced short-term bank lending, have set up some form of safeguard measures for financial stability and have steadily raised their foreign exchange reserves. Of course, there are reasons to be concerned. However, we should not be overly concerned and also look at some aspects on the brighter side.

First of all, FDI inflows, not portfolio inflows, have become the most important source of foreign capital flow to Asian economies after the crisis (Table 10.1). Although a part of FDI inflows can be driven by short-term financial motives and thus behave just like speculative portfolio investments, FDI as a source of finance offers advantages over other sources of foreign finance to developing host countries. It has proved to be more stable than other types of financial flows, as reflected in the Asian financial crisis and the Mexican crisis of the mid-1990s. Direct investors show a longer-term commitment to host economies than lenders (particularly short-term lenders) and speculative portfolio investors. FDI is also easier to service than commercial loans, since profits tend to be linked to the performance and business cycles of the host economy.

Perhaps for some direct investors there is a genuine choice between entering a host country through greenfield FDI and entering it through M&As. However, the two modes of entry are not always the only realistic alternatives for either TNCs or host countries, as for example when a telecommunication network is privatized or a large ailing firm needs to be rescued and no domestic buyers can be found. Thus, as was witnessed by many cases in the crisis-hit countries in Asia, when the only realistic alternative for a local firm is a closure, cross-border merger or acquisition can serve as a life preserver.

There is also a study which indicates that the volatility of capital flows in most Asian countries declined in the 1990s. Measuring financial instability or volatility by the coefficient of variation (standard deviation divided by mean), instead of standard deviation itself, Nunnenkamp (2001) finds that the financial volatility in Asia as a whole declined from the 1980s to the 1990s. The major source of financial instability (and an important cause of the Asian financial crisis in 1997) was found to be the private bank lending. But this effect was mitigated by the positive effect (i.e., declining volatility) of FDI and somewhat neutral effect of portfolio investment. Since the share of bank lending shrank to a minimum in Asia (see Table 10.1) after the financial crisis, the financial instability should not be seen as the major problem in Asia, following Nunnenkamp's approach[7].

Finally, whether FDI has a positive or negative impact on the host country's balance-of-payments depends on the following factors (WIR, 2000, p. 165): the size of FDI inflows, net of disinvestments; the outflows of direct investment income; the export and import propensities of foreign affiliates; the indirect impact of FDI on the export and import propensities of domestic firms; and the indirect impact of FDI on import demand by consumers in the host country. However, the balance-of-payments effects of FDI and the country distribution of the value added by foreign affiliates can also be affected by transfer pricing – the pricing of intra-firm transactions across national boundaries. This is the area where Asian economies should pay closer attention, because TNCs have frequently considerable freedom in assigning prices in these transactions, particularly when there are no comparable prices to serve as reference.

In sum, while keeping a close watch is still important, we should not be too worried about this new trend as it relates to the financial stability in these countries.

Domestic Investment and Growth

The assets that the FDI bundle comprises are many: capital, technology, market access, employment, skills and management techniques, etc. FDI brings in financial resources to host countries. The inflows are more stable and easier to service than commercial debt or portfolio investment. FDI can also bring modern technologies, some not available without FDI, and they can raise the efficiency with which existing technologies are used. Moreover, it can stimulate technical efficiency in local firms, suppliers, clients and competitors, by providing assistance, acting as role models and intensifying competition. FDI by TNCs can provide access to export markets, both for existing activities and for new activities that exploit the host economy's comparative advantages. FDI can also generate employment and transfer skills and management techniques (WIR, 1999, p. 317).

True, when a country is poor and saves little, additional capital from outside can help it realize investment opportunities. But over time, as a country becomes better integrated with the rest of the world, a dollar of foreign capital raises investment less than it did in the past. This shift has several explanations, among which Mishra *et al.* (2001, p. 3) point out that the composition of capital flows is changing. More specifically, they argue that foreign direct investment is being used less for 'greenfield' projects (construction of new factories), while mergers and acquisitions have become more common. At the same time, the share of portfolio capital in total inflows tends to be increased[8]. As M&As increasingly replace greenfield FDI, this may involve smaller benefits or larger negative impacts from the perspective of host country development. The financial resources provided by M&As do not always go into additions to the capital stock for production, while in the case of greenfield FDI they do. Hence a given amount of FDI through M&As may correspond to a smaller productive investment than the same amount of greenfield FDI, or to none at all (WIR, 2000, p. xxiv). In other words, the commercial objectives of TNCs and the development objectives of host economies may not necessarily coincide.

In any case, private capital flows are found to have a significant impact on domestic investment, with the relationship being strongest for foreign direct investment and international bank lending and weaker for portfolio flows. A comprehensive study by Bosworth and Collins (1999) provides evidence on the effect of capital flows on domestic investment for 58 developing countries during 1978–95. The authors distinguish among three types of inflows: FDI, portfolio investment and other financial flows (primarily bank loans). By using capital inflows and domestic investment expressed as percentages of GDP, they find that an increase of a dollar in capital flows is associated with an increase in domestic investment of about 50 cents.

However, there are significant differences among different types of inflow. FDI appears to bring about a one-for-one increase in domestic investment; there is virtually no discernible relationship between portfolio inflows and investment (i.e., little or no impact); and the impact of loans falls between those of the other two.

In connection with the implications of foreign investment on domestic investment in the East Asian context, it is worthwhile to note the following arguments that refute the validity of the 'flying geese' hypothesis for East Asian growth. The first is an argument put forward by Bernard and Ravenhill (1995), in that many Asian economies are lacking absorptive capacity. They argue that the flying geese model of development cannot be applied to most Asian economies, except maybe Korea and Taiwan, because export manufacturing in these economies relies entirely on foreign technology and components and is carried out for the most part by subsidiaries of transnational corporations[9]. In a slightly different context, Borensztein *et al.* (1998) also find that the FDI inflows increase economic growth when the level of education in the host country – a measure of its absorptive capacity – is high, which is not the case for many Asian economies. The second is an argument put forward by Masuyama and Vandenbrink (2001), in that there has been a global paradigm shift from industrial technology to information technology. They argue that, with the recent development of cross-border M&As and the closer integration of economies around the globe, the full-set component of production, which has been the trade-mark of East Asian growth, is fast losing its relevance[10].

CONCLUSION: FUTURE PROSPECTS OF FOREIGN INVESTMENTS IN ASIA

We have attempted to find the changing nature of foreign investments in developing Asian countries especially after the financial crisis in this chapter. As a first step, we have looked at changing supply and demand conditions of foreign investments in the region in the past few years. On the supply side of FDI inflows, we examined a change in international capital flows that has been geared towards FDI and portfolio investments rather than bank lending or grants, and a change in international production system where the role of TNCs has increasingly been strengthened. On the demand side of FDI inflows, an increased competition for external source of funds in Asia and the resulting acceleration of deregulations on FDI inflows, as well as a reduction in production costs (particularly wages and rents) were examined. From these changes in the conditions of foreign investments, the following changes in the characteristics of FDI in East Asia after the financial crisis were noted: 1) the regional composition of FDI was changed in such a way that the share of FDI from Western countries of the USA and Europe increased while that from Japan decreased; 2) cross-border M&As became an important mode of FDI entry in Asia; 3) sectoral composition of FDI also changed in such a way that more investments were directed to the services sector, particularly to financial industries. Finally, we have ventured to find the implications of these changing conditions and characteristics on the industrial structure, the financial stability and the domestic investment of Asian economies.

What then can be said of the future prospects of foreign investment in developing countries of East Asia? The future prospects of foreign investment in East Asia will primarily be determined by the growth prospect of these countries. The most important reason why there was a continuous rise of FDI inflows to East Asia in the 1980s and 1990s before the financial crisis was the strong and dynamic economic growth of these countries. Again, the sharp rise of FDI inflows to Asia in 1999 and 2000 was not coincidental with a strong (V-shape) rebound of growth in many of these economies, where economic growth plunged immediately after the financial crisis. In short, economic growth and FDI are mutually dependent on each other, so that a change in FDI inflow affects growth at the same time economic growth affects the inflow of FDI. However, the future prospects of foreign investment in Asia will also be affected by other factors, in both positive and negative ways, among which the following should be given closer attention.

Changing Global Trends

We have already mentioned the ongoing worldwide trends that have already been affecting industrial restructuring, and consequently economic transformation, of the East Asian economies. These are a shift from industrial to information technology, a trend towards liberalization and deregulation in trade and investment, and especially a continuing globalization of capital markets. To some extent these trends are interrelated and their combination is spearheading economic globalization. For instance, an advance in information technology and a relaxation of national controls on foreign exchange and financial markets make the free flow of foreign investment possible, with little regard for national boundaries. Indeed, the cross-border production network is being forcefully carried out by FDI of the TNCs. The future strength of these global trends will certainly affect the future supply condition of foreign investments in a significant way.

Economic Restructuring

The economic growth, which is affected by FDI inflows, is also dependent on how well and how fast restructuring efforts in the corporate, financial, labour and public sectors of these countries are progressing in East Asia. Basically, economic restructuring affects economic growth by reducing waste and raising efficiency. But, it also affects entry conditions of foreign investment in the process. For example, restructuring the financial sector by selling off inefficient banks or financial institutions and by accelerating deregulations will have a positive influence on foreign investors to take part in this process.

Vulnerability to External Shocks

One of the major lessons of the financial crisis was that excessive reliance on foreign resources or markets leaves growth prospects extremely vulnerable to external shocks. After the Asian financial crisis, policy makers in the crisis-hit countries rightly rejected a retreat into protectionism. But it would be just as wrong for them to allow global market forces to dictate future growth and development. In fact, there is a nationalistic sentiment within East Asian economies that foreign TNCs are ruthlessly invading markets of crisis-hit Asian countries.

As domestic savings is likely to remain high, a need or dependence on foreign capital will be that much less. Therefore, greater attention also needs to be given to domestic sources of growth, such as higher social spending. There is a major role for public investment and the involvement of a development state, with new policy agendas. Regional economic ties are likely to remain important and should be strengthened, *inter alia*, though collective defence mechanisms against systematic financial instability and contagion (Trade and Development Report, 2000, VII). As this kind of sentiment prevails, the demand for foreign capital or investment will be affected in a negative way.

Rivalry among Asian Economies and the China Factor

As more and more developing countries opt for outward-oriented development strategies, both the vulnerability to trade shocks and the risk of fallacy of composition tend to increase. This applies to both trade and investment dimensions. In this respect, today's conditions are quite different from those prevailing in the 1960s and 1970s when only a handful of East Asian countries were pursuing outward-oriented strategies, had easy access to the markets of industrial countries and faced no major challenge from other third-world producers or from the importing countries themselves. Today, there is a rivalry among Asian economies – especially between China and the rest of Asia – for foreign investment or for export markets. The rivalry may work against a particular country in its attempt to attract foreign investment. Thus, there might be a regional distribution problem of FDI inflows. But in the region as a whole, more investments would be forthcoming as a result of an increased competition from China[11]. In fact, the continued inflow of foreign investment to China contributed to the total inflow of FDI to East Asia not falling sharply immediately after the crisis in 1998.

NOTES

1. *World Investment Report 2000.*
2. Woo (2001), p. 279.
3. Defined as the acquisition of more than 10 per cent equity share (*World Investment Report 2000*, p. 10).
4. *World Investment Report 2000*, p. 52.
5. It is important to note, however, that it is not possible to determine precisely the share of cross-border M&As in FDI inflows. M&As can be financed locally or directly from international capital markets; neither is included in FDI data. FDI data are reported on a net basis, M&A data are not. Moreover, payments for M&As (including those involving privatizations) can be phased over several years (UNCTAD, *World Investment Report 1999*, p. 8).
6. For more detail on the general implications of M&As, see *World Investment Report 2000*, pp. 14–15.
7. However, his approach should be balanced by other studies and approaches (Fernandez-Arias and Hausmann, 2000, for example), some of which lead to different conclusions.
8. Other explanations by Mishra *et al.* for this shift include the following. First, countries have recently built up larger foreign exchange reserves, partly in response to the greater need for liquidity to ward off financial crises resulting from sudden flights of private capital. Second, capital outflows are apparently increasing. Outflows are not well captured in international statistics, but it appears that traditional 'flight' of domestic capital and 'round-tripping' (that is, when capital flows out and then flows back in) to escape domestic taxes are not the only reasons for outflows. Some part of the capital flows represents a diversification of investment portfolios by domestic residents and, ultimately, benefits both the residents and the global economy (Mishra *et al.*, 2001, p. 3).
9. 'The predominance of foreign firms in many sectors of manufacturing in Southeast Asia and the continued dependence of such firms on technology and component inputs from overseas casts doubt on the relevance of the flying geese analogy for Southeast Asia. Certainly, even if the different regional, global and technological environments in which industrialization is occurring are ignored, the pattern of manufacturing development in these countries – the overwhelming dependence on foreign firms, export-oriented manufacturing that does not build on an import-substituting base, and the lack of linkages with local components

suppliers – is very different from that experienced by Japan or by Korea and Taiwan' (Bernard and Ravenhill, 1995, p. 199).

10. 'With the progress of globalization and the IT revolution, the flying geese model is becoming less relevant to describe the pattern of development in East Asia. Differences in the adaptability of East Asian economies to globalization and IT are disturbing the order of the flying geese. The flying geese pattern of economic and industrial development in East Asia had two components: the traditional sequential development of individual 'full-set' industrial structures, as seen in Japan and Korea, and the production networks through FDI. With the closer integration of economies around the globe, the full-set component is losing significance and the network component is becoming dominant' (Masuyama and Vandenbrink, 2001, p. 39).
11. There is an argument that Asian countries are composed of economies at various stages of development with different qualities of comparative advantage, which makes FDI inflow to a certain country complementary, not competitive, to other countries in the region. It is also sceptical to believe China's official FDI numbers, because of 'round-tripping' of mainland investment disguised as FDI: 'At more than $40 billion annually, China's FDI numbers look impressive.' But much of China's FDI comes from Taiwan and Hong Kong, at least some of which represents the round-tripping of mainland investment disguised as FDI. Errors and omissions in China's balance of payments last year also amounted to $11.89 billion (*Far Eastern Economic Review*, 2001).

REFERENCES

Bernard, M. and J. Ravenhill (1995), 'Beyond product cycles and flying geese: regionalization, hierarchy, and the industrialization of East Asia', *World Politics*, **47**, 171–209.

Borensztein, E., J. De Gregorio and J.-W. Lee (1998), 'How does foreign direct investment affect economic growth?', *Journal of International Economics*, **45**, 115–35.

Bosworth, B.P. and S.M. Collins (1999), 'Capital flows to developing economies: implications for saving and investment,' *Brookings Papers on Economic Activity*: 1, Brookings Institution, 143–69.

Far Eastern Economic Review, Aug. 2, 40–43.

Fernandez-Arias, E. and R. Hausmann (2000), *Is FDI a Safer Form of Financing?*, Inter-American Development Bank, Working Paper 416, Washington, D.C.

Japan External Trade Organization (JETRO) (2000), *White Paper on Foreign Investment*.

Masuyama, S. and D. Vandenbrink (2001), 'Industrial restructuring in East Asian economies for the twenty-first century', in S. Masuyama, D. Vandenbrink and C. S. Yue (eds), *Industrial Restructuring in East Asia towards the 21st Century*, Nomura Research Institute and Institute of Southeast Asian Studies, Tokyo and Singapore, 3–54.

Mishra, D., A. Mody and A. Panini Murshid (2001), 'Private capital flows and growth', *Finance and Development*, June, 2–5.

Nunnenkamp, P. (2001), 'Too much, too little, or too volatile? International capital flows to developing countries in the 1990s', *Journal of International Economic Studies*, Korea Institute for International Economic Policy (KIEP), **5** (1), 119–47.

Park, Y.H. (2000), *The Expansion of Global Conglomerates into Asia after the Economic Crisis and Its Implications*, Korea Institute of Economic Policy (KIEP).

UNCTAD (2000), *World Investment Report: Cross-border Mergers and Acquisitions and Development - Overview*, UN: New York and Geneva.

Woo, C. (2001), 'Industrial upgrading of Korea: process, prospects and policies', in S. Masuyama, D. Vandenbrink and C.S. Yue (eds), *Industrial Restructuring in East Asia towards the 21st Century*, Nomura Research Institute and Institute of Southeast Asian Studies, Tokyo and Singapore, 256–304.

World Bank (2000), *Trade and Development Report*.

World Bank (2001 and 2003), *Global Development Finance*.

APPENDIX

Table A10.1 FDI inflows, by host region and economy, 1988–1999 (US$ million)

	1988–93 (yr. ave.)	1994	1995	1996	1997	1998	1999
World	190,629	255,988	331,844	377,516	473,052	680,082	865,487
Developed	140,088	145,135	205,693	219,789	275,229	480,638	636,449
EU	78,511	76,866	114,387	108,604	128,574	248,675	305,058
USA	44,781	45,095	58,772	84,455	105,488	186,316	275,533
Japan	737	912	39	200	3,200	3,192	12,741
Developing	46,919	104,920	111,884	145,030	178,789	179,481	207,619
S, E, SEA	27,113	65,954	71,654	87,952	93,518	87,158	96,148
E.&SEA	26,407	64,345	68,670	84,398	88,582	83,455	92,918
China	8,852	33,787	35,849	40,180	44,236	43,751	40,400
H.K.	3,689	7,828	6,213	10,460	11,368	14,776	23,068
Korea	956	991	1,357	2,308	3,088	5,215	10,340
Singapore	3,982	8,550	7,206	8,984	8,085	5,493	6,984
Taiwan	1,160	1,375	1,559	1,864	2,248	222	2,926
Indonesia	1,269	2,109	4,346	6,194	4,677	–356	–3,270
Malaysia	3,320	4,581	5,816	7,296	6,513	2,700	3,532
Philippines	770	1,591	1,459	1,520	1,249	1,752	737
Thailand	1,899	1,343	2,000	2,405	3,732	7,449	6,078
Cambodia	44	69	151	294	168	121	135
Laos	10	59	88	128	86	45	79
Myanmar	137	126	277	310	387	315	300
Vietnam	319	1,936	2,349	2,455	2,745	1,972	1,609

Source: UNCTAD, *World Investment Report 2000*.

Table A10.2 Cross-border M&A sales, by region/economy of seller, 1987, 1990, 1995–1999 (US$ million)

Region / Economy	1987	1990	1995	1996	1997	1998	1999
Total world	74,509	150,576	186,593	277,023	304,848	531,648	720,109
Developed economies	72,804	134,239	164,589	188,722	234,748	445,118	644,590
EU	12,761	62,133	75,143	81,895	114,591	187,853	344,537
USA	51,765	54,697	53,237	68,069	81,707	209,548	233,032
Japan	27	148	541	1,719	3,083	4,022	15,857
Developing economies	1,704	16,052	15,966	34,700	64,573	80,755	64,550
S, E, SEA	256	3,960	6,278	9,745	18,586	15,842	25,003
E&SEA	256	3,953	5,854	8,374	16,390	13,094	24,156
China		8	403	1,906	1,856	798	2,155
H.K.	181	2,620	1,703	3,267	7,330	938	3,152
Korea			192	564	836	3,973	9,057
Singapore	21	1143	1,238	593	294	468	2,060
Taiwan		11	42	50	601	24	2,070
Indonesia	29		809	530	332	683	1,112
Malaysia		86	98	768	351	1,096	1,101
Philippines	25	15	1,208	462	4,157	1,905	1,637

Source: UNCTAD, *World Investment Report 2000.*

11. Foreign Direct Investment as a Factor in Asian Regional Development

Nathalie Aminian

INTRODUCTION

An important issue in the debate over the necessity of free capital mobility for developing countries is whether capital inflows have significant effects on real economy. Proponents of capital account liberalization invoke the growth-promoting attributes of capital inflows as an important factor in the process of financial integration and regional development. It is worth noting that the attitudes in developing countries toward capital flows have shifted over time. In the 1970s many countries maintained a rather cautious position with respect to foreign capital. In the 1980s, the attitudes shifted radically toward a more welcoming stancc in policy. Developing countries have indeed adopted policies conducive to the liberalization of their capital account, although the pace was quite different from one region to another in conjunction with the diversity of countries' experiences. Asia, contrary to Latin America, is a frequently cited example of a 'partial' and 'cautious' liberalization. Most Latin American economies were relatively open even in the 1960s and the progress toward capital account liberalization was continued until the early 1980s and reversed at the time of the debt crisis. In Asia, the pattern has been different, with a steady decline in the number of countries imposing capital account restrictions since the late 1970s, and no increase around the time of the debt crisis. In the early 1990s, the process of the capital account liberalization was accelerated. Not only did capital flows to Asia increase more rapidly, but their composition changed substantially as well. Foreign direct investment and portfolio flows (bonds and equities) replaced commercial bank debt as the dominant sources of foreign capital. These capital inflows in Asia increased domestic investment, and increased investment contributed to achieving higher growth. Good economic performances drew further capital inflows. A 'virtuous cycle' of capital flows and economic growth was actually an important part of the Asian development. However, the Asian currency crisis in the late 1990s and the shocks of volatile capital outflows increased doubts about the benefits of such flows. Since then, Asian countries' demand for external capital has declined. Empirical studies underlined this new scepticism; implying a weak relationship between capital inflows and the performance of developing countries. But still, conventional wisdom suggests that foreign direct investment is the most favourable form of capital inflows because it is supposed to be more stable compared to alternatives, especially bank lending. Direct investment is, indeed, more costly to reverse and less sensitive to economic shocks.

As empirical literature provides diverging outcomes about the real effects of private capital inflows, it is relevant to investigate the role of capital inflows in the economic development in Asia and specifically, to examine the link between foreign direct investment and growth in the long run to leave out business-cycle fluctuations and short run shocks.

This chapter characterizes the capital inflows in selected East Asian countries (China, Indonesia, South Korea, Malaysia, the Philippines, Singapore and Thailand) before and after the Asian financial crisis, and empirically investigates the impact of capital inflows on economic variables over the 1980–2000 period.

The chapter is structured as follows. The second section provides an overview of the discussion of the contribution of capital inflows to increased economic growth. The third section presents a descriptive analysis of capital flows (direct investment and portfolio investment) in selected East Asian countries. The fourth section presents an empirical investigation and discusses the regression results. A final section concludes.

THEORETICAL ISSUES

The contribution of foreign direct investment (FDI) to economic growth has been debated quite extensively in the literature. This debate has clarified the channels through which FDI may help to raise growth in the recipient country. Two main channels have been emphasized: the process of technological diffusion and capital accumulation in the host country.

Technology Diffusion

Recent developments in growth theory have highlighted the importance of technological change for economic growth[1]. The growth rates of developing countries are supposed to be highly dependent on the extent to which these countries can adopt and implement new technologies available in developed countries. Thus, growth rates in developing countries are explained by a 'catch-up' process in the level of technology. Technology diffusion can take place through different channels that involve the transmission of ideas and new technologies: importation of high-technology products, adoption of foreign technology and acquisition of human capital. Among these channels, FDI[2] by multinational corporations (MNCs) is considered to be the most important. MNCs are among the most technologically advanced firms and are supposed to invest heavily in research and development, which is why their FDI may exert a positive influence on the process of technological change in the host country[3]. This knowledge spillover leads to higher productivity of capital and labour in the host country, and the main contribution of FDI is therefore in terms of improving total factor productivity.

The new growth literature has provided a framework in which to improve empirical studies. But the evidence is not clear: there is both positive and negative impact of FDI on growth[4]. Gupta and Islam (1983) try to explain growth with a set of pooled cross-country and time series data for a large group of developing countries over several sub-periods during 1950-73. They conclude to a non -significant coefficient of the FDI variable. Husain and Jun (1992) use a similar method for pooled data for the ASEAN countries over 1970-88. They find a positive effect for the FDI variable. Borensztein *et al.* (1995) study the impact of FDI from industrial countries to 69 developing countries. They find that FDI contributes to growth in less-developed countries through technology transfer. FDI is thus considered to contribute relatively more to growth than domestic investment, by implementing technologies with higher productivity. Given a sample of eight Asian countries (four NIES and ASEAN 4) from 1976 to 1997, Ito (1999) finds a positive link between annual growth rate and one year lagged FDI when controlling for the change in the yen/dollar exchange rate, Japan's growth rate and the US growth rate. He shows that the weighted average of growth rate of Asian economies tends to increase when the yen appreciates from the preceding year, and higher growth in Japan and the United States helps the growth of the selected countries. For individual economies, results are quite different: the FDI effect on growth is evident for Hong Kong, Thailand and Malaysia; the yen/dollar exchange rate seems to influence growth in Korea, Taiwan, Thailand and Malaysia; the Japanese growth has a positive effect on Korea, Taiwan and Thailand, while the US growth has a positive effect only on Taiwan. Regressions for Singapore, Indonesia and the Philippines do not produce any meaningful results.

To understand better the relationship between capital flows and economic growth, other studies emphasize that FDI does exert a positive influence on growth only given certain characteristics of the economy in the host country. They suggest that whether FDI boosts growth is contingent on additional factors within the host country, e.g. the initial level of development, human capital development, trade policy, financial development, legal system development, etc. De Mello (1999) speaks of the 'absorptive capacity' of the recipient country. Some studies do explicitly examine such factors. Balasubramanyam *et al.* (1996) test the hypothesis that foreign trade and FDI are complements for 46 developing countries. To do that, they take into account the trade orientation of countries, and thus divide the sample into countries pursuing export promoting policies and those pursuing import substitution policies. They stress that FDI is more likely to promote growth in countries that are export oriented, and moreover FDI is negatively related to growth in countries which are import-oriented. Borensztein *et al.* (1998) show that the effect of FDI on economic growth is dependent on the level of human capital available in the host economy. There is a strong positive interaction between FDI and the level of educational attainment, used as proxy for human capital. De Mello and Fukasaku (2000) studied the relationship between foreign trade and FDI in selected Latin American and Southeast Asian economies over the period 1970–94. They found that the impact of FDI on the trade balance is more significant in trade-oriented economies, i.e. in Southeast Asian countries rather than in Latin American ones. Edison *et al.* (2002) investigate the impact of international financial integration on real variables for 57 countries over the period 1980–2000, and show that this relationship depends on the level of economic development, financial development, legal system development, government corruption and macroeconomic policies. However, they find that capital flows are not robustly related to economic growth even when they take into account the economic, financial, institutional and macroeconomic characteristics.

Capital Accumulation

Capital inflows may enhance economic growth by augmenting capital accumulation in the host country. Net capital inflows increase resources that the recipient country can use. Thus, capital inflows have been associated with a rise in domestic investment in many developing countries. Investment is believed to promote economic growth and higher growth, in turn, invites more investment, exhibiting a 'virtuous cycle'. The link between capital flows and investment depends on the nature of the capital flows and on the domestic investment climate. Long-term capital flows – such as FDI – are strongly and positively associated with domestic investment; short-term flows – such as PFI – have little impact related to investment. FDI is often supposed to be a preferred form of capital inflows for host countries. Compared to bank lending or portfolio bonds, it is more difficult to withdraw investment that has become real assets.

FDI may increase investment and then economic growth on condition that it does not 'crowd out' equal amounts of investment from domestic sources by competing in product markets or financial markets. But it is worth noting that, conversely, FDI may support the expansion of domestic firms by complementing production or by increasing productivity through the spillover of advanced technology. In other words, FDI may generate either 'crowding-in' or 'crowding-out' effects on domestic investment. Jansen (1993) distinguishes three major explanations of the positive effect of FDI on domestic investment. First of all, FDI is part of private investment, so any increase in FDI may contribute to an increase in private investment. Second, new FDI projects may induce complementary domestic private investments 'that provide inputs to, or use outputs of, the foreign firm'. Third, an important part of foreign investment projects is actually financed from domestic financial markets[5].

However, FDI can also have adverse effects, as the 1994 Mexican and 1997 Asian crises illustrated. For example, foreign capital flows may complicate monetary policy and drive up real exchange rates when the size of capital inflows becomes exceptionally large. This is inconvenient in countries which have adopted a fixed exchange rate mechanism. Ito (1999) considers that capital flows to Asian countries have been too important – relative to the current account deficits – in the 1990s, sometimes exceeding 10 per cent of GDP. Moreover, these countries have adopted a *de facto* dollar peg. Thus, the logic of 'virtuous cycle' worked in reverse, generating a 'vicious cycle'.

Otherwise, Feldstein (1994) stresses that the impact of FDI inflows on domestic investment is ambiguous. Foreign capital may indeed raise domestic investment, but it may also increase imports and thus can dampen domestic production and investment. From a more general perspective, it is worth noting that analysing the effect of FDI on local investment requires taking into account the possibility that capital outflows may be induced. Furthermore, in a world of high capital mobility, an increase in inflows may have no impact on local investment because funds would move only to finance investment demand without increasing that demand. Feldstein considers that the close relationship between FDI and local investment suggests a lack of deep integration in the financing of investment projects: when almost all domestic savings goes to domestic investment, international capital inflows will not be significantly offset by international outflows and aggregate domestic investment will be close to the full amount of the inflows. But as financial integration increases, the link between FDI and domestic investment will weaken. East Asia and Latin America are more integrated into the global economy and the financial markets than other developing regions and are considered as the most important FDI recipients. The link between FDI and local investment may thus be weaker than in other regions[6].

The relationship between FDI and domestic investment may also depend on a variety of domestic factors such as the depth of financial markets, human capital and political stability. These factors define a country's ability to translate FDI into domestic investment.

The complex relationship between FDI and domestic investment requires empirical answers, which a growing body of research on emerging economies has attempted to provide. Feldstein (1994) found that a dollar of capital inflows is associated with a one-dollar rise in local investment. Borensztein *et al.* (1998) highlight similar results. They also find some evidence of a crowding-in effect, i.e. FDI is complementary to domestic investment. Bosworth and Collins (1999) consider that capital flows have a strong impact on domestic investment, especially as far as FDI is concerned. In contrast, PFI has a positive but statistically insignificant impact on investment.

In addition, the association between FDI and domestic investment became noticeably weaker in the 1990s, reflecting increased integration of some countries into the international financial markets: hence, domestic savings and investment decisions are less correlated. Moreover, during the 1990s, cross-border mergers and acquisitions (M&A) activity accounted for an increasing fraction of FDI[7]. Greenfield FDI is positively correlated to productive capacity, whereas M&A is not. According to World Bank studies (2001), M&A activity in East Asia increased by 34 per cent in 1998 and about 45 per cent in 1999, owing to the easing of government barriers to such transactions and the fall in the foreign currency value of assets after the currency depreciation induced by the financial crisis. These increases in M&A activity make understanding and the measure of the relationship between FDI and domestic investment more difficult.

Regional Development

An aspect of the impact of FDI on growth and economic development for less developing countries that remains under-studied is that of regional integration and membership in trade blocs. Haveman *et al.* (2001) tried to consider the impact of trade flows, inward FDI, preferential treatment of less-developed countries and membership in trade blocs. They find that openness and FDI inflows do lead to increased growth, membership in a trade bloc facilitates growth and the dispersion of income in the trade bloc also encourages faster growth among member countries.

These results highlight the significant role of regional integration in the growth process and represent an important issue and a challenge particularly for East Asian countries.

DESCRIPTIVE ANALYSIS

This section presents the evolution of FDI and PFI flows to Asian selected countries. FDI and PFI variables represent respectively the ratios of FDI and PFI to GDP.

From Figure 11.1, it is striking that all selected countries significantly increased FDI flows during the 1990s. However, the composition of capital flows is different across countries. China and Malaysia are countries that encouraged and received FDI. Their PFI inflows are small or even negative in the case of Malaysia. Korea is the single country where not only does PFI outweigh FDI but, in some subperiods, FDI net flows are negative. Thailand is the main recipient of capital flows (FDI and PFI) between 1993 and 1996, but PFI magnitude is higher than FDI. To get further examination of the composition of capital flows in Asia, it is useful to look at PFI. PFI consists of equities, bonds and other securities investment. Figure 11.2 shows two types of PFI: equity and fixed income (bonds) investment. We can notice that in the 1980s equity foreign portfolio investment (EFPI) was almost non-existent in any country. In the early 1990s, EFPI increased in each country, showing their financial integration. EFPI is a prominent variable because it is supposed to have a positive direct effect on macroeconomic performance in emerging economies (Durham, 2004).

It is worth noting that the Asian crisis was preceded by a strong boom in capital flows, particularly PFI flows. The reversal in 1997 – for the affected Asian countries[8] – corresponded predominantly to a fall in PFI inflows, and specially fixed income foreign portfolio investment. It is also notable that FDI inflows continued during the crisis, moderating only slightly. This is why we can consider FDI as a factor of economic recovery and development in this region. Contrary to other capital inflows, FDI is quite independent from financial fluctuations.

EMPIRICAL INVESTIGATION

This section seeks to shed light on the relationship between capital inflows (FDI and PFI) and real variables.

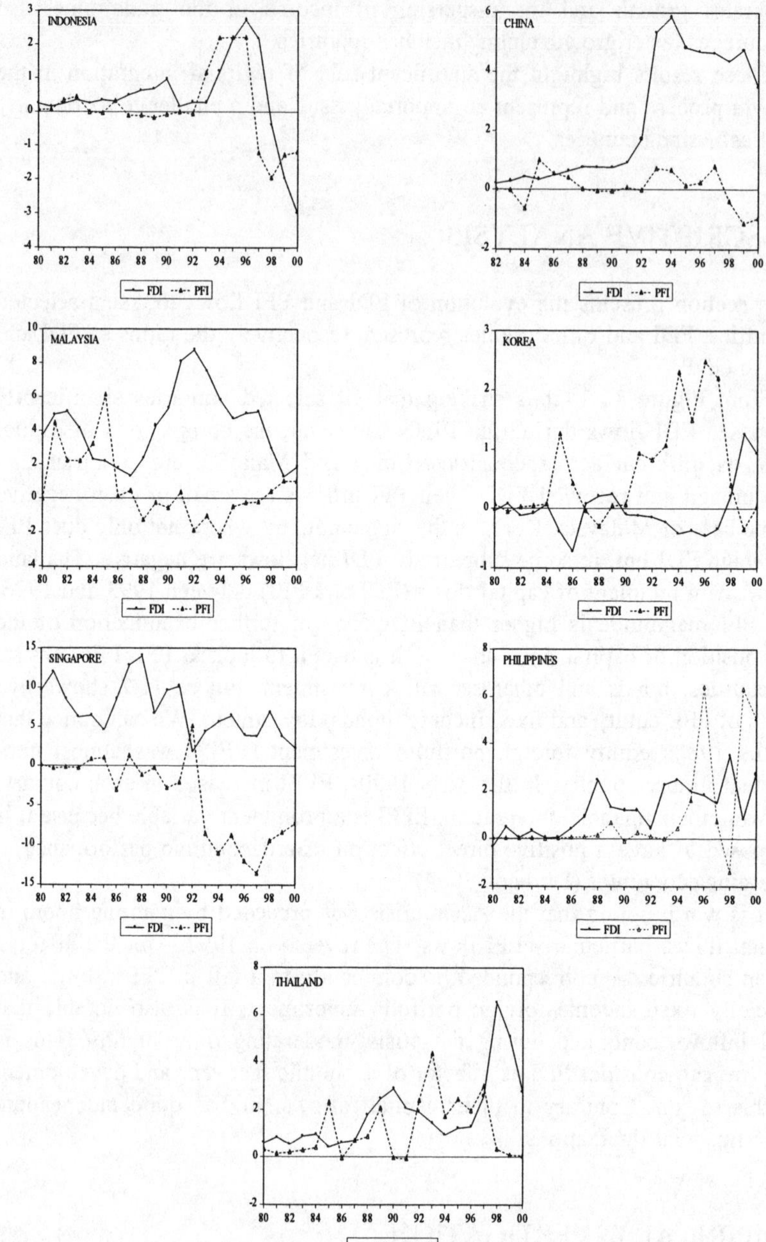

Figure 11.1 Net FDI and PFI inflows (as a share of GDP) to selected Asian countries

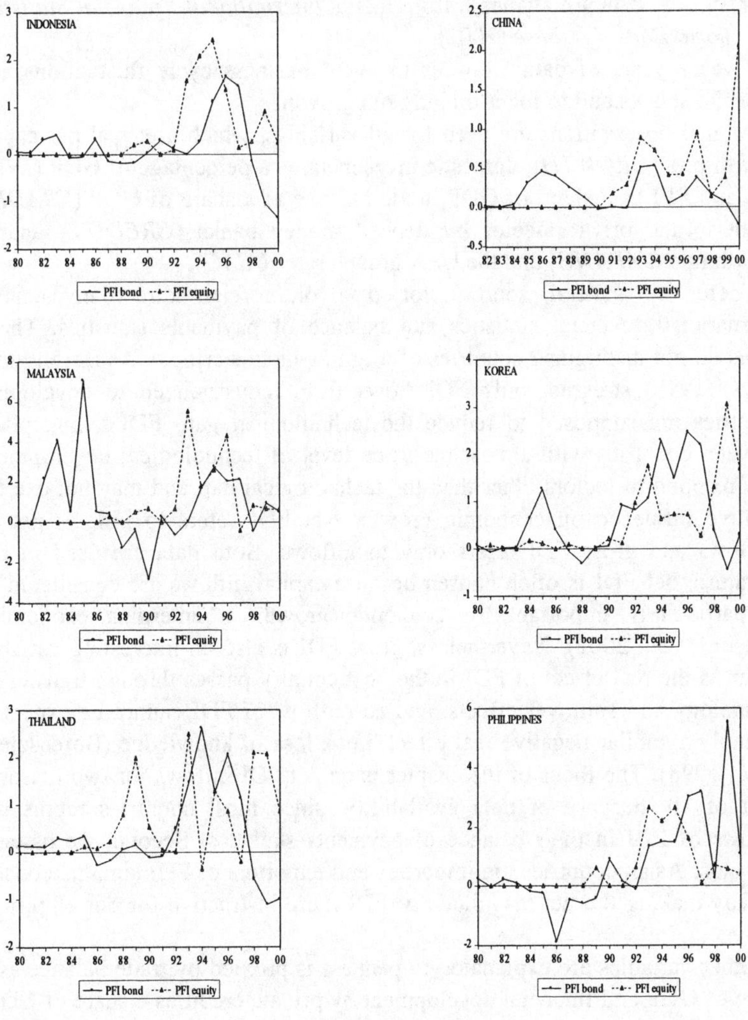

Note: Data are not available for Singapore.

Figure 11.2 Composition of PFI (bond and equity as a share of GDP) in selected Asian countries

The Data

The data used in this chapter span 1980 through 2000 except for China (1982–2000), reflecting the problem of the availability of data for this country. The data are available from IMF's *International Financial Statistics and World Bank database* (2002).

Twenty years of data allow us to avoid business cycle fluctuations and financial shocks and to focus on long run growth.

Annual observations are used for all variables, which are: real per capita growth rate (*GROWTH*), domestic investment as a percentage of GDP (*INV*), FDI and PFI as a share of GDP, trade balance as a share of GDP (*TRADE*), credit to the private sector by deposit money banks (*CREDIT*), Japan's growth rate (*JAPANG*) and the USA growth rate (*USAG*).

There are several sources for data on foreign direct investment: international financial statistics and balance of payments statistics. These series do not distinguish countries of origin, which is critical. As Borensztein *et al.* (1998) stressed, only FDI flows from industrialized to developing countries are supposed to reduce the technological gap. FDI taking place between countries with almost the same level of technological development may respond to factors other than the technological gap and may not exert a positive influence on economic growth. Net FDI refers to inflows net of outflows and gross FDI refers only to inflows. Both data are used in the literature: net FDI is often chosen because capital inflows are considered to be particularly important for economic growth in emerging economies (Edison *et al.*, 2002). Nevertheless, gross FDI is also an interesting variable as far as the real effect of FDI in the host country passes through transfer of technology and spillover effects, and an outflow of FDI cannot be expected to imply a similar negative real effect, i.e. a loss of knowledge (Borensztein *et al.*, 1998). The focus of the chapter is on net FDI inflows for two reasons. First of all, because of data availability, since most countries report net inflows of FDI in their balance of payments statistics. Second, we assume that most Asian countries are importers and exporters of FDI simultaneously, thereby making the net magnitude of FDI more instructive for our empirical study.

Other variables are explanatory: openness is proxied by trade balance as a share of GDP and financial development by private credit as a share of GDP. The significance of Japan's growth rate and the USA growth rate for Asian economic performances is discussed in Ito (1999). Indeed, the most important trade partners for Asian countries are Japan and the United States. Therefore, the income effect of the Japanese and the US growth should have a positive impact on growth performances of Asian economies.

Unit Root Tests

As for preliminary stationary analysis, the integration properties of the data are assessed using conventional unit root tests. The results of the unit root tests are summarized in Table 11.1.

Causality Tests

The statistics reported in Table 11.2 are conventional *F*-tests of the null hypothesis that *T Granger does not cause F*. The causal knowledge is instructive for the examination of the relationship between variables, and allows for the analysis of causation when the variables are cointegrated.

Results show the existence of feedback effects and suggest a strong association between variables. Paradoxically, in Indonesia, FDI does not Granger-cause domestic investment and in the Philippines FDI does not Granger-cause economic growth. We assume that no meaningful results would be shown for the Philippines as far as even domestic investment does not Granger-cause growth.

Econometric Methodology and Regression Results

To assess empirically the effect of capital inflows on economic growth, we use the following basic formulation:

$$GROWTH = \alpha_0 + \alpha_1 X + \alpha_2 Y + \xi$$

where *X* and *Y* are vectors of variables and ξ is an error term, *X* is a vector of capital inflows (FDI or PFI as a share of GDP), *Y* is a vector of variables that are generally supposed to be important to explain economic growth (*INV*, *CREDIT*, *TRADE*) or economic growth in East Asia (*JAPANG*, *USAG*).

Long run regression results are shown in Tables 11.3 and 11.4, and concern each country separately. Our results do not robustly support the idea that FDI boosts economic growth:

- The FDI effect on the growth is evident only for Malaysia; FDI inflows have a negative impact on growth in China, Indonesia and Thailand.
- Regressions for Korea, the Philippines and Singapore did not produce any meaningful result.
- PFI seems to influence positively growth in Indonesia, the Philippines and Thailand, and negatively in Malaysia.

Table 11.1 Unit root tests

	Level	Difference	Level	Difference	Level	Difference	Level	Difference	Level	Difference	Level	Difference
CHINA	−3.3441**	−4.9530***	−1.7936	−2.9842*	−1.4333	−4.1165***	−1.9810	−3.8107**	−1.2345	−3.6373**	−0.1646	−3.0706**
INDONESIA	−2.6979*	−4.6052***	−2.4168	−3.4275**	−3.4444**		−2.5477	−3.0963**	−0.9807	−4.1338***	−0.3113	−4.2319***
KOREA	−3.2372**		−1.9323	−3.4291**	−2.6955*	−3.6028**	−1.9660	−3.1856**	−0.6251	−6.2346***	0.7316	−3.5972**
MALAYSIA	−2.8413	−4.0689***	−2.2399	−2.9136*	−2.5267	−2.9124*	−1.7784	−3.5718**	0.6231	−3.8980***	−0.9733	−3.9456***
PHILIPPINES	−3.3099**		−2.7302*	−3.6055**	−1.5176	−4.0236***	−2.5952	−8.4419***	0.0790	−3.3923**	−1.3732	−3.7061**
SINGAPORE	−4.1091***		−1.8651	−2.9414*	−2.3899	−4.8266***	−1.3075	−4.5504***	−2.8653*	−3.4897**	−2.0696	−2.5971
THAILAND	−2.3306	−3.5519**	−2.4551	−3.0133**	−2.5654	−3.7780**	−2.4537	−4.1706***	1.6291	−5.0928***	−2.0783	−3.0527*

Note: The numbers reported are augmented Dickey–Fuller statistics, significant at 10%, 5% and 1%, respectively.

Table 11.2 Granger causality tests

Country	Null hypothesis FDI → GROWTH	Null hypothesis GROWTH → FDI	Null hypothesis FDI → INV	Null hypothesis INV → FDI	Null hypothesis INV → GROWTH	Null hypothesis GROWTH → INV
CHINA	0.4086	1.3205	3.7941	4.4787**	1.2210	0.6452
INDONESIA	2.62042	7.2573**	5.2215**	0.9100	0.6045	12.9352**
KOREA	0.2016	4.6183**	0.1081	2.3833	2.3369	0.9025
MALAYSIA	0.3281	5.9347**	2.1527	1.6266	1.3776	10.6707***
PHILIPPINES	4.4364**	1.5583	0.3175	2.0842	4.4364**	1.5583
SINGAPORE	0.9320	0.1578	1.2071	0.4139	1.4651	0.3237
THAILAND	1.9834	1.1149	0.6427	1.4131	2.0524	19.1940***

Note: ** and *** significant at 5% and 1%, respectively. The results were obtained using two lags for each variable, otherwise the number of lags is specified in parentheses. The number of lags was chosen by the Schwartz criterion.

- The Japanese economic growth has a positive spillover effect on Malaysia and Thailand, while the US economic growth does not exert any influence on Asian economies.

Table 11.5 shows the regression results about the relationship between FDI and domestic investment. The FDI inflows have a positive spillover effect on Indonesia, the Philippines and Thailand. We propose to get to the core of this relationship by distinguishing the 1980s and the 1990s. The regression results by decade (1980–90 and 1991–2000) are presented in Tables 11.6 and 11.7. The positive effect of FDI on domestic investment is more obvious in the 1980s than in the next decade, except for China and Indonesia. The results are very little as far as PFI inflows are concerned.

CONCLUDING REMARKS

This chapter presents the capital flow characteristics of selected East Asian economies between 1980 and 2000, and examines the linkages between capital inflows and real variables. Our empirical study does not support the theoretical claim that foreign capital inflows *per se* accelerate economic growth. In fact, we find that FDI is not robustly linked with economic growth. However, our results do not imply that capital inflows are completely unassociated with the real economy. Indeed FDI is mostly, positively associated with domestic investment especially in the 1980s, but this tendency weakens in the 1990s. This evidence can be explained by three possibilities:

- As countries become more integrated into international markets, domestic saving and investment decisions are less correlated, and thus the link between capital flows and investment weakens.
- The increasing importance of M&A as part of FDI – which has less relationship with investment – induces a weaker relationship between FDI and investment.
- The excessive amount of capital inflows in Asia.

Our results are consistent with evidences shown in the literature and confirm diverging outcomes about the relationship between capital inflows and economic performances. That is why we assume that it is important to take into account the diversity of experiences among countries in terms of openness to international capital markets, kind of capital inflows and economic development. Moreover, we consider that both the celebration of

Table 11.3 Foreign direct investment and economic growth

Dependent variables	CHINA	INDONESIA	KOREA	MALAYSIA	PHILIPPINES	SINGAPORE	THAILAND
FDI (–1)	–2.3780**	–6.1451***	–0.2243	3.1318***	–0.8786	–0.6046	–5.2533***
INV	4.0019***	4.1374***	5.1029***	–1.9302*	4.4407***	1.9283*	–
CREDIT	–2.5973**	1.2328	–2.8272**	–1.0964	–0.8848	–1.6730	–4.1882***
TRADE	1.8160	–4.0152***	1.4062	2.5094**	1.1521	0.5155	5.8033***
JAPANG	–	1.0223	–0.0969	3.2776***	1.1768	0.3300	4.9344***
USAG	–	1.6960	–0.4346	0.6848	–1.6157	0.7468	0.3988
R^2	0.6270	0.8617	0.8677	0.6802	0.7287	0.4411	0.8595
Adjusted	0.8027	0.7926	0.8067	0.5327	0.6036	0.1617	0.8054
F-statistic	5.0441**	12.4666***	14.2180***	4.6099***	5.8221***	1.5786	15.8983***

Note: *GROWTH* is the dependent variable. Amount of observations in regressions is: 20 (except for China: 18). The method of estimation was simple ordinary least squares. *, ** and *** denote significance at the 10%, 5% and 1% level, respectively. A blank entry indicates that the regression was not significant at the 5% level.

Table 11.4 Portfolio investment and economic growth

Dependent variables	CHINA	INDONESIA	KOREA	MALAYSIA	PHILIPPINES	SINGAPORE	THAILAND
PFI (–1)	0.4187	3.7422***	–0.6229	–2.0379*	2.2801**	–0.4852	2.6132**
INV	3.7307***	1.3042	5.6634***	–1.4373	4.2940***	1.1988*	–
CREDIT	–3.0527***	2.2716**	–2.9965***	–2.9674**	–1.7243*	–1.8621*	–3.6185***
TRADE	–0.6749	–1.8436*	1.4067	2.8114**	2.2111**	0.4066	3.3318***
JAPANG	–	0.3783	0.0277	1.5074	–0.3719	0.3061	3.2672***
USAG	–	1.454	–0.5834	0.2636	–1.9239*	0.8036	0.3238
R^2	0.6043	0.8690	0.8713	0.6333	0.7589	0.4351	0.7122
Adjusted R^2	0.4725	0.8036	0.8119	0.4500	0.6477	0.1527	0.6015
F-statistic	4.5831**	13.2692***	14.6684***	3.4552**	6.8231***	1.5410	6.4352***

Note: *GROWTH* is the dependent variable. Amount of observations in regressions is: 20. The method of estimation was simple ordinary least squares. *, ** and *** denote significance at the 10%, 5% and 1% level, respectively. A blank entry indicates that the regression was not significant at the 5% level.

Table 11.5 Foreign direct investment and domestic investment

	CHINA	INDONESIA	KOREA	MALAYSIA	PHILIPPINES	SINGAPORE	THAILAND
FDI	3.4283***	3.4166**	–2.9874***	4.1767***	1.4762	–1.3305	–1.2321
R^2	0.4234	0.4071	0.3300	0.5216	0.1198	0.0895	0.0777
Adjusted R^2	0.3874	0.3722	0.2943	0.4917	0.0641	0.0389	0.0265
F-statistic	11.7533***	11.6734***	8.9248***	17.44***	2.1791	1.7704	1.5182

Note: *INV* is the dependent variable. Amount of observations in regressions is: 20. The method of estimation was simple ordinary least squares. *, ** and *** denote significance at the 10%, 5% and 1% level, respectively. A blank entry indicates that the regression was not significant at the 5% level.

Table 11.6 FDI and domestic investment, by decade

	1980–1990				1991–2000			
	FDI	*CREDIT*	Adjusted R^2	*F*-statistic	*FDI*	*CREDIT*	Adjusted R^2	*F*-statistic
CHINA	–0.0346	–0.1268	–0.2886	0.1591	6.0984***	2.4501**	0.8751	24.5254**
INDONESIA	-0.6151	1.3754	0.6740	8.2734**	7.8030***	–1.1831	0.9336	49.800***
KOREA	1.9758*	1.1460	0.3675	2.0339	0.4244	–2.6260**	0.6716	10.2047***
MALAYSIA	3.6450***	–7.2198***	0.9594	104.8309***	2.3397*	1.0661	0.3498	3.4214
PHILIPPINES	1.0456	4.0542***	0.6719	11.7223***	0.3580	0.6597	–0.1238	0.5040
SINGAPORE	–2.8687**	–0.8505	0.4005	4.3412**	0.5490	0.3756	–0.2063	0.2303
THAILAND	4.6970***	0.4066	0.8943	43.30***	–3.9248***	0.1695	0.6222	8.4125**

Note: The method of estimation was simple ordinary least squares. *, ** and *** denote significance at the 10%, 5% and 1% level, respectively. A blank entry indicates that the regression was not significant at the 10% level.

Table 11.7 PFI and domestic investment, by decade

	1980–1990				1991–2000			
	PFI	CREDIT	Adjusted R^2	*F*-statistic	PFI	CREDIT	Adjusted R^2	*F*-statistic
CHINA	0.8444	–0.6924	–0.1318	0.5339	1.4210	2.0917*	0.2132	2.2119
INDONESIA	2.5272**	5.8227***	0.7627	17.0758***	1.2449	–1.1316	0.3229	3.1469
KOREA	–1.4165	1.0806	0.0158	1.0710	0.5307	–3.0491**	0.6762	10.3984***
MALAYSIA	-0.8361	–8.6713***	0.8905	37.6050***	–1.9016*	–0.1609	0.2360	2.3905
PHILIPPINES	0.5177	4.3551***	0.6502	10.2955***	–1.2477	1.4088	–0.0638	1.3066
SINGAPORE	1.2668	0.4721	–0.0128	0.9364	0.0749	0.3744	–0.2582	0.0792
THAILAND	–0.9010	4.4335***	0.6394	9.8664***	2.2129*	–1.2023	0.2886	2.8357

Note: The method of estimation was simple ordinary least squares. *, ** and *** denote significance at the 10%, 5% and 1% level, respectively. A blank entry indicates that the regression was not significant at the 10% level.

capital inflows in the early 1990s and the subsequent scepticism were both excessive. The economic reality is more complex and therefore requires a more nuanced conclusion. The question on whether international capital flows have long-term impact on economic performances or whether international financial integration offers real benefits may not have a binary answer, to the extent that, in the process of integration with international markets, capital flows can bring significant benefits but transition also implies costs in real terms.

NOTES

1. Grossman and Helpman (1991); Barro and Sala-i-Martin (1995).
2. The difference between FDI and other capital flows is that FDI is not just a transfer of funds, but consists of a range of factors such as capital, new technologies, etc. FDI can thus contribute to the transfer of technology and the increase of productivity. The point is that these effects are very difficult to show up and to measure.
3. Findlay (1978) stresses that FDI increases the rate of technical progress in the host country through a 'contagion' effect from the advanced technology, new varieties of capital goods and management skills.
4. For a survey of the empirical literature see Haveman *et al.* (2001).
5. See Heilleiner (1987). According to this author, the access to local financial markets by foreign investors gives them the opportunity to reduce the investment risk and to obtain cheap finance, particularly when local financial markets are 'repressed'.
6. The World Bank's investigation (2001) shows that the relationship between FDI and investment in Sub-Saharan Africa has been even stronger than in East Asia and the Pacific or in Latin America and the Caribbean.
7. FDI can be capitalized as greenfield investment, i.e. building new capacity, or as acquisition of assets of existing local firms. In principle, the balance of payments statistics that record FDI include both forms, although they do not differentiate between them.
8. Thailand, Malaysia, the Philippines, Indonesia and Korea.

REFERENCES

Balasubramanyam, V.N., M. Salisu and D. Sapsford (1996), 'Foreign direct investment and growth in EP and IS countries', *Economic Journal*, **106**, 92–105.

Barro, R. and X. Sala-i-Martin (1995), *Economic Growth*, Cambridge, MA: McGraw-Hill.

Borensztein E., J. De Gregorio and J.-W. Lee (1995), 'How does foreign direct investment affect economic growth?', *NBER Working Paper* 5057, Cambridge.

Borensztein E., J. De Gregorio and J.-W. Lee (1998), 'How does foreign direct investment affect economic growth?', *Journal of International Economics*, **45**, 115–35.

Bosworth and Collins, (1999), 'Capital Flows to Developing Economies: Implications for Saving and Investment', *IMF Seminar Series N° 1999–21*, 1–44.

De Mello, L.R. (1999), 'Foreign direct investment-led growth: evidence from time series and panel data', *Oxford Economic Papers*, **51**, 115–35.

De Mello, L.R. and K. Fukasaku (2000), 'Trade and foreign direct investment in Latin America and Southeast Asia: temporal causality analysis', *Journal of International Development*, **12**, 903–24.

Durham, J. B., (2004), 'Absorptive capacity and the effects of foreign direct investment and equity foreign portfolio investment on growth', *European Economic Review*, **48**, 285–306.

Edison, H.J., R. Levine and L. Ricci (2002), 'International financial integration and economic growth', *Journal of International Money and Finance*, **21**, 749–76.

Feldstein, M. (1994), 'The effects of outbound foreign direct investment on the capital stock', *NBER Working Paper* 4668, Cambridge.

Findlay, R., (1978), 'Relative backwardness, direct foreign investment, and the transfer of technology: a simple dynamic model', *Quarterly Journal of Economic*, **92**, 1–16.

Grossman, G. and E. Helpman, (1991), *Innovation and Growth in the Global Economy*, Cambridge: MIT Press.

Gupta, K.L. and M.A. Islam (1983), *Foreign Capital, Savings and Growth: An International Cross-Section Study*, Dordrecht: Reidel Publishing.

Haveman, J.D., V. Lei and J.S. Netz (2001), 'International integration and growth: a survey and empirical investigation', *Review of Development Economics*, **5**, 289–311.

Helleiner, G., (1987), 'Direct foreign investment and manufacturing for exports: A review of issues', in V. Cable and B. Persaud (eds), *Developing with Foreign Investment*, London: Croom Helm, 67–83.

Husain, I. and K.W. Jun (1992), 'Capital flows to South Asian and ASEAN countries: trends, determinants and policy implications', *World Bank Working Paper WPS 842*, Washington DC.

Ito, T. (1999), 'Capital flows in Asia', NBER, *Working Paper* 7134, Cambridge.

Jansen, K., (1993), 'Direct foreign investment and adjustment: The case of Thailand', *Working Paper*, Series on Money, Finance and Development, The Hague: Institute of Social Studies.

Summers, L. (2000), 'International financial crises: causes, prevention and cures', *American Economic Review Paper and Proceedings*, **90**, 1–16.
World Bank (2001), *Global Development Finance*.

12. The Korean Market: A Political Economy Perspective

You-il Lee

INTRODUCTION

Perhaps the most striking feature of the Korean economy in the late 20th century has been its rise to and fall from economic eminence. During the 1970s and the 1980s the Republic of Korea (hereafter Korea) achieved the most spectacular economic growth among the developing countries. Yet, in the latter part of 1997, Korea became the first country among the 'East-Asian Miracles' to receive what was then a record-breaking US$58 billion rescue package from the International Monetary Fund (IMF) to remedy its ailing economy.

Since early 1997 the Korean economy had exhibited some critical symptoms that signalled the imminence of its collapse. In January 1997, what was formerly the 14th largest business group, Hanbo, particularly Hanbo Steel (a major business of Hanbo Group), collapsed under US$6 billion of debt and in March 1997 another leading business (Sammi Steel) of Sammi Group fell. Furthermore, in July of that year, Kia, Korea's third largest car maker, suffered a severe credit problem. It was nationalized in October as a result of the Korean banks' refusals to provide more loans. Thus the stability of the banking sector was threatened and the viability of their lending policies exposed to scrutiny. As a consequence, the spectre of overseas loan defaults emerged as the Korean foreign exchange rate plummeted to a long-time low.

As a result of these events, the Korean government, on 21 November 1997, officially requested the IMF for emergency help to restore its sick economy. This marked the end of the country's unimpeded advance as a leading newly industrializing country, and of its progress towards becoming an advanced industrial country. Korea has then re-acquired emerging economy status alongside Asian peers such as Thailand, Vietnam and Indonesia. With the Stand-by Agreement with the IMF on 3 December 1997, Korea like Indonesia, officially fell under the IMF control. The much-vaunted *Miracle on the Han River* has become inappropriate for the Korean economy during the IMF loan era.

Although the IMF loans were paid-off in mid 2001, the post-1997 era meant a painful prospect for the Korean economy. The conditions of the rescue package imposed by the IMF certainly demanded a fundamental overhaul of the Korean political economy where one finds state-driven market and industrial policies, a strong nationalist policy towards inflow of foreign direct investment (FDI) and market/economy dominance including distribution by a tight cabal of a small number of family (mostly) owned conglomerates or *chaebol*. On the other hand, this new environment offers more opportunities than risks to foreign investors. The first part of this chapter offers a brief theoretical survey on the Korean financial and political crises, which were revealed via the so-called '97 Asian Crisis. This section is followed by an analysis of the impact of the Korean crisis, which brought about changes in the Korean market environment. It will also provide some strategic insights for existing and potential foreign investors, offering invisible challenges as well as the prevailing opportunities of the Korean market.

This study is in part based on the author's pre-existing and working knowledge of the Korean political economy and a number of fieldwork exercises made during the period between 1997 and 2002 in Korea conducting over 80 face to face interviews with senior executives, mainly chief executive officers (CEOs) of multinational corporations (MNCs) operating in Korea1. Major issues that were examined in this study include:

- The nature of the Korean crisis: a political economic perspective;
- The Korean market opportunity triggered by the crisis;
- Strategic implications of the Korean crisis and its consequences for the MNCs.

KOREAN CRISIS: SOME THEORETICAL CONSIDERATIONS

Market or State?

The major determinants of Korea's phenomenal economic success and 1997 financial crisis have been the subject of debate among economists, political scientists (and political economists) and institutionalists. Literature advances a range of explanations, from market mechanisms to the strong role of the State and the role of the state policy in facilitating private and public sector co-ordination. Liberal market economists or neo-classical theorists have attributed the newly industrializing countries' (NICs) phenomenal economic growth in the last three decades to the pursuit of export-oriented industrialization (EOI) along with policies that favour a market orientation and minimal state intervention (Westphal, 1978; Krueger, 1982; Riedel, 1988; Little, 1990; Westphal, 1990).

The World Bank, a champion of the neo-classical school, expands the above view. It believes that 'effective but limited State activism' is one of the most important factors contributing to the success of the so-called HPAEs or high performing Asian economies (Korea, Singapore, Taiwan, Hong Kong, China, Indonesia, Malaysia and Thailand) (Chowdury and Iyanatul, 1993, pp. 1–27; World Bank, 1994, pp. 1–26). It argues that in the market friendly strategy, 'the appropriate role of State is to ensure adequate investments in people, provide a competitive climate for private enterprise, keep the economy open to international trade, and maintain a stable macro-economy' (Chowdury and Iyanatul, 1993, p. 10).

While the neo-classical approach attempts to explain the success of the Korean economy over the last three decades in terms of the shifting patterns of comparative advantage and its management, a new breed of scholars, known as statists, began to look into domestic political processes and structures in Korea in relation to its rapid economic growth. In spite of the considerable debate about the character of the post-war Korean state, the common consciousness of the literature is perhaps most evident in its view on the State dominance over economy, market and labour. In their view, what really matters in the context of Korea's economic success is the domestic political structure that shapes policy choices and implementation and ultimately determines economic outcomes (Jones and Sakong, 1980; Kuznets, 1985; Cheng and Moon, 1987; Moon, 1988; Wade, 1988; Chu, 1989; Haggard and Moon, 1990; Woo, 1991; Wade, 1992).

What they suggest is that rather than emphasizing policy itself, the nature of economic policy-making should first be analysed in examining the nature of Korean economic development. Accordingly, the adoption of an export-oriented industrialization (EOI) strategy was not a result of market forces, but of a conscious state choice to realize economic and political objectives. The State's consistent and coherent implementation has been facilitated by State strength unique to Korea. Political insulation of the economy, which is essential to the continuation of an export-oriented growth, was possible through the hegemonic developmental coalition and the exclusion of the popular sector.

The above two distinct theories (neo-classical and statist) on the success of NICs have their own unique explanations. While the neo-classical school treats the Asian model as a classic economic model that shows the virtues of the western capitalist system, the State or institutionalist school sees the Asian model as a different paradigm from the western, and that *difference* is the key to its economic triumph (Frankel, 1998). However, how do they explain the current crisis given that Korea's economic success has been rooted either in the nation's adherence to the market principles and minimal State intervention or the so-called western capitalism or in the strong capacity of the State? Why has the Korean economy under such circumstances suddenly collapsed?

Economists, although to some extent it differs from country to country, tend to contribute various macroeconomic (capital inflows, real exchange rate application) and microeconomic (credit expansion, financial regulation and supervision) factors to the current crisis (Radelet and Sachs, 1998). Some also argue global and international shocks and structural flaws led to the crisis. Common causes behind the current crisis that can be found among economic literature include accumulation of current account deficits, sustained appreciation of the currency value, mismanagement of the financial institutions and excessive short-term, and foreign currency-denominated debt, etc. (Corsetti *et al.*, 1998; Radelet and Sachs, 1998). Corsetti *et al.*'s (1998) empirical work on the Asian crisis suggests that the Asian economic crisis is rooted in the inconsistency of policies aimed at simultaneously sustaining growth, investment and risk-taking, maintaining stable exchange rates and providing guarantees to underregulated financial institutions. In the absence of fully developed and sophisticated securities markets, these policies caused large account imbalances.

Similarly, Radelet and Sachs (1998) argue that the inherent instability of the international financial markets hit by several international macroeconomic shocks including the abrupt reversal of the long-term trend towards appreciation of the yen vis-à-vis the US dollar during the mid-1990s also played a critical part in causing the current Asian economic crisis. More importantly, they argue that IMF bailout programs applied to Mexico, Argentina and countries of East Asia have to a large extent contributed to the significant increase of new moral hazards in international lending (Radelet and Sachs, 1998).

Krugman (1998) suggests that applying the currency-crisis models to the current Asian crisis is partially accurate. He argues that the Asian crisis may have been only incidentally about currencies but it was mainly about bad banking and its consequences. In particular, Krugman places a problem of moral hazard/asset bubble, which created severe inflation – not of goods but of asset prices such as land and stock – as a major contender for a leading role in the crisis (Krugman, 1998).

However, the economic literature seems to put too much emphasis on institutional functions and 'good governance' and less recognition of the role played by the State (Robison and Beeson, 1998). Unlike the neo-classical economists, State-centred theorists, while they see the crisis as financial in origin, tend to analyse the problems and causes in relation to capacity of the developmental State. Weiss and Hobson (1998) argue that the 1997 meltdown of Asian currencies is fundamentally rooted in the vulnerability of State capacity to strong winds of global finance. In other words, the State power is the most critical variable in explaining both the sources of the crisis and its ensuing severity. Chang (1998) and Chang and Yoo (1998) in their study on the deep causes of the Korean financial crisis show how the transitional (rather weakening) State capacity, especially the Kim Young Sam regime (1993–1998) in relation to its relationship with business and institutions led to the crisis. Haggard *et al.* (1999) also argue that despite Korea's political tradition of strong presidents, the inconsistency between the government and policymaking process under the Kim Young Sam administration led to the depth of the current crisis. Chang (1998) sees the solution to the crisis, contrary to the IMF bailout packages that are to break crony capitalism and to reduce the State power, in strengthening, not weakening the 'co-ordinating function' of the State. Lee and Kim (1998) provide a similar view that cessation of State involvement in the Korean economy can hardly occur even in the IMF era unless market democratization is fully realized.

But most of all, the dominant paradigm among social scientists (economists, political scientists and political economists) on the 1997 crisis is to either reverse or modify their earlier verdicts of *Asian model* either as a triumph of western capitalism or the superiority of Asian developmental States in implementing economic liberalization. It is important to note that major international financial institutions like the World Bank and the IMF up until the outbreak of the Thai crisis (July 1997) were the major protagonists of Asian capitalism. State theorists such as Weiss and Hobson (1998), Haggard and Moon (1983), Haggard (1988) and Wade (1988) too, put a strong emphasis on the relative autonomy of the developmental states of East Asia in explaining their economic success.

The Korean financial crisis should not be treated solely as an economic crisis or as a crisis of State capacity. Instead, Korea's post-1997 currency meltdown should be understood as a structural crisis of the Korean post-war political economy (Kim, 1999). This crisis is an unexpected but inevitable result of Korea's fast economic growth in which various but detrimental factors that eventually led to the collapse of the miracle were embedded in the institutions that stimulated growth. It is a result of an accumulated structural crisis of the Korean political economy, which represents the State's unlimited market intervention, chronic corruption rooted in the State–*chaebol*–bank tight alliance, over-reliance on a small number of *chaebol* groups, misconception and mis-implemention of globalization policy led by the State and the *chaebol*, and the accumulation of discrepancy between economic and social progress.

Chaebol

Korea is to a large extent a command economy and the mechanism by which economic commands are effected is the *chaebol*. Until very recently, the Korean State chose to favour the *chaebol* over most business affairs as a means of accelerating the national priority of rather fast economic growth. This tight collusion between State and business inevitably created inequality between the *chaebol* and small and medium-sized companies, between social classes, and between industrial sectors. It may be true that such a protection was necessary at the beginning of economic development. However, this practice continued to exist over the last three decades. More importantly, much more emphasis has been given to political favours rather than economic efficiency (Choi, 1998).

Yoo (1998) argues the root of the *chaebol* problem that led to the 1997 financial crisis can be found in six major failures: failure of corporate governance; failure of the financial sector; failure of the exit market; excessive political influence of *chaebol* economic power over government policy making; popular misconception of the nature of big business or 'too big to fail perception'; and the State's failure to provide adequate regulatory enforcement. As is well known since the IMF bailout, the *chaebol* had engaged in indiscrimate borrowings from both domestic and foreign sources to expand their projects. Critically, these foreign borrowings were made with short-term maturities. Consequently, as the Korean economy went into bad track in early 1997, weak foundations of these groups and tight alliance between State and business caused foreign investors to lose their confidence. Equally important, these *chaebol* groups managed in a very non-transparent fashion, further undermining the confidence of the foreign investors.

These companies (*chaebol*) exist in a similar way to the pre-Second World War zaibatsu groups in Japan, a highly centralized family (mostly) controlled system. They exercise monopolistic and oligopolistic control across product lines and industries. *Chaebol*, like the *zaibatsu*, are prestigious, powerful and influential and their corporate behaviour largely determines the competitive climate. Because of their size and state protection, the *chaebol* have been able to borrow at advantageous rates. Not only that, but they take extended credit and thus delay payments by considerable periods through the device of issuing promissory notes to their suppliers. This resulted in chaebol having numerous advantages that rendered them resistant to certain types of competitive threat. The *chaebol* have always been on the top of the State priority list. In turn, the *chaebol* prioritized quantitative rather than qualitative growth. Consequently, a number of *chaebol* groups neglected long-term technological innovation and instead focused on the short-term goal of expanding their business lines into diverse lines. The following is a typical impression of the *chaebol* volunteered by a chief executive officer of one of the leading MNCs operating in Korea:

> When you read of the vision statements of the major chaebol you have to be impressed with the boldness of their visions. They talk about tripling their size within a five-year period where most MNCs are reluctant to set long-term objectives embodying more than 15–20 per cent annual growth. Generally speaking risk profiles and levels of aggressiveness differ markedly between Korean and most other foreign companies. Major Korean companies also have supported state initiatives to establish strategic industries, for example shipbuilding and electronics, etc.

The distribution system in Korea reflects some of the characteristics peculiar to the Korean market that provide difficulties for foreign investors. The most frequently spoken word among interviewees during interviews is *chaebol*. Retail outlets in Korea are controlled by the *chaebol*, creating vertically integrated linkages between manufacturers and retailers. The top thirty *chaebol* dominate retail sectors, ranging from cosmetics, toiletries to cars and computers. For example, by 1996, the total number of subsidiaries owned by the top thirty *chaebol* were 668 in almost every industrial sector, ranging from primarily consumer goods, automobiles, finance, machinery, electronics, engineering, construction, cosmetics to insurance and securities. Among these 668 subsidiaries, 55 are controlled by Samsung, 46 by Hyundai and 48 by LG respectively (New Industry Management Academy, 1997).

Implications for Multinational Companies

Traditionally, it has always been a big challenge for foreign companies in Korea to compete with the *chaebol*. The *chaebol* have typically been unwilling to see a competitor's products on the same shelf in the same store, thus effectively locking out the foreign product, absorbing 15 per cent of the country's Gross Domestic Product (GDP). It is estimated by one of the interviewed consumer products companies that imported consumer electronics and home appliances, in particular, have generally had access to only about 10 per cent of the retail market. However, Korea's credit crisis has forced the *chaebol* to commit most of their available cash flow to paying off their excessive debt. The top 30 *chaebol* groups were found to have piled up debts averaging about 4.5 times their assets in 1997. The debt-to-equity ratio averaged 449.4 per cent in 1997 (Chun, 1997). The top 30 *chaebol* groups accumulated a total debt of 249.67 trillion won (US$177 billion). Among the heaviest borrowers were the big five *chaebol*, Hyundai, LG, Daewoo, Sunkyung and Samsung. The CEO from a foreign company operating in Korea provides some insight:

> MNCs never took those loan commitments. They don't have any financial problem. So MNCs are more or less watching and seeing how serious this [debt crisis] is going to be. Korean companies, on the other hand, don't have money, so even if they need research, or even if they need to do something like advertising, they are just cutting marketing support below the level appropriate for their market share. It is absolutely long-term suicide for a company.

The *chaebol*'s desperate need for cash albeit the strong government and market pressure to reform, which will boost mergers and acquisitions (M&As) of Korean firms by foreign firms, and their size and vision may present foreign companies with their greatest market opportunities. In 1998 for example, foreign M&As through the purchase of outstanding stock rose by 77 per cent, from US$699 million to $1241 million. Foreign experts on M&As estimate the approximate value of assets for sale would exceed US$10 billion, including big Korean companies such as Mambo Machinery, Halla Heavy Industries and Korea Heavy Industries and Construction (EAAU, 1999). Another outstanding development of *chaebol* behaviour in the post-'97 era is their involvements in strategic alliances with MNCs. *Chaebol* like LG, Samsung, Hyundai and Hanhwa have made strategic alliances with MNCs such as Philips, Hitachi, Renault and Sony in industries ranging from venture to cosmetics (SERI, 2001).

Attitude

The outbreak of the currency crisis and its seriousness to the Korean economy resulted in a striking transition in Korea's attitude towards foreign companies and products. A survey of 1000 Koreans (June 1998) conducted by Sofres FSA, a French market research company, revealed that 75 per cent of the surveyed people said it was all right for foreigners to buy into Korean companies and 86 per cent of workers in industrial facilities said they were willing to accept a merger with a foreign company (The Economist Conferences, 1998).

To turn the distorted Korean economy into a healthy economy, the Kim Dae Jung government (or DJ government, 1998–2002) has shown a strong commitment by making decisive reform efforts in sectors, mostly the finance and the corporate (*chaebol*) restructuring. The aim was to eliminate Korea's chronic disease, which is tight government–business collusion, to enhance transparency and supervision, and to restore market confidence. It is generally accepted by the former DJ and now Roh Moo Hyun administration and the Korean people since the eruption of currency meltdown that foreign capital is critical to the Korean economy. Not only does FDI in Korea stabilize the foreign exchange market but also it eventually helps in restructuring the economy and increasing economic efficiency. The November 1998 Foreign Investment Promotion Act, which has been endorsed by the DJ government, streamlined laws and regulations of FDI, abolished restrictions on the foreign ownership of land and hostile cross-border M&As, and allowed foreign participation in large public enterprises and key industries (EAAU, 1999).

Government

A crux of the DJ administration's reform policies during the period between 1998 and 2002 was to uproot crony capitalism; non-transparent financial practices involving government, the *chaebol* and major banks; and the prolonged but rapid wage increase that outstripped the gains in labour productivity, which all contributed to the erosion of Korea's international competitiveness.

However, according to principles of market economy, government's role must be limited to providing and establishing necessary legal infrastructure for banking restructuring and incentives for corporations to work within the framework. For Korea, this is the most difficult task to achieve. The Korean model has not been, and is not, like the liberal model, where excessive intervention of government in the market is absent.

The Korean government still seems remained as a 'god father', presiding over most aspects of economic affairs. Korea's political and economic structures are still under government influence. Korean financial sectors, over the last four decades, have been under the government umbrella. Key figures in the major banks used to be appointed by the president himself and all the financial matters were dealt with by the Ministry of Finance (now the Ministry of Finance and Economy). Although there has been some change in terms of the government and president's perception towards the bank roles since the IMF involvement in the Korean economy, it seems hard to argue that the above tradition has disappeared. It is natural in a sense that Korean politicians, bankers and even the Korean people are still preoccupied with strong leadership, which is provided by the government. Ironically, despite the IMF's free-market mandate, it is imperative that progress be closely monitored by the government if liberalization is to be achieved successfully. Perhaps a combination of imposed free-market principles and Korean-style capitalism makes it necessary for the government in some ways to continue to play a more active role than a government might elsewhere. This is partly why the role of the government and bureaucrats seems contradictory to many foreign investors in Korea. While most existing and potential foreign investors welcome the measures that have been taken by the Kim Dae-Jung administration, they appear to have doubts about the exact role of the government.

The author's survey, conducted in 1998 of 24 MNCs that developed business presence in Korea, revealed that 71 per cent of the CEOs said they were somewhat confident with the government's ability to restructure the financial system. On the other hand, 42 per cent of the CEOs expressed no confidence with the Korean government's ability to deal with the chaebol issue. 58 per cent said they were somewhat confident. None of the respondent companies said they were 'very confident', which contrasts with their view on government ability to deal with financial sectors. This result shows the still dominant position of the *chaebol* groups in the Korean economy.

KOREAN MARKET: STRATEGIC IMPLICATIONS FOR MULTINATIONAL COMPANIES

According to a survey in *the Far Eastern Economic Review and Asia Business Review* (Far Eastern Economic Review, 1998), Korea was ranked as the least favourable destination among Asian countries in which to invest and affords the second greatest level of social instability. The poll conducted in early 1998, among business leaders in 10 Asian countries marked Korea on the second highest position in terms of political risk.

Table 12.1 corroborates an earlier survey of Korea's investment climate, conducted by the International Statistics Research Centre. That review was performed in October 1996 on 324 foreign MNCs out of 1519 companies operating in Seoul. According to that survey more than 19 per cent of the respondents claimed to be considering moving out of Seoul. The main determinant behind this is the ever-increasing wage level and 75 per cent of the respondents listed the complex and difficult procedure with bureaucracy as a major barrier to investing in Korea.

A late 1998 survey of the MNCs in Korea conducted by the author echoed these results. This segment of the survey received the greatest response of all sections, with a response rate of 100 per cent. Each participant was asked to rank eighteen items, which appear to be difficult areas for foreign investors in doing business in Korea, in order of severity (e.g. 18-most difficult, 1-least difficult). Two thirds of respondent companies believed strong Korean nationalism, foreign exchange risk, bureaucracy and difficulty in obtaining information from government and regulatory bodies to be major impediments to doing business in Korea. Other major impediments to doing business include: *chaebol*'s dominance in domestic market; Korean business culture, poor outlook for economic growth; and corruption.

Table 12.1 Overall ranking of investment climate in Asia, 1998

Rank	Best place	Worst place	Political instability	Social instability
1	Australia	Korea	Indonesia	Indonesia
2	China	Indonesia	Korea	Korea
3	Malaysia	Thailand	Thailand	Thailand
4	Taiwan	Japan	Philippines	China
5	Thailand	Malaysia	Australia	Philippines
6	Philippines	China	Singapore	Singapore
7	Singapore	Australia	Hong Kong	Australia
8	Korea	Taiwan		Malaysia
9	Japan	Singapore		Hong Kong
10	Indonesia	Taiwan		Japan

Source: Far Eastern Economic Review (1998).

Table 12.1 shows two particular features of past and present Korean market environment. Firstly, 50 per cent of foreign companies ranked Korea's strong nationalism as the most difficult aspect in doing business in Korea. Korea has had a long history of economic nationalism stimulated by negative experiences as a result of earlier interactions with foreign regimes (Michell, 1999). A strong belief in self-sufficiency has inevitably resulted in a tough business climate, seemingly especially hostile to foreign companies. Secondly, eleven managers saw Korea's regulatory environment such as government red-tape and bureaucracy as another major impediment to their investment and business operations in Korea. In fact, those are difficult even for Korean firms. Other major factors impeding investment included: regulatory controls over movement of capital (including repatriation of profits); poor outlook for economic growth, recession, post crisis; Korean business culture; and corruption. A new area for the mangers' concern in their business is the current crisis. 42 per cent of companies cited foreign exchange risk through devaluation of the *won*.

Despite these barriers, the reality, manifest from the author's field research and survey, is that the market potential dwarfs the obstacles and other issues that hinder MNC operations in Korea. The associated cost of foreignness such as unfamiliarity with local economic, cultural and political rules, regulations and business norms has not and ought not to deter foreign MNCs. The market and size of the economy coupled with its potential are much more persuasive determinants in making decisions to invest in the Korean market. Each participant was asked to mark one or two of the most important motives among items in Table 12.2. Table 12.3 provides a breakdown of major motives behind the company's initial decision to invest in Korea.

The market (48 million people) and size of the Korean economy coupled with its potential turned out to be the most persuasive factors in companies' actual decision to invest in the Korean market. Another important discovery of this study combined with pre-existing knowledge with the intensive field work exercises conducted in Korea is that the depicted knowledge of the Korean market in the media as well as in Korea related literature, which was with a full of negative colour is rather superficial and incomplete. There are various evidences that support the argument. For example, the rapidly increasing figure and continuity of the inflow of foreign capital in Korea is one of the vivid proofs. In particular, during the four year period after the crisis (1998 to 2001), Korea has attracted around US$52 billion in FDI which is almost more than double the entire amount of the previous four decades (Kim and Choo, 2002, p. 30); by 2000 more than 1100 business sectors of Korea had been fully opened up to foreign investors (Economist Intelligence Unit, 2002, p. 29). It is important to recognize that unlike the previous years where FDI into Korea was dominated by firms from the United States and Japan, current FDI into Korea is in large part made by European countries such as Germany, the Netherlands and the United Kingdom (EAAU, 1999). A key force behind this was their increasing awareness of the growing Korean market. Further investment de-restrictions coupled with a lower value of the currency (won), declining status of the chaebol, and the government capacity which resulted from the 1997 financial crisis may make investments more attractive. This also ties these unknown entities (to the West) to the perceptions and realities experienced by senior executives charged with the responsibility of running foreign companies in Korea. Overwhelmingly, 75 per cent of participating CEOs in the survey said they would encourage other foreign companies to invest in Korea. The major reason for the encouragement was the market and size of the Korean economy coupled with its potential.

Table 12.2 Major impediments to doing business in Korea

Impediments	Major factor		Minor factor	
	Number	%	Number	%
Korea's strong nationalism	12	50	6	25
Bureaucracy and difficulty in obtaining information from government and regulatory bodies	11	46	7	30
Foreign exchange risk	10	42	8	34
Korean business culture	9	37		13
Corruption	9	38	4	17
Regulatory controls over movement of capital (including repatriation of profits)	8	33		13
Poor outlook for economic growth, recession, post crisis	8	33	3	13
Anti-competitive practices in tendering	7	29	5	21
Poor intellectual property protection	7	30	3	11
Chaebol's dominance in domestic markets	6	25	5	21
Lack of infrastructure	5	21	4	17
Difficulty in obtaining finance	5	21	4	17
Lack of motivation among Korean employees	5	21	3	13
Communication (language)	3	13	10	42
Slowness in the reform process	3	13	7	29
Lack of information about potential opportunities		13	5	21
Political instability	3	13	3	13
High company and personal taxes	2	8	4	17

Note: Score ranked by foreign management for major factor ranges from 18 to 14 and for minor from 13 to 9.

Table 12.3. Motives behind a company's initial decision to invest in Korea

Description of motives in the initial decision to invest	Major reason	
	Number	%
Already a major market and local presence important	16	66
As a part of company's globalization strategy	9	38
To explore a new market	4	16
To establish a beachhead for market expansion	3	12
Approached by Korean partner	1	4
To produce products for export to third market		
To increase productivity by using low cost labour		
To acquire local technology		

Note: Companies were given the opportunity to provide more than one motive behind their initial decision to invest in Korea. Thus, responses add to greater than 24 and percentages greater than 100.

Striking Difference

Enriching the pre-existing knowledge and exploring a new frontier like this study is always challenging. There is also a danger in extracting definite conclusions. This is because of the nature of the topic, which is limited and the nature of the topic's cultural, institutional and political sensitivity. However, this study reveals critical implications for the various forms of foreign investment behaviour, particularly in the process of the firm's advancing to the Korean market. One of the most striking differences of the Korean market from the rest of the Asian counterparts is found in its revolutionary nature in market development and the influence of the government and a small number of conglomerates, the *chaebol* on the overall economic and market behaviour. This study has shown that the Korean government has been and is playing 'producer', 'director' and 'player' in socio-economic, political and institutional matters. This is a significant aspect of Korean political economy because either recognition or disregard of this highly invisible area often plays a part as an important barometer for the firm's fate in a foreign operation. Not surprisingly, the majority of interviewees cited that most multinational conflicts and related issues are found in the company's ignorance of the impact of the dynamic nature of the Korean capitalism on multinational business. For example, there is no place like Korea in the globe, where the economy is influenced and controlled by the *chaebol*. As detailed in various places in this chapter, the *chaebol*'s big hand over almost every business field, and the distribution system in particular, is not comparable with any other economy. This dominance, at the same time, provides the greatest market opportunities for the MNCs.

Current/Future Strategy

The implication of the above is clear: know the market before the decision is made. But as it is always applied to every occasion, theory is not necessarily accompanied by reality. The author's survey result echoed this hypothesis. Two thirds of respondents overwhelmingly regarded market understanding including patience, culture, people and long-term vision as the *most* precious lesson they learnt from doing business in Korea. This result corroborates the 1996 survey of 156 (the number of respondents) MNCs conducted by Frank Small & Associates (Marketing and Research Consultants). A major finding of the survey was that market understanding was identified as the single most important issue (84 per cent) in having a successful business venture in Korea. Two other critical issues standing out as being the most critical were human resources and government regulations.

Despite this, there still remain challenges, constraints and even possible crises in realizing a successful business in a foreign market.

Overall, the assessment of the Korean market requires a multidisciplinary approach. There is nothing to be disregarded. This means that the business success in a foreign land must be accompanied with a multi-faceted picture of the market. Therefore, the exploration of a dynamic market like Korea requires a lot of perspiration, patience, capital, preparation; but it is highly profitable and should be a long-term oriented target.

CONCLUSION

This chapter has shown that Korea's rapidly changing market environment should not be treated solely as a consequence of the economic crisis or a political crisis but as a result of structural crisis of the Korean political economy. It is clear, however, that the post-1997 era, which seemingly brought about a fundamental overhaul of the structure of the Korean political economy, contributed to the change of the Korean market image among multinational corporations, and offered a watershed for foreign investors with long-term implications for market opportunities.

Equally important, maintenance of Korea's competitive advantages in attracting foreign capital such as a rich market potential, a strong industrial base, an abundance of highly educated workforce, an excellent communication infrastructure, a high savings rate, a record of growth and high market value in terms of strategic business location will surely be dependent on the newly elected Roh Moo Hyun government's (2003 and onwards) capacity in dealing with ongoing bold reform measures initiated by the Kim Dae Jung administration (1998–2002) in the financial, corporate, labour and public sectors.

NOTE

1. These high level executives are from 3M Korea Ltd, A.C. Nielsen Co., ACCOR Asia Pacific, Andersen Consulting, B.M.G. (Hankook) Music Co., Ltd, Bain and Company, BASF Korea, Ltd., BNFL Korea Liaison Office, BP Korea Ltd, Bristol-Myers Squibb Pharmaceutical Group, British Airways, Cathay Pacific Airways, Ltd., Ciba-Geigy Korea Ltd, Citibank, N.A. Seoul Branch, Clorox Korea Ltd, Dentsu Inc., Deutsche Bank AG, Seoul Branch, Deutsche Morgan Grenfell, Dow Chemical Korea Ltd, Eastman Chemical Korea Ltd, Ericsson Korea Ltd, Euro-Asian Business Consultancy Ltd, European Union Chamber of Commerce in Korea, Ford International Business Development Inc, Ford Motor Company of Korea, Friedrich-Ebert-Stiftung, GFT Korea Co, Ltd, Glaxo-Wellcome Korea Ltd, Grand Hyatt Seoul, Han-Dok Pharmaceuticals, Co, Ltd, Hanseng Foods Ltd, Henkel Korea Ltd., Hewlett-Packard Korea Ltd, Hong Kong Telecom Korea Representative Office, ICI Korea Ltd, ING Bank, Intel Korea Ltd, International Distillers Korea, J Walter Thompson Korea Ltd, Japan Chamber of Commerce & Industry, Japan External Trade Organisation (JETRO), Johnson & Johnson Korea Ltd, Johnson & Johnson Medical Ltd, Kia Ford Credit Financial Company, Kodak Korea Ltd, Korea Illies Engineering Co, Ltd, Korea Johnson Co Ltd, KOREABEN, Korean-German Chamber of Commerce, Lego Korea Co Ltd, Levi Strauss Korea Ltd, Louis Vuitton Korea Ltd., Lux Korea Ltd, MAN B&W Korea Ltd, Management Frontiers Pty Ltd, Marks & Spencer Korea Franchise D&S Ltd., McKinsey Incorporated, Merck Korea Ltd., Morgan Grenfell Korea Ltd, Myungmy Cosmetics Co, Ltd, Nokia Mobile Phones, Korea Branch, Overlook Investments, PRK Distribution, Royal Copenhagen Korea Ltd, Schlumberger Technologies Korea, Seoul Hilton, Sulzer Korea Ltd, Sunrider International Korea, Swarovski, Texas Instruments Korea Ltd, The Prudential Life Insurance Company of Korea Ltd, Unilever Korea, Volvo Korea Ltd, American Chamber of Commerce in Korea, BHP Steel North Asia Ltd, MSAS Cargo International, ANZ Banking Group, Frank Small & Associates, Jardine Fleming Securities Ltd, Johnson Matthey, BHP Minerals Asia Inc.

REFERENCES

Bank of Korea (1993), *Weekly Report on FDI*, Seoul: Bank of Korea.

Bank of Korea (1995), *Economic Statistics Yearbook*, Seoul: Bank of Korea.

Bank of Korea (1996), *Economic Statistics Yearbook 1996*, Seoul: Bank of Korea.

Chang, H. (1998), 'South Korea: the misunderstood crisis', in K.S. Jomo (ed.), *Tigers in Trouble*, London: Zed Books, pp. 223–31.

Chang, H. and C. Yoo (1998), 'The triumph of the rentiers?', *Challenge*, **43** (1), 105–24.

Cheng, T. and J. Moon (1987), *Newly Industrializing Asia in Transition*, Berkeley: Institute of International Studies.

Choi, J.J. (1998), 'Korea's political economy: search for a solution', Korea Focus, **6** (2), 1–20.

Chowdury, A. and I. Iyanatul (1993), *The Newly Industrializing Economies of East Asia*, London: Routledge.

Chu, Y. (1989), 'State structure and economic adjustment of the East Asian newly industrializing countries', *International Organization*, **43** (4), 647–72.

Chun, S. (1997), 'Large conglomerates face dissolution under demand', *Korea Herald*, Seoul, 4 December.

Corsetti, G., *et al.* (1998), 'Paper tigers? A preliminary assessment of the Asian crisis', paper presented at the conference on *NBER–Bank of Portugal International Seminar on Macroeconomics*, Lisbon, 14–15 June.

East Asia Analytical Unit (1999), *Korea Rebuilds: From Crisis to Opportunity*, Canberra: Department of Foreign Affairs and Trade (Australia).

Economist Intelligence Unit (2002), *Magnet or morass?: South Korea's prospects for foreign investment*, Hong Kong: EIU.

Far Eastern Economic Review (1998), 'Asian executive poll', *Far Eastern Economic Review*, 15 January.

Frankel, J. (1998), 'The Asian model, the miracle, the crisis and the fund', paper delivered at the US international trade commission, 16 April.

Haggard, S. (1988), 'The Newly Industrialising Countries in the International System', *World Politics*, **38** (2), 343–70.

Haggard, S. and C. Moon (1983), 'The South Korean state in the international economy: liberal, dependent, or mercantile?', in J. Ruggie (ed.), *The Antinomies of Interdependence*, New York: Columbia University Press, pp. 131–90.

Haggard, S. and C. I. Moon (1990), 'Institutions and Economic Policy: Theory and a Korean Case Study', *World Politics*, **42** (2), 210–35.

Haggard, S., D. Pinkston and J. Seo (1999), 'Reforming Korea Inc.: the politics of structural adjustment under Kim Dae Jung', *Asian Perspective*, **23** (3), 201–35.

Jones, L. and I. Sakong (1980), *State, Business, and Entrepreneurship in Economic Development: The Korean Case*, Cambridge: Havard University Council.

Kim, W.S. and M. Choo (2002), *Managing the Road to Globalzsation: The Korean Experience*, Seoul: Korea Trade-Investment Promotion Agency.

Krueger, A. (1982), 'Newly industrializing economies', Economic Impact, vol. 40.

Krugman, P. (1998), 'Will Asia bounce back?',

Internet: http://web.mit.edu/krugman/www/suisse.html.

Kuznets, P. (1985), 'State and economic strategy in contemporary South Korea', *Pacific Affairs*, **58** (1), 44–67.

Lee, Y. and H. Kim (1998), 'The dilemma of liberalization: financial crisis and the transformation of capitalism in South Korea', paper presented at the conference on *From Miracle to Meltdown: the End of Asian Capitalism?*, Asia Research Centre, Murdoch University, Perth, Australia.

Little, I. (1990*), Economic Development, Theory, Policy and International Policy*, New York: Praeger.

Michell, T. (1999), 'Business environment: Korean business culture in transition', in East Asia analytical unit, *Korea Rebuilds: From Crisis to Opportunity*, Canberra: Department of Foreign Affairs and Trade (Australia), 99–118.

New Industry Management Academy (1997*), The Analysis of Financial Affairs of the Top Thirty Chaebol*, Seoul: NIMA.

Radelet, S. and J. Sachs (1998), 'The East Asian financial crisis: diagnosis, remedies, prospects', paper presented at the conference *on Brookings Panel*, Washington D.C., USA, 26–27 March.

Riedel, J. (1988), 'Economic development in East Asia: doing what comes naturally?', in H. Hughes (ed.), *Achieving Industrialization in East Asia*, Cambridge: Cambridge University Press.

Robison, R. and M. Beeson (1998), 'Globalization, crisis and the future of Asian capitalism', paper presented at the conference *on From Miracle to Meltdown: The End of Asian Capitalism?*, Asia Research Centre, Murdoch University, Perth, Australia.

SERI (Samsung Economic Research Institute) (2001), *Report on the Korean Economy*, Seoul: SERI.

The Economist Conferences (1998), 'Summary of the economist conferences: sixth roundtable with the government of the Republic of Korea', 22–24 June.

The European Union Chamber of Commerce in Korea (1997*), Trade Issues 1997*, Seoul: The European Union Chamber of Commerce in Korea.

Wade, R. (1988), 'State intervention in outward-looking development' in G. White (ed.), *Developmental States in East Asia*, London: MacMillan Press.

Wade, R. (1992), 'Review Article: East Asia's Economic Success-Conflicting Perspectives, Partial Insights, Shaky Evidence', *World Politics*, **44** (2), 270–320.

Weiss, L. and J. Hobson (1998), 'State power and economic strength: revisited: What's so special about the Asian crisis?', paper presented at the conference on *From Miracle to Meltdown: the End of Asian Capitalism*, Asia Research Centre, Murdoch University, Perth, Australia

Westphal, L. (1978), 'The Republic of Korea's experience with export-led industrial development', *World Development*, **6** (3), 347–82.

Westphal, L. (1990), 'Industrial policy in an export-propelled economy: lessons from South Korea's experience', *Journal of Economic Perspectives*, **4** (3), 41–59.

Woo, J. (1991), *Race to the Swift: State and Finance in Korean Industrialization*, New York: Columbia University Press.

World Bank (1994), *The East Asian Miracle: Economic Growth and Public Policy*, Oxford: Oxford University Press.

World Media (1996), *Directory: Foreign Companies in Korea 1996/7*, Seoul: World Media.

Yoo, S.-M. (1998), 'Democracy, efficiency, equity and Chaebol Reform', *Korea Focus*, **6** (4), 1–15.

APPENDIX

Table A12.1 Critical business issues in South Korea

Issues	Critical (%)	Most critical (%)
Market understanding	84	32
Human resources	68	12
Government regulations	63	13
HQ understanding	63	13
Cultural understanding	64	5
Networking	50	3
Distribution	47	2
Financial issues	37	2
Form of corporate structure	28	4
Intellectual property rights	28	4

Source: Frank Small & Associates (Korea), 1996.

13. Which Exchange Rate Policy to Help Boost Foreign Direct Investment-Led Growth in ASEAN?

Françoise Nicolas

INTRODUCTION

In the wake of the financial crisis, the slowdown of foreign direct investment (FDI) inflows into ASEAN has become a major matter of concern in the region, while competition from China seems to compound the problem. FDI in the region remained below pre-crisis level in 2001 mainly as a result of large divestments in Indonesia. In response, most governments are searching for ways of reviving FDI flows as well as rebalancing the composition of capital inflows away from short-term and toward longer-term equity holdings (Nicolas 2000). FDI continues to be perceived as a powerful engine of growth and of technology diffusion, and this is why one of the priorities of Southeast Asian economies is to maintain or enhance their attractiveness for foreign investors.

It is usually believed that a regional approach to the problem is warranted in an attempt to avoid beggar-thy-neighbour competition for FDI. As a complement to co-operative schemes such as the ASEAN Investment Area which aims at encouraging intra-regional FDI flows, other policies may have a role to play in boosting FDI inflows into the region. While exchange rate policy is often assessed with the specific objective of preserving export orientation (and thus competitiveness), in the case of ASEAN countries, attracting FDI may also rank high among its objectives. It is the aim of the present chapter to examine which role exchange rate policies may have in this respect. To that purpose it will examine what the economic literature has to say on the impact of exchange rate factors on FDI inflows and try to derive possible policy implications for ASEAN economies.

The chapter opens with a survey of the possible impacts of exchange rate variables on FDI inflows, from both a theoretical and an empirical perspective. While the mere existence of an exchange rate impact is no longer a matter of controversy, the direction of this impact and the channels through which it operates are ambiguous both theoretically and empirically, leaving any firm policy implications badly wanting. The second section provides a discussion of the past ASEAN experience with FDI and exchange rate policy, and closes with suggestions for the future.

HOW DO EXCHANGE RATES AFFECT FDI INFLOWS: WHAT THE LITERATURE HAS TO SAY

Theoretical Considerations

For a long time, the conventional wisdom was that exchange rates did not matter for FDI. Because these investments could be treated like the acquisition of a financial asset, the need to first convert the home currency into foreign currencies and later convert the foreign currency return back to home currency could be handled in the spot and forward markets at the time of the purchase. Yet this argument is now widely believed to be a fallacy (Feenstra, 1998). Exchange rate considerations do play a role in FDI decisions because there are no hedging possibilities for such long-term investment.

Several reasons can be given for the existence of an impact of exchange rate fluctuations. It should however be emphasized at this stage that exchange rates are merely secondary factors affecting FDI. Such explanations are complements to the standard theoretical literature on the determinants of FDI. In other words, exchange rate variables are thought to account for the volatility of FDI around a supposed historical trend (Bayoumi and Lipworth, 1997). Moreover, as pointed out by Kogut and Kulatilaka (1988) for instance, exchange rate factors are more likely to affect sequential FDI rather than initial FDI.

In this section, a distinction will be made between the impacts of exchange rate changes and of exchange rate variability[1].

Exchange Rate Changes

While the mere existence of an impact of exchange rate changes on FDI flows is no longer a matter of controversy, the direction of the impact is theoretically indeterminate. In particular, a devaluation can theoretically have any impact on a country's direct investment abroad, depending on the particular configuration of the foreign investors' activities and thus on the alternative effects of exchange rate changes on the costs and revenues of the firms.

A first group of theoretical models come to the conclusion that a real depreciation of the host country's currency is expected to exert a positive impact on FDI inflows. There are several channels through which real exchange rates may affect FDI in this way (Goldberg and Klein, 1997).

i) In the developing country context, the most important channel may be that a depreciation of the real exchange rate reduces the cost of domestic labour (and other productive inputs) relative to foreign production costs. The rising labour demand and employment thus raises the return on capital. As a result, greenfield FDI is expected to increase in response to a depreciation. This channel is usually referred to as the competitiveness (or relative wage) effect.

ii) Among industrial economies, the link between exchange rates and FDI may be based either upon the purchase of knowledge (Feenstra, 1998) or of firm-specific assets (Blonigen, 1997). In these two cases, exchange rates enter the calculation because the purchase and returns are in differing currencies, and a real depreciation of the host country's currency makes FDI more likely. This explanation fits the case of mergers and acquisitions (M&As) particularly well.

iii) Exchange rates may also affect FDI through an imperfect capital market channel. Froot and Stein (1991) emphasize the wealth effects of exchange rate changes as the dominant channel for exchange rate effects. A real depreciation of the domestic currency raises the wealth of foreign investors and reduces the price of domestic assets, thus stimulating FDI inflows. By way of illustration, as stressed by Bayoumi and Lipworth (1997), the appreciation of the yen in the late 1980s enabled Japanese firms, whose book values rose compared with those of foreign companies, to collateralize assets to finance new investment more easily than could their competitors in countries with depreciated currencies. This channel is obviously relevant for FDI through M&A as well as for greenfield investments.

Wealth effects and competitiveness effects work in the same direction but one or the other channel may dominate depending on the form of FDI (greenfield versus M&A) and, more importantly, on the nature of the host economy. Yet, the positive impact described above holds true both for firms who aim at serving the local market and for those whose objective is to take advantage of better production conditions abroad in order to re-export.

A second group of models highlight alternative possibilities, suggesting an inverse relationship between a real exchange rate depreciation and FDI.

i) First, a negative effect is perfectly possible if imported capital goods or intermediate goods are important in the production process. As a result of the depreciation of the host country's currency, imports are made more expensive and the production costs will increase making the location of production less attractive (Caves, 1988; Cushman, 1985, 1988).

ii) Moreover, the impact may also be reversed if the effects on government policy are taken into account. For example an exchange rate depreciation is likely to improve a country's trade balance and thus lead to decreasing pressures for the implementation of protectionist policies. In this context, FDI may be reduced if it was used as a tariff-jumping strategy (Benassy-Quéré *et al.*, 2001a).

Exchange Rate Volatility and Uncertainty

With the advent of floating exchange rates, exchange rate volatility prevailed and with it new sources of concern for internationally-oriented firms. The international environment has indeed been characterized by high instability for the past 25 years, well beyond expectations. The risks associated with that variability have an impact on the decision making process of MNCs to the extent that it affects the conditions under which they make decisions about pricing, sourcing, financing and the location of production and investment. While some types of risks associated with exchange rate variability may be hedged by firms (short-term transaction risk for instance), such is not the case for longer-term risk associated with changes in competitive relationships between alternative locations that arise from changes in real exchange rates (Whitman, 1984).

Conventional wisdom may suggest that there is a negative relationship between uncertainty and FDI, but this is not necessarily the case. Reasons for greater exchange rate volatility to both stimulate and hinder FDI have been pointed out in the literature (Ito *et al.*, 1996). The ambiguous impact of exchange rate uncertainty depends in particular on the location of FDI and on the orientation of these investments.

As recalled by Cushman (1985, 1988), some initial theoretical work analysed the impact of exchange rate risk on FDI in a portfolio theory framework. In this context, FDI may help in the diversification of real assets by a multinational, as a result, increased risk is expected to have a negative impact on FDI because of the rise in a foreign subsidiary's market risk.

Eventually, most models adopted another approach, emphasizing the decision to produce abroad. The theoretical models usually focused on the case of the horizontally integrated firm, which is assumed to produce a final good either domestically or abroad.

A first set of models (Broll and Gilroy, 1986; Calderon-Rossell, 1985) analysed the impact of exchange rate risk on the choice between domestic and foreign production, and hence between domestic and foreign investment. The MNC has the choice between producing domestically or abroad through a subsidiary. In their framework, the level of sales is unaffected by the exchange rate risk but the MNC trades off profits to reduce risk through allocation of production. Theoretically, the impact of exchange rate risk is ambiguous; it depends on the relative cost structure between the two locations of production. Itagaki (1981) suggests that the impact of exchange rate uncertainty on foreign production depends on whether a firm's exposure is positive or negative.

Cushman (1985, 1988) departs from the previous models in a number of ways, in particular because he considers the effects of exchange rate uncertainty on capital and labour levels rather than on production levels. Moreover he focuses on real rather than nominal exchange rate risk. The model assumes a two-period time frame, where the firm implements capital investment this period in order to realize profits next period, for which price levels, the nominal exchange rate, and hence the real exchange rate are uncertain. The firm is assumed to be risk averse.

In this model, the impact of exchange rate uncertainty is shown to depend crucially first on the firm's expectations about the future exchange rate and second on the behaviour of marginal costs. The conclusion is that any result is possible, depending on the production structure of the firm. Cushman identifies four possibilities.

In the first case, the MNC produces exclusively abroad for the foreign market. In this context, an expected appreciation of the foreign currency is found to lower the cost of capital, thus raising FDI; at the same time a rise in exchange rate risk increases the cost of capital and lowers FDI.

In a second case, FDI is a substitute for exports, in other words, the firm supplies the foreign market either through exports or through local production. In this case, exchange rate uncertainty provides a strong incentive to raise FDI as a partial substitute for reduced exports. Direct investments abroad may be seen as a means of risk diversification.

By contrast, if part of the production by the MNC is re-exported to the home country, the positive impact of exchange rate uncertainty vanishes and the impact is ambiguous. The effect of risk depends on whether exchange risk exposure is positive or negative, and on the relative strength of the capital and the labour cost effects.

Finally, if output can be produced in either location and sold in either location, a rise in risk is likely to encourage FDI. The condition for such a positive impact to obtain is that the capital cost effect should not be strong.

Other authors have addressed the same issue but under different assumptions. Goldberg and Kolstad (1995) show a positive impact of short-term exchange rate volatility on FDI even in the presence of risk aversion, when investment flows substitute in part for trade. Their model assumes an intertemporal decision making process but there is no *ex post* adjustment of a variable productive factor. Exchange rate volatility tends to stimulate the share of investment activity located on foreign soil, yet this does not necessarily imply that domestic investment is depressed as a result. This leads to the conclusion that exchange rate volatility can contribute to the internationalization of production activity without depressing economic activity in the home market.

In Nicolas (1991), risk neutrality is also assumed. Yet, because the decision making process is taken to be intertemporal, the exchange rate enters the profit function in a non-linear fashion, and exchange rate uncertainty is shown to have a positive impact on FDI flows. This can be explained by the existence of an asymmetry in the cost of 'being wrong'. When the objective of the multinational firm is to target the foreign market, exchange rate uncertainty stimulates FDI because it is a means of diversifying or of avoiding losses due to declining market shares. The model thus illustrates a situation of loss aversion rather than risk aversion.

Aizenman (1992) also describes the case of risk neutral agents, but emphasizes the production flexibility argument. In his model, both a negative or a positive correlation may obtain between exchange rate volatility and FDI, depending on the nature of the shocks. Similarly, Aizenman and Marion (2001) develop a model where exchange rate volatility raises horizontal FDI but discourages vertical FDI.

Overall, these models suggest that exchange rate uncertainty tends to exert a positive impact on FDI in the standard case of the horizontally-integrated MNC, which fits intra-OECD FDI flows. By contrast, the impact is much more ambiguous in other cases.

Another strand of the literature points exactly in the opposite direction. Various reasons may explain the contrasted effect. A first set of models emphasize the irreversible nature of investments which discourages investors from undertaking a foreign investment project that involves too high a sunk cost. The value of waiting is expected to rise with the degree of uncertainty, making investment decisions less likely (Dixit, 1987). This negative impact of uncertainty is more likely to obtain when FDI is a greenfield investment, or when it involves long-term involvement such as the development of a distribution network or the establishment of brand recognition (Ito *et al.*, 1996).

More recently, Benassy-Quéré *et al.* (2001a) developed a theoretical model in which exchange rate volatility is shown to impact FDI inflows negatively when these investments are not of the market-seeking kind but of the efficiency-seeking kind. As in most other models, the exchange rate is the only source of uncertainty; moreover the firm is supposed to be risk averse and to operate in a two-period framework: the investment decision is made as a first step (while the future exchange rate is unknown) and the production decision as a second step. Yet, this model departs from Cushman's in many respects. In particular, the emphasis is on the choice between two alternative locations of production in the developing world. The point is to sell on the investor's market and not on the foreign market. The two host countries compete for attracting FDI and exchange rate uncertainty is shown to reduce the attractiveness of one location compared to the other more stable environment.

To sum up, the theory does not provide any clear-cut conclusion as to the direction of the impact of exchange rate uncertainty on FDI flows. This is thus an empirical issue. The only firm conclusion is that the type of FDI (vertical integration versus horizontal integration) appears to be paramount. Because emerging economies tend to attract vertical FDI, while OECD countries tend to attract horizontal FDI, the impact of uncertainty can be expected to vary across different locations of production, it is negative in the former case and positive in the latter.

Empirical Observations

Past empirical studies confirm a strong influence of exchange rate movements on FDI. Changes in exchange rates directly affect factor prices of host countries vis-à-vis home countries, thus representing a major criterion whereby MNCs decide their FDI. In line with the conclusions of the models presented earlier, there is ample evidence that exchange rate depreciations boost FDI inflows in a number of cases, whether host countries are industrial economies (Cushman, 1985, 1988; Caves, 1988; Froot and Stein, 1991; Nicolas, 1991; Klein and Rosengren, 1994; Crabb, 2001; Mac Dermott, 2002), or developing economies (Ito *et al.*, 1996; Bayoumi and Lipworth, 1997; Goldberg and Klein, 1997; Seo *et al.*, 2002, Urata and Kiyota, 2002). Using firm-level data, Dewenter (1996) or Blonigen (1997) come to the same conclusion. By contrast, few analyses fail to find a significant impact of exchange rates on FDI (Stevens, 1998, or Healy and Palepu, 1993).

Empirically, longer-term exchange rate fluctuations as well as uncertainty about the duration of the over(under)valuation of a currency appear to be major sources of concern for the firms, rather than short-term volatility. Overall, exchange rate uncertainty is usually expected to be more detrimental to emerging or developing economies than to industrial economies (Kawai and Takagi, 2000): while the expected negative impact of exchange rate variability on trade flows could not be firmly established empirically for industrial countries, by contrast the expected negative impact appears more clearly for developing countries (Caballero and Corbo, 1989; McKenzie, 1999). There is a presumption that the asymmetry in the impacts of exchange rate variability between emerging and industrial economies also holds true for FDI flows. This may have something to do with the type of FDI conducted in the two different groups of countries.

Most empirical studies dealing with FDI flows among industrial countries confirm the expected positive impact of exchange rate uncertainty as described by Cushman (1985, 1988), Nicolas (1991), Goldberg and Kolstad (1995). In other words, increased exchange rate risk tends to stimulate outward direct investment if the point is to serve the foreign market[2]. Experimenting with different measures of exchange rate uncertainty (both short-run variability and long-run misalignment), Bailey and Tavlas (1991) by contrast do not confirm these results, although they do not come up with a negative impact either.

Aizenmann and Marion (2001) find that real effective exchange rate volatility has significant and differential effects on FDI into mature and emerging markets. The correlation is positive and significant for high income countries, but insignificant for lower income countries. In very much the same vein, Urata and Kiyota (2002) find that higher real exchange rate volatility discourages FDI inflows into emerging East Asian economies, although the impact is quite weak. Bénassy-Quéré *et al.* (2001b) also observe a negative impact of nominal exchange rate volatility when tested on FDI flows from industrial countries to developing or emerging economies.

These differentiated empirical findings confirm that the kind of FDI plays a key role in the direction of the impact of exchange rate uncertainty on FDI flows.

General Policy Implications

As far as exchange rate levels are concerned, the policy implications of the theoretical models presented above are quite clear: avoiding a real appreciation should be a primary objective for a FDI-seeking economy. As a result, pegging to a depreciating currency may be an optimal strategy (Takagi, 1996). Such is the case because a depreciation of the host country's currency is shown to boost FDI whatever the objectives of the foreign investors. Preserving price competitiveness appears to be an overriding objective for countries eager to attract FDI inflows.

With regards to exchange rate volatility, the implications are not as clear-cut. An optimal exchange rate regime depends very much on the kind of FDI a country is willing to attract. Most theoretical models emphasize the case of industrial economies, that is to say the case of horizontally-integrated MNCs wishing to invest abroad in order to serve the foreign market. In these conditions, FDI is a substitute for exports, and it may be stimulated by exchange rate variability because it helps diversify risk. Seeking exchange rate stability is hence not necessary to attract FDI.

Bénassy-Quéré *et al.* (2001a) and Urata and Kiyota (2002) are the only authors who address explicitly the issue of the optimal exchange rate regime for a developing country wishing to attract export-oriented FDI. They come to the following conclusions in terms of exchange rate policy.

i) There is a necessary trade-off between price competitiveness and nominal exchange rate stability, targeting one is necessarily at the expense of the other. By construction, what they describe as a 'successful currency board' is the first-best solution because it allows simultaneously to preserve competitiveness and avoid nominal volatility. Their model also shows that the impact of a loss in competitiveness in the absence of nominal volatility is negative, while maintaining competitiveness by allowing some nominal volatility is less harmful. As a result, a crawling peg or a strategy of managed floating is a second-best solution which helps maintain competitiveness with limited volatility.

ii) With regards to the choice of an optimal anchor, they conclude that an emerging economy should stabilize its exchange rate vis-à-vis the currency of its major FDI provider, and that the best solution is to choose to peg to a depreciating currency[3].

iii) Finally, when the issue is addressed from a strategic point of view, another conclusion is that there are global gains in differentiating exchange rate policies across countries. As a result, monetary regionalism may be a way of increasing FDI to emerging countries because it would allow foreign investors to diversify the exchange rate risk across various locations4.

Of course, other considerations may reverse these conclusions. In particular, if a 'fixed' exchange rate encourages foreign currency debt transactions, it may crowd out FDI and equity flows, yet a credible peg may also encourage equity inflows by reducing exchange rate risk (Lane and Milesi-Ferretti, 2000). The respective importance of these two impacts is again an empirical issue.

An additional difficulty is due to the fact that other objectives may be targeted through exchange rate policy, while FDI attractiveness may also be enhanced through other means than exchange rate policy.

FOREIGN DIRECT INVESTMENT AND EXCHANGE RATE POLICIES IN SOUTHEAST ASIA

FDI Trends and Patterns in Southeast Asia

The four major ASEAN economies (Indonesia, Malaysia, Thailand and the Philippines) have collectively been among the most important destinations for FDI outside the OECD area. As a group, they have been the fifth most popular host to FDI world-wide in the 1990s, though a long way behind China (OECD, 1999). These countries differ to some extent in terms of the origin of their inward investment, reflecting differences in their economic structure as well as in their historical ties to investor countries. Yet, FDI inflows tend to be dominated by Japanese FDI[5] although the NIEs as a group account for about the same proportion[6]. Another important point to mention at this stage is that ASEAN economies also tend to import primarily from Japan and to export primarily to the USA.

Table 13.1 FDI inflows to ASEAN, 1995-98 (million of US dollars, % of total)

Investors	1995	1996	1997	1998	Total
Japan	4263	4955	5810	4056	19085
	(18.1)	(19.2)	(19.5)	(18.5)	(18.9)
USA	2119	4586	3669	3427	13801
	(9.0)	(17.7)	(12.3)	(15.6)	(13.6)
EU 15	5607	6231	5542	5344	22725
	(23.8)	(24.1)	(18.6)	(24.4)	(22.5)
ASEAN	3516	3121	3962	2073	12674
	(14.9)	(12.1)	(13.3)	(9.5)	(12.5)
Asian NIEs*	2033	2029	3387	1803	9252
	(8.6)	(7.8)	(11.4)	(8.2)	(9.1)
Total (incl. Others)	23540	25848	29780	21899	101067

Note: * Hong Kong, Korea and Taiwan only.
Source: ASEAN Secretariat, ASEAN FDI Database.

The Japanese domination in the region is all the more important because Japanese investors can be shown to exhibit distinct behaviours compared to other investors. First, Japanese FDI is found to be a substitute rather than a complement to domestic investment in Japan: FDI is thus a means of restructuring Japanese industries (Nakamura and Oyama, 1998). Japanese firms tend to go for vertical integration, thus fuelling the dynamics of a regional division of labour. Japanese FDI can be said to be mostly efficiency-seeking (and not market-seeking) although the situation may vary slightly from one host country to the next. Malaysia and Thailand are probably sometimes seen as potential markets, while this is not yet the case for Indonesia or the Philippines.

Japanese FDI in Asia is also found to have strong trade expansion effects, while this is rarely the case with US FDI. This is the major reason why Japanese FDI is usually perceived as a powerful engine of regional integration (Goldberg and Klein, 1997). First, imports from Japan are found to respond positively to FDI from Japan (while imports from the USA do not respond to FDI from the USA). In addition, exports to Japan are sometimes, but not systematically found to respond positively to FDI from Japan. Overall Japanese FDI in ASEAN is primarily for re-export purposes to third markets rather than to Japan.

Another difference between Japanese and US FDI flows in ASEAN relates to how they reacted in the past to various factors, and in particular to exchange rate changes. First, empirical evidence (Ito *et al.*, 1996) suggests that Japanese FDI in East Asia is strongly affected by changes in real bilateral exchange rates, while this is not always the case for FDI from the USA[7]. In addition, this observation holds true for ALL East Asian countries, including ASEAN economies (Nakamura and Oyama, 1998). Various explanations can be offered. A first possibility is that US FDI is quite heavily involved in non-manufacturing activities. This explanation is however not fully convincing because Japanese FDI is also strongly concentrated in non-manufacturing activities, with another major portion of the flows in the electrical industry. Another explanation is related to the characteristics highlighted earlier: Nakamura and Oyama (1998) suggest that the exchange rate sensitivity of FDI flows is smaller for local market-oriented FDI inflows (mostly US) and stronger for export-oriented FDI (mostly Japanese). In very much the same vein, Bayoumi and Lipworth (1997) argue that the main driving forces for Japanese FDI are domestic conditions and the exchange rate because these flows appear to be focused more on outsourcing.

In a comparative analysis of the determinants of FDI in East Asia and Latin America over the period 1989–98, Urata and Kiyota (2002) find the expected positive impact of a depreciation of the host country's currency on FDI inflows. Yet, both Japanese and US firms apparently make FDI decisions by considering exchange rate movements vis-à-vis the dollar, probably as a result of their export orientation to the USA. This point is examined at some length in the next section.

An Assessment of Pre-crisis Exchange Rate Policies

When examined in more detail, the exchange rate policies adopted in the region during the period 1985–97 were not absolutely identical, even if they produced relatively similar results. Indonesia and the Philippines let their currencies systematically depreciate in nominal terms vis-à-vis the dollar throughout the whole period. This policy was justified by the systematically higher domestic inflation which would have otherwise led to a strong real appreciation. These two countries paid apparently very little attention to the movements in their bilateral yen exchange rates. As a result of the prevailing inflation differentials, the rupiah ended up depreciating in real terms with respect to the yen but not to the dollar, while the peso appreciated in real terms both against the dollar and the yen. By contrast, Malaysia and Singapore opted for an asymmetric strategy when confronted with a depreciating or an appreciating yen. While Malaysia tended to let the ringgit move more closely with a depreciating yen, suggesting a heavy emphasis on export promotion, the Singapore dollar moved more closely with an appreciating yen in an attempt to preserve price stability. Finally, the Thai baht systematically followed the dollar in nominal terms irrespective of whether it was appreciating or depreciating vis-à-vis the yen.

The result of these strategies, with the exception of Singapore, was a combination of real stability vis-à-vis the dollar[8] and nominal volatility with respect to the yen (with a nominal depreciation until 1995 and an appreciation afterwards). Yet overall, the common exchange rate strategy adopted by ASEAN economies was a *de facto* nominal peg to the dollar. A number of studies provide ample empirical evidence on this policy (Kawai and Akiyama, 2000; McKinnon and Schnabl, 2002).

Pegging to the dollar made perfect sense for these countries when the dollar was weak because it was a neat way of preserving competitiveness on the US market and enhancing their attractiveness as production locations for Japanese investors. This strategy is usually justified by the alleged willingness, on the part of ASEAN countries, to preserve the competitiveness of their exporting firms and thus to privilege export promotion, even at the expense of price stability. As underlined earlier, volatility did not seem to impact Japanese FDI negatively in the past; this may be because the potential negative impact was more than offset by the gain in competitiveness resulting from the real depreciation of these countries' currencies vis-à-vis the yen, as well as by the perspectives of export penetration on the US market.

The asymmetry in the reactions to exchange rate changes on the part of Japanese and US foreign investors had certainly an impact on the way ASEAN countries chose to solve the trade-off between competitiveness and volatility, and provided an appropriate rationalisation for maintaining the peg to a depreciating dollar.

The depreciation of the host countries' currencies with respect to the yen led to an increase in Japanese FDI in Southeast Asia. Exchange rate changes apparently induced Japanese MNCs to move offshore those parts of their operations in which they were losing comparative advantages. This fits with the standard explanation that exchange rate changes impact on production costs thus changing the comparative advantages of certain goods between two countries and thus encouraging the transfer of production bases from one country to another. Yet a major difficulty is for the host countries to eventually manage to preserve their attractiveness as locations of production, in particular in a highly competitive environment.

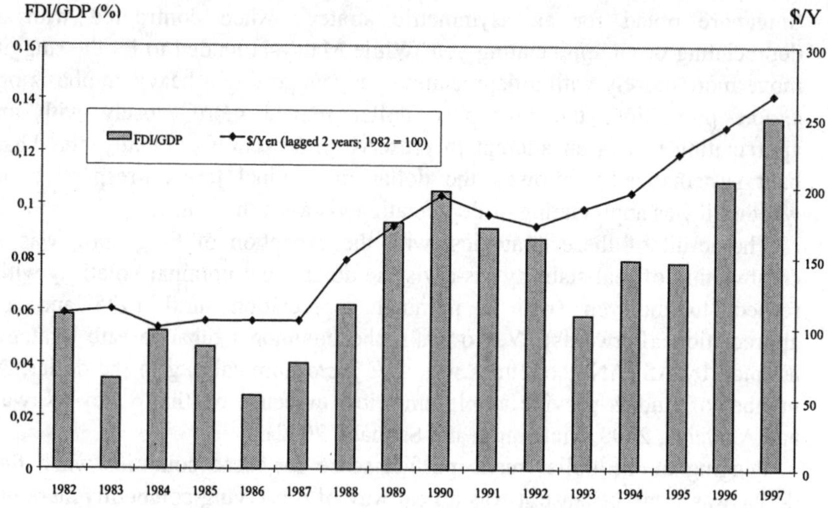

Source: Ministry of Finance, Japan.

Figure 13.1 Japanese direct investment in ASEAN 4

The appreciation of the yen with respect to the dollar also probably raised Japanese FDI in SEA, although this is a matter of controversy. Figure 13.1 confirms for instance anecdotal claims that Japanese export industries (especially labour-intensive industries) shifted their production bases to Southeast Asian countries in response to the significant appreciation of the yen against the US dollar from 1985 on. In a regression of the aggregate FDI flows from Japan to eight Asian countries on the yen/dollar exchange rate lagged one period, Ito (1999) shows more formally that FDI from Japan tends to increase as the yen appreciates. Yet, according to Nakamura and Oyama (1998), the impact of a strong yen vis-à-vis the dollar is found to be marginal on Japanese FDI flows to the region.

Pegging to the dollar was a way of preventing competitiveness losses vis-à-vis the dollar-dominated markets, which are the main outlets for ASEAN producers, and of avoiding uncertainty. Because export and FDI promotion ranked high in the list of priorities, the link to the dollar turned out to be an optimal strategy while the dollar was depreciating. It must be stressed that the peg to the dollar was not an optimal strategy *per se* but turned out to be optimal until mid-1995 given the circumstances, namely given the systematic depreciation of the dollar vis-à-vis the yen. Maintaining nominal exchange rate stability with respect to the dollar was appropriate up to a certain point. When the dollar started appreciating with respect to the yen, the strategy of pegging to the dollar all of a sudden lost its usefulness as a means of preserving competitiveness and the costs of the policy became overwhelming. These costs had been present all along (in terms of excessive borrowing for instance because there was no perceived risk[9]) but they were more than offset by the positive impact of the policy on competitiveness, exports and growth, which helped sustain the ability to go on piling up more debt.

Another benefit of the *de facto* dollar peg was to help maintain a consistent exchange rate policy throughout the region and thus to avoid beggar-thy-neighbour phenomena. Yet, this result was coincidental rather than the result of a deliberate co-operative strategy. The choice of the dollar peg may not have been optimal for all the countries in the region, but it was maintained probably as the result of a co-ordination failure. Although the objective of intra-regional exchange rate stability should rank high on the priority list of the ASEAN economies in the future, this target should not simply be reached as the result of an inadvertent and uncoordinated policy.

For these various reasons, the former strategy cannot be taken as a model for further policy, although its observed impact may shed light on the possible directions for exchange rate policy in ASEAN in the future.

Lessons for the Future

In the discussion about the optimal exchange rate policy for East Asian emerging economies, avoiding the return of financial crises is very often privileged. Yet in this respect exchange rate policy cannot be the single answer, it is one among many instruments and it can only be really helpful when combined with other policy measures. Its major impact is likely to be merely indirect to the extent that it may help rebalance capital inflows in favour of longer-term flows. Other more direct measures are also called for and are likely to have a much more direct impact. Such is the case for reforms of the financial sector, for enhanced supervision of the banking sector, for phased financial liberalization, etc.

Attracting FDI inflows has always ranked high in the priority list of ASEAN governments, and there is no reason to believe that a policy change is likely to occur in this respect. As argued by Artus (1999), using FDI to finance growth avoids excessive external debt, leads to a better analysis of investment projects, is more stable, transfers new technology and does not incur real currency over-valuation. The expansion of FDI inflows into ASEAN was also instrumental in promoting a regional division of labour, in tightening intra-regional trade linkages and in fuelling the so-called Asian miracle. Finally, by providing stability to the growth dynamics, larger FDI inflows may also help reduce the risk of a renewed currency crisis. A number of authors (Frankel and Rose, 1996; Park and Rhee, 1998) indeed show that a low level of net FDI correlates closely with the incidence of currency crisis. In other words, it can be shown empirically that higher inflows of FDI lower the odds of a crisis.

The theoretical and empirical literature (including empirical evidence about FDI flows to Southeast Asia) suggest that exchange rate factors do matter for FDI decisions, and thus that the choice of an exchange rate regime is not neutral. While the choice of an exchange rate policy cannot be determined exclusively by the authorities' desire to stimulate FDI inflows, the impact such a choice may have on these flows should be taken into consideration. The major policy implications from the literature reviewed above is that an exchange rate strategy allowing to preserve competitiveness while minimizing nominal volatility could be instrumental in luring foreign investors. The way the trade-off was made between these two objectives in the pre-crisis period cannot be repeated successfully given the current yen/dollar exchange rate.

The above analysis calls for some form of exchange rate management and not for any of the so-called corner solutions. The first conclusion to be derived is that one of the corner solutions, namely pure floating, should be clearly out of the question for ASEAN countries since it can help achieve neither of the two objectives highlighted above. Under a free float, substantial volatility should be expected, while there would be no guarantee that competitiveness will be preserved. The other extreme solution, namely a currency board cannot be a very palatable option either in the case of ASEAN, because there is no 'natural' country to which these economies should peg their currency. If ASEAN economies chose the dollar as an anchor currency, they would gain in stability vis-à-vis the dollar but not vis-à-vis the yen, while they would lose or gain in terms of competitiveness vis-à-vis Japanese and US investors depending on which direction the exchange rate moves. Given the complexity of their trade and capital linkages with the rest of the world, this cannot be expected to be an optimal strategy.

Among the intermediate options left to the countries in the region, pegging to a basket of currencies is probably the best choice, given their relatively balanced but complex set of partners, although the definition of a basket that would appear suitable to all partners may be a tricky task. But this may not be the only difficulty. As argued by Kawai and Takagi (2000), there is a strategic interdependence in the choice of exchange rate regimes for neighbouring countries that compete for exports in third markets and for FDI inflows. Because such is the case within ASEAN, a common exchange rate policy is an optimal choice in order to avoid the risk of beggar-thy-neighbour strategies. When countries tend to be in competition in third markets as well as for FDI, exchange rate policies in each country are suspected of having significant effects on the economic prospects of other countries in the region, potentially resulting in a non-co-operative equilibrium. The recent return to a *de facto* dollar peg in ASEAN[10] is probably such an example. The only possibility for ASEAN countries to drop the *de facto* dollar peg for a currency basket peg is to do it collectively. Otherwise, because there is uncertainty as to the evolution of the exchange rates of the three major world currencies, there is always a risk that moving unilaterally would place a country at a disadvantage vis-à-vis its competitors, neighbours and partners. When switching from the dollar peg to a basket peg, a country would face more volatility vis-à-vis the dollar, less volatility vis-à-vis the other currencies within the basket and an unknown competitiveness impact. In order to avoid a possible loss, the country will be tempted to stick to the same policy as its competitors, even if it is deemed sub-optimal. This situation is typical of a prisoner's dilemma in game theory, and the only way to induce all countries to move simultaneously is for them to realise how costly the non-co-operative equilibrium is, or how beneficial the co-operative outcome would be. If economic integration is pursued further, this change in the pay-off matrix may finally materialize.

Following the financial crisis, the need for tighter co-operation is much stronger today than it was perceived in the past. ASEAN countries have the objective of going ahead more forcefully on the road to regional integration. This implies the implementation of the ASEAN Free Trade Area (AFTA) as well as the further promotion of the ASEAN Investment Area (AIA). Intra-regional exchange rate stability should thus be a priority if these objectives are to materialise. But this requires more commitment and determination than ASEAN countries have been ready to show so far.

CONCLUDING REMARKS

Exchange rate policy is only one among many instruments that may play a role in an overall strategy aiming at attracting FDI inflows. It is merely an enhancing factor, while providing an enabling competitive environment is key.

In spite of a generally favourable stance towards FDI, ASEAN economies proved highly selective until recently. They can be said to have adopted a dualist policy of aggressively promoting export-oriented FDI, while protecting the economy from market-seeking investment. This was reflected in particular through the imposition of numerous restrictions on foreign investors' activities, in the form of ownership limitations, outright prohibition in some sectors, performance requirements, etc. The perceived threat of investment diversion away from ASEAN and towards China had begun to push ASEAN policies towards FDI in a more liberal direction even before the crisis, but the crisis has definitely given a new impetus to the liberalization[11]. In parallel, it is important that these countries choose an exchange rate policy which is not at odds with this priority.

In this respect, the exchange rate policy may also be instrumental in helping strengthen a coherent regional bloc. As far as ASEAN is concerned, co-operation in the monetary sphere may be the only way out for countries who can no longer afford to go it alone. As a result, rather than the type of exchange rate policy, ensuring the consistency of this policy at the regional level may be what really matters.

NOTES

1. The impact of exchange rate changes has been initially analysed in the context of fixed but adjustable exchange rates. The first analyses date back to the mid-1970s (Kohlhagen, 1977 for instance).
2. The same conclusion is reached by Nicolas (1991).
3. Yet this option is not a real solution since it would imply switching anchors according to the evolution of the exchange rate, a highly costly and complicated strategy.
4. These conclusions hinge however very much on the assumption the foreign investor has to choose between two alternative locations, and this may not necessarily be the case.
5. The Philippines is the only exception where US investors clearly dominate.
6. At the level of East Asia as a whole, FDI is approximately balanced across the three main foreign investors, Japan, the US and the EU (with 10 per cent each). Next to them, the 3 NIEs (Hong Kong, Taiwan and Korea) are the most important investors, trusting about 40 per cent.
7. A parallel phenomenon could not be observed in Latin America. FDI into that region, from both the US and Japan was not found to respond to real exchange rate changes (Goldberg and Klein, 1997).
8. Malaysia and Thailand also managed to basically maintain the stability of their nominal exchange rate vis-à-vis the dollar.
9. Nominal exchange rate stability favoured indebtedness in dollars or at least gave the impression that such indebtedness was not a risky strategy.

10. Empirical evidence on this point is provided by McKinnon and Schnabl (2002) among others.
11. Competition from China should probably not be overestimated. Although China is used as an outward processing region for goods developed elsewhere in Asia and thus in direct competition with some ASEAN countries, it is also perceived as a future market. As stressed by Feenstra (1998), companies such as Boeing, General Motors and Motorola certainly see their investments in China as part of a global strategy to secure sales in China over the long-term but not necessarily resulting in short-term reduction of production costs.

REFERENCES

Aizenman, J. (1991), 'Foreign direct investment, productive capacity and exchange rate regimes', NBER Working Paper, No 3767.

Aizenman, J. (1992), 'Exchange rate flexibility, volatility and the patterns of domestic and foreign direct investment', *NBER Working Paper*, No 3853.

Aizenman, J. and N. Marion (2001), 'The merits of horizontal versus vertical FDI in the presence of uncertainty', *NBER Working Paper*, No 8631, December.

Artus, P. (1999), 'The role of foreign direct investment in financing growth and in stabilizing exchange rates', *mimeo*, December.

Bailey, M. and G. Tavlas (1991), 'Exchange rate variability and direct investment', *The Annals of the American Academy of Political and Social Science*, **516**, 106–16.

Bayoumi, T. and G. Lipworth (1997), 'Japanese foreign direct investment and regional trade', *IMF Working Paper*, 97/103, August.

Benassy-Quéré, A., L. Fontagné and A. Lahrèche-Revil (2001a), 'Exchange rate strategies in the competition for attracting FDI', *Journal of the Japanese and International Economies*, **15**, 178–98.

Benassy-Quéré, A., L. Fontagné and A. Lahrèche-Revil (2001b), 'Stratégie de change et attraction des investissements directs en Méditerranée', mimeo, Novembre.

Blonigen, B. (1997), 'Firm-specific assets and the link between exchange rates and foreign direct investment', *The American Economic Review*, **87** (3), 447–65.

Broll, U. and M. Gilroy (1986), 'Auslandsproduktion und Wechselkursrisiko: ene einfache theoretische Analyse', *Diskussionsbeiträge, Universität Konstanz*, March, Serie I, **215**.

Caballero, R. and V. Corbo (1989), 'The effect of real exchange rate uncertainty on exports: empirical evidence', *The World Bank Economic Review*, **3**, 263–78.

Calderon-Rossell, J. (1985), 'Towards the theory of foreign direct investment', *Oxford Economic Papers*, **37**, 282–91.

Caves, R.E. (1988), 'Exchange rate movements and foreign direct investment in the United States', *Discussion paper*, n°1383, Harvard Institute of Economic Research, Harvard University.

Crabb, P. (2001), 'Exchange rates and investment by multinational corporations: a firm-level test of the imperfect capital markets result', *mimeo*, September.

Cushman, D. (1985), 'Real exchange rate risk, expectations and the level of direct investment', *Review of Economics and Statistics*, **67**, 297–308.

Cushman, D. (1988), 'Exchange rate uncertainty and foreign direct investment in the US', *Weltwirtschaftliches Archiv*, **124**, 322–36.

Dewenter, K. (1996), 'Do exchange rate changes drive foreign direct investment', *Journal of Business*, **68**, 405–33.

Dixit, A. (1987), 'Entry and exit decisions of firms under fluctuating real exchange rates', *mimeo*, Princeton University, October.

Feenstra, R. (1998), 'Facts and fallacies about foreign direct investment', University of California, Davis, *Department of Economics working paper*, 98/04.

Frankel, J. and A. Rose (1996), 'Currency crashes in emerging markets: empirical indicators', *NBER Working Paper*, No 5437, January.

Froot, K. and J. Stein (1991), 'Exchange rates and foreign direct investment: an imperfect capital markets approach', *Quarterly Journal of Economics*, **106**, 191–217.

Goldberg, L. and M. Klein (1997), 'Foreign direct investment, trade and real exchange rate linkages in Southeast Asia and Latin America', *NBER Working Paper*, No 6344.

Goldberg, L. and C. Kolstad (1995), 'Foreign direct investment, exchange rate variability and demand uncertainty', *International Economic Review*, **36** (4), 855–73.

Guérin, J.-L. and A. Lahrèche-Revil (2001), 'Volatilité des changes et investissement', *Economie Internationale*, **88**, 5–22.

Healy, P. and K. Palepu (1993), 'International corporate equity acquisitions: who, where and why?', in K. Froot (ed.), *Foreign Direct Investment*, Chicago and London: The University and Chicago Press, pp. 231–53.

Itagaki, T. (1981), 'The theory of the multinational firm under exchange rate uncertainty', *Canadian Journal of Economics*, **14**, 276–97.

Ito, T., *et al.* (1996), 'Exchange rate movements and their impact on trade and investment in the APEC region', *IMF Occasional Paper*, n°145, IMF, Washington, D.C., December.

Ito, T. (1999), 'Capital flows in Asia', *NBER Working Paper*, No 7134, May.

Kawai, M. and S. Akiyama (2000), 'Implications of the currency crisis for exchange rate arrangements in emerging East Asia', *mimeo*, June.

Kawai, M. and S. Takagi (2000), 'Proposed strategy for a regional exchange rate arrangement in post-crisis East Asia', *Policy Research Working paper*, World Bank, n°2503, December.

Klein, M. and E. Rosengren (1994), 'The real exchange rate and foreign direct investment inn the US: relative wealth vs relative wage effects', *Journal of International Economics*, **36**, 373–89.

Kogut, B. and N. Kulatilaka (1988), 'Multinational flexibility and the theory of foreign direct investment', *Working Paper*, Wharton School of the University of Pennsylvania, July.

Kohlhagen, S. (1977), 'Exchange rate changes, profitability and direct foreign investment', *Southern Economic Journal*, **44**, 376–83.

Lahrèche-Revil, A. and A. Benassy-Quéré (2002), 'China in a regional monetary framework', *mimeo*, Kobe Research Project, April.

Lane, P. and G.M. Milesi-Ferretti (2000), 'External capital structure : theory and evidence', *CEPR Working Paper*, n°2583, October 2000.

Mac Dermott, R. (2002), 'Real exchange rate fluctuations and foreign direct investment', Rutgers University, *mimeo*, April.

McKenzie, M. (1999), 'The impact of exchange rate volatility on international trade flows', *Journal of economic Surveys*, **13**, 71–106.

McKinnon, R. and G. Schnabl (2002), 'Synchronized business cycles in East Asia: fluctuations in the yen/dollar exchange rate and China's stabilizing role', *mimeo*, 19 August.

Nakamura S.-y. and T. Oyama (1998), 'The determinants of foreign direct investment from Japan and the United States to East Asian countries, and the linkage between FDI and trade', *Bank of Japan Working Papers*, 98-11, November.

Nicolas, F. (1991), *Exchange Rate Uncertainty and Direct Foreign Investment - An Imperfect Competition Approach*, PhD Dissertation, Imprimerie Nationale, Genève.

Nicolas, F. (2000), 'Capital flows and exchange rate regimes in East Asia : lessons from the crisis', in Council for Asia-Europe cooperation (CAEC), 'Asia-Europe Cooperation: Beyond the Financial Crisis', *Les Cahiers de l'Ifri*, n°31.

OECD (1999), *Foreign Direct Investment and Recovery in Southeast Asia*, Centre for Cooperation with Non-Members, OECD, Paris.

Ogawa, E. (2001), 'Monetary integration in East Asia', *The Journal of East Asian Affairs*, **Fall–Winter**, 344–68.

Ohno, K. (1998), 'Exchange rate management in developing Asia – reassessment of the pre-crisis Soft Dollar Zone', *mimeo*.

Park, D. and C. Rhee (1998), 'Currency crisis in Korea: could it have been avoided?', *mimeo*, April.

Seo, J.-S., S. Tarumun and C.-S. Suh (2002), 'Do exchange rates have any impact on foreign direct investment flows in Asia: experiences of Korea', *mimeo*, presented at the First Annual Conference of the AKES, July.

Stevens, G. (1998), 'Exchange rates and foreign direct investment: a note', *Journal of Policy Modelling*, **20**, 393–401.

Takagi, S. (1996), 'The yen and its East Asian neighbors, 1980-95: cooperation or competition?', *NBER Working Paper*, No 5720, August.

Urata, S. and K. Kiyota (2002), 'Exchange rate, exchange rate volatility and foreign direct investment', *mimeo*, Kobe Research Project, April.

Whitman, M. (1984), 'Assessing greater variability of exchange rates: a private sector perspective', *American Economic Association Papers and Proceedings*, **74**, 298–304.

PART III

International Trade and Investment in Regional Economic Integration

14. Economic Integration, Regions and Trade: The Experience of the Iberian Peninsula

João Dias

INTRODUCTION

The 'New Economic Geography' rediscovered the importance of space in economic activity. Of course, the relations within and between the space units depend very much on the existence of institutional arrangements. For example, in the case of Iberian countries, Portugal and Spain had practically no economic relations before 1986. But the Southern enlargement of the European Union to include these countries also induced strong economic integration in the Iberian Peninsula itself.

In fact, formal integration of the area, though demanding new responses by economic agents in this era of globalization, entailed a redistribution of economic activity in this new global regional market. The effective construction of this market was achieved not only by the elimination of formal impediments to factor movements but also through the creation of physical infrastructures and the implementation of policies designed to facilitate these movements.

The purpose of this chapter is to analyse some of the effects of Iberian integration on the trade relations between Portugal and Spain, using data at a regional level. This spatial dimension is particularly important when, as is the case in Spain, economic and politically strong regional powers tend to emerge, influencing the localization of economic activities.

The chapter is structured as follows. The next section briefly surveys trade relations between Portugal and Spain, before and after EU membership. The following section analyses trade relations at the regional level. This analysis is further elaborated in the fourth section with the application of a gravity-type equation to trade between continental Spain's provinces and Portugal. The final section concludes.

TRADE RELATIONS BETWEEN PORTUGAL AND SPAIN

Portugal and Spain form, together, a well-defined geographic entity in Europe, the Iberian Peninsula. Strangely, however, economic links between Portugal and Spain were extremely weak until the mid-eighties. As a clear example of this, in 1970 Spain absorbed less than 2 per cent of total Portuguese exports and supplied only 4 per cent of imports. These are very low figures indeed when account is taken of the fact that Spain is the only neighbour of Portugal. As far as Spain is concerned, Portugal was also a very weak trade partner, particularly on the import side (the figures involved were 2.8 and 0.4 per cent, for exports and imports). This has no parallel in other OECD countries, as the shares of neighbour partners in this area are usually much higher (see Table A14.1).

All this changed dramatically after 1986, when these two countries joined the European Community (see Figures A14.1 and A14.2). For Portugal, Spain became increasingly a major partner and this country ranks now first either in exports or (particularly) in imports. Compared to the situation in the last year before integration, the share of Spain increased by a factor of five and four, for exports and imports respectively. For Spain, the importance of Portugal is more modest. Even so, Portugal ranks third for exports but declines to ninth as a partner in Spain's imports. In this case, the increase in trade was four times for exports and three times for imports (Table 14.1).

Table 14.1 Share of selected partners in the external trade of Portugal and Spain (%)

	Exports				Imports			
				Portugal				
	Spain	France	EU15	EU14*	Spain	France	EU15	EU14*
1985	4.2	12.7	68.8	64.6	7.4	8.1	48.3	40.9
2000	19.3	12.6	79.5	60.2	25.3	10.6	74.1	48.8
				Spain				
	Portugal	France	EU15	EU14**	Portugal	France	EU15	EU14**
1985	2.2	15.5	53.9	51.7	0.8	9.3	39.2	38.4
2000	8.9	19.2	68.4	59.4	2.5	17.7	64.5	62.0

Notes: * EU without Spain.
** EU without Portugal.

Source: Calculated with data from IMF, DOTS, 1992 and June 2001.

Naturally, EU membership changed substantially the share of the European Union in the total trade of the Iberian countries. For Portugal, the EU now represents about 80 per cent of Portuguese external trade. However, these changes occurred almost exclusively with Spain. In fact, the percentage of the other member states has even declined from 65 to 60 percentage points in the case of exports, and increased only from 41 to 49 points in the case of imports. In the case of France, for instance, there is practically no change. This is understandable due to the fact that Portuguese exports benefited already, before EU membership, from substantial facilities in the European market. So, integration meant, above all, opening the Portuguese market to EU products. For Portugal, a very important side effect of membership was the normalization of trade relations with Spain. For Spain, the figures are somewhat different. The importance of previous EU-members increased but, again, this increase is particularly marked on the import side, after the suppression of trade barriers to EU products.

Trade between Portugal and Spain is rather asymmetrical, in the sense that Spain's exports to Portugal are much higher (2.7 times more, in year 2000) than its imports from Portugal. This is curious as Spain, like Portugal, runs an important deficit vis-à-vis all its major partners. And this is not due to a particular group of products; rather it happens in the large majority of items, even in many of those goods exported by Portugal. There are some important reasons for this, in many cases linked to the economic integration of the Iberian Peninsula itself, following EU enlargement. One reason is related to the strategies of multinational firms and the way they tend to conceive the Iberian space. For them, the preferred localization of economic activity is in Spain, a larger market and with a more central position in relation to other markets. Many of these firms have, after integration, transferred their productive plants from Portugal to Spain and supply the minor Portuguese market from there. In this case, the ongoing integration of the two markets has permitted important economies of scale. A second reason is due to bilateral capital movements and investment decisions, particularly after the Single Market. The dominant capacity of Spanish firms has been translated into significant investments in Portugal (Caetano, 1998), in many cases in order to supply this market with products imported from the headquarters in Spain. Another explanation is related to significant structural changes in the agricultural sector in both countries, combined with major changes in the distribution sector in Portugal, where a dramatic increase in the importance of large supermarket chains took place. These large chains tend to concentrate their supply sources in large competitive markets like Spain, particularly in terms of agriculture and other food related products. In fact, the share of these products (SITC section 0) in total Spain's exports to Portugal increased from around 5 per cent in 1994 to about 15 per cent in recent years.

Table 14.2 Share of intra-industry trade in Portugal–Spain: manufactures (%)

	SI	GL	GLC
1988	58	53	77
1998	63	47	84

Notes: GL and GLC stands for Grubel–Lloyd index, standard (GL) and corrected for trade imbalances; SI is for Finger–Kreinin similarity index, here applied to both vectors of imports and exports.

Source: Calculated with data from OECD, ITCS.

It is well known that, in general terms, economic integration, in Europe and elsewhere, has tended to promote a specialization not between industries but within industries. That is, economic integration has given rise more to intra-industry rather than inter-industry trade. Table 14.2 shows the classical indicators for the analysis of two-way trade for the case of Portugal and Spain. While there seems to be a reasonable overlap of bilateral imports and exports, the evolution has not been dramatic and according to EU patterns, there is large room for improvement. After fifteen years of integration, these two neighbouring economies still have an important share of inter-industry type trade. Besides, they tend to concentrate in traditional products, with low technology content (Table 14.3). In fact, for both countries, only the 'standard' group has significantly increased in importance. This is not intended to imply that only 'high-technology' is good and 'low-tech' is bad.

The data nevertheless are consistent with a strong persistence of production structures. Modernization of both economies has been spurred by formal economic integration but changes have not been dramatic as yet.

Table 14.3 Decomposition of trade in manufactures of Portugal and Spain according to technology content (%)

		High	Intermediate	Standard
Exports from Spain	1988	15	56	29
to Portugal	1998	19	43	38
Exports from Portugal	1988	8	48	44
to Spain	1998	8	40	52

Source: Calculated with data from OECD, ITCS. Classification of exports according to Foders (1996).

REGIONS AND BILATERAL TRADE

Regions in Spain (*Comunidades Autónomas*) now have significant powers and their local governments have specific prerogatives and the possibility of intervention in various domains. This is not the case in Continental Portugal where macro regions do not have independent authorities. Rather, they have only minimalist structures directly dependent on the central government. The situation in Spain also explains, in some cases, the aggressiveness of local governments in the promotion of regional products in external markets, thereby achieving a superior performance in their external trade. *Cataluña* is an example of this (Broder, 1998).

How have the different communities in Spain succeeded in promoting economic links, particularly with respect to trade, with other regions in Portugal? Of course, this seems to be particularly important for those regions in Spain and Portugal that share a common border. Unfortunately, we do not have data concerning trade between regions, except for a particular case.

A priori, it would also seem quite plausible that, after the normalization of economic (and political) relations and reinforced links between Portugal and Spain following EU accession in 1986, neighbouring regions in both cases would lead the process of regional integration. So, flourishing of economic activity might be expected somewhere near the frontier. However, it so happens that both population and economic activity are located, in Portugal, near to the sea and, in terms of regions, mainly concentrated in the regions of *Lisboa e Vale do Tejo* and *Norte*. The other regions are less important and less developed, particularly in those areas near the frontier.

The case of Spain is not different; that is, those regions near the frontier with Portugal are less developed, less populated (with a partial exception of some areas in *Galicia*), and less active economically. A clear example, from both sides, is *Alentejo* in Portugal and its neighbour *Extremadura* in Spain. This clearly reduces the dynamism of those areas and the possibilities of joint synergies and economies of scale. An important exception is the *Norte*-Portugal and *Galicia*-Spain.

Tables A14.2 and A14.4 show the contribution of each region to the exports and imports of Portugal and Spain. As shown, the regions near the border (Figure A14.4) make a marginal contribution to the exports and imports of Portugal. The exception is, of course, the *Norte*, which is the country main exporting region.

Does proximity/neighbourhood matter in trade relations between regions in Portugal and Spain? Recent studies applying the gravitational model for provinces in Canada and states in the USA have revealed an unexpectedly high importance of proximity in determining the levels and shares of trade between regions.

In Portugal, all of the regions in the Centre and South, with extensive borders with Spain, have a high share of trade with Spain (Table 14.4). As referred to above, they share also the characteristics of low levels of development and industrial activity, particularly in the border subregions.

Table 14.4 Share of Spain in total trade of Portuguese regions (%)

	Exports		Imports	
	1993	1999	1993	1999
Algarve	22	36	36	51
Centro	20	24	22	30
Alentejo	23	27	22	42
Lisboa e Vale do Tejo	20	19	18	25
Norte	9	13	16	22
Continental Portugal	14	17	18	25

Source: Data from Instituto Nacional de Estatística, Lisbon.

However, it seems that we have here a puzzling contrast between the other two regions *Lisboa e Vale do Tejo* and *Norte*. The first region is the only one with no border with Spain. The *Norte* region has an extensive border with Spain: the entire north and east frontier. Yet, it is this last region, largely industrialized and comprising about half of total Portuguese exports that has a lower share of trade with Spain. Breaking down the data using subregions resolves the apparent puzzle. First, the large subregions sharing a border with Spain (see Figure A14.3) are again, less populated and industrialized. In fact, the most extensive subregions *Alto Trás-os-Montes* and *Douro* represent, together, less than 1 per cent of *Norte*'s total exports and the potential to export is also limited by the structure of production in these areas. This means that the diversity of goods that these subregions can offer to Spain is very scarce. Besides, the neighbour subregions in Spain are not very different. So, the share of manufactures in total exports of *Alto Trás-os-Montes* and *Douro* to Spain is, usually, less than 50 per cent (see Table A14.3).

All this means that, after all, the core of economic activity is not, in the *Norte* region, distinguishably less distant from the rich regions in Spain than the region *Lisboa e Vale do Tejo*. Still, even here distance matters. In spite of the almost complete isolation of Portugal from Spain in the past, the recent integration of both economies has permitted a gradual and increasing interaction between the region *Norte* in Portugal and *Galicia* in Spain, even though *Galicia* has its own peculiarities in terms of development. In fact, recent region-to-region data collected specifically for these two regions (INE-IGE, 2000) show that most of the imports of *Galicia* from Portugal are indeed supplied by the *Norte* and almost half of the exports to Portugal have the *Norte* region as destination (Table 14.5). On the other hand, *Galicia* is not so exceptionally important for the trade of *Norte*, but even so that region has a high share of almost one quarter of total exports and imports of *Norte* with Spain. There has been some diversification in recent years but half this trade, in both directions, is still concentrated in the agriculture, livestock, fishing, textiles and clothing products.

Table 14.5 Trade between Galicia and Norte region, 1997 (%)

Share of *Norte* in total trade of *Galicia*	
Exports	12.0
Imports	8.4
Share of *Norte* in trade of *Galicia* with Portugal	
Exports	45.8
Imports	66.3
Share of *Galicia* in total trade of *Norte*	
Exports	3.4
Imports	6.3
Share of *Galicia* in trade of *Norte* with Spain	
Exports	23.9
Imports	22.7

Source: Data from Instituto Nacional de Estatística e Instituto Galego de Estatística, *Comércio Intracomunitário da euro-região Galiza-Norte de Portugal*, Porto, 2000.

What about regions in Spain? Table 14.6 presents some data showing the importance of Portugal for these regions. In general terms neighbouring regions trade more than distant ones. Thus, a very high share of 40 per cent of all exports and imports of *Extremadura* has Portugal as partner. It is true that its neighbouring region, *Alentejo*, is a poor one and cannot explain such a high share. However, the most important market, in Portugal, is *Lisboa e Vale do Tejo*. This region represents around two thirds of all Portuguese imports, either from Spain or the rest of the world. And it is, like all the other regions, not far away from the frontier.

The importance of Portugal for *Galicia* follows the same rule: the more proximate, the higher the share. This is not a strict rule, though. For instance, *Andalucia*, which is closer than *Catalunã*, has a lower share of exports to Portugal than the more distant region. Overall, however, working with Spanish data on a subregion (province) basis for 1999 shows a reasonably high correlation coefficient of –0.6 between distance from Portugal and the share of exports going to this market with a coefficient of –0.5 for the share of imports and distance.

Table 14.6 Share of Portugal in total trade of each region of Continental Spain (%)

	Exports		Imports	
	1995	2000	1995	2000
Andalucia	7	9	4	4
Aragon	9	11	3	3
Asturias	9	12	3	3
Cantabria	7	8	1	2
Castilla la Mancha	14	21	3	4
Castilla y Leon	10	10	7	4
Cataluna	8	9	1	2
Extremadura	36	40	32	40
Galicia	19	17	8	9
Madrid	12	13	3	2
Murcia	4	5	2	1
Navarra	6	6	2	2
Pais Vasco	6	6	2	2
La Rioja	9	14	5	6
Valencia	5	7	4	3
Spain *	8	10	3	3

Note: * Includes Baleares and Canarias but excludes Ceuta and Melilla.
Source: Calculated with data from Aduanas e Impuestos Especiales, Madrid.

AN APPLICATION OF THE GRAVITY-TYPE EQUATION TO TRADE BETWEEN PROVINCES IN SPAIN AND PORTUGAL

Since the pioneering work of Tinbergen (1962), Poyhonen (1963) and specially Linnemann (1966), the application of the so-called gravity equation to empirical trade studies has been highly successful. The basic formulation may be represented as:

$$X_{ij} = AY_i^{b_1} y_i^{b_2} Y_j^{b_3} y_j^{b_4} D_{ij}^{b_5} e^{u_{ij}} \tag{14.1}$$

This equation explains the transactions between any two countries (*i* and *j*) as a function of some attraction forces (the 'mass' Y = GDP and y = GDP per head, preferential arrangements, etc.) and repulsion ones (D = distance). Recent applications include the works of McCallum (1995), Wall (2000) and Hillberry (2002) on trade between Canadian provinces and US states.

This section provides estimates of a model in the spirit of the gravity equation, applied to trade between 47 provinces of Continental Spain and Portugal. Unfortunately, no data on a province-to-province basis is available, so the model used is:

$$X_{EP} = AY_E^{\beta_1} y_E^{\beta_2} D_{EP}^{\beta_3} \ e^{u_{EP}} \qquad (14.2)$$

or, after applying logarithms,

$$\log X_{EP} = \beta_0 + \beta_1 \log Y_E + \beta_2 \log y_E + \beta_3 \log D_{EP} + u_{EP} \qquad (14.3)$$

where, in this case, the variables *X*, *Y* and *y* are the exports (imports) of a province in Spain to (from) Portugal, and the GDP and GDP per head of that province. Distance is calculated as the shortest distance by road used by trucks between the capital of the province and Portugal. As far as Portugal is concerned, a possibility is to consider Lisbon, on the grounds that the major volume of trade is made with this region (*D1*). However, a considerable group of provinces (for instance in *Galicia*) trades essentially with the Norte Region, and Oporto arises as another possibility (*D2*). A third option adopted here is to calculate the minimum distance between a province and either Lisbon or Oporto (*D3*).

The possibility of an additional influence of sharing a border may be taken into account by the inclusion of a dummy variable, and the equation becomes:

$$\log X_{EP} = \beta_0 + \beta_1 \log Y_E + \beta_2 \log y_E + \beta_3 \log D_{EP} + \beta_4 Border_{EP} + u_{EP} \qquad (14.4)$$

where the variable *Border* takes the value one if a province shares a frontier with Portugal and zero otherwise.

A priori, it is expected that the signs of *Y* and *y* are both positive and that distance has a negative coefficient. The influence of a common border on the exports or imports of two areas is, in principle, positive, although in this case it is not clear if it should be significant.

Table 14.7 presents some results for equations (14.3) and (14.4) using *D3* as distance. The results using *D1* and *D2* are not substantially different, although some multicollinearity problems are apparent when we use *D1*. In any case, *D3* has only marginally better statistical properties. The model passes the usual tests of heteroscedasticity and other tests. As is usual in other applications, the gravity model fits the data quite well.

Table 14.7 Estimation of the gravity equation for trade between the provinces of Continental Spain and Portugal

	Exports				Imports			
	1995		1999		1995		1999	
Constant	−0.46 (−0.24)	−1.59 (−0.68)	0.34 (0.22)	−0.88 (−0.47)	0.12 (0.06)	−1.45 (−0.63)	−1.35 (−0.62)	-3.92 (-1.51)
Log *Y*	1.21 (10.9)	1.22 (10.9)	1.04 (11.7)	1.05 (11.7)	1.12 (9.99)	1.13 (10.1)	1.18 (9.29)	1.19 (9.57)
log *y*	2.77 (5.07)	2.80 (5.10)	2.24 (5.11)	2.27 (5.19)	1.91 (3.49)	1.96 (3.58)	1.52 (2.45)	1.59 (2.61)
log *D*	−1.36 (−5.42)	−1.20 (−3.84)	−1.10 (−5.42)	−0.93 (−3.68)	−1.30 (−5.17)	−1.08 (−3.47)	−1.23 (−4.27)	−0.87 (−2.47)
Border		0.32 (0.86)		0.34 (1.16)		0.44 (1.20)		0.72 (1.75)
N	47	47	47	47	47	47	47	47
$\bar{R}^2$	0.77	0.77	0.81	0.81	0.73	0.73	0.69	0.71
F	53.00	39.70	64.60	49.20	41.40	31.80	35.70	28.80
BP	0.13	0.02	0.20	0.00	0.01	0.11	2.21	3.81

Note: *t*-ratios in parentheses. Data from Aduanas e Impuestos Especiales, Madrid. BP = Breusch–Pagan statistic for testing heteroscedasticity.

The results confirm the importance of the level of development in creating trade. *Ceteris paribus*, a 1 per cent increase in the market size increases exports to Portugal by a similar percentage. But the bigger markets are also, as is the case in *Catalunã* and Madrid, the richer ones. And this makes a big difference, as the elasticity of exports vis-à-vis GDP per head is much higher. This is understandable. More developed regions, particularly if they coincide with big agglomerations and with the concentration of industrial production, have the means, the scale, the networks, links and contacts, logistics, initiative and a large panoply of advantages which permits them to export more than other regions (Stolper, 2000; Shatz and Venables, 2000). This tends to be the case in Spain where, in addition, these more developed and populated regions tend also to be the production and distribution headquarters of multinational firms to all the Iberian area.

The high significance and the level of the coefficients of GDP and GDP per head do not change with the inclusion or exclusion of the *Border* variable. The elasticity of the distance variable is more sensitive to the specification (14.3) or (14.4), although the changes are not dramatic. In any case, the distance coefficient is highly significant and negative, as expected. That is, the findings of the second section are confirmed here: distance remains a considerable obstacle to trade.

An interesting result is the reduction in the GDP, GDPC and distance elasticities, between 1995 and 1999 (with the only exception of GDP in the case of imports). This clearly points to a reinforcement of integration between Portugal and Spain, after the implementation of the Single Market in 1993. Of course, the case of distance reflects also the reduction in transportation costs with the improvement in roads and road transports in the Peninsula.

Contrarily to other applications of the gravity model, the border does not have the high impact it has when we are considering neighbour countries. But, again, the results for the border coefficient found in this section are in accordance with what has been already emphasized in the previous section, namely the low level of development and industrial activity of neighbouring provinces in Spain and Portugal. However, the increasing concern in both countries about these poor interior regions has motivated specific development programs for them and some structural changes are already in progress. This, in turn, is paving the way for stronger economic links between provinces from both sides of the border. The somewhat different results for 1995 and 1999 obtained here concerning the border variable are in line with this. The border coefficient is slightly increasing and, for the import equation, besides being positive as expected, it is significant at the 10 per cent level in 1999.

Of course, we may have some specification problems here (although some tests, like RESET, suggest the opposite), in particular through the variables 'level of development' and 'border'. Indeed, it may be more adequate to include another variable expressing the share of industrial products in exports, as a more adequate proxy for the capacity to sell abroad.

As is usual in some branches of economics and particularly in the 'new economic geography' (Fujita, Krugman and Venables, 1999), it is often convenient to consider agriculture as an immobile sector and industry as a mobile one. So, State intervention to counterbalance economic forces, that lead naturally to agglomeration, may have already attained some goals. This, combined with central authorities' policies towards a more even distribution of national income may, in one way or another, introduce some bias in the hypothesized direct link between exports, GDP per head and the border effect. If we include this new variable, that is, the percentage of industrial products in the exports to Portugal, its own coefficient is significant at the 5 per cent level and the border coefficient also becomes significant at the 10 per cent level, in 1999. This does not change our results much, but more work needs to be done in order to obtain a completely satisfactory specification of the determinants of trade between regional entities in Spain and Portugal.

CONCLUSIONS

Departing from a situation of practically ignoring each other until the eighties, Portugal and Spain have now become very important economic partners. In the past, it was politics that promoted isolation. It was necessary to wait for European integration to promote the 'normalization' of economic relations between the Iberian countries. In a sense, the integration in the European Union corrected the distortions of decades of isolation. This same integration also accelerated time, as this correction was made very rapidly.

Now some of the forces described by the 'new economic geography', concerning the localization of economic activity in the Iberian Peninsula, are in process. Some of them tend to concentrate production in Spain and may lead to the marginalization of Portugal (or large areas in both Portugal and Spain) in terms of industrial activity.

However, there are also institutional forces in motion to counteract the purely economic ones, tending to impose a more even distribution of population and economic activity over the Iberian space. As a result of the operation of both types of forces, we now have a reasonably high integration of the Iberian territory, in particular at the regional level. An important aspect of this institutional intervention is the slow but persistent integration of the neighbouring regions from both sides and the operation of distance in an economically consistent way.

REFERENCES

Broder, A. (1998), *Histoire économique de l'Espagne contemporaine*, Paris: Economica.

Caetano, J.M. (1998), *Portugal–Espanha: Relações Económicas no Contexto da Integração Europeia*, Lisbon: Celta.

Foders, F. (1996), 'Mercosur: a new approach to regional integration?', *Kiel Working Paper* 746.

Fujita, M., P. Krugman and A.J. Venable (1999), *The Spatial Economy*, Cambridge and London: MIT Press.

Hillberry, R.H. (2002), 'Aggregation bias, compositional change, and the border effect', *Canadian Journal of Economics*, **35** (3), 517–30.

INE-IGE (2000), *Comércio Intracomunitário da Euro-Região Galiza-Norte de Portugal*, Oporto: INE-DRN.

Linnemann, H. (1966), *An Econometric Study of International Trade Flows*, Amsterdam: North-Holland.

McCallum, J. (1995), 'National borders matter: Canada–U.S. Regional trade patterns', *American Economic Review*, **June**, 615–23.

Poyhonen, P. (1963), 'A tentative model for the volume of trade between countries', *Weltwirtschaftliches Archiv*, **90** (1), 205–19.

Shatz, H.J. and A.J. Venables (2000), 'The geography of international investment', in G.L. Clark., M.P. Feldman and M.S. Gertler (eds), The *Oxford Handbook of Economic Geography*, New York: Oxford University Press.

Stolper, M. (2000), 'Globalization, localization, and trade', in G.L. Clark, M.P. Feldman and M.S. Gertler (eds), *The Oxford Handbook of Economic Geography*, New York: Oxford University Press.

Tinbergen, J. (1962), *Shaping the World Economy*, New York: Twentieth Century Fund.

Wall, H.J. (2000), 'Gravity model specification and the effects of Canada–U.S. Border', *Federal Reserve Bank of St. Louis, Working Paper* 2000-024A.

APPENDIX

*Table A14.1 Share of a neighbour in a country's exports and imports**

	Exports		Imports	
	1985	1998	1985	1998
Canada–USA	77.6	83.6	69.8	66.8
Norway–Sweden	9.4	10.6	19.2	16.9
Finland–Sweden	12.5	8.9	12.8	12.9
Netherlands–Germany	28.2	18.8	24.5	19.0
Ireland–UK	34.4	22.6	46.0	38.2
Austria–Germany	30.3	33.2	43.9	44.4
Austria–Italy	9.2	9.7	8.5	8.7
Portugal–Spain	3.9	15.8	7.2	25.0
Spain–France	15.7	19.6	10.4	19.2
Spain–Portugal	2.2	8.8	0.8	2.8
Greece–Italy	12.5	12.2	10.5	17.3

Note: * For each pair, % of second country in the external trade of first country.
Source: Data from CEPII-Chelem.

Table A14.2 Share of each region in total exports and imports of Continental Portugal (%)

	Exports		Imports	
	1993	1999	1993	1999
Algarve	0.4	0.2	0.3	0.4
Centro	11.9	14.3	6.6	8.5
Alentejo	2.4	3.0	0.8	1.1
Lisboa VT	34.2	37.6	66.1	65.1
Norte	51.2	44.8	26.1	25.0

Source: Data from Instituto National de Estatística, Lisbon.

Table A14.3 The Norte region and its two larger subregions, 1995 (%)

	Norte	*Douro*	*Alto TM**
% of *Norte's* exports	100	0.2	0.3
% of Spain in total exports	11.2	2.0	11.9
% of Spain in total imports	19.6	16.7	46.1
Decomposition of exports to Spain			
Agric./food/beverages/minerals	11.6	60.6	48.3
Other products	88.4	39.4	51.7

Note: * Alto TM = Alto Trás-os-Montes.
Source: Calculated with data from *Anuário Estatístico* 1998, Instituto Nacional de Estatística (Lisbon) and Junta de Castilla y León (Spain).

Table A14.4 Share of each Comunidad in total exports and imports of Continental Spain (%)

	Exports	Imports
Andalucia	8.3	7.5
Aragon	4.2	3.1
Asturias	1.4	1.2
Cantabria	1.2	0.9
Castilla la Mancha	1.5	2.0
Castilla–Leon	6.9	5.2
Cataluña	27.7	29.6
Extremadura	0.6	0.2
Galicia	6.9	5.5
La Rioja	0.7	0.4
Madrid	11.5	25.2
Murcia	2.6	2.5
Navarra	4.3	2.4
Pais Vasco	9.6	6.3
Valencia	12.7	7.7
Spain	100.0	100.0

Source: Calculated with data from Secretaria de Estado de comercio y Turismo, Madrid.

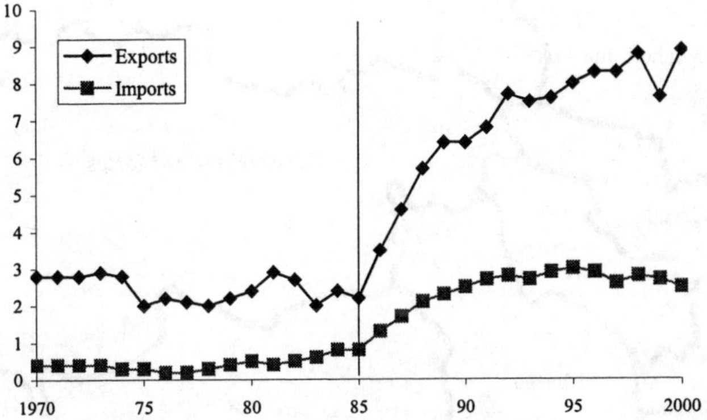

Source: Own calculations with data from CEPII-Chelem and IMF, Direction of Trade Statistics, various issues.

Figure A14.1 Share of Spain in total exports and imports of Portugal, 1970–2000 (%)

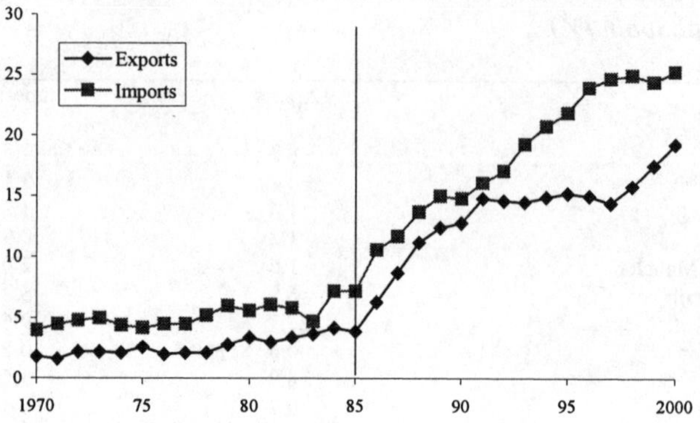

Source: See Figure A14.1.

Figure A14.2 Share of Portugal in total exports and imports of Spain, 1970–2000 (%)

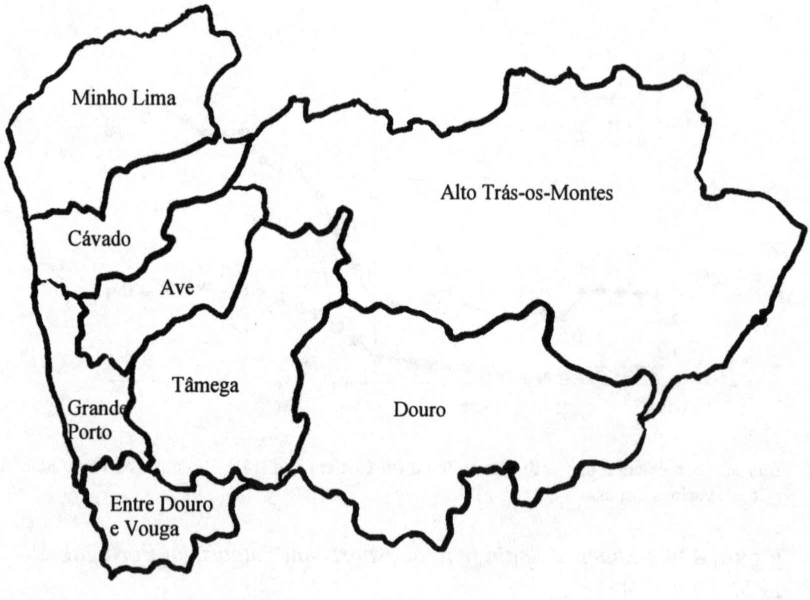

Source: Freehand drawing by the author.

Figure A14.3 The subregions of Norte

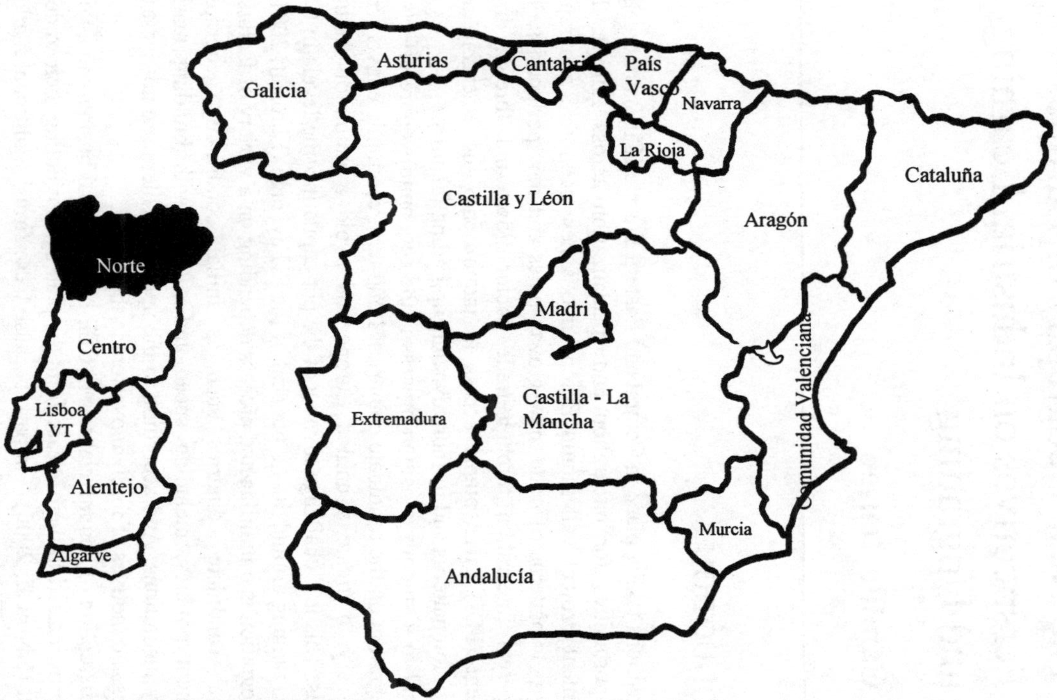

Source: Freehand drawing by the author.

Figure A14.4 Regions of Continental Portugal and Spain

15. The New Geography of Europe: Perspectives on Industrial Learning and Upgrading

Camilla Jensen

INTRODUCTION

The transitions taking place in Central and Eastern Europe (CEE) are creating new opportunities for integration and specialization across Europe. The Enlargement Project will mould Europe into a new economic geography, creating new patterns of trade, new growth poles and new peripheries. The ongoing real integration through trade, factor flows and foreign direct investment (FDI) gives ample access to inquire into the emerging new specialization patterns and its more dynamic upgrading features.

Critical to a smooth transition process is the economic welfare effects of real integration on the candidate countries. Long-term economic convergence is necessary to create a unified Europe and avoid a union of multiple standards. This is a challenge in view of the per capita income levels in CEE countries ranging around 30–60 per cent of the EU average (Eurostat, 2001a). Real integration is a multifaceted process depending on a variety of factors in individual candidate countries such as initial conditions, geography, government policies, including speed and success with building market economy institutions. And according to the upgrading literature not least the strategies and motives of foreign investors in the region.

The disruption of commercial ties in CEE has left local business in a void. Many firms reacted to their release from the plan by reorienting their trade to the West (UN/ECE, 2000) – in part, because these firms' traditional markets had collapsed. FDI has reinforced this process of reorientation with the EU markets as the new gravitating centre. FDI provides opportunities for learning and upgrading in industrial production through technology transfer and capabilities accumulation. However, there is also the great danger that some host countries are incorporated as end-nodes in multinational networks providing them little opportunity for indigenous learning and hence upgrading.

Focus in this chapter is on the relative changes in the competitive position of bilateral CEE exports to the EU in the period 1993–2000. The research question being whether FDI in any significant way has contributed to industrial upgrading.

However, industrial upgrading is a loosely defined new catchword in the development literature with many different connotations and practices. Hence the chapter starts with a short review of the theoretical literature in international economics providing us with a set of perspectives on upgrading processes: inter-industry types of upgrading and intra-industry types of upgrading. Subsequently these terms are for simplicity named industry and quality upgrading respectively. The different types of upgrading are tested using econometrics in later sections of the chapter. Much of the current literature on upgrading in transition is *ad hoc* and strictly empirical according to the review in the third section. Most authors suggest that FDI has played a large role for the observed upgrading processes in CEE according to this section, but none have yet provided for specific tests thereof in a cross-country framework. The chapter sets out to do this in order to clarify the developmental role of FDI in a broader CEE perspective than the single-country case. The empirical contribution sets out with data presentation in the fourth section, followed by regression results in the fifth section. Finally, the results obtained in the chapter are juxtaposed with the theoretical perspectives and past results.

THEORY ON INDUSTRIAL UPGRADING

This section will review two theories that take an explicit focus on economic upgrading and with emphasis on the possible tutorial role of FDI in a development perspective. The particular advantage of these theories compared to other theories in international economics incorporating FDI is their explicit focus on dynamic perspectives of FDI and industrial upgrading.

The two theories reviewed here have been developed in relative isolation as they stem from different social science traditions. The first derives from an eclectic approach to international business and economics and relates to the eclectic OLI paradigm (Dunning, 1981) on explaining multinational enterprise. The second derives from a distinct sociological approach (Gereffi,

1996) to global commodity chains in the post-war economy. First the two theories are briefly introduced and explained, but emphasis in this review is placed on their predictions about upgrading in view of host country FDI.

Upgrading Along the Investment Development Path (IDP)

The Investment Development Path (IDP) is derived from the OLI paradigm (Dunning, 1993; Dunning and Narula, 1996; Narula, 1996) describing the interaction between inward and outward FDI at different stages of development. It builds around country cases, explaining how initial host countries to FDI go through different stages of development and eventually become outward investors or home countries to FDI along this path.

Originally the IDP includes four stages, where stage one and two are marked by inward FDI carried by traditional motivations of mainly natural resource-seeking FDI including simple location advantages such as cheap labour. Stage three is the take off stage where the host country has accumulated critical endowment along with providing a certain market size. At this stage the tutorial role of FDI is crucial in manufacturing industries (Dunning, 1993) and motives will start to exhibit features of the market-seeking type and possibly also with elements of a more knowledge exploratory type. It is around stage two and stage three that upgrading becomes critical and where FDI ignite and reinforce accumulation of created assets (as opposed to natural endowments) with local firms of the knowledge-based type (human capital and entrepreneurial capital).

Stage four is marked by a shift from net-inward position of FDI to a net-outward position based on the host country firms' own accumulated ownership advantages. Finally, stage five is added later (Narula, 1996) because of the rise in strategic asset-seeking FDI and the fact that the net investment position of the host country may turn to negative anew since its highly developed location advantages associated with local innovation activities become increasingly enticing to investor nations at similar levels of development. Hence the IDP centres on multinational firms as carriers of knowledge (technology), from home to host countries until stage four and mainly in the reverse direction at stage five. According to the IDP, multinational activity is an important complement to the national development effort.

The centrally dynamic feature of this theory is that endowments are not fixed along the IDP, but change considerably over time as countries move to the next stage, from natural resource endowments at stage one and two, to physical capital endowments at stage three and with knowledge-based assets as the most important ingredient in the development of the firm and location after stage three. FDI is a central feature along this path entering endogenously in the process of accumulating created and mainly knowledge-assets.

Accumulation of created assets with a country's firms is hence central to the story of upgrading contained with the IDP. According to the predictions of the IDP, FDI will lead to upgrading if it supports the host country's accumulation processes at its particular stage of development, implying that there is a match between the location advantages offered by the host country and the ownership advantages of types of investors that are also likely to support an accumulation of created assets in the local environment. The ownership advantages of the multinational firm may catalyse the development of local firms' ownership advantages through various types of spillover effects. Gradually these spillovers may also upgrade the location advantages of the host country through for example agglomeration effects (Dunning and Narula, 2000). Upgrading is more likely to occur if there are unexplored combinations of ownership advantages from the home country and location advantages (endowments) in the host country that also combines or entices with accumulation of local ownership advantages in the host economy (Ozawa, 1992). A virtuous process of learning and knowledge spillovers from multinational firms to local firms will start to support host country development in a rapidly changing and dynamic environment. Movement from stage two through stage three is central in this respect. Dunning (1993) describes upgrading to take place in practice through various micro-type spillovers and linkages starting to develop between the multinational firm and firms in the domestic market, for example, through training of domestic employees and managers, and creation of backward and forward linkages with indigenous firms.

The IDP predicts the following central features of the host country's trade patterns under a scenario of upgrading (Dunning, 1993; Dunning and Narula, 2000):

- Shifts in export patterns away from primary towards secondary (manufacturing) industries and later on from secondary towards tertiary (service) industries.
- Shifts in specialization patterns towards more technology-intensive (skill and R&D intensive) industries along the path.
- Shifts in investor strategies from natural resource-seeking to market-seeking including efficiency-seeking FDI and eventually to strategic asset-seeking.

Hence the IDP is a macroeconomic theory of upgrading that emphasizes inter-industry shifts in export patterns as upgrading takes place. According to the IDP multinational firms are not isolated to any specific type of industry or activity.

The ultimate test of upgrading is the graduation to stage four, where the host country becomes an outward investor itself. However, it is beyond the present empirical case to look into outward FDI, even though there is some sign of increasing outward FDI from the most reformed and advanced transition countries (UNCTAD, 2002).

The emphasis on spillovers in relation to the IDP provides a strong bridge to a very large and mainly empirical literature on the topic of spillovers related to FDI in host developing nations (Blomström et al., 2001). This literature proposes for example that spillovers are more difficult to achieve the larger the technology gap between multinational and local firms, but less so if the host country is endowed with human capital. Spillovers in less developed countries will always tend to be relatively shallow in knowledge content (such as competition-based demonstration effects) when motives are exploitative rather than explorative (strategic asset-seeking) and vice-versa. Strategic asset-seeking FDI is more likely to include spillovers of the highest quality type such as entering of strategic alliances between the multinational and domestic firms.

Propositions from the empirical literature on spillovers often provide a less optimistic picture as to the automatic progression on the IDP (Dunning and Narula, 2000), since it would appear that it is much more likely to benefit from FDI when being a highly developed country with all the opportunities to attract high quality FDI with very strong spillover effects. Hence, more recent contributions to the IDP suggests that it is possible to be locked-in on the IDP or even fall back from stage three to stage two if upgrading is unsuccessful. Small qualitative differences in the process of accumulating created assets locally appear to be decisive to whether countries end up in a good or a bad equilibrium on the IDP. From an empirical perspective it remains less researched when and exactly why a country experiences upgrading on the IDP, e.g. when there are unexplored endowment opportunities. However, many recent contributions from various types of literature suggest that accumulation of human capital is particularly decisive to upgrading (e.g Borenzstein *et al.*, 1995), a proposition that also follows naturally from most of the microeconomic literature on spillovers referred to above.

Upgrading in Global Commodity Chains (GCC)

The theory about global commodity chains (GCC) takes departure from a structuralist perspective on international trade (Gibbon, 2001) and a sociological approach to the mechanisms ruling relations between firms. As opposed to the transaction cost literature, the GCC approach does not emphasize differences in the inter-firm power relations depending on whether firms are governed under the same umbrella of owners or not. This means that subsidiary–parent relationships can be marked by divergence in development objectives just as a licensor and a licensee. Rather the GCC framework describes relationships between firms as those of leader and follower roles. However, it is possible that the ability to exert power is greater in those types of relationships that international business normally perceive as intra-firm (parent–subsidiary relations). But the main point of the GCC analysis is that the way lead firms choose to exert power through choice of relationships depends rather on the nature of industry competition in relation to core competencies of firms and barriers to entry than power (ownership) as such (Gereffi, 2001)[1].

Gereffi maintains that the GCC approach is different from related concepts such as global value chains (see for example UNCTAD, 2002) because of its explicit focus on the distribution of power in the GCCs and because of its differential level of analysis being international or global as opposed to national[2]. But often it is also based on American corporate strategies driven by a large home market foremost (Gereffi, 2001) and hence not necessarily representative of European firms that are typically still confined to smaller and more fragmented markets.

The GCC approach is based on industry cases at the international level (Gereffi, 1999). Based on industry studies the GCC framework distinguishes between at least two types of GCCs with different principles of organization, coordination and networking: the buyer-driven chains and the producer-driven chains (Gereffi, 1999; Gibbon, 2001). The GCC framework predicts that it is mainly in the producer-driven chains that FDI plays a central role while the buyer-driven chains typically are organized internationally according to other more decentralized governance principles. The producer-driven chains are characteristic for capital- and technology-intensive industries such as automobiles, computers and heavy machinery. The buyer-driven chains are oppositely organized internationally through trade mainly and described by decentralized production networks that typically source their materials, inputs and semi-manufactures in developing countries. The buyer-driven chains are characteristic for labour-intensive industries such as garments, footwear, toys and consumer electronics. Hence the GCC approach suggests that FDI is an exclusive phenomena to certain industries and hence also exclusive to any relationship between FDI and upgrading within these.

A major hypothesis of the GCC approach is that upgrading will be almost impossible for countries that are incapable of linking up with the most significant global players of the industry. Hence it poses a rather bleak scenario of development, confined to countries capable of linking up to the

GCCs, confined to specific local firms in those countries and furthermore upgrading being confined to those firms that are able to increase their power and hence their rents through the GCCs over time. Firms that do not upgrade over time are unlikely to maintain their position in the GCC in the longer run. The theory offers little possibility of horizontal type of spillovers whereby local firms may empower themselves without the GCCs. A proposition that is well in accordance with empirical results for transition countries (Smarzynska, 2002). The main source to improvement of a firm's position in the commodity chain is organizational learning, however, a learning process that may also be subordinate to the concerns of the leading firms in the industry. A country's position in the GCC can be improved through backward linkage creation from the multinational firm to local suppliers (Gereffi, 1999).

The GCC predicts the following central features of the host country's trade patterns under a scenario of upgrading (Gereffi, 1999):

- Upgrading through organizational learning in the individual subsidiary.
- Upgrading through the creation of backward linkages to domestic suppliers.

Hence the GCC approach is mainly concerned with upgrading of an intra-industry type, whereas the inter-industry dimension of upgrading relates specifically to the fact that FDI is the result of different fundamental ways of organizing the GCCs.

In this section two different theoretical perspectives on upgrading have been presented. The theories are largely complementary even though they tend to focus on or stress two different aspects of industrial upgrading – namely inter-industry versus intra-industry types of upgrading. In the following sections these will be referred to for simplicity as industry (inter-industry) and quality (intra-industry) upgrading. But while the IDP approach is generally positive towards the tutorial role of FDI during decisive stages of a country's development path, where the upgrading processes are tantamount, the GCC approach is more sceptical in particular about quality upgrading whereas industry upgrading associated with FDI is by this theory seen as largely a result of different international organizational and transactional modes applied by the multinational firm.

STUDIES OF INDUSTRIAL UPGRADING IN TRANSITION COUNTRIES

Quite a few empirical studies have been made that assess the extent to which the newly created trade ties with the EU have been beneficial from the viewpoint of CEE producers. Specialization studies belong to this category, even though it is relatively rare to find studies on specialization that discuss issues of upgrading explicitly. Most studies on upgrading focus on price quality gaps in East–West trade or what in this chapter is termed quality upgrading. Increasing specialization in up-market goods fetching a relatively higher unit price is taken as an indicator of quality upgrading based on sophistication of skills and access to technology necessary to produce such higher quality goods. Such studies reveal how East European produces are situated in a scheme of vertical product differentiation as described below followed by a discussion of available studies on the industry composition or specialization pattern of CEE exports. Finally, reference is made to studies that explicitly have aimed to connect upgrading with FDI in transition countries.

Quality Upgrading of Trade

The pioneering study by Landesmannn and Burgstaller (1997) shows that price quality gaps are very large in CEE exports, meaning that CEE producers are vertically differentiated in the low quality segments on EU markets. Landesmann and Burgstaller find that CEE producers are underrepresented in the high quality segments also when compared to the South EU countries. Further, the study evidences that upgrading is taking place at a quite high pace (higher than for other benchmark groups) in exports to the EU over the periods 1988–1990 and 1992–1994. But the picture is also found to be quite diverse for Central European and other CEE producers, where the former are lead recipients of FDI in the region. A closure of price quality gaps is found to take place, including consolidation of market shares for many branches of the engineering-based industries in Central Europe. Findings that conform well to the studies on specialization discussed below.

A later study by Freudenberg and Lemoine (1999) reports similar evidence. However, they take a two-fold perspective on upgrading: namely distinguishing goods by stages of production (primary, intermediate, capital and consumption goods) and by price quality gaps as in the Landesmann and Burgstaller study. They also include all the ten candidate countries in their study. Freudenberg and Lemoine (1999) find that intermediate products form the largest and most dynamic part of East European exports, while the opposite is true for capital goods and in most cases also for consumption goods. However, consumption goods are also increasing, especially in exports from Central Europe. While the position of the Baltic States is also improving in this respect, the study reveals that Baltic exports are much more traditional and still highly dependent on primary products. Over 90 per cent of trade flows between the Baltic States and the EU may be characterized as inter-industry trade. Freudenberg and Lemoine (1999) confirm the findings of the early study and for a somewhat later period (1993–1996) – considerable upgrading can be observed to take place in CEE exports through gradual closure of price quality gaps. The situation is not confirmed for two of the Baltic States. Only Estonia exhibits as much upgrading, but starting also from a lower level in terms of initial price quality gaps. The results of Freudenberg and Lemoine (1999) indicate a very strong convergence between productive structures in Central Europe and the EU. Both the Balkan and Baltic countries are lagging considerably behind in this process.

The last study for review is by Graziani (2003). The focus is explicitly on upgrading and again using price quality gaps as indicator. Graziani's study includes some slightly longer time spans than the other studies. Also focusing on the ten candidate countries, he finds that two countries, Hungary and Slovenia, have fared best in the upgrading process, while the experiences of an intermediate group are more mixed (including Poland) where some downgrading has taken place in combination with severe contractions in certain industries. In Graziani's study it is also evident that the Baltic States have fared the worst in regard to upgrading. While there has been upgrading in several important Estonian industries, the quality has actually worsened in the majority of exports from Latvian and Lithuanian industries. Finally, Graziani's study analyses differences in price quality gaps across statistics on Outward Processing Trade (OPT) and non-OPT trade (from the COMEXT database). It should be noted that OPT trade by definition refers to inter-firm vertically integrated trade rather than intra-firm trade. This particular type of trade has been governed by a particular set of trade policies during the 1990s granting EU producers tariff free access from within sensitive industries such as textiles when re-importing their own goods after processing in CEE countries (UN/ECE, 2000). Meticulously comparing the upgrading in these two types of distinct trade flows Graziani finds that upgrading is largely driven by OPT trade from specific industries such as textiles, clothing, footwear in general and from electrical machinery exports in the case of Poland and Estonia. Thus the study questions whether this is really a process of upgrading, e.g. it cannot be verified that the higher quality standards really spill over on autonomous producers.

Industry Upgrading of Trade

A large number of studies on emerging export specialization from CEE to EU have also been made. Only a few of them are mentioned here. Among the early studies CEE producers were found to have comparative advantage coming from within labour intensive industries such as textiles and footwear (Collins and Rodrik, 1991). A somewhat later EBRD study confirms these observations, with trade patterns and comparative advantages reflecting the pre-transition specialization patterns having grown and gradually evolved on EU markets since the 1970s (EBRD, 1997). A study by Brenton and Gros (1997) also confirms these findings since they observe that early trade reorientation was possible without much upgrading having taken place.

Later studies tend to find a much less sticky trade pattern and especially for data after 1993 (Freudenberg and Lemoine, 1999). The clearest examples of emerging new comparative advantages are from within engineering-based industries such as consumer electronics and automobiles. A relatively large number of studies based on more recent trade data starts confirming that industry upgrading is taking place (UN/ECE, 2000; EBRD, 2001). Carlin and Landesmann (1997) document increasing export shares from within skill and R&D intensive industries over time for the Czech Republic, Hungary, Slovenia and to some extent Poland. The latest available EBRD study of trade specialization confirms that an industry upgrading process is taking place regarding the composition of exports and particularly in Central Europe (EBRD, 1999).

Compared to Central Europe, the Baltic States, the Balkans and CIS are exhibiting a much more traditional and sticky specialization pattern. Freudenberg and Lemoine (1999) find that in the more peripheral states further away from EU borders industrial restructuring has not yet become visible in trade patterns. Trade here still assumes a very traditional role based on inter-industry patterns. Exports from the peripheral regions are to a much greater extent based on primary products or labour-intensive manufactures. Some countries and in particular the Baltic States have an export basket strongly skewed towards primary products such as crude materials (Eurostat, 2001b).

Foreign Direct Investment and Upgrading

Only a few studies have tested explicitly for the role of FDI on upgrading. All of the studies mentioned here undertake analysis for the role FDI has played to industry upgrading since no studies have investigated for quality upgrading.

Most available studies in this area have been made for Poland where evidence is not quite conclusive depending on the type of data used. Jensen (2002) using UN trade data and Polish FDI data finds that FDI has upgraded the product composition of the Polish export basket after 1992 towards the more technology intensive (capital and skill intensive) industries and activities. Another study (Weresa, 2001) based on decomposition of Polish industry data by ownership points to FDI creating RCA from within a few industries such as food products and transport equipment while in some industries multinational firms have also relied on existing Polish comparative advantages on EU markets. A World Bank study confirms that FDI has aided in a successful industry upgrading process especially toward the more skill intensive industries even though export specialization is still relatively higher for the pure labour intensive industries (Kaminski and Smarzynska, 2001).

Kaminski (2000) provides ample and convincing stylized facts on the relationship between FDI and trade restructuring in the case of Hungary. First generation firms of the local type succeeded in reorienting basic labour intensive exports to the EU markets, while second generation firms are driven by foreign capital and increasingly emerge from within the skill intensive industries.

Other country case studies of FDI's developmental role in general document that multinational firms in the transition countries are more export intensive than their domestic counterparts (Eltetö, 2000) and hence likely to have a large influence on the industrial composition of trade.

DATA

This section introduces the data variables used in the subsequent regression analysis. Both trade and FDI data are treated as endogenous to the analysis, e.g. time series data is made available. However, because of limited data availability, the subsequent analysis assumes that other explaining variables such as level of development (relative GDP per capita) along with other absolute or relatively stationary variables (geographic distance and population) are exogenous to the analysis. When relevant a data point in the middle of the period analysed has been chosen for these exogenous variables. The data were collected for the ten candidate countries including Russia and Ukraine to make some comparisons across sub-regions in CEE possible. Following the categories of the EBRD (EBRD, 2002) the cross-section of countries is grouped accordingly.

CEB: The eight accession countries from Central Europe (Czech Republic, Hungary, Poland, Slovenia and Slovakia) and from the Baltic countries (Estonia, Latvia and Lithuania).
SEE2: Two countries from South Eastern Europe: Bulgaria and Romania.
CIS2: Two countries from the CIS: Russia and Ukraine.

The potential data set involves 12 CEE countries' trade with 15 EU countries allowing for a total of 168 observations in a dynamic cross-section analysis similar to a first difference equation technique. However, due to the relatively late accession of Austria, Finland and Sweden these bilateral flows could not be included in the analysis covering the period 1993–2000, but only in the later period covering 1997–2000. The latter results are reported in the Appendix only (Tables A15.2 and A15.3). Hence the number of observations is reduced to 132 in the analysis covering the full period. Concerning quality upgrading there are further missing observations since some types of goods are not always traded bilaterally.

Data Sources and Manipulation

The trade data were obtained from Eurostat's COMEXT database that contains information on bilateral trade between each EU country (the reporting country) and all intra and extra EU partners. On the basis of the 2-digit and 8-digit product information respectively quoted in the Combined Nomenclature (CN) subsequent variables were calculated. Hereafter reporting country and partner country are referred to as home and host country respectively. The relative factor intensities of industries pertaining to products at the 2-digit level are assigned using information hereon from Landesmann (1996) based on a self-elaborated concordance table from the NACE to the CN nomenclature. Hence trade is assigned to five groups of relative factor intensities: labour intensive, capital intensive, skill intensive and R&D intensive, where the latter three are referred to under one as technology intensive also.

From the trade data different types of product shares are calculated to shed light on upgrading based on the relative factor intensities of their respective industries. The first step is to distinguish manufacturing from non-manufacturing (primary) exports. As a rule all those activities not included under manufacturing industry in Landesmann (1996) are categorized as primary exports in the CN nomenclature. However, some primary exports will slip through by this procedure since the CN nomenclature at the 2-digit level is not always very accurate, e.g. tin and manufactures of tin belong to the same 2-digit code. Three indicators of the industry composition of CEE exports are calculated for 1993, 1997 and 2000: share of manufactured exports (SM), share of capital intensive exports (SK) and share of technology intensive exports (ST).

Price quality gaps are also calculated for the same three years departing from the trade data. As in Freudenberg and Lemoine (1999) prices are calculated as unit values at the 8-digit level. Average prices in intra and extra EU imports respectively are then adopted to calculate relative prices. Note that while the price quality gap benchmarked by external trade measures the quality level relative to third countries' trade with the EU, the price–quality gap as benchmarked by internal prices is a reflection of the CEE quality level relative to that prevailing on the internal market. Then according to the relative price at the 8-digit level up-market (high quality) and down-market (low quality) goods in bilateral manufacturing exports are classified as those taking a value of below and above one respectively. Finally, the measure of the price quality gap is taken as the share of up-market relative to down-market goods in bilateral exports. Besides the differently weighted aggregate measures of price quality gaps in CEE exports, more disaggregate measures are also calculated at the level of group of industries with similar factor intensities: PGIL (price quality gaps in labour intensive industries), PGIK (in capital intensive industries), PGIH (in skill intensive industries) and PGIRD (in R&D intensive industries).

Information on bilateral inflows of FDI from the EU to the CEE countries was obtained from the OECD's *International Direct Investment Statistics Yearbook 2000* (OECD, 2001). This source includes data on outward flows and positions (stocks) for almost all the EU member countries. In some cases the stock had to be estimated by simple aggregation of the historical flows. Data for 1999 FDI stocks by home and host country can be seen in Table A15.1 in the Appendix. The Baltic countries are a special case since they are included as one listing in the OECD source. It was therefore necessary to calculate a weight for each EU country's investment in each of the three Baltic States on the basis of the information available herein in UNCTAD (2000). There is no information published by international source on FDI stocks broken down in combination by industry and host country. It is therefore not possible to separate out FDI flows that have gone into manufacturing industries. That is a serious bias in the data since in some cases the FDI stock in manufacturing industries may be strongly overestimated.

The FDI *stocks* used in the regression analysis are the bilateral FDI per capita stocks in pairs of home and host countries whereby the FDI stock better reflects relative importance to the host country's industrial restructuring process. For example, the absolute FDI stock in Russia is the largest in the sample, but the smallest relatively when controlling for host country size. Hence the likely impact on industrial restructuring is much smaller in Russia than other countries.

Another general problem with the FDI and trade data in combination is that the effect of FDI flows on the host country's trade with third partners cannot be accounted for (or the effect third country FDI may have on exports to the home country). It is a matter of choice whether the analysis should be made for bilateral or aggregate partners, each type of analysis offers advantages and disadvantages. The bilateral analysis is in principle more accurate but hence also comes at the cost of losing some important aspects of the relationship between trade and FDI. The bilateral analysis only reveals that part of upgrading associated with FDI that affects re-exports to the home country. Hence it only sheds partial light on possible effects of FDI on the upgrading of host country exports. Finally, the analysis does not take into account the possible effect that CEE FDI outflows could have on their export performance. The latter problem is not too serious in the period concerned since outflows at this time are still very small.

Other explaining variables are included into the analysis. To avoid observing a spurious relationship between trade patterns and FDI some additional variables are included to explain upgrading of exports. National effort in terms of education and R&D may be equally important explanatory factors of upgrading. Besides the original value of the dependent variable in 1993 and a measure for the *FDI stock*, the primary equation includes a measure of human capital endowment HCE (taken from World Bank, 2002 as the average of the population having received tertiary schooling in 1980 and 1997). Also, a dummy is adopted for countries having used direct sales as *privatization method* since this may reflect a higher quality of firms resulting from transition (EBRD, 2001, Country Tables). As a measure of indigenous R&D activity is taken the part of gross expenditure on R&D undertaken by private business in 1998: GERD *by business enterprise* (Eurostat, 2000b but for Ukraine the estimates come from UNESCO, 2000).

To avoid another aspect of spurious relationships or a so-called simultaneity bias a 2SLS estimate procedure is used where factors that directly may affect the host country's ability to attract *FDI* are accounted for with a secondary equation. The lagged value of the endogenous variable *FDI* stock is taken as instrument. For example, any positive correlation between FDI and upgrading may be because of a third factor explaining both. One of the variables used to explain the *FDI stock* is overlapping with the exogenous variables in the primary equations: human capital endowment (HCE). A *reform progress indicator* is used to reflect the influence that the progress with building market economy institutions may have on transition host countries ability to attract FDI. As a measure hereof is used the summary EBRD indicator for progress with reform for 1998 taken from the Appendix tables published in Falcetti *et al.* (2002). The geographical distance *Geo distance* is taken as a proxy for the possible dampening effect that physical and cultural distance may have on reducing FDI and especially of the market-seeking type. The distance is calculated as the distance between the capitals of pairs of countries at www.indo.com/distance. Finally, the *relative GDP per capita* as seen from the viewpoint of host countries is taken from the Eurostat sources (Eurostat, 2000a, 2001a) as a measure of the relative level of development of the host country vis-à-vis the home country. These data are for 1998 also.

All variables that are absolute rather than shares or relatives are transformed by logarithm.

Stylized Data Facts

Some stylized facts of the data are presented in Tables 15.1 and 15.2. Table 15.1 shows the stylized facts of industry upgrading whereas Table 15.2 reproduces the aggregate measure for quality upgrading. Before turning to the analysis of the bilateral data these aggregate data facts are briefly discussed.

Comparing the stylized facts on upgrading shown in Table 15.1 (industry) and Table 15.2 (quality) suggests that the transition countries have followed different paths in the transition of their exports. The most successful countries in terms of upgrading follow a stable path of upgrading, gradually increasing their shares of technology-intensive imports and gradually closing price quality gaps. To this group of countries belong the Czech Republic, Slovakia, Hungary, Russia and Slovenia. Except for Russia and Slovakia it is noteworthy that these countries all start upgrading from a relatively fortunate position – their share of technology-intensive exports is already high in 1993 and price quality gaps are rather low or non-existing already at this stage of transition. Both Hungary and the Czech Republic have had a high FDI stock per capita throughout this period.

Another group of countries follow a more ruptured process, these are Estonia, Poland and Romania, starting from a lower level they increase their share of technology-intensive exports, while their upgrading process is U-shaped, first quality goes down and then up. Estonia and Poland are major recipients of FDI, with Estonia being among one of the largest three recipients in per capita terms along with Hungary and the Czech Republic. This less stable pattern may be related to a major rupture with the old export structures. Shifting towards new export activities may very likely involve some trade-off in relation to an aggregate quality concept. The last group of countries consist in what must be termed unsuccessful or slow upgraders, to

Table 15.1 Descriptive statistics, industry upgrading by host country

Host country	1993	1997	1999
Estonia	0.507	0.493	0.609
Latvia	0.472	0.506	0.508
Lithuania	0.495	0.582	0.491
Poland	0.536	0.630	0.648
Czech Republic	0.710	0.759	0.828
Slovakia	0.653	0.776	0.788
Hungary	0.703	0.792	0.878
Romania	0.437	0.471	0.525
Bulgaria	0.554	0.631	0.582
Ukraine	0.536	0.641	0.642
Russia	0.394	0.442	0.463
Slovenia	0.689	0.666	0.766

Note: Average share of relative technology-intensive exports in bilateral exports to the EU, %.
Source: Own calculations based on the COMEXT datebase.

Table 15.2 Descriptive statistics, quality upgrading by host country

Host country	1993	1997	1999
Estonia	0.702	0.110	0.267
Latvia	0.416	0.330	0.129
Lithuania	0.051	0.196	0.157
Poland	0.311	0.224	1.009
Czech Republic	1.103	1.112	1.848
Slovakia	0.456	0.508	1.436
Hungary	2.118	2.212	2.790
Romania	0.830	0.729	1.628
Bulgaria	0.839	0.393	0.510
Ukraine	0.101	0.603	0.119
Russia	0.081	0.082	0.109
Slovenia	2.289	2.234	2.693

Note: Average share of 'above average' quality products in bilateral exports to the EU, % weighted by prices in internal EU trade (PGI).
Source: Own calculations based on the COMEXT database.

this group belong Latvia, Lithuania, Bulgaria and Ukraine. In this last group, countries either lose shares in technology-intensive exports and/or experience quality downgrading over the period 1993–1999. Possibly it would be more correct to include Russia into this latter group since progress on both types of upgrading is very slow. All these countries are characterized by relatively low stocks of FDI per capita.

REGRESSION ANALYSIS

The results of the analysis of industry upgrading are shown in Table 15.3. The first three columns in Table 15.3 show results for the primary equation where the dependent variables are different aspects of industry upgrading. The final columns in Tables 15.3 and 15.4 are the secondary equation in the 2SLS system.

The results in Table 15.3 show that the composition of exports is relatively path dependent even though the coefficients are below one half in all cases for a total period of eight years. The FDI stock is a poor explanatory factor of upgrading. So is the human capital endowment which is observed to have if any a strictly negative direct impact on upgrading and also the ability of countries to attract FDI. It is possible that the human capital endowment is overestimated for some countries in the way it is measured here (the average of the population having received tertiary schooling in 1980 and 1997). But the results suggest that some of the formerly accumulated skills and knowledge under socialism are rendered redundant by the market economy. The very differential speed and success with introducing market economy institutions may also bias the validity of a historical human capital indicator. It is also possible that populations having received lesser formal education under socialism fare better during transition, e.g. entirely divorcing the relationship between formal education under socialism and actual skills relevant in a market economy.

The indigenous R&D effort performs slightly better especially in regard to lifting the share of technology-intensive exports for this cross-section of countries. Hence it is also analysed whether the FDI stock in combination with human capital produces upgrading, or also if the group of countries matters, for example, Central Europe and the Baltic countries (CEB) have much more preferential access to the EU. Only in the latter quite restricted case is it found that FDI has helped to upgrade the industry composition of exports towards more technology intensive types of products and the impact being quite small. Those CEB countries relatively well-endowed with human capital stand out as the only group apparently affected positively by FDI in this aspect of industry upgrading.

With the results in Table 15.4 the issue of quality upgrading and FDI is analysed. There appears to be inconsistency in these results concerning for example path dependence (second row in Table 15.4). Aggregate measures of price quality gaps *PGI* and *PGE* reveal quite high path dependency in goods quality whereas the disaggregate measures do not. This must be explained by underlying industry composition of those goods, e.g. switching between similar quality goods that belong to different industry groups in regard to relative factor intensities. Correspondingly the models explaining aggregate

Table 15.3 Regression results, industry upgrading by host country, 1993–2000 (2SLS)

Dependent variable:	SM 2000	SK 2000	ST 2000	Log FDI stock
Explaining variables				
Intercept	2.212***	0.001	1.113***	13.395**
	(7.84)	(0.00)	(3.14)	(2.46)
SM 1993/SK 1993/ST 1993	0.219***	0.326***	0.232***	
	(3.36)	(3.78)	(3.14)	
Log FDI stock	–0.016	–0.015	–0.008	
	(–1.08)	(–1.01)	(–0.47)	
Log FDI stock x Log HCE	0.006	0.001	–0.002	
	(1.36)	(0.40)	(–0.53)	
Log FDI stock x Log HCE x CEB	0.001	–0.000	0.009**	
	(0.46)	(–0.04)	(2.24)	
Log HCE (human capital end.)	–0.231***	0.070	–0.217***	–1.031
	(–3.68)	(1.22)	(–3.19)	(–1.24)
Log GERD by business enterprise	0.006	–0.013*	0.020**	
	(0.83)	(–1.68)	(2.25)	
Privatization method	0.024	0.053*	0.052	
	(0.75)	(1.65)	(1.41)	
Reform progress indicator				3.685***
				(4.36)
Log Geo distance				–2.841***
				(–6.67)
Relative GDP per capita				–4.075***
				(–3.20)
R^2 (adjusted)	0.297	0.143	0.234	0.459
N	132	132	132	132

Notes: * The coefficient is significant at the 10% level.
** The coefficient is significant at the 5% level.
*** The coefficient is significant at the 1% level.

Table 15.4 Regression results, quality upgrading by host country, 1993–2000 (2SLS)

Dependent variable:	PGI 2000	PGE 2000	PGIL 2000	PGIK 2000	PGIH 2000	PGIRD 2000	Log FDI stock
Explaining variables							
Intercept	5.636***	9.830***	1.126	2.946**	0.477	12.923***	14.779**
	(3.37)	(4.98)	(1.10)	(1.99)	(0.05)	(2.25)	(2.45)
PGX 1993	0.678***	0.435***	0.068***	0.262***	–0.198	0.086	
	(5.16)	(3.57)	(4.41)	(2.76)	(–0.62)	(0.43)	
Log FDI stock	–0.182	–0.239	0.102	0.036	–2.932***	–0.101	
	(–1.48)	(–1.70)	(1.37)	(0.34)	(–4.03)	(–0.24)	
Log FDI stock x Log HCE	0.035	0.038	–0.014	–0.042	0.654***	–0.132	
	(0.99)	(0.96)	(–0.63)	(–1.31)	(2.97)	(–1.04)	
Log FDI stock x Log HCE x CEB	0.028	0.049	–0.027	0.010	0.109	0.142	
	(0.98)	(1.45)	(–1.40)	(0.38)	(0.59)	(1.34)	
Log HCE	–1.645***	–2.761***	–0.254	–0.646	0.556	–3.133*	–1.526*
	(–3.51)	(–5.06)	(–0.88)	(–1.55)	(0.20)	(–1.94)	(–1.72)
Log GERD by business enterprise	0.110*	0.123	0.052	–0.000	–0.041	–0.200	
	(1.81)	(1.78)	(1.32)	(–0.01)	(0.11)	(–0.89)	
Privatization method	–0.033	0.021	0.104	–0.249	1.271	0.191	
	(–0.13)	(0.07)	(0.65)	(–1.06)	(0.80)	(0.21)	
Reform progress indicator							3.693***
							(4.15)
Log Geo distance							–2.760***
							(–5.92)
Relative GDP per capita							–4.654***
							(–3.53)
R^2 (adjusted)	0.375	0.378	0.160	0.083	0.087	0.000	0.458
N	118	118	118	118	118	118	118

Notes: * The coefficient is significant at the 10% level.
** The coefficient is significant at the 5% level.
*** The coefficient is significant at the 1% level.

price quality gaps perform much better than the models explaining those for industry groups that are relatively labour intensive, capital intensive, skill and R&D intensive respectively. FDI has played no or a negative role for quality upgrading according to the aggregate models. Within groups of industries there is hardly any effect of FDI on quality upgrading.

The only group for which an impact is captured with the regression analysis is for the skill intensive industries. FDI plays a generally negative role in these industries for quality upgrading, except in those countries relatively well-endowed with human capital where there is a positive impact of FDI on quality upgrading. These results are not significantly different across the whole group of countries analysed, e.g. the CEB group does not stand out from the other countries in this aspect.

Results for the period 1997–2000 that include the latest three entrants to the EU confirm or strengthen the above results and observations according to Appendix Tables A15.2 and A15.3.

DISCUSSION AND CONCLUSION

Departing from two different macro theoretical approaches to industry upgrading the objective of the chapter is to evaluate the role if any that FDI has played in respect to industry and quality upgrading of exports from the transition countries.

With respect to industry upgrading the results confirm the theoretical predictions and the few available single country studies of the same issue. FDI is found to be associated with those types of structural changes associated with industry upgrading of the composition of the export basket towards more technology-intensive industries. However, this is only generally true for a specific group of countries, namely the candidate countries in Eastern Europe or those that are labelled CEB consisting of Central Europe and the Baltic countries. Furthermore, FDI has only played a significant role for industry upgrading within this group of countries in those cases that they are relatively well endowed with human capital as measured by formal schooling in this study. According to the IDP predictions this may be because only these countries have been successful in advancing from Stage 2 to Stage 3 on the IDP (before or after transition) or maintaining their Stage 3 position during post-socialism. According to the GCC predictions, industry upgrading should follow automatically with FDI involvement. The latter may not be the case because FDI is relevant in a larger group of industries that those normally included as impacted by FDI in the GCC approach. European markets are more fragmented and hence European multinational strategies in Eastern Europe may reflect a greater multitude of motives and activities also within more traditional industries.

For quality upgrading, results are largely negative or inconclusive. The results confirm the GCC prediction that FDI may play a very selective upgrading role. The results also confirm those obtained by Graziani (2003) suggesting that FDI plays a marginal role to quality upgrading in transition countries. A lot of noise is introduced in the data because of the structural changes taking place within manufacturing. The most successful transition countries appear to be those capable of gradually increasing quality levels whilst undergoing structural changes. It is not often that quality upgrading has been aided by FDI according to the results in this study. Only from within the skill intensive industries and for those countries relatively well endowed with human capital are positive results obtained on the developmental role of FDI through upgrading the quality of exports.

Results are preliminary and should be read with reservations due to the aggregate nature of the data and the fact that only a portion of reality is captured when focusing on upgrading processes in bilateral trade and investment relationships of pairs of countries. It is tantamount to obtain FDI data at the more disaggregate level to further investigate and understand the differential upgrading role of FDI in different types of industries and countries. Finally, a human capital indicator singularly reflecting formal historical education may not be the best proxy for skills relevant to manufacturing industry in the transition countries.

NOTES

1. 'What distinguishes lead firms from their followers or subordinates is that they control access to major resources that generate the most profitable returns in the industry', Gereffi, 2001, p.1622.
2. *Ibid.*

REFERENCES

Blomström, M., A. Kokko and S. Globerman (2001), 'The determinants of host country spillovers from foreign direct investment: a review and synthesis of the literature', in Barell, R. and N. Pain (eds), *Inward Investment, Technological Change and Growth – The Impact of Multinational Corporations on the UK Economy*, London: Palgrave and the National Institute of Economic and Social Research.

Borenzstein, E., J.D. Gregorio and J.-W. Lee (1995), 'How does foreign direct investment affect economic growth?', *NBER Working Paper Series*, 5057, Massachussets: National Bureau of Economic Research.

Brenton, P. and D. Gros (1997), 'Trade reorientation and recovery in transition economies', *Oxford Review of Economic Policy*, **13** (2), 65–76.

Carlin, W. and M. Landesmannn (1997), 'From theory into practice? Restructuring and dynamism in transition economies', *Oxford Review of Economic Policy*, **13** (2), 77–105.

Collins, S.M. and D. Rodrik (1991), *Eastern Europe and the Soviet Union in the World Economy*, Washington: Institute for International Economics.

Dunning, J.H. (1981), *International Production and the Multinational Enterprise*, London: Allen & Unwin.

Dunning, J.H. (1993), *Multinational Enterprises and the Global Economy*, Harlow: Addison Wesley.

Dunning, J.H. and R. Narula (1996), 'The investment development path revisited: some emerging issues', *Foreign Direct Investment and Governments: Catalysts for Economic Restructuring*, London: Routledge.

Dunning, J.H. and N. Rajneesh (2000), 'Industrial development, globalization and MNEs', *Oxford Development Studies*, **28** (2), 141–67.

EBRD (1997), *Transition Report 1997 – Enterprise Performance and Growth*, London: European Bank for Reconstruction and Development.

EBRD (1999), *Transition Report 1999 – Ten Years of Transition*, London: European Bank for Reconstruction and Development.

EBRD (2001), *Transition Report update 2001*, London: European Bank for Reconstruction and Development.

EBRD (2002), *Transition Report 2002 – Agriculture and Rural Transition*, London: European Bank for Reconstruction and Development.

Eltetö, A. (2000), 'The impact of FDI on the foreign trade of CECs', in H. Gabor (ed.), *Integration through Foreign Direct Investment*, Cheltenham: Edward Elgar.

Eurostat (2000a), 'Per capita GDP below 75 per cent of the EU average in 50 of the 2110 EU regions', *Statistics in Focus*, Theme 1 (1/2000), Brussels: Statistical Office of the European Communities.

Eurostat (2000b), 'Research investment more limited in the candidate countries than in the EU', *Statistics in Focus*, Theme 9, (3/2000), Brussels: Statistical Office of the European Communities.

Eurostat (2001a), 'Central European candidate countries: Per capita GDP in 41 out of 53 regions below 50 per cent of the EU average in 1998', *Statistics in Focus*, Theme 1 (31/2001), Brussels: Statistical Office of the European Communities.

Eurostat (2001b), 'Specialization of the candidate countries in relation to EU', *Statistics in Focus*, Theme 6 (6/2001), Brussels: Statistical Office of the European Communities.

Falcetti, E., M. Raiser and P. Sanfey (2002), 'Defying the odds: initial conditions, reforms, and the growth in the first decade of transition', Journal of Comparative Economics, **30** (2), 229–50.

Freudenberg, M. and F. Lemoine (1999), 'Central and Eastern European countries in the international division of labour in Europe', *CEPII Document de Travail*, **5**, Paris: Centre d'Etudes Prospectives et d'Informations Internationales.

Gereffi, G. (1996), 'Global commodity chains: new forms of coordination and control among nations and firms in international industries', *Competition and Change*, **1** (4), 427-39.

Gereffi, G. (1999), 'International trade and industrial upgrading in the apparel commodity chain', *Journal of International Economics*, **48**, 37–70.

Gereffi, G. (2001), 'Shifting governance structures in global commodity chains with special reference to the internet', *American Behavioral Scientist*, **44** (10), 1616–37.

Gibbon, P. (2001), 'Upgrading primary production: a global commodity chain approach', *World Development*, **29** (2), 345–63.

Graziani, G. (2003), 'Product quality upgrading and the next EU enlargement', *Papeles del Este*, No. 6, Electronic Internet Journal published by Universidad Complutense, Madrid.

Jensen, C. (2002), 'Foreign direct investment, industrial restructuring and the upgrading of Polish exports', *Applied Economics*, **34**, 207–17.

Kaminski, B. (2000), 'Industrial restructuring as revealed in Hungary's pattern of integration into European Union markets', *Europe-Asia Studies*, **52** (3), 457–87.

Kaminski, B. and B.K. Smarzynska (2001), 'Foreign direct investment and integration into global production and distribution networks: the case of Poland', *Policy Research Working Paper*, 2646, Washington: The World Bank.

Landesmannn, M. (1996), 'The pattern of East–West European integration: catching up or falling behind?', in R. Dobrinsky and M. Landesmann (eds), *Transforming Economies and European Integration*, Cheltenham: Edward Elgar.

Landesmannn, M. and J. Burgstaller (1997), 'Vertical product differentiation in EU markets: the relative position of East European producers', *WIIW Research Report* (234a), Vienna: The Vienna Institute for Comparative Economic Studies.

Narula, R. (1996), *Multinational Investment and Economic Structure*, London: Routledge.

OECD (2001), *International Direct Investment Statistics Yearbook 2000*, Paris: Organization for Economic Co-operation and Development.

Ozawa, T. (1992), 'Foreign direct investment and economic development', *Transnational Corporations*, **1** (1), 27–55.

Smarzynska, B.K. (2002), 'Does foreign direct investment increase the productivity of domestic firms? In search of spillovers through backward linkages', *Policy Research working Paper*, 2923, Washington: The World Bank.

UN/ECE (2000), *Economic Survey of Europe, 2000* (1), Paris: United Nation's Economic Commission for Europe.

UNCTAD (2000) *World Investment Report 2000 – Cross-Border Mergers and Acquisitions and Development*, New York and Geneva: United Nations Conference on Trade and Development.

UNCTAD (2002), *World Investment Report 2002 – Transnational Corporations and Export Competitiveness*, New York and Geneva: United Nations Conference on Trade and Development.

UNESCO (2000), *1999 Statistical Yearbook*, Paris: United Nations Educational, Scientific and Cultural Organization.

Weresa, M. (2001), 'The impact of foreign direct investment on Poland's trade with the European Union', *Post-Communist Economies*, **13** (1), 71–83.

World Bank (2002), *World Development Indicators*, Washington: The World Bank.

APPENDIX

Table A15.1 Bilateral FDI stocks from the EU to Eastern Europe, 1999, in million EURO

Home country	Host country												
	BL	CZ	EE	HU	LV	LT	PL	RO	SK	SI	RU	UI	CEE*
Austria	34	1302	11	1324	7	0	507	149	455	570	129	24	27
Bellux	117	1420	2	780	0	18	616	68	56	0	219	0	3
Denmark	0	175	40	81	103	86	659	0	0	27	54	0	3
Finland	0	18	93	19	12	62	89	0	0	0	114	0	1
France	24	463	10	757	0	0	2350	651	83	137	519	26	2
Germany	106	4547	44	4809	114	30	6117	346	835	291	704	238	2
Greece	0	0	0	0	0	0	0	2	0	0	0	0	20
Ireland	0	0	0	0	0	0	0	0	0	0	0	0	0
Italy	8	110	5	272	1	5	918	87	24	37	93	3	1
Netherlands	10	2028	17	1294	24	9	3020	112	198	12	1007	23	3
Portugal	2	1	0	6	0	0	161	2	0	0	0	0	2
Spain	63	50	0	52	0	0	175	16	0	2	6	1	0
Sweden	6	413	600	88	92	346	658	45	81	9	75	35	3
UK	0	1282	69	762	28	51	882	139	12	29	64	11	1
EU share of total CEE inflow (%)	15	69	53	58	18	30	54	29	48	79	29	13	

Note: * Share of total outflow.
Sources: OECD (2001), EBRD (2001) and UNCTAD (2000).

Table A15.2 Regression results, industry by host country, 1997–2000 (2SLS)

Dependent variable:	SM 2000	SK 2000	ST 2000	
Explaining variables				
Intercept	2.376***	–0.165	0.666***	6.131
	(10.08)	(–1.16)	(3.45)	(1.39)
SM 1997/SK 1997/ST 1997	0.038***	0.661***	0.543***	
	(2.80)	(10.35)	(8.39)	
Log FDI stock	–0.000	–0.001	–0.004	
	(–0.05)	(–0.14)	(0.34)	
Log FDI stock x Log HCE	0.005	–0.001	–0.001	
	(1.08)	(–0.31)	(–0.36)	
Log FDI stock x Log HCE x CEB	–0.002	0.000	0.008***	
	(–0.61)	(0.34)	(2.45)	
Log HCE (human capital end.)	–0.188***	0.074*	–0.135***	–1.000
	(–2.86)	(1.88)	(–2.63)	(–1.40)
Log GERD by business enterprise	0.015*	–0.002	0.014**	
	(1.73)	(–0.39)	(2.21)	
Privatization method	0.016	0.024	0.020	
	(0.44)	(1.08)	(0.73)	
Reform progress indicator				3.826***
				(5.11)
Log Geo distance				–1.986***
				(–7.32)
Relative GDP per capita				–3.497***
				(–2.98)
R^2 (adjusted)				0.456
N				168

Notes: * The coefficient is significant at the 10% level.
** The coefficient is significant at the 5% level.
*** The coefficient is significant at the 1% level.

Table A15.3 Regression results, quality upgrading by host country, 1997–2000 (2SLS)

Dependent variables:	PGI 2000	PGE 2000	PGIL 2000	PGIK 2000	PGIH 2000	PGIRD 2000	Log FDI stock
Explaining variables							
Intercept	3.806***	14.057***	0.839	1.771**	–0.961	10.853	5.865
	(2.84)	(7.28)	(0.97)	(2.03)	(–0.13)	(1.35)	(1.27)
PGX 1993	0.839***	0.123***	0.178**	0.249***	0.792***	2.153**	
	(7.97)	(3.53)	(2.19)	(5.31)	(3.42)	(2.46)	
Log FDI stock	–0.226	–0.198	0.077	0.027	–2.651***	0.121	
	(–2.20)	(–1.31)	(1.13)	(0.41)	(–4.60)	(0.19)	
Log FDI stock x Log HCE	0.067**	0.035	–0.029	0.013	0.617***	0.014	
	(2.23)	(0.77)	(–1.38)	(0.66)	(3.54)	(0.08)	
Log FDI stock x Log HCE x CEB	–0.007	0.006	–0.003	–0.037**	0.078	–0.194	
	(–0.29)	(0.18)	(0.19)	(–2.18)	(0.54)	(–1.20)	
Log HCE	–1.134***	–3.908***	–0.177	–0.365	0.063	–2.492	–1.106
	(–3.02)	(–7.22)	(–0.73)	(–1.48)	(0.03)	(–1.10)	(–1.48)
Log GERD by business enterprise	0.108**	0.137*	0.052	0.025	0.312	–0.254	
	(2.22)	(1.85)	(1.57)	(0.74)	(1.06)	(–0.81)	
Privatization method	0.094	0.208	0.082	–0.159	1.689	0.891	
	(0.48)	(0.69)	(0.60)	(–1.16)	(1.45)	(0.71)	
Reform progress indicator							3.873***
							(5.06)
Log Geo distance							–1.885***
							(–6.63)
Relative GDP per capita							–3.947***
							(–1.48)
R^2 (adjusted)	0.448	0.332	0.058	0.180	0.148	0.024	0.443
N	155	155	155	155	155	155	155

Notes:
* The coefficient is significant at the 10% level.
** The coefficient is significant at the 5% level.
*** The coefficient is significant at the 1% level.

16. The Changing Pattern of Intra-regional Trade in Northeast Asia

Young-il Park

INTRODUCTION

For two decades or so before the economic crisis, East Asian economies continued to experience miraculous growth[1]. The World Bank report (1993) pointed out that it was due to good fundamentals such as high saving ratios, keen interests in education, diligent work habits and active entrepreneurship, an outward looking industrialization strategy and government's strong commitment to economic growth. However, it is important to note that most East Asian economies did not grow independently, but their growth was interrelated with each other through steady expansion of the regional trade and investment. An expanding regional economy has been both a cause and an effect of national economic growth. While the technological diffusion and increased specialization facilitated by an expanding regional trade provided considerable stimulus to the growth of an economy, that economy's growth, in turn, promoted closer regional trade relations through its increased demand for foreign goods, capital and technology. This process created a virtuous circle of exports and investment at the regional level. Though the virtuous circle appeared to change to a vicious one with the economic crisis and Asia's dynamic growth fell into a trap, the structure has not changed, as evidenced by the fact that growth of exports has been the most important driver in bouncing back from the crisis[2].

One of the consequences of the dynamic growth is the emergence of Northeast Asia as the third pole of the global economy. Over the last two decades Northeast Asian economies have grown at an average rate of 6.7 per cent annually, compared with 2.8 per cent for the world economy. This outstanding growth led to the great ascension of Northeast Asia in the world economy. Its weight rose from 13 per cent to 21 per cent in world GDP, from 10 per cent to 17 per cent in world exports and from 10 per cent to 16 per cent in world imports. Now, Northeast Asia forms an economic pole – comparable with North America and Europe – with its population and economic dynamism exceeding those of both North America and Europe.

Another consequence is a rapidly deepening interdependence among the regional economies, resulting in a greater capability of self-sustained growth of the region. Over the last two decades intra-regional trade in Northeast Asia trade has increased from 16 per cent to 38 per cent. Instead, the share of US and European markets in the trade of Northeast Asian countries has been declining. Peculiarly, the greater intra-regional trade was achieved through market forces at the private level without any institutional framework at the government level. Now, Northeast Asian economies have come to trade intensively with each other to a extremely high degree.

Theoretically, the increase in intra-regional trade in a particular region results from three broad factors: the increase in the region's share in world trade; the underlying complementarity between the commodity structures of regional countries' global trade; and differential degrees of trade resistances between trading routes diverting trade flows. The three factors have played their own part in the high degree of and rapid increase in intra-regional trade in Northeast Asia. Although all regional economies have increasingly depended upon extra-regional sources for raw materials and fuels, and have commonly specialized in exports of manufactures, their industrial structures have been highly complementary with each other. The relative endowments of productive factors speak for themselves: highly capital and technology-abundant Japan; moderately capital and technology-abundant newly industrializing economies (NIEs), such as Korea, Taiwan, Hong Kong; and labour-abundant China. In addition, the rapid increase in the region's share in world trade and improved market access to each other have also contributed a lot to this increase in intra-regional trade. Nevertheless, the trade relationship between regional countries has not yet fully fledged, as evidenced in relatively low country bias indexes.

Recently, the Northeast Asian region has gained a greater momentum for regional cooperation and conciliation at institutional level. Given the high degree of market-led integration based on high complementarity, the institutional arrangements have intensified further intra-regional trade by increasing country bias between regional countries. First of all, there was the historic summit between the South and North Koreas. The summit would remove the legacy of the Cold War that is one of the most serious obstacles to Northeast Asian economic cooperation. Another important development was China's joining to the World Trade Organization (WTO) in 2001. Lastly, various attempts have been made to form an institutional framework and promote regional cooperation since the crisis. Now, the proposal for a Korea–Japan trade agreement is under discussion among economists and policy makers of both countries and addressed to the public in a series of seminars[3]. The Korea–Japan Free Trade Agreement will be open to China. This means a significant transition in commercial policy of the regional countries that have never committed to a regional preferential trade arrangement. In the monetary sector, on the other hand, a swap agreement has been concluded between ASAN+3 members under the Chiang Mai Initiative (CMI). All of these efforts will conduce to a rapid increase in country bias, and hence, trade intensity between the regional countries.

The main purpose of this chapter is to explain the changing level and pattern of intra-regional trade flows in Northeast Asia, focusing on bilateral trade between Korea, Japan and China. Emphasis will be put on two elements: trade potentials resulting from the commodity composition of each country's global trade in the absence of trade resistances; and deviation of actual trade from potential trade resulting from the differential degree of trade resistances.

THEORETICAL BACKGROUND

Studies which analyse the determinants of the size and pattern of bilateral trade flows can be classified into two independent approaches, the gravity approach and the intensity approach[4]. The former assumes that a particular trade flow is independent from other trade flows and is concerned with the absolute rather than the relative level of bilateral trade[5]. Alternatively, the intensity approach, which is adopted in this study, recognizes interdependence among bilateral trade flows and seeks to explain the relative level of a particular bilateral trade flow. It calculates an 'index of trade intensity', which measures the extent to which a pair of trading countries trade more or less intensively with each other than they do with the rest of the world.

Initially, studies on bilateral trade refer little to the mainstream trade theory. This is largely because the traditional trade theory has focused on the size and pattern of a country's total trade in the two-country framework. Hence, there is no room to make allowance for bilateral and regional trade flows in a multi-country real world. Nevertheless, one can draw implications from the theory to understand the determinants of bilateral trade flows, since bilateral trade between a particular pair of trading countries evolves as an aspect of their global trade.

The implications of the trade theory for bilateral trade flows vary across theories. The neoclassical theory of comparative advantage regards international trade as a mechanism making up national deficiency in production factors and predicts that the level and pattern of a country's trade are determined by its comparative advantage, originated from the relative endowment of production factors such as labour, capital, natural resources and technology. Accordingly, this view implies that at a given point of time, the greater the differences in relative factor endowments between a pair of countries, the larger the potentiality to trade with each other. In other words, dissimilarity of factor endowments is the main source of bilateral trade. On the other hand, new theories regard international trade as a mere extension of the internal market and emphasize the role of scale economies in international trade (Linder, 1961; Hufbauer and Chilas, 1974). Thus, the story is different: the greater the similarity of factor endowments between a pair of countries, the higher the potentiality to trade with each other. The former theory is useful to explain the determinants of inter-industry trade which have been important for the traditional trade between Northeast Asian countries, while the latter is suitable for explaining the determinants of intra-industry trade which becomes more general between the developed countries and has recently come to prosper between Northeast Asia countries.

The above expectation needs to be modified due to transaction costs. Generally, trade theories neglect the transaction costs of trade. But, transaction costs are essential to overcome trade resistances. These costs hinder the free flows of commodities by reducing the difference between border prices and pre-trade domestic prices and deviate the actual trade flows from those expected from the production costs. Trade resistances broadly comprise natural resistances and artificial resistances. Natural resistances are those impeding trade, such as geographical and psychic distance. The latter are closely associated with differences in customs, language, history and culture between countries. Artificial resistances are created, maintained and removed by government and private action. The government-initiated resistances include trade embargo, preferential trade agreement and trade policy, and the privately initiated inducements which are created by joint ventures, technology licence agreements and international subcontracts.

It is useful to divide the influence of trade resistances on trade flows into two categories: those which are uniform across all the trading routes, do not discriminate across the bilateral trading routes and have an effect on a country's global trade by causing a diversion of transaction between domestic markets and foreign markets as a whole; and those which differ between trading routes and cause a diversion between the trading route[6]. In a multi-country real world the latter are more general. This has a profound impact on the geographical distribution of trade: trade flows tend to divert towards the route with relatively low degree of trade resistance away from the one with high trade resistance. There can be an extreme case where differentials in transaction costs to overcome trade resistances may even nullify comparative advantages based on the production costs.

In summary, a pair of countries in a multi-country real world trade more or less intensively with each other than they do with the rest of the world because of the factors affecting the commodity composition of their global trade and because of their geographical proximity, cultural familiarity, historical and political ties, and special institutional arrangements. The influence of the former is measured by 'complementarity' index, and that of the latter by 'country bias' index[7]. The concept and logic of trade indexes are described in the Appendix. Success in calculating indexes of complementarity and country bias requires commodity groups to be classified at a significant level of detail, so that each commodity group includes reasonably homogeneous sub-commodities. In this study, commodities are classified up to the 3-digit Standard International Trade Classification (SITC) level[8]. The number of commodity groups amount to as many as 183.

THE CHANGING PATTERN OF GLOBAL TRADE IN NORTHEAST ASIA

Relative Factor Endowment

Economic characteristics of the five Northeast Asian countries are presented in Table 16.1, which implies the comparative advantage of each individual country. The first three columns show the absolute sizes of population, land area and gross national product (GNP). Table 16.1 highlights an immense diversity of economic size within the region. For example, China has an enormous size of land area and population. China commands 95 per cent of Northeast Asian land and 86 per cent of population. On the other hand, Japan accounts for 69 per cent of the region's GNP.

The fourth and fifth columns show population density and GNP per capita, in order to indicate relative factor endowments. Population density is assumed to be negatively correlated with the combined availability of natural resources, arable land and other economically useful natural endowments[9]. Table 16.1 shows that Northeast Asian economies are extremely poor in natural resources and have a comparative disadvantage in producing natural resource-based primary goods. Even China, which has a huge land area and is known as a country relatively well endowed with natural resources, has a population density three times as high as the world average, indicating that China is a natural resource-poor country.

Per capita GNP is used as a proxy for the ratio of capital to labour. The relevant concept of capital, here, is broadly defined as all man-made resources to contribute to improvement of labour productivity. Therefore, it includes not only physical capital equipments, but also social capital, human skills, technological and organizational knowledge, and other intangible productive factors, following Johnson's concept (1968), while labour is defined in the narrow sense of human labour time availability. This concept enables value-added per worker to be used as a measure of the overall capital intensity of production10. Table 16.1 shows that Northeast Asian economies are very diverse in capital stock per head: extremely abundant Japan; moderately abundant NIEs; very poor China. The last column presents an average annual rate of growth over the period 1980–1999, in order to indicate economic dynamism. The growth performance has varied with individual countries, depending on their stage of economic development and the opening time to international trade. There is a clear tendency that the higher the per capita income, the lower the growth rate.

Table 16.1 Characteristics of Northeast Asia economies

	Population (million)	Area (1000 km^2)	GNP (US$, billion)	Population density	GNP per capita (US$)	Average annual growth rate of GDP (1980–1999)
Japan	127	378	4079	336	32230	2.8
Korea	47	99	398	475	8490	7.6
Taiwan	22	36	289	605	13250	7.3
H.K.	7	1	162	6946	23520	5.4
China	1250	9597	980	134	780	10.4
World	5975	133572	29232	46	4890	2.8

Source: World Bank (2000).

The Krueger's two-sector three-factor model explains best the changing pattern of trade in Northeast Asian economies[11]. A poor country opening up to international trade will tend to specialize in the production and exports of primary products in exchange for manufactures. As its stock of capital accumulates and hence, its wages and income grow more rapidly than the other countries, its export specialization will gradually switch away from primary products to manufactures, with increasing importance of capital-intensive manufacturing activities over time. The earlier the switch and the more labour-intensive manufactured goods initially exported, the lower the country's natural resources per worker. This is because the resource-poor country's wage will be low in the initial stage, and the low wage will give the country an international competitiveness in unskilled labour-intensive manufactures. At the same time, the faster the gradual change of exports towards more capital-intensive manufactures, the higher the growth rate. Active attraction of foreign direct investment into the poor country tends to accelerate the above process.

An entrance of the poor country to international markets with export specialization in labour-intensive manufactures will have two opposing impacts on the trade pattern of existing exporters. One is the intensifying competition in the international market for the concerned products. The other comes from the newcomer's increasing demand for more capital-intensive products, such as intermediates and capital goods to produce their exports. Both impacts become driving forces for the existing exporters to upgrade their production and exports, in addition to rising wage domestically. These impacts are likely to be stronger in countries situated near the newcomer because of the influence of trade resistances, since lower transaction costs in a particular bilateral trading route or little difference in transaction costs to a given third market tends to cause minor differences in production costs to be reflected in the trade pattern. This process of industrialization leads to a sequential interplay between complementarity and competition between the regional countries and to an increasing interdependence of industrial structures[12].

The Changing Pattern of Trade Specialization

The theoretical implication strongly supports the changing pattern of production and trade in Northeast Asia. In the process of economic development there cannot be structural change without a change in size. Hence, before looking at the changing pattern of trade specialization, changes in trade size should be considered.

As a natural consequence of export-led growth, the rapid growth of GDP in Northeast Asian economies was closely associated with their high growth rate of trade[13]. Figure 16.1 presents the trend of shares of Northeast Asian economies as a whole and individually in the world trade. The exports and imports of Northeast Asian countries as a whole have risen annually at an average rate of 9.0 per cent and 7.5 per cent respectively over the period 1980-1999, compared with the growth rate of 5.7 per cent of the world trade. Thus, the share of Northeast Asia in the world trade increased from 11 per cent to 19 per cent for exports and from 11 per cent to 15 per cent for imports. The import share reached a peak of 18 per cent in 1996 prior to a drastic fall during the economic crisis. The faster growth of their exports compared to their imports produced an ever growing surplus of their current account against the rest of the world[14].

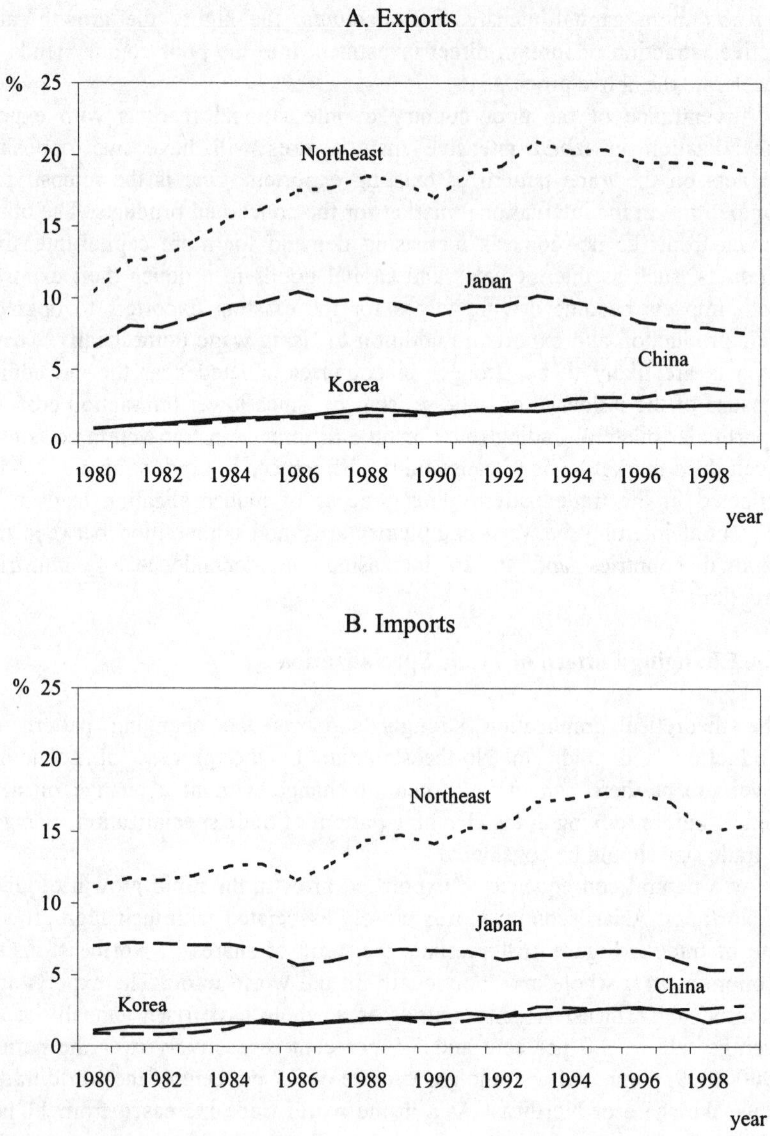

Source: International Economic Data Bank, ANU, Canberra, Australia.

Figure 16.1 Shares of Northeast Asian economies in world trade

There has been a distinct trade performance among the regional countries. Japan has been losing its weight, while four developing countries have gained weight. The developing countries have compensated more than the share lost by Japan to increase the weight of Northeast Asia as a whole in the world trade. Exports of the four developing countries were only 58 per cent of those of Japan in 1980, but now have become 1.5 times as large as those of Japan.

The most important contributor to the increased share of Northeast Asia was China. China's exports have grown at an annual rate of 13 per cent and imports at the rate of 12 per cent during the period 1980–1999. Consequently, China's share has more than quadrupled from 0.9 per cent to 3.9 per cent in world exports and tripled from 0.9 per cent to 2.9 per cent in world imports. The contribution of three NIEs is slightly less remarkable. Their exports grew at a rate of 11 per cent and imports at 10 per cent, but the growth rate has slowed down in the 1990s. Their combined share rose from 2.9 per cent to 7.9 per cent in exports and from 3.2 per cent to 7.2 per cent in imports.

Japan's poor performance is striking. Until the mid-1980s, Japan's trade performance was outstanding, but the Plaza Agreement that doubled the yen–dollar rate from 265 to 138 yen per dollar in a year was a turning point in Japanese international competitiveness. Japan's exports grew rapidly at an annual rate of 8.3 per cent in the first half of the 1980s, but subsequently, dropped to 4.7 per cent. On the other hand, Japan's imports, which contracted at an annual rate of –1.6 per cent in the first half of 1980s, grew at a rate of 13.5 per cent annually, but the growth rate reduced to 3.1 per cent in the 1990s because of the severe recession[15]. Hence, Japan's share in world exports rose rapidly from 6.6 per cent in 1980 to 10.5 per cent in 1986, but plunged to 7.5 per cent in 1999. Japan's share in world imports declined from 7.0 per cent to 5.7 per cent in the first half of the 1980s, but again rose to 6.8 per cent by 1989 and then declined to 5.5 per cent by 1999. The radical decline of import demand affected most adversely its neighbouring Asian countries[16].

The rapid growth of trade in Northeast Asian countries accompanied a huge change in the commodity composition. The change in commodity composition reflects the changing pattern of comparative advantage. As explained in the Appendix, the trade specialization index measures the relative competitiveness of a certain country in a certain commodity, compared with the country's average competitiveness in all the other commodities, or compared with the average competitiveness of the rest of world in the commodity. Thus, the export specialization index is widely used as an index of the revealed comparative advantage[17].

Table 16.2 shows export and import specialization indexes over the period 1980–1998 in four broad commodity groups of agricultural products, mineral products, capital-intensive manufactures (CIMs) and labour-intensive

Table 16.2 Trade specialization index numbers by broad commodity group of Japan, Korea and China

		Exports						Imports					
		1980–82	1983–85	1986–88	1989–91	1992–94	1995–97	1980–82	1983–85	1986–88	1989–91	1992–94	1995–97
Japan	Agricultural	0.12	0.11	0.08	0.07	0.06	0.06	1.04	1.14	1.47	1.34	1.46	1.10
	Mineral	0.12	0.11	0.14	0.12	0.15	0.19	3.14	3.15	2.60	2.28	2.00	1.86
	Manufacture	1.48	1.47	1.33	1.38	1.35	1.38	0.31	0.38	0.55	0.64	0.68	0.80
	C-intensive	1.73	1.74	1.65	1.73	1.69	1.80	0.28	0.34	0.50	0.59	0.62	0.81
	L-intensive	0.93	0.80	0.47	0.50	0.52	0.39	0.37	0.40	0.59	0.76	0.86	0.75
Korea	Agricultural	0.50	0.33	0.34	0.31	0.30	0.25	1.04	0.89	0.90	0.85	0.79	0.59
	Mineral	0.21	0.23	0.23	0.19	0.25	0.35	1.87	1.74	1.50	1.51	1.69	1.80
	Manufacture	1.35	1.38	1.26	1.32	1.29	1.30	0.70	0.82	0.91	0.92	0.90	0.95
	C-intensive	0.80	0.80	0.93	1.04	1.17	1.40	0.75	0.80	1.09	1.10	1.06	1.19
	L-intensive	4.00	4.15	2.90	2.96	2.26	1.37	0.57	0.43	0.42	0.43	0.50	0.42
China	Agricultural	1.26	1.24	1.21	0.96	0.78	0.51	1.76	0.96	0.82	0.90	0.62	0.66
	Mineral	1.53	1.41	1.20	0.73	0.55	0.60	0.20	0.32	0.35	0.42	0.62	0.77
	Manufacture	0.77	0.79	0.90	1.05	1.13	1.20	0.98	1.17	1.16	1.13	1.16	1.13
	C-intensive	0.33	0.29	0.38	0.60	0.58	0.79	1.05	1.30	1.34	1.26	1.32	1.34
	L-intensive	2.68	3.00	2.82	3.10	3.56	2.66	0.93	0.84	0.76	0.96	0.95	0.68

Note: Agricultural products: SITC 0 (33 commodity group at 3-digit level), 1 (4), 4 (4), 21 (2), 22 (1), 23 (1), 24 (4), 25 (1), 26 (7), 29 (2), total 59 groups.
Mineral products: SITC 3 (5), 27 (6), 28 (6), 68 (9), 661, 662, 663, 667, 671, total 31 groups.
Capital-intensive manufactures: SITC 5 (18), 7 (18, exc. 735), 62 (2), 64 (2), 67 (8, exc. 671), 69 (9), 86 (4), 891, 892, 896, 897, total 65 groups.
Labour-intensive manufactures: SITC 61 (3), 63 (3), 65 (7), 81 (1), 82 (1), 83 (1), 84 (2), 85 (1), 664, 665, 666, 735, 893, 894, 895, 899, 951, total 28 groups.

Source: International Economic Data Bank, RSPacS, ANU, Canberra, Australia.

manufactures (LIMs) for Japan, China and Korea. The indexes are the weighted averages of index values in each 3-digit SITC commodity group, which is calculated for 183 commodity groups, seen in the notes to Table 16.2. At a glance, the table confirms that the trade specialization pattern of each country reflects the relative factor endowments presented in Table 16.1. Broadly, all countries of the region have a comparative advantage in manufactures and a comparative disadvantage in primary products. But there is great variation in the degree of comparative advantage in LIMs and CIMs between countries. The table also shows huge change in the trade specialization pattern, representing a radical shift in comparative advantages. China experienced the most rapid change in trade specialization, while Japan the least.

Japan has strongly specialized its exports in CIMs alone and its imports in primary products. Japan entered international markets with strong export specialization in LIMs in the 1950s and already upgraded its structures of production and exports to CIMs by the 1970s, and highly specialized in imports of a variety of primary products. This pattern has hardly changed. The only notable change is that Japan's comparative advantage in LIMs shifted rapidly from being moderately weak to being extremely weak during the period. The value of Japan's export specialization index in LIMs declined from 0.93 to 0.39, while that of the import specialization index rose from 0.37 to 0.75. In addition, the value of Japan's import specialization index in mineral products substantially shrank from 3.14 to 1.86, while that in CIMs rose from 0.28 to 0.81. Consequently, Japan switched from being a trader, dominated by inter-industry trade between manufactures and primary products, to being a trader increasingly undertaking intra-industry trade within manufactures. Indeed, one of the most important developments in Japan's trade was the rapid increase in imports of manufactures, especially from the East Asian developing countries (Park, 1998).

The three NIEs, the second runner group of relay of economic growth in Northeast Asia, entered into the international markets in the 1960s. They took Japan's economic success as a model and pursued an outward looking strategy of industrialization. They exploited dynamic gains from rapidly growing exports based on their comparative advantage to achieve an outstanding economic performance. They enjoyed an annual rate of 10 per cent of economic growth by the late 1980s, and their factor endowment has transformed from labour abundance to labour shortage. Hence, their comparative advantage has been gradually transformed from LIMs to CIMs, identical to Japan during the previous two decades.

Korea has experienced considerable change in its trade pattern. The most prominent change occurred within manufactured goods: the value of export specialization index in LIMs declined from 4.00 to 1.37, while that in CIMs rose significantly from 0.80 to 1.40. Now, Korea's exports are more specialized in CIMs than in LIMs. Korea's imports have been continuously specialized in primary products, but the trend is on the decline. Instead, the degree of Korea's import specialization in CIMs has increased considerably from 0.75 to 1.19. Now, Korea's exports and imports are simultaneously specialized in CIMs and undertaking increasingly intra-industry trade in CIMs. At the same time, the declining degree of import specialization in agricultural products is closely associated with the decreased degree of export specialization in LIMs since the activities processing agricultural materials are largely labour-intensive.

China's trade pattern has experienced a huge change from being an exporter of primary products to being an exporter of manufacturing goods. Being impressed by the achievements of Japan and the three NIEs, China, the third runner in Northeast Asia, implemented decisively economic reform and open door policy in 1978. Liberalization and market opening reform measures have been steadily and gradually introduced. Initially, China came to the international market by exporting primary products in exchange for manufactures. China is not necessarily abundant in natural resources and introduced actively capital, technology, marketing and management expertise through foreign direct investment. This led to a rapid shift in China's comparative advantage from primary products towards manufactures in less than one decade after opening up.

China has increasingly specialized its exports in LIMs in the initial stage of industrialization, but rapidly upgraded its comparative advantage towards more capital-intensive activities. The value of China's export specialization index in LIMs was 2.68 in the beginning of 1970s, rose further to 3.56 in the early 1990s, and thereafter started to drop to 2.66, while that in CIMs gradually increased from 0.33 to 0.79. In import trade, China was initially specialized only in agricultural products alone because of food shortage. However, on implementing economic reform and opening-up, the strong specialization in agricultural products weakened. This weakened specialization was due to the initial introduction of market forces into the rural economy to increase production of foodstuffs. Instead, import specialization swiftly shifted to CIMs. Subsequently, China's strong specialization in CIMs has remained unchanged. At the same time, as industrialization has spreaded and deepened, the value of import specialization index in mineral products has steadily risen from 0.20 to 0.77. At present, China exports LIMs in exchange for CIMs with increasing imports of mineral products.

These changes in trade specialization pattern of Northeast Asian countries have created economic forces that led to a greater interdependence of industrial structures among regional countries, with greater dependence of natural resources upon the extra-region. In this process, there has been a continual rise and fall in the degree of comparative advantage in a certain commodity group for individual countries. This has led to complementary relationship on the one hand and competitive relationship on the other hand between countries.

This interdependent feature between Northeast Asian countries in the process of industrialization is well documented in Anderson and Park (1989) for the textile industry. Japan entered the export-led growth path in the 1950s. Until the mid-1960s Japan had a strong comparative advantage in labour-intensive textile products. In the mid-1960s, the NIEs entered the international market and improved their comparative advantage in the labour-intensive textiles and clothing to replace Japan's exports. Japan upgraded its production and exports to upstream textiles including synthetic and regenerated fibres. The adjustment has been repeated since China came to the world market to follow the NIEs. As the NIEs improved their comparative advantage towards more capital-intensive upstream, Japan upgraded its textile industry to the high-tech activities and finally became to lose its comparative advantage in a variety of textile products. This process led Northeast Asian countries as a whole to capture a greater share of world textile exports. The same story is featured in electrical and electronic machinery, apparatus and appliances. Japan was the first to strengthen its comparative advantage in the industry. As the NIEs entered to export markets, Japan began to lose comparative advantage in the most labour-intensive segments and upgrade its production and exports of products needing inputs of more capital and sophisticated technology. Close on the heels of the NIEs was China, whose growth rate in the exports of electrical and electronic products was even higher than those of the NIEs. Now, Northeast Asia has a gigantic share in world exports of electrical and electronic machinery, apparatus and appliances.

Most dynamic development in the interplay of complementarity and competition among regional countries in the process of sequential industrialization occurred in the latter half of 1980s. Previously, Japan was the only major supplier of machinery and equipments and their components and parts, embodied with sophisticated technology and high quality intermediates. The NIEs' comparative advantage in those products was not developed yet. However, the yen's steep appreciation, following the Plaza agreement, swept the pattern of comparative advantage in the Northeast Asian countries to strengthen competitiveness of the NIEs in those products. Now, the NIEs increasingly became to compete with Japan that began to lose its international competitiveness in a larger range of more capital and technology-intensive activities, and in turn, left labour-intensive activities to China. This development was accelerated by the active foreign direct investment within the region, making another driving force to increase interdependence between the regional countries[18].

THE INCREASED INTRA-REGIONAL TRADE

The Changing Pattern of Intra-regional Trade

The sequential outward-looking economic development of Northeast Asian countries not only raised the region's weight in the world trade, but also rapidly increased intra-regional trade. As seen in Figure 16.2, intra-regional trade between the Northeast Asian economies more than doubled over the period 1980–1998. The ratio increased from 17 per cent to 33 per cent in export trade and from 15 per cent to 39 per cent in import trade. Most prominently, intra-regional trade increased more rapidly in their imports. Given the facts that most Northeast Asian countries are heavily depending for natural resources upon extra-regional sources and strongly specializing their imports in natural resources, it implies that their imports of manufactured products have increasingly come from the regional countries, while their exports continued to go to the extra-regional markets[19].

Figure 16.3 presents the trend of each country's share in other regional countries trade. There has been a significant change in patterns of intra-regional trade: Japan lost its importance as a trading partner, while China and Korea gained their weight.

In Korean trade, Japan's weight fell while that of China increased (Figure 16.3 A). China emerged as Korea's third largest trading partner with its share of 8.8 per cent in Korean exports and 7.0 per cent in imports. Contrarily, Japan lost its importance though it remains as the most important source of Korean imports and the second largest market for Korean exports. Japan's share has more than halved from 17.3 per cent to 8.8 per cent in Korea's exports and declined from 26 per cent to 19 per cent in Korea's imports. However, the decline was not uniform. Japan's share reached a peak of 34.4 per cent in Korea's imports in 1986 and 21.6 per cent in Korea's exports in 1989. Now, Japan has almost the same importance as China in Korean export markets[20].

The importance of Korea and China increased considerably as Japan's trading partners over the period 1980–1998 (Figure 16.3 B). Korea's share in Japan's exports increased from 4.1 per cent to 7.1 per cent in 1996 prior to a sharp decline during the economic crisis, while China's share rose from 3.9 per cent to 5.2 per cent. On the other hand, Korea's share in Japan's imports rose from 2.1 per cent to 4.3 per cent, while China's share

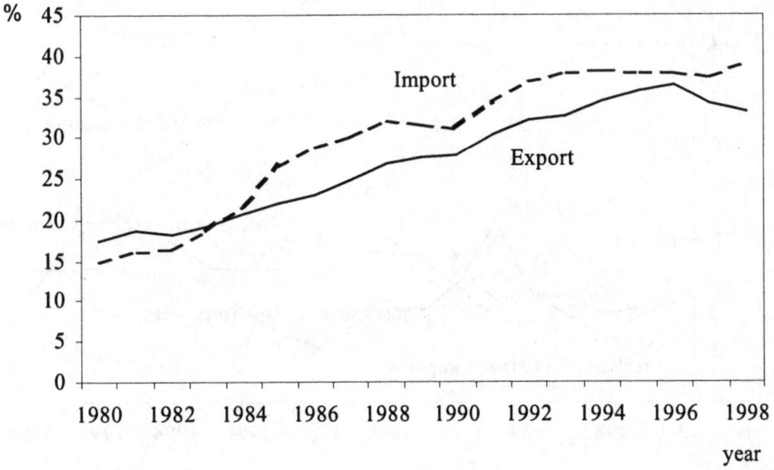

Source: IMF, Direction of Trade Statistics.

Figure 16.2 The trend of intra-regional trade in Northeast Asia

A. In Korea's trade

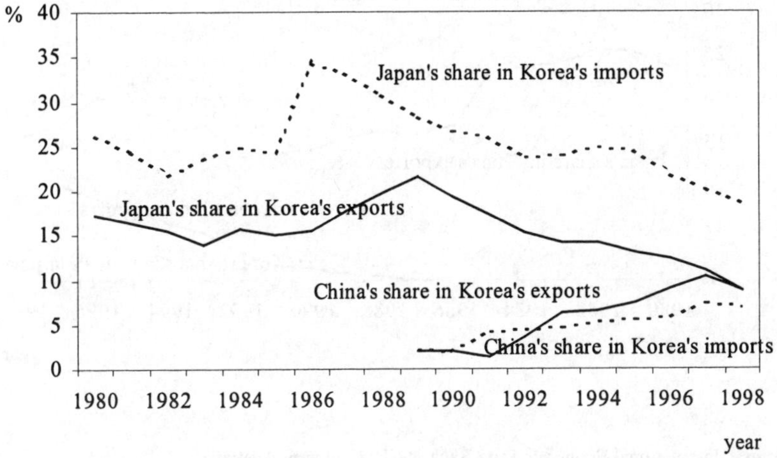

Figure 16.3 Each country's share in the other regional country's trade

B. In Japan's trade

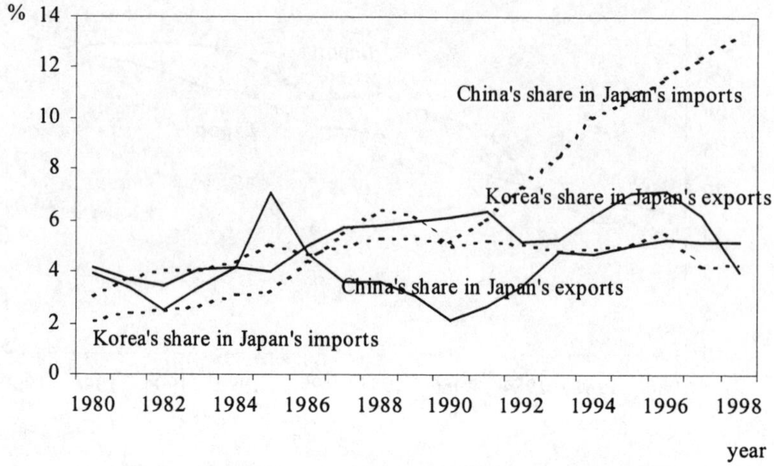

C. In China's trade

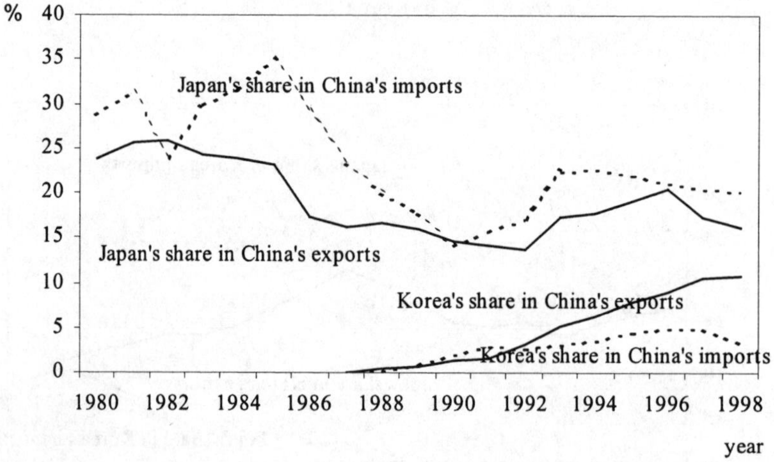

Source: International Economic Data Bank, ANU, Canberra, Australia.

Figure 16.3 (continued)

increased from 3.1 per cent to 13.3 per cent. As Japan's major trading partner there are two distinctive features between Korea and China. Firstly, Korea is more important as a market for Japan's exports than as a source of Japan's imports, while China is far more important as import source than export market. At the same time, Korea is more important than China as an export market for Japan, while China is far more important than Korea as a source of Japan's imports. Secondly, the increasing trend is different between Korea and China. In Japan's exports, Korea's share rose in the latter half of the 1980s and mid-1990s and declined in the early and late 1990s, while China's share rose sharply in the first half of 1980s and 1990s and declined drastically in the latter half of the 1980s. In import trade, Korea's share experienced a sharp rise in the late 1980s but declined in the 1990s, while China's share rose steeply in the 1990s after a gentle increase in the 1980s. The distinction is likely to reflect differential structure of trade specialization between Korea and China. Korea is rather competitive with Japan, while China is complementary to Japan. As China's trading partner, there has been a contrasting trend between Korea and Japan (Figure 16.3 C). Korea's weight rose dramatically while Japan's weight fell considerably. Korea emerged as the fourth largest trading partner of China to supply 10. 8 per cent of China's imports and absorb 5.0 per cent of Chinese exports. Contrastingly, Japan's weight declined considerably from 23.8 per cent to 16.1 per cent in China's exports and from 28.7 per cent to 20.3 per cent in China's imports, though with a huge fluctuation during the period.

Change in a country's share in a particular partner's trade results from three broad sets of factors: rapid growth of the regional countries' share in world trade; complementarity increase between their trade specialization patterns; and reduced trade resistances in the regional trading route relative to the other routes. Since the first factor has been discussed earlier, the following discussion focuses in the last two factors, which determine the degree of trade intensity.

Increasing Trade Intensity

Trade intensity index measures the extent to which a pair of trading partners trade more or less intensively with each other than they do with the rest of the world by netting out the effects of different size of each trading country. The trade intensity is separated into complementarity index, which measures the potential trade intensity resulting from the correspondence of commodity composition of each country's global trade, and country bias index, which measures the deviation of actual trade from the potential trade because of the differential degree of trade resistances across trading routes. These trade indexes are measured for each direction in a particular bilateral trade flow in a multi-country, multi-commodity world since each trading route faces a different degree of competition and substitution from the alternative trading routes. That is, in trade between Korea and Japan, the degree of value of trade indexes in Korea's export trade with Japan is different from those in the opposite direction, Japan's export trade with Korea.

Figures 16.4 to 16.6 chart the trend in trade intensity, complementarity and country bias indexes in bilateral trade between Korea–Japan, Korea–China and Japan–China. Several notable features emerge from the figures. First, the degree of trade intensity between the regional countries is significantly high. The second feature is a pre-eminently high degree of complementarity in every trading route, which reflects the distinctive pattern of comparative advantage among the regional countries. The different degree of comparative advantage in manufacturing sector is the main source of complementarity. The third picture is the low country bias in almost all trading routes. Given the geographical proximity, cultural familiarity and common separation from the major centres of world trade, this implies that the regional trade relationship has been greatly influenced by political factors. Lastly, there is further room to exploit the high trade potentials through government-initiated measures.

Korea–Japan trade

Bilateral trade between Korea and Japan has always been very important to each country. Until the normalization of Korea–China trade, each country was the most proximate to the other in terms of geographical, historical, psychic and cultural distance. At the same time, they have shared a common political and strategic interest in the region as members of alliance under the leadership of the USA. At the same time, their industrial structures are complementary to each other, based on the difference in stage of industrialization, though both countries have been increasingly competing in international markets of a variety of CIMs.

The value of trade intensity index in Korea's exports to Japan is much lower than that in Japan's exports to Korea (Figures 16.4 A and B). The former rose sharply in the latter half of the 1980s to reach a peak of 3.1 in 1989 because of the increasing complementarity, but subsequently, fell drastically due to the rapid decrease in the country bias index. On the other hand, the trade intensity in Japan's export trade with Korea has tended to decline slightly over the last two decades. The trend corresponded largely to the country bias index, which has declined since the late 1980s, while the complementarity index remained around 2.7 after a sharp rise to a peak of 3.0 in the early 1980s.

The complementarity index has always been much higher between Japan's exports and Korea's imports, compared to that between Korea's exports and

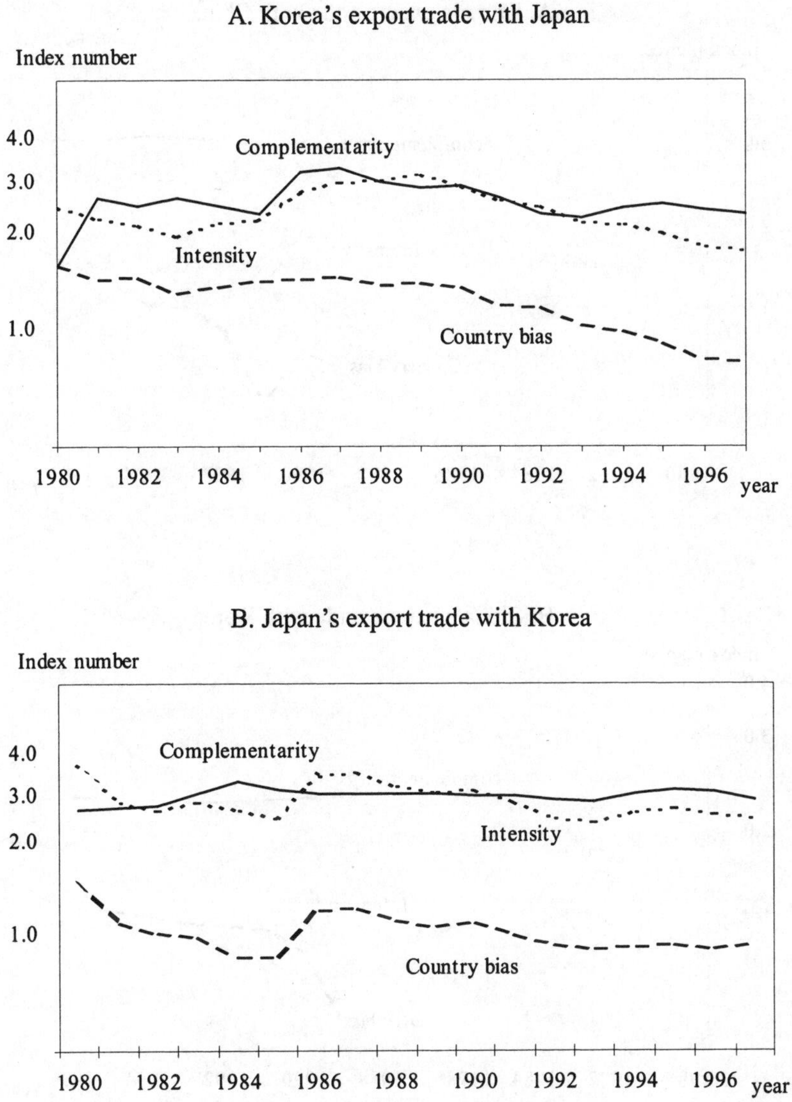

Source: International Economic Data Bank, ANU, Canberra, Australia.

Figure 16.4 Trend of trade indexes between Korea and Japan

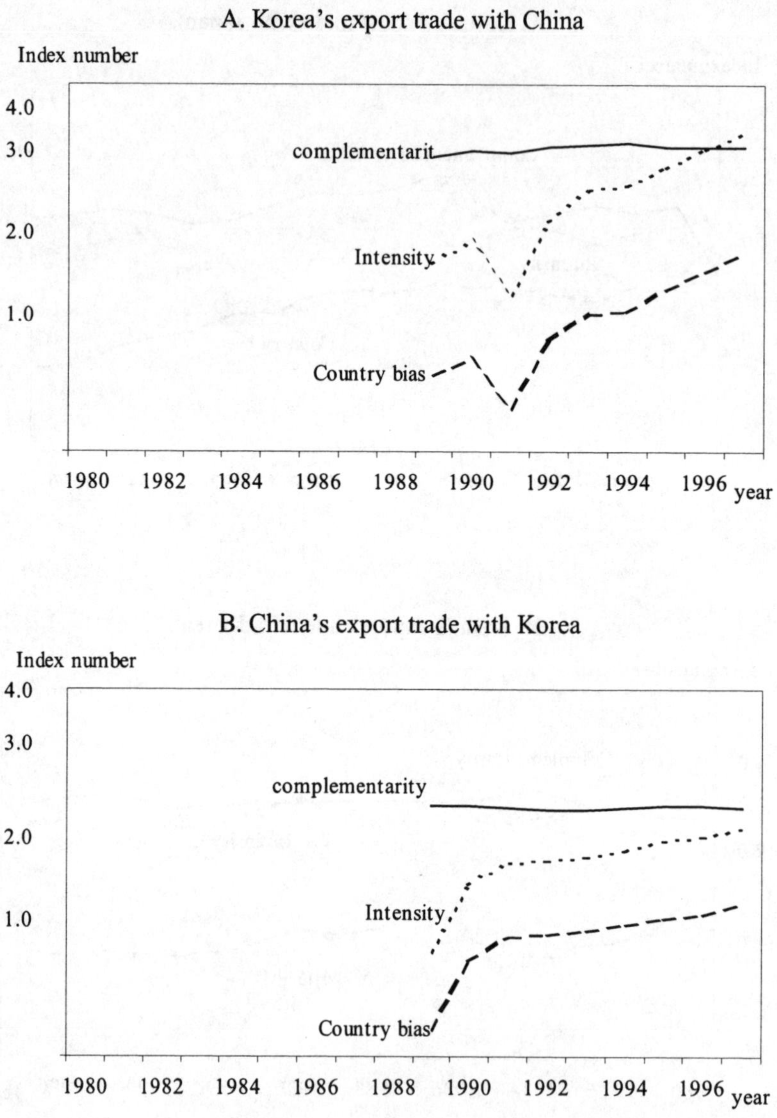

Source: International Economic Data Bank, ANU, Canberra, Australia.

Figure 16.5 Trend of trade indexes between Korea and China

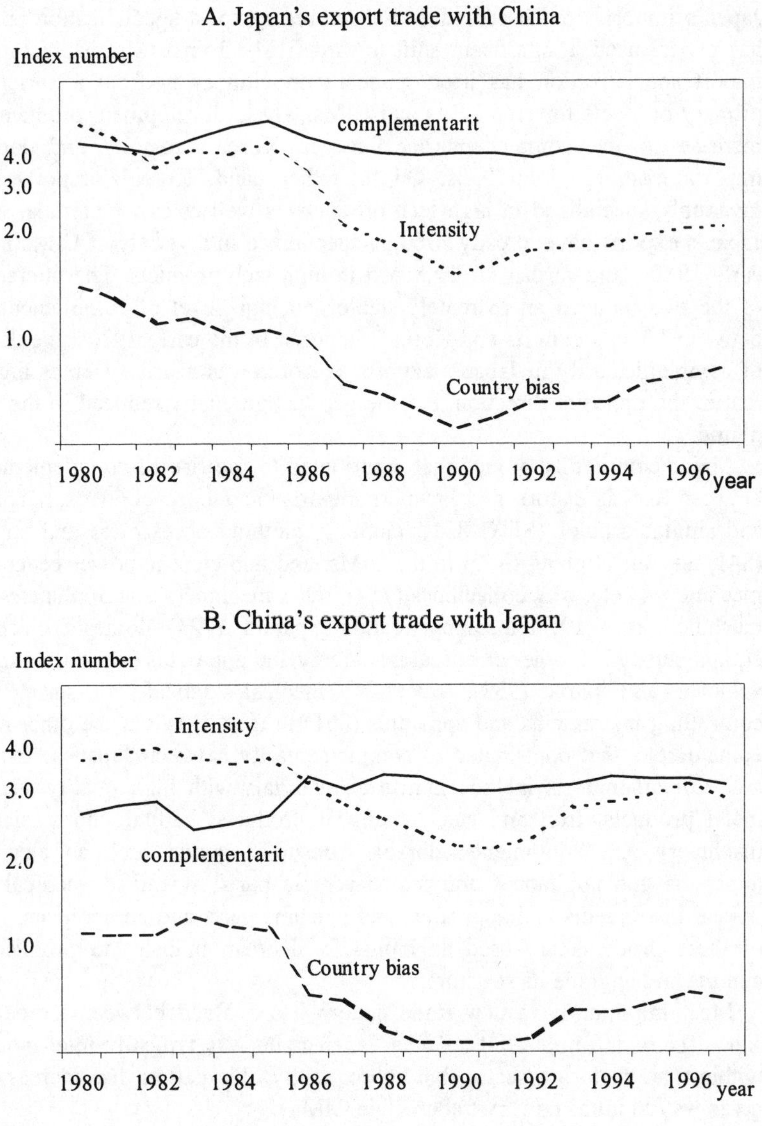

Source: International Economic Data Bank, ANU, Canberra, Australia.

Figure 16.6 The trade indexes between Japan and China

Japan's imports. As discussed earlier, Korea's export specialization pattern has experienced a significant shift toward CIMs from LIMs, while Japan's import specialization has been gradually moving away from a variety of primary products towards LIMs and CIMs. These development produced an increase in the complementarity between Korea's exports and Japan's imports from the mid-1980s. On the other hand, Korea's imports have invariably specialized in high tech products as well as raw materials, while Japan's exports have already strongly specialized in a variety of CIMs in the early 1980s, and further strengthened in high tech products. The interaction of the two induced an extremely stable and high level of complementarity between Japan's exports and Korea's imports. In the early 1980s, the degree of complementarity in Japan's exports to Korea was nearly twice as high as that in the opposite direction, but the gap has gradually reduced in the later period.

Major commodity groups that contributed to the rise of complementarity between Korean exports and Japanese imports include travel goods, handbags and similar articles (SITC 831), clothing, clothing accessories and apparel (841) and fur clothing (842) in the LIMs; and non-electric power generating machinery (711), office machines (714), other machinery and appliances and machine parts (719), telecommunication apparatus (724), domestic electrical equipments (725), other electrical machinery and apparatus (729), road motor vehicles and parts (732), scientific, medical, optical, measuring and controlling instruments and apparatus (861) in the CIMs. On the other hand, commodities that contributed to complementarity between Japanese exports and Korean imports include industrial materials with high quality such as metal products, iron and steel, chemical products; capital goods such as machinery and equipments; durable consumer goods such as electrical apparatus and appliances and motor vehicle parts; scientific, medical and optical instruments and apparatus; and machine parts and components. Most of these products are used as inputs for Korean industry to produce its exports and upgrade its structure.

Most importantly, a new trade pattern has evolved between Korea and Japan. Until the mid-1980s, Korea–Japan trade was typically inter-industry within manufacturing sector, but subsequently, this pattern has increasingly given way to intra-industry trade within CIM.

Country bias indexes in Korea–Japan trade have shown a long-term trend of decline in both directions. Generally, the trend in country bias in Korea–Japan trade is negatively correlated with that in Korea–China trade. Besides, the index value was much higher in Korea's export to Japan than vice versa until the early 1990s, but this trend was reversed in the late 1990s.

Change in country bias in Korea–Japan trade was closely associated with China's entry into the regional trade. China's greater role as a source of

Japan's imports directed low country bias in Korea's exports to Japan. Because of the geographical and psychic proximity to Japanese markets, previously Korea was the major supplier of fresh and simply preserved fish (031), prepared and preserved fish (032), fresh and frozen vegetables (054, 055) in agricultural products, and clothing (841), travel goods (831), footwear (851) and other manufactured articles (899) in LIMs, and technologically standardized CIMs. But as China improved its capacity to export and Japanese firms established affiliates and subsidiaries in China, Korea's access to Japanese markets has deteriorated, compared to China's access.

On the other hand, Korea diverted its import sources away from Japan toward China in a variety of primary products and labour-intensive products. Previously, Japan enjoyed a competitive edge in Korean markets due to geographical, historical and cultural proximity, but Korea–China trade diverted away from Japan. Major commodity groups in which Korea's imports have been diverted toward China comprise: meat preparations (013), cheese and curd (024), eggs (025), fresh fruit and nuts (051), tea and mate (074), tobacco manufactures (122) and fur clothing (842). At the same time, Korea's import diversification scheme away from Japan is worth mentioning with regard to the long-term decline in country bias in Japan's exports to Korea. The scheme imposed restriction on imports of machinery and equipments, and electrical apparatus and appliances from Japan, and hence, the discriminating effect became greater as Korea's imports of those products increased.

The sustained difference in trade intensity between two directions throws light on the causes of a chronical issue of trade imbalance between Korea and Japan. Within the framework of trade intensity, bilateral imbalance between a pair of trading partners originates from two sources: imbalance in each country's global trade and difference in the degree of trade intensity between two ways. Both of these factors contributed to imbalance in Korea–Japan trade. Korea's global balance has fluctuated between deficit and surplus, while Japan's balance has been in huge surplus. This implies that the bilateral balance is favourable to Japan. The effect was much more magnified by the sustained higher degree of trade intensity in Japan's exports to Korea than in Korea's exports to Japan. And the higher trade intensity resulted from the higher degree of complementarity between Japan's exports and Korea's imports than between Korea's exports and Japan's imports. However, the effect is partly neutralized by the higher country bias in Japan's imports from Korea than vice versa. This suggests that Korea would suffer trade deficits in the near future until both countries pattern of trade specialization experience another transformation.

Korea–China trade

The trade intensity between Korea and China has experienced a spectacular rise (Figures 16.5 A and B). Until the late 1980s, the formal trade was prohibited for political reasons. But, within a decade after the trade relationship was normalized, China emerged as Korea's third most important trading partner and Korea became China's fourth largest trading partner. Now China's share in Korea's exports is almost four times as large as is expected from its share in world imports, and Korea's share in China's exports is twice as large as its share in world imports. The trade intensity index values reached 3.9 in Korea's export trade with China and 1.9 in the opposite direction. The high degree of trade intensity was solely originated from the high degree of complementarity between both countries' comparative advantages. The country bias in Korea–China trade has increased rapidly since the normalization of trade relationship, but still remains low under unity. Notably, the trade intensity in Korea's export to China is twice as high as that in China's export to Korea.

As discussed earlier, China's export specialization has rapidly shifted from primary products toward LIMs and recently, toward CIMs. Its import specialization remained strong in a variety of CIMs over the last two decades. China's increasing export specialization in LIMs has been closely correlated with its increasing import specialization in CIMs such as intermediates and capital goods. This changing pattern produces a high degree of complementarity in Korea–China trade, where Korea's comparative advantage has moved to production and exports of more CIMs.

Complementarity between Korea's exports and China's imports are extremely high throughout the period and shows further increasing tendency over time. Commodities which have contributed to a high degree of complementarity are those such as synthetic fibres (266), yarns (651) and fabrics (652, 653) in LIMs, and organic chemicals (512), nitrogenous fertilizers (561), plastic materials (581), non-electric power generating machinery (711), office machines (714), other machinery and appliances and machine parts (719), telecommunication apparatus (724), domestic electrical equipment (725), other electrical machinery and apparatus (729), road motor vehicles and parts (732), scientific, medical, optical, measuring and controlling instruments and apparatus (861) in CIMs. On the other hand, complementarity between China's exports and Korea's imports has been moderately high and stable at a level of 2.4 to 2.5. Both China's increasing export specialization in LIMs and Korea's decreasing import specialization in LIMs did not produce further increase. Major commodities that contributed to complementarity throughout the whole period are those such as unmilled maize (044), other crude minerals (276), crude petroleum (331), petroleum products (332), fur skins (613), pig iron (671), lead (685), tin (687), machinery and appliances and machine parts (719), electric power machinery (722), telecommunications apparatus (724), other electric machinery and apparatus (729). In the 1990s, the contribution of machinery and appliances gained in importance while that of primary products lost in importance.

Country bias indexes rose rapidly in trade between Korea and China. Until the late 1980s, when prohibitively high government-initiated trade resistances overwhelmed the low natural resistances, the high degree of trade complementarity produced no actual trade flows. However, the removal of trade embargo prompted rapid rise of country bias, thanks to the low natural resistances of geographical, historical and cultural adjacency. However, the country bias indexes were still low under unity, implying unfledged trade relationship yet. The index value was still under unity of 0.79 in China's export trade with Korea, and it was not until 1997 that the value became to exceed unity in Korea's export trade with China.

One interesting feature is the difference in country bias between directions, since government-initiated trade resistances are reciprocal and hence, unlikely to persist with inequality in access to partner's markets. This puzzle can be understood by taking the commodity composition of each trading route into consideration. Differences in commodity composition created differential country bias in three ways: asymmetric economic distance between two ways because of the presence of third countries competing with the partners; different potential trade volume causing difference in traders' market orientation and outlook; and different impact of individual trade resistances varying with commodity groups[21]. Considering the presence of Japan, Taiwan, Hong Kong, Singapore and other ASEAN countries, it is likely that China has been confronting more intense competition in access to Korean markets than Korea has in access to Chinese markets.

The difference in trade intensity between two directions is a major cause of bilateral imbalance in Korea–China trade. Korea has enjoyed huge surplus in the bilateral trade with China throughout the whole period. Trade specialization pattern induced both the higher degree of complementarity between Korea's exports and China's imports than China's exports and Korea's imports, and the higher degree of country bias in Korea's exports to China than the opposite route because of less competition from the third countries.

Japan-China trade

The degree of trade intensity between Japan and China has experienced a long-term trend of decline with significant fluctuation in both directions over the last two decades (Figures 16.6 A and B). The index value in Japan's export trade with China fell drastically from 4.1 to 1.3 during the 1980s and it regained to 1.9 in the 1990s. In contrast, the index value in China's export trade with Japan was extremely high (3.5 in the early 1980s) but declined considerably in the latter half of the 1980s, and rose again in the 1990s. The trend largely corresponded to the up and down of country bias index, since the degree of complementarity has been very high and stable. The country bias index in Japan–China trade was very high in the first half of the 1980s, but in the latter half of the 1980s declined substantially and then rose again in the 1990s. Trade complementarity between Japan and China remained extremely high in both directions throughout the whole period. Complementarity between Japan's exports and China's imports rose significantly from 3.5 to 4.2 in the first half of the 1980s, but subsequently declined to 3.0 by 1997. Given the sustained high degree of Japan's strong export specialization in a variety of CIMs, a huge shift in China's import specialization pattern towards industrial intermediates and capital goods caused increase in complementarity in the first half of the 1980s. As China's exports became increasingly specialized in LIMs, however, it strengthened import specialization further in industrial intermediates from which Japan's exports diverted to machinery and equipments. This resulted in a drastic decline in the late 1980s. Commodity groups which contributed ups and downs in complementarity in the 1980s, include synthetic textile fibres (266), yarns (651), fabrics (652, 653), organic chemicals (512), nitrogenous fertilizers (561), iron and steel bars, rods, angles and shapes (673), plates and sheets of iron or steels (674). Commodities which contributed to steady increase are those such as non-electric power generating machinery (711), office machines (714), metal working machinery (715), textile and leather machinery (717), other machinery and appliances and machine parts (719), telecommunication apparatus (724), domestic electrical equipment (725), other electrical machinery and apparatus (729), scientific, medical, optical, measuring and controlling instruments and apparatus (861) in CIMs with the high level of technology.

On the other hand, complementarity has remained stable in the plateau ranging from 2.8 to 3.1 after a sharp rise in the first half of the 1980s. China's increasing export specialization in the primary products immediately after its opening up to world markets, and then transformation to LIMs contributed to the high degree of complementarity with Japan's imports, which has been increasingly specialized in the primary products and LIMs. However, as China's exports have shifted gradually from LIMs toward CIMs, complementarity between China's exports and Japan's imports began to decline.

In Japan–China trade, the most remarkable development was the reduced country bias. Country bias index in both directions was substantially high in the early 1980s, fell sharply until the early 1990s and then turned to rise. The decline of country bias during 1980s largely attributes to the normalization of China's trade relationship with Korea and Taiwan and accompanies the rapid increase in country bias between China and the two NIEs. On the other hand, the increase in the 1990s has much to do with the Japanese direct investment towards China, leading to a privately initiated trade resistance, which gives competitive edges to Japanese traders. The active Japanese direct investment in the mid-1990s favoured Japan's access to China's imports of capital goods, components, and intermediates and China's exports to Japanese markets in a variety of primary products and LIMs.

Trade intensity is higher in China's export trade with Japan than in Japan's export trade with China. The asymmetry is due to the higher degree of both complementarity and country bias in China's export trade with Japan than vice versa. Especially, the changed pattern of China's trade specialization produced much more complementarity in its export trade than import trade with Japan, so that complementarity which was much higher in Japan's exports to China than in the opposite direction in the early 1980s, approached to almost the same level in two directions.

CONCLUSION

This chapter aimed to explain the sources of the rapid growth of bilateral trade between the Northeast Asian countries by using the intensity approach. Over the last two decades the Northeast Asian economies have experienced miraculous growth through the outward-looking industrialization policy. The strategy raised not only their weight in the world production and trade, but also trade flows between regional countries. The intra-regional trade has more than doubled from 16 per cent to 38 per cent, while their dependence on extra-region declined considerably. The expansion of regional trade has been both a cause and an effect of economic growth of individual countries to form a virtuous circle and to increase the degree of interdependence among the regional economies, resulting in a greater capability of self-sustained growth.

Primarily, greater intra-regional trade results from three broad sets of factors: the increase in the region's share in world trade; underlying complementarity between the commodity structures of regional countries' global trade; and the differential degree of trade resistances between trading routes causing trade diversion. This chapter confirms that the three factors played their role in the greater intra-regional trade of Northeast Asia. The share of Northeast Asian countries as a whole rose from 10 per cent to 19 per cent in world exports and from 11 per cent to 15 per cent in world imports.

However, there has been important variation between the regional countries. Japan's weight in world and regional trade has fallen incredibly, while the NIEs and China's weight rose amazingly.

Trade complementarity has been strikingly high between the regional trade. One might have supposed that all Northeast Asian countries are poor in natural resources, have comparative advantage in the manufacturing sector, and hence, are competitive with each other. However, this study shows that complementarity is extremely high and has increased further as their comparative advantage strengthened in the manufacturing sector. This is a consequence of increasing interdependence of industrial structures in the process of sequential industrialization from the regional countries. The gradual upgrading of individual countries' industrial structure induced the continual interplay between complementarity and competition among regional countries in different stages of industrialization. This contributed to upgrading the structure of comparative advantage towards more capital-intensive and technologically sophisticated industries in which intra-industry trade is prevailing.

Country bias which summarizes the influences of trade resistances has increased rapidly, but is still low. This is a legacy of prohibitively high level of government-initiated trade resistances in the Cold War period, given the geographical proximity and psychic and cultural familiarity between the countries. Until the late 1980 when bilateral trade relationship had been banned between China and the two NIEs, Korea and Taiwan, the regional trade was agglomerated into Japan and the country bias in Korea–Japan trade and Japan–China trade was very high. However, immediately after the trade ban was removed, the country bias in Korea–China trade rose rapidly and that in Japan's trade with the regional countries fell significantly. Currently, despite active foreign direct investment between regional countries that induced intra-regional trade, country bias indexes remain low.

This finding suggests that the increasing integration of Northeast Asian markets has been fundamentally based on market forces, and that institutional regional framework for closer cooperation will further increase the intra-regional trade. So far, in Northeast Asia there has been a pessimistic view to arrange an institution to promote regional trade on political and economic grounds. Politically, there still exists political rivalry and legacy of the Cold War. Economically, there is too little capacity to absorb industrial products and bilateral imbalance. For example, Japan, with the largest markets, has played its role as a principal supplier of capital goods, intermediate inputs and industrial raw materials to its industrializing neighbours, but has not behaved as a market for their manufactured goods. Japan's asymmetric role has been known as a structural problem because of Japan's full set industrialization policy. However, this pattern began to change.

This study also shows that the imbalance of bilateral trade is resolved in the trilateral framework: bilateral imbalance is favourable to Japan in Korea–Japan trade, favourable to Korea in Korea–China trade; and favourable to China in Japan–China trade because of the pattern of comparative advantage of individual countries. It also suggests that an institutional arrangement at the government level would effectively promote regional trade not because of discrimination against outsiders, but because of exploiting the high degree of trade potentials.

NOTES

1. East Asia includes Northeast Asia and Southeast Asia. While Southeast Asia now is relatively well defined with 10 member countries of the Association of Southeast Asian Nations (ASEAN), Northeast Asia is not with diverse definition. The strictest definition of Northeast Asia includes North and South Koreas, Japan, China's northeastern provinces (Liaoning, Jilin and Heilongjian provinces), Russia's Far East and Mongolia. On the opposite end of the spectrum, the broadest geographical definition includes South and North Koreas, Japan, all of China, Hong Kong, Taiwan, Mongolia, and Russia's Far East and Siberia. There are also many other variations between the two. In this chapter Northeast Asia includes five market-oriented economies, such as Japan, South Korea, Taiwan, Hong Kong and China, which experienced dynamic growth over the last generation. The concept of the West Pacific Economic Zone (WPEZ), widely discussed in China, embraces initially these five economies, and then intends to include the ASEAN in the south and the Russia Far East in the north. The miraculous growth of East Asian economy has been considerably differentiated since the economic crisis between industrialized Northeast Asia and less industrialized Southeast Asia. The former has been recovering rapidly with improved export competitiveness whereas the latter was struggling with political and social unstability.
2. Actually, the crisis spreaded promptly over the whole region and dampened exports, which in turn, discouraged investment and consumption with decreased income and uncertain economic prospects for the future. All this development was responsible for a sharp fall of growth in most countries with a negative rate of economic growth in 1998, and also evidenced the high degree of interdependence among the regional countries.
3. A joint study programme between the Institute of Developing Economies, Japan External Trade Organization (IDE–JETRO) and the Korea Institute for International Economic Policy (KIEP) proposed establishing a Korea–Japan Free Trade Agreement (Korea-Japan FTA), similar to the EEC and NAFTA (North American Free Trade Agreement), to bring the Korea–Japan economic relationship closer. For the proposal of the study group, see IDE (2000) and KIEP (2000).
4. Studies on the level and pattern of bilateral trade flows are surveyed by Drysdale and Garnaut (1982).

5. The gravity model was pioneered by Tinbergen (1962), elaborated by Linnemann (1966), and thereafter widely used. It estimates quantitatively and seeks to explain the 'absolute' level of bilateral trade flow by trade potentials representing the size of traders such as GDP and population, and trade resistances such as physical and psychic distances and institutional and historical ties. But it has limitation that assumes independence of each trade flow from others too extremely to catch trade diverting effect between trade flows, which is crucial to understanding a country's bilateral trade relationship.
6. Generally, the influence of trade resistances varies considerably across commodities. Hence, even though a country imposes uniform resistances on all trading routes without any discrimination, their effect is discriminatory through the different influence across commodities. For example, country A's biased protection against imports of foodstuffs will result in discrimination against imports from food exporting countries. This is evidenced in trade between Northeast Asian countries, as seen in the fourth section.
7. Drysdale (1969) greatly enhanced the analytical usefulness of the intensity approach by decomposing intensity of trade into complementarity and country bias.
8. The calculation requires the same commodity classification over the whole period and across all trading routes to enable consistent comparison. In this study, the calculation is based on the International Economic Data Bank (IEDB), held in Asia Pacific School of Economics and Management, the Australian National University. The data are based on the United Nations Commodity Trade Statistics. The author is most grateful to Dr. Kang, manager of IEDB, for the painstaking computation of the indexes.
9. This assumes that natural resources are evenly distributed over the earth's surface. For the usefulness and limitation of using population density as a proxy for relative endowments of natural resource, see Keesing and Sherk (1971) and Bowen (1983).
10. This proxy was first used by Lary (1968) to discuss US imports of manufactured goods from developing countries. However, there is some difficulty with using per capita income for capital stock relative to labour because higher income comes from not only capital stock per head but also abundant natural resources per head. Despite the limitation, however, the proxy is widely used for the ratio of capital to labour.
11. Krueger's model (1977) has two tradable sectors, producing primary products and manufactures, and three factors of production: natural resources which are specific to the primary sector, capital which is specific to the manufacturing sector, and labour which used in both sectors, is intersectorally mobile and exhibits diminishing marginal product in each sector. In her model, at a given set of international prices, the real wage rate is determined by the overall per worker endowment of natural resources and capital, as in the Johnson synthesis, while the pattern of comparative advantage between manufactures and primary products is influenced largely by the relative endowments of capital and natural resources of the country as compared with the rest of the world.
12. For a scheme of dynamic changes in production and trade specialization in a multi-country, multi-commodity setting, see Park (1988).
13. The export-led growth does not necessarily mean that the degree of trade dependence, measured as a ratio of trade to GDP, is high. Japan's trade

dependence is low with 18 per cent in 1999 and even lowered sharply over the last two decade from 31 per cent in 1980. Especially, the extremely low and halved level of Japan's import dependence is a consequence of its full set industrialization under the governmental industrial policy and a cause of increasing trade conflicts with its major trading partners, including United States. China's trade dependence is still lower with 38 per cent in 1999 compared with the average openness of 44 per cent of the world economy, but rapidly rose from 22 per cent in 1980. Only the proportions for the three NIEs are much higher than the world average. Over the last two decades, nevertheless, the ratio lowered from 80 per cent to 67 per cent for Korea and from 111 per cent to 90 per cent for Taiwan, but for Hong Kong, it even rose from 174 per cent to 262 per cent.

14. East Asia as a whole is the largest savings-surplus region in the world and has ample financial resources to handle its financial difficulties. Therefore, one can assume that if there had been a regional institution to promote currency and financial cooperation, East Asia would not have suffered such a crisis. This is one of the most important arguments for institutional arrangement for closer regional cooperation after the crisis.
15. The current recession of the Japanese economy is the longest and deepest in the post-war period. The recession was initiated by a rapid appreciation of yen in 1985, but fundamentally attributable to the failure of Japanese government policy. To offset the reduced external demand in the late 1980s, the Japanese government boosted domestic demand through expansionary monetary and fiscal policies, but this led to skyrocketing land and stock prices to result in a bubble economy. The bubble burst in 1990 and brought everything down. Financial institutions suffered from lowered prices of their mortgage assets and huge non-performing loans. Manufacturers too suffered from lowered asset values and reduced their investment. Consumers cut their expenditures because of radical depreciation of their asset values. These formed a vicious cycle, where less demand led to less production, to less income and to less demand. In this new situation, the traditional Japanese economic system which produced the rapid growth came under the question of its effectiveness. Now, there is increasing doubt as to Japan's full set industrialization which caused a flood of exports and an extremely low level of imports of manufactures.
16. For this reason, Japan has been criticized for the Asian economic crisis and regarded as a large part of problem in recovering from it, far from being part of solution. For the detailed discussion on Japan's negative role during East Asian economic crisis and the subsequent recovering process, see Park (2000).
17. Balassa (1965) recognized that government intervention could compromise the effectiveness of the indexes as an indicator of comparative advantage and treated asymmetrically the export and import specialization indexes, on the ground that the pattern of the import specialization is particularly influenced by government import restrictions.
18. For a detailed discussion on the impacts of yen appreciation upon Japan's foreign direct investment toward and trade with the East Asian developing countries, see Park (1997).
19. This asymmetric feature seems to be a major reason why Northeast Asian economies have been involved with trade friction in the US and European markets. Japan, Korea, China and Taiwan have been the very countries which have faced trade friction most frequently since the 1980s.

20. In 2001, China emerged to as the second largest market for Korean exports, overtaking Japan.
21. For a detailed discussion on the different influence on country bias of different commodity composition between two directions of a bilateral trade relationship, see Park (1987).

REFERENCES

Anderson, K. and Y.I. Park (1989), 'China and the international relocation of world textile and clothing activity', *Weltwirtschaftliches Archiv*, **125**, 129–48.

Balassa, B. (1965), 'Trade liberalization and 'revealed' comparative advantage', *The Manchester School*, **33**, 99–123.

Bowen, H.P. (1983), 'Changes in the international distribution of resources and their impact on U.S. comparative advantage', *Review of Economics and Statistics*, **65**, 402–14.

Drysdale, P.D. (1969), 'Japan and Australia: the prospect for closer economic integration', *Economic Papers*, **30**, 321–342.

Drysdale, P.D. and R. Garnaut (1982), 'Trade intensities and the analysis of bilateral trade flows in a multi-country world: a survey', *Hitotsubashi Journal of Economics*, **22**, 62–84.

Hufbauer, G.C. and J.G. Chilas (1974), 'Specialization by industrial countries: extent and consequences', in H. Giersch (ed.), *The International Division of Labour: Problems and Perspectives*, Germany: Kiel Institute of World Economics.

IMF, *Direction of Trade Statistics Yearbook*, various issues.

Institute of Developing Economies (2000), *Toward Closer Japan–Korea Economic Relations in the 21st Century*, Tokyo: Japanese External Trade Organization.

Johnson, H.G. (1968), 'Comparative cost and commercial policy theory for a developing world economy', Wicksell Lectures, Stockholm.

Keesing, D.B. and D.R. Sherk (1971), 'Population density in patterns of trade and development, *American Economic Review*, **61**, 249–58.

Korean Institute for International Economic Policy (2000), *Toward a Korea–Japan FTA: Assessment and Prospects*, Seoul.

Krueger, A.O. (1977), 'Growth, distortions and patterns of trade among many countries', Special papers in *International Finance*, n° 40, Princeton University.

Lary, H.B. (1968), *Imports of Manufactures from Less Developed Countries*, New York: NBER.

Linder, S.B. (1961), *An Essay on Trade and Transformation*, New York: Wiley.

Linnemann, H. (1966), *An Econometric Study of International Trade Flows*, Amsterdam: North-Holland.

Park, Y.I. (1987), 'Australia's trade redirection: the importance of relative trade resistances', *Pacific Economic Papers*, n° 148.

Park, Y.I. (1988), 'The changing pattern of textile and trade in Northeast Asia', *Pacific Economic Papers*, n° 157.

Park, Y.I. (1997), 'Japan's foreign direct investment toward the East Asia in manufacturing sector and the changing pattern of its trade with the East Asia' (in Korean), *Bulletin of the Institute of Business and Economic Research*, **11**, Inha University, 29–30.

Park, Y.I. (1998), 'The changing pattern of Japanese imports' (in Korean), *Bulletin of the Institute of Business and Economic Research*, **12**, Inha University, 27–59.

Park, Y.I. (2000), 'Japan's role in Asian crisis and its leadership in forming East Asian economic cooperation'(in Korean), *Journal of International Trade and Industry Studies*, **5**., 25–59.

Tinbergen, J. (1962), *Shaping the World Economy: Suggestions for an International Economic Policy*, New York: Twentieth Century Fund.

World Bank (1993), *The East Asian Miracle*, Washington, D.C.

World Bank (2000), *The World Development Report*, Oxford: Oxford University Press.

APPENDIX

This appendix introduces briefly the concept and logic of trade indexes of intensity, complementarity and country bias used in this chapter. The intensity of trade is defined from a two-dimensional *nxn* matrix of international trade flows (*n*: number of countries).

The index of intensity of trade in country *i's* exports trade with country *j* (I_{ij}) is defined as the ratio of the actual value of trade (V_{ij}) to the expected value ($\overline{V_{ij}}$), that is

$$I_{ij} = V_{ij} / \overline{V_{ij}} = \frac{V_{ij}}{V_{i.}} / \frac{V_{.j}}{V_{..}}$$

where V_{ij} : actual exports from *i* to *j*

$\overline{V_{ij}}$: $P_{ij} \times V$

P_{ij} : the probability that *i* exports to $j(P_i \times P_j)$

P_i : the probability that *i* exports (*i*'s share in world exports)

P_j : the probability that *j* imports (*j*'s share in world imports)

$V_{i.}$: *i*'s global exports

$V_{.j}$: *j*'s global imports

$V_{..}$: world trade

The index of intensity of country *i's* export trade with *j* is separated into two effects: complementarity index, C_{ij}, measures the degree of 'match' of commodity composition between country *i*'s global exports and country *j*'s imports; and country bias index, B_{ij}, measures the degree of trade resistances in the trading route relative to those in the alternatives, which causes trade-diversion between trading routes. To illustrate the logic of separation, the two-dimensional matrix, used for illustrating intensity of trade, needs to be extended to a three-dimensional matrix, *nxnxm*, to incorporate the commodity composition (*m*: number of commodities).

The complementarity index in country *i's* export trade with country *j* (C_{ij}) is defined as the intensity of trade expected from the commodity composition of one country's exports and another country's imports, if there were no trade resistances or they were uniform across all trading routes. That is

$$C_{ij} = \frac{\overline{V_{ij}}}{V_{i.}} / \frac{V_{.j}}{V_{..}}$$
$$= \sum_{k=1} \left(\frac{V_{i.k}}{V_{i..}} \times \frac{V_{.jk}}{V_{i.j.}} \times \frac{V_{...}}{V_{..k}} \right)$$
$$= \sum ((V_{..k} / V_{...}) \times S_{i.k} \times S_{.jk})$$

$V_{i.k}$: *i*'s exports of commodity *k*

$V_{.jk}$: *j*'s imports of commodity *k*

$V_{..k}$: world trade of commodity *k*

$V_{i..}(=\sum_{k=1} V_{i.k})$: *i*'s total exports

$V_{.j.}(=\sum_{k=1} V_{.jk})$: *j*'s total imports

$V_{...}(=\sum_{k=1} V_{..k})$: world total trade

$S_{i.k}\left(= \frac{V_{i.k}}{V_{i..}} / \frac{V_{..k}}{V_{...}} \right)$: the index of country *i*'s export specialization in commodity *k*

$S_{.jk}\left(\frac{V_{.jk}}{V_{.j.}} / \frac{V_{..k}}{V_{...}} \right)$: the index of country *j*'s import specialization in commodity *k*

Complementarity index is the weighted sum of products of country *i*'s export specialization index and country *j*'s import specialization index in every commodity *k*, weighted by each commodity *k*'s share in world trade. Trade specialization index measures the relative competitiveness of country *i* in commodity *k*, compared with its average competitiveness in all of the other commodities or compared with the average competitiveness of the rest of the world in commodity *k*. The indexes are generally regarded to reveal a country's comparative advantage, though the terminology given to the indexes varies with authors.

The concept of 'country bias' in bilateral trade measures the extent to which a trading partner has more or less favourable access to the other's markets. Hence, the index of country bias (B_{ij}) is defined as the ratio actual trade flows to the expected ones from both countries' shares of world trade. That is, a weighted average of the indexes B_{ijk}, weighted by the share of the expected trade of each commodity *k* in the total expected trade from *i* to *j*.

$$B_{ij} = \frac{V_{ij}}{\overline{V_{ij}}} = \sum_k \frac{V_{ijk}}{\overline{V_{ij}}} = \sum_k \left(\frac{\overline{V_{ijk}}}{\overline{V_{ij}}} \times \frac{V_{ijk}}{\overline{V_{ijk}}} \right) = \sum_k \left(B_{ijk} \times \frac{\overline{V_{ijk}}}{\overline{V_{ij}}} \right)$$

where

$$B_{ijk} = \frac{V_{ijk}}{\overline{V}_{ijk}} = \frac{V_{ijk}}{V_{i.k}} / \frac{V_{.jk}}{V_{..k}}$$

V_{ijk} = i's exports of commodity k to j

Finally, the intensity of trade is separated into a complementarity and a country bias index, and the index value of intensity is expressed as a product

$$I_{ij} = \frac{V_{ij}}{V_{i.}} / \frac{V_{.j}}{V_{..}} = \left(\frac{\overline{V_{ij}}}{V_{i.}} / \frac{V_{.j}}{V_{..}} \right) \times \frac{V_{ij}}{\overline{V_{ij}}} = C_{ij} \times B_{ij}$$

One important aspect of these indexes is worth stressing. This is associated with the interdependence assumption of the intensity approach. From the standpoint of country i, the weighted average of index value for its various trading routes (or in all commodities) is equal to unity, so that the value of each index in country i's exports to a given trading partner j (or in a given commodity k) is negatively related to the index value in its exports to the other trading partners (in other commodities).

Lastly, the calculation of trade indexes requires detailed trade statistics in the form of annual three-dimensional world trade matrices, disaggregated by a common commodity classification, evaluated at the same currency unit. It should be noted that success in isolating both indexes of complementarity and country-bias requires commodity groups to be classified at a sufficient level of detail, so that each commodity group includes reasonably homogeneous sub-commodities.

17. Korea–Singapore Free Trade Agreement and Analysis of its Economic Impact using a CGE Model

Jong-Hwan Ko and Jung Duk Lim

INTRODUCTION

While the world economy is becoming more integrated on the basis of the multilateral system of the World Trade Organization (WTO), a striking feature of international economic relations at present is the growth of regionalism due to the widening and deepening of regional economic agreements. The past decade has witnessed a flood of regional trade agreements (RTAs). Today, over 170 RTAs are in place[1].

The motives behind this shift towards regionalism are complex: a belief that regional integration is conducive to growth; disillusionment with the framework for global integration; a defensive reaction to the formation and reinforcement of other trading blocs (Greenaway, 1992). Whether regionalism poses a serious threat to multilateralism is a difficult call to make. Although regionalism, in the form of a free trade agreement (FTA) or customs union, is, on the one hand, regarded as a stumbling block to multilateralism due to its perceived undermining of the progress of the multilateral system of the GATT/WTO, Article 24 of the GATT/WTO, on the other hand, acknowledges the formation of FTAs, and the WTO and the OECD, through their official reports, accept regionalism as a building block to multilateralism.

Looking into some examples of RTAs in Western Europe where economic integration arrangements are at their most advanced, the European Union (EU) has formed a single internal market since 1993 and introduced a single currency on 1 January 1999. Alongside this, market widening has occurred with the formation of the European Economic Area (EEA) between the European Community and European Free Trade Association (EFTA) in 1992 and further took place with the accession of central and eastern European countries, such as Poland, Hungary, the Czech Republic, Slovenia, Slovakia, Estonia, Latvia and Lithuania as well as Malta and Cyprus to the EU in May 2004[2].

In North America, the North American Free Trade Agreement (NAFTA) came into effect in January 1994 and is to be extended to a Free Trade Agreement of Americas (FTAA), including 34 countries in North and South America from 2004. In Latin America several sub-regional free trade agreements, such as MERCOSUR, have already been signed.

In Asia, the formation of an FTA among the member nations of the Association of South-East Asian Nations (ASEAN) occurred in 2002. The 18 members of the Asia Pacific Economic Cooperation (APEC) decided via their Bogor Declaration of November 1994 to establish an FTA in the region by 2010 for their higher income members which make up 85 per cent of their trade, and by 2020 for the rest[3].

In addition, there have been many proposals for additional free trade regimes. The most significant by far would be a Trans-Atlantic Free Trade Area (TAFTA), joining Europe and North America[4]. In a similar setting, the Asia-Europe Meeting (ASEM) has been established, since 25 political leaders, from 15 EU countries[5], the President of the European Commission, seven members of ASEAN[6], China, Japan and Korea, gathered for the first time to elaborate the means to improve political and economic cooperation between Asia and Europe in Bangkok on 1–2 March 1996. Furthermore, the ASEM has become institutionalized with the hosting of the second ASEM by the United Kingdom in April 1998, of the third ASEM by Korea in October 2000, and of the fourth ASEM by Denmark in October 2002[7].

Of the world's major trading partners, only Korea, China, Japan and Taiwan were not members of any regional economic arrangements as of September 2001, when the conference was held at which this chapter was presented.

However, Japan has recently assessed the feasibility of FTAs with Mexico and Singapore and formed an FTA with Singapore since January 2002. Korea concluded an FTA with Chile in October 2002. This is the first FTA signed by Korea. The historic agreement is seen as the beginning of Korea's efforts to join the global trend in forming regional trade blocs. Korea's potential next FTA partners include Singapore, ASEAN, China, Japan, Mexico and the United States[8].

Singapore has already inked an FTA with New Zealand and Japan, and is in the midst of working out similar agreements with Australia, Mexico and the United States. Singapore suggested an FTA to Korea in 1999, but Korea responded to it in a reserved manner, because Korea wanted to sign an FTA with Chile in the first place.

However, after its successful negotiation of an FTA with Chile in October 2002, the Korean government recently decided to suggest to Singapore a Joint Study Group to examine the feasibility and desirability of establishing an FTA.

The objective of this chapter is to quantify the potential economic impact of a Korea–Singapore FTA using a multi-region, multi-sector Computable General Equilibrium (CGE) model in order to provide some information needed to assess its economic feasibility and desirability.

The analysis proceeds as follows. The second section provides a brief description of the economies of Korea and Singapore. The third section describes the model structure used for this study. The fourth section shows simulations carried out in this chapter. The fifth section examines the simulation results. A final section concludes with the suggested agenda for a Korea–Singapore FTA.

OVERVIEW OF THE ECONOMIES OF KOREA AND SINGAPORE

Table 17.1 shows the population, GDP, per capita GDP and trade of Korea and Singapore as well as their shares in the world market in 1997. Korea accounts for 0.8 per cent and Singapore 0.1 per cent of world population, respectively. Korea represents 1.5 per cent and Singapore 0.3 per cent of world GDP, which implies that the Korean economy is about five times as large as the Singapore economy in terms of GDP. However, Singapore is approximately twice as rich as Korea in terms of per capita GDP. Korea and Singapore account for 2.5 per cent and 2.1 per cent of world exports and

Table 17.1 Selected indicators for Korea and Singapore in 1997 (1000 persons, US$ million, %)

	Population	GDP	Per capita GDP	Exports*	Imports*
Korea	45,642 (0.8)	445,503 (1.5)	9,761	162,516 (2.5)	158,518 (2.5)
Singapore	3,922 (0.1)	79,822 (0.3)	20,352	131,560 (2.1)	135,495 (2.1)
ROW	5,324,221 (99.1)	28,456,464 (98.2)	5,344	6,115,226 (95.4)	6,115,285 (95.4)
World	5,373,785 (100)	28,981,789 (100)	5,393	6,409,301 (100)	6,409,299 (100)

Note: The figures in parentheses represent percentage shares.
* At market price.

Source: Based on GTAP database version 5, 2001.

imports, respectively, which indicates that these two economies are quite open economies in comparison to their shares of world GDP.

Figure 17.1 illustrates the time series exports between Korea and Singapore during the period 1965–2001. Korea exported goods and services of US$4.08 billion to Singapore and Singapore US$3.01 billion to Korea in 2001. Singapore is the sixth largest export market and the 11th largest import market for Korea. Korea has run a trade surplus with Singapore since 1985.

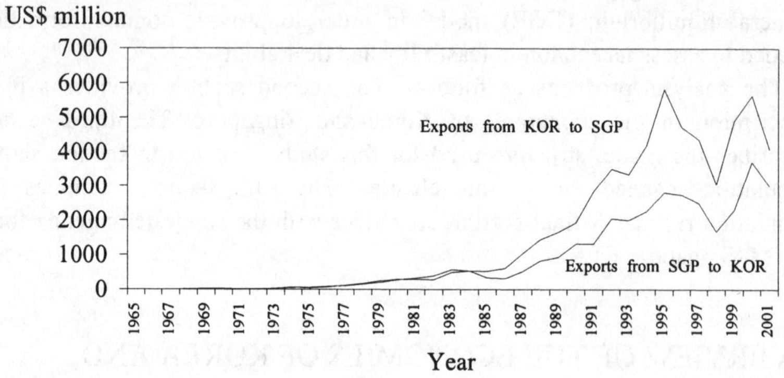

Source: Based on GTAP database version 5, 2001.

Figure 17.1 Exports between Korea and Singapore, 1965–2001

Table 17.2 demonstrates the matrix of exports at world prices of Korea and Singapore and their shares in the world market in 1997, the basis year of the model. Korea's exports to Singapore represent only 3.1 per cent of its total exports, and only 2.6 per cent of Singapore's total exports go to Korea.

Table 17.2 Matrix of exports at world prices and their shares for Korea and Singapore in 1997 (US$ million, %)

	Korea	Singapore	ROW	World
Korea	0.0	4,851 (3,1)	149,986 (96.9)	154,837 (100)
Singapore	3,312 (2.6)	0.0	125,675 (97.4)	128,987 (100)
ROW	155,194 (2.5)	130,569 (2.1)	5,839,625 (95.3)	6,125,388 (100)

Note: The figures in parentheses represent percentage shares.
Source: Based on GTAP database version 5, 2001.

Table 17.3 reports the composition of imports between Korea and Singapore and their bilateral tariff rates, classified into 26 sectors in 1997. It is clear that trade relations between Korea and Singapore are characterized by a great deal of intra-industry trade: the bulk of Korea's exports to Singapore involve electronics products, which is followed by machinery equipment, other services, chemicals, transportation services, and nonferrous metal products; Singapore's exports to Korea are also concentrated in electronics, nonferrous metal products, machinery equipment, chemicals, and iron and steel. There are no grains traded between the two countries.

Of 26 sectors, Singapore levies tariffs on only three products imported from Korea: other agricultural products (OAGR) by 6.1 per cent, livestock by 7.2 per cent, and beverage and tobacco by 8.2 per cent[9]. By contrast, Korea's tariff rate on other agricultural products imported from Singapore is 41.6 per cent and that on processed foods and beverage and tobacco is 29.5 per cent and 28.4 per cent, respectively. Korea also imposes tariffs on all other manufactured imports from Singapore by 2.4 to 7.4 per cent.

Table 17.3 Composition of imports and bilateral tariffs in 1997

	Singapore's imports from Korea			Korea's imports from Singapore		
	Imports (million US$)	Import share (%)	Tariff rate (%)	Imports (million US$)	Import share (%)	Tariff rate (%)
1 Grains	0	0.0	0.0	0	0.0	0.0
2 Othagrprd	2.7	0.1	6.1	8.5	0.3	41.6
3 Livestock	0.1	0.0	7.2	0.4	0.0	9.9
4 Forestry	0.1	0.0	0.0	0.7	0.0	2.7
5 Fisheries	4.3	0.1	0.0	0.8	0.0	9.1
6 Energy	1	0.0	0.0	1	0.0	3.3
7 Procssedfood	20.1	0.4	0.0	24.6	0.7	29.5
8 Bevrg&tobcc	2.1	0.0	8.2	1.6	0.0	28.4
9 Textiles	177.6	3.7	0.0	33.5	1.0	7.4
10 Clothes	15.8	0.3	0.0	2.7	0.1	7.4
11 Leather	13.9	0.3	0.0	1.5	0.0	5.7
12 Woodprd	23.8	0.5	0.0	33.3	1.0	4.5
13 Chemicals	286.7	5.9	0.0	227.0	6.9	7.0
14 Iron&steel	210.5	4.3	0.0	3.8	0.1	6.0
15 NonferrosM	459.8	9.5	0.0	135.2	4.1	2.4
16 FerrousM	60.5	1.2	0.0	9.2	0.3	7.4
17 Autos	43.6	0.9	0.0	12.7	0.4	7.2
18 Othtrnspvhcl	144.4	3.0	0.0	9.9	0.3	3.0
19 Electronics	2608.5	53.8	0.0	1672.3	50.5	7.4
20 Machequip	452.9	9.3	0.0	401.6	12.1	7.0
21 Othmnfcs	36.8	0.8	0.0	17.2	0.5	7.4
22 Construction	0.5	0.0	0.0	0.7	0.0	0.0
23 Trade	58.2	1.2	0.0	90.3	2.7	0.0
24 Transport	47.7	1.0	0.0	174.8	5.3	0.0
25 Finance	20.6	0.4	0.0	7.6	0.2	0.0
26 Other srvcs	158.8	3.3	0.0	441.1	13.3	0.4
Total	4850.9	100.0	0.0	3311.8	100.0	6.0

Source: Based on GTAP database version 5, 2001.

Bilateral imports of other agricultural products and processed food including meat are modest but face a very high average tariff, which implies that agricultural products and processed food are to represent a very sensitive part of a Korea–Singapore FTA. Given the very high tariffs on these products imported from other regions, the incentive for trans-shipment through Singapore is likely to be substantial under the FTA. This raises the prospect of significant enforcement costs associated with the rules of origin for an FTA. For this reason, it is likely that agriculture will be left out of a Korea–Singapore FTA[10].

MODEL STRUCTURE

A multi-region, multi-sector CGE model is used to analyse the potential economic effects of a Korea–Singapore FTA[11]. This model is implemented using the GEMPACK software[12] that solves a model in a linearized form but obtains as accurate a solution for a nonlinear CGE model in the levels form. The database for this model is version 5 of the GTAP database (Dimaranan and McDougall, 2001). Due to the limited space of this chapter, a short general description of a CGE model and some of the distinguishing features of the CGE model used for this study is provided.

A CGE model simulates numerically the general equilibrium structure of an economy. It is built on the Walrasian general equilibrium system in which the central idea is that demand equals supply for all commodities and factors of production at a set of relative prices. A CGE model has a solid micro-foundation which is theoretically transparent. Functional forms are specified in an explicit manner, and interdependencies and feedback of industries are incorporated. Therefore, the model provides a framework by which to assess the effects of policy and structural changes on resource allocation. These characteristics make it possible to differentiate a CGE model from a partial equilibrium model which is not economy-wide, a macro-econometric model which is not multi-sectoral, and an input–output model in which agents don't respond to changes in prices.

The CGE model used for this study is a standard CGE model, which depicts the behaviour of private households, governments and global sectors across each region in the world. Quantities and prices are simultaneously determined on commodity and factor markets by the accounting relationships, the equilibrium conditions specified by the behaviour of economic agents and the structure of international trade.

It is assumed that a representative household determines final demand in each region. Consumers are endowed with primary factors of production, tax revenues and an exogenously specified net transfer from other regions. This income is allocated to private demand, public demand and investment. While private and public demands are determined by utility maximizing behaviour, investment is assumed to be exogenous.

Perfect competition, therefore, constant returns to scale, is assumed in production, while imperfect substitution in goods and services between home and abroad and imperfect substitution among different origins of economies are assumed by the Armington approach, which is one explanation of two-way trade in the same product category, but originating from different nations.

The model includes five factors of production, skilled labour, unskilled labour, capital, land and natural resources. Skilled labour, unskilled labour and capital are used in all sectors, but land is used only in agricultural sectors, and natural resources are utilized in specific industries. Intermediate inputs and capital are traded between regions, whereas labour and land are not traded.

The model includes three regions linked through international trade in 26 sectors. The three regions are Korea, Singapore, and the rest of the world into which all other regions not treated explicitly in the model are aggregated. The 26 sectors are seen from Table 17.3.

SIMULATIONS

In this study, nine different experiments are carried out, based on a baseline scenario of the implementation of the Uruguay Round (UR) Agreement. It is assumed in the baseline scenario that all regions considered in the model reduce tariffs on all imports by 33.3 per cent of their 1995 level. This baseline scenario is a starting point for all other experiments.

Table 17.4 Experiments concerning a Korea–Singapore FTA

	Static effects	Dynamic effects	Total effects
Agricultural products	Experiment 1	Experiment 4	Experiment 7
Manufactured products	Experiment 2	Experiment 5	Experiment 8
All products	Experiment 3	Experiment 6	Experiment 9

Table 17.4 shows nine different experiments done in this study. The experiments are as follows:

- *Experiment 1: In the case of elimination of tariffs only on agricultural products.* In this experiment, the tariffs on agricultural products traded between Korea and Singapore are removed.
- *Experiment 2: In the case of elimination of tariffs only on manufactured products.* In this experiment, the tariffs on manufactured products traded between Korea and Singapore are removed.
- *Experiment 3: Experiment 1 + Experiment 2, that is, in the case of elimination of tariffs on both agricultural and manufactured products*[13].
- *Experiment 4: In the case of an increase in total factor productivity (TFP), as a result of the FTA, only in agricultural sectors.* In this experiment, it is assumed that, as a result of the FTA, an increase in TFP of 5 per cent occurs in agricultural sectors for a period of 10 years, during which the FTA is to be fully implemented, i.e., 0.5 per cent per annum.
- *Experiment 5: In the case of an increase in total factor productivity (TFP), as a result of the FTA, only in manufacturing sectors.* In this experiment, it is assumed that, as a result of the FTA, an increase in TFP of 5 per cent takes place in manufacturing sectors for a period of 10 years, during which the FTA is to be fully implemented, i.e., 0.5 per cent per annum.
- *Experiment 6: Experiment 4 + Experiment 5, that is, in the case of an increase in total factor productivity (TFP), as a result of the FTA, in both agricultural and manufacturing sectors.* In this experiment, it is assumed that, as a result of the FTA, an increase in TFP occurs in agricultural and manufacturing sectors. An increase in TFP of 5 per cent in both the sectors of Korea and Singapore is assumed for a period of 10 years, during which the FTA is to be fully implemented, that is, 0.5 per cent per annum.
- *Experiment 7: Experiment 1 + Experiment 4.*
- *Experiment 8: Experiment 2 + Experiment 5.*
- *Experiment 9: Experiment 3 + Experiment 6.*

The reason why agricultural and manufacturing sectors are differentiated in the scenarios, although an FTA includes in general all sectors, is that it is quite likely that agriculture will be left out of the agreement, as in the Japan–Singapore FTA.

The results of experiments 1, 2 and 3 represent static effects of a Korea–Singapore FTA, those of experiments 4, 5 and 6 refer to its dynamic effects and those of experiments 7, 8 and 9 show its total effects that include static and dynamic effects.

The literature on economic integration traditionally distinguishes between static and dynamic effects. The former represent changes in the allocative efficiency of member states made possible by increased specialization in accordance with the law of comparative advantage, due to the liberalized market of the participating nations, taking their productive capacity as given. By contrast, dynamic effects measure the impact of integration on the productive capacity of member states. Dynamic effects of an FTA could possibly result from (El-Agraa, 1997):

(a) increased productive capacity due to better exploitation of economies of scale made possible by the increased size of the market;
(b) enforced changes in efficiency brought about by intensified competition between firms; and
(c) changes affecting both the amount and quality of the factors of production due to technological advances, encouraged by (b).

Although it is very difficult to estimate the dynamic efficiency effects caused by economies of scale and increased competition as a result of the elimination or reduction of trade barriers among participating nations in an FTA, a relatively clear indication of the presence of the dynamic effects is to be observed in the strong positive correlation between increased output and increased TFP, which can be regarded as an increase in productivity due to economies of scale. In particular, an FTA will facilitate foreign direct investment. An increase in direct investment will expand the level of output, and increased output will enhance productivity as a result of economies of scale. Therefore, an increase in total productivity is used as a proxy variable for dynamic effects in this study. To repeat, an increase in TFP of 5 per cent in relevant sectors of Korea and Singapore is assumed to be in place and this assumption is made for a period of 10 years, during which the agreement is to be fully implemented.

SIMULATION RESULTS

Impact of a Korea–Singapore FTA on Trade

First of all, the effects of a Korea–Singapore FTA on trade are discussed[14]. Table 17.5 reports the impact of nine different experiments of a Korea–Singapore FTA on imports at CIF price. The elimination of tariffs on agricultural products (experiment 1), as a result of the FTA, is expected to lead to an additional increase in imports at CIF price by 0.02 per cent in both Korea and Singapore, implying that tariff elimination in agricultural products will have a negligible impact on imports of these two countries.

The elimination of tariffs on manufactured goods (experiment 2) is expected to result in an additional increase in imports by 0.33 per cent in

Table 17.5 Effects of a Korea–Singapore FTA on imports at CIF price (%)

Region	Exp. 1	Exp. 2	Exp. 3	Exp. 4	Exp. 5	Exp. 6	Exp. 7	Exp. 8	Exp. 9
Korea	0.02	0.33	0.36	–0.06	2.00	2.01	–0.04	2.38	2.44
Singapore	0.02	0.64	0.66	0.01	4.10	4.56	0.02	4.80	5.29
ROW	0.00	0.00	0.00	0.00	0.14	0.31	0.00	0.14	0.30

Source: Authors' own computations.

Korea and by 0.64 per cent in Singapore and the elimination of tariffs on agricultural and manufactured goods (experiment 3) in an additional increase in imports by 0.36 per cent in Korea and by 0.66 per cent in Singapore, which implies that just tariff elimination is to affect imports in the trading partners insignificantly.

However, an increase in TFP, as a result of the FTA, is expected to lead to an increase in imports by more than 2 per cent in Korea and by more than 4 per cent in Singapore in the case of experiments 5 and 6, except experiment 4. In the case of experiment 4, an increase in TFP in agricultural sectors will have an intangible impact on impacts of both economies.

The result of experiment 7 is the sum of the impact of experiment 1 and experiment 4. The results of experiments 8 and 9 can be interpreted as in the case of experiment 7.

Table 17.6 presents the effects of a Korea–Singapore FTA on imports at CIF price by sector in the case of experiments 1, 2 and 3[15]. In the case of experiment 1 (tariff elimination on agricultural products), a negligible impact on imports of agricultural products is expected, except imports of other agricultural products of Korea and Singapore and imports of livestock of Singapore.

In the case of experiment 2 (tariff elimination on manufactured goods), a slight increase in imports of all manufactured goods in both Korea and Singapore is expected. Simulation results of experiment 3 indicate the sum of results of experiments 1 and 2.

In sum, as 3.1 per cent of Korea's exports go to Singapore and 2.6 per cent of Singapore's exports to Korea in 1997, as indicated in Table 17.2, tariff elimination, as a result of the FTA, is expected to have a very limited impact on imports between them.

Table 17.7 shows the impact of a Korea–Singapore FTA on exports at FOB price. In the case of experiments 1, 2 and 3, tariff elimination is expected to exert a similar influence on exports to its impact on imports indicated in Table 17.5, but to a less extent, leading to trade deficits shown in Table 17.8.

For example, Korea is to suffer additional trade deficits of US$13.6 million in the case of experiment 1, US$137.8 million in experiment 2 and

Table 17.6 Effects of a Korea–Singapore FTA on imports at CIF price, by sector (%)

	Exp. 1			*Exp. 2*			*Exp. 3*		
Sectors	Korea	Singap.	ROW	Korea	Singap.	ROW	Korea	Singap.	ROW
1 Grains	0	0	0	0	0	0	0	0	0
2 Othagrprd	2.24	0.49	–0.01	–0.05	0.34	0	2.18	0.83	–0.01
3 Livestock	0	0.54	0	–0.02	0.58	0	–0.02	1.13	0
4 Forestry	0	0	0	–0.01	0.23	0	–0.01	0.23	0
5 Fisheries	0	0	0	0.07	0.2	0	0.07	0.2	0
6 Energy	0	0	0	0	0.22	0	0	0.21	0
7 Procssedfood	–0.04	0.02	0	1.45	0.37	0	1.41	0.4	0
8 Bevrg&tobcc	–0.05	–0.01	0	0.66	0.67	0	0.61	0.66	0
9 Textiles	0.01	0.01	0	0.13	0.38	0	0.14	0.39	0
10 Clothes	–0.02	0.02	0	0.02	0.46	0	0	0.48	0
11 Leather	0	0.03	0	0	0.38	0	0	0.41	0
12 Woodprd	0	0.03	0	0.08	0.53	0	0.08	0.56	0
13 Chemicals	0	0.05	0	0.15	0.31	0	0.15	0.36	0
14 Iron&steel	0	–0.01	0	0.05	0.59	0	0.05	0.58	0
15 NonferrosM	0	0	0	0.11	0.54	0	0.11	0.54	0
16 FerrousM	0	0	0	0.18	0.72	0	0.18	0.73	0
17 Autos	–0.01	0	0	0.21	0.59	0	0.2	0.6	0
18 Othtrnspvhcl	0	0	0	0.03	0.15	0	0.02	0.16	0
19 Electronics	0	0	0	1.63	0.87	0	1.63	0.87	0
20 Machequip	0	0	0	0.41	0.88	0	0.41	0.88	–0.01
21 Othmnfcs	0	0.01	0	0.27	0.45	0	0.27	0.46	0
22 Construction	–0.01	0.01	0	–0.01	0.33	0	–0.02	0.35	0
23 Trade	–0.01	0.03	0	–0.04	0.64	–0.02	–0.05	0.67	–0.02
24 Transport	–0.01	0.03	0	–0.02	0.42	0	–0.03	0.45	0
25 Finance	0	0.06	0	0.01	0.46	0	0.01	0.53	0
26 Other srvcs	0	0.03	0	0	0.46	–0.01	0.02	0.49	–0.01

Source: Authors' own computations.

Table 17.7 Effects of a Korea–Singapore FTA on exports at FOB price (%)

Region	Exp. 1	Exp. 2	Exp. 3	Exp. 4	Exp. 5	Exp. 6	Exp. 7	Exp. 8	Exp. 9
Korea	0.02	0.29	0.31	0.24	9.14	17.44	0.26	9.48	17.83
Singapore	0.01	0.54	0.55	0.02	7.85	11.00	0.03	8.47	11.63
ROW	0.00	0.00	0.00	0.00	–0.13	–0.23	0.00	–0.13	–0.23

Source: Authors' own computations.

Table 17.8 Effects of a Korea–Singapore FTA on trade balance (US$ million)

Region	Exp. 1	Exp. 2	Exp. 3	Exp. 4	Exp. 5	Exp. 6	Exp. 7	Exp. 8	Exp. 9
Korea	–13.6	–137.8	–151.9	404.2	9335.1	19664.7	390.4	9193.7	19513.6
Singapore	5.6	–29.5	–24.4	14.4	2832.5	5168.8	20.4	2819.1	5165.4
ROW	8.0	167.3	176.3	–418.7	–12167.6	–24833.5	–410.8	–12012.8	–24679.0

Source: Authors' own computations.

US$ 151.9 million in experiment 3. By contrast, Singapore is to experience an additional trade surplus of US$5.6 million in experiment 1, but trade deficits of US$29.5 million in experiment 2 and US$24.4 million in experiment 3.

However, an increase in TFP, as a result of the FTA, is to lead to additional trade surpluses of US$ 404.2 million in the case of experiment 4, US$9.3 billion in the case of experiment 5 and US$19.7 billion in the case of experiment 6 for Korea, and US$14.4 million in experiment 4, US$2.8 billion in the case of experiment of 5 and US$5.2 billion in experiment 6 for Singapore. These enormous trade surpluses are due to much greater increases in exports than those in imports in the case of experiments 4, 5 and 6 as shown in Table 17.5 and 17.7.

Table 17.9 reports the effects of a Korea–Singapore FTA on the terms of trade. As a result of tariff elimination (experiments 1, 2 and 3), Korea's terms of trade are expected to be deteriorated and Singapore's terms of trade are to be improved. It is because the elimination of tariffs levied by Korea creates costly trade diversion, with increased imports from Singapore at the expense of lower cost suppliers from the rest of the world (ROW). As the shares of Korea and Singapore in the world trade are no more than 2.5 and 2.1 per cent, tariff elimination between these two economies has a negligible impact on the terms of trade of the rest of the world.

Table 17.9 Effects of a Korea–Singapore FTA on the terms of trade (%)

Region	Exp. 1	Exp. 2	Exp. 3	Exp. 4	Exp. 5	Exp. 6	Exp. 7	Exp. 8	Exp. 9
Korea	–0.01	–0.05	–0.06	–0.05	–1.32	–2.89	–0.06	–1.37	–2.93
Singapore	0.01	0.09	0.11	0.00	–1.37	–2.14	0.01	–1.28	–2.03
ROW	0.00	0.00	0.00	0.00	0.07	0.13	0.00	0.07	0.13

Source: Authors' own computations.

An increase in TFP, as a result of the FTA, will lead to a further deterioration of the terms of trade of Korea and to a shift from their improvement to their deterioration for Singapore, which contributes to a large surge in exports of the two economies in the case of experiments 5 and 6, as indicated in Table 17.7.

Impact of a Korea–Singapore FTA on Welfare and Growth

This section examines the potential effects of a Korea–Singapore FTA on welfare and growth in both countries. An FTA is, by definition, a second-best proposition, since it involves a shift from one protection-ridden situation (with protection against all countries) to another (with protection against non-partners and no protection against partners). Therefore, its welfare consequences are an empirical matter, which depends upon the particular configurations of individual schemes.

Traditional (Vinerian) economic integration theory distinguishes between two welfare effects to be derived from trade creation and trade diversion. In any member state, integration reduces the price of supplies from other FTA members relative to that of supplies from domestic producers, thereby creating trade at the expense of domestic production. At the same time, an FTA drives a wedge between the price of supplies from member and non-member countries, hence diverting from the latter to the former. Trade creation increases welfare, while in general trade diversion has a welfare cost. The net welfare effects of an FTA depend on the relative size of trade creation and trade diversion[16].

Table 17.10 presents the impacts of nine different scenarios of a Korea–Singapore FTA on welfare in terms of per capita utility. In the case of static effects, i.e., experiments 1, 2 and 3, whereas a Korea–Singapore FTA is expected to, as a result of tariff elimination, increase the welfare of Singapore by 0.02 to 0.28 per cent, it is to reduce the welfare of Korea by 0.001 to 0.02 per cent. The corresponding equivalent variation (EV), the change in welfare level converted into income change, is US$16.9 million, US$182.3 million and US$201.6 million for Singapore and –US$20.4 million, –US$126.9 million and –US$148.4 million for Korea in experiments 1, 2 and 3, respectively, as shown in Table 17.11. It is because the elimination of tariffs levied by Korea creates costly trade diversion, with increased imports from Singapore at the expense of lower cost suppliers from the rest of the world (ROW). Therefore, Korea's welfare falls, as does that of the ROW. However, Singapore's welfare rises as a result of the terms of trade gain that it experiences.

Table 17.10 Effects of a Korea–Singapore FTA on welfare (%)

Region	Exp. 1	Exp. 2	Exp. 3	Exp. 4	Exp. 5	Exp. 6	Exp. 7	Exp. 8	Exp. 9
Korea	–0.001	–0.02	–0.02	0.36	3.06	5.97	0.36	3.04	5.95
Singapore	0.02	0.25	0.28	0.02	2.74	5.09	0.04	3.04	5.42
ROW	0	0	0	0	0.02	0.05	0	0.02	0.05

Source: Authors' own computations.

In the case of dynamic effects, i.e., experiments 4, 5 and 6, both Korea and Singapore gain in terms of per capita utility from an increase in TFP as a result of their FTA. The welfare gains of Korea are larger than those of Singapore. In the case of experiment 6 (an increase in TFP in both agricultural and manufacturing sectors), Korea gains the EV of US$20.7 billion and Singapore US$3.4 billion.

Table 17.11 Effects of a Korea-Singapore FTA on equivalent variation (EV) (US$ million)

Region	Exp. 1	Exp. 2	Exp. 3	Exp. 4	Exp. 5	Exp. 6	Exp. 7	Exp. 8	Exp. 9
Korea	–20.4	–126.9	–148.4	570.1	12079.1	20749.9	549.5	11944.8	20588.9
Singapore	16.9	182.3	201.6	11.8	1847.4	3404.6	29.3	2062.5	3641.6
ROW	–12.6	–18.4	–32.1	198.5	6075.3	14687.4	185.8	6060.4	14661.4

Note: Equivalent variation refers to the change in welfare level converted into income change, i.e., the change in GDP equivalent to the change in welfare level.
Source: Authors' own computations.

The welfare effects of experiment 7 are the sum of those of experiment 1 and those of experiment 4. The welfare gains of experiments 8 and 9 can be interpreted as in the case of experiment 7.

In analogue to the welfare effects, the EV effects of experiment 7 are the sum of those of experiment 1 and those of experiment 4. The EV effects of experiments 8 and 9 can be interpreted as in the case of experiment 7.

Table 17.12 indicates the effects of nine scenarios of a Korea–Singapore FTA on their real GDP. Tariff elimination on agricultural products (experiment 1) is expected to lead to a decrease in real GDP of Korea by 0.002 per cent but an increase in real GDP of Singapore by 0.001 per cent. Therefore, it is likely that Korea will request to exclude agricultural goods from the FTA.

Table 17.12 Effects of a Korea–Singapore FTA on real GDP (%)

Region	Exp. 1	Exp. 2	Exp. 3	Exp. 4	Exp. 5	Exp. 6	Exp. 7	Exp. 8	Exp. 9
Korea	–0.002	0.004	0.002	0.32	5.85	11.95	0.31	5.85	11.95
Singapore	0.001	0.044	0.046	0.04	8.63	16.18	0.04	8.72	16.26
ROW	0.000	0.000	0.000	0.00	0.01	0.01	0.00	0.01	0.01

Source: Authors' own computations.

Tariff elimination on manufactured goods (experiment 2) is to result in an increase in real GDP of Korea by 0.004 per cent and Singapore by 0.044 per cent. As a result of tariff elimination on both agricultural and manufactured goods (experiment 3), Korea is to experience an increase in real GDP by 0.002 per cent and Singapore by 0.046 per cent.

The dynamic effects of the FTA are much larger for both countries. An increase in TFP in agricultural sectors (experiment 4) is to contribute to an increase in real GDP of Korea by 0.32 per cent and Singapore by 0.04 per cent. Furthermore, an increase in TFP in manufacturing sectors (experiment 5) is to lead to an increase in real GDP of Korea by 5.85 per cent and Singapore by 8.63 per cent. An increase in TFP in both agricultural and manufacturing sectors (experiment 6) is to result in an increase in real GDP of Korea by 11.95 per cent and Singapore by 16.18 per cent. Here it is to be noted that these GDP gains occur during a period of 10 years, in which a Korea–Singapore FTA is assumed to be fully implemented.

The mechanism of these remarkable positive dynamic effects caused by an increase in TFP on economic growth can be explained as follows. A Korea–Singapore FTA can bring an investment expansion effect, as firms will increase new investment to gain further access to regional market after tariff elimination and shift their production facilities from non-member countries to member states according to the preferential rules of origin. A comprehensive FTA, which includes investment protection clauses, investment liberalization measures and a dispute settlement mechanism, will make trade liberalization policies internationally binding commitments and thus enhance investors' confidence and profitability in partners' investment environment, thereby resulting in an expansion of intra-regional investment. In the long run, economic growth to be achieved by a Korea–Singapore FTA will increase the competitiveness of firms and enable the more efficient allocation of resources, thus stimulating further investment in both economies.

CONCLUSION

This study has tried to quantify the potential impacts of a Korea–Singapore FTA. As seen above, while bilateral tariff elimination only is to have an insignificant impact on trade between the two countries, the FTA is to lead to the following static effects: trade deficits of US$13.6 to 151.9 million for Korea and trade surplus of US$5.6 million to trade deficit of US$24.4 million for Singapore; the deterioration of the terms of trade of Korea and the improvement of the terms of trade of Singapore; welfare loss of Korea and welfare gain of Singapore in terms of per capita utility and equivalent variation; and a slight increase in real GDP for these two economies except experiment 1 for Korea.

By contrast, dynamic effects caused by an increase in total factor productivity as a result of the FTA are projected to be much larger: whereas Korea's imports are to increase by 2 per cent and Singapore's imports by 4.6 per cent, Korea's exports are to rise by up to 17.4 per cent and Singapore's exports by up to 11 per cent, with additional trade surpluses of up to US$19.7 billion for Korea and US$5.2 billion for Singapore facilitated by further deterioration of terms of trade of these two economies. Consequently, Korea and Singapore are to experience welfare gains of much larger extent in terms of per capita utility and equivalent variation compared to the case of tariff elimination only. The real GDP of Korea and Singapore is to increase by up to 12 per cent and 16.2 per cent, respectively.

However, it should be noted that these dynamic effects are based on the assumption that an increase in total factor productivity as a result of the FTA occurs in relevant sectors of the participating economies for a period of 10 years, during which the FTA is assumed to be fully implemented. In order to specify in more detail the causes for its dynamic effects, in addition to the proposed bilateral tariff elimination, other issues such as trade in services, rules governing foreign investment, e-commerce regulations, the streamlining of customs procedures, harmonization of technical standards, etc., should be considered. For example, the impacts of implementing uniform standards for e-commerce in Korea and Singapore, of liberalizing rules governing trade in services and of automating customs procedures in Korea that makes them compatible with the computer-based standards established by Singapore could be taken into account.

In assessing the economic effects of a Korea–Singapore FTA, more attention should be paid to the long run dynamic effects rather than to the short run static. However, in order to avoid the uncertainty of the long run dynamic effects and to secure strong impetus for the pursuit of the FTA, both economies have to seek the means by which to achieve closer cooperation and coordination between them. For example, Korea and Singapore need to standardize and modernize the different trade norms of each other, such as customs procedures, anti-dumping rules, rules of origin, the unification of product classification, etc., in order to lay down the framework for economic integration.

In particular, Korea has to continue to implement its domestic reform policies such as deregulation and governance transparency and its external policies for promoting bilateral cooperation in investment, industry and technology, and pursue the expansion of the exchange of human resources with Singapore. Amidst the current globalization of corporate activities, it is urgently needed to improve the business environment through the liberalization of individual national systems and through their harmonization. In these circumstances, it is very important for Korea to embrace a new commitment to the opening of its markets through further deregulation and pursue an FTA by entering into formal negotiations with Singapore that aims to become a hub of trade and finance in Asia. Singapore has the fourth largest foreign exchange market in the world and plays a very important role as a hub of finance in Asia. Singapore is also a member of ASEAN with which Japan and China are eager to form an FTA. To avoid potential negative impacts of such FTAs, Korea cannot overemphasize the strategic importance of Singapore as a bridge to an FTA with ASEAN in the future.

Last but not least, the version of a Korea–Singapore FTA should be understood as providing an environment in which goods, capital, labour and information move across borders, and enterprises are to be encouraged to extend their horizons and promote global operations in order to stimulate both competition and cooperation in the highly competitive structures of industries between the two economies.

NOTES

1. As of December 2002, the number of regional trade agreements notified to the GATT/WTO is 250 since the establishment of the GATT and that of regional trade agreements notified to the WTO from January 1995 to October 2002 is 130 (WTO, 2003).
2. See Ko (1995a) for an analysis of economic impact of EU trade policy using a CGE model and Ko (2001b, 2001c, 2001d, 2002) for the accession of central and eastern European countries to the EU and its economic impact.
3. See Ko (1994, 1995b) for an analysis of economic impact of trade liberalization in the Pacific Rim countries and APEC using a CGE model.
4. See Bergsten (1996) and Siebert *et al.* (1996) for a description of TAFTA and an alternative to TAFTA.
5. The 15 EU Member States are Austria, Belgium, Denmark, Finland, France, Germany, Greece, Ireland, Italy, Luxembourg, Netherlands, Portugal, Spain, Sweden and UK.
6. The seven members of ASEAN that have participated in the ASEM meetings are Brunei Darussalam, Indonesia, Malaysia, Philippines, Singapore, Thailand and Vietnam. Although Laos and Myanmar joined ASEAN in July 1997 and Cambodia in April 1999, they are not members of ASEM. Refer to the Web site of ASEAN (http://www.asean.or.id) for more details.
7. See Ko (1997, 1998, 2000a, 2000b, 2000c) for the analysis of economic impact of an FTA at the ASEM level.
8. See Ko (2000d) for the analysis of economic impact of a Korea–China–Japan FTA.
9. Applied tariffs in Singapore are now zero for all goods except alcoholic beverages (beverage and tobacco in Table 17.3).
10. Agriculture was left out of the Japan–Singapore FTA.
11. See appendix for a detailed description of the model structure. In addition, see Ko (1993, 1996) for a one-country CGE model for Korea.
12. See Harrison and Pearson (1996) for the GEMPACK software.
13. As indicated in Table 17.3, there are no tariffs on services.
14. Waelbroeck (1976) warned that not too much interest should attach to the effects of economic integration on trade. It is because the primary objectives of economic policy are, according to him, the analysis of its impact on welfare and income distribution. In this paper, however, the effect of a Korea-China-Japan FTA on income distribution is not dealt with explicitly.

15. The simulation results of experiments 4 to 9 are available from the authors on request.
16. The following factors are generally regarded in the economic literature as influencing positively the welfare effects of economic integration: a large number of members; a high proposition of intra-area trade before integration; low transportation costs among members; low common external protection (Balassa, 1987 and Hazlewood, 1987).

REFERENCES

Balassa, B. (1987), 'Economic integration', in J. Eatwell, M. Milgate and P. Newman (eds), *The New Palgrave: A Dictionary of Economics*, London: Macmillan.

Bergsten, C.F. (1996), *Competitive Liberalization and Global Free Trade: A Vision for the Early 21st Century*. APEC Working Paper 96-15, Institute for International Economics.

Dimaranan, B. V. and R. A. McDougall (2001), *Global Trade Assistance and Production: The GTAP 5 Data Base*, Center for Global Trade Analysis, Purdue University.

El-Agraa, A.M. (1997), *Economic Integration Worldwide*, London: Macmillan.

Greenaway, D. (1992), 'Policy forum regionalism in the world economy: Editorial Note', *The Economic Journal*, **102**, 1488–90.

Harrison, W.J. and K.R. Pearson (1996), 'Computing solutions for large general equilibrium models using GEMPACK', *Computational Economics*, **9**, 83–127.

Hazlewood, A. (1987), 'Customs union', in J. Eatwell, M. Milgate and P. Newman (eds), *The New Palgrave: A Dictionary of Economics*, London: Macmillan.

KIEP and IDE (2000), *Toward a Korea–Japan FTA: Assessments and Prospects*, KIEP.

Ko, J.-H. (1993), *Ökonomische Analyse von Energie- und Volkswirtschaft auf der Basis allgemeiner Gleichgewichtsmodelle*, Frankfurt am Main/Berlin/Bern/New York/Paris/Wien: Peter Lang.

Ko, J.-H. (1994), 'General equilibrium analysis of trade liberalization in the Pacific Rim countries in the era of the WTO', *The Review of East Asian Studies*, **1**, (1), 125–56.

Ko, J.-H. (1995a), 'EU trade policy and international trade: a computable general equilibrium model', *The Journal of Contemporary European Studies*, **3**, (1), 133–60.

Ko, J.-H. (1995b), 'Analysis of the effects of trade liberalization in APEC: simulation results of a computable general equilibrium model', Paper presented at Academic Seminar, North-East Asia Socio-Economic

Development, Suekawa Memorial Hall, Ritsumeikan University, Kyoto, Japan (22 Dec. 1995).

Ko, J.-H. (1995c), 'An analysis of economic structure of East-Asian countries in the 21st century and their strategies for regional cooperation' (in Korean), *Pusan International Forum*, 16, Pusan University of Foreign Studies, 46–54.

Ko, J.-H. (1996), 'Analysis of the effects of trade policies under the WTO using a computable general equilibrium model' (in Korean), *Kyong Je Hak Non Jib* (Journal of The Korean Dong-Nam Economic Association), **5** (1), 263–88.

Ko, J.-H. (1997), 'Applied general equilibrium analysis of the effects of trade liberalization between the EU and Asia', Paper presented at the International Conference on *Europe – Asia: The Stakes of Interdependence*, Le Havre, France (September 25–26, 1997).

Ko, J.-H. (1998), 'Economic effects of trade liberalization between Asia and Europe: an applied general equilibrium analysis', *Zeitschrift für Wirtschaftswissenschaften*, 16, Koreanisch-Deutsche Gesellschaft für Wirtschaftswissenschaften e. V.

Ko, J.-H. (2000a), 'Should we be afraid of trade liberalization between Europe and Asia through ASEM?: analysis of its impact using a CGE model', Paper presented at the international conference on *The 3rd Seoul ASEM and Asia-Europe Relations*, organized by the Korean Society of Contemporary European Studies (Seoul, 29–30 September 2000).

Ko, J.-H. (2000b), 'Why not a free trade area between Asia and Europe at the ASEM level?', Paper presented at the international symposium in *commemoration* of the *10th Anniversary of the German Unification: Tasks and Lessons*, organized by Korean–German Association for Social Sciences, Seoul (10 November 2000).

Ko, J.-H. (2000c), 'Why not a free trade agreement between Asia and Europe at the ASEM level?', Paper presented at the Fifth ECSA-World Conference *Enlarging the European Union*, Brussels (14–15 December 2000).

Ko, J.-H. (2000d), 'Analysis of economic effects of a free trade Agreement among Korea, China and Japan', *International Area Studies Review*, **4** (2), 177–209.

Ko, J.-H. (2001a), 'Why not a free trade agreement between Asia and Europe at the ASEM Level?', *The Journal of Contemporary European Studies*, **13**, 134–61.

Ko, J.-H. (2001b), 'The accession of Central and Eastern European countries to the EU and its impact on the Korean economy: a computable general equilibrium approach', *International Area Studies Review*, **5** (2), 125–54.

Ko, J.-H. (2001c), 'Eastern enlargement of the EU and its impact on the global economy', Paper presented at 2001 International Symposium on *The Enlargement of the European Union and its Effects and Prospects:*

with special emphasis in the Korean Peninsula and Germany, organized by Korean–German Association for Social Sciences (KGASS), Seoul President Hotel, Seoul, 2 November 2001.
Ko, J.-H. (2001d), 'Eastern enlargement of the European Union and its economic impact on the EU and Central Europe: a computable general equilibrium approach', Paper presented at the international conference on *Location of Economic Activity, Regional Development and the Global Economy: European and East Asian Experiences*, University of Le Havre, Le Havre, France, 26–27 September 2001.
Ko, J.-H. (2002), 'Eastern enlargement of the EU and analysis of its economic impact using a CGE Model', Paper presented at the international conference on *EU Eastern Enlargement Coming Soon-Strategy of Membership*, University of Gdansk, Sopot, Poland, 19–20 April 2002.
Siebert, H., R.J. Langhammer and D. Piazolo (1996), 'TAFTA: fuelling trade discrimination or global liberalisation?', Kiel Working Paper No. 720. Institut fuer Weltwirtschaft, Kiel.
Waelbroeck, J. (1976), 'Measuring the degree or progress of economic integration', in F. Machlup (ed.), *Economic Integration: Worldwide, Regional, Sectoral*, London: Macmillan.
WTO (2000), *Trade Policy Review: Singapore*, Geneva.

APPENDIX: MODEL STRUCTURE

Nested Production Functions

Leontief production function of commodity i in region r:

(A17.1) $X_i^r = \dfrac{X_{ji}^r}{a_{ji}^r} = \dfrac{VA_i^r}{a_i^{vr}}$ $\quad i = 1,\ldots,26;\ r = 1,\ldots,3$

CES aggregation function of value-added composite in industry i of region r:

(A17.2) $VA_i^r = \psi_i^{vr}\left(\sum_f \delta_i^{vr} F_{fi}^{r\ -\rho_i^{vr}}\right)^{-\frac{1}{\rho_i^{vr}}}$ $\quad i = 1,\ldots,26; f = 1,\ldots,5;\ r = 1,\ldots,3$

where $\sigma_i^{vr} = \dfrac{1}{1+\rho_i^{vr}};\ \rho_i^{vr} \succ -1;\ \sigma_i^{vr} \succ 0\cdot$

Armington aggregation function of composite intermediate good j used in industry i of region r:

(A17.3) $X_{ji}^r = \psi_{ji}^r\left[\delta_{ji}^r XM_{ji}^{r\ -\rho_{ji}^r} + (1-\delta_{ji}^r) XD_{ji}^{r\ -\rho_{ji}^r}\right]^{-\frac{1}{\rho_{ji}^r}}$

$i, j = 1,\ldots,26;\ r = 1,\ldots,3$

where $\sigma_{ji}^r = \dfrac{1}{1+\rho_{ji}^r};\ \rho_{ji}^r \succ 1;\ \sigma_{ji}^r \succ 0\cdot$

CES aggregation function of imported intermediate good j used in industry i of region r:

(A17.4) $XM_{ji}^r = \psi_{ji}^{mr}\left(\sum_s \delta_{ji}^{mr} XM_{ji}^{mr\ -\rho_{ji}^{mr}}\right)^{-\frac{1}{\rho_{ji}^{mr}}}$ $\quad i, j = 1,\ldots,26;\ r = 1,\ldots,3$

where $\sigma_{ji}^{mr} = \dfrac{1}{1+\rho_{ji}^{mr}};\ \rho_{ji}^{mr} \succ -1;\ \sigma_{ji}^{mr} \succ 0\cdot$

CET transformation function of commodity i in region r:

(A17.5) $X_i^r = \psi_i^{tr}\left[\delta_i^{tr} D_i^{r\ \rho_i^{tr}} + (1-\delta_i^{tr}) E_i^{r\ \rho_i^{tr}}\right]^{\frac{1}{\rho_i^{tr}}}$ $\quad i = 1,\ldots,26;\ r = 1,\ldots,3$

where $\sigma_i^{tr} = \dfrac{1}{\rho_i^{tr}-1};\ \rho_i^{tr} \prec 1;\ \sigma_i^{tr} \prec 0\cdot$

Supply function of commodity i to domestic market in region r:

(A17.6) $D_i^r = \delta_i^{tr\ -\sigma_i^{tr}}\left(\dfrac{PX_i^r}{PD_i^r}\right)^{-\sigma_i^{tr}} X_i^r$ $\quad i = 1,\ldots,26;\ r = 1,\ldots,3$

Supply function of commodity i in region r to export market:

(A17.7) $E_i^r = \delta_i^{tr^{-\sigma_i^{tr}}} \left(\frac{PX_i^r}{PE_i^r} \right)^{-\sigma_i^{tr}} X_i^r$ $\quad i = 1,...,26;\ r = 1,...,3$

Factor Demand Functions

Demand function for composite intermediate input *j* used in industry *i* of region *r*:

$X_{ji}^r = a_{ji}^r X_i^r$ [omitted due to (17.1)]

Demand function for value-added composite in industry *i* of region *r*:

$VA_i^r = a_i^{vr} X_i^r$ [omitted due to (17.1)]

Demand function for primary factor of production *f* in industry *i* of region *r*:

(A17.8) $X_{fi}^r = \delta_{fi}^{r^{\sigma_i^{vr}}} \left[\frac{PV_i^r}{PF_f^r (1 + t_i^{fr})} \right]^{\sigma_i^{vr}} VA_i^r$

$i = 1,...,26;\ f = 1,...,5;\ r = 1,...,3$

Demand function for domestic intermediate input *j* used in industry *i* of region *r*:

(A17.9) $XD_{ji}^r = (1 - \delta_{ji}^r)^{\sigma_{ji}^r} \left[\frac{PX_i^r}{PD_{ji}^r (1 + t_{ji}^r)} \right]^{\sigma_{ji}^r} X_{ji}^r$

$i, j = 1,...,26;\ r = 1,...,3$

Demand function for intermediate input *j* imported from region *s*, used in industry *i* of region *r*:

(A17.10) $XM_{ji}^{sr} = \delta_{ji}^{sr^{\sigma_{ji}^r}} \left[\frac{PM_{ji}^r}{PM_{ji}^{sr} (1 + t_{ji}^{msr})} \right]^{\sigma_{ji}^{sr}} XM_{ji}^r$

$i, j = 1,...,26;\ r, s = 1,...,3$

Private and Public Demand

Cobb–Douglas utility function of a representative household:

(A17.11) $U^r = \prod_i C_i^{r^{\alpha_i^{cr}}}$

Armington aggregation of domestic and imported commodities for private demand:

(A17.12) $C_i^r = \left[\delta_i^{cr} CD_i^{r^{-\rho_i^{cr}}} + (1 - \delta_i^{cr}) CM_i^{r^{-\rho_i^{cr}}} \right]^{-\frac{1}{\rho_i^{cr}}}$

$i = 1,...,26;\ r = 1,...,3$

where $\sigma_i^{cr} = \frac{1}{1 + \rho_i^{cr}}$; $\rho_i^{cr} \succ 1$; $\sigma_i^{cr} \succ 0$

Private demand function:

(A17.13) $C_i^r = \dfrac{\alpha_i^{cr} EXP^r}{PC_i^r(1+t_i^{cr})}$ $\quad i = 1,...,26; r = 1,...,3$

Cobb–Douglas aggregation of commodities by public sector in region *r*:

(A17.14) $G^r = \psi^{gr} \prod_i G_i^{r\,\alpha_i^{gr}}$ $\quad i = 1,...,26; r = 1,...,3$

Armington aggregation of domestic and imported commodities for public demand:

(A17.15) $G_i^r = \left[\delta_i^{gr} GD_i^{r^{-\rho_i^{gr}}} + (1-\delta_i^{cr}) GM_i^{r^{-\rho_i^{gr}}} \right]^{-\frac{1}{\rho_i^{gr}}}$

$i = 1,...,26; r = 1,...,3$

where $\sigma_i^{gr} = \dfrac{1}{1+\rho_i^{gr}}$; $\rho_i^{gr} \succ 1$; $\sigma_i^{gr} \succ 0$.

Trade

CES aggregation function across imports from different regions:

(A17.16) $\sum_j XM_{ij}^r + GM_i^r + CM_i^r = \left(\sum_s \delta_i^{msr} M_i^{sr^{-\rho_i^m}} \right)^{-\frac{1}{\rho_i^m}}$

$i = 1,\ldots,26; r, s = 1,\ldots,3$

Cobb–Douglas aggregation function of international transport service:

(A17.17) $\sum_{i,r,s} T_i^{rs} = \psi^t \prod_{i,r} TD_i^{r\,\alpha_i^{tr}}$ $\quad i = 1,\ldots,26; r, s = 1,\ldots,3$

Demand for bilateral imports:

(A17.18) $E_i^{rs} = \delta_i^{ms\,\sigma_i^{ms}} \left[\dfrac{PM_i^s(1+t_i^{mr})(1+p_i^t)}{PE_i^{rs}(1+t_i^{er})} \right]^{\sigma_i^{ms}} M_i^s$

$i = 1,\ldots,26; r, s = 1,\ldots,3$

Income and Expenditure

Consumer expenditure of a representative household:

(A17.19) $EXP^r = \sum_f PF_f^r F_f^r$ (factor income)

$+ \sum_i t_i^{xr}\left(PD_i^r D_i^r + PE_i^r E_i^r\right)$ (indirect taxes)

$+ \sum_{j,i} t_{ij}^r PX_i^r a_{ji}^r X_i^r$ (taxes on intermediate inputs)

$+ \sum_{f,i} t_i^{fr} PF_f^r F_{fi}^r$ (factor tax revenue)

$$+\sum_i t_i^{cr} PC_i^r C_i^r \qquad \text{(consumption tax revenue)}$$
$$+\sum_i t_i^{gr} PG_i^r G_i^r \qquad \text{(public tax revenue)}$$
$$+\sum_{i,s} t_i^{ers} PE_i^r M_i^{rs} \qquad \text{(export tax revenue)}$$
$$+\sum_{i,s} t_i^{msr} \left[PM_i^s M_i^{sr}(1+t_i^{esr}) + P^t T_i^{sr}\right] \quad \text{(tariff revenue)}$$
$$-\sum_i PD_i^r I_i^r \qquad \text{(investment demand)}$$
$$-\sum_i PG_i^r (1+t_i^{gr}) G_i^r \qquad \text{(public demand)}$$

Price Equations

Price of value-added composite in industry i of region r:

$$\text{(A17.20)}\quad PV_i^r = \frac{1}{\psi_i^{vr}} \left\{ \sum_f \delta_{fi}^{r\,\sigma_i^{vr}} \left[PF_f^r (1+t_{fi}^r)\right]^{1-\sigma_i^{vr}} \right\}^{\frac{1}{1-\sigma_i^{vr}}}$$

$i = 1,\ldots,26;\ f = 1,\ldots,5;\ r = 1,\ldots,3$

Price of composite intermediate input j used in industry i of region r:

$$\text{(A17.21)}\quad PX_{ji}^r = \frac{1}{\psi_{ji}^r} \left\{ \delta_{ji}^{r\,\sigma_{ji}^r} \left[PM_{ji}^r (1+t_{ji}^r)\right]^{1-\sigma_{ji}^r} + (1-\delta_{ji}^r)^{\sigma_{ji}^r} \left[PD_{ji}^r (1+t_{ji}^r)\right]^{1-\sigma_{ji}^r} \right\}^{\frac{1}{1-\sigma_{ji}^r}}$$

Price of imported intermediate input j used in industry i of region r:

$$\text{(A17.22)}\quad PM_{ji}^r = \frac{1}{\psi_{ji}^{mr}} \left\{ \sum_s \delta_{ji}^{sr\,\sigma_{ji}^{sr}} \left[PM_{ji}^{sr} (1+t_j^{msr})\right]^{1-\sigma_{ji}^{sr}} \right\}^{\frac{1}{1-\sigma_{ji}^{sr}}}$$

$i, j = 1,\ldots,26;\ r, s = 1,\ldots,3$

Output price of commodity i in region r:

$$\text{(A17.23)}\quad PX_i^r = \frac{1}{\psi_i^{tr}} \left[\delta_i^{tr\,-\sigma_i^{tr}}\, PD_i^{r\,1+\sigma_i^{tr}} + (1-\delta_i^{tr})^{-\sigma_i^{tr}}\, PE_i^{r\,1+\sigma_I^{er}} \right]^{\frac{1}{1+\sigma_I^{er}}}$$

Price of commodity i consumed by private household in region r:

$$\text{(A17.24)}\quad PC_i^r = \left[\delta_i^{cr\,\sigma_i^{cr}}\, PCM_i^{r\,1-\sigma_i^{cr}} + (1-\delta_i^{cr})^{\sigma_i^{cr}}\, PCD_i^{r\,1-\sigma_i^{cr}} \right]^{\frac{1}{1-\sigma_i^{cr}}}$$

$i = 1,\ldots,26;\ r = 1,\ldots,3$

Price of commodity i consumed by public household in region r:

$$\text{(A17.25)}\quad PG_i^r = \left[\delta_i^{gr\,\sigma_i^{gr}}\, PGM_i^{r\,1-\sigma_i^{gr}} + (1-\delta_i^{gr})^{\sigma_i^{gr}}\, PGD_i^{r\,1-\sigma_i^{gr}} \right]^{\frac{1}{1-\sigma_i^{gr}}}$$

$i = 1,\ldots,26;\ r = 1,\ldots,3$

Price of composite import i in region s:

$$(A17.26)\ PM_i^s = \frac{\left\{\sum_r \delta_i^{ms\sigma_i^{ms}} \left[PE_i^{rs}(1+t_i^{ers})\right]^{1-\sigma_i^{ms}}\right\}^{\frac{1}{1-\sigma_i^{ms}}}}{(1+t_i^{mr})(1+t_i^{tr})}$$

$i = 1,...,26;\ r, s = 1,...,3$

Market Clearance Conditions

Domestic output:

$$(A17.27)\ D_i^r = \sum_j XD_{ij}^r + CD_i^r + GD_i^r + I_i^r \qquad i = 1,...,26;\ r = 1,...,3$$

Exports:

$$(A17.28)\ E_i^r = \sum_s M_i^{rs} + TD_i^r \qquad i = 1,...,26;\ r = 1,...,3$$

Imports:

$$(A17.29)\ M_i^r = \sum_j XM_{ij}^r + CM_i^r + GM_i^r \qquad i = 1,...,26;\ r = 1,...,3$$

Primary factors of production:

$$(A17.30)\ FS_f^r = \sum_i F_{fi}^r \qquad f = 1,...,5;\ r = 1,...,3$$

Legend

X_i^r:	Output of commodity i in region r
X_{ji}^r:	Composite intermediate input j used in industry i of region r
VA_i^r:	Value-added composite of commodity i in region r
F_{fi}^r:	Primary factor of production f in value-added composite in industry i of region r
FS_f^r:	Supply of primary factor of production f in region r
XM_{ji}^r:	Imported intermediate input j used in industry i of region r
XD_{ji}^r:	Domestic intermediate input j in industry i of region r
XM_{ji}^{sr}:	Intermediate input j imported from region s, used in industry i of region r
D_i^r:	Supply of commodity i to domestic market in region r
E_i^r:	Supply of commodity i in region r to export market
E_i^{rs}:	Export of commodity i from region r to region s
M_i^s:	Import of commodity i in region s
U^r:	Utility function of a representative household in region r
C_i^r:	Private demand for composite commodity i in region r

CD_i^r:	Private demand for domestic commodity i in region r
CM_i^r:	Private demand for imported commodity i in region r
EXP^r:	Total expenditure of private household in region r
G_i^r:	Public demand for composite commodity i in region r
GD_i^r:	Public demand for domestic commodity i in region r
GM_i^r:	Public demand for imported commodity i in region r
T_i^{rs}:	International transport service for export i from region r to region s
TD_i^r:	International transport service for export i in region r
PX_i^r:	Price of output i in region r
PV_i^r:	Price of value-added composite in industry i of region r
PF_f^r:	Price of primary factor of production f in region r
PX_{ji}^r:	Price of composite intermediate input j used in industry i of region r
PD_{ji}^r:	Price of domestic intermediate input j used in industry i of region r
PM_{ji}^r:	Price of imported intermediate input j used in industry i of region r
PM_{ji}^{sr}:	Price of intermediate input j imported from region s used in industry i of region r
PD_i^r:	Price of commodity i supplied to domestic market in region r
PE_i^r:	Price of commodity i in region r supplied to export market
PC_i^r:	Price of composite commodity i for private demand in region r
PCD_i^r:	Price of domestic commodity i for private demand in region r
PCM_i^r:	Price of imported commodity i for private demand in region r
PG_i^r:	Price of composite commodity i for public demand in region r
PGD_i^r:	Price of domestic commodity i for public demand in region r
PGM_i^r:	Price of imported commodity i for public demand in region r
P^t:	Price of international transport service
a_{ji}^r:	Input coefficient of commodity j used in industry i of region r
a_i^{vr}:	Value-added coefficient in industry i of region r
α_i^{cr}:	Share parameter of Cobb–Douglas utility function of a representative household

α_i^{tr} : Share parameter of Cobb–Douglas aggregation of international transport service

σ_i^{vr} : Elasticity of substitution among primary factors of production in industry *i* of region *r*

σ_{ji}^{r} : Elasticity of substitution between domestic and imported intermediate input j used in industry *i* of region *r*

σ_{ji}^{mr} : Elasticity of substitution between intermediate input j imported from region *s*, used in industry *i* of region *r*

σ_i^{tr} : Elasticity of transformation between composite domestic and export good *i* in region *r*

σ_i^{cr} : Elasticity of substitution between domestic and imported commodity *i* for private demand in region *r*

σ_i^{gr} : Elasticity of substitution between domestic and imported commodity *i* for public demand in region *r*

σ_i^{ms} : Elasticity of substitution between imports from different regions

ρ_i^{vr} : Substitution parameter of Armington aggregation function for value-added composite

ρ_{ji}^{r} : Substitution parameter of Armington aggregation function for composite intermediate input

ρ_{ji}^{mr} : Substitution parameter of Armington aggregation function for imported intermediate input

ρ_i^{cr} : Substitution parameter of private demand function

ρ_i^{gr} : Substitution parameter of public demand function

ρ_i^{tr} : Substitution parameter of CET transformation function

δ_i^{vr} : Distribution parameter of Armington aggregation function for value-added composite

δ_{ji}^{r} : Distribution parameter of Armington aggregation function for composite intermediate input

δ_{ji}^{mr} : Distribution parameter of Armington aggregation function for imported intermediate input

δ_i^{tr} : Distribution parameter of CET transformation function

δ_i^{cr} : Distribution parameter of Armington aggregation function for composite good *i* for private demand in region *r*

δ_i^{gr} : Distribution parameter of Armington aggregation function for composite good *i* for public demand in region *r*

δ_i^{ms}: Distribution parameter of bilateral import function

ψ_i^{vr}: Shift parameter of Armington aggregation function for value-added composite

ψ_{ji}^{r}: Shift parameter of Armington aggregation function for composite intermediate input

ψ_{ji}^{mr}: Shift parameter of Armington aggregation function for imported intermediate input

ψ_i^{tr}: Shift parameter of CET transformation function

ψ_i^{gr}: Shift parameter of Armington aggregation function for composite good *i* for public demand

ψ^{t}: Shift parameter of Cobb–Douglas aggregation function of international transport service

t_i^{fr}: Tax rate on primary factor of production *f* used in industry *i* of region *r*

t_{ji}^{r}: Tax rate on intermediate input *j* used in industry *i* of region *r*

t_j^{msr}: Tariff rate on import *j* from region s used in region *r*

t_i^{mr}: Tariff rate on import *i* in region *r*

t_i^{er}: Export tax rate on commodity *i* in region *r*

t_i^{cr}: Tax rate on private demand for commodity *i* of region *r*

t_i^{tr}: Transport margin of sector *i* in region *r*

18. The Role of Taiwanese Foreign Direct Investment in China: Economic Integration or Hollowing-out?

Chen-Min Hsu and Wan-Chun Liu

INTRODUCTION

The amount of net foreign direct investment in developing countries has climbed more than twelvefold since 1980 according to the IMF data. Long-term foreign investment could provide developing countries with important benefits. Public sector infrastructure projects are in greater demand. However, in the private sphere, the long-term foreign direct investment could expand the capital stock in the host country.

Foreign direct investment (FDI) in the East Asian area has been quite active since 1990. Taiwan, Korea, Hong Kong, Singapore, as well as Japan are the main contributors of FDI flows in this region, while China and the Southeast Asian countries are the demanders of these flows.

The 1997–98 Asian financial crisis has caused the direction of the FDI flows to change. This is particularly clear in the allocation of foreign direct investment funds between crisis countries in East Asia and China. For example, the FDI flows from Taiwan to China increased over the last ten years. The proportion of FDI to China compared with those to the crisis countries increased steadily after 1997.

Although there are several driving forces behind the economic integration in the East Asian region, for example, technology, preference and public policy, it appears that the private enterprises have been playing the main role during the process. The purpose of this chapter is to examine the allocation of the FDI flows in the East Asian region among Southeast Asian countries and

China. In addition, the role of the public policy and the private firms during the foreign direct investment process in the 1990s is also investigated. In particular, we will emphasize the Taiwanese case, since Taiwan has been one of the main contributors in this region. We will show the dynamics of the industry types of foreign direct investment during the 1990s. It appears that foreign direct investment plays the main role in economic integration between Taiwan and China during the process. However, the expansionary outward FDI may cause a hollowing-out of Taiwan's domestic industries. The prospect of this trend will be projected in this chapter.

The investment risk from the firm's prospect will be explored through questionnaires sent to Taiwan firms with investments in China. The balance between economic security or country risk and the individual firm's investment risk will be examined so that policy implications can be drawn from this study.

The remainder of this chapter is organized as follows. The second section describes the pattern of Taiwanese FDI. The third section describes the data characteristics. The fourth section summarizes the empirical results, and a final section concludes the chapter.

THE PATTERN OF TAIWANESE FOREIGN DIRECT INVESTMENT

That the pattern of foreign direct investment differs depending on the source of the investment was suggested by Kojima (1973). He argued that FDI originating in Japan was in line with the host country's comparative advantages and resulted in a trade promotion effect. In contrast, Kojima claimed that FDI originating in the USA did not conform to the host country's comparative advantages and resulted in a trade reduction effect. The difference is that Japanese FDI emanated from competitive industries while the US FDI came from an oligopolistic industry. That is, the differences in the domestic market structure lead to the differences in the overseas operations, which in turn accounts for the various effects of FDI.

Kojima's argument challenges orthodox FDI theory based on Hymer's theorem (1960), which asserts that FDI only comes from oligopolistic firms possessing some kind of intangible asset. According to Hymer, an intangible asset is a prerequisite for FDI because it offsets the disadvantages suffered by a transnational firm when it operates in a foreign country. In contrast, Kojima explained that Japanese firms from competitive industries invested abroad because of changes in macroeconomic conditions in Japan, which made it impossible for firms to continue producing at home. However, Kojima's competitive firms must also possess some industry-specific intangible asset, otherwise these firms would have chosen to switch to a new industry, one which is favoured by the changed macroeconomic conditions at home, instead of venturing abroad to carry on the old business. In this sense, Kojima's firms are not so competitive after all, for any intangible asset generates an economic rent, which is non-existent in a competitive industry. Economic rent is what a FDI firm seeks to internalize through transnational operations when the existing markets do not enable the firm to extract this rent through other arrangements such as licensing or direct export (see Buckley and Casson, 1976).

Kojima's idea that firms investing abroad are competitive ones may stem from the observation that a substantial proportion of Japanese FDI in manufacturing is undertaken by small- and medium-sized firms and on a smaller scale than by American firms.

Likewise, Taiwanese firms started to make substantial direct investments in Southeast Asia in 1980, in China in 1991, and behaved like Kojima's Japanese firms. That is, Taiwanese FDI is dominated by small- and medium-sized firms. The intangible asset possessed by these firms is related to their ability to conduct small-scale and flexible productions. Small-scale firms are able to conduct these productions through the support of an efficient production network encompassing a larger number of highly specialized producers. Firms in the networks are generally independent and are constantly competing among themselves, but they share production and market information that enables them to react quickly and fruitfully to changes in technology and the market (see Perrow, 1992).

In addition, like Japanese FDI firms, Taiwanese firms faced terrible conditions in the domestic investment environment since the late 1980s. Land prices increased sharply and the wage rate rose, while the Taiwan dollar appreciated. Firms attempted to escape from the worsening domestic investment environment and turned to foreign investment to keep their export markets and competitiveness in the industries. That is, FDI appears to play a defensive role in retaining export markets for firms under adverse investment conditions at home. Such kinds of defensive FDI are a substitute for domestic production.

However, from the mid-1990s, Taiwanese firms increased their foreign investment to exploit their assets, such as patents, other technological assets, reputation, skills in production, and marketing and advertising. The FDI plays an expansive role in the international market, and it is quite complementary to domestic production.

Taiwanese FDI is concentrated in less-developed areas, such as China and Southeast Asia. The pattern shifts toward American countries and Europe after 1996 under the 'go slow, be patient' policy, which puts a US$50 million cap on any single investment in China as well as the strike of the Asian financial crisis (see Table 18.1). However, since 2000, Taiwanese FDI towards China surged due to the high economic growth in China and the political instability in Taiwan. It is expected that Taiwanese FDI towards China will continue growing in the next ten years, since the go-slow policy has been abandoned and replaced with the new 'active openness and effective management' policy. According to this new policy, Taiwan entrepreneurs will be allowed to make investment directly in China, except those that may cause damage to Taiwan's national security. In addition, both Taiwan and China of the two sides across the Taiwan Strait have become members of the World Trade Organization since November 2001. Trade related investment will therefore be enhanced.

Table 18.1 Approved Taiwanese outward foreign direct investment

Year	Total (%)	ASEAN (%)	China (%)
1994	1616764 (100)	397731 (24.6)	962209 (57.27)
1995	1356878 (100)	326098 (24.03)	1092713 (80.48)
1996	2165404 (100)	587268 (27.12)	1229241 (56.76)
1997	2893826 (100)	641241 (22.16)	1614542 (55.77)
1998	3296302 (100)	477494 (14.49)	1519209 (46.08)
1999	3269013 (100)	522180 (15.97)	1252780 (38.33)
2000	5077062 (100)	389446 (7.67)	2607142 (51.35)
2001	4391654 (100)	477139 (10.86)	2784147 (63.40)

Note: Unit US*100.
Source: *Taiwan Statistical Data Book*, Council for Economic Planning and Development.

The effect of outward FDI on Taiwan domestic industries is a subject of continuous debate. Using the firm-level data during 1986 to 1994, Chen and Ku (2000) found that FDI strengthened rather than weakened the viability and competitiveness of domestic industries. However, our study will show that this trend is changing. Domestic production and investment in Taiwan decreased over time.

DATA CHARACTERISTICS

The question of whether Taiwanese FDI in China had adversely affected the industry growth in Taiwan has been a serious concern. A negative association of parent production with production of affiliates would suggest a displacement of labour-intensive production to lower-waged countries like China. However, a positive association would suggest either an expanding market share or requiring intermediate goods from the parent company. Theoretically, it is impossible to determine whether the net effect on production is positive or negative.

According to the statistical data from the Ministry of Economic Affairs, the induced export from Taiwan to China due to foreign direct investment in China had been raised to 37.67 per cent of the total export in 2000. In effect, if we follow the official statistics from China, the export of FDI inducement is about 56.22 per cent of the total export from Taiwan to China.

Our research is based on the 2002 survey data which had just been published in August 2002[1]. This is a cross-sectional survey data. The 2002 survey data on foreign investment by manufacturers conducted by the Ministry of Economic Affairs shows that firms investing in China had an increase in the material and intermediate products imported from Taiwan by some 19.60 per cent and 16.56 per cent respectively as compared to the year 2000. While the material and intermediate products purchased from other Taiwanese affiliates in China increased about 34.13 per cent and 26.59 per cent respectively. The samples are in the list of manufacturers that were permitted to make foreign investment by the Investment Commission (Ministry of Economic Affairs). The 2002 survey sample consisted of 3481 manufacturers.

The 2002 sampling data includes 2170 manufacturers excluding those closed, moved out, and withdrawn from investing. Based on this sample, it shows that by the end of 2001, Taiwan foreign investments in China (including Hong Kong), Southeast Asia, and other developed countries (including the USA) accounted for 70 per cent, 12.49 per cent, and 12.40 per cent of the total Taiwanese foreign investment respectively (see Table 18.2). It is worth mentioning that Taiwanese foreign investments in China has an increasing trend. Table 18.3 shows that there is no change on expanding the parent company's production scale following the foreign investments for some 50.89 per cent of the manufacturers in China, while 32.78 per cent show that it has benefited from expanding the parent company's production scale. In addition, Table 18.3 also shows that about 35.85 per cent of the manufacturers in all investment areas benefited on the expanding parent company's production scale after the foreign investments, while 50.65 per cent of the firms show that it has no change and detrimentals were 50.65 per cent.

Table 18.2 Foreign direct investment by areas

Year / Area	1997 (%)	1998 (%)	1999 (%)	2000 (%)	2001 (%)
Developed countries	153 (12.11)	238 (14.65)	251 (12.99)	213 (11.15)	269 (12.40)
China (incl. HK)	842 (66.60)	1048 (64.49)	1345 (69.58)	1343 (70.31)	1519 (70)
Southeast Asia	244 (19.30)	286 (17.60)	272 (14.07)	274 (14.35)	271 (12.49)
Others	25 (1.98)	53 (3.26)	65 (3.36)	80 (4.19)	111 (5.12)
Total	1264	1625	1933	1910	2170

Source: Ministry of Economic Affairs, 1998–2002 Survey on Foreign Investment by Manufactures.

Table 18.3 Foreign direct investment areas and expanding of domestic scale

Domestic scale / Area	Beneficial	No change	Detrimental	Total
Developed countries	146 (54.28%)	113 (42.01%)	10 (3.72%)	269
China (including Hong Kong)	498 (32.78%)	773 (50.89%)	248 (16.33%)	1519
Southeast Asia	90 (33.21%)	149 (54.98%)	32 (11.81%)	271
Others	44 (39.64%)	64 (57.66%)	3 (2.70%)	111
Total	778 (35.85%)	1099 (50.65%)	293 (13.50%)	2170

Note: Developed countries refers to the United States, Canada, Mexico, West European, Japan, Australia and New Zealand.
Southeast Asia refers to Malaysia, Singapore, Thailand, Indonesia, the Philippines and Vietnam.

Source: Ministry of Economic Affairs, *2002 Survey on Foreign Investment by Manufactures*.

Table 18.4 shows that when the causes of investment are: market demand by foreign customers, following Taiwan consumers' incentives from investing areas; cost savings such as land acquirement, material supply, cheap labour; deterioration of domestic investment environment; reduced exchange rate risk; and most favoured nation treatment, the foreign direct investors answer 'no change' on expanding their domestic production scale. In contrast, firms making outward investment because of acquirement of

Table 18.4 Causes of investment and expanding domestic scale

Domestic scale Cause of investment	Beneficial	No change	Detrimental	Total
Market expansion	549 (39.81%)	669 (48.51%)	161 (11.68%)	1379
Demand by foreign customers	299 (41.30)	311 (42.96%)	114 (15.75%)	724
Following Taiwan consumers	202 (34.24)	282 (47.80%)	106 (17.97%)	590
Incentives from investing area	75 (32.19%)	122 (52.36%)	36 (15.45%)	233
Acquirement of technology	57 (52.29%)	49 (44.95%)	3 (2.75%)	109
Acquirement of land	155 (37.53%)	186 (45.04%)	72 (17.43%)	413
Material supply	124 (37.35%)	160 (48.19%)	48 (14.46%)	332
Cheap labour	481 (35.32%)	641 (47.06%)	240 (17.62%)	1362
Capital utilization	131 (47.81%)	114 (41.61%)	29 (10.58%)	274
Deterioration of domestic environment	244 (31.16%)	385 (49.17%)	154 (19.67%)	783
Quota	16 (36.36%)	19 (43.18%)	9 (20.45%)	44
Reduce exchange rate risk	15 (35.71%)	21 (50%)	6 (14.29%)	42
Overcome trade barrier	31 (49.21%)	26 (41.27%)	6 (9.52%)	63
Most-favoured nation treatment	43 (36.13%)	64 (53.78%)	12 (10.08%)	119
Others	8 (12.12%)	53 (80.30%)	5 (7.58%)	66

Source: See Table 18.3.

land, capital utilization, and overcoming trade barriers answer 'beneficial' on expanding their domestic production scale. Table 18.5 shows that most Taiwanese FDI are horizontal-integration orientated, while about 721 firms have adopted the forward or backward integration. The firms stressing horizontal integration and 'irrelevant product' were more inclined to favour 'no change' on expanding the parent company's production, while those stressing vertical integration tended to think it beneficial. Table 18.6 suggests that large, medium and small FDI firms choose either 'beneficial' or 'no change' on expanding the parent company's production.

Table 18.5 Type of production and expanding of parent production

Domestic scale Type of Production	Beneficial	No change	Detrimental	Total
Horizontal division	362 (33.09%)	560 (51.19%)	172 (15.72%)	1094
Vertical division	330 (45.77%)	299 (41.47%)	92 (11.76%)	721
Irrelevant product	86 (24.23%)	240 (67.61%)	29 (8.17%)	355

Source: See Table 18.3.

Table 18.6 Firm size and expanding of parent production scale

Domestic scale Firm size	Beneficial	No change	Detrimental	Total
Small	337 (31.20%)	572 (52.96%)	171 (15.83%)	1080
Medium	154 (36.58%)	215 (51.07%)	52 (12.35%)	421
Large	287 (42.90%)	312 (46.64%)	70 (10.46%)	669
Total	778 (35.85%)	1099 (50.65%)	293 (13.50%)	2170

Source: See Table 18.3.

As for the R&D activities of manufacturers with foreign direct investment, Table 18.7 shows that 79.72 per cent of the firms with FDI in China have a R&D department in their domestic institutes. It suggests that R&D activities of the parent companies are more important to firms, although the counter proportion in developed countries is higher.

Table 18.7 Domestic and foreign R&D department by investment areas

R&D Area	Domestic R&D department		Foreign R&D department	
	no	yes	no	yes
Developed country	17 (6.32%)	252 (93.68%)	134 (49.81%)	135 (50.19%)
China (including Hong Kong)	308 (20.28%)	1211 (79.72%)	492 (32.39%)	1027 (67.61%)
Southeast Asia	65 (23.99%)	206 (76.01%)	108 (39.85%)	163 (60.15%)
Others	19 (17.12%)	92 (82.88%)	68 (61.26%)	43 (38.74%)
Total	409 (18.85)	1761 (81.15)	802 (36.96)	1368 (63.04)

Source: See Table 18.3.

Table 18.8 shows the type of industries by investing areas. As a result, machinery and equipment, computer, communication and video and radio electronic products, electronic parts and components, electrical machinery, supplies and equipment were the major investment industries of Taiwanese foreign investment in China.

Empirical Analysis

Since the survey data used are measured by discrete or ordered scales, we specified regression models with discrete dependent variables to analyse the variation of production and R&D strategies after foreign investments. Expanding the domestic production scale is categorized as 'detrimental', 'no change' and 'beneficial', which is indicated by an ordered scale 0, 1, 2. We specified an ordered probit model to analyse the effects of FDI. We wish to examine the factors that would result in Taiwanese FDIs which might be mainly complementary or a substitute.

The type of investment is divided into four types, i.e. market expansion, technology acquirement, cost savings and others, based on the causes of investment that were described in the questionnaire. Three dummy variables are created to represent four types of investment motivation. Cost savings are classified as defensive investment elements and their expected coefficient signs are thus negative. However, market expansion and technology acquirements are both expansive investing elements and their expected coefficient signs are positive.

Table 18.8 Type of industry by investing area

Investing area / Type of industry	Developed country	China (incl. Hong Kong)	Southeast Asia
08. Food	5	40	9
10. Textile mill products	4	55	20
11. Wearing app. and access.	3	28	20
12. Leather and fur products	1	50	2
13. Wood and bamboo pr.	3	14	11
14. Furniture and fixtures	0	16	9
15. Pulp, paper and paper pr.	1	18	6
16. Printing and rel.support activiv.	0	13	0
17. Chemical material	12	35	12
18. Chemical products	10	49	13
19. Petroleum and coal pr.	0	2	2
20. Rubber products	0	27	7
21. Plastic products	7	80	13
22. Non-metallic mineral pr.	3	33	12
23. Basic metal	6	30	8
24. Fabricated metal products	6	92	25
25. Machinery and equipment	12	179	16
26. Computer communication and video and radio electronic products	100	169	21
27. Electronic parts and components	60	197	17
28. Electrical machinery, supplies and equipment	13	141	17
29. Transport equipment	9	97	20
30. Precision instruments	10	55	0
31. Miscellaneous industrial pr.	4	99	11
Total (Manufacturing)	269	1519	271

Source: See Table 18.3.

The ratio of foreign investment to total investment in 2001 is used as an explanatory variable to the relationship between foreign investment and domestic investment. If FDI has a squeeze impact on domestic investment, then its sign is negative. If it has a supplementary effect, then the sign is positive.

The sales ratio variable is calculated as the foreign operating revenue relative to total operating revenue. We expect that sales ratio has a positive effect on expanding domestic production.

Parent firms with profit are assigned code 1, otherwise 0. It is expected that the parent firms with profit after investing in foreign countries will keep expanding their domestic production. The coefficients of profit status are expected to be positive. As for firm size, it is divided into three types: small, medium and large firms. Two dummy variables are created to represent three types of firm size. Those firms that have more than 200 employees are defined as large firms and are assigned code 1, otherwise code 0. If the number of firm's employees is less than 99, they are defined as small firms. It is expected a large firm tends to expand its domestic production. The coefficient of a large firm is suggested to be positive. However, for a small firm, it may be pushed to a less-developing country due to the deterioration of domestic economic environment, and therefore, the coefficient of a small firm is expected to be negative.

Three variables are created to indicate the characteristics of each firm. One is labour-intensive industry, i.e., those firms whose labour input of foreign production is higher are assigned code 1, otherwise 0. Another is electrical and 'electronics industries'. That is, those firms in computer, communication, and video and radio electronic products, electronic parts and components and electrical machinery, supplies and equipment are denoted electrical and electronics. The other is fabricated metal products industry. The summary statistics for the explanatory variables are reported in Table 18.9.

Table 18.9 Summary statistics for explanatory variables

Variable	Mean	Standard deviation	Minimum	Maximum
Investment area				
Developed countries	0.1240	0.3296	0	1
China (incl. HK)	0.7000	0.4584	0	1
Southeast Asia	0.1249	0.3307	0	1
Ratio of foreign invest.	0.2548	0.2814	0.05	0.95
Profit status	0.4945	0.5000	0	1
Cause of investment				
Market expansion	0.6355	0.4814	0	1
Technology acq.	0.0502	0.2185	0	1
Cost savings	0.6493	0.4773	0	1
Firm size				
Small scale	0.4977	0.5001	0	1
Large scale	0.3083	0.4619	0	1
Sales ratio	0.3109	0.2972	0	0.95
Technology source parent firm	0.8452	0.3618	0	1
Industry				
Labour intensive	0.5747	0.4945	0	1
Electrical&electronic	0.3636	0.4811	0	1
Metal products	0.0571	0.2322	0	1
Type of production				
Vertical integr.	0.3323	0.4711	0	1
Horizontal integr.	0.5041	0.5001	0	1
R&D				
With domestic R&D	0.8115	0.3912	0	1
With foreign R&D	0.6304	0.4828	0	1

Table 18.10 reports the ordered probit model results for domestic production scale strategy. Table 18.10 shows that market expansion and technology acquirement have a significant positive effect, while cost savings have a significantly positive effect on domestic production strategy. It also shows that the FDI in China and Southeast Asia have a significant negative effect. Both the vertical integration and horizontal integration are important factors to parent production strategy. After investing in foreign countries, firm size has little effect on their parent production strategy. It also suggests that the ratio of foreign investment has an insignificantly negative effect on the parent scale. Also, firms with profit have a significantly positive effect on their domestic production strategy. Similarly, the estimated coefficients of labour-intensive and electrical and electronics are significantly positive. Likewise, the parent R&D has significantly and positively affected the parent production scale strategy.

The estimated coefficients should be interpreted in the sense that they affect the probability in such a way that a certain event will occur. This interpretation can be obtained by computing the marginal effects from the estimated model. The marginal effects measure the change in the probability of each choice with respect to a change in an explanatory variable, *ceteris paribus*. Note that the sum of the marginal probabilities of selecting any of the three categories of expanding the domestic production scale equals zero. The results of marginal probabilities are also presented in Table 18.10. It shows that those factors such as market expansion, technology acquirement and cost savings induce firms to expand domestic production scale. The probabilities were 7.10 per cent, 10.74 per cent, and 5.92 per cent respectively. Also, large firms with a high probability expanded domestic production scales only with a probability of 1.09 per cent, while small firms calculated that expansions of production scales would do harm to them. Those firms in labour-intensive and electrical and electronics industries have a high probability to expand their domestic production scales. The probabilities were 9.89 per cent and 11.74 per cent respectively. However, Taiwanese firms in China and Southeast Asia compared with firms in other areas believed that domestic production expansion was detrimental. Those firms with parent R&D, horizontal and vertical integration have a higher probability to expand their domestic production scale.

Due to statistically significant effects from the FDI in China and Southeast Asia on parent company production strategies, we further investigate whether there are any other factors considered on investment in developed countries as compared to Taiwan's enterprises in China and Southeast Asia. The analytical results are shown in Table 18.11. This table suggests that FDI in China with market expansion orientation has positive effects on domestic production, while there are supplementary effects of cost savings motivation.

Table 18.10 Empirical results for ordered probit model

Variable	Coefficient	Marginal effect		
		Detrimental	No change	Beneficial
Intercept	−0.9191*** (−6.992)			
Cause of investment				
Market expansion	0.1940*** (3.487)	−0.0772	0.0062	0.0710
Technology acquirement	0.2794** (2.227)	−0.1104	0.0030	0.1074
Cost savings	0.1616*** (2.573)	−0.0643	0.0051	0.0592
Investment area				
China	−0.3099*** (−3.796)	0.1230	−0.0061	−0.1169
Southeast Asia	−0.1999* (−1.873)	0.0793	−0.0077	−0.0716
Type of production				
Horizontal integration	0.3759*** (4.728)	−0.1491	0.0106	0.1384
Vertical integration	0.6101*** (7.314)	−0.2387	0.0083	0.2305
Firm size				
Small	−0.0204 (−0.283)	0.0081	−0.0006	−0.0076
Large	0.0292 (0.381)	−0.0117	0.0008	0.0109
Ratio of foreign investment	−0.1342 (−1.190)	0.0535	−0.0038	−0.0497
Profit status	0.1794*** (3.301)	−0.0715	0.0051	0.0664
Sales ratio	0.1448 (1.293)	−0.0577	0.0041	0.0536
Industry				
Labour-intensive	0.2698*** (4.605)	−0.1072	0.0084	0.0989
Electrical & electronics	0.3131*** (5.464)	−0.1244	0.0070	0.1174
Fabricated metal products	−0.1239 (−1.065)	0.0493	−0.0045	−0.0448
R&D				
With domestic R&D	0.2518*** (3.405)	−0.0998	0.0098	0.0900
With foreign R&D	−0.0818 (0.059)	0.0326	−0.0022	−0.0304
μ_1	0.3724*** (18.290)			
Log likelihood	−2023.173			
Chi-squared	218.4418			
(degrees of freedom)	(17)			
Number	2170			

Note: ***, ** and * indicate significance at 1, 5 and 10 per cent level, respectively. Numbers in parentheses are *t*-statistics. The estimation software package used is LIMDEP 8.0.

Table 18.11 Empirical results for ordered probit model by area

Variable	Developed countries	China (incl. Hong Kong)	Southeast Asia
Intercept	−2.0394***	−1.0201***	−1.0934***
	(−3.518)	(−6.616)	(−3.323)
Cause of investment			
Market expansion	0.4597**	0.1197*	−0.0154
	(2.298)	(1.811)	(−0.099)
Technology acquirement	0.1770	0.4003**	0.1522
	(0.741)	(2.234)	(0.245)
Cost savings	0.1177	0.1201*	0.3186*
	(0.559)	(1.626)	(1.766)
Type of production			
Horizontal integration	0.5943***	0.2670***	0.4234**
	(2.589)	(2.623)	(2.170)
Vertical integration	0.9383***	0.4949***	0.5318**
	(4.200)	(4.612)	(2.345)
Ratio of foreign inv.	−0.6055	−0.0364	−0.0274
	(−1.166)	(−0.283)	(−0.085)
Profit status	0.2354	0.1853***	0.1264
	(1.327)	(2.884)	(0.793)
Firm size			
Small	−0.5153**	0.1018	−0.2594
	(−2.216)	(1.192)	(−1.258)
Large	0.0306	0.0225	0.2724
	(0.142)	(0.244)	(1.168)
Sales ratio	0.5905*	−0.0022	0.0020
	(1.640)	(−0.017)	(0.006)
Industry			
Labour-intensive	0.2478	0.2806***	0.4735***
	(1.189)	(4.143)	(2.822)
R&D			
With domestic R&D	1.2045***	0.2998***	0.1228
	(2.300)	(3.569)	(0.618)
With foreign R&D	0.0046	−0.0722	0.0416
	(0.026)	(−1.014)	(0.248)
μ_1	0.1178***	0.4404***	0.3419***
	(3.233)	(17.019)	(6.009)
Log likelihood	−184.2430	−1484.9740	−238.5690
Chi-squared (degrees of freedom)	71.8142(13)	84.1054(13)	36.2616(13)
Number	269	1519	271

Note: *** , ** and * indicate significance at 1, 5 and 10 per cent level, respectively. Numbers in parentheses are *t*-statistics. The estimation software package used is LIMDEP 8.0.

The significant and positive effects for FDIs in China and Southeast Asia show that there exists production supplementary for Taiwan exports. Both estimated coefficients of horizontal integration and vertical integration are significant. In addition, except for FDI in developed countries, firm size coefficients are statistically insignificant for FDIs in China and Southeast Asia. It also shows that the ratio of foreign investment coefficients is insignificantly negative. This reflects that FDI has little substitution effect on domestic investment.

In addition to estimating the effect of R&D strategies after foreign investments, a bivariate probit model was applied. The analytical results are shown in Table 18.12. This table shows that large firms will enhance their R&D activities, and firms that are motivated to expand into foreign markets and rely on technology from domestic parent companies are more inclined to conduct R&D activities. Also both horizontal and vertical integration productions have positive effects on conducting R&D activities. In addition, foreign affiliates that rely on the parent company's technology initiate their parent company to conduct more R&D activities. Moreover, the R&D in foreign affiliates is complementary to that in the parent firm.

Table 18.12 The determination of R&D for parent firms

Variable	Coefficient	*t*-statistic
Intercept	0.7336	4.810***
Firm size		
Small	–0.6586	–6.786***
Large	0.2487	2.080**
Investment area		
China	–0.5193	–4.306***
Southeast Asia	–0.4600	–3.164***
Cause of investment		
Market expansion	0.1633	2.281**
Technology acquirement	0.0677	0.379
Cost savings	–0.0607	–0.747
Type of production		
Horizontal integration	0.0481	0.479
Vertical integration	0.2923	2.681***
Technology source parent firm	0.4217	4.271***
Ratio of foreign investment	–0.7600	–6.198***
Industry		
Electrical & electronics	0.4136	5.198***
Affiliate with R&D	0.8639	11.662***
Log likelihood	–845.4015	–
Chi-squared (degrees of freedom)	409.8020(13)	–
Number	2170	–

Note: ***, ** and * indicate significance at 1, 5 and 10 per cent level, respectively. The estimation software package used is LIMDEP 8.0.

Table 18.13 Taiwan exports and imports in the region, 1990–2001

Year		1990	1991	1992	1993	1994	1995	1996	1997	1998	1999	2000	2001
Export	ASEAN 5	67.86	73.48	81.52	88.95	106.84	139	142.1	148.7	104.5	126.8	163.992	128.6
Percentage of Taiwan GDP	(%)	(4.24)	(4.10)	(3.84)	(3.97)	(4.38)	(5.25)	(5.08)	(5.12)	(3.91)	(4.40)	(5.30)	(4.57)
	Singapore	22.03	24.03	25.05	28.9	33.65	44	45.7	48.9	32.6	38.2	54.558	40.515
	Thailand	14.23	14.44	18.09	20.18	24.4	30.7	27.9	25.6	19.3	21	25.623	21.257
	Malaysia	11.03	14.46	16	16.71	22.24	29	29.5	30.4	22.9	28.5	36.117	30.6
	Indonesia	12.46	12.07	12.15	12.85	14.33	18.7	19.6	21.3	10.5	13	17.337	14.8
	Philippines	8.11	8.48	10.23	10.31	12.22	16.5	19.3	22.4	19.3	26.1	30.357	21.5
	Vietnam						10.1	11.8	13	12.1	13.4	16.635	17.3
Percentage of	Hong Kong	85.56	124.31	154.15	184.53	212.62	261.1	267.9	286.9	248.2	260.1	313.363	269.614
Taiwan GDP	(%)	(5.34)	(6.93)	(7.26)	(8.23)	(8.71)	(9.86)	(9.58)	(9.89)	(9.29)	(9.03)	(10.13)	(9.59)
Percentage of	China	32.78	69.28	96.97	127.27	146.53	178.98	191.48	205.18	183.8	212.21	261.44	240.61
Taiwan GDP	(%)	(2.05)	(3.86)	(4.57)	(5.67)	(5.99)	(6.76)	(6.85)	(7.07)	(6.88)	(7.37)	(8.45)	(8.56)
Import	ASEAN 5	40.14	49.09	60.59	67.65	84.21	101.7	107.5	128.6	122.1	140.4	197.162	155.4
Percentage of	(%)	(2.51)	(2.74)	(2.86)	(3.02)	(3.45)	(3.84)	(3.84)	(4.43)	(4.57)	(4.88)	(6.37)	(5.53)
Taiwan GDP	Singapore	14.06	14.45	16.94	18.65	24.12	29.6	27.9	31.5	27	33.1	50.138	33.7
	Thailand	4.47	5.86	8.24	9.73	11.08	14.9	16.7	19.3	19.7	23.8	27.68	21.8
	Malaysia	10.03	14.09	18.29	19.38	23.26	29.5	35.7	42.3	36.2	38.8	53.254	42.1
	Indonesia	9.22	12.34	14.07	16.24	21.14	21.5	18.8	21.8	21	22.9	30.151	25.2
	Philippines	2.36	2.35	3.05	3.65	4.61	6.2	8.4	13.7	18.2	21.7	35.939	32.5
	Vietnam						2.7	3.2	3.9	3.4	3.9	4.689	4.2
	Hong Kong	14.46	19.47	17.81	17.29	15.33	18.4	17	20	19.5	20.9	21.866	18.5
	(%)	(0.90)	(1.09)	(0.84)	(0.77)	(0.63)	(0.69)	(0.61)	(0.69)	(0.73)	(0.73)	(0.71)	(0.66)

Table 18.13 (continued)

Percentage of	China	7.65	11.26	11.19	10.16	18.59	30.91	30.6	39.15	41.11	45.26	62.23	59.02
Taiwan GDP	(%)	(0.48)	(0.63)	(0.53)	(0.45)	(0.76)	(1.17)	(1.09)	(1.35)	(1.54)	(1.57)	(2.01)	(2.104)
Total trade	ASEAN 5	108	122.57	142.11	156.6	191.05	240.7	249.6	277.3	226.6	267.2	361.154	284
Percentage of	(%)	(6.74)	(6.83)	(6.70)	(6.98)	(7.82)	(9.09)	(8.93)	(9.56)	(8.48)	(9.28)	(11.67)	(10.10)
Taiwan GDP	Singapore	36.09	38.48	41.99	47.55	57.77	73.6	73.6	80.4	59.6	71.3	104.696	74.215
	Thailand	18.7	20.3	26.33	29.91	35.48	45.6	44.6	44.9	39	44.8	53.303	43.057
	Malaysia	21.06	28.55	34.29	36.09	45.5	58.5	65.2	72.7	59.1	67.3	89.371	72.7
	Indonesia	21.68	24.41	26.22	29.09	35.47	40.2	38.4	43.1	31.5	35.9	47.488	40
	Philippines	10.47	10.83	13.28	13.96	16.83	22.7	27.7	36.1	37.5	47.8	66.296	54
	Vietnam						12.8	15	16.9	15.5	17.3	21.324	21.5
Percentage of	Hong Kong	100.02	143.78	171.96	201.82	227.95	279.5	284.9	306.9	267.7	281	335.229	288.114
Taiwan GDP	(%)	(6.24)	(8.01)	(8.10)	(9.00)	(9.33)	(10.55)	(10.19)	(10.58)	(10.02)	(9.76)	(10.83)	(10.25)
Percentage of	China	40.43	57.93	74.07	86.89	98.09	114.5	113	114.6	100.1	98	115.7	299.63
Taiwan GDP	(%)	(2.52)	(3.23)	(3.49)	(3.87)	(4.02)	(4.32)	(4.04)	(3.95)	(3.75)	(3.40)	(3.74)	(10.66)

Note: Unit: 100 million US$.
Source: Taiwan Statistical Data Book.

CONCLUDING REMARKS

In this chapter the variation of production and R&D strategies after foreign investment were investigated. We found that market expansion, technology acquirement, cost savings, investment in China and Southeast Asia, type of production, profit status, labour-intensive and electrical and electronics industries, and parent R&D are important factors in parent domestic production strategy after foreign investments. However, the firm size has little effect on expanding domestic production, and FDI has little substitution effect on domestic investment. In addition, we have also found that the driving force of economic integration between Taiwan and China is in technology rather than public policy. Taiwanese FDI toward China plays an important role during the economic integration process. Table 18.13 presents the evolution of Taiwan and China (including Hong Kong) exports and imports of goods and services as a percentage of GDP from 1990 to 2000, as well as those between Taiwan and Southeast Asian countries. The ratios are steady and linear over the last decade, and the average growth rate of trade and exports in two regions are about the same rate, i.e., 6.4 per cent.

It should be noted that the trade pattern of Taiwan's trade in the East Asian region indicates that factors other than free trade agreements (e.g., NAFTA and European Union) are important for increasing regional trade. Taiwan is not a member of the regional free trade area; nonetheless, the share of its trade involving other emerging East Asian countries increased over the last ten years (see Table 18.13). The association of Southeast Asian nations (ASEAN) formed a free trade area in 1992 with an agreement of the Common Effective Preferential Tariff (CEPT). Following the creation of the free trade area, the share of regional trade rose from 14 per cent in 1990 to 18 per cent in 1999 (see IMF's *Direction of Trade Statistics*). Since both Taiwan and China became members of the World Trade Organization in 2002, it is expected the intra-regional trade across the Taiwan Strait will be spurred by an overall reduction in the level of trade barriers.

Recent trade integration across the Taiwan Strait has been technology-driven and it will be accelerated by the WTO agreements in the future. Although defensive Taiwan FDI, especially those labour-intensive industries, seeking cheap labour in the host countries to reduce the cost of production may cause a 'hollowing-out' of domestic industries, this worry cannot be refuted from a microeconomic perspective by utilizing firm data as shown in this study. However, as the non-labour-intensive industry grows and expansionary FDI is undoubtedly beneficial to domestic industries, we will expect larger FDI in this region, including China and Southeast Asian countries. The economic integration will be closer, as the Taiwan government decided to relax the limits on Taiwan outward FDI in China. In fact, direct investments by domestic producers in such sectors as automobiles, semiconductors and chemicals have international diversification effects as well as vertical and horizontal integration effects. However, it should be mentioned that those who lack substantial investments in human capital and become unskilled workers in textiles and apparel for example would restrict trade and outward FDIs in this region, as is given in the Stopler–Samuelson theorem: a decline in the relative wage of unskilled labour-intensive goods. Economic integration in this region needs more supplementary proposals including labour mobility as well as capital mobility policies such as tax agreement and investment security treaty. In the next stage, policy as well as technology will be the driving forces behind the regional economic integration.

NOTES

1. The authors appreciate Professor Hui-Lin Lin of the National Taiwan University who provided this data.

REFERENCES

Buckley, P.J. and M.C. Casson (1976), *The Future of the Multinational Enterprise*, London: Macmillan.

Chen, T. and Y. Ku (2000), 'The effect of foreign direct investment on firm growth: the case of Taiwan's manufactures', *Japan and the World Economy*, **12**, 153–72.

Hymer, S.H. (1960), 'The international operation of national firms: A study of direct foreign investment', Ph.D. Thesis, MIT Press, Cambridge, MA.

Kojima, K. (1973), 'A macroeconomic approach to foreign direct investment', *Hitotsubashi Journal of Economics*, **14**, 1–21.

Perrow, C. (1992), 'Small firm networks', in N. Nohria and R.G. Eccles (eds), *Networks and Organizations: Structure, Form and Action*, Boston, MA: Harvard Business School Press, pp. 445–70.

19. Regional Integration in Northeast Asia: Problems and Prospects

Dong-Chon Suh

INTRODUCTION

Although globalization has been a dominant trend in the recent world economy, there has been a parallel development of regionalism and a proliferation of regional integration arrangements. The deepening of the European Union continued throughout the 1990s with the implementation of the Single European Act and the monetary union arrangement following the Maastricht Treaty. The United States had abandoned its long-held opposition to regionalism and formed the North American Free Trade Agreement with Canada and Mexico in the early 1990s[1]. The move provoked a regional integration movement in South America and a customs union called Mercosur was established. In East Asia, the Association of Southeast Asian Countries (ASEAN) has established the ASEAN Free Trade Area. What is more significant is that a complex web of bilateral free trade agreements has been proposed and studied in the Asia–Pacific region in recent years.

One explanation of such a proliferation of regional arrangements is the domino theory put forward by Baldwin. Establishing a preferential trade area or deepening an existing one produces trade and investment diversion. The diversion generates new political economy forces of pressure for inclusion in nonparticipating nations. If the trade bloc is open to expansion, regionalism spreads like wildfire. If the inclusion is barred, the excluded nations would form a new regional arrangement. Therefore, a single incident of regionalism would trigger a multiplier effect like a row of dominos (Baldwin, 1995).

However, one area that has not been affected by this general trend is Northeast Asia, that accounts for over 20 per cent of the world GDP[2].

Although there have been occasional talks for closer economic cooperation, there has been no serious attempt for institutional integration by the policy makers in the region. None of these countries has ever formed a meaningful bilateral integration agreement with other countries either, except that they have been members of the Asia–Pacific Economic Cooperation (APEC).

The purpose of this chapter is first to explain, why there was a complete absence of regional integration arrangements in Northeast Asia. It then points out that some significant changes have recently taken place in the region's political economy that could have serious impacts on the regional integration. In view of these changes, it considers prospects for the integration and proposes some alternative approaches relevant to Northeast Asia.

For this analysis, regional integration is categorized into three main types. The first is institutional integration that can be achieved by formal negotiation at the government level. Agreements to reduce trade and investment barriers, such as free trade agreements or customs unions, fall into this category. Institutional integration can also be achieved in the monetary area, such as the European Monetary System and the exchange rate mechanism in the European Union.

The second type is market integration. Market integration can be achieved as a result of natural growth of trade and investment by private sector activities. Although there is no exact way to determine the degree of integration, markets can be considered as integrated when they show a higher than normal proportion of intra-regional trade and investment flows or strong interdependence in financial and monetary activities.

The third type is physical integration. In this case, regional countries would cooperate to develop common infrastructures such as regional railways and highways or creation of special economic zones or free trade zones. This type of integration could be achieved either by the government or private market initiatives and would contribute to market integration by facilitating regional trade and investment flows.

WHY WAS THERE NO INSTITUTIONAL INTEGRATION IN NORTHEAST ASIA?

Since the opening of China in the early 1980s, the intra-regional trade and investment expanded rapidly in Northeast Asia. The economies of China, Japan and South Korea were complementary in their economic structures and close economic linkages were forged once the political obstacles to trade and investment were eased.

The rising export dependence among these countries and China's rapid market integration with Japan and South Korea can be seen in Table 19.1.

For instance, China's share in total Japanese exports rose from 3.5 per cent to 6.2 per cent in 1992–2000, and in absolute value terms, recorded an increase of 2.5 times. In the case of South Korea, China's share rose sharply from 3.4 per cent to 10.5 per cent in 1992–2000, an absolute increase of 7.1 times in only eight years. Japan's share in China's exports also rose from 13.7 per cent to 16.9 per cent, recording an absolute increase of 3.5 times in value terms in 1992–2000. South Korea's share in China's exports also rose from 2.8 per cent to 4.4 per cent in 1992–2000, an absolute increase of 4.7 times. As the table shows, however, this rapid expansion experienced a setback in 1998 as the Asian economic crisis hit the region.

Table 19.1 Export dependence (share of total exports, percentages)

From	To	1992	1994	1996	1998	2000	(1992–2000)
Japan	China	3.5	4.7	5.3	5.3	6.2	(2.5)
	S.Korea	5.2	6.1	7.1	3.9	6.2	(1.7)
China	Japan	13.7	17.8	20.4	16.2	16.9	(3.5)
	S.Korea	2.8	3.6	5.0	3.4	4.4	(4.7)
S.Korea	China	3.4	6.4	8.8	9.0	10.5	(7.1)
	Japan	15.1	14.1	12.2	9.3	11.6	(1.8)

Note: Figures in parentheses are absolute increases. China–Korea trade statistics appeared only after the establishment of diplomatic relations in 1991.
Source: IMF, *Direction of Trade Statistics*.

Despite this growing market integration and a rising need to coordinate and manage the economic interdependence, there has been no serious attempt for institutional integration in the region. Physical integration has also been non-existent except the small scale Tumen River Area Development Program promoted by the United Nations Development Program[3]. What were the barriers that hindered institutional integration so far?

Political Barriers

There has been a tendency in recent literature on economic integration that most analyses focus mainly on economic factors and conditions. However, early writers on integration emphasized political factors, and pointed out that political unions preceded commercial unions on many occasions. For example, Viner cited early writers' arguments that, in most instances, the political union led the way and the commercial union grew up from it (Viner, 1950, pp. 94–5). It is well known that the driving force behind the creation of the European Union was the political consensus to avoid the terrible experiences of the two World Wars. The political necessity of forging an alliance in the Cold War era was also responsible for the creation of the economic community in Western Europe.

In Northeast Asia, however, the political conditions for integration have been lacking for the following reasons. First, the tension on the Korean peninsular and the isolation of North Korea had been the main obstacle to reach a political consensus on the regional economic integration including North Korea. North Korea occupies a central position in the region but it had no formal diplomatic relations with South Korea and Japan. The political barrier effectively prohibited normal economic transactions between these countries.

Second, the rivalry between China and Japan hindered any regional move for cooperation in the area. Although Japan provided a considerable amount of foreign aid and private investment to China, there has been deep-rooted rivalry and mutual suspicion in their political and security relations. In the post-war period, Japan was the unchallenged economic power in the region while China was the regional military power. However, this power balance is changing in recent years. On the one hand, Japan is rapidly expanding its military spending to become a regional power. Japan's military expenditure in 1999 exceeded that of China and Japan has provided bases for the US under the joint defence agreement[4].

On the other hand, China has achieved a phenomenal economic growth in the last 20 years. Its GNP in 1999 was 980 billion dollars, which was far below Japan's 4079 billion dollars. However, in terms of exchange rates measured at purchasing power parity, China's GNP reached 4112 billion dollars in the same year. Thus it became the second largest economy in the world, exceeding Japan's 3043 billion dollars (World Bank, 2000)[5]. The changing political and economic powers show the intensity of competition and rivalry between the two countries.

Third, the notion that a geographical proximity and cultural similarities of these countries would create a favourable environment for integration has been illusory. Even though they belong to the Confucian culture, they nevertheless differ markedly in their languages, religions and customs. Furthermore, China and Japan had clashed on the Korean peninsular since the fifteenth century and the experience of Japanese invasion of the continent since the early twentieth century had left these countries with bitter memories of animosities.

Since the end of World War II, South Korea and Japan had normalized relations in the early 1960s by settling on the war compensation and accepting apologies. However, history has never been satisfactorily settled between China and Japan despite the normalization in 1972 and 'Japan–

China Peace and Friendship Treaty' in 1978. Japan has provided a considerable amount of Japanese Overseas Development Assistance fund instead of war reparation. However, when President Jiang Zemin visited Japan in 1998, he raised the history card again and the Japanese responded that they had enough of apologies.

North Korea and Japan have not yet established diplomatic relations and no compensation has been made in any form. This is in stark contrast to the European situation that settled history promptly after the end of the war and created a favourable political condition for integration. Recently, Japan's relations with neighbouring countries suffered another blow when Japanese Prime Minister Junichiro Koizumi visited Yasukuni Shrine where the war criminals were honoured. The government's approval of the history textbook that downplayed Japan's transgressions in the war also caused fury in the neighbouring countries.

Lastly, the US has been an important external actor in shaping the political and security framework in Northeast Asia. The US strategy to maintain stability and influence in Northeast Asia has been to form military alliance with South Korea and Japan and deploy its troops in these countries. As Silver points out, Japan has been at the centre of this strategy to contain China but the US has often played China against Japan in their strategy for maintaining balance in the region (Silver, 2000, pp. 37–40). Unlike Europe where regional regimes such as the North Atlantic Treaty Organization and the Organization for Security and Cooperation in Europe have played a vital role in their security arrangements, the US has maintained that there is no need for a regional security regime in East Asia.

Economic Factors

As evidenced by the fact that none of the countries in Northeast Asia has so far entered any meaningful regional integration agreement, the economic factors for integration were not favourable in this area for the following reasons.

First, economic systems and ideologies were too diverse in the region. Despite the adoption of market principles, China's trade was subjected to various government interventions. The North Korean economy was under rigid central planning while its meagre trade was completely carried out by the state. Economic integration such as free trade agreements does not make sense when trade is under state control because formal barriers such as tariff rates are not as important as they are in the market economy.

Second, the structure of industry and trade was also diverse, reflecting the wide differences in their factor endowments and the stages of development. As is well known in the theory of integration, benefits of integration such as static gains from trade creation and dynamic gains due to economies of scale would be large if the industry and trade structures of member countries are similar. Since the trade arising from differences in factor endowments was already taking place with the exception of North Korea, the additional gains from trade creation by institutional arrangements would not be very large.

Third, although formal trade barriers of China and North Korea are still high, informal barriers such as government guidance, non-transparent business customs and business networks based on personal relations are more important in further trade expansion. As the removal of these barriers requires domestic measures, it cannot be easily negotiated in trade agreements. It would also take time and effort to change domestic institutions that are still under the political constraint of the socialist country.

Fourth, trade diversion effects would be large because a relatively small number of countries will participate in the arrangement and the proportion of intra-regional trade has been low in these countries. Furthermore, as these countries are quite sensitive to the protection of the agricultural sector, comprehensive trade liberalization would be difficult to achieve. Thus, the net static gains from integration would not be large. However, dynamic gains from integration, such as the economies of scale and increase in competition, would be large considering the fact that monopolies and other imperfect competitions are widespread in these countries.

RECENT POLITICAL AND ECONOMIC CHANGES IN NORTHEAST ASIA

The foregoing discussion reveals that the political and economic environments for regional integration were rather immature as evidenced by the absence of cooperative regimes in the area. However, some significant changes have taken place recently.

The East Asian Economic Crisis

East Asia experienced a region-wide economic crisis in 1997–8, which had significant impacts on regional integration.

Impacts of the crisis on the market integration

Trade and investment in East Asia, particularly interaction between Southeast and Northeast Asia, grew rapidly since the mid-1980s and a new trading system emerged in East Asia. The more developed countries in the region such as Japan and the Newly Industrializing Economies have specialized into more capital and technology-intensive industries and the less developed such as China and Southeast Asia into labour-intensive industries.

In Northeast Asia, Japanese and South Korean trade and investment with China grew rapidly since China adopted an open-door policy and normalized diplomatic relations. It revealed that they were natural trade partners possessing complementarity in factor endowments and industry structures. The advantage of geographical proximity, low transport costs and mutual understanding of cultures also contributed to this rapid expansion. However, the expansion trend was arrested at the height of the crisis as the regional countries drastically cut imports. The intra-regional trade decreased due to simultaneous contractions of imports during the crisis while the inter-regional trade with the US and other developed markets increased.

The intra-regional foreign direct investment had been on the rise since the 1980s but the trend was arrested as a result of the crisis. In managing the crisis, the US and the IMF placed a heavy emphasis on reforming the Asian business environment. The Western businesses complained that East Asia was the most difficult area to operate and pointed out that crony capitalism and moral hazard were the main culprits of the crisis. They demanded reforms of business practices, adoption of transparency and rule of law.

In the case of South Korea, what they asked amounted to a virtual dismantling of the *chaebol* structure and a major reform of the business practices in line with the American system. Japan was not directly hit by the crisis but it also experienced a rising inflow of Western capital in the form of mergers and acquisitions into its financial and other ailing sectors. Thus, the Asian crisis has also provided an opportunity for Western businesses to increase their presence in the Asian market via mergers and acquisitions and open up hitherto closed Japanese and South Korean markets. As a result, the market integration process of rising trade and investment linkages among the regional countries was arrested during the crisis.

Impacts on the institutional integration

The crisis has shown the vulnerability of increasing regional trade and investment linkages without a proper mechanism to manage this interdependence. For instance, one of the causes of the crisis had been the mismanagement of exchange rate systems following the devaluation of the Chinese yuan in 1994 and weakening of the Japanese yen from 1995. Had there been a regional exchange rate coordinating mechanism, the total collapse of the regional currencies in 1997 that caused a panic in the Asian financial markets could have been avoided.

The competitive inducements of foreign capital were also responsible for the regional spread of financial instability that led to the financial crisis. The export-oriented growth strategy that centred on a narrow range of labour-intensive products had also resulted in a deceleration of export growth rates and the worsening terms of trade in 1996.

The lack of coordination and cooperation in the region was not only the major cause of the crisis, but also the cause of its severity. The crisis was exclusively managed by outside actors such as the IMF and the US. As is well known in the debate on the IMF prescriptions, the conditions of bailouts such as demand for drastic reforms and high interest rate policies were designed to serve the long-term strategy of the US rather than stabilizing the panic-stricken markets.

There was indeed a regional effort to contain the contagion by creating an Asian Monetary Fund (AMF) in the early phase of the crisis. However, it was strongly opposed by the US on the grounds that it would obstruct the IMF operations[6]. The realization that they were powerless in the crisis prevention and management has awakened regionalism and provided a powerful rationale for the institutional cooperation in the wake of the crisis.

ASEAN initiative on institutional integration and Northeast Asia

Since the early phase of the crisis, the Southeast Asian countries had serious discussions on the institutional integration at their various ASEAN meetings. They agreed on the 'Manila Framework' to start mutual surveillance and cooperation in the financial sector in 1997 and established the 'ASEAN Surveillance System' in October 1998.

However, they soon realized that ASEAN only cooperation would have a very limited value considering the size of their economy and their dependence on the external actors. Thus, they invited three Northeast Asian countries, namely China, Japan and South Korea after their annual consultations, which is subsequently known as the 'ASEAN + 3' formula. This grouping was institutionalized after the Manila summit in 1999 and the cooperation in the context of East Asia such as the Asian Monetary System and Asian Free Trade Area have been under study by ASEAN countries. They also reached an agreement on such monetary cooperation as currency swap and repurchase arrangements in 2000, which is known as the 'Chiang Mai' Initiative. All these proposals are inviting the three Northeast Asian countries.

North–South Relations on the Korean Peninsular

Although the euphoria that followed the North–South summit meeting in June 2000 has now subsided, it was a landmark in the North-South relations on the Korean peninsular. The summit was successful in the sense that it had raised the expectation that the end of half-century hostility on the Korean peninsular was approaching. The historic summit was made possible by the following factors:

(1) The 'sunshine policy' of the South Korean president, Kim Dae Jung.
(2) The North Korean leader, Kim Jong-Il's decision to end the economic isolation and start a carefully managed opening of its economy.
(3) The US policy of engagement based on Perry's Report to ease nuclear and missile threats from North Korea.
(4) China's influence and intermediary efforts to persuade North Korea to improve relations with South Korea and the US[7].

In addition to the highly emotional issue of family reunions, the summit agreed on the following points according to the Joint Declaration:

(1) The basic formula for reunification would be a loose form of federation respecting the principle of 'two countries, two systems'.
(2) Economic cooperation and integration can begin immediately with North Korea providing investment guarantees.
(3) Agreement on the restoration of inter-Korean rail links, which will be extended to Trans-China and Trans-Siberian railways to Europe.

After the summit, North Korea had established diplomatic relations with some European countries and tried a negotiation to normalize relations with the US[8]. However, the move toward a gradual opening of North Korea and reconciliation came to an abrupt halt since George Bush became the US President. North Korea–US relations steadily deteriorated since Mr. Bush called North Korea an axis of evil and reversed the reconciliation policy of the Clinton administration. They both scrapped the Agreed Framework of 1994 and their relations reached a crisis point when North Korea declared to develop its nuclear capability in late 2002.

The political situation on the Korean peninsular as of early 2003 is extremely fluid and uncertain. We can think of three scenarios: (1) war or limited military conflict; (2) tailored containment aimed at the removal of Kim Jong-Il regime; (3) negotiated settlement followed by the reconciliation process. The war option is unthinkable because it means total destruction of the Korean peninsular. The option of containment by an economic sanction is unlikely to be supported by the regional countries. It will be ineffective because North Korea is an extremely closed economy. Thus the only remaining option is a negotiated settlement and reconciliation.

If the reconciliation proceeds smoothly, it will change the regional security environment drastically. As Korea is strategically situated between China and Japan, the division of the Korean peninsular has ironically contributed to the balance of power in the region by providing a buffer zone between the two countries. If the reconciliation leads to an easing of tension or reunification, the regional security framework based on the balance of power on the Korean peninsular would inevitably be modified. A new concept of regional security will be needed and an alternative framework based on the regional regime will be considered in this context.

It will also mark a turning point from a geoeconomic point of view. Since North Korea has been a critical barrier to regional integration, the market integration will gain a new momentum if North Korea moves toward reconciliation and an open economy. However, the institutional integration will still be hindered by remaining ideological differences and historical animosities.

The other promising area would be physical integration. A poor infrastructure has been North Korea's most pressing economic problem apart from food shortages. North Korea has already asked for the supply of electric power to South Korea and talks are underway to construct special economic zones or free trade zones in North Korea. Among physical integration projects, the reconnection of rail lines is of particular importance. Once restored, the inter-Korean railway will be connected further to the Trans-China Railway and Trans-Siberian Railway. Both China and Russia have always shown a keen interest in the project. It will drastically save shipping time and costs from Northeast Asia to Europe[9]. Apart from the badly-needed hard currency revenue that will accrue to North Korea, all countries in the region and the European countries stand to gain by this project: it will spur the development of the hitherto underdeveloped region of Northwestern China and Siberia; North Korea could embark on industrialization with its well-disciplined labour force; the Korean peninsular could well serve as a hub of physical distribution in Northeast Asia.

China's Entry into the World Trade Organization

China finally entered the World Trade Organization (WTO) in 2001. Although China had pursued institutional reforms toward a free-market system since the early 1980s, China's entry marked a watershed in its integration into the global economy.

China has now obtained the MFN (Most Favoured Nations) status, which would guarantee stable access to the industrialized markets. However, China has to comply with the rules of the WTO and the terms of its entry. These terms include a lowering of its tariff rates on industrial and agricultural products, elimination of import quotas, opening of service and telecommunication sectors and liberalization of foreign investments. In addition to trade-related measures, the US and other European countries are pressuring China to embark on fast and sweeping institutional changes such as reforming business practices based on the rule of law and transparency.

China's entry into the WTO would have a profound impact on the regional trade integration. In addition to a lowering of formal trade barriers, its compliance with the WTO system would reduce the informal trade barriers based on the differences in economic and trade systems. Also, China would have to cooperate with the other regional countries in order to exercise its influence in the global trading system.

However, structural adjustments and reforms of the state sector after the entry into the WTO would inevitably worsen the unemployment situation and the income inequality. One way to alleviate these problems is to create employment opportunities by foreign direct investment and to embark on large-scale infrastructure projects with the help of foreign capital. The Chinese government has already given top priority to development projects in its western region and large infrastructure projects such as waterways and highways. As Japan and South Korea already possess the necessary capital and technology in developing infrastructure projects, they will be natural partners in this respect.

Japan's Economic Problems

The Japanese economy is experiencing the longest stagnation in its post-war history. Since the drastic appreciation of the exchange rates after the Plaza Agreement of 1985, the Japanese economy experienced a bubble in the real estate market and the stock market in the late 1980s. Its financial sector suffered a near paralysis after the bursting of the bubble in the early 1990s and it was hit again by the Asian economic crisis in 1997. Government macro-policies to manage this turbulent period have resulted in huge government deficits and near-zero interest rates, which made the fiscal and monetary tools ineffective.

Throughout the 1990s however, Japanese trade and investment have shown a tendency toward a closer integration with the other East Asian economies. Its exports to East Asia exceeded those to the US from the early 1990s and its foreign direct investment to Southeast Asia and China rose steadily as the Japanese companies established regional production networks. Its trade structures are increasingly moving toward the exports of capital goods to the East Asian markets rather than supplying consumer goods to the industrialized markets. Thus, Japan contributed greatly to the shaping of the new division of labour in East Asia but it was an unstable system vulnerable to the fluctuations in the industrialized markets as evidenced by the outbreak of the Asian economic crisis.

In the early phase of the Asian economic crisis, Japan tried to contain it by using its financial resources. Japan proposed the establishment of an Asian Monetary Fund as a regional facility to provide trade finance and balance of payments support to crisis-affected countries in September 1997. The US promptly rejected the idea, however, on the grounds that it would undermine the IMF-centred rescue operation and create another moral hazard. Although Japan provided 43 billion dollars to the IMF rescue packages followed by 30 billion dollars of bilateral aid, known as Miyazawa Plan, it played only peripheral roles in the management of the crisis. This incident was clear evidence that Japan has a limited influence on regional affairs despite its economic power.

Throughout the last decade, the characteristic pattern of the Japanese economy has been high savings, low consumption, trade surplus with the industrialized countries and deficits in the capital account. Ironically however, the capital that Japan invested in the US has been managed by aggressive financiers in Wall Street and the Japanese influence in the global financial markets has been weak despite its financial power. If Japan is to play a more stabilizing role in the global economy, it will have to change this pattern of trade and financial flows with a more balanced and stable position in its trade and capital accounts.

Thus the Japanese economy is moving toward a closer integration with the Asian economies and its economic policy is directed toward creating a more stable regional trade and investment environment. It seems that such a change is a realization that some form of integration with Asian countries could ease its structural problems, such as weak demand and the aging demography. In this context, Japan's decision to form a free trade area with Singapore in 2001 is a marked change in its foreign economic policy. Since the formal trade barriers of Japan and Singapore were already at a low level and no sensitive issue such as agricultural trade was involved, it could not set a meaningful precedent for Japan's trade policy. However, Japan has also taken the initiative to study a similar agreement with South Korea. If it is agreed, it would have a profound impact on the regional politics and economics. Japan would secure a bridgehead to the ASEAN via Singapore and to China and North Korea via South Korea.

Japan also supports monetary and financial cooperation in the wake of the Asian crisis. It supported the 'Chiang Mai Initiative', which proposed a regional network of currency swaps and repurchase agreements. 'ASEAN + 3' nations agreed on this type of financial cooperation to prevent turbulence in the currency markets similar to the crisis that ravaged much of the region. Although Japan has not been successful in creating a yen-currency zone in Asia, it is taking an assertive policy on the Asian monetary cooperation in view of the bi-polarization of the world into the dollar and the euro currency zones.

Changes in US Policy toward Asian Integration

The US is an external actor in Northeast Asia but it has exerted a considerable influence in the geopolitics and geoeconomics of the region. Regarding the formation of a regional regime in Northeast Asia, the US has consistently opposed any attempt to form an Asian only regime. For instance, when Malaysian Prime Minister Mahathir Mohamad proposed the East Asian Economic Caucus (EAEC) in the early phase of the APEC formation, the US strongly opposed the proposal and exerted strong pressures to Japan and Korea to oppose it. As Bergsten (1997) states:

> A central thrust of American foreign policy, including foreign economic policy, has been to avoid any institutional devices that – to use the words of the Secretary of State James Baker – 'would draw a line down the middle of the Pacific and threaten to divide East Asia and North America'. The U.S. has thus firmly and successfully rejected Malaysian and other proposals for the EAEC or any other 'Asian only' devices.

The move by the US to oppose the Japanese proposal of an Asian Monetary Fund in 1997 was consistent with this policy. Although the US feared that it would undermine IMF bailout operations and relax IMF conditions to overhaul the Asian business environment, it also feared that the Asian only institution would weaken US influence in East Asia. It was a clear manifestation of US strategy that East Asia should be kept under the sphere of US influence.

Why is the US so concerned with the regionalization of East Asia? Bergsten provides the following reasons. First, as the game theory and some historical experiences suggest, three-player games are more unstable than two-player games. The reason is that each of the three players fears that the other two will coalesce against it, fostering constant insecurities and pre-emptive strikes to secure tactical advantage. Thus, a world consisting of the three blocs of Europe, America and Asia would be considered as an unstable system.

Second, an effective regional grouping in trade or finance could produce fundamental changes in the world economic system. For instance, Asians would probably be more supportive of using capital controls and aggressive in regulating capital movements. The international institutions such as the IMF could be marginalized and left to manage difficult tasks of inter-bloc relations.

Third, the US rationale for participating in the APEC was to preclude a three-bloc world by linking both sides of the Pacific. The creation of an independent Asian economic entity will undermine the US policy of maintaining a bipolar configuration.

However, Bergsten agrees that Asia's desire for institutional autonomy in the wake of the crisis is fully understandable and points out that there are some positive aspects. For instance, it would enhance financial stability and economic progress and strengthen security by reducing intra-regional conflict. Thus, he recommends that if Asia is determined to start creating its own regional institutions at least in the economic sphere, Americans should accept it as a legitimate goal and work together to orient it in constructive directions that will not disrupt world security and stability (Bergsten, 2000).

A recent task force report sponsored by the Council on Foreign Relations also recommended a positive response to Asian integration. It observed that Japan was playing a leadership role in regional integration negotiations and recommended that the US should work with Japan to make sure that such regional agreements were consistent with the WTO and reinforced multilateral financial systems (Tyson, 2000).

Thus the US position on the regionalization in Northeast Asia is still unclear. Since the end of the Cold War, the superiority of US power has been secure and unchallenged. Its economy has enjoyed unprecedented dynamism while Japanese and other Asian economies have suffered stagnation and financial crises. Triumphant with these changes in the political and economic environment, the US seems to be confident to allow regional integration movements in Asia as long as they do not pose a threat to its hegemony. But on the other hand, as unilateralism has become a hallmark of the post-9/11 US foreign policy, it is reasonable to expect that the US would continue to oppose any Asian only integration.

PROSPECTS FOR ECONOMIC INTEGRATION IN NORTHEAST ASIA

From the foregoing analysis, it is clear that the economic integration in Northeast Asia is entering a new phase. There is a strong economic logic for institutional integration and it seems feasible under the new political and economic environment. Although the changes mentioned above justify a growing optimism that an institutional integration can be launched, the prospects are still uncertain and there are many stumbling blocks to overcome.

(1) Since North Korea declared that it would no longer honour the Agreed Framework of 1994, North Korea–US relations have reached a crisis level in late 2002 and North–South reconciliation is making no progress. The road to reconciliation looks bumpy again, but the obstacle seems to be the political stalemate of short-term nature. Barring the terrible scenario of military conflict, the only remaining option is a negotiated settlement and a process of engagement. The new president of South Korea, Roh Moo-Hyun has made it clear that he would follow the reconciliation approach. North Korea will also resume a gradual and cautious process of economic reform when an assurance to respect its sovereignty is given.
(2) The spirit of community building that will form the socio-cultural basis for institutional integration is still lacking in Northeast Asia and the leadership is coming from nowhere. Japan's relations with its neighbouring countries were strained over the issue of history textbooks and Prime Minister Koizumi's visit to a shrine that honoured militarism. Just why Japan took such steps when their collaboration was badly needed to overcome its economic difficulties was hard to explain. However, as Kahler has observed, the costs of non-cooperative outcomes in terms of prisoner's dilemma have increased and the benefits of interstate cooperation have also increased in the region. As economic growth and good economic management become central to the legitimacy of any governments, it is rational to expect that regionalism rather than nationalism will prevail in Northeast Asia (Kahler, 1994, p. 28).
(3) Under the circumstances, the traditional approach of forming free trade areas or customs unions as a first step toward integration is not relevant in Northeast Asia. The free trade agreement between Japan and South Korea is under study, but economic gains from such arrangements are limited considering the trade flows between the two countries. Rather, it will have politically damaging costs considering Korea's geopolitical situation and intense rivalry between China and Japan. China has also agreed on the formation of a free trade area with the ASEAN while Japan is also considering a comprehensive cooperation scheme with the ASEAN. Such proliferation of bilateral arrangements would not only distort trade and investment flows but also increase unnecessary conflict among the countries in the region. The complex web of bilateral agreements would only be counter-productive, considering the fact that any preferential arrangement would only be the second best solution that may affect member and non-member countries adversely.
(4) Instead, let us consider the following alternative measures. Given the political constraints prevailing in the region, the integration that is

immediately feasible seems to be physical integration focusing on the development of infrastructure. Consider first the case of North Korea. Despite its economic debacle, North Korea has been proud of its *juche* (self-reliance) ideology upon which the whole edifice of the nation has been built. Although it has the willingness to change, its path to opening will be extremely cautious because a drastic change in the people's mindset is needed to accept the open-door policy and pro-market reform. Therefore, North Korea will be more interested in attracting foreign capital into large infrastructure projects than private joint ventures where direct contact with the foreign businessmen is unavoidable. In this context, the re-connection of the inter-Korean railway will provide enormous benefits. First, it will generate much needed hard currency for North Korea. Second, it will construct a regional transportation and physical distribution network facilitating further intra-regional trade and investment. Third, it will also provide faster and cheaper overland passages between Europe and Northeast Asia. Russia and China, the two regional powers surrounding the Korean peninsular, have expressed keen interest in this project and used their leverages to persuade North Korea. Construction of large infrastructure projects is also a priority area in the economic development plan of China. China is attracting foreign participation into the Western development projects and other infrastructures such as a huge North–South waterway project. Since the Japanese and Korean construction industries are suffering from saturation of domestic markets and excess capacities, participation in these projects will be highly complementary and mutually advantageous. Thus, it seems that physical rather than trade integration is the most promising area of cooperation in Northeast Asia.

(5) If the regional countries agree to launch physical integration projects, it would be more appropriate to establish a regional financial institution to manage these projects. In this context, it is noteworthy to mention that the idea of creating a Northeast Asian Development Bank (NEADB) was first proposed in the early 1990s[10]. It was originally intended to develop infrastructure projects such as a gas pipeline system focusing mainly on three states of Northeast China and the Russian Far East. The proposal is still under study but its activity should be expanded to cover North Korea and other parts of China. In the case of North Korea, it will be an ideal instrument because North Korea will be anxious to avoid direct contact with South Korean businessmen due to political sensitivities. In the case of China–Japan relations, Japan has not earned gratitude despite the large transfers of its official development assistance (ODA) funds. As history has shown on many occasions, a bilateral aid is likely to beget ill feelings and resentment on both sides. Japan as a donor has frequently

argued that the Japanese aid should be used as a leverage to influence China, while China has no intention of yielding to such pressures. In view of political and historical animosities prevailing in the region, official aids can be best handled by regional financial institutions. This solution has the advantage of minimizing political conflicts that might arise in the course of regional integration. As the projects will be evaluated by a staff of technocrats, it will increase the efficiency of regional development projects free of political considerations. NEADB can channel its own funds and funds from the other existing multilateral development banks and some ODA funds. It can mobilize funds from international capital markets and private financial institutions interested in the projects can easily participate on the commercial basis. NEADB has the additional advantage in that the external actors such as the US and the other western countries can also participate in this formula, thus mitigating opposition from the US. The bank can also be used as a regional centre for technology transfer and institutional change to facilitate intra-regional trade and investment and further institutional integration. The countries in the region share common problems of institutional underdevelopment and an institutional change toward a market economy based on market principles and rule of law are badly needed. Although they recognize that it is a major challenge for their development, they cannot initiate a serious reform due to the lack of political will to endure short-term pains and resistance from the vested interests. In that case, imposition from without is the best solution and NEADB could serve well as a regional anchor for domestic reforms[11].

(6) In the case that the political constraint on institutional integration can be removed, it can be more fruitfully discussed in a wide framework of East Asia where Southeast Asian countries are included for the following reasons. First, Northeast and Southeast Asian economies are already so intertwined via trade and investment linkages that it is meaningless to separate them. As we have witnessed throughout the Asian economic crisis, their economic activities have been synchronized and needed coordination. Second, although the combined GNP of Northeast Asia was about eight times larger than that of ASEAN, ASEAN countries have been more eager and experienced in regional integration. ASEAN can play the role of intermediary and China–Japan rivalry would be mitigated in a wider framework of East Asia cooperation. ASEAN countries have recognized the importance of Northeast Asian economies in their economies and invited Northeast Asian countries to various post-ASEAN meetings. The 'ASEAN + 3' summit meeting has been annualized since 1999 and various East Asian integration schemes have been discussed in this framework. These include trade cooperation such

as an East Asian Free Trade Area and monetary cooperation such as an Asian Monetary System. Northeast Asian countries that have been sceptical to any institutional arrangement in their own region have shown keen interests and welcomed the initiatives by the ASEAN. China proposed to study the feasibility of free trade agreement between the ASEAN and China and emphasized that it would cooperate with the ASEAN despite the fact that its exports and inflow of foreign capital were highly competitive with ASEAN's.

(7) In conclusion, a more pragmatic approach based on changing political and economic environments in Northeast Asia is a two-track approach: physical integration that can be implemented despite the political constraint and institutional integration that can proceed gradually in a wide framework of East Asian cooperation if the political constraint is removed.

NOTES

1. Bhagwati points out that the main driving force for regionalism in the 1990s is the conversion of the US to regionalism:

   > The conversion of the United States is of major significance. As a key defender of multilateralism through the postwar years, its decision now to travel the regional route (in the geographical and the preferential senses simultaneously) tilts the balance of forces at the margin away from multilateralism to regionalism (Bhagwati, 1993, p. 29).

2. Northeast Asia in this paper refers to China, Japan and North and South Korea.
3. The project will initially connect Hunchun in China, Seonbong and Najin in North Korea and Posjet in Russia. The larger project will connect Yanji in China, Vladivostok in Russia and Chonjin in North Korea.
4. Japan's defence spending in 1999 was estimated as 41 billion dollars while China's as 37 billion dollars in 1998 (Stratfor, 2000).
5. As China continued to record high growth rates, the gap was widened in 2001; China's GNI in PPP was 5505 billion dollars while that of Japan was 3444 billion dollars.
6. For the debates on the AMF and US policy on the crisis management, see Suh (2000).
7. Reported by *Christian Science Monitor* (2000), 'Beijing Unification Priority: Get U.S. Troops out of South Korea' by Kevin Platt.
8. US Secretary of State, M. Albright visited Pyongyang on October and the US removed North Korea from the blacklisted countries. It would have enabled North Korea to receive assistance from international organizations such as the IMF and the World Bank, and the ADB. However, further negotiations have been stalled since the Bush administration reversed the engagement policy.
9. According to South Korea's Ministry of Construction, connecting South Korea to Europe via the Trans-China railway will reduce shipping time from three weeks

by sea to one week by rail. North Korea stands to gain one hundred million dollars a year in railway fees. *Maeil Business Newspaper* estimates that shipping time from Pusan to Berlin will be reduced from 34 days to 20.4 days and transport costs per container will be reduced by 10 to 20 per cent (*Maeil Business Newspaper*, 2001).
10. See Cho and Katz (2001).
11. In China, reformers believe that the entry into the WTO would provide this opportunity. In Japan, it has been frequently argued that only '*gaiatsu*' (foreign pressure) can solve their problems. In South Korea, the strong IMF conditions have served as a catalyst for the major reform after the economic crisis. In North Korea, the opening of its economy will trigger a series of institutional change.

REFERENCES

Baldwin, R.E. (1995), 'A domino theory of regionalism', in R.E. Baldwin, P. Haaparanta and J. Kiander (eds), *Expanding Membership of the European Union*, Cambridge: Cambridge University Press. pp. 25–48.

Bhagwati, J.N. (1993), 'Regionalism and multilateralism: an overview', in J.D. Melo and A. Panagaria (eds), *New Dimensions in Regional Integration*, Centre for Economic Policy Research, Cambridge: Cambridge University Press, pp. 22–51.

Bergsten, C.F. (1997), The Asian monetary crisis: proposed remedies', *Statement Before the Committee on Banking and Financial Services, US House of Representatives*, November 13, http://www.iie.crisis.htm (2000).

Bergsten, C.F. (2000), 'The new Asian challenge', *Working Paper* 00-4, Washington, D.C: International Economics.

Cho, L.J. and S.S. Katz (2001), 'A Northeast development bank?', *NIRA Review*, Winter, pp. 41–7.

Christian Science Monitor (2000), 21 June.

Kahler, M. (1994), 'Institution-building in the Pacific', in A. Mack and J. Ravenhill (eds), *Pacific Cooperation: Building Economic and Security Regimes in the Asia–Pacific Region*, NSW, Australia: Allen and Unwin, pp. 16–39.

Maeil Business Newspaper (2001), 1 January.

Silver, N.E. (2000), 'The United States, Japan and China: setting the course', *Executive Summary*, The Council on Foreign Relations, Washington, D.C.

Stratfor (2000), 'The decade to come: the rise of Japan', http://www.stratfor.com/SERVICES/GIU/FORECAST/decadse to come/asiadecade4.asp

Suh, D.C. (2000), 'U.S. policy toward the East Asian economic crisis', *Studies of the Institute of Comparative Regional Studies*, No. 41, March, Kitakyushu University, Japan, pp. 121–39.

Tyson, L.D. (2000), 'Future directions for U.S. economic policy toward Japan', *Task Force Report*, The Council on Foreign Relations, Washington, D.C.

Viner, J. (1950), *The Customs Union Issue*, New York: Carnegie Endowment for International Peace.

World Bank (2000), World Development Report 2000/2001, Washington, D.C.

Index